ALLARD MOTOR COMPANY
THE RECORDS AND BEYOND

VOLUME ONE

◦ GAVIN ALLARD ◦

ALLARD MOTOR COMPANY
THE RECORDS AND BEYOND

VOLUME ONE

GAVIN ALLARD

Published 2023
ISBN: 978-1-956309-06-5

Printed by Interpress Ltd., Hungary

for the publisher
Dalton Watson Fine Books
Glyn and Jean Morris
Deerfield, IL 60015 USA

www.daltonwatson.com

To my beautiful wife, Sarah – her virtues of professionalism, problem solving and a wonderful glass-half-full attitude carries me to heights I could not have ever imagined.

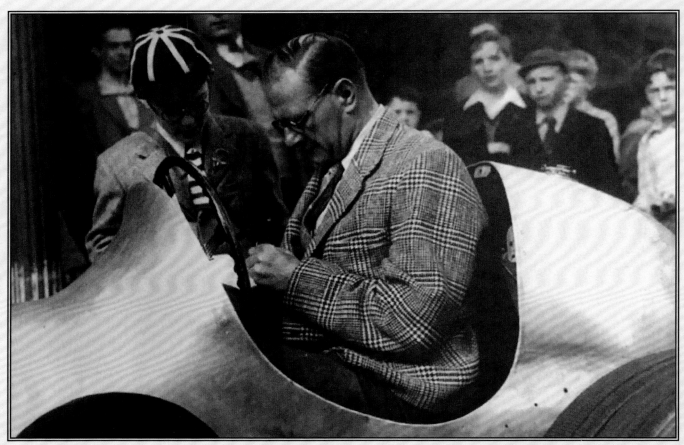

Sydney Allard was always representing the company in public, which included schoolboys dreaming of driving a racing car. Here a boy gets his notebook signed under the envious eyes of his friends.

•CONTENTS•

• PREFACE •

I never met my grandfather Sydney Allard, the founder of first, Adlards, and then the Allard Motor Company, and what I know of him is second-hand, largely from my father Alan, Sydney's son.

Being a boy with a family history of significant merit in British motorsport and manufacturing, it was almost inevitable that I would foster a keen similar interest. My father has often said, 'You are not under the eye of expectation Gavin, you don't have to feel you need to live up to my father's achievements like I did'.

He was right, as my professional career quickly moved into architecture directly from school, but at the same time, the realisation hit that dad's collection of company records in the barn were just the tip of an iceberg that I am still uncovering 35 years later.

Not having a competition history like my grandfather, father or indeed my brother, Lloyd, I expanded my personal motoring interest by nurturing all routes to increase the Allard archive which I curate with great pride today. The Allard archive comprises of my personal collection combined with my father's retained from the Allard Motor Company with him being the last director and inheritor of Sydney's personal items, this is supplemented by the Allard Owners Club collection all of which I maintain in one location.

After planning, organising and hosting a gathering in 1997 in Surrey called 'Allards and the Moving Image', notable names from the old business and most of the Allard family got together to again see Sydney in black and white film and shout out hurrahs as he won the 1952 Monte Carlo rally in the newsreels.

It created an unexpected surge in Allard chat and energy as guests viewed the greatest part of my entire collection brought before them. From that, Sydney's right-hand man, Tom Lush, and author of the much acclaimed 'Allard – The Inside Story' passed into my hands perhaps what

we would call the Holy Grail for safekeeping, the Allard Motor Company car build factory records. They document the details of nearly all the cars built – there is so much visual treasure and surprises within them.

One might assume this sort of written documentation might have been lost, broken up or indeed burnt in the factory fire of 1966, but it was saved by Tom, as was a large bundle of documents. These records form the foundation of this book.

I have reached a point with my collection and in my life that I believe the Allard owner and enthusiast should all have a chance to possess the exact record of a car, including a referencing spreadsheet, just as it was written the day the car was ordered and delivered.

With these records I have added factory photographs recording the models, the advertising, the workshops, the dealers and indeed the workers who built the cars.

Let me share my insatiable enthusiasm for my grandfather's creations; ones that are only existing due to a young man's own extreme determination in a country weary from war, who knew the right people, was in the right place at the right time to achieve success in post-war Britain.

· ACKNOWLEDGEMENTS ·

There are men who have started many good things and never finished; it is with endless thanks to my wife Sarah that when we met in 2018, she did not turn heels and dash in the opposite direction upon learning of my family history in motoring and just how much time that might consume, quite the opposite.

She has been my unrelenting support in pressing on. After completing the scanning phase, it was the turn of the spreadsheet creation, and her teaching background gave her such skills to keep me on the pathway to the finish line with a reassuring yet firm helping hand.

My great friend and indeed huge patron to the archives, Kerry Horan, has over the past 20 years sent packages from around the world, each one an uplifting discovery of all things Allard and many putting joy into a busy workday and now supplying entries to this publication.

Thanks to my father, Alan, and mother, Lynda, for their sympathetic commentary as I follow this route hot on the heels of dad's recent publication 'Allard – The Complete Story'. We both are fulfilling what we set out to do years ago and tell our angle on the Allard legacy.

I also thank the following for their suggestions, support and enthusiasm: my family, Dean Butler for the idea and connections to get this project underway, John Peskett, the Allard Owners Club, Des Sowerby, Captain David Wixon, Chrissie Konig for insight into her father, Goff Imhof, Ian Young for his memories of Allard employment. Dalton Watson's Glyn Morris and Jodi Ellis for their professionalism and determination to bring my thoughts to fruition, as well as Siona Rajshekhar for assisting in table proofing.

If I have missed out anyone then please accept my sincere apologies as an eight-year process is quite the length of time.

Gavin Allard
December 2022

Allardist John Peskett spotted in his natural environment whilst I was out on a recent expedition.

· FOREWORD ·

After many years as archivist for the Allard Owners Club, my son Gavin, with support from other members, has gathered a detailed history of the Allard car sales records.

Gavin is meticulous in his work as a professional Architectural Technician and he has applied this approach to his presentation of the facts and figures in relation to the Allard car sales records from 1946 to 1958 – this being laid out in the form of spreadsheets.

My father's company, the Allard Motor Company, was formed in 1946 and manufactured cars covering a range of distinctive models, from the K1 to the Palm Beach Mk.II.

Gavin has spent many hours researching and compiling these comprehensive Allard manufacturing records, which represent his contribution to the Allard car story.

To many Allard owners and enthusiasts, I am sure these sales records presented in this book, will be of great interest and value in tracing the history of their Allard and the Allard cars of other owners everywhere.

Alan Allard

FAR LEFT: Alan Allard (left) with friend and navigator Rob Mackie (right) in white coats in Cluses, South Eastern France, 1962.

LEFT: Alan Allard (centre) with Rob Mackie (right) in a television interview for the 1962 Monte Carlo rally before the start at Glasgow. He would beat his father's finishing position; they were both in Ford Anglia 'Allardettes'.

ABOVE (BOTH): Alan Allard (left) with navigator Tom Fisk were active competitors in the RAC and Scottish rallies of the late 1960s and early 1970s.

Alan outside the Allard Performance Centre at 51 Upper Richmond Rd, Putney, circa 1970 with a Shorrock supercharger display.

·ALLARD·

• INTRODUCTION •

This book not only records a car's history, but also builds a picture of the dedicated company that constructed Allards and carved its own permanent niche in motoring history.

On page xii, I illustrate how to navigate the factory records using the spreadsheet. These are the seven records books from the day the Allard was ordered and include any subsequent servicing as long as the car was warrantied directly by Allard in London.

The foreign export car reader will not be disappointed, however, as the Allard record cards, starting on page 78, include many exported vehicles and offer even more information such as the name of the ship.

After reading the spreadsheet introduction on page 704, a car's records can be traced by turning to pages 706 to 813. Be careful about what you wish for, as the more entries therein could suggest a car which returned for servicing a few too many times. It was to be expected from a hand-built performance car and Allard had a thriving service department.

The records have all the handwriting nuances of the time, some better than others. They offer delights and surprises that might have never been seen had they not been saved from the flames in 1966.

Offering a page to add notes (pages 820-821, 'Allard Future Discoveries') is not so much an admission that I have not captured everything, as much as a realisation that mystery cars do appear over the years and there is this area to record those findings.

Sydney Allard started building cars a decade before the Allard Motor Company came into being, his firm, Adlards Motors, being a Ford dealership created with his father's original investment. The name was pure coincidence but perhaps deliberately maintained so thus Adlards built twelve pre-war specials. Pages 402-441, 'Adlards Made Allards' and pages 546-575, 'Allards – Without Chassis Numbers', recognise Sydney's road to success was not easy nor overnight and I believe their inclusion is fundamental to understanding a car's heritage.

Some may be surprised to learn that Allard did not have a singular Ford style production line; others will be aware that it was a group of smaller buildings the primary being at Park Hill Clapham, London where the cars came together as a rolling chassis amassing components towards completion. Blocks of orders of specific models were accumulated before production began; the record listings reveal this.

The subsequent pages add the human side of the story showing you where the cars were built. Some photographs see beyond the car in the foreground and show the simple but effective premises which were the backdrop to Allard.

The workforce was dedicated and held incredible specialist skills; they are honoured here.

Dealerships were the worldwide outlets for these special cars and my archive reveals some of those: for export the Allard would be crated in a timber box and for USA orders the engine would be supplied new to the dealer and fitted into the car state-side.

There are drawings, official literature and the original advertising proofs marked up by Sydney who maintained his vision of how Allard was presented globally.

This is all preceded with a wide selection of official Allard Motor Company photographs of the models offered, it is apparent that no one car was the same, indeed some cars were produced as an extra-special order, thus being unique.

The great majority of the images in the book are from an archive formed from my personal and my father's collections, as well as a handful from the Allard Owner's Club, of which I am the archivist/historian. Only photographs and documents from other sources are noted with the caption.

As with much of the British car industry, Sydney could not keep up with car development as he wished and even though his 1952-55 model the Palm Beach did sell in some numbers its demise was set with Triumph's TR series launch. Production did not stop so much as fade until just a single car remained in a corner uncompleted: a Palm Beach Mk.II model, the end of an incredible run.

One might have thought a small firm would fold at this point, not so with Allard. Sydney merely put his time into his Ford and commercials dealership and the supercharging business he already operated. His motorsport interests were still satisfied with international rallying (along with his son) and the emerging drag racing sport which Sydney brought from the USA with his friend and associate Dean Moon.

Lastly, the long-lasting admiration of Allard was embodied in Capt. David Wixon's 'Allard Grace' on page 822. Does Sydney exist somehow outside this world carrying on his genius to this day or is this just human whimsy? I like to think he does.

· HOW TO VIEW THE CAR RECORDS ·

You, as an Allard owner or inquisitive reader, will be eager to find where a car appears in the following records. Here is a guide to what they are and how to view them.

The first two records are the Allard Allocation Book I, pages 1-57 and Allard Allocation Book II, pages 58-77. All the information from these would have been recorded as the car was allocated from the customer order and progressively filled out until the car was delivered; that customer could have been an individual, company or dealership and indeed in one case a nation (an Embassy ordered a car).

The Allard Record Cards, pages 78-167, were principally prepared for exported cars. The index cards were actually small, empty envelopes sealed, then placed in the typewriter and treated as if a piece of card. The information would include many extra export details such as the name of the ship, shipping costs and consignees.

The fourth record is the Allard Warranty Book, pages 168-201 and contains the name and address details of the owner who took delivery of the car from the factory/dealership in London.

The last records, the fifth, sixth and seventh, are the Allard Service Records I, pages 202-259, Allard Service Records II, pages 260-349 and Allard Service Records III, pages 350-393. They show the Allard cars that came back into the London dealership for anything from regular servicing with lubricant replacement to rather robust repairs and alterations. For me, these hold the most fascinating entries and, in some cases, display the determination to get absolute satisfaction from their wonderful Allard. In many cases these will be the only remaining record of the vehicle after production. The reader should be made aware that there is a gap between service records from 1952 to 1955 and I am not aware of their existence, it is highly likely they were destroyed in the office fire of April 1966.

The example (opposite, page xiii) is an allocation record and these, unlike all the other records, do cover all the cars constructed, minus the twelve pre-war cars built by Adlards, 1936-1945 (refer to section 'Adlards Made Allards', pages 402-441) and Allard specials/competition vehicles and side projects (refer to section 'Allards – Without Chassis Numbers', pages 546-575).

Therefore, to start with, please see the Appendices section entitled 'Appendix 2 – Allard Chassis Number Spreadsheets' on page 704, from pages 706-813 the cars are listed in numerical order and within that listing every single page on which the car is mentioned. It should be noted that in some instances, the model field will reflect the model as stated in the Allocation Book records, and not necessarily the usual, current terminology. For instance, some cars are shown as a J model, but are now considered as a J2.

Alternatively, use the 'Appendix 3 – Registration Number Index' (pages 814-819) for locating a car. The numbers gathered are those known within the original records or the historian's 'Domesday' Book record compiled in the last three decades shown in Appendix 1 (pages 678-703).

Enjoy your adventure.

·EXAMPLE RECORD·

1 **Chassis No.** The Allard chassis plate displays this generally in two lines, with the first being the model number and the second the chassis number, i.e. 81M 851.

2 **Engine No.** The most commonly used Ford sidevalve engine has a prefix '7'.

3 **Chassis type** J, K, L, M, P. The first J had the suffix '1' added later after the J2 was launched.

4 **Body type** Tourer, 2 Seater, Coupe generally or also 'chassis' including the wings and bonnet.

5 **Body colour** Simple colour description.

6 **Interior colour** Normally leather but recorded as 'frame' if car is chassis only.

7 **Hood colour** Most Allards were convertibles but sometimes a soft-top was not noted.

8 **Wheel colour** Rarely any information here, most solid wheels were silver.

9 **Remarks** Nuggets of information recorded here including remarks by Tom Lush's hand.

10 **Allocated to** An individual, dealership or country or multiples of these noted.

11 **Delivered** Date the vehicle arrived at the dealership or arrived with the first owner.

ALLARD
ALLOCATION BOOK I

1947-1952
CHASSIS 101-2299

The reader should note that the numbering does not mean there are 100 cars missing, but rather that Sydney likely decided that it reads better to have chassis 101 and not chassis 001. Twelve Allards had come before that, and would have made that numbering inaccurate.

Chassis No.	Engine No.	Chassis Type	Body Type	Body Colour	Interior Colour	Hood Colour	Wheel Colour		Remarks	Allocated To		Date Delivered
97												
98												
99												
100												
102	S2/7783/E	L	Tourer	Red	Red Leather				Demo.			18/3/194
101			Experimental									
100												
103	BOB 32/103	J₁	2 Seater	Blue	Blue Leather				Demo. HUG 430			22/3/194
104	S/27726 E	K	2 Seater	Red	Red Leather				Belgium		X	22/10/4
105	S/27732 E	L	Tourer	Grey					Argentine		X	29/11/4
106	K12311	J₁	2 Seater	White					A. G. Imhof (Allard)			25/7/4
107	4145849	M	D.H. Coupe	Maroon	Red Leather	MRB 441			Demo.			
108	7079928	K	2 Seater	White	Red Leather				I drove to Southampton for shipment Monday 31.	U.S.A.	X	31/3/194
109	K 12312	J₁	2 Seater	White					KHW 100	K.E.O. Burgess (Allard)		5/7/46
110	K 12313	J₁	2 Seater	White						J.H. Appleton (Allard) 3-9-46		3/9/4
111	S/27194 E	J₁	2 Seater	Black						G.H. Mansell (Allard) 31-10-46		31/10/4
112	S/270035	J₁	2 Seater	Black						Jersey	X 19-12-46	19/12/4
113												
114							HLF 601		Special built at S1. some welding & other work at Park Hill under this numb.			
115	7079927	L	Tourer	Red	Red Leather				Belgium		X 10-1-47	10/1/4
116	7079932	L	Tourer	Blue	Blue Leather				Dagenham Motors (Richards)		15-4-47	15/4/4
117	EOM 32/1025/AM	J₁	2 Seater	Metallic	Blue Leather				K-/W 331 ?	Maurice Wick (Allard)		3/4/4
118												
119												
120												
121	7079931	M	Coupe	Frame	Body					Adlards (Lucas)		
122	7079929	L	Tourer	Red	Red Leather				I drove to Newhaven for shipment Monday 10 March	Switzerland	X 10-3-47	10/3/4
123	7079953	L	Tourer	Grey	Grey Leather					Nunn	13-5-47	13.3.
124	7079926	L	Tourer	Blue	Blue Leather	Black				Palestine	X 12-3-47	12/3/
125	7079954	L	Tourer	Black Green	Brown Leather	Fawn				Frew (Tomas) 29-4 47		29/4/
126	7079941	L	Tourer		Blue Leather	Grey				S. Africa (Hotchkiss)	X	
127	7079952	L	Tourer	Red	Red Leather					Adlards		
128	7079934	L	Tourer	Blue	Blue Leather					Dagenham Motors (Crozia)		

CHASSIS NO.	ENGINE NO.	CHASSIS TYPE	BODY TYPE	BODY COLOUR	INTERIOR COLOUR	HOOP COLOUR	WHEELS COLOUR	REMARKS	ALLOCATED TO.		DATE DELIVERED
129	7079930	L	Tourer	Skeleton Body					Dagenham Motors (Sanders Garage)		21/4/47
130	7079923	L	Tourer	Maroon	Red Leather				U.S.A	✗	15/5/47
131										✗	
132	7079947	L	Tourer	Skeleton Body					Belgium	✗	10/1/47
133	7079563	L	Tourer	Maroon	Red Leather				Jersey	✗	1/7/47
134	7125295	L	Tourer	Skeleton Body					Belgium	✗	17/1/47
135	7125299	L	Tourer	Skeleton Body					Belgium	✗	17/1/47
136	7125302	L	Tourer	Maroon	Red Leather Maroon				Taylors		9·10·47
137	7125293	L	Tourer	Skeleton Body					Universal (Premier Garage)		8/5/47
138	7125297	L	Tourer	Skeleton Body					Universal (Premier Garage)		23/3/1947
139	7125301	L	Tourer	Skeleton Body					Universal (Premier Garage)		24/4/47
140	7125300	L	Tourer	Maroon	Red Leather	Maroon	Red Wells		Malta Adlards	✗	31/7/47
141	7125291	L	Tourer	Maroon	Red Leather	Maroon	Red Wells		Adlards Goulds (Durling)		25/4/47
142	7079950	K	2 Seater	Blue	Blue Leather				Hughes (L. Watkins)		23/4/47
143	7079939	K	2 Seater	Red	Red Leather				Argentine Palestine English	✗	25/8/4
144	7124860	K	2 Seater	Black	Red Leather				Goulds (Currie)		16/5/4
145	K-145	K	2 Seater	Skeleton Body					Adlards (MacPhee)		6/4/47
146	7116824	K	2 Seater	Blue	Blue Leather			(Totham)	Switzerland	✗	15/5/4
147	7125292	K	2 Seater	Green	Blue Leather				Taylors (Horace Roberts)		18/7/47
148	S2-773138	Ti	Chassis					HRH 472	Universal Car Co. (Premier Garage)		4/3/47
149	7179622	K	2 Seater	Red	Grey Leather				Harwoods Argentine (Fox)	✗	9/6/4
150	7479628	K	2 Seater	Maroon	Red Leather	Maroon	Red Wells		Bristol St. Motors (H.C. Bradshaw)		25/5/47
151	7179623	K	2 Seater	Black	Brown Leather	Red to	Red Wheels	(collected by Silcox & Collings)	Taylors (Barton)		30/7/4
152	T152	Ti	Chassis					5152 ... Service shows 5 GP 474 June 20 47/25/8/1956	Allard (L. Potts)		28/3/47
153	7125303	M LH	Coupe	Lt Blue	Red	Grey		This chassis number was quoted when FGP 290 was re-registered as HPX 57, letter & photo shows "solid" front axle. MR DORNER	Brazil	✗	14·3·1
154	7179627	K	2 Seater	White	Blue Leather	Blue	Blue Wheels		Belgium (Bunn)	✗	22/6/4
155	7179564	K	2 Seater	Chassis Red	Blue Leather				R.F. Hamilton (R. Baird)		10/3/194
156	7179617	K	2 Seater	Maroon White	Grey Leather Green Leather	Maroon Green	Maroon Wells Green Wells	Experimental.	Allard		12·12·1
157	7179626	K	2 Seater	Maroon	Red Leather	Maroon	Red Wells		U.S.A. Gibraltar	✗	5·12·47
158	7179625	K	2 Seater	Blue	Blue Leather	Blue	Blue Wells		U.S.A Monterey 1990 U.S.A Built (photo)	✗	8·8·47
159	7179562	K	2 Seater	Skeleton Body					Goulds (Bonallack)		28·4·4
160	7179565	K	2 Seater	Red	Red Leather				Argentine Harwoods (Fox)	✗	9·7·4

CHASSIS NO	ENGINE No	CHASSIS TYPE	BODY TYPE	BODY COLOUR	INTERIOR COLOUR	HOOD COLOUR	WHEELS COLOUR	REMARKS	ALLOCATED TO		DATE DELIVERED
161	7199604	K	2 Seater	Black	Blue leather			U.S.A. 11/92 ...	Hughes	(Central Garage)	20.8.47
162	7199546	K	2 Seater	Maroon	Grey leather				Argentine Dag Motors (Mr Hall) ✗		26.7.47
163	7199084	K	2 Seater	Red	Red leather	Beige Hood			Patterson		15.9.47
164	7199877	L	Tourer	Black Red	Brown leather Brown				Adlards	(Capt Richards)	9.7.47
165	7179876	K	2 Seater	Maroon	Red				U.S.A.	✗	8.8.47
166											
167											
168											
169											
170											
171											
172											
173											
174											
175											
176											
177											
178											
179											
180											
181											
182											
183											
184											
185											
186											
187											
188											
189											
190											
191											
192											

CHASSIS NO	ENGINE NO	CHASSIS TYPE	BODY TYPE	BODY COLOUR	INTERIOR COLOUR	HOOD COLOUR	WHEELS COLOUR	REMARKS	ALLOCATED TO		DATE DELIVERED
193											
194											
195											
196											
197											
198											
199											
200	7179554	L	Tourer	Cordoba Grey	Red Leather				Harris	(Edwards)	28.7.47
201	7179891	L	Tourer	Maroon	Brown Leather				Dag. Motor	(Craddock)	16.9.47
202	7179618	L	Tourer	Red	Red Leather				English	(Morton)	12.9.47
203	7179889	L	Tourer	Maroon	Red Leather	Beige Hood			Hartwelle	(Frey)	15.8.47
204	7179887	K	2 Seater	White	Blue Leather				U.S.A. Brazil argentine	X	29.10.47
205	718034	K	2 Seater	Blue	Grey Leather	Grey	Blue		Adlards	(Oldham) X	6.10.47
206	7179890	K	2 Seater	Black	Red Leather				Goulds		12/9/47
207	7179881	K	2 Seater	Skeleton	Body				Adlards	(Wayne)	16/5/47
208	7179886	M	Coupe Chassis		Dolphin Special Body	LBH 856		Service Station on 13/9/48 new chassis! Sub-Bonnet scuttle only	Adlards Motors (Stormont Eg.)		29.4.47
209	7180025	L	Tourer	Maroon	Grey Leather	Grey Hood.			U.S.A	X	8.8.47
210	7180045	L	Tourer		Blue	Grey Beige		Untrimmed	Nunns		6.11.47
211	7180041	L	Tourer	Chassis					Tate of Leeds		30.4.47
212	7179884	L	Tourer	untrimmed	Grey	Grey		Brass W/screen deficient	Tate of Leeds		15.10.47
213	7180043	K	2 Seater	Maroon	Maroon	Grey Hood	Maroon	L.H. Steering	Brazil	X	5.11.47
214	7180027	M	Coupe	Skeleton Chassis				JGV 4	Adlards Mrs Imhof (Somin) (Imhof) JGV4		14/7/47
215	7180038	M	Coupe	Skeleton Chassis					Adlards	(Burges)	30/6/47
216	7180050	M	Coupe	Chassis					Goulds		3/6/47
217	7180033	M	Coupe	Skeleton Chassis					Adlards	(Imhof) JGVS	2/7/47
218	7180036	L	Tourer	Maroon	Maroon	Maroon			Gibralter	X	5.12.47
219	7180044	K	2 Seater	Chassis					Tate		4/6/47
220	7180125	K	2 Seater	Chassis					Hamilton		7/5/47
221	7180126	K	2 Seater	Red	Grey Leather	Grey Hood			George + Jobling		25.8.47
222	7180121	K	2 Seater	Maroon	Red Leather				Hamilton		7.8.47
223	7180128	L	Tourer	Chassis					Hamilton		19/5/47
224	7180127	L	Tourer	Blue	Blue Leather	Grey Hood			Dag C.		26.7.47

·ALLARD·

Chassis No	Engine No	Chassis Type	Body Type	Body Colour	Interior Colour	Hood Colour	Wheels Colour	Remarks	Allocated To		Date Delivered
225	7180140	L	Tourer	Chassis				8114	Dagenham Motors (Pleaner)		3/6/47
226	7180195	L	Tourer	Blue	Grey	Grey			Furrows		21.11.47
227	7180139	L	Tourer	Blue	Blue	Grey			George & Jobling		28.11.47
228	7180201	M	Coupe	Chassis					Dag. Motors (Adlards)		26/6/47
229	7180194	M	Coupe	Chassis				One sub-bonnet supplied only.	Adlards (Stormont)		25/7/47
230	7180200	M	Coupe	Maroon	Blue	Blue			Australia (Clement Shaw)		17.12.47
231	7180191	M	Coupe	White	Red	Maroon			Dagenham		19.12.47
232 X	7180138	M	Coupe	Maroon					Perris	48	24.3.48
233	7180190	K	2 Seater	Skeleton Body					Dagenham Motors (Hams)		14/6/47
234	7180198	K	2 Seater	Skeleton Body					Universal (Premier)		17.7.47
235	7180193	K	2 Seater	Blue	Red Leather	Black Hood			Nunn		12.9.47
236	7180259	K	2 Seater	Skeleton Body					Frew		26/4/47
237	7180196	K	2 Seater	Maroon	Maroon Leather	Beige			Australia (Clement Shaw)		17.12.47
238	7180197	K	2 Seater	Blue	Grey Leather	Grey Hood		Evans Shewan	Brazil		26.9.47
239	7180224	K	2 Seater	Black	Maroon Leather	Beige			Hartwells		17.11.47
240	7180225	K	2 Seater	Chassis					Bristol St. Motors		1.10.47
241	7180262	K	2 Seater	Black	Red Leather	Black Hood		after long storage. note quote body No Intrigue? Sold July 1980(or 9) Cosling engine by Sotheby Auction Bonnet straps / air scoops on bonnet	Brazil		29.10.47
242	7180261	K	2 Seater	Black	Blue Leather	Black Hood	Reg No SH 9025		Alexanders		13.10.47
243	7180260	L	Tourer	Red	Grey	Grey			Demo.	48	4.2.48
244	7180258	L	Tourer	Blue	Grey Leather	Grey			Mann Egerton		7.11.47
245	7180257	L	Tourer	Red	Red	Beige			Tate		6.12.47
246	7180263	L	Tourer	Chassis					Dag. Motors (Saunders)		30.7.47
247	7180264	L	Tourer	Untrimmed	Red	Ridley	Grey	Glass w/screen deficient	George & Jobling		15.10.47
248	7180291	K	2 Seater	Chassis					Hartwells (R H Fleming)		8.7.47
249	7180298	K	2 Seater	Chassis					Dag. Motors (Saunders)		27/6/47
250	7180299	K	2 Seater	Blue	Blue Leather	Grey Hood			Bristol St. Motors (Fleming)		10.10.47
251	7180296	K	2 Seater	Chassis					Tate		18.7.47
252	7180293	K	2 Seater	Chassis					Hartwells (W J Fleming)		8.7.47
253	7180295	L	Tourer	Brown	Brown	Beige		Untrimmed LUB 652 AWLOCK CROYDON ROE NIL 9/9 1967	Tate of Leeds		17.10.47
254	7180294	L	Tourer	Chassis					Furrows (Oatleys)		1.10.47
255	7180292	L	Tourer	Red	Grey	Grey			Australia (Clement Shaw)		17.12.47
256	7180266	L	Tourer	Chassis					Dag. Motors (Featherstone)		15.7.47

Chassis No	Engine No	Chassis Type	Body Type	Body Colour	Interior Colour	Hood Colour	Wheels Colour	Remarks	Allocated To	Date Delivered
257	7180301	L	Tourer	Chassis					Dagenham (Dr Du Fang)	13.8.47
258	7180310	K	2 Seater	Chassis					Adlards (J Burns)	6.8.47
259	7180303	K	2 Seater	Chassis					Patterson	1.10.47
260	7180270	K	2 Seater	chassis					Adlards (Salford)	3.10.47
261	7180302	K	2 Seater	Chassis					Bristol St. motors	1.10.47
262	7180308	K	2 Seater	Chassis					Dag. Motors	3.10.47
263	7180299	M	Coupe	Black	Blue	Black			Frew	28.11.47
264	7180305	M	Coupe	Chassis					Gould (wreck)	10.11.47 24.8.4
265	7180304	M	Coupe	Black	Blue	Beige			West. Africa (Thomson) X	9.1.48
266	7180306	M	Coupe	Chassis	-				Tate (Emerson)	11.11.4
267	7180300	M	Coupe	Chassis					Hughes	4.7.4
268 A	7180312	L.H. M.	Coupe	Maroon	Brown	Maroon			Adlards	14.4.48
269	7180313	M	Coupe	Grey	Red	Grey			Nunns	22.4.48
270	7180317	L.H. M.	Coupe	Maroon		Maroon			Frew	
271	7195529 7186429	L.H. M.	Coupe	Grey	Grey	Grey		Hot type windows	Nunns	22.6.48
272	7180315	M	Coupe	Red	Maroon				Nunns.	27.4.48
273	J-273	J.	2 Seater	Chassis				NPC 640	L. Potter (Allards)	29.9.47
274	J-274	J.	2 Seater	Chassis					Taylors (Roberts)	5/9/47
275	J-275	J.	2 Seater					KBP 242 R/S	L. Potter	22.1.48
276	7191968	K	2 Seater	Blue					Frew	
277	7188842	K	2 Seater	Chassis					Bristol St Motors	21.10.47
278	7180309	L.H. L	Tourer	Blue	Grey	Grey			Adlards	21.11.48
279	7186425	L.H. L	Tourer	Blue	Grey	Black Beige			Tate	21.11.48
280	7186444	L.H. L	Tourer	Maroon	Brown				Nunns	23.4.48
281	7180316	L.H. L	Tourer	Blue	Grey	Grey		W. r M.	Nunns	22.11.48
282	7186641	L	Tourer	Black	Maroon	Maroon Beige			Nunns	28.4.48
283	7187082	L	Tourer	Chassis					Bristol St. Motors	1.10.47
284	7186688	L	Tourer	Untrimmed	Blue in cut	grey	2 Battery	Lido & Brass w/screen deficient	Hartwells	20.10.47
285	7187006	L	Tourer	Chassis					Bristol St. motors	1.10.47
286	7186959	L	Tourer	Blue	Grey	Grey			Patterson	24.11.47
287	7186448	L	Tourer	Blue	Blue	Beige			S. Africa (Batters)	15.12.47
288	7186633	L	Tourer	Chassis					Hughes	2.10.47

CHASSIS	ENGINE	TYPE	BODY	COLOUR	INTERIOR	HOOD	WHEELS	— REMARKS	ALLOCATED TO		DATE DELIVERED
289	7186664	M	Coupe	Chassis					A. E. Gould		5/9/47
290	7180811	M	Coupe	Chassis					Bristol St. Motors		1.10.47
291	7180307	M	Coupe	Chassis					Bristol St. Motors		1.10.47
292	7187003	M	Coupe	Chassis					George & Jobling		3/9/47
293A	7186888	M L.H.	Coupe	Maroon	Brown	Maroon			Tate		1.5.48
294	7180097	M L.H.	Coupe	Chassis					Gibralter	X	8.12.48
295	7186894	M L.H.	Coupe	Blue	Blue	Grey			Taylor (Roberts)		26.4.48
296	7188004	M L.H.	Coupe	Chassis					~~Gaylor~~	X	3.5.48
297	7186856	M	Coupe	Grey	Brown	Grey			Adlards (Moss & Sawton)		13.#.48
298	7188839	L	Tourer	Chassis					Mann Egerton (Layton)		15.10.47
299	7188846	L	Tourer	Chassis					Battersons (Crabtree)		15.10.47
300	7188052	L	Tourer	Chassis				2 Battery lids deficient	George & Jobling		20.10.47
301	7188035	L	Tourer	Chassis					Alexanders		29.10.47
302	7188044	L	Tourer	Chassis					Adlards (Linnery)		11.11.47
303	7186193	M	Coupe	Chassis				2 Battery lids deficient	Furrows		20.10.47
304	7188841	M	Coupe	Chassis				2 Battery lids deficient	Furrows		20.10.47
305	M-305	M	Coupe	Chassis & Body				Untrimmed	Universal (Tongue)		9.12.47
306	7188847	M	Coupe	Chassis				2 Battery lids deficient	Goulds		20.10.47
307	7188840	M	Coupe	Chassis					Dagenham Motors		27.10.47
308	7188845	M	Coupe	Chassis				—	Harris		24.10.47
309	7188843	M	Coupe	Chassis					Goulds		21.10.47
310	7188055	L	Tourer	Chassis					Bristol St. Motors		29.10.47
311	7188034	L	Tourer	Chassis					Adlards (Rogers)		4.11.47
312	7187074	L	Tourer	Chassis					Dag. Motors (Bentley)		4.11.47
313	7187967	L	Tourer + Body	Blue	Grey			Untrimmed	Hartwells		21.11.47
314	7190989	L	Tourer + Body	Grey	Beige			Untrimmed	Allards (Bent)		20.11.47
315	7188054	L	Tourer	Black	Brown	Beige			Hamilton		5.1.48
316	7186646	M	Coupe	Chassis					English (Dibben)		7.11.47
317	7187049	M	Coupe	Chassis					Gould (Lovell)		5.11.47
318	7188078	M	Coupe	Chassis					George & Jobling		6.11.47
319	7187949	M	Coupe	Chassis					Dag. Motors (Mowbray)		6.11.47
320	7187904	M	Coupe	Chassis					Dag. Motors (Foxhunt)		6.11.47

CHASSIS	ENGINE	TYPE	BODY	COLOUR	INTERIOR	HOOD	WHEELS	REMARKS	ALLOCATION	DELIVERED
321	7187960	M	Coupe	Chassis					George & Jobling	7. 11. 47
322	7187943	M	Coupe	Chassis					Dag. Motors (Regent Park)	7. 11. 47
323	7187952	M	Coupe	Chassis					Hughes	7. 11. 47
324	7191992	M	Coupe	Chassis					Goulds (Leigh)	10. 11. 47
325	7191969	M	Coupe	Chassis					Goulds (K. Hole)	10. 11. 47
326	7191961 / 7191838	M	Coupe	Chassis					Goulds (K. Hole)	10. 11. 47
327	7188002	M	Coupe	Chassis					Dag. Motors (Bentley)	12. 12. 47
328	7167945	M	Coupe	Chassis					Dag. Motors (Bentley)	25. 11. 47
329	7191967	M	Coupe	Chassis					~~Hemn~~ Tate (Harrison)	20. 11. 47
330	7191965	M	Coupe	Chassis					Dag. Motors (Kroyer)	11. 11. 47
331	7194839	M	Coupe	Grey	Blue			Reg No JLK 957 / Derelely Road Test M.C. Rally	Changed from 340 Lewis	20. 7. 48
332	7191966	L	Tourer	Chassis + body		Untrimmed			Tate	28/11/47
333	7190966	L	Tourer	Chassis					Adlards (Turner)	24. 11. 47
334	7188078	L	Tourer	Chassis					Taylors (Whitladys)	28. 11. 47
335	7191971	L	Tourer	Chassis + body	Grey	Grey	Untrimmed		Tate	11. 12. 47
336	7191962	L	Tourer	Chassis + body	Blue	Grey	Untrimmed		English	31. 12. 47
337	7191840	L	Tourer	Chassis + body	Grey	Grey	Untrimmed		Tate	11. 12. 47
338	7179880	L L.H.	Tourer	Chassis + body	Brown	Beige	Untrimmed		Tate	11. 12. 47
339	7188003	K	2 Seater	Black					Hoffman	20. 11. 47
340	7191889	M	Coupe	Maroon	Red	Beige		Changed from 331	Nunns (Lord)	2. 2. 48
341	7191850	M	Coupe	Jade	Blue	Beige			English	23. 2. 48
342	7187938	M	Coupe	Blue	Grey	Blue			Nigeria	12. 2. 48
343	7190964	M	Coupe	Chassis					Tate (Harrison)	12. 12. 47
344	7191970	L	Tourer	+ body	Blue	Grey	Untrimmed		Tate	11. 12. 47
345	7186856	L	Tourer	Chassis + body	Grey	Grey	Untrimmed		Nunns	18. 12. 47
346	7188549	L	Tourer	Chassis + body	Brown	Beige	Untrimmed		Bristol St.	17. 12. 47
347	7188846	L	Tourer		Maroon	Brown Beige			Bristol St	30. 1. 48
348	7188850	L	Tourer	Chassis	Brown	Beige	Untrimmed		Bristol St	12. 1. 48
349	7188892	L	Tourer	+ body	Grey	Black	Untrimmed		Frew	5. 1. 48
350	7186919	L	Tourer	Maroon Black	Brown	Beige			Alexander	15. 1. 48
351	7186944	L	Tourer	Chassis		Beige	Untrimmed		Material supplied Dag. motors	31. 12. 48
352	7188169	M	Coupe	Chassis					Taylors	15. 12. 47

Chassis	Engine	Type	Body	Color	Interior	Hood	Wheels		Remarks		Allocation		Delivered
353	7188124	M	Coupe	Chassis							Adlards (Bowrinas)		27.1.48
354	7188043	M	Coupe	Chassis							Adlards (Clayton) Mears Bros.		25.3.48
355	7187965	M L.H.	Coupe	Black	Blue	Grey					Italy X		14.2.48
356	7186890	L	Tourer	Blue	Grey	Black					Universal		30.1.48
357	7193179	L	Tourer	Black	Brown	Beige					Mann Egerton		12.2.48
358	7186647	L	Tourer	Chassis							Universal (Hall)		29.12.47
359	7186892	L	Tourer	Chassis							Taylors (Whiteladies)		23.1.48
360	7193638	L	Tourer	Chassis							Taylors (Whiteladies)		22.12.47
361	7186640	L	Tourer	Chassis							Taylors (Whiteladies)		5.1.48
362	7193586	L	Tourer	Chassis							Patterson		2.1.48
363	7193629	L	Tourer	Chassis							Taylors (Whiteladies)		9.1.48
364		J											
365	7193369	K	2 Seater	Black	Red						Adlards (Bligh)		24.3.48
366	7188053	K L.H.	2 Seater	Gunmetal	Grey	Black					Brazil X		19.3.48
367	7193623	K	2 Seater	Chassis							Dag. Motors (Abbott)		13.1.48
368	7193088	K	2 Seater	Black	Mar.	Beige							
369	7193630	K	2 Seater	Chassis							Tate		2.2.48
370	7188550	K	2 Seater										
371	7193144	K	2 Seater	Maroon	Maroon						Hamilton		6.4.48
372	7193092	K	2 Seater	Red	Red	Beige					Furrows (C.C)		5.4.48
373	7193803	K	2 Seater	Chassis							Mann Egerton (Lee)		15.1.48
374	7193633	K	2 Seater	Red	Red						Dag. Motors		4.4.48
375	7193370	K	2 Seater	Blue	Grey						Tate		6.4.48
376	7191636	M	Coupe	Chassis							Nunns (Wynroe)		20.1.48
377	7186648	M	Coupe	Chassis							Alexander (Arthur)		30.1.48
378	7193829	M	Coupe	Chassis							Adlards (Allen)		27.1.48
379	7190967	M	Coupe	Chassis							Dag. Motors (Bedford) Tate (Bancroft)		30.1.48
380	7195147	M	Coupe	Chassis							Hughes (Wrigley)		2.2.48
381	7193261	M	Coupe	Chassis							Tate (Harrison)		30.1.48
382	7193519	M	Coupe	Blue	Grey	Blue					Forte (Bone)		16.2.48
383	7193089	M	Coupe	Maroon	Red	Maroon					Taylors		23.2.48
384	7193140	M	Coupe	Grey	Grey	Grey					Universal (Southall)		2.3.48

CHASSIS	ENGINE	TYPE	BODY	COLOR	INTER.	HOOD	WHEELS	REMARKS	ALLOCATION		DELIVERER
385A	7193816	M	Coupe	Grey	Blue	Blue Grey		Ace discs, and...	headlighter, ... C. Edwards	Gold Coast	7. 2. 48
386		J	2 Seater	Brown	Beige						
387	7193852	L	Tourer	Chassis + Body				Untrimmed		Tate	27. 1. 48
388	7195170	L	Tourer	Blue	Grey	Grey				Gould	23. 2. 48
389	7187951	L	Tourer	Chassis + Body	Grey Grey			Untrimmed	Tate		3. 2. 48
390	7195114	L	Tourer	Chassis + Body				Untrimmed	no materials supplied Dag Motors (Bentley)		13. 2. 48
391	7193621	L	Tourer	Maroon	Brown	Beige			Patterson		16. 3. 48
392	7193107	L	Tourer	Grey	Grey	Grey			Hughes	(Brown)	10. 3. 48
393	7193620	L	Tourer	Chassis + Body				Untrimmed	no materials supplied Dag Motors (Bentley)		11. 2. 48
394	7195199	L	Tourer	Chassis + Body Brown Beige				Untrimmed	Tate		13. 2. 48
395B	7195131?	L	Tourer	Chassis					Taylors (Whitbladen)		30. 1. 48
396		J	2 Seater								
397A	7193812	M	Coupe	Maroon	Grey	Maroon			Goulds	(Richard Bros)	3. 3. 48
398A	7193624	M	Coupe	Black	Red	Beige			Bristol St.	(Erskine)	12. 3. 48
399A	7193087	M	Coupe	Black	Red	Beige			Alexanders	(Dr. Patterson)	8. 3. 48
400	7195655	M	Coupe	Grey	Grey	Grey			Adlards	(Decca)	5. 4. 48
401	7194902	M	Coupe	Maroon	Red	Maroon			Hamilton		24. 3. 48
402	7193817	K	2 Seater	Chassis					Tate	(Harrison)	2. 2. 48
403	7193837	K	2 Seater	Grey					Clarke	(Freightright)	30. 4. 48
404	7195746	K	2 Seater	Grey					Tate	Letter G Gardner 25/4/68 LV13 906 (Kent)	20. 4. 48
405	7195784	M	Coupe	Chassis				...	Adlards (Johnson)		25. 3. 48
406	7195528	L	Tourer	Chassis + Body				Untrimmed	...		17. 2. 48
407	7195526	L	Tourer	Chassis + Body				Untrimmed	... Nunns		18. 2. 48
408A	7195545	M	Coupe	Blue	Grey	Grey			George + Jobling		16. 3. 48
409	7187961	M	Coupe	Maroon	Red	Maroon			Mann Egerton	(Youngman)	15. 3. 48
410	7146144	M	Coupe	Red	Grey	Grey Beige			Harras	(Edwards)	19. 3. 48
411	7195710	L	Tourer + Body					Untrimmed	Dag Motors		24. 2. 48
412	7195784	L	Tourer + Body Brown Beige					Untrimmed	George + Jobling		24. 2. 48
413	7195838	M	Coupe	Black	Brown	Beige			Patterson	(Harvey-Every)	18. 3. 48
414	7195842	M	Coupe	Chassis					Tate	(Harrison)	24. 12. 48
415		J						the front car	NPG 250		
416	7193804	K	2 Seater	Maroon	Maroon	Maroon		1 Gear?	Bristol St		8. 6. 48

Grey don 1537

Chassis	Engine No.	Type	Body	Colour	Interior	Hood	Wheels	Remarks		Allocation		Delivered
417	7196782	K	2 Seater	Grey	Brown	Grey				Patterson		14. 5. 48
418	7196910	K	2 Seater	Grey	Brown	Grey				Taylors		14. 5. 48
419	7196924	K	2 Seater	Grey	Grey					Nunns		7. 5. 48
420	7197000	M	Coupe	Chassis						Goulds	(Lynn)	28. 2. 48
421	7196931	M	Coupe	Chassis						Adlards	(Putney)	1. 3. 48
422	7197015	L	Tourer	Chassis - Body	Blue grey			Untrimmed		Tate		23. 3. 48
423	7196928	L	Tourer	Chassis + Body				Untrimmed	No. Material	Nunns		31. 3. 48
424	7197009	K	2 Seater	Grey	Red	Grey				Tate		13. 5. 48
425	7196998	K	2 Seater	Blue	Blue	Black				Dag. Motors		15. 6. 48
426	7196999	L	Tourer	Chassis + Body				Untrimmed	No. Leather	English		25. 3. 48
427	7195658	M	Coupe	Chassis						Hughes	(Western)	12. 3. 48
428	7196610	M	Coupe	Chassis						Dag. Motors	(Robertson)	16. 3. 48
429	7196723	L	Tourer	Chassis						Taylors	(Whittachers)	12. 3. 48
430	7196603	M	Coupe	Chassis	Reg. No. LUM896 special body allocated 14" coupled end of Pontiac Cabs "Coplan says made by Len Francis" 11/12/48					Tate		11.12
431	7197341	M	Coupe	Chassis						Bristol St.	(Steele)	16. 3. 48
432	7195692	L	Tourer	Chassis						Taylors	(Whiteladies)	16. 3. 48
433	7196755	M	Coupe	Black	Red	Beige				Dag. Motors		14. 5. 48
434	7196744	M	Coupe	Black	Brown	Beige		NND 990 Letter from Englewood	USA	Goulds		20. 5. 48
435	7196744	K	2 Seater	Grey	Grey	Black				Nunns		19. 5. 48
436	7197339	K	2 Seater	Black	Red	Beige				George & Jobling		5. 5. 48
437	7196750	L	Tourer	Chassis						Universal		19. 3. 48
438	7197269	K	2 Seater	Maroon	Maroon	Maroon				Nunns		14. 6. 48
439	7197265	K	2 Seater	Primrose	Maroon	Maroon				L. Watkins		4. 6. 48
440	7195588	K L.H.	2 Seater	Black Maroon	Maroon	Beige			Mr Haworth (Rbort Germany)	Wooquay (Solomn)		22. 8-49
441	7197488	L L.H.	Tourer	Maroon	Maroon	Maroon				U.S.A. X		3. 6. 48
442	7191286	L	Tourer	Blue	Blue	Black				Universal		29. 5. 48
443	7197466	K	2 Seater	Chassis						Nunns	(Thompson Foxey)	5. 4. 48
444	7197496	K	2 Seater	Black	Brown	Beige				English		15. 6. 48
445	7197468	K	2 Seater	Grey	Red	Grey				George & Jobling		9. 6. 48
446	7197495	L	Tourer	Red	Red	Beige				Dag. Motors (Ferrari) Demo		6. 4. 48
447	7197656	M	Coupe	Chassis						Dag. Motors	(Ferrari)	6. 4. 48
448	7197470	K	2 Seater	Blue	Blue	Grey				Taylors	(Rexall)	21. 6. 48

Chassis	Engine	Type	Body	Colour	Interior	Hood	Wheels	Remarks		Allocation			Delivered
449	7197664	L	Tourer	Chassis + Body	Red	Maroon				Dag. Motors			5. 5. 48
450	7196743	M	Coupe	Maroon	Maroon	Maroon				Tate			11. 5. 48
451	7196783	M	Coupe	Black	Red	Black				English			13. 5. 48
452	7197469	M	Coupe	Grey	Grey	Grey				Patterson			16. 6. 48
453	7197486	M	Coupe	Maroon	Maroon	Maroon				Alexanders			26. 6. 48
454	7197659	M	Coupe	Grey	Grey	Green				Adlards (Mills)			5. 07. 48
455	7197658	L	Tourer	Chassis + Body	Red	Maroon		Untrimmed		Dag. Motors			3. 5. 48
456	7197713	L	Tourer	Chassis + Body	Brown	Beige		Untrimmed		Tate			23. 4. 48
457	7197711	K	2 Seater	Maroon	Maroon	Maroon				Tate			8. 6. 48
458	7197712	K	2 Seater	Blue	Blue	Blue				Tate			29. 6. 48
459	7197716	M	Coupe	Chassis	Grey	Grey				Goulds (Linfield)			5. 4. 48
460	7197714	L	Tourer	Chassis + Body				GGG 831 (1949)	Classed as 1949 mods.	George & Jobling (Callender)	see letter on file from Jackson.		5. 5. 48
461	7197662	K L.H.	2 Seater	Black	Brown	Beige				Nunns			1. 7. 48
462	7197850	K	2 Seater	Chassis						Portugal X X			21. 4. 48
463	7197611	M	Coupe	Grey	Grey	Grey				Hong Kong			22. 6. 48
464	7197815	M L.H.	Coupe	Grey	Grey	Grey				Adlards (Armitage)			19. 7. 48
465	7197769	M	Coupe	Maroon	Maroon	Beige				Egypt <			21. 6. 48
466	7197461	M	Coupe	Maroon	Maroon	Beige			New Gear	Taylors			23. 7. 48
467	7197808	K	2 Seater	Grey	Grey	Grey				~~Patterson~~ Adlards (Ratcliffe Sq.)			5. 7. 48
468	7197847	M	Coupe	Maroon	Maroon					Bristol St.			15. 6. 48
469	7198245	M	Coupe	Chassis						Bristol St.			23. 4. 48
470	7197743	M	Coupe	Grey	Grey	Grey				Adlards (McDowell)			2. 6. 48
471	7197807	M L.H.	Coupe	Maroon	Maroon	Maroon				Universal			18. 6. 48
472	7197829	M	Coupe	Blue	Grey	Blue				Nunns			22. 7. 48
473	7197848	L	Tourer	Chassis + Body	Maroon	Maroon		Untrimmed		Bristol St.			28. 4. 48
474	7198130	L	Tourer	Chassis						Nunns (Thomas)			19. 4. 48
475	7198113	L	Tourer	Chassis						Shennan (I.O.M.)			26. 4. 48
476	7197816	K	2 Seater	Black	Red	Beige				Bristol St.			5. 7. 48
477	7198131	K	2 Seater	Grey	Grey	Grey				~~Adlards~~ ~~( )~~ Patterson			23. 6. 48
478	7198117	L	Tourer	Chassis						Taylors (Whiteladies)			26. 4. 48
479	7198232	L	Tourer	Chassis						Taylors (Whiteladies)			27. 4. 48
480	7198283	K	2 Seater	Chassis						Taylors (Fisher)			26. 4. 48

Chassis	Engine	Type	Body	Colour	Interior	Hood	Wheels	Remarks		Allocation		Delivered
481	7198292	K̶	2 Seater	Grey	Grey	Grey				Bristol St		29. 6. 48
482	7197861	K	2 Seater	Grey to Brown	Grey Beige				(conversion to 2/H)		EGYPT	K	
483	7198317	L	Tourer	Chassis + Body					Untrimmed		George + Jobling		18. 5. 48
484	7198351	L	Tourer	Blue	Blue	Grey					Dag. Motors	(Mr Drawe)	24. 6. 48
485	7198210	K	2 Seater	Grey	Grey	Grey					Nunns		9. 7. 48
486	7198390	L	Tourer	Chassis + Body	maroon	maroon					Nunns		25. 5. 48
487	7198347b	K̶	2 Seater	Grey	Grey	Grey					Bristol St		9. 7. 48
488	7198187	K	2 Seater	Black	Maroon	Black	Maroon				Adlards	(E.D. abbott)	6. 8. 48
489	7191968	K	2 Seater	Chassis					Altered from K-276	Proto.	Whitiladies Garage		19. 7. 48
490													
491													
492													
493													
494													
495													
496													
497													
498													
499													
500	7188022	L	Tourer	Blue	Grey	Beige					George + Jobling		10. 2. 48
501	7196141	M	Coupe	Chassis							Dag. Motors	(Archway)	6. 2. 48
502	7196143	M	Coupe	Blue	Blue	Blue					Hartwells	(Mr Woolfe)	12. 3. 48
503	7196230	M	Coupe	Red	Maroon	Maroon					Hughes		25. 3. 48
504		M	Coupe	Chassis					less Engine +	Gear Box	Adlards (Archdale)		4. 2. 48
505	7195953	M	Coupe	Chassis							Adlards (Hall)		22. 3. 48
506	7196140	M	Coupe	Light Blue	Blue	Dark Blue					Nunns		12. 5. 48
507	7196121	M	Coupe	Blue	Blue	Grey					Furrows	(Barker)	53. 3. 48
508	7195693	L	Tourer + Body	maroon	maroon				Untrimmed		George + Jobling		
509	7195952	L	Tourer	Black	Brown	Beige			Tyresoles service record show on 26.5.48	mileage was 2089 "Dick Bartin"	Adlards	(Thompson)	2. 4. 48
510	7195768	K	2 Seater	Black							Demo... Sold		
511	7195140	K	2 Seater	Chassis							George + Jobling		13. 2. 48
512	7195855	L	Tourer	Chassis							Universal (Brooke...)		

Chassis	Engine	Type	Body	Colour	Interior	Hood	Wheels	Remarks		Allocation		Delivered
513	7196123	L	Tourer	Maroon light	Maroon	Maroon Dark				Nunns.		5. 5. 48
514	7198529	×M	Coupe	Blue	Blue	Blue				Demo		16. 7. 48
515	7195539	M	Coupe	Maroon	Brown Maroon	Beige			Old Type	Furrows		12. 6. 48
516	7195546	L	Tourer + Body						Untrimmed		Bristol St.		9. 3. 48
517	7195836	M	Coupe	Grey	Grey	Grey				Dag. Motors		7. 4. 48
518	7195659	K	2 Seater Chassis					Nov. 1985 Letter from E.J. Stutt, Auckland	N. Zealand — Paris out there.	Taylors	(Roberts)	1. 3. 48
519	7195653	K	2 Seater	Black	Maroon	Beige				English		29. 4. 48
520	7195654	L	Tourer	Blue	Blue	Grey				Taylors	31.3 48	31. 3. 48
521	7196602	L	Tourer Chassis							Dag. Motors	(Austin Garage)	4. 3. 48
522	7195837	M	Coupe Chassis							Bristol St.	(Riverley)	12. 3. 48
523	7195656	M	Coupe Chassis							Adlards	(Harrison)	15. 3. 48
524	7196231	L	Tourer Chassis + Body	Maroon	maroon	maroon		Untrimmed		Dag. Motors		7. 4. 48
525	7196745	L	Tourer Chassis + Body					Untrimmed	No Material	Nunns.		23. 3. 48
526	7196598	×M	Coupe	Black	Brown	Beige				Taylors		19. 5. 48
527	7196599	M L.H.	Coupe	Grey	Grey	Blue	NFC 139 This car used with Barkley caravan in U.S.A. in stock on Sept. 30, 1949 Experimental model.	Alan Gould 1949 Monte C. Rally (Back page 81) Cromwell Rd. with Canham + Shula Panter	Hartwells	× Regn. J.LW 489	12. 4. 48
528	7196910	M	Coupe	White	Green					U.S.A.		30. 3. 48
529	7198916	M	Coupe	Maroon	Maroon	Beige				KL0122 Allard (Demo.)		17. 2. 50
530	7198189	M	Coupe	Black	Brown	Beige				Hamilton		23. 6. 48
531	7198300	M	Coupe	Blue						Hamilton		23. 6. 48
532	7198192	M	Coupe Chassis							Gould		24. 4. 48
533	7198363	×M	Coupe Chassis							Tate	(Harrison)	14. 5. 48
534	7198346	M	Coupe Chassis							Tate	(Harrison)	7. 5. 48
535	7198532	M	Coupe Chassis							Few.		23. 4. 48
536	7198355	M	Coupe	Blue	Grey	Grey				Gould		28. 6. 48
537	7198364	M	Coupe	Blue	Blue	Blue	Stolen in London August 1967	Regn. JFS 293	Hughes		24. 6. 48
538	7198354	L	Tourer	Navy Blue	Grey	Grey				Gould's		14. 6. 48
539	7198350	K	2 Seater	Maroon	Maroon					Hartwells		
540	7198362	K	2 Seater Body + Chassis							Gert	× (broken down)	3.8.48
541	7198392	M	Coupe	Maroon	Red	Beige				English		20. 7. 48
542	7198393	M	Coupe	Blue	Blue	Blue				English		2. 7. 48
543	7198394	L	Tourer	Maroon	Maroon	Maroon				Canada	(Howard)	18. 6. 48
544	7198395	K	2 Seater	Maroon	Maroon	Maroon		FUG 257	B.J. Bennett now Hereford 4/9 1967	Taylors		30. 7. 48

Chassis	Engine	Type	Body	Colour	Interior	Hood	Wheels	Remarks			Allocation		Delivered
545	7198523	K	2 Seater	Red	Red						Hughes		26.7.48
546	7198515	M	Coupé	Maroon	Maroon	Maroon		Letter from T.G Moore to Sydney of Poor steering etc. not fitted with M'every 4	March 1959 Ballasalla, Isle of Man.		Taylors		30.6.48
547	7198538	M	Coupé	Black	Red	Beige					Mann Egerton		12.7.48
548	7198834	L	Tourer	Black	Brown	Beige					Frew	(Aitkin)	12.7.48
549	7198897	L	Tourer	Maroon	Red	Beige					Hartwells	(Cookson)	9.7.48
550	7198389	M	Coupé	Maroon	Maroon	Maroon					Dag. Motors		1.7.48
551	7198902	M	Coupé	Maroon	Maroon	Maroon					Nunns		16.7.48
552	7198904	M	Coupé	Black	Grey	Grey					Tate		6.7.48
553	7198514	K	2 Seater	Red	Red						Hughes		16.8.48
554	7198835	K	2 Seater	Red	Red	Beige					Furrons		23.8.48
555	7198903	M	Coupé	Black	Blue	Beige					Frew	X	6.7.48
556	7198900	M	Coupé	Black	Brown	Beige					New Zealand	(Ian Brown)	9.7.48
557	7198898	L	Tourer	Maroon	Brown	Beige					Patterson		19.7.48
558	7198905	K	2 Seater	Red	Red	Beige					Dag. Motors	X	16 12 49
559	7198906	K L.H.	2 Seater	Grey	Red	Grey					Uruguay (Salem - Emelas)		30 - 3 - 49
560	7198233	L	Tourer	Red	Brown	Beige					Dag Motors		23.7.48
561	7198824	M	Coupé	Grey	Grey	Grey					Dag. Motors	X	19.7.48
562	7199047	M L.H.	Coupé	Blue	Blue	Blue					Pakistan (Rowley)		19.7.48
563	7198907	M L.H.	Coupé	Maroon	Red	Beige					Nunns		22.7.48
564	7198901	M	Coupé	Grey	Blue	Blue					Adlards (Armitage)		22.7.48
565	7199064	M	Coupé	Chassis							Frew		22.5.48
566	7199076	M	Coupé	Chassis							Tate		8.6.48
567	7199272	M	Coupé	Chassis							Nunns	(Thomas)	26.6.48
568	7199071	M	Coupé	Grey	Blue	Blue					Hartwells	X	19.7.48
569	7199181	M	Coupé	Maroon	Maroon	Beige					Australia	X	7.7.48
570		L	Tourer	Chassis					Less Engine			Nunns	(Thomas Motors)	18.6.48
571	7199157	K	2 Seater	Chassis							Gould	(Gray)	29.5.48
572	7199206	K L.H.	2 Seater	Grey	Red	Grey					Uruguay (Salem - Emelas)		30 - 3 - 49
573	7199160	M	Coupé	Chassis							Adlards	(Stormont)	8.6.48
574	7199197	M L.H.	Coupé	Blue	Blue	Blue					Denmark	X	17.8.48
575		M	Coupé	Chassis					Less Engine			Nunns	(Thomas Motors)	10.6.48
576	7199435	M	Coupé	Chassis							Tate	(Tate)	

CHASSIS	ENGINE	TYPE	BODY	COLOUR	INTERIOR	HOOD	WHEELS	REMARKS		ALLOCATION		DELIVERED
577	7199260.7	K	2 Seater	Black	Maroon	Beige	Maroon			English	Monterey 1990 U.S.A McManus (notes)	28.7.48
578	7199439	M	Coupe	Chassis						Taté		25.6.48
579	7199371	M	Coupe	Maroon	Maroon	Beige			New Gear	George + Jobling		23.7.48
580	7199436	M	Coupe	Chassis						Universal		9.6.48
581	7199448	K	2 Seater	Grey	Brown	Grey				Dag. Motors		11.8.48
582	7199374	M	Coupe	Blue	Blue	Blue				Taylors		12.8.48
583	7199387	M	Coupe	Blue	Blue	Blue				Bristol St.		10.8.48
584	7199372	M	Coupe	Blue Grey	Blue Grey	Blue				Nunns		19.7.48
585	7199449	K	2 Seater	Blue	Blue	Grey			Export Mombassa	Creswick	✗	3.9.48
586	7199370	K	2 Seater	Grey	Brown	Grey	Grey			Hartwells		29.7.48
587	7199452	M	Coupe	Chassis						Central Motors	I.O.M	8.6.48
588	7199471	M L.H.	Coupe	Chassis						Taté		16.6.48
589	7199673	M	Coupe	Grey	Grey	Grey			Old Type	Hoffman		19.8.48
590	7199065	L	Tourer	Chassis						Taté	(Clarke)	15.6.48
591	7199664	K	2 Seater	Blue	Blue	Blue				English	1953 Now owned by Frost of Rochdale	8.9.48
592	7199220	K	2 Seater	Grey	Red					English	(Waring)	17.8.48
593	7199712	M	Coupe	Chassis						Adlards	(Putney)	16.6.48
594	7199499	M	Coupe	Blue Light	Blue	Blue				Demo. J4K272	This HD for Potters Loaned on Jubilee 49 Months.	Pay 97 book
595	7199438	K	2 Seater	Blue	Blue			see exposed. Purchased S/H in 1953 and shipped to California 12/53	Alpine?	J4K438 (Reg No) ✗ Shipped 10th July	24-7.48
596	7199676	L	Tourer	Chassis						Bristol St.		16.6.48
597	7199748	M	Coupe	Chassis						Dag. Motors	(Knox)	21.6.48
598	7199699	M	Coupe	Grey	Grey	Green				Australia	✗(Everett)	10.8.48
599	7199688	K	2 Seater	Blue	Blue	Black				English		
600	7199671	K	2 Seater	Blue	Blue	Blue				Dag. Motors		31.8.48
601	7199663	L	Tourer	Blue	Blue	Grey				English		4.8.48
602	7199788	L	Tourer	Chassis						George + Jobling		29.6.48
603	7199755	M	Coupe	Black	Red	Black				English		19.8.48
604	7199762	M	Coupe	Grey	Grey	Blue				Taté		12.8.48
605	7199273	K	2 Seater	Grey	Brown	Grey				Rhodesia	✗(Hundley)	20.12.48
606	7199993	M	Coupe	Chassis						Dag. Motors	(Ferrani)	24.6.48
607	7200060	K	2 Seater	Grey Blue	Brown Blue	Grey				Dag. Motors		
608	7200052	K	2 Seater	Maroon	Maroon	Maroon				Taté	S.O.R Taté	17.10.48

Chassis	Engie	Type	Body	Colour	Interior	Hood	Wheels	Remarks.			Allocation		Delivered
609	7199780	M	Coupe	Grey	Grey	Grey					Furrows		16.8.48
610	7199789	M	Coupe	Black	Red	Black					Harris		18.8.48
611	7199996	L	Tourer	Chassis							Taylor (Whiteladies)		7.7.48
612	7199989	K	2Str.	Maroon	Maroon	Maroon					Bristol St.		22.9.48
613	7199985	M	Coupe	Chassis							Adlards (Stevens)		8.7.48
614	7200014	M	Coupe	Black	Red	Black					Adlards (Okell)		9.9.48
615	7200061	M	Coupe	Black	Brown	Beige					Adlards (Turner)		19.8.48
616	7200000	L	Tourer	Blue	Blue	Grey				two gear	Tate		13.9.48
617	7200184	K	2Seater	Grey	Brown	Grey		MR RICE CKD 0760		two gear	Bristol St		16.9.48
618	7200071	M	Coupe	Black	Red	Beige					Adlards (Dr. Compton)		1.9.48
619	7200166	M	Coupe	Black	Brown	Beige					Goulds		24.9.48
620	7200187	M	Coupe	Maroon	Red	Beige		Tot		TOM TURNER. 1989	S. Rhodesia (Mr Ian Douglas)		23.8.48
621	7200193	K	2Seater	Grey	Blue	Blue					Alexanders		29.9.48
622	7200193	K	2Seater	Maroon	Maroon	Maroon					Demo.		6-9-50
623	7200158	M	Coupe	Maroon	Red	Beige					Universal (Bartholomew)		27.8.48
624	7200148	M	Coupe	Grey	Blue	Blue					George & Jobling		27.8.48
625	7200168	M	Coupe	Maroon	Red	Beige					Adlards (Stewart)		6.9.48
626	7200203	L	Tourer	Maroon	Maroon	Beige			Chis alt	No. altered 16 1510	Denmark. U.S.A. (Moss)		27.8.48
627	7200186	M	Saloon	Green	Orange			KLO 123			Adlards	Demo	8-12 68
628	7200216	M	Coupe	Chassis							Adlards (Potter)		10.7.48
629	7200291	K	2Str.	Grey	Blue	Blue					Kenya (Carnegie)		14.12.48
630	7200147	M	Coupe	Black	Red	Black					Hughes		9.9.48
631	7200208	M	Coupe	Grey	Blue	Blue		Blue after Shutton			Dag. motors		27.8.48
632	7200470	L	Tourer	Black	Red	Beige					George & Jobling		1.9.48
633	7200466	K	2Seater	Maroon	Maroon	Maroon					Bristol St.		26.11.48
634	7200345	M	Coupe	Chassis							Taylors (Blades)		16.7.48
635	7200149	M	Coupe	Grey	Grey	Green					Bristol St.		31.8.48
636	7200409	M	Coupe	Grey	Grey	Green					Hughes		3.9.48
637	7200473	L	Tourer	Chassis							Taylors (Whiteladies)		22.7.48
638	7200767	K	2Seater	Grey	Brown	Grey					Tate		9.9.49
639	7200952	K	2Seater	Grey	Brown						Adlards (Keswick)		20-5-49
640	7200374	M	Coupe	Grey	Blue	Blue					Patterson		30.8.48

Chassis	Engine	Type	Body	Colour	Interior	Hood	Wheels	Remarks		Allocation		Delivered
641	7200665	M	Coupe	Chassis					H G	Nunns		10. 8. 48
642	7200563	L	Tourer	Grey New Green	Grey	Grey		{ Allard O Club Newsletter Oct. 1986. Car now in Switzerland		Furrows	(Stevens)	7. 9. 48
643	7200816	K	2 Seater	Grey	Brown	Grey					English S.O.R.	26 11 48
644	7200970	K	2 Seater	Grey	Brown Light	Grey				English		23. 12. 48
645	7189886	M	Coupe	Black	Blue	Black				Frew		6. 9. 48
646	7200672	M	Coupe	Maroon	Red	Beige				English.		1.
647	7200763	K	2 Seater	Grey	Brown	Grey				Dagenham Mr	S.O.R Tate	14 . 11 . 47
648	7200817	K	2 Seater	Grey	Brown	Grey.				Bristol St.	S.O.R Central Motors	22 - 2 - 49
649	7200390	M	Coupe	Chassis						Frew		31.7.48.
650	7200944	M	Coupe	Black	Blue	Beige				Alexanders		3. 9. 48
651	7200951	M	Coupe	Black	Maroon	Black				Taylors		8. 9. 48
652	7200762	L	Tourer	Grey	Grey	Grey				English		18. 10. 48
653	7200754	K	2 Seater	Grey	Brown	Grey				Dag. Motors	(Chaseside Motors)	6. - 5 - 49
654	7200757a	K	2 Seater	Maroon	Maroon	Maroon		Ray N Letter, now Peter Bland U.SA Jan. 1972		Nunns.	Central Motors S.O.R	28 . 12 . 49
655	7200783	K	2 Seater	Maroon	Maroon	Maroon				Bristol St		3. 12. 48.
656	7200774	M	Coupe	Maroon	Red	Maroon				Dag. Motors		16. 9. 48
657	7200946	M	Coupe	Black	Red	Beige				Harris		9. 9. 48
658	7200939	M	Coupe	Maroon	Maroon	Beige				Hughes		16. 9. 48
659	7200478	M	Coupe	Chassis						Nunns.		21. 7.48
660	7200661	M	Coupe	Chassis						Bristol St.		21.7.48
661	7200745	M	Coupe	Chassis						Bristol St		21.7.48
662	7200702	M	Coupe	Chassis						Nunns		20. 7.48
663	7200694	M	Coupe	Chassis					new gear	Tate		30.7.48
664	7200669	M	Coupe	Chassis					new gear	Tate		29.7.48
665	7187957	M	Coupe	Chassis					new gear	Tate		29.7.48
666	7200748	M	Coupe	Chassis					new gear	Taylors		24. 8. 48
667	7200722	M	Coupe	Chassis					new gears	Taylors		12. 8. 48
668	7200692	M	Coupe	Chassis				Bonnet fitted	new gear	Kenya		20. 8. 48
669												
670	7200768	L	Tourer	Grey	Grey	Grey		SOLD TO: Mr D.R. SIMPKIN "THE RED HOUSE" QUORN LEICESTERSHIRE.		Demo. K.G.C.895.		TUE: 21 JUNE 49
671	7200738	L	Tourer	Red	Maroon	Beige				English		7. 10. 48
672	7200765	L	Tourer	Chassis				?		Taylors		1. 9. 48

Chassis	Engine	Type	Body	Colour	Interior Hood	Hood Wheels	Remarks		Association		Delivered
673	7200943	M	Coupé	Maroon	Maroon	Beige	1995		Taylors		16.9.48
674	7200770	M	Coupé	Black	Grey	Grey	Under restoration in Minehead		Dagenham Motors		9.9.48
675	7200943	L L.H.	Tourer	Maroon	Maroon	Beige			U.S.A (Illinois Hamill)		23.8.48
676	7202305	M L.H.	Coupé	Chassis					Denmark (Returned & Broken down)		17.8.48
677	7202507	M	Coupé	Blue	Blue	Blue			Egypt Universal (Standhill)		4-2-49
678	7200982	M L.H.	Coupé	Blue	Blue	Blue			Tate		21.9.48
679	7200978	L	Tourer	Black	Red	Beige			U.S.A (Hoffman)		30.8.48
680	7200776	K	2 Seater	Chassis					Nunns		27.8.48
681	7200976	K	2 Seater	Maroon	Maroon	Maroon			Universal		28.11.49
682	7200766	M	Coupé	Maroon	Red	Beige			Bristol St.		17.9.48
683	7200769	M	Coupé	Maroon	Red	Maroon			English		13.9.48
684	7200771	M	Coupé	Maroon	Red	Beige			Tate		17.9.48
685	7200746	K	2 Seater	Blue	Blue	Blue	Show	new gear	Mann Egerton (W.H. King)		15.11.48
686	7202521	K	2 Seater	Bronze	Red	Beige	Show		Adlards Kenya (Abbott)		14.12.48
687	7200743	M	Coupé	Grey	Grey	Grey	Show		Furrows		25.11.48
688	7200693	L	Tourer	Maroon	Maroon	Maroon	Show		Adlards		24.11.48
689	7200755	L	Tourer	Black	Blue	Grey			Dag. Motors (Alderton)		30.9.48
690	7200223	L	Tourer	Grey	Grey	Grey			Goulds		15.10.48
691	7202186	K	2 Seater	Maroon	Maroon	Maroon			Furrows Wayne Grt.K.		1 12 48
692	7200736	M	Coupé	Blue	Blue	Blue			Hartwells		22.9.48
693	7200698	M	Coupé	Blue	Blue	Blue			Furrows		24.9.48
694	7200490	L	Tourer	Grey	Red	Grey			Nunns		25.10.48
695	7202236	L	Tourer	Blue	Blue	Grey			Showroom Dag. Motors		8-11-48
696	7200475	K	2 Seater	Maroon	Maroon	Maroon			Adlards		
697	7200697	M	Coupé	Blue	Blue	Blue			Universal		17.9.48
698	7200982	M	Coupé	Black	Grey	Grey	colour alteration agreed		Goulds		27.9.48
699	7202238	K	2 Seater	Grey	Blue	Blue Grey	Greyhill (Demo) Germany	Cancelled By of R. authority sent to Japan Germany			22-8-49
700	7200683	L	Tourer	Grey	Grey	Grey			Kenya		15.12.48
701	720080	M	Coupé	Blue	Blue	Blue			Nunns		30.9.48
702	7202468	M	Coupé	Maroon	Red	Maroon			Tate		27.9.48
703	7200881	M	Coupé	Maroon	Red	Maroon			Nunns		9.10.48
704	7200772	M	Coupé	Chassis					Tate of Leeds		13.9.48

Chassis	Engine	Type	Body	Colour	Interior	Hood	Wheels	Remarks	Allocation	Delivered
705	7200726	M	Coupe	Maroon	Brown	Maroon			Bristol St.	29.9.48
706	7200728	M	Coupe	Black	Grey	Grey			Frew	1.10.48
707	7200727	M	Coupe	Black	Grey	Grey			Alexanders	30.9.48
708	7200402	K	2Seater	Chassis					Goulds	14.9.48
709	7202469	M	Coupe	Black	Grey	Grey			Adlards (Shaffer)	2.10.48
710	7202462	M	Coupe	Green	Brown	Green			Nunns	15.10.48
711	7202488	M	Coupe	Black	Brown	Grey			Hartwells	1.10.48
712	7202514	M	Coupe	Grey	Blue	Blue			George + Jobling	11.10.48
713	7200761	K	2Seater	Grey	Brown	Grey			Universal	
714	7202450	M	Coupe	Green	Grey	Grey			Furrows	15.11.48
715	7202486	M	Coupe	Grey	Grey	Blue Grey			Furrows	12.10.48
716	7202454	M	Coupe	Maroon	Red	Buge			Dag Motors ~~Goulds~~ Tate M	28-2-49
717	7200764	K	2Seater	Grey	Brown	Grey			Tate ~~Tate~~	5.11.47
718	7200471	L	Tourer	Grey	Grey	Black			Frew	1.11.48
719	7200691	M L-H	Coupe	N.Blue	Blue	Black		Special 2 seater	Demo.	
720	7202506	M	Coupe	Black	Grey	Grey			Adlards	11.48
721	7202491	M	Coupe	Blue	Buge	Blue			Adlards (Dr Pearlman)	2.12.48
722	7202949	M	Coupe	Grey	Grey	Grey			English	12.10.48
723	7202946	M	Coupe	Grey	Maroon	Grey			Taylor	12.11.48
724	7200557	K	2Seater	Maroon	Maroon			Tonneau cover, Spare Wheel Lock	Nunns	17-1-49
725	7202444	M	Coupe	Chassis					Adlards	6.10.48
726	7202971	M	Coupe	Black	Grey	Grey			Adlards.	14.10.48
727	7202988	M	Coupe	Chassis				less Head lamps, Bulkhead, Petrol	Pickering (George Jobling)	4.10.48
728	7202528	K	2Seater	Blue	Blue	Blue			Goulds	23.1.50
729	7202315	L	Tourer	Cream	Brown	Black			Frew	13.12.48
730	7202464	M	Coupe	Black	Maroon	Buge			Adlards (Barkers)	14.10.48
731	7202466	M	Coupe	Chassis					Universal (Lindley)	14.9.48
732	7202447	M	Coupe	Chassis					Bristol St	23.9.48
733	7202998	M	Coupe	Grey	Blue	Blue			Patterson	15.10.48
734	7202999	M	Coupe	Grey	Grey	Blue Grey			Hartwells	16.10.48
735	7203004	M	Coupe	Grey	Grey	Blue Grey			Dag Motors	15.10.48
736	7202944	M	Coupe	Chassis					Bristol St.	22.9.48

4/11/48

Chassis	Engine	Chassis	Body	Colour	Interior	Hood	Wheels	Remarks	Remarks	Allocation	Delivered
737	7202953	M	Coupe	Chassis						Nunns	24.9.48
738	7202979	M	Coupe	Maroon	Brown	Beige				Taylors	20.10.48
739	7202951	M	Coupe	Blue	Grey	Blue				English	1.11.48
740	7202960	M	Coupe	Maroon	Maroon	Beige				Demo	6-5-49
741	7203195	M	Coupe	Chassis						Furrows	30.9.48
742	7202408	K	2 Seater	Blue	Blue	Blue				Hughes	21-1-49
743	7202527	L	Tourer	Maroon	Brown	Beige		Tonneau Cover		Harris	2.12.48
744	7202987	M	Coupe	Maroon	Maroon	Beige				Nunns	28.10.48
745	7202936	M	Coupe	Maroon	Maroon	Beige		Tylees service records show Chis... MRB 441		Universal	22.10.48
746	7203157	M	Coupe	Maroon	Brown	Beige				Tate	29.10.48
747	7202978	M	Coupe	Maroon	Brown	Beige				Adlards (Seddon)	26.10.48
748	7203194	M	Coupe	Chassis					Bonnet fitted	George Jobling	22.10.48
749	7203591	M	Coupe	Chassis						Tate	15.10.48
750	7202562	M	Coupe	Black	Brown	Beige				English	14.11.48
751	7202168	M	Coupe	Blue	Blue	Blue				Dag. Motors	
752	7203450	M	Coupe	Blue	Blue	Blue				Frew	
753	7242593	M	Coupe	Grey	Grey	Grey				Goulds	19.11.48
754	7203627	M	Coupe	Chassis						~~Furrows~~ Dag. Motors	17.11.48
755	7202175	K	Seater	Red	Red	Beige				Bristol St.	21-4-49
756	7203506	M	Coupe	Blue	Blue	Blue				Harris	9.11.48
757	7202218	L	Tourer	Maroon	Maroon	Beige				English	26.11.48
758	7203465	M	Coupe	Grey	Grey	Grey				Frew	8.12.48
759	7203491	M	Coupe	Black	Grey	Beige				Nunns	10.11.48
760	7203768	M	Coupe	Chassis						Adlards (Young)	18.11.48
761	7203589	M	Coupe	Black	Brown	Black				Mann Egerton (W.King)	17.11.48
762	7203590	M	Coupe	Black	Brown	Black				Dag. Motors	17.11.48
763	7202313	K	2 Seater								
764	7203644	M	Coupe	Black	Grey	Beige				Taylors	3.12.48
765	7203605	M	Coupe	Blue	Blue	Blue				Taylors	5.11.48
766	7203774	M	Coupe	Chassis						Bristol St.	21.10.48
767	7203610	M	Coupe	Blue	Blue	Blue				Adlards (Skin)	9.11.48
768	7203625	M	Coupe	Maroon	Maroon	Beige			English		25-1-49

CHASSIS	ENGINE	TYPE	BODY	COLOUR	INTERIOR	HOOD	WHEELS	REMARKS		ALLOCATION		DELIVERIES
769	7203789	M	Coupe	Chassis					Bonnet fitted	Harris		23.11.48
770	7202514	K	2 Seater	Maroon	Maroon	Maroon		~~Fitted~~		USA (Alenkes)	S.O.R. Gould	26.1.50.
771	7202538	L	Tourer	Maroon	Maroon	Buge		Mr. Jarratt.		Italy		6.12.48
772	7202171	L	Tourer	Maroon	Brown	Buge		at 51, "Rich Red on 12-1-57" "Prepare for clocks"	NSTEI Ray's Roadster 85 New Member 772 W.Chisholm Hollywood reg L GY 397	Dag. Motors		22.12.48
773	7200408	L	Tourer	Maroon	Brown	Buge				Bristol St		1.12.48
774	7221938 / 7202514	K2 (LH)	2 Seater	Red nose	Red	Maroon			Coil Springs	Uruguay.	ADC Newsletter June 96 Racing in Montevideo!	9.2.50
775	7200477	K	2 Seater	Blue	Blue	Blue				Tate		15.7.48
776	7203624	M	Coupe	Grey	Grey	Blue Grey				Nunns		8.12.48
777	7203623	M	Coupe	Maroon	Maroon	Buge		Fatal Crash 4 child	Number transferred	Patterson	Lammoga JM 792	28.11.48
778	7203643	M	Coupe	Grey		Blue Grey				Nunns.		7.12.48
779	7203784	M	Coupe	Chassis				?		~~Hartwells~~ Furrows		18.11.48
780	7203766	M	Coupe	Black	Maroon	Buge				George & Jobling		17.11.48
781	7203884	M	Coupe	Blue	Blue	Blue				Harris		11.12.48
782	7203893	M	Coupe	Chassis				Bonnet fitted		George & Jobling	(Stobcross)	15.11.48
783	7203734	M	Coupe	Grey	Grey	Grey				English		17.11.48
784	7203883	M	Coupe	Grey	Grey	Grey				Bristol St.		17.11.48
785	7203735	M	Coupe	Maroon	Maroon	Buge				Hughes	(Dr Scarborough)	25.11.48
786	720733	M	Coupe	Chassis				Eng No. Invoice by	711-C. 7203733.	Hartwells		30.11.48
787	7203885	M	Coupe	Chassis		Black		Bonnet fitted		Tate		23.11.48
788	7203948	M	Coupe	Maroon	Maroon	Beige				George & Jobling		3.12.48
789	7203953	M	Coupe	Blue	Blue	Blue				English		17.12.48
790	7203954	M	Coupe	Maroon	Maroon	Buge				Tate		2.12.48
791	7203882	M	Coupe	Chassis						Furrows.		17.11.48
792	7204181	L	Tourer	Black	Blue	Beige				Hughes.		18.8.49
793	7204083	M	Coupe	Maroon	Maroon	Buge				Dag. Motors		7.12.48
794	7204089	M	Coupe	Maroon	Maroon	Buge				~~Furrows~~ Patterson	(County Garage)	17.1.49
795	7203943	M	Coupe	Chassis nose						English		8.11.48
796	7204739	K	2 Seater	Blue	Blue	Blue				Bristol St.		31-3-50
797	7204084	M	Coupe	Blue	Blue	Blue				Nunns		3.12.48
798	7204067	M	Coupe	Maroon	Maroon	Beige				Alexanders		13.12.48
799	7203959	M	Coupe	Chassis						Hartwells		9.11.48
800	7204759	L	Tourer	Blue	Brown	Buge				Adlards (Grime)		17.12.48

CHASSIS	ENGINE	TYPE	BODY	COLOUR	INTERIOR	HOOD	WHEELS	REMARKS		ALLOCATION		DELIVERIES
801	7204090	M	Coupe	Grey	Grey	Blue				Bristol St		23 - 2 - 49
802	7204091	M	Coupe	Classis	Grey	Grey				Bristol St Dag Motors	Cancelled	4 - 2 - 49
803	7204094	M	Coupe	Maroon	Maroon	Beige				Hartwells		
804	7204233	M	Coupe	Black	Red	Black				Goulds		23. 12. 48
805	7204248	M	Coupe	Blue	Blue	Blue				Universal		8 - 12 - 48
806	7203958	M	Coupe	Grey	Red	Grey			Export Malaya	M Plunkett		18 - 3 - 49
807	7204738	L	Tourer	Blue	Blue	Beige				Tate	see Ghoulds	5 11 49
808	7204186	M	Coupe	Blue	Blue	Blue				Bristol St		14 12 48
809	7204312	M	Coupe	Blue	Blue	Blue				Nunns		10. 12. 48
810	7204257	M	Coupe	Charcoal				Bonnet	fitted			15. 12. 48
811	7204491	K	2 Seater	Black	Maroon	Maroon			Gear on stearing	Dag. Motors	(Richards)	3 - 5 - 49
812	7204304	M	Coupe	Red	Red	Beige				Malta		28 - 12 - 48
813	7204368	M	Coupe	Grey	Blue	Blue				English		4 - 1 - 49
814	7203464	M	Coupe	Grey	Maroon	Grey				Adlards Furrows (Nuffield)		23 - 2 - 49
815	7203384	L	Tourer	Maroon	Maroon	Maroon				Dagenam Mtr.		11 . 11 . 49
816	7204111	M	Coupe	Black	Brown	Beige				Alexanders		17 - 3 - 49
817	7204415	M	Coupe	Maroon	Maroon	Beige				Tate		7 - 3 - 49
818	7204333	M	Coupe	Black	Red	Black				Germany Adlards		9 - 2 - 49
819	7204313	M	Coupe	Black	Blue	Black				Kenya		17. 12. 48
820	7204413	M	Coupe	Maroon	Maroon	Beige				Hughes		17 - 1 - 49
821	7204461	M	Coupe	Black	Brown	Beige				Universal		18 - 2 - 49
822	7204731	L	Tourer	Grey	Blue	Black		LONDON To SEKIN RALLY 1960	Kate & John Morley-Tucker	Dag. Motors	see Wrenbotsut	20 - 5 - 49
823	7204436	M	Coupe	Black	Red	Black				Furrows		21. 12. 48
824	7204450	M	Coupe	Blue	Blue	Blue				Patterson		16. 12. 48
825	7204525	M	Coupe	Black	Brown	Beige				Nunns		17 - 2 - 49
826	7204737	K	2 Seater	Blue	Blue	Blue				Adlards	(Peacocks)	3 - 2 - 49
827	7204466	M	Coupe	Blue	Blue	Blue				Nunns		23. 12. 48
828	7204074	M	Coupe	Grey	Blue	Blue				Universal		13 - 1 - 49
829	7204526	M	Coupe	Grey	Blue	Blue				Tate		11 - 1 - 49
830	7204740	L	Tourer	Grey	Grey	Grey				Hartwells Patterson		7. 6. 49
831	7206817	M	Coupe	Chassis				Bonnet	No Bonnet	Furrows		10 - 3 - 49
832	7204556	M	Coupe	Black	Brown	Beige				English		22 - 2 - 49

CHASIS	ENGINE	TYPE	BODY	COLOUR	INTERIOR	HOOD	WHEELS	REMARKS		ALLOCATION		DELIVERIES
833	7204527	M	Coupe	Blue	Blue	Blue			~~Dag. Motors~~	Nunns		31-1-49
834	7204486	M	Coupe	Black	Maroon	Black		9SF, 756		~~Furrows~~	Alexanders		27-1-49
835	7204573	M	Coupe	Grey	Grey	Blue				Hamilton		7-1-49
836	7204587	M	Coupe	Chassis				Bonnet fitted	Adlards (Welbecks)	Heavy Type rear spring	17.12.48
837	7204735	L	Tourer	Blue	Blue	Beige			Dag. Motors		16 12 48
838	7204597	M	Coupe	Black	Blue Red Maroon	Black			George + Jobling		23.12.48 21 Jan 49. Warranty
839	7204586	M	Coupe	Maroon	Red Maroon	Beige			Bristol St		18-1-49 20 Jan 49. Warranty
840	7204658	M	Coupe	Chassis				Bonnet taken off	~~Bonnet fitted~~ Tate		19-1-49
841	7223840	*K2 LH	2 Seater	Grey	Grey	Grey		Coil Springs	Uruguay		9.2.50
842	7204598	M	Coupe	Grey	Blue	Blue			Mann Egerton (W King)		3-1-49
843	7204589	M	Coupe	Grey	Blue	Blue			Bristol St		10-1-49
844	7204847	M	Coupe	Chassis				Bonnet taken off	~~Bonnet fitted~~ Furrows		23-3-49
845	7204736	L	Tourer	Grey	Grey	Grey			Hartwells		25-2-49
846	7206530	M	Coupe	Blue	Blue	Blue			~~Coil Springs~~ Bristol St.		16-2-49
847	7206593	M	Coupe	Blue	Blue	Blue			Bristol St.		16-2-49
848	7204668	M	Coupe	Black	Grey	Black			Frews		23.12.48
849	7204665	M	Coupe	Black	Red	Beige			Tate		23.12.48
850	7204756	M	Coupe	Black	Grey	Black			Alexanders		30-12-48
851	7206589	M	Coupe	Grey	Grey	Grey			Universal		2-3-49
852	7206928	L	Tourer	Maroon	Maroon	Beige			Adlards		19-3-49 1-48
853	7204657	M	Coupe	Grey	Grey	Blue			Dag. Motors		22 Jan. 49.
854	7204769	M	Coupe	Grey	Red	Grey			Nunns		21-1-49
855	7206586	M	Coupe	Black	Maroon	Black		?	George + Jobling		18-2-49
856	7207042	L	Tourer	Blue	Blue	Black			Uruguay Salem		8 12 49
857	7204742	M	Coupe	Grey	Grey	Blue		First NNU 326 Sabon Goalan NNU 326	Adlards (Haynes)		11-1-49
858	7204635	M	Coupe	Maroon	Maroon	Beige		Since reced ally 22-2-50 service accident-repair 19-9-52	Universal (Fletcher)		28-1-49
859	7207238	M	Coupe	Grey	Grey	Maroon			~~Adlards~~ English		23-2-49
860	7206952	L	Tourer	Blue	Blue	Grey			TATE OF LEEDS. BAWTRY MOTOR Cº		6-5-49
861	7204641	M	Coupe	Maroon	Red Maroon	Beige			Taylors		18-1-49
862	7204819	M	Coupe	Blue	Grey	Grey			English		21-1-49
863	7202150	M	Coupe	Maroon	Maroon	Beige			~~Nunns~~ ~~English~~ Nunns		21-1-49
864	7204615	M	Coupe	Blue	Blue	Blue			Tate		25-1-49

CHASSIS	ENGINE	TYPE	BODY	COLOUR	INTERIOR	HOOD	WHEELS	REMARKS		ALLOCATION	DELIVERIES.
865	7204624	M	Coupe	Maroon	Red	Beige				George Jobling	19-1-49
866	7206963	L	Tourer	Grey	Grey	Black				Dag. Motors	3-9-49
867	7207204	L	Tourer	Maroon	Red	Beige				Adlards (Soames & ...)	24-8-49
868	7207804	L	Tourer	Grey	Grey	Black		steering column gear change		Nunns	17-10-49
869	7204812	M	Coupe	Maroon	Red	Beige				Tate	21-1-49
870	7204844	M	Coupe	Black	Maroon	Beige				Bristol St	28-1-49
871	7204805	M	Coupe	Blue	Blue	Blue				Dag. Motors	19-1-49 Warranty 20 Jan 49
872	7206520	M	Coupe	Blue	Blue	Grey				Patterson	12-2-49
873	7206587	M	Coupe	Blue	Grey	Grey				Adlards (Hawthys Hudgley)	27-1-49
874	7206612	M	Coupe	Black	Maroon	Black Beige				Dag. Motors (Mann Egerton)	28-1-49
875	7204934	M	Coupe	Blue	Blue	Blue				Adlards (Peacock)	25-1-49
876	7204973	M	Coupe	Black	Blue	Black				Dag. Motors	28-1-49
877	7206613	M	Coupe	Blue	Blue	Blue				Mann Egerton	27-1-49
878	7206526	M	Coupe	Black	Blue	Grey				Universal	2-2-49
879	7206667	M	Coupe	Black	Maroon	Beige				Goulds	27-1-49
880	7206627	M	Coupe	Grey	Blue	Blue				English	7-2-49
881	7206811	M	Coupe	Grey	Blue	Blue				Dag. Motors	2-2-49
882	7206591	M	Coupe	Grey	Grey	Grey				Furrows	2-2-49
883	7206...	M	Coupe	Black	Brown	Beige				English	2-2-49
884	7206...	M	Coupe	Black	Brown	Beige		HVE57A	M.HILL REIGATE AOC NIL 8/9 1967	Tate	2-2-49
885	7206...	M LH	Coupe	Grey	Grey	Grey				Tate	10-2-49
886	7186429	K	2 Seater	Chassis						Portugal	16.12.48
887	7206871	M LH	Coupe	Grey	Grey	Grey				U.S.A. (Forbes)	4-5-49
888	20074 / 7205936	J	2 Seater	...	Red					Ref to S.M.A. KXC 170 Built after June 1949	23.3.51
889	7206771	M	Coupe	Blue	Grey	Grey				Adlards (Mrs. Wild)	21-2-49
890	7206864	M	Coupe	Maroon	Maroon	Beige				Dag. Motors (Dr. Watton)	11-2-49
891	7206776	M	Coupe	Maroon	Maroon	Beige				Tate	15-2-49
892	7207010	M	Coupe	Maroon	Maroon	Beige				Tate	10-2-49
893	7206635	M	Coupe Grey	Grey	Grey	Black				Frew	14-2-49
894	7207143	M	Coupe	Maroon	Red	Beige				George & Jobling	14-2-49
895	7207122	M	Coupe	Maroon	Maroon	Beige				Bristol St	25-2-49
896	7207271	M	Coupe	Blue	Blue	Blue				Mann Egerton (W. King)	14-2-49

CHASSIS	ENGINE	TYPE	BODY	COLOUR	INTERIOR	HOOD	WHEEL SPTS.	DISPOSITION	H.P.	DELIVERIES
897	7207123	M	Coupe	Maroon	Red	Beige		Tate		25 - 2 - 49
898	7207288	M	Coupe	Maroon	Red	Beige		Frew		28 - 2 - 49
899	7207148	M	Coupe	Grey	Blue	Blue		Dag. Motors.		23 - 2 - 49
900	7207110	M	Coupe	Blue	Blue	Blue		Tate		8 - 3 - 49
901	7207201	M	Coupe	Maroon	Maroon	Beige		Tate		9 - 3 - 49
902	7207805	L	Tourer	Red	Red	Beige		Kenya.	E.1.E	29 - 3 - 49
903	7207826	L	Tourer	Blue	Grey	Beige		Dagenham Mtrs		14 11 49
904	7207818	L	Tourer	Maroon	Red	Beige		Venezuela	L. Bockh.	8 12 49
905	7207822	L	Tourer	Maroon	Red	Beige		Adlards	(Mr. Adkin)	24 2 50
906										
907	—	Continued at 1,000 series [the M coupe] March 1949								
908										
909										
910										
911										
912										
913										
914										
915										
916										
917										
918										
919										
920										
921										
922										
923										
924										
925										
926										
927										
928										

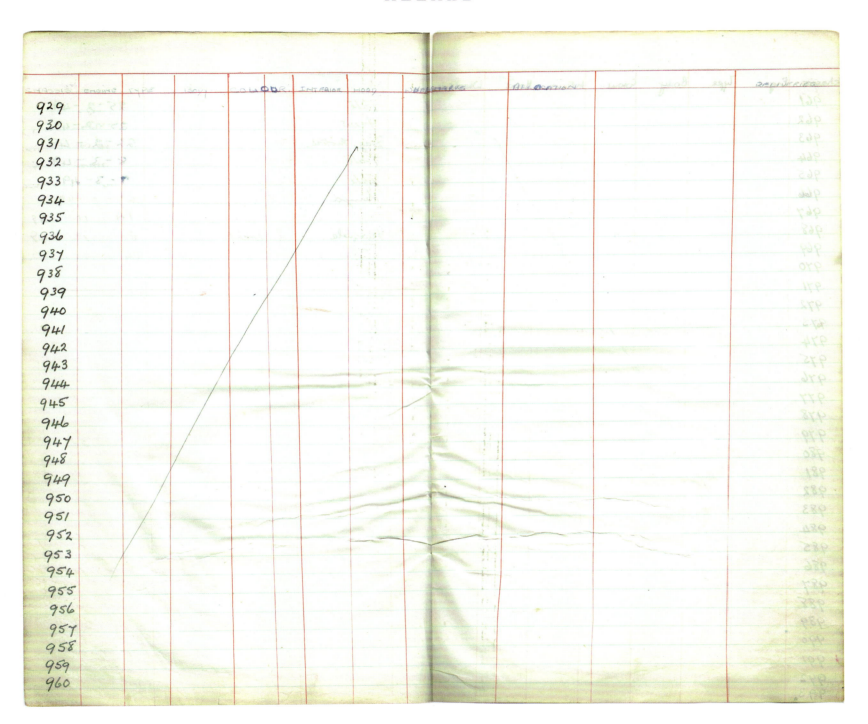

CHASSIS	ENGINE	TYPE	BODY	COLOUR	INTERIOR	HOOD	TRIMMINGS	ALLOCATION				REGISTERED
929												
930												
931												
932												
933												
934												
935												
936												
937												
938												
939												
940												
941												
942												
943												
944												
945												
946												
947												
948												
949												
950												
951												
952												
953												
954												
955												
956												
957												
958												
959												
960												

chassis	Engine	Type	Body	Colour	Interior	Hood	Wheels	ts	Allocation			Delivered	
961													
962													
963													
964													
965													
966													
967													
968													
969													
970													
971													
972													
973													
974													
975													
976													
977													
978													
979													
980													
981													
982													
983													
984													
985													
986													
987													
988													
989													
990													
991													
992													
993													

Chassis	Engine	Type	Body	Colour	Interior	Hood	Wheels	Remarks	Allocation		Deliveries
993											
994											
995											
996											
997											
998											
999											
1000	7207230	M	Coupe	Blue	Blue	Blue			Tate		7 - 3 - 49.
1001	7207231	M	Coupe	Blue	Blue	Blue			Dag. Motors	(H.C. Paul)	5 - 3 - 49.
1002	7207111	M	Coupe	Grey	Blue	Grey			English		11 - 3 - 49
1003	7207144	M	Coupe	Grey	Blue	Blue			Adlards	(W. Straker)	9 - 3 - 49.
1004	7207582	M	Coupe	Blue	Grey	Blue			English		9 - 3 - 49.
1005	7207734	M	Coupe	Black	Grey	Black			Adlards	(L.H. Mitchell)	2 - 3 - 49.
1006	7207750	M	Coupe	Blue	Blue	Blue			Adlards	(Hartley & Midgley)	4 - 3 - 49.
1007	7207733	M	Coupe	Grey	Grey	Blue			Adlards		5 - 3 - 49.
1008	7207021	M	Grey	Grey	Black	Grey			Tate		11 - 3 - 49
1009	7207938	M	Coupe	Grey		Grey					11 - 3 - 49
1010	7207779	M	Coupe	Grey	Blue	Blue			Export Kenya	(Capt. Mc.Rea)	31 - 3 - 49
1011	7207362	M	Coupe	Grey	Grey	Blue			Furrows.		17 - 3 - 49
1012	7207297	M	Coupe	Black	Grey	Black			English		21 - 3 - 49
1013	7207757	M	Coupe	Black	Maroon	Golden Brown			Dag. Motors		23 - 3 - 49
1014	7207258	M	Coupe	Black	Red	Black			Alexanders		17 - 3 - 49
1015	7206832	M	Coupe	Grey	Grey	Blue			English		23 - 3 - 49
1016	7209290	M	Coupe	Grey	Maroon	Grey			Adlards	(Clark)	29 - 3 - 49
1017	7209271	M	Coupe	Black	Brown	Brown			Dag. Motors	(m. Baker)	18 - 3 - 49
1018	7209273	M	Coupe	Black	Maroon	Beige			Germany		26 - 3 - 49.
1019	7209286	M	Coupe	Maroon	Red	Beige			English		21 - 3 - 49
1020	7209291	M	Coupe	Maroon	Maroon	Beige			Adlards	(Phillips)	18 - 3 - 49
1021	7209281	M	Coupe	Maroon	Maroon	Beige			Dag. Motors	(Offord)	18 - 3 - 49
1022	7209287	M	Coupe	Maroon	Maroon	Beige			Adlards.	(Hartley & Midgley)	23 - 3 - 49
1023	7209393	M	Coupe	Maroon	Maroon	Beige			Bristol St.		21 - 3 - 49.
1024	7209269	M	Coupe	Blue	Blue	Blue			Marmon Egerton		23 - 3 - 49.
1025	7209387	M	Coupe	Blue	Blue	Blue			Bristol St.		22 - 3 - 49.

Chassis	Engine	Type	Body	Colour	Interior	Hood	Wheels	Remarks	Allocation		Delivered
1026	7209399	M	Coupe	Blue	Red	Blue			Nunns		22 - 3 - 49
1027	7209272	M	Coupe	Blue	Blue	Blue			Universal		28 - 5 - 49
1028	7209388	M	Coupe	Cream	Red	Beige			E.T.E. Kenya		29 - 3 - 49
1029	7209396	M	Coupe	Grey	Red	Grey			Alexanders	(Black)	29 - 3 - 49
1030	7207815	M	Coupe	Grey	Blue	Grey			~~Gray~~ Adlards	(Peacocks)	29 - 3 - 49
1031	7206840	M	Coupe	Blue	Blue	Blue			Nunns	(R. Holt)	19 - 4 - 49
1032	7207281	M	Coupe	Grey	Grey	~~Blue~~ Blue			Addards	(Mears)	1 - 4 - 49
1033	7209682	M	Coupe	Grey	Grey	Grey			Hartwells		31 - 3 - 49
1034	7209609	M	Coupe	Grey	Grey	Blue			Bristol St.		2 - 4 - 49
1035	7209616	M	Coupe	Black	Maroon	Beige			Universal		30 - 3 - 49
1036	7209611	M	Coupe	Black	Maroon	Beige			Bristol St.		11 - 4 - 49
1037	7209615	M	Coupe	Black	Blue	Black			Frews		5 - 4 - 49
1038	7209747	M	Coupe	Black	Blue	Black			English		4 - 4 - 49
1039	7209762	M	Coupe	Black	Maroon	Beige			English		13 - 4 - 49
1040	7209403	M	Coupe	Maroon	Red	Maroon			George & Jobling		8 - 4 - 49
1041	7209743	M	Coupe	Maroon	Maroon	Beige			Bristol St.		9 - 4 - 49
1042	7209744	M	Coupe	Maroon	Red	Beige			English		5 - 4 - 49
1043		M									
1044											
1045											
1046	7209760	M	Coupe	Maroon	Brown	Brown			Universal		13 - 4 - 49
1047	7209749	M	Coupe	Blue	Blue	Blue			Adlards	(Hungerford Motors)	14 - 4 - 49
1048	7209933	M	Coupe	Maroon	Red	Beige			Tate		20 - 4 - 49
1049	7209882	M	Coupe	Blue	Grey	Blue			~~Dag Motors~~ Tate		19 - 7 - 49
1050	7209894	M	Coupe	Blue	Grey	Blue			Dag. Motors		13 - 4 - 49
1051	7209892	M	Coupe	Blue	Grey	Grey			Adlards	(Pearsons)	7 - 7 - 49
1052	7209991	M	Coupe	Grey	Grey	Grey			Hartwells		21 - 4 - 49
1053	7209941	M	Coupe	Blue	Blue	Blue			Dag. Motors		25 - 4 - 49
1054	7209897	M	Coupe	Grey	Blue	Blue	LTV 218	D.A. Drew Coventry 1967	Universal		19 - 5 - 49
1055	7209955	M	Coupe	Grey	Grey	Blue			Frews		6 - 5 - 49
1056	7210550	M	Coupe	Maroon	Red	Beige			Adlards	(D. Rowe)	14 - 5 - 49
1057	7210568	M	Coupe	Grey	Grey	Grey			English		26 - 5 - 49

Chassis	Engine	Type	Body	Colour.	Interior	Hood Wheels		Remarks		Allocation	Delivered
1058	7210579	M	Coupe	Black	Grey	~~Grey~~ Black		(Mr. Craig)		Dag. Motors	28-4-49
1059	7210551	M	Coupe	Maroon	Red	Beige				Bristol St.	4-5-49
1060	7210523	M	Coupe	Black	Brown	~~Black~~ Brown				George & Jobling	29-4-49
1061	7210555	M	Coupe	Black	Brown	Brown				George & Jobling	9-5-49
1062	7210565	M	Coupe	Grey	Grey	Grey				Adlards.	4-5-49
1063	7210570	M	Coupe	Black	Red	Black				Frew	29-4-49
1064	7210700	M	Coupe	Maroon	Red	Beige				Hartwells	26.5.49
1065	7210747	M	Coupe	Black	Red	Beige				Bristol St.	29-4-49
1066	7210708	M	Coupe	Maroon	Red	Beige				Dag. Motors	23.5.49
1067	7210710	M	Coupe	Blue	Blue	Beige				Bristol St.	9-5-49
1068	7210744	M	Coupe	Blue	Blue	Blue				Dag. Motors.	1 June 49
1069	7210821	M	Coupe	Maroon	Maroon	Beige		(Rowe)		Adlards	16-5-49
1070	7210933	M	Coupe	Blue	Grey	Grey				Bristol St. Motors.	22.6.49
1071	7210988	M	Coupe	Blue	Blue	Grey		(Mr. Jack Varley)		Adlards	19-5-49
1072	7210925	M	Coupe	Blue	Blue	Blue		(Mr Hallard)		Adlards (Demo)	
1073	7210931	M	Coupe	Grey	Grey	Grey		HARTWELLS			11 June 49
1074	7210937	M	Coupe	Grey	Grey	Grey		Philips Garages F. Limited		Adlards.	16 June 49
1075	7210934	M	Coupe	Grey	Red	Grey		Adlards	(Coombs)		18.5.49
1076	7210698	M L.H.	Coupe	Blue	Blue	Blue		Uruguay	(Salim)		29-4-49
1077	7210709	M L.H.	Coupe	Blue	Blue	Blue		Uruguay	(Salim)		29-4-49
1078	7210935	M	Coupe	Grey	Blue	Grey		Dr Pereira.		Dag. Motors	21 June 49
1079	7210811	M	Coupe	Grey	~~Grey~~ Red	Grey		Alexanders			26.5.49
1080	7210823	M	Coupe	Black	Red	Black.		Harris	(Ivor L Roberts)		27.5.49
1081	7210810	M	Coupe	Black	Brown	Black		Adlards.	(Coombs Service Station Guildford)		14 June 49
1082	7212057	M	Coupe	Black	Brown	Brown		George & Jobling			11 June 49
1083	7212029	M.	Coupe	Black	Red	Black		George & Jobling			1.6.49
1084	7212070	M	Coupe	Grey	Grey	Blue		Dag. Motors			30.5.49
1085	7212113	M	Coupe	Grey	Blue	Black		Universal	(Lincolnshire Motors)		30.5.49
1086	7212059	M	Coupe	Black	Grey	Grey		Malaya	(Export.		21 June 49
1087	7212145	M	Coupe	Black	Grey	Black		New Engine, gear Box & wings, Coms, gate, Bumper &c.		Universal ~~Hartwells~~ (Universal coach)	15.7.49
1088	7210924	M	Coupe	Maroon	Red	Beige		Collected 16.6.49		Dag. Motors	16 June 49
1089	7212094	M	Coupe	Maroon	Red	Beige		Tested 10/6/49		Dag. Motors	10 June 49

Chassis	Engine	Type	Body	Colour	Interior	Hoods	Wheels	Remarks		Delivered
1090	7210930	M	Coupe	Maroon	Maroon	Beige			Bristol St.	8 . 7 . 49
1091	7212013	M	Coupe	Grey	Grey	Grey			Goulds.	11 . 7 . 49
1092	7212020	M	Coupe	Grey	Red	Grey			Goulds.	7 . 7 . 49
1093	7212113	M	Coupe	Grey	Blue	Blue			Dag. Motors Nunns	22 . 7 . 49
1094	7212331	M	Coupe	BLACK	RED	BLACK			Dag motors	5 . 7 . 49.
1095	7212354	M	Coupe	Black	Brown	Black			Tate	4 . 8 . 49.
1096	7212352	M	Coupe	Black	Red	Black			Nunns Dag. Motors	19 . 7 . 49
1097	25539·132	M	Coupe	Grey	Grey	Grey		(Price)	Allards	25 . 6 . 49.
1098	7212297	M	Coupe	Maroon	Red	Beige			Nunns.	2 . 8 . 49.
1099	7212353	M	Coupe	Maroon	Maroon	Beige			Tate	9 . 8 . 49.
1100	7212112	M	Coupe	Grey	Grey	Blue			Adlards	28 . 9 . 49
1101	7209282. 81.M	Coupe	Chassis				For W.R. Davies (Motors) Ltd	Chassis Only.	Furrows Shrewsbury	25 . 6 . 49.
1102	7212148	M	Coupe	Grey	Blue	Blue			George & Jobling	19 . 8 . 49
1500	7207388	P	Saloon	Green	orange				George & Jobling	24 . 10 . 49
1503	7212114	P	Saloon	Black Green	Brown				Furrows (St Jerom)	21 . 9 . 49.
1504	7212336	P	Saloon	Green	Orange				Nunns	23 . 9 . 49
1505	7200691	P	Saloon	Green	Orange				Bristol St.	11 . 10 . 49.
1506	7212146	P	Saloon	Green Morning Blue	Orange			?	Dag motors	11 . 10 . 49
1507	7212127	P	Saloon	Green	Red			new Lamps. George Jobling Show model		8 . 12 . 49
1508	7212076	P	Saloon	Green	Orange Green				Tate	11 . 10 . 49
1509	7200761	P	Saloon	Green	Orange				Bristol St.	26 . 10 . 49
1510	5345/33 L.H.	L X	Tourer	Red grey Silver	light Red Blue	Beige Maroon		transferred from 626. Export (George Joseph)	U.S.A. U.S.A	26 . 5 . 50
1511	R571372 P.	M	Coupe	Maroon				MRB No.	Experimental	
1512	D 198.	J L.H.	2 Seater	Blue	Blue		Export		Uruguay	30 . 1 . 50
1513	3953/52	J L.H.	2 Seater	Silver	Red		Export	(Bull) U.S.A.		2 . 3 . 50
1514		J	2 Seater	Silver	Red	less Engine	Export	first J. Oxford	Tom Cole U.S.A.	13 . 10 . 49
1515		J.	2 Seater	Silver	Red	less Engine	Export	Duntov Telemo car KUC 31 1989. Tom Turner.	Ardun U.S.A.	24 . 8 . 49
1516	7193088	P	Saloon	Grey	Blue Grey				Goulds	10 . 11 . 48
1517	7217525	P	Saloon	Black	Maroon				Furrows	26 . 11 . 49
1518	7215392	P	Saloon	Black	Maroon				Adlards (Bully)	25 . 11 . 49
1519	7217522	P	Saloon	Black	Red	Maroon			Adlards (Butterfly)	9 . 11 . 49
1520	7217520	F	Saloon	Black	Brown				Harris	26 . 11 . 49
1521	7209742	M	Coupe	Blue	Blue	Blue		Cold Spring	Dag. Motors Patterson	30 . 8 . 49
1501	7202295	P	Saloon	Green	orange				English	21 . 10 . 49
1502	7202115	P	Saloon	Green	orange					16 . 9 . 49

Chassis	Engine	Type	Body	Colour	Interior	Hood	Wheels	Remarks	Allocation		Deliveries
1522	7210822	M	Coupe	Maroon (Grey/Black)	Maroon (Grey/Red)	Beige (Blue/Black)		Coil Springs	Adlards		7-10-49
1523	7215400	M	Coupe	(Black)	Red			Coil Springs	Adlards		28-9-49
1524	7215392	M	Coupe	Grey	Blue	Blue		Coil Springs	Adlards	(L.G. Johnson)	20-9-49
1525	7215388	M.	Coupe	Maroon	Maroon	Beige		Coil Springs	New Central Garage	Demo.	13-12-49
1526	7215399	M	Coupe	off Beige	off-white	Blue Maroon	new lamps	Coil Springs	George & Jobling	Show model	8-12-49
1527	7215393	M	Coupe	Black	Red	Black		Coil Springs	Nunns	(E.J. Gaskell)	8-9-49
1528	7215512 / 7125512	M	Coupe	Grey	Grey	Grey		Coil Springs	Dag. Motors		12-9-49
1529	7215524	M	Coupe	Blue	Blue	Blue		Coil Springs	Universal		20-9-49
1530	7215521	M	Coupe	Black/Blue	Blue	Black		Coil Springs	Nunns		7-10-49
1531	7215523	M	Coupe	Blue	Blue	Blue		Coil Springs	Dag. Motors		17-10-49
1532	7212357	M	Coupe	Grey	Blue	Blue		Coil Springs	Adlards	(Phillips)	23-9-49
1533	7202305	M	Coupe	Maroon	Maroon	Beige		Coil Springs	Patterson	(S.W. Wood)	13-10-49
1534	7217523	M	Coupe	Blue/Grey	Blue	Blue		Coil Springs	Dag. Motors		29-10-49
1535	7217529	P.	Saloon	Black	Brown				Nunns		16-11-49
1536	7217643	P	Saloon	Grey	Grey				Patterson		22-11-49
1537	7217637	P	Saloon	Black	Red				English		7-11-49
1538	7217638	P	Saloon	Grey	Blue				Dag. Motors		2-12-49
1539	7212149	P	Saloon	Grey	Maroon				Mann Egerton		2-12-49
1540	7202519	P	Saloon	Show Blue	Red				Harris Goulds		8-12-49
1541	7206959	P	Saloon	Black	Red				Goulds (Adlards)		10-12-49
1542	7217705	P	Saloon	Maroon	Maroon				Harris Bristol St.		13-12-49
1543	7217634	P	Saloon	Black	Red				Hamilton		19-12-49
1544	7219356	P	Saloon	Maroon	Red				George & Jobling		5-1-50
1545	E429845P	M (L.H.)	Coupe	Red	Natural	Beige	new lamps Export	Coil Springs	U.S.A.	(Grancor)	7-1-50
1546	7228019	K1 (L.H.)	2 Seater	Blue	Blue		New York Show — Prototype see file letter PAUL JAMES April 93 Show New York	Coil Springs			20-3-50
1547	7219362	P	Saloon	Maroon	Maroon				Universal		30-12-49
1548	7219361	P.	Saloon	Black (Grey)	Brown				Adlards		23-12-49
1549	7219357	P	Saloon	Black	Red				English		30-12-49
1550	7222478 / 7202313?	P (L.H.)	Saloon	Black	Grey		Export		Uruguay		6-1-50
1551	7219363	P	Saloon	Maroon	Maroon				Dag. Motors		19-12-49
1552	7219818	P	Saloon	Green	Brown				Dag. Motors		10-1-50
1553	7219819	P	Saloon	Green	orange				Hughes		10-1-50

Chassis	Engine	Type	Body	Colour	Interior	Hood	Wheels	Remarks			Allocation	Deliveries		
1554	7221926	P	Saloon	Green	Orange						Bristol St.	16	1	50
1555	LAK0107	J L.H.	2 Seater	Silver	Red			Caddy mods ½ Engine	Export (Grancor)		U.S.A.	7	1	50
1556	153 29411	J L.H.	2 Seater	Red	Red	for goldsmidt.	Wire wheels	Was Watkins Glen 23/9/50				24	3	50
x 1557	3957/32	"J"	2 Seater	Silver			CWG 12	own Engine	(R. Clarkson)		Halstead Motor Co.	28	2	50
x 1558	3956/90/E283 3958/60	J	2 Seater			Motor 1900 see Service Job 39-7 20-12-51 also sold 8-2-71	KOF 999	OS 7525 14/1	J.A.Lone-George Wonthorpe (mr. Clark)	(mr. Matt)	Tate Bristol St.	14	4	50
x 1559	3957/41	J	2 Seater	Red			P 8034Z				Patter George & Jobling	15	4	50
1560	7219817	P L.H.	Saloon	Grey	Maroon				Export		Venezuela	23	1	50
1561	7219823	P L.H.	Saloon	Black	Red				Export		Uruguay	17	1	50
1562	7219814	P L.H.	Saloon	Black	Brown				Export		Uruguay	17	1	50
1563	7221934	P	Saloon	Green	Orange				(Francis Garage)		Furrows	26	1	50
1564	7221924	P	Saloon	Green	Orange						Universal	19	1	50
1565	7221923	P	Saloon	Grey	Grey						Nunns	23	1	50
1566	7222123	P	Saloon	Grey	Grey						Patterson	25	1	50
1567	7222084	P	Saloon	Grey	Blue						Goulds	19	1	50
1568	7222086	P	Saloon	Grey	Blue						Tate	26	1	50
1569	7222083	P	Saloon	Grey	Blue						Bristol St.	26	1	50
x 1570	3930/108	J	2 Seater	Black	Red	MWE 254 Registered 11951 Sept 87 fitted with 60s Lee Engine + Gear Box	in May 88 ex2 Newbolt Ford OHV 289 + box Rev. Combe	(T.C. Harrison)		Tate	26	1	50
1571		J L.H.	2 Seater	Black	Green			(J.F. Sleigh) (mr. Sleigh) (mr. Hewitt)		U.S.A Universal Tate	24	4	50
x 1572	5341/29	J	2 Seater	Green				(mr. Hewitt) (mr. Curtis)		Universal Patterson	4	5	50
x 1573	5355/40	J	2 Seater	Grey	Maroon	Red Wls	NUB 862					11	5	50
x 1574	3933/114	J	2 Seater	Blue			OBB 377	(mr. Curtis)		Patterson	85	5	50
x 1575	5343/31	J	2 Seater	Poly. Steel Grey	Mr. Hill	Serviced no 51 11/8/52 BJV 365		(mr. Hyde)		Nunns	15	6	50
x 1576	5335/23	J	2 Seater	Green				Peter Moore 1958 KLJ 2 (mr. Way Hope)		English	26	5	50
1577		J	2 Seater	Black		The 8 Ball		mr. J Wacker. Tom Cole (mr. Watkins)		U.S.A.	8	6	50
1578		J L.H.	2 Seater	Green	ex SHA, 1950 Le Mans car	Shipped to	Seddon RP Imp order't Cw Co N.Y	without engine - special Caddy to be fitted on 1517 for orders the Watkins Glen		U.S.A.	30	8	50
1579		J L.H.	Chassis			Plus Total gearbox ali Cyl. Heads & Induction, Dual Carb	Less Gear Box So. springs clshields, Exhaust Tubes			SPAIN	21	4	50
1580	7222111	P	Saloon	Grey	Grey						Harris (Edwards)	27	1	50
1581	7222487	P	Saloon	Chassis				coupe Bulkhead Cowl, & Bonnet fitted.			Patterson	11	1	50
1582	7222493	P	Saloon	Black	Brown						Nunns	2	2	50
1583	7222477	P	Saloon	Dark Blue	Maroon						Frew	1	2	50
1584	7202313	P L.H.	Saloon	Black	Brown						Hartwells	3	2	50
1585	7223833	P L.H.	Saloon	Show Blue	Blue				(Export)		Peru	22	2	50

Chassis	Engine	Type	Body	Colour	Interior	Hood	Wheels	Remarks		Allocation	Deliveries
1586	7222488	P	Saloon	Black	Blue				(Cleales)	Dag. Motors	3 · 2 · 50 ·
1587	7223852	P.	Saloon	Black	Red				(Avery)	Adlards	9 · 2 · 50.
1588	7223857	P	Saloon	Grey	Red					English	13 · 2 · 50.
1589	7223823	P	Saloon	Show Blue	Red					Universal	13 · 2 · 50
1590	7223880	P	Saloon	Green	Brown					Dag. Motors	13 · 2 · 50
1591	7223879	P	Saloon	Green	Orange				(Haynes)	Adlards	16 · 2 · 50
1592	7223878	P	Saloon	Cream	Maroon				Export.	Chile	22 · 2 · 50
1593	7223889	P.	Saloon	Green	Orange					Goulds	17 · 2 · 50.
1594	7223836	P	Saloon	Green	Orange					Bristol St	20 · 2 · 50
1595	7188852	P	Saloon	Black	Brown					Demo. Adlards	21 – 3 – 50
1596	7224160	P	Saloon	Dark Blue	Blue				(Cameron Campbell)	George & Jobling	23 · 2 · 50
1597	7224156	P	Saloon	Grey	Grey				(Rowe)	Adlards	21 · 2 · 50
1598	7224198	P	Saloon	Grey	Maroon					Mann Egerton	24 · 2 · 50
1599	7224197	P	Saloon	Grey	Blue					Universal	25 · 2 · 50
1600	7224155	P.	Saloon	Grey	Grey					Dag. Motors	8 · 3 · 50
1601	7224205	P L.H	Saloon	Green	Red			Export	(Los Angeles.)	U.S.A.	0
1602	7225864	P	Saloon	Dove Grey	Green			Export		Sweden	13 – 3 – 50
1603	7225837	P	Saloon	Grey	Blue					Dag. Motors	9 – 3 – 50.
1604	7225843	P	Saloon	Show Blue	Blue					Furrows	10 – 3 – 50
1605	7225839	P	Saloon	Black	Brown					Nunns	9 – 3 – 50
1606	7225896	P	Saloon	Black	Red				(Cleales)	Dag. Motors	13 – 3 · 50
1607	7225886	P	Saloon	Black	Brown					Nunns	14 – 3 – 50
1608	7226137	P	Saloon	Grey	Blue					Tate	17 – 3 – 50
1609	7226083	P	Saloon	Blue	Blue					~~Dag. Motors~~ Bristol St.	16 – 3 – 50
1610	7226141	P	Saloon	Black	Brown					Universal	16 – 3 – 50
1611	7226136	P	Saloon	Black	Brown					~~Dag. Motors~~ Furrows	21 – 3 – 50
1612	7226082	P	Saloon	Black	Maroon					Nunns	21 – 3 – 50
1613	7226135	P	Saloon	Grey	Red					English	20 – 3 – 50
1614	7226077	P	Saloon	Black	Brown					Goulds	25 – 3 – 50
1615	7226085	P	Saloon	Blue	Blue					English	30 – 3 – 50
1616	7226076	P	Saloon	Blue	Blue					Tate	28 – 3 – 50
1617	7228009	P	Saloon	Grey	Blue					Tate	31 – 3 – 50

Chassis	Engine	Type	Body	Colour	Interior	Hood	Wheels	Remarks		Allocation	Delivered
1618	7228018	P	Saloon	Black	Brown					Mann Egerton	3 – 4 – 50
1619	7228015	P	Saloon	Green	Green					Taté Portugal	5 – 4 – 50
1620	5340-28 7228237	P L.H.	Saloon	Maroon	Maroon				(Oxford)	Venezuela	26 – 4 – 50
1621	7228247	P	Saloon	Blue	Blue		Letters from Welwin, Sheffield Wed Nov 65 Jan Oct 66, also Reg May 8	End Bellshill Lanark quotes extensive comp histy reg No USM 704.		Universal	12 – 4 – 50
1622	7224205	P	Saloon	Black	Brown					George & Jobling	11 – 4 – 50
1623	7233881 7228242	P	Saloon	Black	Maroon					Mann Egerton	13 – 4 – 50
1624	7228241	P	Saloon Coupé	Grey	Blue		[See Stock Card]	P Chrom. special cpé Ardun engine Cab		Harris	14 – 4 – 50
1625	799T-1423980 7228240	P	Saloon	Grey Black	Grey Red				Columbia rev sale	Sweden	24 – 8 – 50
1626	7228238	P	Saloon	Grey	Grey					Bristol St.	13 – 4 – 50
1627	7228017	P	Saloon	Blue	Maroon					Nunns	14 – 4 – 50
1628	7228520 7228250	P	Saloon	Blue	Blue					Bristol St.	19 – 4 – 50
1629	7228525	P	Saloon	Grey	Blue					Taté	21 – 4 – 50
1630	7228510	P	Saloon	Grey	Blue				(Haylor & Root)	Adlards	19 – 4 – 50
1631	7228518	P	Saloon	Grey	Grey					Furrows	21 – 4 – 50
1632	7228907	P	Saloon	Black	Brown			KYP.640.	Deme.	Adlards	22 – 4 – 50
1633	7228924	P	Saloon	Grey	Blue					Bristol St.	25 – 4 – 50
1634	7228904	P	Saloon	Black	Brown					Bristol St.	28 – 4 – 50
1635	7228918	P	Saloon	Grey	Blue				(Owen)	Adlards	25 – 4 – 50
1636	7228517	P	Saloon	Black	Brown					Nunns	4 – 5 – 50
1637	7228905	P	Saloon	Blue	Blue					Dag. Motors	1 – 5 – 50
1638	7228239	P L.H.	Saloon	Grey	Grey					Universal	21 – 8 – 50
1639	7228917	P	Saloon	Black	Brown				(Cott Jackson)	Frew	4 – 5 – 50
1640	7228509	P	Saloon	Black	Brown				(Holbrook)	Adlards	4 – 5 – 50
1641	7229717	P	Saloon	Grey	Grey					Patterson	4 – 5 – 50
1642	7229762	P	Saloon	Grey	Blue					Universal	11 – 5 – 50
1643	7229764	P	Saloon	Grey	Grey					Taté	9 – 5 – 50
1644	7229765	P	Saloon	Black	Brown					Nunns	19 – 5 – 50
1645	7229693	P	Saloon	Black	Brown					George & Jobling	13 – 5 – 50
1646	7229718	P	Saloon	Black	Brown					Universal	23 – 5 – 50
1647	7229759	P	Saloon	Grey	Red				(Rootes)	Dag. Motors	16 – 5 – 50
1648	7229713	P	Saloon	Black	Brown					Bristol St.	16 – 5 – 50
1649	7229739	P	Saloon	Black	Brown					Dag. Motors	15 – 5 – 50

Chassis	Engine	Type	Body	Colour	Interior	Hood	Wheels		Allocation		Deliveries
1650	7229903	P	Saloon	Black	Red (maroon)				Adlards	(Mr Grundy)	19 - 5 - 50
1651	7229920	P	Saloon	Grey	Blue				English		14 - 5 - 50
1652	7229726	P	Saloon	Black	Brown				Adlards	(Cowling)	25 - 5 - 50
1653	7229916	P	Saloon	Black	Maroon				Tate		25 - 5 - 50
1654	7229904	P	Saloon	Grey	Grey				Patterson		22 - 5 - 50
1655	7231831	P	Saloon	Black	Brown				Bristol St		31 - 5 - 50
1656	7231834	P	Saloon	Grey	Blue				Universal		26 - 5 - 50
1657	7231838	P	Saloon	Black	Blue Brown				Adlards	(Salwood)	2 - 6 - 50
1658	7231852	P	Saloon	Black	Brown				Adlards	(Horton)	2 - 6 - 50
1659	7231829	P	Saloon	Grey	Red				Frew		7 - 6 - 50
1660	5342/30 7229913	P	Saloon	Black	Brown				Nunns	(Webb)	8 - 6 - 50
1661	7229853	P	Saloon	Blue	Blue				Nunns		6 - 6 - 50
1662	7229911	P	Saloon	Black	Red				Goulds		7 - 6 - 50
1663	7229772	P	Saloon	Grey	Blue				Harris		13 - 6 - 50
1664	7232476	P	Saloon	Black	Brown				English	(6. Cox)	10 - 6 - 50
1665	7232436	P	Saloon	Black	Brown				Hamilton		13 - 6 - 50
1666	7232462	P	Saloon	Black	Brown				George & Jobling	(Grosvenor)	17 - 6 - 50
1667	7232479	P	Saloon	Black	Brown				Universal		16 - 6 - 50
1668	7233186	P	Saloon	Black	Brown				George & Jobling		16 - 6 - 50
1669	7233207	P	Saloon	Grey	Maroon				Mann Egerton		22 - 6 - 50
1670	7233210	P	Saloon	Black	Brown				Harris		17 - 6 - 50
1671	7228240	P	Saloon	Black	Brown				Bristol St		21 - 6 - 50
1672	7232488	P	Saloon	Black	Brown				Adlards	(Wymer)	1 - 7 - 50
1673	7233173	P	Saloon	Grey	Blue		Partially restored, under restoration. Stolen in London August 1967	Reg No LGX 678	Tate		27 - 6 - 50
1674	7233157	P	Saloon	Blue	Blue				Tate		29 - 6 - 50
1675	7233183	P L.H.	Saloon	Mid Blue	Blue				Bristol St		25 - 8 - 50
1676	7233217	P L.H.	Saloon	Black	Red				Bristol St		25 - 8 - 50
1677	7242409	P	Saloon	Black	Red				Harris		3 - 2 - 51
1678	7232560	P	Saloon	Black	Brown				Adlards		1 - 7 - 50
1679	7233167	P	Saloon	Black	Brown				Furrows		4 - 7 - 50
1680	7231846	P	Saloon	Black	Maroon				English	Reg No JAA 500 ?check	4 - 7 - 50
1681	7232480	P	Saloon	Black	Brown				George & Jobling		19 - 7 - 50

Chassis	Engine	Type	Body	Colour	Interior	Hood	Wheels	Allocation	Deliveries
1682	7233192	P	Saloon	Grey	Grey			Patterson	10 – 7 – 50
1683	7229913	P	Saloon	Grey	Grey			Universal	11 – 7 – 50
1684	7235353	P	Saloon	Ming Blue	Blue			Nunns	11 – 7 – 50
1685	7233193	P	Saloon	Blue	Blue			Bristol St	10 – 7 – 50
1686	7233689	P	Saloon	Grey	Grey			Dag. Motors	11 – 7 – 50
1687	7233680	P	Saloon	Black	Brown			Nunns	13 – 7 – 50
1688	7233678	P	Saloon	Grey	Maroon			Adlards	19 – 7 – 50
1689	7235793	P	Saloon	Grey	Red			English	1 – 8 – 50
1690	5336/24	J L.H.	2 Seater	Blue	Red		Export	Sweden	5 – 7 – 50
1691	5354/39	J L.H.	2 Seater	Silver	Red.		Export	Peru	22 – 6 – 50
1692	5356/41	J L.H.	2 Seater	Red	Red.	Cotal 3.m see Export card	Export card	Portugal	23 – 5 – 50
✗ 1693	2005	J	2 Seater	Green	D.Butler – Ardun still ✓	Sept '67 A.O.C Newsletter Reg.no LLP 797 owned by Perkett, of Leicester		Narronago Adlards	7 – 10 – 50
1694	5350/38	J L.H.	2 Seater	Silver	Red.		Export	Portugal	7 – 6 – 50
✗ 1695	7219817	J	2 Seater	Green				Watkins	22 – 8 – 50
1696		J L.H.	2 Seater	Red	Red.		Export (Gibbs)	U.S.A.	25 – 7 – 50
● 1697	5348/36	J L.H.	2 Seater	Red	Red.	see Export Card. Sup. Ardun	Less Engine Export Ardun unit?	Denmark	25 – 7 – 50
1698	8M 931v	J	2 Seater	Red	Red	" " see letter in file from Jackson not dated.	Export Cadillac unit	Australia	26 – 1 – 51
✗ 1699	2008X	J L.H.	2 Seater	Blue			Export (Gardner)	Australia	18 – 1 – 51
1700	7228029	K2 L.H.	2 Seater	Light Blue	Tan	Beige	Export	Canada	9 – 5 – 50
1701	7226140	L L.H.	Tourer	Silver Grey	Light Blue	Maroon	Export Nuns	U.S.A. last L built	27 – 4 – 50
1702		K2 L.H.	2 Seater	Black	Red		Export Woodhull (Forbes)	U.S.A. V.S.A.	31 – 5 – 50
1703	7228922	K2 L.H.	2 Seater	Blue	Blue	Blue	Export (Forbes)	U.S.A.	14 – 5 – 50
1704		K2 L.H.	2 Seater	Blue	Blue		Less Engine Export	U.S.A.	5 – 7 – 50
1705		K2 L.H.	2 Seater	Blue	Blue		Export	U.S.A.	27 – 7 – 50
1706	—	K2 L.H.	2 Seater	Grey	Blue		Export	U.S.A.	21 – 8 – 50
1707		K2 L.H.	2 Seater	Grey	Red	Special = de Dion axle	Export	U.S.A.	9 – 11 – 50
1708		K2 L.H.	2 Seater	Black	Red.		Export	U.S.A.	19 – 9 – 50
1709	B18F 7200263	M-2	Coupe	Black		Black LXR 942	"No 6 whole"?	ADLARDS LTD	18 6 51
1710	7235800	P	Saloon	Blue	Blue		see 2000/2001	Universal	18 – 7 – 50
1711	7235798	P	Saloon	Black	Brown			Harris	21 – 7 – 50
1712	7235796	6P	Saloon	Black	Brown			Dag. Motors	20 – 7 – 50
1713	7235794	P	Saloon	Grey	Blue			Bristol St	25 – 7 – 50

Chassis	Engine	Type	Body	Colour	Interior	Hood	Wheels		Allocation	Deliveries
1714	7233679	P	Saloon	Black	Brown				Nunns	27-7-50
1715	7233880	P	Saloon	Grey	Grey				Dag. Motors	27-7-50
1716	7233677	P	Saloon	Black	Brown				George & Jobling	31-7-50
1717	7233681	P	Saloon	Grey	Blue				Tate	29-7-50
1718	7235801	P	Saloon	Black	Brown				Universal	31-7-50
1719	7235354	P	Saloon	Grey	Maroon				Mann Egerton	31-7-50
1720	7240741 ~~7228242~~	P	Saloon	Black	Maroon				Adlards	28-7-50
1721	7233877	P	Saloon	Grey	Grey				Bristol St	1-8-50
1722	7235795	P	Saloon	Black	Bright red				Adlards	3-8-50
1723	7235359	P	Saloon	Black	brown				Goulds	2-8-50
1724	7235799	P	Saloon	Black	brown				Dag. Motors	1-8-50
1725	7235797	P	Saloon	Maroon	maroon				Nunns	21-8-50
1726	7233903	P	Saloon	Grey	red				Nunns	21-8-50
1727	7233878	P	Saloon	Black	brown				Adlards	17-8-50
1728	7233902	P	Saloon	Grey	red				English	21-8-50
1729	7233156	P	Saloon	Blue	blue				Bristol St	18-8-50
1730	2006X ~~2005~~	J	2 Seater	Blue			Chassis only. Show counter Allards (Daus)		U.S.A.	
1731	5338/26	J	2 Seater	Red	Red	✗ Taken from export card.	Export		Australia	8-8-50
1732	—	L.H. J	2 Seater	Black	Red		Export		U.S.A.	2-8-50
1733		L.H. J	2 Seater	Blue	Red.	K2. Wings/bumpers Sean Davidson	Export		U.S.A.	9-50
1734	—	L.H. J	2 Seater	Red	Blue		Export		U.S.A.	15-8-50
1735	5349/37 ~~11861~~	2029Z J	2 Seater	Green				L.P. 798. Healey Eng. B. Jobbe	U.S.A.	
1736	.	L.H. J	2 Seater	Red	Red.		Export		U.S.A.	3-9-50
1737	5347/35	J	2 Seater	Red	Red		Export		~~U.S.A.~~ Canada	14-8-50
1738	—	J	2 Seater ~~Red~~	Red	Red.		Export		U.S.A.	25-8-50
1739		L.H. J	2 Seater	Red	Red		Export		U.S.A.	19-9-50
L2X/1740	Caddy	L.H. K	2 Seater	Grey	Red	Tourer body in P chassis K2 Front grille.	Export	Photo in file: special for de Dion, Caddy engine	Sweden	29-9-50
1741		K2	2 Seater	Green	Red		Export		U.S.A.	13-10-50
1742		L.H. K2	2 Seater	Grey	Red.		Export.		U.S.A.	6-9-50
1743	7250830	L.H. K2	2 Seater	Blue	Red		Export		Sweden	12-3-51
1744		L.H. K2.	2 Seater	Grey			Export		U.S.A.	9-10-50
1745	8607/154	K2	2 Seater	Black			Export		Australia	6-12-50

Chassis	Engine	Type	Body	Colour	Interior	Hood	Wheels		Allocation	Deliveries
1746	7237910	P	Saloon	Black	Brown				Furrows	24 - 8 - 50
1747	7237911	P	Saloon	Grey	Maroon				Taylors	24 - 8 - 50
1748	7237908	P	Saloon	Grey	Grey				New Central	25 - 8 - 50
1749	7237913	P	Saloon	Black	Brown				Adlards	29 - 8 - 50
1750	7237914	P	Saloon	Grey	Grey				Patterson	31 - 8 - 50
1751	7226140	P	Saloon	Grey	Blue				Adlards	30 - 8 - 50
1752	7238774	P	Saloon	Blue	Blue			(a gall.)	Dag. Motors	4 - 9 - 50
1753	7238767	P	Saloon	Grey	Blue				Harris	2 - 9 - 50
1754	7238756	P	Saloon	Black	Brown				Adlards	2 - 9 - 50
1755	7238765	P	Saloon	Grey	Blue				Universal	4 - 9 - 50
1756	7238759	P	Saloon	Black	Brown				Dag. Motors	4 - 9 - 50
1757	7238770	P	Saloon	Black	Brown				Dag. Motors	6 - 9 - 50
1758	7238777	P	Saloon	Blue	Blue				English	6 - 9 - 50
1759	7238763	P	Saloon	Blue	Blue				Bristol St	7 - 9 - 50
1760	7238464	P	Saloon	Blue	Blue				Nunns	11 - 9 - 50
1761	7238761	P	Saloon	Black	Maroon				Adlards	8 - 9 - 50
1762	7238779	P	Saloon	Black	Brown				Dag. Motors	14 - 9 - 50
1763	7238800	P	Saloon	Grey	Blue				Bristol St	13 - 9 - 50
1764	7238768	P	Saloon	Blue	Blue				Tate	15 - 9 - 50
1765	7238783	P	Saloon	Grey	Maroon				English	22 - 9 - 50
1766	7238782	P	Saloon	Blue	Blue				Taylors	20 - 9 - 50
1767	7240049	P	Saloon	Black	Maroon				Tate	19 - 9 - 50
1768	7240041	P	Saloon	Black	Maroon				Universal	20 - 9 - 50
1769	7240030	P	Saloon	Black	Maroon				Bristol St	30 - 9 - 50
1770										
1771										
1772										
1773										
1774										
1775										
1776										
1777										

Chassis	Engine	Type	Body	Colour	Interior	Hood	Wheels		Allocation	Deliveries
1778										
1779										
1780	8	J	2 Seater	Maroon	Blue		Export		U.S.A.	4 - 9 - 50
1781	5339/27	J	2 Seater	Blue	Blue		Export		Australia	6 - 10 - 50
1782	5307/61	J	2 Seater	Blue	Blue		~~Saut~~ Export		Australia	13 - 11 - 50
✗ 1783	2009 Y	J	2 Seater	Blue	Blue	NCV 942	Hood Screen wire whls. close ratio	Ken Watkins. Dr. MANTON NEW CAVENDISH ST W.	New Central	6 - 2 - 51
✗ 1784	2004 X	J	2 Seater	Red	Red.				Adlards	9 - 1 - 51
1785	~~2004~~	J	2 Seater				Export	Show	Turkey	22 - 1 - 51
1786	5357/42	L.H. J	2 Seater	Blue	Blue		Export		Portugal	22 - 9 - 50
1787		L.H. J	2 Seater	Silver	Natural		Export		U.S.A.	21 - 11 - 50
1788		L.H. J	2 Seater	Black	Red		Export		U.S.A.	21 - 11 - 50
1789		L.H. J	2 Seater	Bronz.			Export		U.S.A.	7 - 11 - 50
1790	7240048	P	Saloon	Black	Maroon				Goulds	30 - 9 - 50
1791	7238824	P	Saloon	Black	Brown				Tate	27 - 9 - 50
1792	7246023	P	Saloon	Grey	Maroon				Adlards.	7 - 10 - 50
1793	7240038	P	Saloon	Black	Maroon				Nunns	21 - 9 - 50
1794	7238766	P	Saloon	Grey	Grey				Dag. Motors	27 - 9 - 50
1795	5369/44	P	Saloon	Black	Maroon		Large Engine		Nunns	2 - 10 - 50
1796	7238822	P	Saloon	Grey	Grey				George & Jobling	28 - 9 - 50
1797	7238786	P	Saloon	Black	Maroon				Frew	29 - 9 - 50
1798	7238801	P	Saloon	Blue	Blue				Nunns	4 - 10 - 50
1799	7240739	P	Saloon	Grey	Blue				Bristol St	27 - 9 - 50
1800		L.H. K2	2 Seater	Ivory	Tan		Export		U.S.A.	28 - 12 - 50
1801		L.H. K2	2 Seater	Green	Green		Export		U.S.A	28 - 11 - 50
1802		L.H. K2	2 Seater	Bug's Blue	Red		Export		U.S.A.	11 - 12 - 50
1803	7240932	K2	2 Seater	Blue	Blue			Show	Bristol St	10 - 11 - 50
1804		L.H. K2	2 Seater	Blue			Export		U.S.A	1 - 12 - 50
1805	5344/12	L.H. K2	2 Seater	Grey	Red		Export		Peru	21 - 12 - 50
1806	5346/34	K2	2 Seater	Cream			Export		U.S.A.	18 - 12 - 50
1807	8606/151	K2	2 Seater	Red	Natural Leather	?	Export		U.S.A.	12 - 12 - 50
1808		L.H. K2	2 Seater	Grey			Export		USA	5 - 1 - 51
1809		L.H. K2	2 Seater	Black	Red		Export		U.S.A.	3 - 1 - 51

Chassis	Engine	Type	Body	Colour	Interior	Hood			Allocation	Delivered
1810	7240732	P	Saloon	Black	Maroon				English	3 - 10 - 50
1811	7240727	P	Saloon	Black	Brown				Universal	3 - 10 - 50
1812	7240730	P	Saloon	Grey	Blue				Tate	5 - 10 - 50
1813	7240933	P	Saloon	Grey	Blue				Adlards	14 - 10 - 50
1814	7240935	P	Saloon	Black	Maroon				Mann Egerton	9 - 10 - 50
1815	7240943	P	Saloon	Black	Brown				Dag. Motors	10 - 10 - 50
1816	7240726	P	Saloon	Grey	Blue		Show		Allard Motor Co	2 - 2 - 51
1817	7240930	P	Saloon	Grey	Grey				Alexanders	14 - 10 - 50
1818	7240936	P	Saloon	Black	Maroon				Bristol St	13 - 10 - 50
1819	7240931	P	Saloon	Grey	Grey				New Central	18 - 10 - 50
1820	7242158	P	Saloon	Black	Brown				Adlards	11 - 10 - 50
1821	7242134	P	Saloon	Grey	Grey				Nunns	18 - 10 - 50
1822	7242159	P	Saloon	Black	Brown				Taylors	19 - 10 - 50
1823	7242408	P	Saloon	Black	Maroon				Adlards	18 - 10 - 50
1824	7242135	P	Saloon	Black	Red				Adlards	19 - 10 - 50
1825	7242436	P	Saloon	Blue	Blue				Tate	20 - 10 - 50
1826	7242427	P	Saloon	Black	Maroon				Nunns	20 - 10 - 50
1827	7242415	P	Saloon	Blue	Blue				Nunns	27 - 10 - 50
1828	7242419	P	Saloon	Grey	Blue				Universal	2 - 11 - 50
1829	7242414	P	Saloon	Black	Red				Dag. Motors	27 - 10 - 50
1830	7242449	P	Saloon	Grey	Maroon				Nunns	31 - 10 - 50
1831	7242157	P	Saloon	Black	Brown				Adlards (Isle of Man)	31 - 10 - 50
1832	7242160	P	Saloon	Maroon	Maroon				Nunns	31 - 10 - 50
1833	7240728	P	Saloon	Black	Brown				Dag. Motors	3 - 11 - 50
1834	7242146	P	Saloon	Blue	Blue				Universal	13 - 11 - 50
1835	7242421	P	Saloon	Grey	Red				Taylors	6 - 11 - 50
1836	7242413	P	Saloon	Grey	Grey				English	6 - 11 - 50
1837	7242988	P	Saloon	Black	Brown				Harris	6 - 11 - 50
1838	7242992	P	Saloon	Green	Green				Dag. Motors	13 - 11 - 50
1839	7242985	P	Saloon	Grey	Blue				Ferrours	8 - 11 - 50
1840	7244921	K2	2 Seater	Bronze	Beige		Export		U.S.A.	17 - 1 - 51
1841	9059/80	K	2 Seater	Black			Export		U.S.A.	12 - 12 - 50

Chassis	Engine	Type	Body	Colour	Interior	Hood			Allocation		Delivered
1842		K2 L.H.	2 Seater	Green	Red			Export	R/P Imported Motors	U.S.A.	16 - 1 - 51
1843		K2 L.H.	2 Seater	Black	Red.			Export	R/P Imported Motors	U.S.A.	17 - 1 - 51
1844	LESS ENG.	K2 L.H.	2 Seater	Silver	Red			Export		U.S.A.	5 · 3 · 51
1845	~~~~	K2 L.H.	2 Seater	Black	Red			Export	R/P Imported Motors	USA	3 · 4 · 51
1846		K2 L.H.	2 Seater	Red	Red.			Export	R/P Imported Motors	U.S.A.	16 - 1 - 51
1847		K2 L.H.	2 Seater	Green	Red			Export	R/P Imported Motors	U.S.A.	18 - 1 - 51
1848		K2 L.H.	2 Seater	Ivory	Blue			Export	R/P Imported Motors	U.S.A.	18 - 1 - 51
1849	Less original Caddy motor	K2 L.H.	2 Seater	Export file shows Royal Blue	Red	Letter from Roy M Dees '92 owner requested information			R.P. Imported.	U.S.A.	31 · 1 · 51
1850		J L.H.	2 Seater	Primer	Red			Export	British Motor Car Coda	U.S.A.	25 · 1 · 51
1851		J L.H.	2 Seater	BLUE	BLUE				British Car Sales	USA	30 - 1 - 51
1852	LESS ENG.	J L.H.	2 Seater	Green	Red	Brad schumber min 1951? M. BRADBROOK letter 9/88	2nd PERUNA CAR?	Export	R/P IMPORTED	U.S.A.	5 · 3 · 51
1853		J L.H.	2 SEATER	RED	RED)				BILL C?	U.S.A	31 - 1 - 51
1854		J LH	2 SEATER	GREEN	RED			Export	CUSTOM AUTO: TEXAS	U.S.A.	14 · 5 · 51.
1855	2015/2	J LH	2 SEATER	GREEN	RED			Export	GEO. WALES GARAGE	GENEVA	14 · 5 · 51.
1856											
1857		J L.H.	2 Seater	Bronze	brown		new york show		(SAN FRANCISCO)		
1858		J L.H.						Export	CALIF: SPORTS CAR CO.	U.S.A.	21 · 2 · 51
1859	LESS ENG.	J L.H.						Export	R/P IMPORTED	U.S.A.	5 · 3 · 51
1860		P L.H.	Saloon	Silver	Red			Export	R/P Imported Motors	U.S.A	18 - 1 - 51
1861	7242991	P	Saloon	Grey	Grey				Bristol St		10 - 11 - 50
1862	7242986	P	Saloon	Grey	Grey				New Central		14 - 11 - 50
1863	7242987	P.	Saloon	Blue	Blue				Bristol St		14 - 11 - 50
1864	7242990	P	Saloon	Black	maroon				Tate		14 - 11 - 50
1865	7244325	P	Saloon	Green	Orange				Harris		17 - 11 - 50
1866	7244327	P	Saloon	Blue	Blue				George + Jobling		17 - 11 - 50
1867	7244328	P	Saloon	Grey	Grey				English		16 - 11 - 50
1868	7244326	P	Saloon	Blue	Blue				Mumms		22 - 11 - 50
1869	7244333	P	Saloon	Grey	Grey				Hartwells		20 - 11 - 50
1870	7244323	P	Saloon	Grey	Blue				English		22 - 11 - 50
1871	7244329	P	Saloon	Black	Red				Goulds		20 - 11 - 50
1872	7244485	P	Saloon	Grey	maroon				Mann Egerton		24 - 11 - 50
1873	7244484	P	Saloon	Black	maroon				Adlards		27 - 11 - 50

Chassis	Engine	Type	Body	Colour	Interior	Hood				Allocation	Delivered
1874	7244501	P	Saloon	Grey	Grey					Dag. Motors	24-11-50
1875	7244481	P	Saloon	Black	Grey					Bristol St.	28-11-50
1876	7244482	P	Saloon	Blue	Blue					English	29-11-50
1877	7244506	P	Saloon	Black	Maroon					Alexanders	30-11-50
1878	7244504	P	Saloon	Grey	Red					Goulds	1-12-50
1879	7244958	P	Saloon	Grey	Grey					Nunns	30-11-50
1880	7244929	P	Saloon	Black	Maroon					Adlards (Putney)	1-12-50
1881	7244920	P	Saloon	Black	Maroon					Adlards	1-12-50
1882	7244981	P	Saloon	Show Grey	Blue					George & Jobling	7-12-50
1883	7244972	P	Saloon	Grey	Grey					Dag. Motors	11-12-50
1884	7244934	P	Saloon	Green	Orange					Adlards	7-12-50
1885	7244956	P	Saloon	Grey	Maroon					Bristol St	13-12-50
1886	7233877	P	Saloon	Grey	Grey					Universal	11-12-50
1887	7244998	P	Saloon	Show Grey	Blue					Adlards	12-1-51
1888	7246360	P	Saloon	Show Grey	Blue					Nunns	1-1-51
1889	7246359	P	Saloon	Black	Maroon					Bristol St.	13-12-50
1890	7244999	P	Saloon	met Grey	Red					Dag. Motors	14-12-50
1891	7246358	P	Saloon	Black	Brown					Frews	14-12-50
1892	7246427	P	Saloon	Cream	Red			Export		E.I.E (Nairobi)	25-1-51
1893	7246430	P	Saloon	Black	Brown					English	18-12-50
1894	7246428	P	Saloon	Black	Maroon					Nunns	21-12-50
1895	7246470	P	Saloon	Blue	Blue					Tate	22-12-50
1896	7246469	P	Saloon	Grey	Blue					Dag. Motors	21-12-50
1897	7246479	P	Saloon	Blue	Blue					Universal	28-12-50
1898	7246514	P	Saloon	Black	Maroon					Harris	29-12-50
1899	7246503	P	Saloon	Show Grey	Blue					George & Jobling	27-12-50
1900	7246502	P	Saloon	Grey	Grey					New Central	18-1-51
1901	7246494	P	Saloon	Black	Brown					Adlards	15-1-51
1902	7246506	P	Saloon	Grey	Grey			Export		E.I.E (Nairobi)	25-1-51
1903	7246519	P	Saloon	Blue	Blue					Nunns	13-1-51
1904	7246817	P	Saloon	Grey	Blue					Dag. Motors	8-1-51
1905	7246895	P	Saloon	Blue	Blue					Bristol St	5-1-51

Chassis	Engine	Type	Body	Colour	Interior	Hood			Allocation	Delivered
1906	7246816	P	Saloon	Show Grey	Blue				Patterson	8 - 1 - 51
1907	7246914	P	Saloon	Show Grey	Red				George & Jobling	10 - 1 - 51
1908	7246896	P	Saloon	Black	Red				English	15 - 1 - 51
1909	7246880	P	Saloon	Black	Red				Universal	12 - 1 - 51
*1910	8M 861 Cadillac	J	2 Seater	Green	Green	Hutchison Le Man	DVT 983	Le Man? for → (Hutching)	Nunns	1 - 4 - 51
1911	8M 580	J	2 Seater Green	Green	Green		JMO 120		Collins	29 - 3 - 51
1912	2019-Z	J	2 Seater	Grey			Wreck LXY 15	Served ab 51 V.R.R. 9 August 1951 mileage 6,954	Allards - Wick	10 - 4 - 51
1913	7246897	P	Saloon	Show Grey	Blue				Frews	15 - 1 - 51
1914	7246826	P	Saloon	Blue	Blue				George & Jobling	16 - 1 - 51
1915	7246818	P	Saloon	Black	Brown				Dag. Motors	18 - 1 - 51
1916	7246930	P	Saloon	Grey	Grey				Nunns	18 - 1 - 51
1917	7246916	P	Saloon	Black	Red				Adlards	24 - 1 - 51
1918	7246844	P	Saloon	Blue	Blue				Adlards	26 - 1 - 51
1919	7246894	P	Saloon	Blue	Blue				Harris	20 - 1 - 51
1920	7246931	P	Saloon	Black	Red				Adlards	24 - 1 - 51
1921	7246915	P	Saloon	Grey	Grey				Bristol St.	22 - 1 - 51
1922	7246917	P	Saloon	Black	Red				Adlards	4 - 4 - 51
1923	7244921	K2	2 Seater	Green	Green				Bristol St	19 - 2 - 51
1924	7249344	K2	2 Seater	Show Blue	Blue				Dag. Motors	21 - 2 - 51
1925	9088/144 / 7249391	K2	2 Seater	Dark Green	Green	For Blackley LXT335	Service record 14 March 1951 (500 service)		Adlards (Watney)	19 - 2 - 51
1926	7246913	P	Saloon	Grey	Grey				Adlards	27 - 1 - 51
1927	7249402	P	Saloon	Black	Brown				Harris	29 - 1 - 51
1928	7249341	P	Saloon	Black	Maroon				Tate	6 - 2 - 51
1929	7249342	P	Saloon	Black	Brown				Dag. Motors	29 - 1 - 51
1930	7249401	P	Saloon	Show Grey	Blue				Patterson	7 - 2 - 51
1931	7249408	P	Saloon	Black	Maroon				Nunns	7 - 2 - 51
1932	7249599	P	Saloon	Grey	Maroon				Dag. Motor	5 - 2 - 51
1933	7249375	P	Saloon	Blue	Blue				Bristol St	9 - 2 - 51
1934	7249410	P	Saloon	Show Grey	Blue				Universal	10 - 2 - 51
1935	7249351	P	Saloon	Blue	Blue				Nunns	10 - 2 - 51
1936	7249651	P	Saloon	Grey	Grey				New Central	10 - 2 - 51
1937	7249594	P	Saloon	Dark Green	Grey			Export	Australia	28 - 2 - 51

Chassis	Engine	Type	Body	Colour	Interior	Hood				Allocation	Delivered
1938	7249652	P	Saloon	met grey	Maroon					Harris	1.3.51
1939	7249440	P	Saloon	Black	Brown					George & Jobling	22.2.51
1940	7249601	P	Saloon	Black	Brown					Dag. Motors	19.2.51
1941	7249597	P	Saloon	met grey	Maroon					Nunns	20.2.51
1942	7250064	P	Saloon	Show grey	Blue					Tate	19.2.51
1943	7250061	P	Saloon	met grey	Red					Alexanders	19.2.51
1944	7250067	P	Saloon	Black	Maroon					Bristol St.	20.2.51
1945	7250054	P	Saloon	Black	Brown					Dag. Motors	21.2.51
1946		J					Single Seater				
1947		J					Single Seater				
1948	7250056	P	Saloon	Black	Maroon					Harris	22.2.51
1949	7249400	P	Saloon	Black	Maroon					Patterson	22.2.51
1950	7250049	P	Saloon	met grey	Blue					Nunns	26.2.51
1951	7250065	P	Saloon	met grey	Red					Dag. Motors	26.2.51
1952	7250062	P	Saloon	met grey	Blue					Bristol St.	28.2.51
1953	7250059	P	Saloon	Black	Brown					Goulds	28.2.51
1954	7249596	P	Saloon	Show grey	Red					Frews	1.3.51
1955	7250060	P	Saloon	Brown	Beige		leathercloth			Nunns	4.3.51
1956	7250845	P	Saloon	Black	Maroon			Export	New Zealand		22.3.51
1957	7250837 7250857	P	Saloon	met grey	Red	FPN 300				Adlards	5.3.51
1958	7251628	P	Saloon	met grey	Blue			Export	New Zealand		22.3.51
1959	7250851	P	Saloon	Black	Orange					Nunns	13.3.51
1960	7250831	P	Saloon	Blue	Blue					Bristol St.	9.3.51
1961	7250980	P	Saloon	Black	Maroon					English	12.3.51
1962	7250978	P	Saloon	Black	Maroon					Tate	14.3.51
1963	7250977	P	Saloon	Grey	Maroon					Adlards	12.3.51
1964	7250979	P	Saloon	Black	Maroon		used S/H in Monte E Rui 1953 LXR 946			Adlards	10.3.51
1965	7252602	P	Saloon	Grey	Maroon			Lying derelict in garage at Dalmeny Scotland, Sept '81		Alexander	19.3.51
1966	7252809	P	Saloon	Blue	Blue					George & Jobling	21.3.51
1967	7252761	P	Saloon	Blue	Grey					Goulds	9.3.51
1968		K2 L.H.	2 Seater	Burg Blue	Red			Export	U.S.A.		3.3.51
1969		K2 L.H.	2 Seater	spring Blue	Red			Export	U.S.A.		3.4.51

Chassis	Engine	Type	Body	Colour	Interior	Hood			Allocation		Delivered
1970		K2 L.H.	2 Seater	Black	Swang				Export	U.S.A. Wayne Adams 1992/3	3.3.51
1971	1456291	J	2 Seater	Green			Targa + M. Mighli cat LXR 949		S.H.A.		7.9.51
1972		J	2 Seater	Blue	Red		Converted to X spec at 51, 12-11-55 LXT 5.		LXT 5.	Imhof.	17.3.51
1973	2010/Z	J	2 Seater	Red	Red		Recorded U. Service JOD 97 18-6-51 Reg Nº. MGC 570 571 X-5-6-51		Export.	Argentine	4.6.51
1974		J L.H.	2 Seater	Blue	Blue				EXPORT.	U.S.A.	30.3.51
1975	HIL	J L.H.	" "	Dove Grey	red	black			Export	U.S.A.	13.7.51
1976		K2 L.H.	2 Seater	Grey	Red				EXPORT	USA	12.3.51
1977		K2 L.H.	2 Seater	Green	Green				Export	U.S.A.	12.3.51
1978		K2 L.H.	2 Seater	Blue	Blue				Export	U.S.A.	12.3.51
1979		K2 L.H.	2 Seater	Red. M.G.	Red				Export .	U.S.A.	30.3.51
1980		K2 L.H.	2 Seater	Red	Red				Export	U.S.A.	21.4.51
1981		K2 L.H.	2 Seater	Bronze	Brown	Black.			Export	U.S.A.	28-7-51
1982		K2	2 Seater	Black					EXPORT	USA	20.4.51
1983	LESS ENG	K2	2 SEATER	DOVE GREY	RED HIDE				EXPORT.	U.S.A.	16.4.51
1984	"	K2		BLUE	BLUE	"			Export	U.S.A.	16.4.51
1985		K2 L.H.		Grey	Black		Caddy. mods.		Export	U.S.A	21.6.51
1986	LESS ENG.	K2 L.H.	2 SEATER.	DOVE GREY	RED HIDE				Export	U.S.A.	21.4.51
1987.	4G-69244F R.H.	P.	Saloon	Cream Black	Red Brown				Export	Peru Frews.	18.6.51.
1988	7252736	P.	Saloon	Black	Grey				Matage.		20.3.51
1989		P	Saloon	Chassis only					Adlards.		28.2.51
1990	7252738	P	Saloon	Black	Brown				Universal		22.3.51
1991	7252737	P	Saloon	Blue	Blue				New Central		21.3.51
1992	7252760	P	Saloon	Blue Grey	Blue				Bristol St.		28.3.51
1993	7252759	P	Saloon	Grey	Red				English		29.3.51
1994	7252765	P	Saloon	Black	Brown				Day Motors		29.3.51
1995	7252773	P	Saloon	Blue	Blue				Mimms		24.51
1996	7252739	P	Saloon	Black	Maroon				Mimms		30.3.51
1997	7252805	P	Saloon	Grey	Maroon				Harris		3.4.51
1998	7252813	P	Saloon	Blue	Blue				Tate		6.4.51.
1999	7252812	P	Saloon	Black	Brown				Taylors		6.4.51
2000	8-7483/2	M-2	Coupe	Grey	Red		Leviathan (whale) Type		Australia N.S.W		3.51
2001	7246933	M-2	Coupe	Green	natural	Tan	whale	EXPORT.	U.S.A.		4.6.51

Chassis	Engine	Type	Body	Colour	Interior	Hood					Allocated	Delivered
2002	O·Y	M2				Black						
2003	7268856	L.H. M2	Coupé	Green	Red	Beige	The Whale Type?		600×16	Support	Japan. U.S.A.	10-3-52
2004		M2?	(J2004?)			A.S. Price Blk	See card index - shown as 52 ...					25-12-50
2005	7260708	M2 L.H.	Coupé	Cream	Red	The Whale	Export.	600×16 tyres	Venezuela.		30. 8.51.
2006	S 39953 E. L.H.	M2X	Coupé	Grey	Natural	Tan		M.P. 116.	Adlards		27. 4. 51.
2007		M2	Coupé	Sunshine	Orange						
2008		M2									
2009		M2									
2010	8M-988	J	2 Seater	Blue	Blue	Lightweight windscreen	Hood Close Screen Roofed	HW WHYTE	LYV 366 Serviced oblgs 22.7.52 mileage 336 S.H.A.	1951 Le Man car see Xport card	
2011		J	2 Seater			Lengthened Chassis		To table to Engine - special F.H. Coupé body (LXN5)		Mr. Imhof.	
2012	2020/2	J	2 Seater	Bronze	Brown	for address see warner book - Adlards	Ortheffleix	Tatham NK77 Serviced at 51, mileage 4354 on 23/6/52	Adlards	28.6.51.
2013		J								
2014	2N 939	J2X	2 Seater	Green	Green	Involved in crash at Monaco 12 Drum hms outburst Brigslt	T.T. car New tangent paint	S.H.A. Mr P. Collins MGF 850	note export card ref 4 chassis S 2137	
2015	2017/2	J	2 Seater			Lengthened chassis	long w.b. Saloon body Chrysler GJB1		Godsall	2.4.51
2016	2013/2	J L.H.	2 Seater	Ivory	Red		Export		Finland	20.4.51.
2017	2014/2	J L.H	. .	CREAM.			Export		Finland	25.4.51.
2018	NIL.	J	" "	red	blue	black.	Export		U.S.A.	12.9-51
2019	NIL	J	. "	DARK BLUE.	RED	BLACK	L/H Export		U.S.A.	18-8-51.
2020	NIL	J	2 seater.	red	red		Export		U.S.A.	13-9-51
2021	7252811	P	Saloon	Black	Maroon				Taylors	9.4-51
2022	7252810	P	Saloon	met. Grey	Maroon				Dag. Motors	9-4-51
2023	7252814	P	Saloon	Grey	Grey	Export			Australia	9-4-51.
2024	7252815	P	Saloon ~ Chassis						Nurns.	3. 4. 51
2025	7252774	P	Saloon	Black	Brown				Dag. Motors	9-4-51
2026	7252806	P	Saloon	Black	Red				Adlards	26.4. 51.
2027	7254519	P	Saloon	Show Grey	Maroon				Adlards	9-4-51
2028	7249391	K2	2 Seater	Blue	Red	Blue	Eng no 3958/60	Chassis number changed to K2194	SWITZERLAND	16.4.51.
2029	7018/87	K2	. .	Blue	Rec	Black	Export	Export	Holland	4.6.51.
2030	NIL	K2	" "	beige	black.	black	Export		U.S.A.	12.4.51
2031	7252888	K2	2 Seater	RED	RED HIDE GREEN	BLACK	Export		U.S.A.	12.5.51
2032	7256167	K2	2 Seater	GREEN	BLACK	BLACK	Export		U.S.A.	12.5.51

Chassis.	Engine	Type	Body.	Colour	Interior	Hood.					Allocated.	Delivered.
2033	9615-86	K2	2 Seater	Short Grey	Blue						George Jobling	9-4-51
2034	7249391	K2	2 Seater	Red	Red						Dag. Motors	4.6.51.
2035	7246933	K2	2 Seater	Blue	Blue						Bristol St.	4.6.51.
2036		K2										
2037	less engine	K2	2 Seater	Black	Red			Export		U.S.A.		24·5·51.
2038	7252989	P	Saloon	met Grey	Red						Mann Egerton	*10-4-51
2039	7254520	P2	Saloon	Black	Blue						Alexander	*10-4-51
2040	7252985	P	Saloon	met Grey	Maroon		LXY·16.	to customer 13/7/51 demo.			Adlards	10-4-51
2041	7252956	P	Saloon	met Grey	Blue						Goulds	19.4.51
2042	7252881	P	Saloon	met Grey	Maroon						Nunns	20.4.51
2043	7254552	P	Saloon	Blue	Blue						Nunns	20.4.51
2044	7254581	P	Saloon	Black	Maroon						Trate	25.4.51
2045	7254578	P	Saloon	Black	Blue						Adlards	27.4.51
2046	7254682	P	Saloon	met Grey	Maroon						Hartwells	30.4.51
2047	7254579	P	Saloon	Black	Red			Export		Australia		15·5·51
2048	7254772	P	Saloon	Black	Maroon						Nunns	15·5·51
2049	7254684	P	Saloon	Cream	Red			Export		Australia.		15·5·51
2050	7254761	P	Saloon	Blue	Blue						New Central	30.4.51
2051	7256025	P	Saloon	Short Grey	Blue						Patterson	1·5·51
2052	7256032	P	Saloon	met Grey	Red Maroon			Export		Australia		15·5·51.
2053	7256036	P	Saloon	met Grey	Blue						Bristol St.	4·5·51
2054	7254754	P	Saloon	met Grey	Blue						Nunns	8·5·51
2055	7256187	P	Saloon	Black	Grey						English	5·5·51
2056	7256026	P	Saloon	Blue	Blue						Nunns	9·5·51.
2057	7256176	P	Saloon	Black	Red						Nunns	11·5·51.
2058	E1-U500	P2	Safari	Bronze	Brown natural			SL-87-4500	YXA555 SHA august 9.4 8ov. sale to dealer	Amber Picture		April 16th 1952
2059	2017/X 2020/2	J	2 Seater	Red	Red	for home use registered UK	be fine export LYV 364	Export	NSU975 April 1939 - car at Bhms Auction	Australia N.Z.		4·5·51·
2060	7256022	P	Saloon	met Grey	Blue						Bristol St.	9·5·51
2061	7256225	P	Saloon	met Grey	Red						Adlards	15·5·51
2062	7256177	P	Saloon	met Grey	Blue						George Jobling	15·5·51
2063	7256161	P	Saloon	Black	Red Maroon						Bristol St.	16·5·51
2064	7256029	P	Saloon	Blue	Blue					102	Trate	16·5·51

Chassis	Engine	Type	Body	Colour	Interior	Hood			Allocated		Delivered
2065	7252955	P	Saloon	met. Grey	Red: Maroon				Kenns		5.51
2066	7254685	P	Saloon	Black	Red Maroon				Hamilton		24.5.51
2067	7254553	P	Saloon	met Grey	Blue			Export	Singapore		21.5.51
2068	7252890	P	Saloon	Black	Brown				Frew		24.5.51
2069	7256164	P	Saloon	met Grey	Grey			Export	Malaya		21.5.51
2070	7256171	P	Saloon	Blue	Blue				George Jobling		28.5.51
2071	7254760	P	Saloon	met Grey	Blue				Harris		29.5.51
2072	7256764	P	Saloon	met Grey	Grey				Harris		29.5.51
2073	7256774	P	Saloon	Green	Orange				Goulds		4.6.51
2074	7256767	P	Saloon	met Grey	Red				Dag. Motors		4.6.51
2075	7256765	P	Saloon	Black	Maroon				Bristol St.		11.6.51
2076	7256766	P	Saloon	Black	Brown				Adlards		
2077	7256773	P	Saloon	Blue	Blue				New Central		7.6.51
2078	7256791	P	Saloon	Black	Brown			Export	Japan		8.6.51
2079	12105/155	P L.H.	Saloon	Grey	Red			Export	Finland		25.6.51
2080	7260024	K2	2 Seater	Bronze	Brown	R/W			Kenns		39.8.51
2081	LESS ENGINE	K2 L.H.	2 Seater	Black	Beige			Export	U.S.A.		24.5.51
2082	9618/86	K2 L.H.	2 Seater	met green	Green	grey		EXPORT	U.S.A.		4.6.51
2083		K2 L.H.	2 Seater	Cream	Black			Export	U.S.A.		28.7.51
2084	Cadly Spec.	K2 L.H.	2 Seater	Blue	Brown			Gen Curtis Le May (afterward Griswold)	shipped gear, USAF Transport plane	8.8.51	
2085		K2 L.H.	2 Seater	Green	grey			Export	U.S.A.		30.8.51
2086		J	2 Seater	Red	Red		Front Washer.	Export	U.S.A.		20.4.51
2087											
2088	2018.Z.	J	2 Seater	Maroon	Maroon	Black		Export (Donavon)	New Zealand		24.5.51
2089	12104/154	J L.H.	2 Seater	Red	Red			Export	Cuba		31.7.51
2090	12018.Z.	J	2 Seater	Royal Blue	Blue		at Monterey 1996 (Cordell Dahm) OLG 601		Tate		13.7.51
2091	7258575	K2	2 Seater	Grey	Grey				English		26.6.51
2092	7258571	K2	2 Seater	Blue	Red				Furrows		27.6.51
2093	7252887	K2	2 Seater	Cream	Red	grey		(Export)	4 Lee Malaya		28.6.51
2094	7252807	P	Saloon	met Grey	Grey			Export	Australia		14.6.51
2095	7258538	P	Saloon	Black	Maroon				Kenns		18.6.51
2096	7258085	P	Saloon	Black	Maroon				Alexander		22.6.51

Chassis	Engine	Type	Body	Colour	Interior	Hood			Allocated	Delivered
2097	7258770	P	Saloon	Black	Brown				Mann Egerton	9-7-51
2098	7258540	P	Saloon	met Grey	Blue				Tate	21.6.51
2099	7257941	P	Saloon	met Grey	Blue				Frews	21.6.51
2100	7258039	P	Saloon	Black	Blue				Harris	25.6.51
2101	7258040	P	Saloon	Black	Maroon				Tate	27.6.51
2102	7258098	P	Saloon	met Grey	Blue				new Central	24.6.51
2003	7258087	P	Saloon	Black	Brown		Rad		Dag. Motors	29.6.51
2104	9616/83	K	2 Seater	BLACK	RED			EXPORT	N. ZEALAND!	1...11.6.51
2105	2023.Z	K2 LH	2 Seater	Black	Red			Export	U.S.A.	28-7-51
2106	2024.Z	K2 LH	2 Seater	Red	Red			Export	U.S.A	28-7-51
2107		K2	2 Seater	met Green	Green				Tate	23.6.51
2108	LESS ENGINE	K2	2 Seater	Red	Red			EXPORT	Australia	20.8.51
2109	7259626	K2	2 Seater	Black	red				Dagenham Motors	26-7-51
2110	7258084	P	Saloon	met Grey	Blue				Nunns	2-7-51
2111	7258765	P	Saloon	Blue	Blue				George & Jobling	4-7-51
2112	7259012	P	Saloon	Blue	Blue				Nunns	9-7-51
2113	7258766	P	Saloon	Black	Brown		600 x 6 tyres		George & Jobling	11-7-51
2114	7259220	P	Saloon	Black	Tan		600 x .6 "		Bristol St	11-7-51
2115	7259227	P	Saloon	Black	Tan		600 x 6 "		Harris Nunns	17-7-51
2116	7256771	P	Saloon	met Grey	Maroon		600 x 6 "		Bristol St	13-7-51
2117	7258542	P	Saloon	met Grey	Grey		600 x 6 "		Adlards	18-7-51
2118	7258711	P	Saloon	Black	Maroon		600 x 6 "		Nunns	18-7-51
2119	7259636	P	Saloon	Grey met	blue	remote gearchange lever			Tate of Leeds	20-7-51
2120	2022.Z	J	2 Seater	Red	Red	white wire wheels T. Tillington Belfast			Hamilton	11.9.51
2121	2026 Z	J	2 Seater	met Grey	Blue				Nunns / DAGENHAM MOTORS	27.8.51
2122	2027 Z	J	2 Seater	Bronze	Brown	To Bristol St S.O.R 7/9/51	Transferred to Dagenham Motors (sold 1-5-52) No further record		Bristol St	9.51 / 1.5.52
2123	LESS ENG.	J LH	2 Seater	Blue	Red			EXPORT	Woods Motors USA	31-8-51
2124	2030 Z	J LH	2 Seater	Cream	Red			Export	Finland	11-9-51
2125	2025 Z	J LH	2 Seater	Blue	Blue			Export	Denver Colorado	10-1-52
2126	7258720	P	Saloon	Black	Red		600 x 16 tyres		Adlards Sheffield	2-8-51
2127	7258764	P	Saloon	Blue	Blue		600 x 16 tyres		Goulds	17-7-51
2128	7259272	P	Saloon	Black	Maroon				Bristol St	20-7-51

Hol 3218

CHASSIS	ENGINE	TYPE	BODY	COLOUR	INTERIOR	HOOD				ALLOCATED	DELIVERED
2129	7259717	P	Saloon	Black	Red					Nunns	31.7.51
2130	7259721	P	Saloon	Black	Brown		6.00 x 16 Tyres.			Universal	24.7.51
2131	7259634	P	Saloon	Show Grey	Red					Knivs	25.7.51
2132	7259013	P	Saloon	Black	Blue					Universal	31.7.51
2133	7259 275/726	J	Saloon	Dk blue	Blue	New Zealand	— Single	R/H	Export	New Zealand Singer	30.7.51
2134	7259286	P	Saloon	Nat. Grey	Blue	New Zealand	— Single	R/H	Export	New Zealand Singer	30.7.51
2135	7259281	P	Saloon	Black	Maroon	New Zealand	— Single	R/H	Export	New Zealand Singer	31.7.51
2136	2003	J	Chassis	—		— 1950 Chassis: show chassis	R/H.		Export	Gardeners Motors	6.7.51
2137	8M.988.(Cad)	J	2 Seater	Green		Radcliffe MGT. 850			Export (SHEA Simmonds)	Persse	25.7.51
2138	2028 Z	J2/x	2 Seater	Green	Black	Black	Fitted Farquam with Cadd engine John Williams			Adlards	4.9.51
2139	7259285	P	Saloon	Show grey int.	Maroon	New Zealand	— Single	R/H	Export	New Zealand Singer	31.7.51
2140	7259014	P	Saloon	Grey Show grey	Grey			R/H	Export	New Zealand Singer	11.8.51
2141	7259287	P	Saloon		Blue	NEW ZEALAND	— 6.00 x 16	R/H	Export	New Zealand Singer	13.8.51
2142	7259282	P	Saloon	Black	Maroon		6.00 x 16.	R/H		New Zealand Bristol St.	16.8.51
2143	7259221	P	Saloon	Show Grey	maroon		6.00 x 16 Tyres			Patterson	11.8.51
2144	7259632	P	Saloon	Blue	blue		6.00 x 16 Tyres.			Tate of Leeds	17.8.51
2145	7259628	P	Saloon	Black	maroon					Universal	1.9.51
2146	7259718	P	Saloon	int. Grey	Grey					Bristol St	21.8.51
2147	7259727	P	Saloon	int. Grey	Blue					Dag. Motors	11.9.51
2148	7260148	P	Saloon	int. Grey	Grey					English	13.9.51
2149	7260352	K2	2 Seater	Motif Green	Green	Blk.				Bristol St	2.8.51
2150	7260147	K2	2 Seater	Grey	Grey	Grey.				Nunns Yowel	5.8.51
2151	7260116	K2	2 Seater	Bronze	Brown	Blk.				Nunns	1.8.51
2152	7260669	K2 LH.	2 Seater	Pacific Green	Green				Export	Australia	24.8.51
2153	I. 2103/153	K2 LH.	2 Seater	Cream	Red	L/H.			Export	Finland	11.9.51
2154	Less Engine	K2 LH.	2 Seater	Green	Red	Black not removed.				Seddon U.S.A.	11.12.51
2155	2131 Z LH.	J	2 Seater	Red	Red	Service record booked in by Car Mark	no defects, mileage 174 14/5/52		:	DAGENHAM MOTORS	30.4.52
2156	Less Engine	J	2 Seater	Black	Red				Export	U.S.A.	
2157	2033 Z LH.	J	2 Seater	Ivory	Red				EXPORT	VENEZUELA.	11.10.51
2158	NEo. ENGINE	P	Saloon	Green	Red		6.00 x 16 Tyres.		Export	U.S.A	
2159	7260137	P	Saloon	int. Grey	Blue					Nunns	31.8.51
2160	7260146	P	Saloon	int. Grey	Blue					Tate	8.9.51

CHASSIS.	ENGINE.	TYPE	BODY	COLOUR	INTERIOR	HOOD.			ALLOCATED	DELIVERED.
2161	7260376	P	Saloon	met. Grey	Grey				Dag. Motors	30.8.51
2162	7261353	P	Saloon	Black	Brown				Luxurous	13-9-51
2163	7260356	P	Saloon	Primer	blue		6.00x6.	Export	Australia	6.9.51
2164	7260377	P	Saloon	Primer	maroon		6.00x16 Tyres	Export	Australia	6.9.51
2165	7260026	P	Saloon	Blue	Blue	radio.			New Central	15-8-51
2166	7260707	P	Saloon	Primer	grey.		600x.6	Export	Australia	4.9.51
2167	7261710	P	Saloon	Black	Green				Nunns	18-9-51
2168	7260729	P	Saloon	Primer	Maroon		6.00x16	Export	Australia	8.9.51
2169	7261750	P	Saloon	met Grey	Blue				Nunns	20-9-51
2170	7260025	P	Saloon	Primer	grey blue		600x.6	Export	Australia	4.9.51
2171	7261748	P	Saloon	Green	orange				Frew	22-9-51
2172	7260670	P	Saloon	Primer	blue		600x.6	Export	Australia	8.9.51
2173	7261749	P	Saloon	Black	maroon				Adlards Simut	16-10-51
2174	7261367	P	Saloon	Black	Brown				Universal	25-9-51
2175	7261983	P	Saloon	Blue	Blue		Follow Prox.		Adlards	1-10-51
2176	7261972	L.H. P	Saloon	Green	orange			Export	Brazil	4-10-51
2177	7261966	L.H. P	Saloon	Black	Red.			Export	Brazil	4-10-51
2178										
2179	Less	L.H. J	2 Seater	Black	Red	Last J2!		Export	U.S.A.	17-10-51
2180	Less Engine	L.H. J2X	2 Seater	Green	Red	Black 1951 Show Model.		Export	U.S.A.	21-11-51 3-10-51
2181	46 16377 F.	L.H. P	Saloon	met Grey	Red			Export	Finland	3-10-51.
2182	3G99168F	L.H. P	Saloon	maroon	Red			Export	Finland	10-10-51.
2183	14241/133	L.H. P	Saloon	met Blue	Blue	Ran in 1952 M/Carlo Rally from Stockholm	MR ONNI WINKES	Export	Finland	24-10-51
2184	7260369	P	Saloon	Black	Brown				Bristol St.	26-9-51.
2185	7260728	P	Saloon	met Grey	Red				Hartwells	26-9-51.
2186	7261360	P	Saloon	Black	maroon				Nunns.	1-10-51.
2187	7261359	P	Saloon	Black	Brown				Dag. Motors	4-10-51.
2188	7261352	P	Saloon	Blue	Blue				New Central	12-10-51.
2189	7262013	P	Saloon	met Grey	Blue				Tate	10-10-51.
2190	7261709	P	Saloon	Grey	Red				Nunns	14-11-51
2191	Less Engine	L.H. J2X	2 Seater	Blue	Blue	Black Jean Davison France.		Export (?)	USA	29-11-51
2192	Less Engine	J2X	2 Seater	Grey	Red			Export (Wood)	USA	22-1-52

CHASISS	ENGINE	TYPE	BODY	COLOUR	INTERIOR	HOOD				ALLOCATED	DELIVERED
2193	Less Engine	L.H. J2X	2 Seater	Blue	Red	Black		Export (Moss)		U.S.A. Switzerland	14-12-51
2194	7259720	K2	2 SEATER	RED	BROWN HIDE		Changed from (see) K2028	Export		~~SINGER N. ZEALAND~~	15.8.51
2195	~~7261757~~ LESS ENGINE	K2	2 Seater	Red	Red			Export		U.S.A.	
2196	7261789	K2	2 Seater	GREEN A-GREY	GREEN					BRISTOL ST. MOTORS	29-8-51
2197	2036.2.	L.H. K2 ELECT.	2 Seater	Blue	Blue			Export		U.S.A.	10-1-52
2198	LESS ENGINE	L.H. K2 ELEC	2 Seater	BLUE	BLUE	BLACK	LHD	Export		SEDDON. U.S.A	3-1-52
2199	LESS ENGINE	L.H. K2	2 Seater	Blue	Red	Black		Export		SEDDON U.S.A.	7-2-52
2200	7262943	K2	2 Seater	Silver Grey	Grey					English	19-10-51
2201	7264458	K2	2 Seater	Blue	Blue					Blue	
2202	7264732	K2	2 Seater	Red	Red	Black				Dag. Motors	20-11-51
2203	7269801	K2	2 Seater	light-met. Grey	Grey	Black	Believed to be first JK2X chassis	driven by Dunlop in Belgium MPL117		Adlards	21.3.52
2204	7261753	P	Saloon	Blue	Blue					George & Jobling	11-10-51
2205	7262460	P	Saloon	Black	Brown					Nunns	23-10-51
2206	7262392	P	Saloon	Blue	Blue					Bristol St.	15-10-51
2207	7262343	P	Saloon	met. Grey	Blue		Radio			Goulds	17-10-51
2208	7262561	P	Saloon	met Grey	Maroon					English	23-10-51
2209	7262957	P	Saloon	met Grey	~~Blue~~ Blue					Nunns.	24-10-51
2210											
2211											
2212											
2213											
2214											
2215											
2216											
2217											
2218											
2219	Less Engine	L.H. J2X	2 Seater	Red	Red			Export (Goldsmith)		U.S.A	29-1-52
2220											
2221	Less Engine	L.H. J2X	2 Seater	Red	Black	Black		Export (Seddon)		U.S.A.	23-1-52
2222	Less Engine	L.H. J2X	2 Seater	Blue	Red			Export (Seddon)		U.S.A.	23-1-52
2223	Less Engine	J2X	2 Seater	Grey	Red			Export		Peters	29-12-51
2224	2017/2	J2X	Chassis				Special Wide Chassis Col. Geer			Aero Essex	14-1-52

CHASSIS	ENGINE	TYPE	BODY	COLOUR	INTERIOR	HOOD				ALLOCATED TO	DELIVERED.
2225	7262939	P	Saloon	Blue	Blue		new small grille & heater			Tate	29-10-51.
2226	7262937	P	Saloon	Black	Brown					Bristol St.	27-10-51.
2227	7262952	P	Saloon	Blue	Blue					Nunns	1-11-51.
2228	7261992	P	Saloon	met Grey	Grey					Bristol St.	29-10-51
2229	7262385	P	Saloon	met Grey	Maroon					~~Nunns~~ Nunns.	~~27-11-51~~
2230	7262468	P	Saloon	met Grey	Blue					Bristol St.	1-11-51.
2231	7262389	P	Saloon	Black	Blue					Tate	1-11-51.
2232	7262934	P	Saloon	Black	Brown					Dag. Motors	6-11-51.
2233	7262479	P	Saloon	met Blue	Blue					Tate	8-11-51.
2234	7264457	P	Saloon	Show Grey	Blue					Tate	8-11-51.
2235	7262462	P	Saloon	Black	Maroon					Bristol St.	7-11-51.
2236	7264506	P	Saloon	met Grey	Maroon					Tate	8-11-51.
2237	7262374	P	Saloon	Black	Tan					Bristol St.	7-11-51.
2238	7263582	P	Saloon	met Grey	Red					Bristol St.	13-11-51.
2239	7264733	P	Saloon	met Grey	Blue				Export	New Zealand	10-11-51.
2240	7264494	P	Saloon	met Grey	Blue				Export	New Zealand	13-11-51.
2241	7264542	P	Saloon	Blue	Blue				Export	New Zealand	13-11-51.
2242	7262014	K2	2 Seater	Bronze	Brown					Bristol St.	3-10-51.
2243		K	2 Seater								
2244											
2245											
2246	7264696	P	Saloon	Black	Tan				Export	New Zealand	13-11-51.
2247	7264547	P	Saloon	met Grey	Blue				Export	New Zealand	13-11-51.
2248	7262928	P	Saloon	Black	Tan				Export	New Zealand	13-11-51
2249	7262954	P	Saloon	Blue	Blue					Frews	20-11-51.
2250	7262969	P	Saloon	met Grey	Red					Nunns	1-12-51
2251	7262955	P	Saloon	met Grey	Grey					Goulds	21-11-51.
2252	7263584	P	Saloon	Blue	Blue					Adlards	1-12-51
2253	7265181	P	Saloon	Black	Brown				Export	New Zealand	4-12-51.
2254	7265177	P	Saloon	Black	Blue					New Central	29-11-51
2255	7265163	P	Saloon	Black	Maroon					Bristol St.	30-11-51
2256	7265164	P	Saloon	Blue	Blue					Adlards	28-11-51.

CHASSIS	ENGINE	TYPE	BODY	COLOUR	INTERIOR	HOOD			ALLOCATED TO	DELIVERED
2257	7265763	P	Saloon	met Grey	Red				Hartwells	4-12-51
2258	7265700	P	Saloon	met Grey	Grey				Dag. Motors	3-12-51
2259	7265777	P	Saloon	Blue	Blue				Dag. Motors	5-12-51
2260	7265761	P	Saloon	Blue	Blue				Dag. Motors	5-12-51
2261	7265860	P	Saloon	met Grey	Blue				Hamilton	10-12-51
2262	7264737	P	Saloon	show Grey	Blue				George & Jobling	6-12-51
2263	7264876	P	Saloon	Blue	Red				Adlards	15-12-51
2264	7263696	P	Saloon	Black	Brown				Dag. Motors	15-12-51
2265	7264881	P	Saloon	Black	Blue		Export		New Zealand	14-12-51
2266	7264738	P	Saloon	Black	Maroon				George & Jobling	13-12-51
2267	7266394	P	Saloon	met Grey	Red				Hartwells	18-12-51
2268	7265169	P	Saloon	met Grey	Blue		Export		New Zealand	18-12-51
2269	7265037	P	Saloon	met Grey	Maroon	Radio			Adlards	8-1-52
2270	7266551	P	Saloon	Blue	Blue				George & Jobling	2-1-52
2271	7266542	P	Saloon	Blue	Blue		Export		New Zealand	20-12-51
2272	7266396	P	Saloon	Black	Brown				New Central	28-1-52
2273	7265701	P	Saloon	Black	Maroon				Bristol St.	21-12-51
2274	7265854	P	Saloon	Black	Brown				Dag. Motors	31-12-51
2275	E408	PIX	Saloon	met Blue	Blue		S.H.A. Monte Car checked			
2276	7265770	P	Saloon	Black	Blue				Bristol St.	3-1-52
2277	7266553	P	Saloon	met Grey	Maroon		Export		New Zealand	4-1-52
2278	7265855	P	Saloon	met Grey	Red		Export		New Zealand	4-1-52
2279	7266539	P	Saloon	met Grey	Maroon		Central Motors Leicester		Universal	28-1-52
2280	7266441	P	Saloon	Blue	Blue				Tate	6-3-52
2281	7264458	P	Saloon	Blue	Blue				Adlards	2-2-52
2282	7266389	P	Saloon	Blue	Blue		S.O.R.		Henns	13-3-52
2283	7268037	P	Saloon	Black	Blue				Tate	2-2-52
2284	7268026	P	Saloon	Black	Maroon				Furrows	5-2-52
2285	E409	PIX	Saloon	met Grey	Maroon		S.H.A. Miss Adlards Monte Car		Adlards	13-3-52
2286	7268378	P	Saloon	Black	Brown				New Central	1-2-52
2287	7268364	P	Saloon	met Grey	Red	Black Brown	WILSON AMALGAMATED. RETURNED		see 3100 and export Card	18.3.53
2288	7268379	P	Saloon	met Grey	Blue		(BANKET AREAS LTD. GOLD COAST)		Goulds	9-2-52

CHASSIS	ENGINE	TYPE	BODY	COLOUR	INTERIOR	HOOD			ALLOCATED TO	DELIVERED.
2289	7268369	P	Saloon	met Grey	Maroon				Dag. Motors	19-2-52.
2290	7268860.	P	Saloon	Blue	Grey				Nuw Central	15-2-52.
2291	7268850.	P	Saloon	Blue	Grey				Bristol St.	25.2.52.
2292	7268851	P	Saloon	Black	Brown				Nuw Central	15-2-52.
2293	7269443	P	Saloon	Black	Maroon				Patterson	20-2-52
2294	7269434	P	Saloon	Black	Brown				Dag. Motors	26.2.52.
2295	7265176 ~~E~~	M2X	Coupe	Blue	Blue	Black			Adlards	28-11-51
2296	7262377	M2X	Coupe	Cream	Brown	Fawn			Tate	6-11-51.
2297	7265766	M2X	Coupe	Grey	Blue	Black			Bristol St.	11-12-51.
2298	Less Engine L.H.	M2X	Coupe	Blue	Red	Beige L.E.		Export (Sidden)	U.S.A	24-1-52.
2299	7265691	M2X	Coupe	met Grey	Red	Black			Dagenham Motors AB	21-12-51.
2300										
2301										
2302			Continued at Chassis No 3012							
2303										
2304										
2305										
2306										
2307										
2308										
2309										
2310										
2311										
2312										
2313										
2314										
2315										
2316										
2317										
2318										
2319										
2320										

NOTE:

Address from unknown source quotes chassis
L2X/1740 : STEN TELLANDER
HÄSTHOVSGATAN 13   Fjällgatan 55D
GOTHENBURG O   Borås
SWEDEN.   Sweden

Later: Letter from Sören Frosberg
Jan. 1994   in files with photographs.
Car totally destroyed in fire.

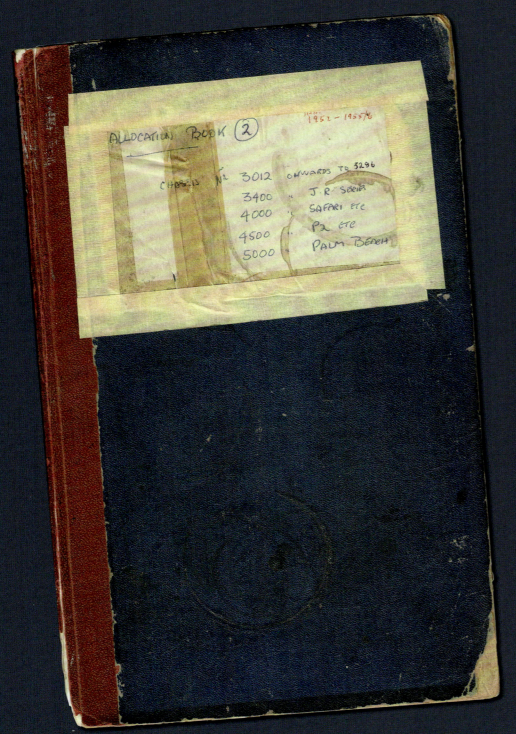

ALLARD
ALLOCATION BOOK II

1952–1955/6

CHASSIS:
3012–3286
3401–3407
4000–4009
4500–4513
5000–5201

Palm Beach = 5000 chain Nº
Safari 4000
P.2 4500

CHASSIS Nº	ENGINE	TYPE	BODY	COLOUR	INTERIOR	HOOD			ALLOCATION	DELIVERED
3000	5337/25	P2	Safari				Ec.4001	MKA 554 1st D.A.	19-12-55 at 51 from Silverstone mileage 47,987	
3001										
3002										
3003										
3004										
3005										
3006										
3007										
3008										
3009										
3010										
3011										
3012	7266391	M2X	Coupe	met. Grey	Red	Black		S.C.R.	English Dag. motors	20-2-52
3013	7266552	M2X	Coupe	Black	Brown	Black			Dag. motors	31-1-52
3014	7266545	M2X	Coupe	Blue	Blue	Black	Santin.		Dag. motors	1-1-52
3015	7268025	M2X	Coupe	Black	Brown	Black			Dag. motors	25-1-52
3016	7268373	M2X	Coupe met. light Blue	light Blue	Blue	Black			Dag. motors	25-1-52
3017	Less Engine	K3	2 Seater	Ivory	Black	Black	3c Dion axle	Imoterg	U.S.A	12-3-52
3018	Less Engine	K2	2 Seater	Grey	Red	Black		(Seddon)	U.S.A	14-3-52
3019	Less Engine	K2	2 Seater	Red	Black	Black		(Seddon)	U.S.A	6-3-52
3020	LESS ENGINE	K2	2 Seater	FRENCH GREY	BLACK	BLACK			U.S.A	3-4-52
3021	LESS ENGINE	K2	2 Seater	B. GREY	RED	BLACK			U.S.A	31-4-52
3022	LESS ENGINE	K2	2 Seater	M.G. RED	BLACK	BLACK		(SEDDON)	U.S.A	6-5-52
3023	LESS ENGINE	K2	2 Seater	GREEN	GREEN	BLACK		(Seddon)	U.S.A	4-5-52
3024	LESS ENGINE	K2	2 Seater	CREAM/BLACK	BLACK	BLACK			U.S.A	22-4-52
3025	LESS ENGINE	K2	2 Seater	RED	B.RED	BEIGE		(Seddon)	U.S.A	26-5-52
3026	2R-558	K2	2 Seater	MET. BLUE	ORANGE	BEIGE		GEN CURTIS.	U.S.A	9-5-52
3027	LESS ENGINE	K2	2 Seater	GREEN	GREEN	BLACK				31-5-52
3028	LESS ENGINE	K2	2 Seater	RED	RED	BLACK		(KerR motors)	U.S.A	9-7-52
3029	LESS ENGINE	K2	2 Seater	GREEN	RED	BLACK			U.S.A	17-6-52
3030	C52/8/45973	K-3	3 Seater	Blue	Red		1952 Show car.	(General Griswold)	U.S.A. NGP 170	3-11-52
3031	Less Engine	K2	2 Seater	PRIMER				DISTRIBUIDORA DE AUTOS	U.S.A.	8-12-52
3032	15870/146	K	2 Seater	GREEN	GREEN	BLACK		(DR. MAHAFFY)	PANAMA	11-8-52

CHASSIS No	ENGINE No	TYPE	BODY	COLOUR	INTERIOR	HOOD				ALLOCATION		DELIVERED
3033	7275022	K2	2 SEATER	M-BLUE	MAROON	BLACK			(U.S. EMBASSY)	JOHN. CHARLES. KLAFFENBACH		30.7.52
3034	LESS ENGINE	K2	2 SEATER	BLACK	RED	BLACK				NOEL KIRK MOTORS U.S.A		15.7.52
3035	7277942	K2	2 SEATER	RED	RED	BLACK				A. LOUIS STRAUS. U.S.A.		3.9.52
3036	7277954	K2	2 SEATER	CREAM	BLACK	BLACK				A. LOUIS STRAUS.		3.9.52
3037	Less Engine	J2X L.H.	2 Seater	Red	Black	Black		Export	(Seddon)	U.S.A.		29-1-52
3038	less Engine	J2X L.H.	2 Seater	Blue	Red			Export	(Seddon)	U.S.A.		12-2-52
3039	less Engine	J2X L.H.	2 Seater	Blue	Red	Black		Export	(Denver)	U.S.A.		14-2-52
3040	LESS ENGINE	J2X L.H.	2 SEATER	BLACK	RED	BLACK		Export	(CALIFORNIA)	U.S.A.		25.2.52
3041	Less Engine	J2X L.H.	2 Seater	Ivory	Red	Black		R/P. IMPORTED California	U.S.A			6-3-52 ~~24-2-52~~
3042	LESS ENGINE	J2X	2 SEATER	RED.	RED	BLACK		Export	R/ Imported	U.S.A.		29.2.52
3043	LESS ENGINE	J2X	2 SEATER	GREEN	GREEN	BLACK		Export	SEDDON	U.S.A.		29.2.52
3044	LESS ENGINE	J2X L.H.	2 Seater	RED	RED				(Denver)	U.S.A		26.3.52
3045	LESS ENGINE	J2X L.H.	2 Seater	ROYAL BLUE	BLUE				(Three)	U.S.A.		27.3.52
3046	~~LESS ENGINE~~	J2X	2 Seater	RED.	RED.				(California)	U.S.A		29.3.52
3047	LESS ENGINE	J2X	2 Seater	GREEN.	RED.	BLACK			SEDDON	U.S.A		2.4.52
3048	LESS ENGINE	J2X L.H.	2 Seater	WHITE	BLACK	BLACK						2.4.52
3049	CHR-151	J2X L.H.	2 Seater	Light de Man body British R. Green			Chrysler Engine	4 Speed Box owsch Change rear end.	Le Man car	(Curtis)	Rebuilt as Piston spec MXF 974	
3050	LESS ENGINE	J2X L.H.	2 Seater	BRIGHT RED	RED.	BEIGE			(Harry Steele)	U.S.A.		1.5.52
3051	LESS ENGINE	J2X L.H.	2 Seater	RED	RED				(California)	U.S.A.		17.4.52
3052	LESS ENGINE	J2X L.H.	2 Seater	BLUE	BLUE?		Cadillac		(CALIFORNIA)	U.S.A.		18.4.52
3053	C-150	J2X	2 Seater	B.R RED ✓ Green	Tan	BLACK.		4 speed Box Fred Demodeau	(Watkins)	New Central ORL 320		9.5.52
3054	LESS ENGINE	J2X	2 Seater	BLUE	BLUE	BEIGE			(Craigu)	Nairobi		26.5.52
3055	CHR-100	J2X L.H.	2 Seater de Man body	Green	Chrysler engine retained = car shipped with Cadillac mountings		Le Man car (S.H.A)		R/P. IMPORTED MTR CO.	U.S.A. MXF 969		13.8.52
3056	LESS ENGINE	J2X L.H.	2 Seater	BUGAT BLUE	RED	BLACK			(Seddon)	U.S.A.		6.5.52
3057	LESS ENGINE	J2X L.H.	2 Seater	BLACK.	RED.				(Seddon)	U.S.A.		24.8.52
3058	LESS ENGINE	J2X	2 Seater	RED.	RED	BEIGE			(Seddon)	U.S.A.		24.5.52
3059	LESS ENGINE	J2X L.H.	2 Seater	GREEN	WHITE	BLACK			IMPORTED MOT	U.S.A.		26.6.52
3060	LESS ENGINE	J2X	2 Seater	CREAM	BLUE				(Seddon)	U.S.A		24.5.52
3061	LESS ENGINE	J2X L.H.	2 Seater	GREEN	GREEN	BLACK			(Seddon)	U.S.A.		14.6.52
3062	LESS ENGINE	J2X	2 Seater	IVORY	RED	BLACK			NOEL KIRK	U.S.A.		25.6.52
3063	20412	J2X L.H.	2 Seater	BRONZE	BROWN	BEIGE			(George Lee)	Singapore		10.6.52
3064	LESS ENGINE	J2X	2 Seater	GREEN	RED	BLACK			(Seddon)	U.S.A.		2.7.52
3065	LESS ENGINE	J2X	2 Seater	Royal BLUE	RED	BLACK				U.S.A.		2.7.52

·ALLARD·

CHASSIS No	ENGINE No (CHRYSLER)	TYPE	BODY	COLOUR	INTERIOR	HOOD			ALLOCATION	DELIVERED
3066	C.52-8-46975	J2X	2-SEATER. (Le Mans body)	M-BLUE	RED	BLACK			CAPTAIN LESLIE. U.S.A.F. (U.S.A.)	2.12.52
3067	LESS ENGINE	J2X	2 SEATER.	WHITE	GREEN	GREEN			R/P. IMPORTED MOTOR CAR CO:	18.8.52
3068	LESS ENGINE	J2X	2 seater	BLACK	RED	BLACK			CALIFORNIA SPORTS.	15.7.52.
3069	LESS ENGINE	J2X	2 seater.	BLUE	BLUE	BLACK			CALIFORNIA SPORTS. CAR	15.7.52.
3070	2040 Z	J2X	2 Seater	RED	RED	BLACK	Le Mans body? letter from Bueda 17-1-87		Nairobi	24.6.52.
3071	LESS ENGINE.	J2X	2 Seater	RED	RED	BLACK			NOEL KIRK MOTORS.	6.1.53
3072	LESS ENGINE	J2X	2 SEATER	LIGHT BLUE	RED	BLACK			MOTORSPORT INC; U.S.A.	22.7.52.
3073	LESS ENGINE	J2X	2 SEATER	BLACK	BROWN				SPEEDCRAFT ENTERPRISES	9.9.52.
3074	LESS ENGINE	J2X	2 SEATER	PRIMER	RED				CALIFORNIA SPORTS CAR CO.	25.9.52.
3075	LESS ENGINE	J2X	2 SEATER	RED	RED				NOEL KIRK MOTORS. U.S.A	1.9.52.
3076	LESS ENGINE	J2X	2 SEATER	RED	RED	BLACK			SHAWNEE MOTOR CO: (U.S.A)	30.9.52.
3077	LESS ENGINE	J2X	2 SEATER	GREY-RED	HIDE INT.				NOEL KIRK MOTORS.	4.10.52.
3078	7269845	P	Saloon	met. Grey	Red				Nunns	14-3-52.
3079	7269838	P	Saloon	met. Grey	Blue	MON 831	Miss L Rado Birmingham	AOC N/L 1967	Bristol St.	0--8-52.
3080	7269839	P	Saloon	met. Grey	Maroon				Adlards	3.4.52.
3081	7269433	P	Saloon	Black	Brown				New Central	13-3-52.
3082	7269840	P	Saloon	Black	Brown				Adlards	26.3.52 / 19.3.52
3083	7270578	P	Saloon	Black	Maroon				Harris	19.3.52
3084	7270583	P	Saloon	Black	Brown				Furrows	4.4.52
3085	7270581	P	Saloon	Bronze	Maroon				George & Jobling	18.4.52.
3086	7271485	P	Saloon	met. Grey	Maroon				Universal	14.4.52
3087	7271089	P	Saloon	Black	Brown				Patterson	9.5.52
3088	7273164	P	Saloon	Black	Brown				Adlards	16.5.52.
3089	7268377	M2X	Coupé	met. Grey	Blue	Black			Goulds	31-1-52
3090	7268859	M2X	Coupé	met. Grey	Maroon	Black	Discovered in Bar. rec AOC New letter April 88		Tate	7-2-52.
3091	7268855	M2X	Coupé	met. Grey	Maroon	Black			Bristol St	9-2-52.
3092	7269430	M2X	Coupé	Red Green Black	Brown	Black			Adlards	14-3-52.
3093	7269429	M2X	Coupé	Black	Brown	Black			Patterson	29.3.52.
3094	Less Engine	M2X L.H.	Coupé	Blue	Red	Blue		Sedden	U.S.A.	17-3-52
3095	7269844	P X	Coupé	lt. Blue	Blue BROWN	Blue	Sold at Cape £10,500 25 July 1985.			0--3-52
3096	7270599	M2X	Coupé	met. Grey	Maroon	Black			Mann Egerton	1.5.52
3097	7271488	M2X	Coupé	met. Grey	Maroon	Black			Adlards	26.4.52
3098	7274426	M2X	Coupé	Blue	Grey	Black			Adlards	4.6.52

CHASSIS Nº	ENGINE Nº	TYPE	BODY	COLOUR	INTERIOR	HOOD			ALLOCATION	DELIVERED
3099	7271156	P	Saloon	met. grey	maroon		with central remote gear change.		English. (Coxdo)	9.5.52
3100	12F 7268369 mech.	P	Saloon	Black	Brown		Transferred & shipped under 2287		Tarkwa (Gold Coast)	13.3.53
3101	7280981	P	Saloon	met. grey	maroon				BRISTOL STREET MOTORS	1.10.52
3102		P	Saloon	Black	Brown					
3103	E1-U-5101	P	Saloon	BLUE	RED			SWEDEN	MME. JOCOLYN. HJELME-LUNDBERG.	23.7.52
3104	7275028	P	Saloon	Blue	Blue	‚		(508)	George & Jobling	
3105		P	Saloon							
3106		P	Saloon							
3107	9424 B.	L.H. P	SALOON	BLACK	BLUE				INGVAR BERGENGREN	2.10.52
3108										
3109										
3110										
3111										
3112										
3113										
3114										
3115										
3116										
3117										
3118										
3119	7280348	M2X	Coupe	Black	Brown	Black	Black Record cards show exported to Sydney N.S.W	Reg Nº YMH692 19/9/56 Mr M Couch	Dag. Motors	12.9.52
3120	7271486	M2X	Coupe	Black	brown	black			Munns (Webbs)	8.5.52
3121		M2X	Coupe	Black	brown					
3122	7274428	M2X	Coupe	Blue	Blue	Black		(Allard)	Dominions Export	14.6.52
3123		L.H. M2X	Coupe	met. grey	maroon	Black				
3124	15868/105	M2X	Coupe	Cream	Red	Red			Stockholm	6.8.52
3125	LESS ENGINE	K2	2 SEATER	TORQ. BLUE	GREY	BLACK			NOEL KIRK MOTORS.	18.9.52
3126	LESS ENGINE	K2	2 SEATER	RED	RED	BLACK			NOEL KIRK MOTORS.	22.9.52
3127	LESS ENGINE	K2	2 SEATER	BEIGE	BROWN				NOEL KIRK MOTORS.	7.10.52
3128	15869/108 LESS ENGINE	K	2 SEATER	CREAM GREY	RED RED	BLACK			JUAN RIU. PANAMERICAN IMPORT NOEL KIRK MOTORS.	27.10.52
3129										
3130	LESS ENGINE	K2	2 SEATER	CREAM	TAN	BLACK			RIVIERA MOTORS INC.	10.10.52
3131										

·ALLARD·

Chassis Nº	Engine Nº	Type	Colour	Body	Interior	Hood			Allocation	Delivered
3132				2-Seater.						
3133	Less Engine.	K2	Blue	Blue	Blue.	Black		Noel Kirk Motors	U.S.A.	6.11.52.
3134										
3135										
3136										
3137										
3138										
3139										
3140	Less Engine	J2X	White.	Le-Mans. 2-Seater	Red.				Speedcraft Enterprises, U.S.A.	24.12.52.
3141	Less Engine.	J2X	Red Primer	Le Mans 2-Seater	Brown/or Pig-Skin				Allard Motor Co., Inc. U.S.A.	9.1.53
3142	Less Engine	J2X	Green	2 Seater	Tan Pig-Skin	Black			Sports Car Inc. U.S.A.	27.3.53
3143	Less Engine	J2X	Red	Black	Black	Black			Noel Kirk Motors.	10.10.52
3144	Less Engine	J2X	O/White.	2-Seater	Black	Black			Noel Kirk Motors (U.S.A).	19.11.52.
3145	Less Engine	J2X	Red	2-Seater	Black	Black			Noel Kirk Motors (U.S.A.)	19.11.52.
3146	Less Engine	J2X	Cream	2-Seater	Red	Black			Noel Kirk Motors (U.S.A).	20.11.52.
3147	Less Engine	J2X	Red	2-Seater	Tan				Sports Car Inc (U.S.A.)	13.3.53.
3148	Less Engine.	J2X	Red.	2-Seater	Black	Black			Noel Kirk Motors (U.S.A.)	29.11.52.
3149	Less Engine.	J2X	Biscuit	Le Mans 2-Seater	Red.	Black.			Noel Kirk Motors (U.S.A.)	7.1.53.
3150	8R.144 Cadillac	J2X	Red	2 Seater.	Red	Red.			Juan Riu. Pan American.	24.10.52
3151	Less Engine	J2X	Black	2-Seater.	Red				Noel Kirk Motors.	6.1.53
3152	Less Engine.	J2X	Green	Le Mans. 2-Seater	Green	Black			Sports Cars Inc.	24.2.53
3153	S334(Chrysler)	J2X	White	Lemans. 2-Seater.	White.	Black			Norman K. Patton. U.S.A.	14.5.53.
3154	Less Engine.	J2X	Primer	2-Seater.	Red.	Black.			Allard Motor Co. Inc. U.S.A	9.1.53.
3155	Less Engine	J2X	Red	Le Mans 2-Seater.	White Black	Black		Query? Correspondence with J.C McGregor Springfield Ohio claiming 1980/83 + Davis record cards - establishes this car as Ed Schilling Le Mans type, red + red. - shippers data correct. but is A.M.C New York	Sports Cars. Inc.?	8.4.53
3156	Less Engine	J2X	Red	2-Seater	Red	Black			Ingvar Bergengren. U.S.A	6.3.53.
3157	Less Engine	J2X	Red	2 Seater	Red	Black			R.S. Robinson. Firestone Tire Rubber.	10.12.52
3158	Less Engine	J2X	Red	2-Seater.	Red.	Black.			Sports Cars Inc. U.S.A.	22.4.53
3159										
3160										
3161	Less Engine	J2X	Red	2-Seater	Red	Black			Shawnee Motor Co. U.S.A.	2.5.53.
3162	Less Engine.	J2X	Gun Metal	2-Seater. Red.	Red.	Black.		Bob Lytle	Sports Car. Inc. U.S.A.	3.2.53
3163	Less Engine	J2X	Blue	2-Seater	Red				Custom Automotive U.S.A.	2.5.53.
3164	S5028(Chrysler)	J2X	Red	2-Seater	Red	Black			Basil K. Evans. (Allard)	24.9.53.

Chassis Nº	Engine Nº	Type	Body	Colour	Interior	Hood			Allocation		Delivered
3165	LESS ENGINE	K3	SPORTS. M-BLUE	M-BLUE	BLUE	BLACK.			ALLARD MOTOR CO. INC. U.S.A.		7.1.53.
3166	LESS ENGINE	K3	SPORTS. 3-SEATER	SILVER GREY	RED	BLACK			SPORTS CAR INC. U.S.A.		23.2.53
3167	LESS ENGINE	K.3	3-SEATER	PRIMER	BLACK	BLACK			OVERSEAS EQUIPMENT CORPORATION. U.S.A.		12.1.53.
3168	LESS ENGINE	K3	3-SEATER	CREAM	BLACK	BLACK			ALLARD MOTOR CO; INC; U.S.A.		24.12.52.
3169	LESS ENGINE	K3	3-SEATER	CREAM	RED	BLACK			WM. W. VALENTINE U.S.A.		2.3.53.
3170	LESS ENGINE	K3	3-SEATER	BLACK	RED	BLACK			SPORTS CARS INC U.S.A.		14.3.53
3171	1458 614 CARBON	K.3	3-SEATER	LIGHT GREY	RED	BLACK			VAUXHALL MOTORS LTD. U.S.A.		24.2.53.
3172	LESS ENGINE	K.3	3-SEATER	M-BLUE	RED.	BLACK			ALLARD MOTOR CO; INC. U.S.A.		4.1.53.
3173	LESS ENGINE	K3	3-SEATER	M-BLUE	RED	BLACK			JORGE BARRANCO MEXICO		27.3.53
3174	LESS ENGINE	K.3	3-SEATER	M.GREY	RED	GREY			SPORTS CARS INC. U.S.A.		18.3.53
3175	GEARBOX LESS ENGINES	K.3	3-SEATER	ROYAL BLUE	RED.	BLACK			BRITISH MOTOR CAR DISTRIBUTORS. U.S.A.		5.2.53.
3176	LESS ENGINE.	K3.	3-SEATER	M-BLUE	BLUE	BLACK			NOEL KIRK MOTORS. U.S.A.		4.2.53
3177	GEARBOX LESS ENGINES	K3	3-SEATER	MAROON	RED	BLACK			NOEL KIRK MOTORS. U.S.A.		4.2.53.
3178	LESS ENGINE	K3.	3-SEATER	M.G.RED.	BLACK	BLACK.			ALLARD MOTOR CO. INC. U.S.A.		8.1.53.
3179	LESS ENGINE.	K3.	3-SEATER	RED.	BLACK	BLACK.			SPORTS CARS INC. U.S.A.		14.5.53.
3180	LESS ENGINE.	K3	3-SEATER.	M.BLUE.	RED.	BLACK			SPORTS CAR INC. U.S.A.		3.2.53.
3181	LESS ENGINE.	K3	3-SEATER.	M-GREY	GREY	BLACK			SPORTS CAR INC. U.S.A.		12.5.53.
3182	LESS ENGINE	K3	3-SEATER	RED.	BLACK	BLACK			NOEL KIRK MOTORS U.S.A.		25.6.53.
3183	LESS ENGINE	K3.	3-SEATER	M-GREY	RED	BLACK			SPORTS CAR INC. U.S.A.		24.2.53.
3184	LESS ENGINE	K3	3-SEATER.	BRONZE	TAN	BLACK.			SPORTS CARS INC. U.S.A.		5.5.53.
3185	LESS ENGINE.	K3.	3-SEATER.	GREEN	TAN	BLACK.			SPORTS CARS INC. U.S.A.		22.4.53.
3186	LESS ENGINE	K3	3-SEATER	TURQUOISE	BLUE	BLACK.			NOEL KIRK MOTORS U.S.A.		27.5.53.
3187	LESS ENGINE	K3	3-SEATER	CREAM	BLACK	BLACK			SPORTS CARS INC. U.S.A.		18.3.53
3188	LESS ENGINE	K3	3-SEATER	M.GREEN	TAN	BLACK.			JORGE BARRANCO & CO. MEXICO.		15.3.53.
3189	LESS ENGINE	K3	3-SEATER	M-GREY	GREEN	BLACK.			SPORTS CAR INC. U.S.A.		14.3.53.
3190	LESS ENGINE	K3	3-SEATER.	BRONZE	TAN	BLACK			SPORTS CAR INC. U.S.A.		19.3.53
3191	LESS ENGINE	K3	3-SEATER	SILVER GREY	RED.	BLACK			BRITISH MOTOR CAR U.S.A.		24.4.53.
3192	LESS ENGINE	K3	3-SEATER.	GREEN	GREEN	BLACK.			NOEL KIRK MOTORS. U.S.A.		10.7.53.
3193	LESS ENGINE.	K3.	3-SEATER.	CRIMSON.	TAN	BLACK.			NOEL KIRK MOTORS. U.S.A.		10.7.53.
3194	LESS ENGINE	K3	3-SEATER	MAROON	BLACK	BLACK			SPORTS CAR INC. U.S.A.		8.4.53
3195	LESS ENGINE	K3	3-SEATER	BLUE	RED				NOEL KIRK MOTORS U.S.A.		20.8.53.
3196	LESS ENGINE	K3	3-SEATER	M-BLUE	BLUE	BLACK			KIRK MOTORS. U.S.A.		27.4.53.
3197	LESS ENGINE	K3	3-SEATER.	M-BLUE.	BLUE	BLACK.			SPORTS CARS INC. U.S.A.		5.5.53.

CHASSIS Nº	ENGINE Nº.	TYPE	BODY	COLOUR	INTERIOR	HOOD			ALLOCATION.	DELIVERED
3198	LESS ENGINE	K3	2-SEATER SPORTS	BRONZE	TAN	BLACK			SPORTS CARS INC U.S.A.	4.6.53.
3199	LESS ENGINE	K3	3-SEATER	BRONZE	TAN	BEIGE			SPORTS CARS INC., U.S.A.	25.6.53.
3200	LESS ENGINE	J2X	2-SEATER	RED	RED	BLACK.			SPORTS CARS INC. U.S.A.	16.4.53.
3201	LESS ENGINE	J2X Le Man B.	2-SEATER	RED.	BLACK			U.S.A.	MERRIMACK ST GARAGES	15.10.53.
3202	LESS ENGINE	J2X Le Man B.	2-SEATER	GREEN	RED	BLACK			SHAWNEE MOTOR CO. U.S.A.	22.4.53.
3203	Nº TRANSFERD TO 3211				.					
3204										
3205	D.50.1013	J2X	2-SEATER	RED	RED	BLACK.		U.S.A	ALLARD MOTOR CO. LTD. U.S.A.	16.6.54
3206										
3207										
3208	LESS ENGINE	J2X	2-SEATER	RED	BLACK				BRITISH MTR. CAR. DIST. U.S.A.	24.8.53.
3209	LESS ENGINE.	J2X	2-SEATER SPORTS	BEIGE	RED.				BUDD & DYER. LTD. CANADA.	16.5.53.
3210										
3211	V.8. 3211	J2X	2-SEATER SPORTS	RED	RED				ARIMANY & CO. LTD. GUATEMALA	26.8.53.
3212										
3213	9T.136 CAD.	J2X Le Man Body	2-SEATER SPORTS	RED	BLUE	GREY.			ANTIONIO IZQUIERDO. B COLUMBIA.	24.8.54.
3214	LESS ENGINE.	J2X	2-SEATER.	RED	RED.				P. WHITESIDE. U.S.A	29.11.54
3215										
3216										
3217										
3218										
3219										
3220										
3221										
3222										
3223										
3224										
3225										
3226										
3227										
3228										
3229										
3230										

CHASSIS NO.	ENGINE NO.	TYPE	BODY	COLOUR	INTERIOR	HOOD			ALLOCATION	DELIVERED
3231										
3232										
3233										
3234										
3235										
3236										
3237										
3238										
3239										
3240										
3241										
3242										
3243										
3244										
3245										
3246										
3247										
3248										
3249										
3250	LESS ENGINE	K3	3-SEATER	M-BLUE	RED	BLACK			SPORTS CARS INC; U.S.A.	29.4.53
3251	95-1509	K3.	3-SEATER	BLUE.	RED	BLACK.	conflicts with export cards		BRIG-GEN. KERN. D. METZGER. U.S.A.F.	22.5.53.
3252	8.R.394.	K.3.	3seater	Biscuit	Red	BLACK	NLHE Rome 641. export		Brig Gen. J.P. McDonnell. U.S.A	6.2.53.
3253	LESS ENGINE	K3	3-seater	M.GREEN	GREEN	BEIGE	See letter 2 June 1981 from Waffe		SPORTS CARS INC U.S.A.	24.9.53
3254	LESS ENGINE	K3	3-SEATER	RED	GREY	BEIGE			MOTORESEARCH CO., U.S.A.	26.6.53.
3255	LESS ENGINE.	K3	3-SEATER	RED	BLACK	BLACK.			CUSTOM AUTOS. U.S.A.	16.9.53.
3256	7797600 CHRYSLER	K.3	3seater	Black	Red	GREY.	home export		Mrs K. Sarabhai India	29.5.53.
3257	C.53/8/1033	K.3.	3-SEATER.	BISCUIT	TAN	BEIGE			MR J. BURRELL. LOS ANGELES.	2.4.53.
3258										
3259	LESS ENGINE	K3	3-SEATER	PRIMER	TAN	FAWN			MR. HARRY STEELE	6.8.53.
3260	LESS ENGINE	K3	3-SEATER.	RED	TAN				NOEL KIRK MOTORS. U.S.A	24.8.53.
3261	LESS ENGINE	K3	3-SEATER	MET.BLUE	BLUE	BLACK			NOEL KIRK MOTORS. U.S.A	16.9.53.
3262	LESS ENGINE.	K3.	3-SEATER	M.GREEN	GREEN	BLACK.			SPORTS CARS INC.	16.9.53.
3263										
3264										

CHASSIS NO	ENGINE NO	TYPE	BODY	COLOUR	INTERIOR	HOOD			ALLOCATION	DELIVERED
3265										
3266	LESS ENGINE	K3	3-SEATER	WHITE	BLACK	BLACK			SPORTS CARS INC. U.S.A.	20.7.53
3267	LESS ENGINE	K3	3-SEATER	WHITE	BLACK	BLACK		Stuffed in yellow with P. Beard Z 5139	SPORTS CARS INC	6.8.53
3268	LESS ENGINE	K3	3-SEATER	METALLIC BLUE	RED				NOEL KIRK MOTORS. U.S.A.	24.8.53
3269	LESS ENGINE (CAD)	K3	3-SEATER	PRIMER	BLACK	BLACK			SPORTS CARS INC. U.S.A	20.7.53
3270	2N.23/1460088	K3	3-SEATER	M.BLUE	RED	BLACK		PAUL.E.COUSIN	BELGIUM	30.5.53
3271										
3272										
3273										
3274									LT-COL ALAN.C.		
3275	18F/1254986	K3	3-SEATER	GREEN	TAN	BLACK			SHANNEE CONWAY GERMANY	24.7.53
3276										
3277	LESS ENGINE	K3	3-SEATER	RED	BLACK	BEIGE			A.M.C. INC. U.S.A	21.9.53
3278	LESS ENGINE	K3	3-SEATER	RED	BLACK				NOEL KIRK MOTORS. U.S.A	13.11.53
3279									VENEZUELA	
3280	25.584	K3	3-SEATER	CREAM	RED				MR.BERNADO.R.CASANOVA	18.2.54
3281	25.499	K3	3-SEATER	BLUE	Red/Black	Black			WESTMOUNT GARAGE. CANADA	4.12.53
3282	LESS ENGINE	K3	3 Seater	Black	Red			Show car	NOEL KIRK MOTORS	13.11.53
3283	LESS ENGINE	K3	3-SEATER	GREEN	GREEN				HOUSE OF ALLARD U.S.A	5.4.54
3284	LESS ENGINE	K.3	3-SEATER	OFF WHITE	BLACK	BLACK			WESTMOUNT GARAGE REGD. CANADA	11.6.54
3285										
3286	4290334	K-3	3 Seater	Ming Blue	GREY	BLACK			Mr. J.P. Carstairs	8.10.54
3287										
3288										
3289										
3290										
3291										
3292										
3293										
3294										
3295										
3296										
3297										

JR

CHASSIS NO.	ENGINE NO.	TYPE	BODY	COLOUR	INTERIOR	HOOD			ALLOCATION	DELIVERED.
3397										
3398										
3399										
3400						1986				
3401	LESS ENGINE	JR	2-SEATER RED	RED	RED	Bland Mark				
3402	2S-316.CAD	JR	2-SEATER	BLUE	BLUE		Number when crashed QF 9066	NLN 652	A.E. GOLDSCHMIDT U.S.A.	28.3.53.
3403	2S-433.CAD	JR	2-SEATER	BLUE	BLUE	Syd Schism			COL. DAVE SCHILLING U.S.A.F.	25.4.53.
3404	CAD.25439.	JR	2-SEATER	BLUE	BLUE.	Dean Butler		NLN 650	COL. READE TILLEY U.S.A.	5.8.53.
3405	EXT-X2	JR	Chassis only for Tommy Sopwith			OLT 101	Sapphire Allard Sphinx		GEN. CURTIS E. LE MAY, U.S.A. 1963 1985 BRIAN CROOT TO FRANCE - NAME?	19.6.53.
3406		JR					1982 - DU BROL. 1986.		Moffat Larinaga / '86 - Shape	
3407	Caddy OVT 983	JR	GREEN/TAN (Fairing behind drivers seat for spare tanks)							
3408										
3409										
3410										
3411										
3412										
3413										
3414										
3415										
3416										
3417										
3418										
3419										
3420								NLN 650		
3421										
3422										
3423										
3424										
3425										
3426										
3427										
3428										
3429										

JR

3401 GOLDSCHMIDT - BLAND Rebuilding

3402 Schilling rebuild - (Grill Caps) NLN 652   Running   MARSII

3403 Tilley - SYD Schieman NLN 650   Running

3404 Le May - Shawnee. Dean Butler Rebuilding

3405 Sphinx? Believed sold in France

3406 Moffat Du Brol   1988 Jack Bokstrom 1991 Bland out 1991 J Bland out 1991 Brian Shorts

3407 Larinaga - Brian Shorts In Concours condition

SAFARI

CHASSIS NO.	ENGINE NO.	TYPE	BODY	COLOUR	INTERIOR	HOOD				ALLOCATION	DELIVERED
3992											
3993											
3994											
3995											
3996											
3997											
3998											
3999		Safari chassis No.	3000 / 4506 / 4507				Photograph & feature article in Autocar April 16, 1952		Delivered?		
4000	E1/U500	SAFARI	NATURAL WOOD	BRONZE			This chassis built under No 2058		SHA MXA 555 full length doors/rear		1952
4001	5337/25	SAFARI	" "		MW Vitton		This chassis built under 3000		Dennis MXA 554	short doors & tailgate.	
4002	7275054	P2	SAFARI	BRONZE & NAT WOOD	Sold to MR Lane Ord Willaston	The Laurel		NKC 461		NUNNS OF MANCHESTER D.A. COUTROUBIS (GREECE)	14.7.52. 28.1.53.
4003	H 259/80 SR-406 LGF 36587E	P2	Safari	Bronze & nat. wood.	BROWN		2137500 steel heads	C.S.C. O.H.V. engine not to be mentioned	WORCESTER WINDSHIELDS CO. Owen Wright of W. Hampton New Shops, Broadway 8½	15.11.52.	
4004											
4005	9L-2643 (CAD)	P2.	MONTE·CARLO SALOON	MAROON	LIGHT·BEIGE	see Woodward book Dag. Motors			DR. REID TWEEDIE (MALAYA)	15.1.53.	
4006	7274425	P2	Safari	Bronze & natural wood.			Ian Campbell Traig? Argyll	on scholarship A U.S.A. Vintage dealer in ERIE 8GNN - 3970 UPMYNDEN	Dag. Motors	6.8.52.	
4007	7244928	P2.	SAFARI	GREY & NATURAL WOOD					CARVILL, NAIROBI	28.8.52.	
4008	LESS ENGINE	P2	SAFARI	Bronze		The Needle			JORGE BARRANCO MEXICO	30.3.53.	
4009	7287341	P2	Safari	natural wood.	Brown	OEU 79 June 1982 Mr Nickolson	Radio & aerial KEPPING, MANCHESTER A.D.O. Club (Central Garage Fair Oaks) Mot 8 November 1986/April 88 letter from Mrs J Cronbes london ford Shrewsbury			Bristol St. Motors	28.1.54.
4010											
4011							[see notes on P2 saloon record pages]				
4012	4513										
4013		P2	Safari	White	Brown		seen at Monterey 1990				
4014											
4015											
4016											
4017											
4018											
4019											
4020											
4021											
4022											
4023											
4024											

CHASSIS NO.	ENGINE NO	TYPE	BODY	COLOUR	INTERIOR	HOOD			ALLOCATION	DELIVERED
4487										
4488										
4489										
4490										
4491										
4492										
4493										
4494										
4495										
4496										
4497			See also chassis No. 4555								
4498										
4499										
4500	LESS ENGINE 7287263	P.2.	SALOON	BLACK	RED.		Allard book file on file to N York letter on file June 76 — now Chrysler engined Reg No. OLC 655.		LAWRENCE. A. HART. U.S.A.	11. 4. 53
4501	7287623	P2	SALOON	BlacR	Red				Mortlake of Putney	23. 12. 53
4502	M-821-B-(Linum)	P2.	SALOON	BLUE	BLUE.	A.O.E News letter July 88 — now Chrysler saloon lim.			INGVAR BERGENGREN. SWEDEN	24. 9. 53
4503	5162H5972.	P2	Saloon	Blue	BLUE (Sliding roof) Bentley grey MOG 160		Show Car		PAUL. E. COUSIN. Belgium	11. 11. 53
4504	18/F1283424	P.2.	SALOON.	Blue Bentley Grey.	RED.	Restored but for sale at £1500 July 7912	Q.H.D. No. 226229.		Hon. Mrs Laine.	16. 6. 53.
4505	9 T 163	P.2	Saloon	Oxford Blue	Maroon		Blue Wheels.	TZ 300 St.	Hamilton	24. 8. 54
4506	LESS ENGINE	P.2.	SAFARI	CREAM	RED			DENVER IMPORTED MOTORS	COLORADO	21. 12. 53
4507	Y2847681	P2	SAFARI	GREEN	GREEN		letter 20 Dec 1956 from London solicitor ref client in N. Suffolk, quote reg No OXE 475	THOS. MOTORS LTD.	RHODESIA.	14. 4. 54
4508	B18-7293228	P2	Saloon	Blue	Blue		1972 Robbins of Kingsferford	W. E. Wyatt. (Barton's Radio)	New Guinea	31. 8. 55
4509	7289179	P2	Saloon	Bristol Fawn	Red	BLK. Wls.			Dagenham Motors	30. 6. 54
4510	A.V. 6644	P.2.	Saloon	Black	Grey		Dean Butler, March 1993	Westmount Garage	CANADA.	2. 2. 55
4511										
4512	Caddy. ?	P2	SALOON	BLUE	BLUE		SHA 17 OCT 1956 ERIC ALEXANDER JOHN WILLIAMS TGT 703.	Reg Oct 12 1956		28.4.54
4513	Plymouth not confirmed	P.C.2	Safari		see letter from Pat Hyde	Sept-Oct 88	Seen at Montlhéry in 1990 see AOE Newsletter April 92			X
4514										
4515			Undated sales list from RH Zack vintage dealer in USA, quotes Safari P2, 4506 + K2037 confirmed by letter dated August 1960.				NOTE: letter dated March 26 1956 from J. WHEELER NEW HOUSE RHODES UNIVERSITY GRAHAMSTOWN S. Africa	Imported in crate (bad condition) by Zarmeyer, 1979		
4516										
4517										
4518			Now (1982) in process of restoration by R Lammaga							
4519										

Upper right notes:

This car seen and photographed in Montlhéry, 1990
Owner now (2' or 3") trying to sell, and
claim car was sent over less engine..
and first owner now 90 years old and
still races car occasionally ...

letter weight ticket presumably shows Lincoln engine / auto gearbox
Safari shipped from Liverpool in Feb 1956 ??
thought to be for Canada [Ecor chassis T. Zard]
and proves clearly remembered that car was shown at Earls Court, 1955
now classified by roadholder that car was shown at Earls Court, 1955 — no record in book

all this now clarified by letter to Pat Hyde (Sept 1983) from present owner — Victoria B. Columbia
Chassis 4513

PALM
BEACH

CHASSIS No.	ENGINE No.	TYPE	BODY	COLOUR	INTERIOR	HOOD			ALLOCATION	DELIVERED
4982										
4983										
4984										
4985										
4986										
4987										
4988										
4989										
4990										
4991										
4992										
4993										
4994										
4995										
4996										
4997										
4998										
4999								Prototype to Graham Paige Company ref Mr Larry Richards (page 141 in back)		
5000	A 4442	21Z	Sports	cream	Black			S.A.	G. Paige	29-3-52
5001	—	21Z	"							
5002		21C	"							
5003	EOTA 48095	21C	"	Blue	Grey.	Grey.		U.S.A.	C. Guerra	9.9.52.
5004	EOTA 40646	21Z	"	RED.	BLUE	BLACK.		~~U.S.A.~~ Juan Riu. Colombia.		19.5.53.
5005										
5006	EOTA 40545	21C	"	CREAM	RED	BLACK.		U.S.A.	SPORTS CARS INC.	20.4.53.
5007										
5008										
5009	EOTTA 3823	21Z	3 seater	Bronze	Brown.				Demo . NGN567	?
5010										
5011										
5012										
5013										
5014										

CHASSIS NO:	ENGINE NO:	TYPE	BODY	COLOUR	INTERIOR	HOOD.				ALLOCATION	DELIVERED
5015											
5016											
5017	EOTA 54355	21 C	3-SEATER SPORTS.	RED	RED	BLACK.				INGVAR. BERGREN. SWEDEN	12. 5. 53.
5018											
5019											
5020											
5021											
5022											
5023											
5024											
5025.	EOTTA 15804	212 SPORTS.	3 seater SPORTS 3-SEATER	BLUE.	RED	BLACK	Used in Danny Kay Film with special effect. Fake replica used in England for Continuity			MAJOR. H.G. FISHER. U.S.A.F.	8. 11. 52.
5026	EOTTA 37844	212	SPORTS. 3-SEATER	GREEN.	GREEN	BLACK				BRIG-GEN. S.F.GIFFIN. U.S.A.F.	17. 4. 53.
5027	EOTTA-3285	212 SPORTS	SPORTS 3-SEATER.	RED	GREY	BLACK				AUTOHALL SERVETTIE S.A. GENEVA, SWITZERLAND	4. 3. 53
5028	EOTTA 13954	212 SPORTS	SPORTS.	BRONZE.	BROWN	BLACK				SPORTS CAR INC. U.S.A.	23. 2. 53
5029	EOTTA 28012	212 SPORTS	3seater SPORTS.	NIGHTBLUE.	BLUE.	BLACK.				SPORTS CAR. INC. U.S.A.	5. 2. 53.
5030											
5031											
5032											
5033											
5034											
5035											
5036											
5037											
5038	EOTTA-24657.	212	3 seater P.B. SPORTS	NIGHT BLUE	TAN	BLACK				OVERSEAS EQUIPMENT CORP; NEW YORK, U.S.A.	22. 12. 52
5039	EOTTA-36423	212	3-SEATER P.B. SPORTS.	RED	RED.	BLACK				SPORTS CARS INC. U.S.A.	22. 4. 53.
5040											
5041											
5042											
5043											
5044											
5045											
5046											
5047											

CHASSIS NO	ENGINE NO	TYPE	BODY	COLOUR	INTERIOR	HOOD					ALLOCATION		DELIVERED.
5048													
5049													
5050													
5051													
5052													
5053													
5054	EOTTA 51009	212	3-SEATER	MAROON	TAN	BLACK					NOEL KIRK MOTORS.		6.8.53
5055													
5056													
5057													
5058													
5059													
5060													
5061	212.EOTTAH4766	212.	3-SEATER	BLUE.	BLUE.	BLACK.					LIBERTO PIJOL	MAYNOU. MEXICO.	20.6.53.
5062													
5063												CANADA.	
5064	EOTTA- 212- 52035	212	3-SEATER	BLUE	RED	BLACK.					CLARK SIMPKINS.		9.8.53.
5065													
5066													
5067													
5068													
5069													
5070	212-44759.	212.	3-SEATER	BLUE	RED	BLACK					JUAN RIU. PANAMERICAN IMPORT. COLOMBIA.		24.6.53.
5071	212-EOTTA61241	212	3-SEATER.	BLUE	GREY						NOEL KIRK MOTORS. U.S.A.		20.10.53
5072													
5073													
5074	EOTTA 36426	212	3-SEATER	GREY	WHITE	BLACK					AMC SPORTS CARS.		9.4.53
5075	EOTA 81337	21C	3-SEATER	GREY	RED	BLACK					AUTOHALL SERVETTE		17.3.53
5076													
5077													
5078													
5079	EOTTA-47126	212.	3 seater	red	red	BLACK	R.H.D	AUGUSTIN LEGORRETA. MEXICO.	EXPORT	MEXICO			1.7.53
5080	EOTTA.49589.	21.Z.	3 seater	ming blue.	grey	BLACK.	R.H.D	John Padly Castairs	Dag. Motors				14.7.53

CHASSIS No	ENGINE No	TYPE	BODY	COLOUR	INTERIOR	HOOD					ALLOCATION		DELIVERED
5081	EOTA.144570 85180	21.C.	3 seater	light blue	light blue			Home. Mr Scott Fuller.			EXPORT. (New York)		20.4.53.
5082													
5083													
5084													
5085													
5086													
5087													
5088													
5089													
5090													
5091													
5092													
5093													
5094													
5095													
5096													
5097													
5098													
5099													
5100	EOTTA.49587	21. Z.	3 seater	ming blue	blue	BLACK.	R.H.D.		Ardwick Motors.	Nunns.			16.7.53.
5101													
5102	EOTTA 37380	21. Z.	3 Seater	Black	Red	BLACK	R.H.D	KOK 56.	J. Scott	Nunns Quicks.			11.4.53.
5103	EOTTA 226228	21 Z	3-SEATER	BLACK	RED	BLACK				W. J. HOOD AUSTRIA V4 Embassy VIENNA			28.7.53.
5104	EOTTA-5104E	21 Z	3 Seater	Bronze	Brown			Sep 1992 Letter from Australia N.E. Stainsfield Brisbane	NYO 66 (R. J. Canham)	Adlards.			?
5105	EOTTA-61181	21 Z	3 Seater	ming Blue	Grey			Dunlop Tyres Chrome Blue piping wire file	Show Car. S.L.B.	Tate			?
5106	EOTTA-55382	21 Z	3 Seater	ming Blue	Grey	BLACK			TRACTOR SPECIALITIES	NEW ZEALAND			14.9.53.
5107	EOTTA-63603	21 Z	3 seater	Black	Red	Black		Red wheels		Frews.			Nov 53.
5108	EOTTA-71017	21 Z	3 seater	Dark Green	Buge	Buge		Buge Wls.	(Petersham Garage)	Dag. motors			8.1.54
5109	EOTTA-122656	21 C	3 seater	ming Blue	Grey	BLACK		Wire wheels		Hamilton (Belfast)			6.2.54
5110	EOTTA-71016	21 Z	3 seater	Chassis				white piping Tonneau cover overdrive special Head lamp. Heater, Radio + lamp. Perspex side seens Shot		Abbotts of Farnham (for saloon body)			6.1.54
5111	EOTTA-81368	21 Z	3 seater	ming Blue	Black	Black			(Mr Knight)	Dag. motors			1.4.54
5112		21	3 seater										
5113		21	3 seater										

CHASSIS No.	ENGINE No.	TYPE	BODY	COLOUR	INTERIOR	HOOD		ALLOCATION	DELIVERED
5114		21	3 seater						
5115		21	3 seater						
5116		21	3 seater						
5117	EOTTA 47137	212	3-Seater	CREAM.	RED	BLACK.		SWEDEN. INGVAR BERGENGREN	8.7.53.
5118	EOTTA 84132	212	3-SEATER	GREEN	GREEN			H. WESTMOUNT GARAGES CANADA.	6.4.54
5119	EOTTA-68598	212	3-SEATER	GREEN	GREEN			HOUSE OF ALLARD U.S.A.	6.4.54
5120	EOTTA.68600	212	3-SEATER	GREY	RED			HOUSE OF ALLARD U.S.A. S.AMERICA	5.4.54
5121	EOTTA-65636	212	3-SEATER.	BLACK	RED.			MR.N.WINLOUGH BY.	25.11.53.
5122	EOTTA-86249	212	3-SEATER	BRONZE	BLUE	BLACK.		ANTONIO IZQUERDO S.AMERICA.	6.5.54
5123	EOTTA-87198	212	3-SEATER	SILVER	RED	BLACK		ANTONIO IZQUIERDO. S.AMERICA.	6.5.54
5124	EOTTA-90976	212	3-SEATER	RED	GREY	BLACK.		TRACTOR SPECIALTIES. NEW ZEALAND	21.5.54
5125	EOTTA-91995	212	3-SEATER	RED	GREY	BLACK		TRACTOR SPECIALTIES. NEW ZEALAND	21.5.54
5126	EOTTA-94306	212	3-SEATER	OFFWHITE	RED	BLACK		MR.D.SIONER. VENEZUELA.	17.6.54
5127	EOTTA-98324	212	3-SEATER	GREEN	RED	BLACK		ANTONIO IZQUIERDO. S.A.	5.8.54
5128	EOTTA-93835	212	3-SEATER	GREEN	BROWN	BLACK.		TRACTOR SPECIALTIES LTD NEW ZEALAND	4.6.54.
5129	EOTTA-96041	212	3-SEATER	BEIGE	TAN	BLACK		WESTMOUNT GARAGES CANADA RKGD	22.4.54
5130	EOTTA-105816	21Z	3 Seater	Blue	Red	BLACK	no 13 be changed from 5154	Madagasca	11.10.54
5131	EOTTA-97184	21Z L.H.	3-SEATER	GREY	RED	BLACK		HERBERT.N.BERGE (USA)	10.8.54.
5132		21Z L.H.	3 Seater						
5133									
5134	EOTTA-103929.	212	3-SEATER.	IVORY	RED	BLACK		ANTON.O IZQUIER-DO SOUTH AMERICA.	23.11.54
5135	EOTTA-101665	212	3-Seater.	Ivory.	Maroon	Black.		L.H. PALACIOS (NV) INC. NETHERLANDS W.INDIES	21.9.54.
5136	EOTTA-108970	212	3-SEATER	SMOKE GREY	MAROON	BLACK.		L.H. PALACIOS NV (INC) WEST INDIES	23.11.54
5137	EOTTA-52047	21Z	3-SEATER	IVORY	BLACK			NOEL KIRK MTRS. U.S.A	20.8.53.
5138	EOTTA-42899	21Z	3-SEATER	M-GREY	RED	BLACK	TRACTOR SPECIALITIES	NEW ZEALAND	28.5.53.
5139	EOTTA-52046	212	3-SEATER	WHITE	BLUE	BLACK		SPORTS CARS INC. U.S.A	5.8.53
5140	EOTA 100359 EOTTA-52036	21C	3 Seater	Brown	Brown	BLACK	R.H.D.	hunns	31.7.53.
5141	EOTA-100359	21Z	3 Seater	Blue	Blue	BLACK	R.H.D.	Dagenham Motors New Zealand	6.8.53.
5142	EOTTA-54624	21Z	3 Seater	Blue	Blue	BLACK.	R.H.D.	Tractor S. hunns New Zealand	14.9.53.
5143	EOTA-100347	21.C	3 seater	Red	Red	BLACK	R.H.D	Bankltop hunns	1.7.54
5144	EOTTA-55564	21Z	3 seater	Red	Red	Black.		SWEDEN INGVAR BERGENGREN	9.9.53.
5145	EOTTA-58513	212	3-SEATER	RED	BLUE	BLACK		SWEDEN INGVAR BERGENGREN	24.9.53.
5146	EOTTA-62299	2	3-SEATER	BLUE	BLUE.			NOEL KIRK MOTORS	3.11.53.
5143/3	EOTTA-53258 LH 21Z		3 Seater	Dark Blue	RED	BLACK	GENERAL UNDER HILL	JAPAN	28.8.53.

CHASSIS NO	ENGINE NO:	TYPE	BODY	COLOUR	INTERIOR	HOOD			ALLOCATION	DELIVERED.
5147.	EOTTA-63599	21Z	3-SEATER	BLACK	TAN		wire wheels 1988 Tom Turner.		NOEL KIRK MOTORS.	12.11.53.
5148	EOTTA-61149	21Z	3-SEATER.	IVORY	RED.				BRITISH MOTOR CAR DIST.	20.10.53.
5149	EOTTA-80288	212	3-SEATER	CREAM	GREEN				HOUSE OF ALLARD. USA	6.4.54
5150	Less engine	21.H L.H.	Chassis				Flown to Paris Sept 16 1953 (Flight 130)		Farel (France)	15-9-53.
5151	D-44/8387	21D	3 Seater	Red	RED.		Red Ram Dodge Engine OGY 456		MR. J. WOLFENSON. ARG.	2.4.54
5152	EOTTA-65634	212	3-SEATER	BLUE	RED.				NOEL KIRK MOTORS.	20.11.53.
5153	EOTTA-85213	21Z	3 Seater	Pod Green	Green	Beige			Bristol St.	9.4.54
5154	EOTTA-96029	21Z	3 Seater	Blue	Red	BLACK	No to be changed from 5130		New Zealand Tractor Spec.	27.8.54.
5155	EOTTA-137335	21Z	3-Seater	Red.	BLUE.			London Motors Ltd	New York. U.S.A.	16.4.55.
5156	EOTTA-108596	212	3-Seater	RED	RED	BLACK.		New York.	John J. Voates.	12.1.55.
5157	EOTTA-146322	212	3-Seater	White	Red	Black.		New York	U.S.A.	5.8.55.
5158	EOTTA 155308	21Z	A O C Newsletter, July 1972:	Letter from			John McLennon, Lower Hutt, N.Z. who owns this car, but registered in 1956.			
5159			> Nov 1983/and April 89 "				George STUTT PAKURANGA, N.Z " now " " "			
5160										
5161										
5162										
5163							March 89 Said car now in Finland. Delivered "Spring" 1956			
5164	Pencil rubbing of chassis plate!	21Z		Red	(Letter from S. Forresberg	Gotenburg	Sept 1985 see EXPORT CARD)			
5165										
5166										
5167										
5168										
5169										
5170										
5171										
5172										
5173										
5174										
5175										
5176										
5177										
5178										
5179										

CHASSIS No.	ENGINE No:	TYPE	BODY	COLOUR	INTERIOR	HOOD.				ALLOCATION	DELIVERED
5180											
5181											
5182											
5183											
5184											
5185											
5186											
5187											
5188											
5189											
5190											
5191											
5192											
5193											
5194											
5195											
5196											
5197											
5198											
5199											
5200	EOTA·9bb71	21.C.	Saloon	Maroon & silver		=		NYF.595	L.A.C. Lands	A.E.BATTS. letter, Oct 73 15 GREENLEAZE AV. DOWNEND, BRISTOL 560105 BS16·6LN	17. 7. 53.
5201	EOTA·9bb70	21.C.	Saloon	Maroon.				HXY.451.	L.A.C. Lands		10. 7. 53
5202											
5203											
5204											
5205											
5206											
5207											
5208											
5209											
5210											
5211											
5212	6.53H										

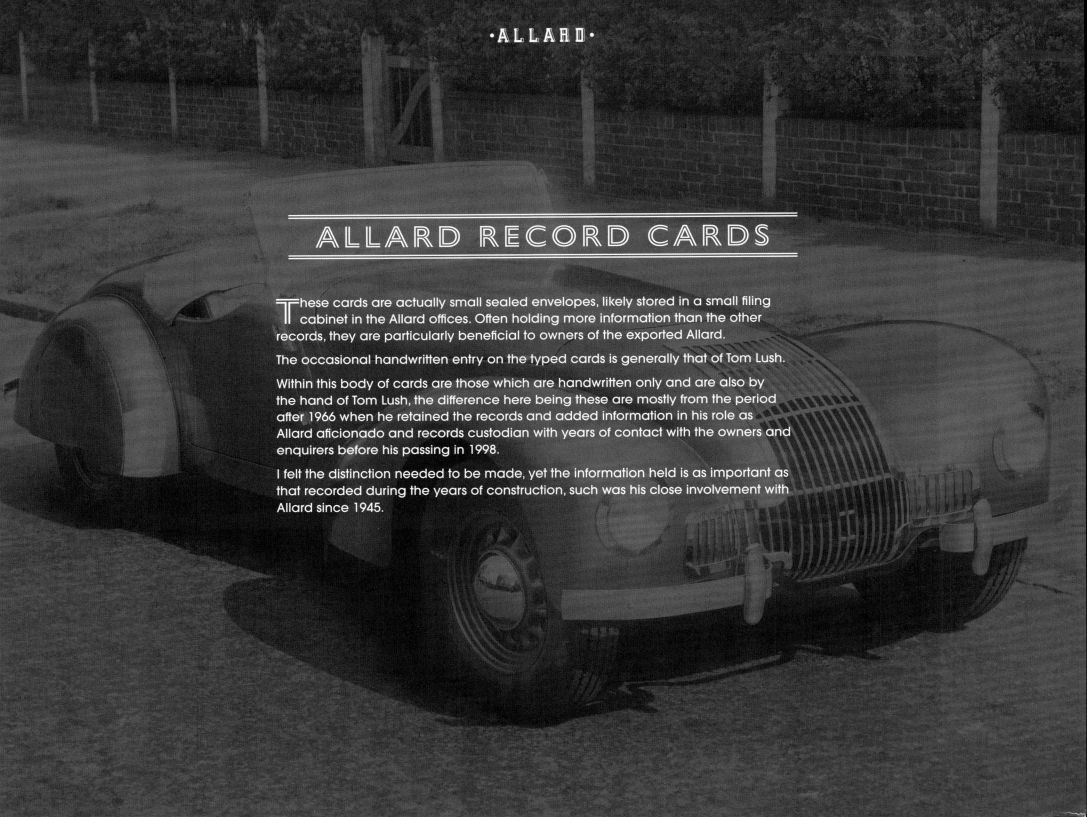

ALLARD RECORD CARDS

These cards are actually small sealed envelopes, likely stored in a small filing cabinet in the Allard offices. Often holding more information than the other records, they are particularly beneficial to owners of the exported Allard.

The occasional handwritten entry on the typed cards is generally that of Tom Lush.

Within this body of cards are those which are handwritten only and are also by the hand of Tom Lush, the difference here being these are mostly from the period after 1966 when he retained the records and added information in his role as Allard aficionado and records custodian with years of contact with the owners and enquirers before his passing in 1998.

I felt the distinction needed to be made, yet the information held is as important as that recorded during the years of construction, such was his close involvement with Allard since 1945.

Ardun Engineering Corporation.,
37 East 28th Street,
New York 16., N.Y.   File No.

Ordered 17-8-49. Invoice S-1090. CD3 FF- ...... Dlvd 9-9-49.
ALLARD K-TYPE TWO SEATER LHD: Black, maroon leather upholstery.
                                Engine No. 7193088.
                                CHASSIS NO. K-368.

J.C. MOUNT.   ss AM. MERCHANT.   Closing 9-9-49.
Freight £60.   Docs   12-9-49.

Richard B. Parker., 31 Hermon St, Belmont., Massachusetts.

                                        YB 14/6/54

82 AMERICA Ardun/ Parker/   K-368.

M. Salem & Cia,
Calle Tucuman 2575, BUENOS AIRES, ARGENTINE.

EMELAS & CIA, Rincon 661, MONTEVIDEO., URUGUAY.

Ordered 9-3-49   Delivered 21-4-49

K-TYPE 2 SEATER.; Colour grey, red leather upholstery.

Chassis No. K-559. LHD.   Engine No. 7198906

74 URUGUAY   K-559

R.M. Overseas Motor Sales Co.,
Volklingerstrasse 24.,
Dusseldorf., Germany.   File No.

Ordered 31-5-49. Invoice S-1019. CD3 FF- ...... Dlvd 22-8-49
ALLARD K-TYPE TWO SEATER RHD: Maroon, maroon leather upholstery.
                                Engine No. 7195783.
                                CHASSIS NO. K-440.

Exported to Germany via Dover Ferry 23-9-49.

F.J. Havenith, Military Security Board, Industrial Division.,
          83 HQ. CCG (B.E), Wuppertal., B.A.O.R.
and c/o Stansfield, 'Eskdale', Cottam Hall Lane, Ingol, Lancs.

79 GERMANY Myhill / Havenith/   K-440.

EMELAS & CIA,
Rincon 661,
MONTEVIDEO,
URUGUAY.

Ordered 9-3-49   Delivered 20-4-49

K-TYPE 2 SEATER LHD.; Colour Red, red leather, grey hood.

Chassis No. K-572.   Engine No. 7199206.

78 URUGUAY   K-572

Andrew Crookston., Esq.
c/o Egyptian Phosphate Co.,
38, Grosvenor Gardens.,
London. S.W.1.   File No.

Ordered 23-6-49. Invoice S-1031. CD3 FF- .... Dlvd 4-9-49
ALLARD K-TYPE TWO SEATER LHD: Grey, grey leather upholstery.
                                Fitted Andre Tele-Controls.
                                Engine No. 7197861.
                                Registration No. KUW 556.
                                CHASSIS NO. K-482.

Shipped via Dover Ferry 5-9-49. (Export to Egypt)

                        YB 14/6/54

77 EGYPT Crookston/   K-482.

Anthony F.M. Luscombe,
816e Valencia Avenue,
Burbank, California.   File No. 653.

Ordered 24-7-48. Invoiced L. Potter. CD3 PP-889086. Dlvd 17/12/
                                                              53.
ALLARD K1 TYPE 2 SEATER RHD: Light Blue, blue leather.
                               CHASSIS NO. K-595.
                               ENGINE NO. 7199438.
                               REGISTRATION NO. JYK 438.

Originally sold to Leonard Potter for entry in the 1948 Alpine
Rally. Purchased secondhand from Car Sales, High St, Egham,
Surrey by Mr. Luscombe on the 24th July, 1953.

PALL MALL DEPOSIT. ss LOCH AVON. Closing 17-12-53
Freight £   Docs   -12-53

UK address: 238 Collier Row Lane, Romford, Essex. (Emmigrant)

517 AMERICA Luscombe/   K-595

R/M OVERSEAS MOTOR SALES CO.,
c/o W. Seidel.,
Volklingerstrasse 24.,
Dusseldorf., Germany.   File No. 80.

Ordered 14-6-49.   Invoice S-1348.   Delivered 22-8-49.
ALLARD K-TYPE 2 SEATER RHD: Grey, blue leather upholstery.
                             Engine No. 7203238.
                             CHASSIS NO. K-699.

J.R. Miles., Education Advisor, Harver Barracks,
          APO 800., Kitzigen Sub Post Office, U.S. Army.

Lt. Richard K. Patton., 2735 Pike Road., Birmingham 8., Alabama.
                                        ys 14/6/54

80 GERMANY R/M. /Miles/ Patton/   K-699

MOSS MOTORS LTD,   ORDER. NO. 2.   1
3210, West Olympic Boulevard,
LOS ANGELES 6., CALIFORNIA. U.S.A.
                                   S-1177
Ordered 17-1-50   Invoiced 18-1-50   Delivered 26-1-50

K-TYPE 2 SEATER RHD.; Colour maroon, maroon leather, maroon hood.

Chassis No. K-770.   Engine No. 7202511.   C.D.3. DD 352832.

93 AMERICA Moss   K-770

L. BOCKH & CIA LTDA,   ORDER NO. 1.
Apartado 3756,
San Ididro A San Julian 11,
CARACAS., VENEZUELA.

Ordered 5-1-50   Invoiced 10-1-50   Delivered 23-1-50

K-TYPE 2 SEATER RHD.; Colour blue l., blue leather upholstery.

Chassis No. K-728.   Engine No. 7202526   C.D.3. DD 352831.

Freight £87.10.   From:- London Docks.

91 VENEZUELA Bockh   K-728

EMELAS & CIA LTDA,
Rincon 661,
MONTEVIDEO., URUGUAY.   S-1136

Ordered 16-11-49   Invoiced 1-12-49   Delivered 9-2-50.

K-TYPE 2 SEATER LHD.; Colour red, red leather, maroon hood.

Chassis No. K-774.   Engine No. 7221938.   C.D.3...........
          Coil Springs.

96 URUGUAY Salem   K-774

A.G. Tilton,   - 37 Melrose Street,
Wakool Hotel,   Parkdale,
Wakool, N.S.W.   Melbourne, S.12.
Australia.   File No. n/a

ALLARD K-1 TYPE 2 SEATER RHD: Red, red leather upholst.
                                 Eng. No: 7202176.
                                 CHASSIS NO: K-755.

Pall Mall Deposit. m.v. HIMALAYA. Closing 16-11-54
Freight £   Docs   -11-54

Note:-   AMC acting solely as shippers on behalf of
         consignee, Mr. A.G. Tilton. Car purchased
         secondhand from independent source.

540 AUSTRALIA Tilton/   K-755.

EMELAS & CIA LTDA,
Rincon 661,
MONTEVIDEO., URUGUAY.   S-1136

Ordered 16-11-49   Invoiced 1-12-49   Delivered 9-2-50

K-TYPE 2 SEATER LHD.; Colour grey, grey leather, grey hood.

Chassis No. K-841.   Engine No. 7223840.   C.D.3...........

95 URUGUAY Salem   K-841

·ALLARD·

EMELAS & CIA.,
Rincon 661, MONTEVIDEO - URUGUAY.

Ordered 16-11-49   Invoiced 1-12-49   Delivered 15-1-50

4-SEATER TOURER LHD.;   Colour grey, grey leather, grey hood.

Chassis No. L-856.   Engine No. 7207042.

84   URUGUAY   L-856

George Joseph Mercantile Co.,
Joseph Building.,
161 E. Main Street,
Trinidad., Colorado.   File No. 21.

Ordered 14-4-50. Invoice S-1316. CD3 FF-891339. Dlvd 25-5-50
ALLARD L-TYPE TOURER LHD: Maroon, maroon leather upholstery.
                           ENGINE NO. 5345/33 LH.
                           CHASSIS NO. L-1510.

1st owner: E.V. Shugart, Council Bluffs., Iowa.
2nd owner: Andrew A. Griffin, 1250 York St, Des Moines., Iowa.

EVAN COOKS LTD.   ss AM. MERCHANT.   Closing 25-5-50
Freight £60.   Docs   27-5-50

112 AMERICA G. Joseph Co./Shugart/Griffin/   L-1510

ENGINEERING & INDUSTRIAL EXPORTS (E.A) LTD.,
Private Bag.,
Nairobi., Kenya., E. Africa.   File No. 66.

Ordered 21-3-49 Invoice S-829.   Delivered 21-4-49.
ALLARD L-TYPE TOURER RHD: Colour red, red leather upholstery.
                           ENGINE NO. 7207805.
                           CHASSIS NO. L-902.

Joseph C. Mount.   ss ....   Closing 21-4-49.
Freight £   Docs   26-4-49.

C.G. Fane., P.O. Kabete., Kenya Colony., East Africa.
R. Ainsworth., c/o Directorate of Civil Aviation.,
            P.O. Box 5163., Nairobi., Kenya., E. Africa.
                                   YB 14/6/54

66 EAST AFRICA E.I.E./Fane/ Ainsworth/   L-902

Moss Motors Limited.,
3210 West Olympic Blvd,
Los Angeles, California.   File No. 9.

Ordered 9-9-50. Invoice S-1204. CD3 FF-156810. Dlvd 24-4-50.
ALLARD L-TYPE TOURER LHD: Colour Silver, blue leather upholstery.
                           Less engine. Cadillac modification.
                           CHASSIS NO. L-1701.

J.C. MOUNT.   ss DRINA.   Closing 26-4-50.
Freight £58.-6.-4d.   Docs   30-4-50.   YB 14/6/54

Howard A. Bosken, 3135 Mozart, Cincinnati 11., Ohio.
                        (Chassis No. unverified)

105 AMERICA Moss Motors/ Bosken/   L-1701

L. BOCKH & CIA,
Apartado 3756, San Isidro A San Julian 11,
CARACAS., VENEZUELA.

Ordered 11-11-49   Invoiced 1-12-49   Delivered 31-12-49.

4-SEATER TOURER LHD.;   Colour maroon, maroon leather, maroon hood.

Chassis No. L-904.   Engine No. 7207818.

85 VENEZUELA   L-904

W.R. Plunkett., Esq.
c/o P.W.D. Segarrat,
Johore., Malaya.   File No.

Ordered 19-1-49. Invoice S-950. HOME DELIVERY 18-3-49.
ALLARD M-TYPE D/HD COUPE RHD: Colour Grey, red leather upholst.
                              Engine No. 7203958.
                              CHASSIS NO. M-806.

                              REGISTRATION NO. KLP 818

London Transport & Freight. ss DUNBAR CASTLE. Closing 17-9-49
Freight £   Docs   19-9-49

                              YG 14/6/54

70 MALAYA Plunkett/   M-806.

Engineering & Industrial Exports (E.A) Ltd.,
Private Bag,
Nairobi., Kenya Colony.   File No.

Ordered 22-2-49. Invoice S-830. HOME DELIVERY 29-3-49.
ALLARD M-TYPE D/HD COUPE RHD: Grey, blue leather upholstery.
                              Engine No. 7207779.
                              Registration No. KLP 819.
                              CHASSIS NO. M-1010.

L.T. & FREIGHT.   Dunnotar Castle.   Closing 18-10-49.
Freight £   Docs   23-10-49.

Capt. R.H. McBean, Outspan., Nyeri., Kenya Colony, E. Africa.

                              YG 14/6/54

73 KENYA E.I.E./ Capt. McBean/   M-1010.

Capt. H.R. Sykes.,
H.Q. Land North Rhine, Westphalia.
Frontier Control Service.,
Krefeld., B.A.O.R., Germany.   File No. 64.

Ordered 7-11-48. Invoice S-922. Delivered 9-2-49.
ALLARD M-TYPE D/HD COUPE RHD: Black, red leather upholstery.
                              HMV Radio. Burglar device horn.
                              Engine No. 7204333.
                              CHASSIS NO. M-818.

Delivered to Dover/Calais Ferry Boat 9-2-49.

64 GERMANY Sykes/   M-818.

British & Overseas Merchants Ltd.,
175 Piccadilly,
London. W.1.   (Mr. Cole)   File No. 65.

DEALER:- R.M. Overseas Motor Sales Co.,
         c/o W. Seidel., Volklingerstrasse 24., Dusseldorf.,
                                                Germany.
Ordered 19-2-49. Invoice S-839. CD3 FF- ...... Dlvd 19-3-49.
ALLARD M1 D/HD COUPE RHD: Black, maroon leather upholstery.
                          ENGINE NO. 7209273.
                          CHASSIS NO. M-1018.

Temporary use in U.K. prior to export to Germany ../../49.

65 GERMANY R.M./Cole/   M-1018

John W. Forbes.,
Room 827.,
60 State Street.,
Boston., Massachusetts.   File No. 75.

Ordered 19-11-48. Invoice S-872. CD3 FF- ...... Dlvd 6-5-49.
ALLARD M1 D/HD COUPE LHD: Colour silver grey, grey leather.
                          ENGINE NO. 7206871.
                          REGISTRATION NO. KLY 15.
                          CHASSIS NO. M-887.

DAVIES TURNER. ss. AMERICAN MERCHANT. Closing 14-6-49.
Freight £60.   Docs   15-6-49.

W.H. Leathers, Hingham., Massachusetts. (182 North Street)
                              YG 14/6/54

75 AMERICA Forbes/ Leathers/   M-887

Engineering & Industrial Exports Ltd,
Private Bag,
Nairobi, Kenya.   S-828

Ordered 12-2-49.   Delivered 29-3-49.

Chassis No. M-1028. Engine No. 7209388.

4-SEATER DROPHEAD COUPE: Colour cream, red leather.

132 EAST AFRICA E.I.E.   M-1028.

M. Salem & Cia, Calle Tucuman 2575, Buenos Aires, ARGENTINE.

Ordered 9-3-49   Invoiced   Delivered 30-3-49

DROPHEAD COUPE   Colour light blue, blue leather, blue hood.

Chassis No. M-1076   Engine No. 7210698.

71   URUGUAY   M. Salem & Cia.   M-1076

Grancor Automotive Specialists.,
5652 North Broadway.,
Chicago 40., Illinois.   File No. _____

Ordered 4-10-49. Invoice S-1155. CD3 FF- ...... Dlvd 12-1-50.
ALLARD M-TYPE D/HD COUPE LHD: Red, natural leather upholstery.
                               Mercury Engine No. E-429845-P.
                               CHASSIS NO. M-1545.

J.C. MOUNT.   ss AM. MANUFACTURER.   Closing 12-1-50.
Freight £60.   Docs   14-1-50.

Lieut. L.W. Leslie M.D., AO 2213096., 3902D Medical Group.,
                        Offutt Air Force Base, Omaha, Nebraska.

87   AMERICA   Grancor/ Lt. Leslie M.D./   M-1545.

M. Salem & Cia,
Calle Tucuman 2575, Buenos Aires, ARGENTINE.

Ordered 9-3-49   Delivered 29-4-49

DROPHEAD COUPE   Colour light blue,maroon, maroon, maroon.

Chassis No. M-1077   Engine No. 7210709.

72   URUGUAY   M. Salem & Cia .   M-1077

Kyle Palmer & Co.,
P.O. Box 289.,
Kuala Lumpur., Malaya.   File No. _____

Ordered 6-5-49. Invoice S-896.   HOME DELIVERY 21-6-49.
ALLARD M-TYPE D/HD COUPE RHD: Black, grey leather upholstery.
                               Engine No. 7212059.
                               Registration No. SV 1655.
                               CHASSIS NO. M-1086.

J.C. MOUNTS & CO.   ss DUNBAR CASTLE   Closing 23-12-49
Freight £   Docs   28-12-49

James L. Ross., P.O. Box 289., Kuala Lumpur., Malaya.

                                 YB 14/6/54

76   MALAYA   Kyle Palmer/ Ross/   M-1086.

Card 1:

Julian E. Hill.;
The Wolds.,
4 Woonona Avenue.,
Wahroonga., N.S.W.   File No. 46.

also Aust. Estates, Forbes., New South Wales., Australia.
" " The Grange., Ashwell., Baldock., Herts., England.

Ordered 16-8-50. Invoice S-1812. Delivered 20-5-51.
ALLARD M2 D/HD COUPE RHD: Colour Grey, red leather upholstery.
" The Leviathan type "   Engine No. Mercury 7483/2.   LXY 20
                             CHASSIS NO. M-2000.

DAVIES TURNER.   ss STRATHMORE ....   Closing 31-8-51.
Freight £155. 0. 2d.   Docs   4-10-51.

E. Neely., 2 Station Street, Wentworthville., N.S.W., Australia.

223 AUSTRALIA Hill/ Neely/   x   * M-2000.

Card 2:

R/P IMPORTED MOTOR CAR COMPANY,   39
147 West 54th Street,
NEW YORK 19., N.Y.
U. S. A.   File No. 63.

Ordered 3-10-50. Invoice S-1800. CD3 HH-886250. Dlvd 4-6-51.

ALLARD M2 CONVERTIBLE LHD: Green, green leather.
                           Chassis No. M-2001. Cadillac mod.
                      Port Wyndham
DAVIES TURNER: ss PORT ADELAIDE - KGV Dock. (shut out through dock strike)
                Freight £97.18.7.   Docs recd. 21.7.51.

226 AMERICA Seddon.   M-2006.(?)

Card 3:

M2 COUPE "WHALE"   SHIPPED U.S.A. 4-6-51
ENSINE 7246933   Nᵒ EXPORT RECORD CARD

Similar car reported in 1975. in letter from Don
                                        Milligan

Phone call 2 July 88 from Brian Sharpe saying he had
purchased car (unseen) and was awaiting delivery.
Seen at Brian's April 1989

                              M2# 2001

Card 4:

R/P IMPORTED MOTOR CAR CO.,
147 West 54th Street,
New York 19., N.Y.   File No. 218.

Ordered 26-11-51. Invoice S-2086. CD3' JJ-88664. Dlvd 24-1-52.
ALLARD M2X D/HD COUPE LHD: Royal Blue, red leather upholstery.
                           Less engine. Cadillac modification.
                           CHASSIS NO. M#2298.

DAVIES TURNER.   ss AMERICAN PRESS%   Closing 25-1-52.
Freight £69-14-7d.   Docs   6-2-52.

D.W. Lockard., 2905 "Q" Street, N.W. Washington., D.C.

                                        y/b 21/6/54

282 AMERICA Seddon/ Lockard/   M-2298.

Card 5:

L. Bockh & Cia.,
San Isidro a San Julian 11.,
Caracas., Venezuela.   File No. 124.

Ordered 24-2-51 Invoice S-1932 CD3 HH-886278 Dlvd 29-8-51.
ALLARD M2 COUPE LHD: Colour Sunshine, orange leather upholstery.
("The Whale")   Engine No. 7260708.
                      CHASSIS NO: M2-2005.

LEP TRANSPORT   ss BARRANCA   Closing 29-8-51
Freight £88-4-8.   Docs   10-9-51

Mr. Geza Benedek, P.O.Box 934, Caracas, Venezuela.
also Bitucotex C.A., Apartado 4025, Caracas., Venezuela.

2nd: Fred Nordstrom, Corp. Venezolana del Motor,
     Apartado 74, Pilita a Mamey, 154. Caracas, Venezuela.

263 VENEZUELA Bockh/ Benedek/Nordstrom/   x   *M2-2005.

Card 6:

Messrs. Ingvar BERGENGREN.,
Lindhagensplan.,
Stockholm., Sweden.   File No. 361.

Ordered 24/5/52. Invoice S-2241. Reynolds delivery 6-8-52.
ALLARD M2X COUPE LHD: Portland stone, red leather, red l. hood.
                      CHASSIS NO. 3124. Engine No. 15868/105.

LEP TRANSPORT. ss MALMO. Closing 6-8-52.
Freight £33. 0. 2.   Docs ...7-8-52.

361 SWEDEN Bergengren.   2xM-3124.

NEW YORK MOTOR SHOW.   ORDER. NO.12.   3

Moss Motors Ltd, 3210 West Olympic Blvd, Los Angeles 6, Calif.
     S-1286
Invoiced 1-3-50.   Delivered 21-3-50

Chassis No. K-1546   Furl. K2 [coil spring
                                   new body + front]
Freight £60.

                            NEW YORK SHOW.

102   AMERICA   Moss. NYS   2K-1546

John W. Forbes., Esq.
Room 827.,
60 State Street,
Boston 9., Massachusetts.   File No.

Ordered 25-2-50. Invoice S-1253. CD3 FF-156815. Dlvd 4-4-50.
ALLARD K-TYPE TWO SEATER LHD: Dk Blue, blue leather upholstery.
                               Engine No. 7228922.
                               CHASSIS NO. K-1703.

DAVIES TURNER.   ss AM. HARVESTER.   Closing 4-4-50.   1/8 14/6/54
Freight £54. 0. 0.   Docs   9-4-50.
Paul D. Broderick, 367 Walnut Avenue, Roxbury., Massachusetts.
2nd Owner: Norman W. Kalat, 108 Prospect St, Shrewsbury, Mass.
3rd Owner: Jim Thatcher, 420 Defiance Avenue, Findlay, Ohio.

108 AMERICA Forbes/ Broderick/ Kalat/Thatcher/   K-1703

Charmbury of Victoria Ltd,
P.O. Box 234.,
Victoria B.C., Canada.   File No.

Ordered 27-1-50. Invoice S-1294. CD3 FF-891338. Dlvd 9-5-50.
ALLARD K-TYPE TWO SEATER LHD: L. Blue, blue leather upholstery.
                               Engine No. 7228629.
                               CHASSIS NO. K-1700.

DAVIES TURNER.   ss EMPRESS OF CANADA.   Closing 9-5-50.
* Sold direct to Trident Motors, 2868 Dufferin St, Toronto, Ont.
1st Owner: Revd. John K. Moffatt, 52 Simcoe Street South,
                             Oshawa., Ontario., Canada.
2nd Owner: B. Pallant, 9 Lapp Street, Toronto., Ontario.

                                    1/8 14/6/54

109 CANADA Charmbury/ Trident/Moffatt/Pallant/   * K2-1700

R/P IMPORTED MOTOR CAR COMPANY,   ORDER NO.26.   2
147 West 54th Street,
NEW YORK 19, N.Y.
U. S. A.

Ordered 5-5-50   Invoiced S-1351   Delivered 5-7-50

Chassis No. K-1704 LHD.   C.D.3. FF 891348
Less engine. Blue., blue.   cad. mod.

SHIPPERS: Thomas Meadows & Co. Ltd.

119 AMERICA   Seddon   K-1704

J.C. Woodhull, Inc.   ORDER NO. 20.
20, Mercer Street,
DOVER, N.J.
U. S. A.   S-1293

Ordered 24-4-50   Invoiced S-1293   Delivered 30-5-50

Chassis No. K-1702 LHD.   C.D.3. FF 891335
Less engine.   Black, red leather

SHIPPERS.   Messrs Evan Cook'(Packers Ltd).

            Freight £60.

111 AMERICA   Woodhull   2K-1702

R/P IMPORTED MOTOR CAR COMPANY,   ORDER NO. 25.   1
147 West 54th Street,
NEW YORK 19, N.Y.
U. S. A.

Ordered 15-5-50   Invoiced S-1372   Delivered 27-7-50

Chassis No. K-1705 LHD.   C.D.3. FF 891349
Less engine. Blue., blue.   cad. mod.

SHIPPERS. THOMAS MEADOWS & CO. LTD.

            FREIGHT. £60.

118   AMERICA   Seddon   K-1705

rds

MOSS MOTORS LIMITED.,
3210, W. Olympic Boulevard.,
Los Angeles 6., California.   File No. 33.

Ordered 4-7-50. Invoice S-1387. CD3 FF-891356. Dlvd 22-8-50.
ALLARD K-TYPE 2 SEATER LHD: Colour Silver grey, blue leather.
                            Less engine. Modified to accomodate
                                      clients 186 bhp Mercury.
                            CHASSIS NO. K-1706.

MEADOWS & CO.   ss AM. MERCHANT.   Closing 23-8-50.
Freight £60.   Docs   30-8-50.

Dr. Henry M. Ure., 1218 Highland Ave., Manhattan Beach., Calif.

124 AMERICA MOSS/Dr. Ure/   K-1706

Gunnar Bengtson., Esq.
c/o J.A. Kjellber & Soner A/B.,
Goteborg 2., Sweden.   Order No. 23.

Ordered 29-4-50. Invoice S-1358. CD3 DD-352828. Dlvd 28-9-50.
ALLARD K2 TOURER RHD: ** Special body having K2 front and L-type
                         Tourer rear. De Dion rear axle. André.
                         Two spare tyres. Cadillac No. 8M-895.
                         CHASSIS NO. K-1740. Grey, red leather.
                                   L2X-1740

THOMAS MEADOWS: ss MALMO.   Closing 29-9-50.
Freight £38. 0. 0d.   Docs   30-9-50.

136 SWEDEN Bengtson/   L2X-1740.

                                                          9
R/P Imported Motor Car Company,
147 West 54th Street,   Order No. 32.
NEW YORK 19., N.Y.

Ordered 21-8-50.   Invoiced S-1389.   Delivered 9-11-50.

Chassis No. K-1707.   C.D.3. FF 891354.   Cadillac modification.
                      De Dion rear axle.

K2 TWO SEATER LHD: Colour grey, red leather upholstery.

ss AMERICAN IMPORTER.   B £3.25 recd Thomas Meadows
                        Sent to Westminster Bank 16-11-50
                        Putney - 16-11-50

   FREIGHT £60.

137 AMERICA Seddon   2 K-1707

                                                          10
R/P Imported Motor Car Company,
147 West 54th Street,   Order No. 35.
NEW YORK 19., N.Y.

Ordered 10-7-50.   Invoiced S-1427.   Delivered 13-10-50

Chassis No. K-1741.   C.D.3. FF 891367.   Cadillac modification.

K2 TWO SEATER : LHD.   Colour Green, red leather upholstery.

ss AMERICAN FARMER.

SHIPPERS? LEP TRANSPORT LTD. FREIGHT. £60.

138 AMERICA Seddon   2 K-1741

R/P IMPORTED MOTOR CAR CO.,
147 West 54th Street,
New York 19., New York.   File No: 34.

Ordered 10-7-50. Invoice S-1426. CD3 FF-891364. Dlvd 13-9-50
ALLARD K-TYPE 2 SEATER LHD: Colour Black, red leather upholstery.
                            Less engine. Cadillac modification.
                            CHASSIS NO: K-1708.

EVAN COOKS.   ss AMERICAN MILLER.   Freight £60. 0. 0
Closing 14-9-50.   Docs 19-9-50.

1st Owner:
2nd Owner: G. Donald Dyne, 133 Lakeview Terrace, Ramsey., N.J.

130 AMERICA Seddon/ Dyne/   *K2-1708

R/P IMPORTED MOTOR CAR COMPANY,   ORDER. NO. 42.   6
147 West 54th street,
NEW YORK 19., N.Y.

Ordered 8-8-50   Invoiced S-1409   C.D.3. FF 891369

Delivered 6-9-50   Shipped AMERICAN MERCHANT - Evan Cooks Ltd.

K-TYPE 2 SEATER LHD.   Colour Grey, red leather.   less engine

SHIPPERS. MESSRS EVAN COOK'S BACKERS LTD.

        FREIGHT. £50.

128 AMERICA Seddon   2? K-1742

MOTORTILLBEHOR.,
Wallingatan 38,
STOCKHOLM.,
SWEDEN.

Order No. 44.

Ordered 4-8-50. Invoice S-1696. CD3 n/a. Delivered 12-3-51.
ALLARD K2 TWO SEATER: Colour blue, red leather upholstery.
Chassis No. K-1743. Engine No. 7250830.

LEP TRANSPORT. ss Leo. Freight £27-13-6. Docs rec'd........

188 SWEDEN Motortillbehor. 2K-1743.

R/P IMPORTED MOTOR CAR COMPANY,
147 West 54th Street,
NEW YORK 19., N.Y.

ORDER NO.45. 11

Ordered 14-8-50. Invoiced S-1430. C.D.3. No- FF 891368
Delivered 9-10-50.

Chassis No. K-1744. LHD. (FORD engine to be fitted in U.S.A)

K-TYPE 2 SEATER: Colour French grey, red leather.

SHIPEERS. MESSRS LEP TRANSPORT LTD. FREIGHT.£50.

142 AMERICA Seddon K-1744.

ORDER NO. 47

WANGARATTA MOTORS PTY LTD,
15, Reid Street,
WANGARATTA, VICTORIA.
AUSTRALIA.

Ordered 16-8-50. Invoice S-1526. Delivered..6-12-50..........

K2 TWO SEATER RHD: Colour (~~primer only~~).Black, red leather.

Chassis No. K-1745. Engine No.8607/154 (overbored Mercury).

ss ..Taranaki..... LEP TRANSPORT. FREIGHT £70.

151 AUSTRALIA Wangaratta 2K-1745

ORDER NO.48. 12

R/P IMPORTED MOTOR CAR CO,
147 West 54th Street,
NEW YORK 19., N.Y.

Ordered 21-8-50. Invoice S-1473. C.D.3. FF-891379.
Delivered..29-11-50..........

K2 TWO SEATER LHD: Colour Ivory, tan leather.

Chassis No. K-1800. Modified to accomodate Cadillac.

ss..American Leader.. LEP TRANSPORT. Docs recd 7/12/50

FREIGHT.£50.

Robert Ellis, Millburn Service Center, 175 Main Street,
Millburn., New Jersey.

152 AMERICA Seddon /Ellis/ 2K-1800

R/P IMPORTED MOTOR CAR CO,
147 West 54th Street,
NEW YORK 19, N.Y.

ORDER NO.49. 13

Ordered 21-8-50. Invoice S-1474. C.D.3. FF-891378.

K2 TWO SEATER LHD: Colour Green, green leather.

Chassis No. K-1801. Cadillac modification.

ss..American Leader.... LEP TRANSPORT. Docs recd 7/12/50

Delivered..28/11/50.....

FREIGHT £50.

153 AMERICA Seddon. 2K-1801

R/P IMPORTED MOTOR CAR CO.,
147 West 54th Street,
New York 19., N.Y.

File No: 50.

Ordered 21-8-50 Invoice S-1474. CD3 FF-891380 Dlvd 11-12-50
ALLARD K2 TWO SEATER LHD: Bugatti blue, red leather upholstery.
Less engine; Cadillac modification.
CHASSIS NO: K-1802.

LEP TRANSPORT ss AMERICAN MILLER Closing 15-12-50
Freight £60.-0.-0d. Docs 27-12-50

Mr. Arthur J. Ferguson, 6242 S.W. 27th St, Miami 32., Florida.
(Goodbody & Co, 14 Northeast 1st Ave., Miami 32., Florida.)

154 AMERICA Seddon/Ferguson/ 2K-1802

ORDER NO. 53.   9

MOSS MOTORS LIMITED,
3210 West Olympic Boulevard,
LOS ANGELES 6., CALIFORNIA.

Ordered 1-9-50.   Invoice S-1479.   C.D.3. HH-537899.
                                      Delivered...3-12-50...

K2 TWO SEATER LHD: Colour Danube blue, blue.

Chassis No. K-1804. (less engine) - American Ford installation.

ss LOCH GARTH - LONDON.   LEP TRANSPORT. (Docs read 20/12/50)

        FREIGHT £60.

150   AMERICA   Moss   LK-1804.

Motor City Inc.,
1221 N.E. Sandy Boulevard.,
Portland., Oregon.   File No. 56.

Ordered 18-9-50. Invoice S-1539. CD3 HH-537892. Dlvd 12-12-50.
ALLARD K2 TWO SEATER LHD: Red, natural leather upholstery.
                    Mercury Engine No. 8606/151.
                    CHASSIS NO. K-1807.

DAVIES TURNER.   ss BRAZILIAN PRINCE.   Closing 12-12-50.
Freight £60. 0. 0d.   Docs   14-12-50.

John Wallace Graham (Professor Violin).,
Route 2., Box 209., Salem., Oregon.   17/6/54

155   AMERICA   Motor City/ Graham/   LK-1807.

ORDER NO. 55.

SOCIEDAD MERCANTIL INTERNACIONAL S.A.,
Jiron Ayacucho 266.,
LIMA., PERU.

Ordered 4-9-50.   Invoice S-1547.   CD3 No. HH 5737891.
                                       Delivered..21st.December.1950.

K2 TYPE 2 SEATER LHD: Colour Silver grey, red leather.

Chassis No. K-1805.   Engine No. 5344-32.

Shipped & crated by Davies Turner & Co.   Ship..KEMUTA........

        FREIGHT. £81.3.0.

158   SOMERIN   PERU   LK-1805

ORDER NO.59.

WOOD MOTORS,
9925 Whittier,
DETROIT 24., MICHIGAN. U.S.A.

Ordered 26-9-50.   Invoice S-1575.   CD3 No. HH-537888.

K2 TWO SEATER LHD: Gunmetal, red leather.

Chassis No. K-1808.   Modified to accomodate Oldsmobile engine.

SHIPPERS : Davies, Turner & Co.

Delivered for crating....4-1-51.   Ship..American Clipper..
                £104-13-4   Docs received..26-1-51...

160   AMERICA   Wood   LK-1808

Motor City Inc.,
1221 N.E. Sandy Boulevard.,
Portland., Oregon.   File No. 57.

Ordered 18-9-50. Invoice S-1538. CD3 HH-537894. Dlvd 12-12-50
ALLARD K2 TWO SEATER LHD: Cream., red leather upholstery.
                    Mercury Engine No. 5346/34.
                    CHASSIS NO. K-1806.

DAVIES TURNER.   ss BRAZILIAN PRINCE.   Closing 12-12-50.
Freight £60. 0. 0d.   Docs   14-12-50.

Clifton A. Priest., 608 S.E. Tacoma Street, Portland 2., Oregon.
        also at 1112 Seldcorr, Portland, Oregon.
                                        17/6/54

156   AMERICA   Motor City / Priest/   LK-1806

R/P IMPORTED MOTOR CAR COMPANY.,
147 West 54th Street,
NEW YORK 19., N.Y.   Order No. 60.

Ordered 29-9-50.   Invoice S-1576.   HH-537886. Dlvd 3-1-51
ALLARD K2 TWO SEATER LHD : Colour black, red leather upholstery.
                    Less engine.   Cadillac modification.
                    CHASSIS NO. K-1609.

LEP TRANSPORT : AM. HARVESTER.   Closing 9-1-51.
Freight £60. 0. 0.   Docs ..11-1-51.

159   AMERICA   Seddon.   LK-1809

All

Card 17 — ORDER NO. 76

R/P IMPORTED MOTOR CAR COMPANY,
147 West 54th Street,
NEW YORK 19., N.Y.

Ordered 13-11-50   Invoice S-1599.   CD3 HH-537884

K2 TYPE 2 SEATER LHD: Colour bronze, beige leather.

Chassis No. K-1840.   Cadillac mod: Delivered 16-1-51.

SHIPPERS: Davies Turner.   ss AMERICAN CLIPPER.

£60-0-0   Docs received..26-1-51.......

F.M. Zeder, Vice Pres. Eng., Chrysler Corpn.
Raymond C. Jennings, 118 Hill St, Naugatuck. Mod.

164   AMERICA   Seddon   2K-1840

Card 16 — ORDER NO. 68

R/P IMPORTED MOTOR CAR COMPANY.,
147 West 54th Street,
NEW YORK 19., N.Y.

Ordered 9-10-50.   Invoice S-1601.   CD3 HH-886398.

K2 TWO SEATER LHD: Brewster (dark) green, red leather upholstery.

Chassis No. K-1843.   Cadillac mod: Delivered 17-1-51.

SHIPPERS: Lep Transport.   ss AMERICAN CLIPPER.

FREIGHT £60.   Docs received.....25/1/51   (£165-7-6)
                                          2 cars.

162   AMERICA   Seddon   2K-1843

Card — File No. 58

Motor City Inc.,
1221 N.E. Sandy Boulevard.,
Portland 2., Oregon.   File No. 58.

Ordered 18-9-50. Invoice S-1537. CD3 HH-537895. Dlvd 12-12-50.
ALLARD K2 TWO SEATER LHD: Colour Black, natural leather upholstery.
                          Mercury Engine No. 9089/80.
                          CHASSIS NO. K-1841.

DAVIES TURNER. ss BRAZILIAN PRINCE. Closing 12-12-50.
Freight £60. 0. 0d.   Docs   14-12-50.

F.D. Mayer., Attorney at Law.,
F.D. Mayer Office Building., Lebanon., Oregon.

157   AMERICA   Motor City / Mayer /   2K-1841.

Card 28 — Order No. 95

R/P IMPORTED MOTOR CAR COMPANY,
147 West 54th Street,
NEW YORK 19., N.Y.   Order No. 95.

Ordered 8-1-51.   Invoice S-1692.   CD3 HH-886383.
ALLARD K2 TWO SEATER: Colour silver, red leather upholstery.
Chassis No. K-1844.   Cadillac modification.   Delivered 3-3-51.

DAVIES TURNER: ss American Inventor.   Freight ....
                                         Docs rec'd............

184   AMERICA   Seddon.   2K-1844.

Card 18 — ORDER NO. 77

R/P IMPORTED MOTOR CAR COMPANY,
147 West 54th Street,
NEW YORK 19., N.Y.

Ordered 13-11-50.   Invoice S-1600.   CD3 No. HH-537885.

K2 TWO SEATER LHD: Colour Green (dark), red leather upholstery.

Chassis No. K-1842.   Cadillac mod: Delivered 18-1-51.

SHIPPERS: DAVIES TURNER.   ss AMERICAN CLIPPER.
£60   Documents received...26-1-51.........

165   AMERICA   Seddon   2K-1842.

Card 29 — Order No. 96

R/P IMPORTED MOTOR CAR COMPANY,
147 West 54th Street,
NEW YORK 19., N.Y.   Order No. 96.

Ordered 8-1-51.   Invoice S-1691.   CD3 HH-537882.   Dlvd 30-3-51.
ALLARD K2 TWO SEATER: Colour black, red leather upholstery.
Chassis No. K-1845.   Cadillac modification.

DAVIES TURNER: ss ....   Docs received 14-4-51.
Freight £53-17-0.

186   AMERICA   Seddon.   2K-1845.

R/P IMPORTED MOTOR CAR COMPANY,
147 West 54th Street,
NEW YORK 19., N.Y.   ORDER NO.78. 19

Ordered 13-11-50.   Invoice S-1598.   CD3 HH-537883.

K2 TWO SEATER LHD: Colour red, red leather upholstery.

Chassis No. K-1846.   Cadillac mod: Delivered 16-1-51.

SHIPPERS: Davies Turner.   ss AMERICAN CLIPPER
          £59-6-0   Docs received 26-1-51........

166   AMERICA   Seddon   LK-1846

R/P IMPORTED MOTOR CAR CO.,
147 West 54th Street.,
New York 19., N.Y.   File No.

Ordered 2-1-51. Invoice S-1624. CD3 HH-886393. Dlvd 31-1-51.
ALLARD K2 TWO SEATER LHD: Royal Blue, red leather upholstery.
                            Less engine. Cadillac modification.
                            CHASSIS NO. K-1849.

DAVIES TURNER.   ss AM. IMPORTER.   Closing 31-1-51.
Freight £56-3-7d.   Docs   10-2-51.

F.D. Heastand., 86 Third Street, San Francisco 3., California.

175 AMERICA   Seddon/ Heastand/   LK-1849.

R/P IMPORTED MOTOR CAR CO.,
147 West 54th Street,
New York 19., N.Y.   File No. 83.

Ordered 2-1-51. Invoice S-1603. CD3 HH-886399. Dlvd 17-1-51.
ALLARD K2 TWO SEATER LHD: Dark Green, red leather upholstery.
                         Less engine. Cadillac modification.
                         CHASSIS NO. K-1847.

LEP TRANSPORT.   ss AM. CLIPPER.   Closing 17-1-51.
Freight £105-7-6d.   Docs   25-1-51.

Carl G. Schmidt., 103 N. Home Avenue, Park Ridge., Illinois.

169 AMERICA   Seddon / Schmidt /   LK-1847.

R/P IMPORTED MOTOR CAR COMPANY,   31
147 West 54th Street,
NEW YORK 19., N.Y.   Order No. 85.

Ordered 2-1-51.   Invoice S-1690.   CD3 HH-886379.   Dlvd 3-3-51.
ALLARD K2 TWO SEATER: Colour bugatti blue, red leather.
Chassis No. K-1968.   Cadillac modification.

LEP TRANSPORT :   ss American Inventor.   Freight...........
                                          Docs received............

189   AMERICA   Seddon.   LK-1968.

R/P IMPORTED MOTOR CAR COMPANY,   ORDER NO. 82.   20
147 West 54th Street,
NEW YORK 19., N.Y.

Ordered 2-1-51.   Invoice S-1612.   CD3 No. HH-886397.

K2 TWO SEATER LHD: Colour Ivory, blue leather.

Chassis No. K-1848.   Cadillac mod: Delivered 18-1-51.

SHIPPERS : DAVIES TURNER.   ss AMERICAN CLIPPER.
           £59-0-6   Documents received 26-1-51.........

168   AMERICA   Seddon   LK-1848.

R/P IMPORTED MOTOR CAR COMPANY,   32
147 West 54th Street,
NEW YORK 19., N.Y.   Order No. 86.

Ordered 2-1-51.   Invoice S-1689.   CD3 HH-886378.   Dlvd 3-4-51.
ALLARD K2 TWO SEATER: Colour blue, red leather upholstery.
Chassis No. K-1969.   Cadillac modification.

DAVIES TURNER: ss ....   Docs received 14-4-51.
                                    Freight £55-19-6.

190   AMERICA   Seddon.   LK-1969.

R/P IMPORTED MOTOR CAR CO.,
147 West 54th Street,
New York 19., N.Y. File No. 87.

Ordered 2-1-51. Invoice S-1686. CD3 HH-886384. Dlvd 3-3-51.
ALLARD K2 TWO SEATER LHD: Black, Ivory leather upholstery. Less engine. Cadillac modification. CHASSIS NO. K-1970.

DAVIES TURNER. ss AM. INVENTOR. Closing 3-3-51.
Freight £70. 0. 0d. Docs 7-3-51.

David H.H. Felix., 1416-18 South Penn Square, Philadelphia 2.

YB 17/6/54

179 AMERICA Seddon/ Felix/ 2K-1970.

4

CALIFORNIA SPORTS CAR CO.,
1460 Pine Street,
SAN FRANCISCO., CALIF. Order No. 93.

Ordered 8-1-51. Invoice S-1666. CD3 HH-886387.
ALLARD K2 TWO SEATER: Colour Light blue, blue leather.
Chassis No. K-1978. Cadillac modification. Delivered 15-3-51.

LEP TRANSPORT. ss LOCH GARTH. Freight £62-8-3.
Packed by Reynolds. Docs received 25-4-51.

183 AMERICA California Sports. K-1978

2

CALIFORNIA SPORTS CAR CO.,
1460 Pine Street,
SAN FRANCISCO., CALIF: Order 91.

Ordered 8-1-51. Invoice S-1667. CD3 HH-886386. DWD 15-3-51
ALLARD K2 TWO SEATER: Colour silver grey, red leather upholstery.
Chassis No. K-1976. Cadillac modification.

LEP TRANSPORT: ss LOCH GARTH.; Freight 62-8-3 Docs 25/4/51

181 AMERICA California Sports. 2K-1976.

California Sports Car Co.,
1460 Pine Street,
San Francisco., California. Order No. 94.

Ordered 8-1-51. Invoice S-1694. CD3 HH-537881. Dlvd 30-3-51.
ALLARD K2 TWO SEATER LHD: Colour Red, red leather upholstery. Less engine. Cadillac modification. CHASSIS NO. K-1979.

LEP TRANSPORT. ss LOCH GARTH. Closing 23-4-51.
Freight £62-8-3d. Docs 26-4-51.

O. Wallace., c/o Walt Disney Studios., Hollywood., California.

17/4/54

192 AMERICA Calif Sports/ Wallace/ K-1979.

California Sports Car Co.,
1460 Pine Street,
San Francisco., California. File No. 92

Ordered 8-1-51. Invoice S-1665. CD3 HH-886388. Dlvd 15-3-51.
ALLARD K2 TWO SEATER LHD: Pacific Green, green leather upholstery. Less engine. Cadillac modification. CHASSIS NO. K-1977.

LEP TRANSPORT. ss LOCH GARTH. Closing 16-3-51. (Packed Reynold)
Freight £ Docs 20-3-51.

Harry Mhoon Fair., F.E. Booth Co, Inc.
280 Battery Street, San Francisco 11., Calif.

182 AMERICA CALIF SPORTS/ Mhoon Fair/ K-1977

37

R/P IMPORTED MOTOR CAR COMPANY,
147 West 54th Street,
NEW YORK 19., N.Y.

Ordered 21-2-51; Invoice S-1711; CD3 HH-886240.
Allard K2 TWO SEATER: Colour M.G. Red, red; modified for Cadillac.

DAVIES TURNER: "MUNCASTER CASTLE" Delivered 21-4-51.
Freight £52-3-6. K-1980. Docs rec'd 1-5-51.

217 AMERICA Seddon. K-1980.

rds

Card 1 (top left):

R/P IMPORTED MOTOR CAR COMPANY,
147 West 54th Street,
NEW YORK 19, N.Y.
U. S. A.   File No. 125.   36

Ordered 27-2-51. Invoice S- 1779. CD3 HH-886245.
ALLARD K2 TWO SEATER LHD: Bronze, brown leather.

Chassis No. K-1981. Modified for clients FORD ENGINE.

LEP TRANSPORT - ss ASIA - Delivered 29-7-51.
Freight £........) Docs received 7./8/51.
                  ₤ and P. 2.58.

209 AMERICA Seddon.   K-1981.

Card 2 (top right):

R/P IMPORTED MOTOR CAR CO,
147 West 54th Street,
NEW YORK 19., N.Y.   35

Ordered 8-1-51. Invoice S-1685. CD3 HH-886380. Dlvd 16-4-51.
ALLARD K2 two seater: Colour dark blue, blue leather.

ss "AMERICAN SCIENTIST"...LEP...Freight £53-3-0...Docs recd 25-4-51.

(spare wheel in right wing, model)

195 AMERICA Seddon.   K-1984.

Card 3 (middle left):

K 1982.   193 AMERICA SEDDON   33

R/P IMPORTED MOTOR CAR COMPANY,
147 West 54th Street,
NEW YORK 19., N.Y.

Ordered 8-1-51. Invoice S-1688. CD3 HH-886377. Dl'vd 21-4-51.
K2 ALLARD 2 SEATER : Colour black, red; Chassis No. K-1982.

DAVIES TURNER : "MUNCASTER CASTLE" Docs received 1-5-51.
                        Freight £54-4-0

Stanley L. Peterson, 809 Quincy Street, Reno 2., Nevada.

195 AMERICA Seddon. /Peterson/   K-1982.

Card 4 (middle right):

Custom Automotive.,
2122 North Pearl Street.,
Dallas., Texas.   File No. 174.

Ordered 5-6-51. Invoice S-1684. CD3 HH-886258. Dlvd 22-6-51.
ALLARD K2 TWO SEATER LHD: Grey, black leather upholstery.
                          Less engine. Cadillac modification.
                          CHASSIS NO. K-1985.

DAVIES TURNER. ss DALEBY. Closing 22-6-51. (delayed by Strike)
Freight £60-14-0d.   Docs   14-7-51.

Major R.A. Duncan USAF., Box 133 OMS., APO 207., c/o P.M., New York.

196 AMERICA Custom Auto/ Duncan/   K-1985.

Card 5 (bottom left):

R/P Imported Motor Car Co.,
147 West 54th Street,
New York 19., New York.   File No: 98.

Ordered 8-1-51. Invoice S-1687. CD3 HH-886376. Dlvd 16-4-51.
ALLARD K2 TWO SEATER LHD: Colour Grey, red leather upholstery.
                          Less engine. Cadillac modification.
                          CHASSIS NO: K-1983.

DAVIES TURNER.   ss AMERICAN SCIENTIST   Closing 17-4-51
Freight £53.-3.-6d.   Docs   27-4-51.

194 AMERICA Seddon/   K-1983.

Card 6 (bottom right):

R/P IMPORTED MOTOR CAR CO.,
147 West 54th Street,
New York 19., N.Y.   File No. 84.

Ordered 2-1-51. Invoice S-1572. CD3 HH-886391. Dlvd 20-4-51.
ALLARD K2 TWO SEATER LHD: Colour Grey, red leather upholstery.
                          Less engine. Cadillac modification.
                          CHASSIS NO. K-1986.

LEP TRANSPORT.   ss MUNCASTER CASTLE. Closing 25-4-51.
Freight £52-17-5d.   Docs   27-4-51.

Dr. E.J. Bien M.D., 1165 Park Avenue, New York 28., N.Y.

187 AMERICA Seddon/ Dr. Bien/   K-1986.

SALON DE L'AUTO.,
1, Place du Lac.,
GENEVA., SWITZERLAND.   Order No. 107.

Ordered 19-1-51.   Invoice S-1693.   CD3 HH-886385.
ALLARD K2 TWO SEATER: Colour bronze, brown leather upholstery.
Chassis No. K-2028.   Engine No. 7249391.   Delivered 26-2-51.

LEP TRANSPORT: Train Ferry Truck No. 708997.
Freight £62-4-6 (delv'd to Stand).   Docs received. (NATURAL le Coult

CAR RETURNED TO U.K. via Harwich...... 8th May 1951.

185   SWITZERLAND   Geneva Show.   (see K-2194)   K-2028.

All Sports Inc.,
Excelsior., Minnesota.   File No. 112

Ordered 8-2-51. Invoice S-1773. CD3 HH-886244. Dlvd 8-4-51.
ALLARD K2 TWO SEATER LHD: Colour Red, red leather upholstery.
                          Engine No. 7252888.
                          CHASSIS NO. K-2031.

LEP TRANSPORT.   ss SEABOARD STAR.   Closing 9-4-51.
Freight £48-8-3d.   Docs   22-5-51.

Don P. Schoenert, R.F.D., Route 3., Box 278A., Excelsior., Minnesota

204   AMERICA   All Sports/ Schoenert/   K-2031.

N.V. Haarlemsche Auto Centrale,
Haarlem., Holland.   File No. 172.

Ordered 4-6-51. Invoice S-1832. CD3 HH-886256. Dlvd 7-6-51.
ALLARD K2 TWO SEATER LHD: Royal Blue, red leather upholstery.
                          * De Dion rear axle. 6 wire wheels.
                          * Spare wheels in front wings.
                          * Mercury engine No: 7018/87.
                          CHASSIS NO: K-2029.

McCullan delivery to the Hook of Holland via Harwich. Carnet.

G.J. Th. A. Van Wuck, Wilhelminastr. 97, Osten (N.Br.), Holland.

229   HOLLAND   Haarlemsche/Wuck/   K2-2029.

ALL SPORTS INC;
EXCELSIOR.,
MINNESOTA., U.S.A.   File..113.

Ordered 8-2-51.   Invoice S-1774. CD3 HH-886243. Dlvd 8-4-51.
K2 TWO SEATER : Chassis No. K-2032. Engine No. 7256167.
                 Colour green, green leather.

LEP TRANSPORT : ss Seaboard Star.
                 Freight..£48-8-3   Docs rec'd..22-5-51.

205   AMERICA   All Sports   K-2032.

R/P IMPORTED MOTOR CAR COMPANY,
147 West 54th Street,
NEW YORK 19., N.Y.   File No. 108.

Ordered 25-1-51. Invoice S-1843. CD3 HH-886260. Dlvd 11/7/51.
ALLARD K2 TWO SEATER LHD; Red, black leather, red wheels.
                 . De Dion rearend; 6 wire wheels; spare
                         wheels in wings.
Chassis No. K-2030. Cadillac modification. Delivered 11 July 1951

LEP TRANSPORT. ss Washington.... Closing 15th July 1951
Freight £134-13-4) 7018 Docs received..21-7-4
         1975 (3 cars on same account)

233   AMERICA   Seddon.   K-2030

MOSS MOTORS LIMITED.,
4675 West Pico Boulevard,
LOS ANGELES 6., CALIF.   File No. 130.

Ordered 16-3-51. Invoice S-1781. CD3 HH-886248. Dlv'd 21-5-51.
ALLARD K2 TWO SEATER LHD: Colour black, red leather.
                 Chassis No. K-2037. Cadillac mod.

DAVIES TURNER : ss Corrientes. Delivery Liverpool Docks (Coach).
                 Freight £77-13-3..   Docs received..6-6-51.
                 (£48-16-7)

211   AMERICA   Moss.   K-2037.

MOSS MOTORS LIMITED.,
4675 West Pico Boulevard,
LOS ANGELES 6., CALIF.   File No. 131.

Ordered 16-3-51. Invoice S-1782. CD3 HH-886247. Dlv'd 21-5-51.
ALLARD K2 TWO SEATER LHD: Colour black, white leather.

                    Chassis No. K-2081. Cadillac mod.

DAVIES TURNER: ss Corrientes. Loading Liverpool Docks. (coach.)
                Freight £.48-16-7. Docs rec'd. 6-6-51....

212   AMERICA   Moss.   K-2081.

General Curtis E. Le May.,
Offutt Air Force Car Club.,
Offutt Air Force Base.,
Omaha., Nebraska.   File No. (nemo)

Ordered 8-5-51.   (collected by USAF transport 8-8-51)
ALLARD K2 TWO SEATER LHD: Metallic blue, brown leather uphlstry.
                           Less engine. Cadillac modification.
                           CHASSIS NO. K-2084.

General F.H. Griswold., Offutt AFB., Omaha., Nebraska.

3rd owner. T.P. Bauschard., 721 Park Avenue South., Erie., Pa.

249   AMERICA   Gen. Le May/Griswold/Bauschard/   K-2084.

IMPORT MOTORS,
575 Spring Street,
ATLANTA., Georgia.
U. S. A.   File No. 171.

Ordered 31-5-51. Invoice S-1819. CD3 HH-886254. Dlvd 4-6-51.

ALLARD K2 TWO SEATER LHD: Pacific green, green leather.
                    Chassis No. K-2082. Engine No. 9518/86.
                                         (4375 Mercury)
                    Bert Wyndham
DAVIES TURNER: ss PORT ADELAIDE - KGV Dock. shut out through Dock Strike
                Freight £.59-7-6. Docs recd...24-7-51...

225   AMERICA   Import Motors   K-2082.

Custom Automotive.,
2122 North Pearl Street,
Dallas., Texas.   File No. 204.

Ordered 15-8-51. Invoice S-1919. CD3 HH-886275. Dlvd 3-9-51
ALLARD K2 2 SEATER LHD: Pacific Green, grey leather upholstery.
                         LESS ENGINE. CHASSIS NO. K-2085.

LEP TRANSPORT. ss DALEBY. Closing 3-9-51.
Freight £49-13-6.   Docs   12-9-51.

Col. Paul W. Tibbetts Jr, H.Q. 3200th Proof Test Group,
(1st Atom Bomb pilot)   Eglin Air Force Base, Florida.

2nd. Owner: Philip Guedel,   Los Angeles.

3rd owner: Fred Berryhill, Fred Berryhill Equipment Co Inc.,
                                         Lubbock., Texas.
John C. Myers, President, Northrop Aviation Corpn.

255   AMERICA   Custom Auto/Tibbetts/Guedel/Berryhill/   K-2085.

R/P IMPORTED MOTOR CAR COMPANY,   42
147 West 54th Street,
NEW YORK 19., N.Y.
U. S. A.   File No. 195.

Ordered 20-7-51. Invoice S-1887. CD3 HH-886268.
ALLARD K2 TWO SEATER LHD: Cream, black leather & wings.

Chassis No. K-2083. Modified for normal FORD ENGINE.

DAVIES TURNER: ss ASIA. Delivered 30-7-51.
Freight £.36-14-7...   Docs recd 3-8-51.

244   AMERICA   Seddon   K-2083.

George Lee Motors.,
200 Clemenceau Avenue.,
Singapore., Malaya.   File No. 155.

Ordered 11-4-51. Invoice S-1797. Delivered 28-5-51.
ALLARD K2 TWO SEATER RHD: Cream, red leather upholstery.
                           Engine No. 7252887.
                           CHASSIS NO. K-2093.

DAVIES TURNER. ss BEN LOMOND. Closing 28-5-51.
Freight £100-18-1d.   Docs   13-6-51.

C. Haddon Cave., The United Sua Betong Rubber Estates Limited.,
            Yong Peng Estate, Yong Peng P.O., Johore, Malaya.

219   SINGAPORE   George Lee/ Haddon Cave/   K-2093.

R.A. Gibbons & Co.,
66 S. Eastbourne.,
York Bay., Wellington., N.Z.   File No. 157.

Ordered 20-4-51. Invoice S-1840. Delivered 11-6-51.
ALLARD K2 TWO SEATER RHD: Colour Black, red leather upholstery.
                          Engine No. Mercury 9616/83.
                          CHASSIS NO. K-2104.

Dr. V.B. Cook., Hutt Hospital., Lower Hutt., New Zealand.

LEP TRANSPORT.   ss RANGITOTA.   Closing 27-6-51.
Freight £127-7-0d.   Docs   14-7-51.

2nd Owner: W. Hegarty., P.O. Box 139., Gisborne., New Zealand.

230 NEW ZEALAND Gibbons/ Dr. Cook/ Hegarty/   K-2104.

Gardiners Motor Service.,
297/299 Stanmore Road.,
Petersham., N.S.W.   File No. 135.

Ordered 27-5-51. Invoice S-1914. Dlvd Reynolds 20-8-51.
ALLARD K2 TWO SEATER RHD: Colour Red, red leather upholstery.
                          Less engine. (Mercury modification ?)
                          CHASSIS NO. K-2108.

LEP TRANSPORT.   ss ATHENIC.   Closing 21-9-51.
Freight £86-16-1d. plus packing.   Docs received 25-9-51.

R.G. Cioccarelli., 80 Proctor Parade., Chester Hill., N.S.W.
(purchased car secondhand in February 1954 - Mercury 5307-61 fitted
                                        ?   ?   ?

1st Owner:

247 AUSTRALIA Gardiner/ Cioccarelli/   K-2108.

Lamb's Auto Supply Co.,
405 Mahoning Road N.E.,
Canton 4., Ohio.   File No. 167.

Ordered 22-5-51. Invoice S-1850. CD3 HH-886262. Dlvd 30-7-51.
ALLARD K2 TWO SEATER LHD: Colour Black, red leather upholstery.
                          ARDUN Engine No. 2023-Z.
                          CHASSIS NO. K-2105.

DAVIES TURNER.   ss RAVNESJELL.   Closing 30-7-51.
Freight £145-16-6.   Docs   13-8-51.

Jim Hoover., HOOVER MANUFACTURING CO., Cleveland., Ohio.
James C. Hoover., 1400 N. Dearborn Parkway., Chicago., Illinois.
THE HOOVER COMPANY., Mid-Western Division, 1417 Merchandise Mart
              Plaza., Chicago 54., Illinois.
Main Factory: THE HOOVER COMPANY., North Canton., Ohio.

234 AMERICA Lamb's Auto/ Hoover/   K-2105.

Gardiners Motor Service.,
297/299 Stanmore Road.,
Petersham., N.S.W.   File No. 169.

Ordered 26-3-51. Invoice S-1915. Delivered 15-8-51.
ALLARD K2 TWO SEATER RHD: Pacific Green, green leather upholstery.
                          Engine No. 7223308.
                          Australian Registration No. VIC GAN 582
                          CHASSIS NO. K-2152.

LEP TRANSPORT.   ss ATHENIC.   Closing 20-9-51. (packed)
Freight £86-16-1d.   Docs   25-9-51.

Haig Hurst., Manchester Supplies., Box 4., Fairfield.,
                             Melbourne., Victoria., Australia.
        and:
          'Glenrise', Falls Rd, Kalorama, Victoria.

251 AUSTRALIA Gardiner/ Haig Hurst/   K-2152.

LAMB'S AUTO SUPPLY COMPANY.,
405 Mahoning Road, N.E.
CANTON 4., OHIO.

Ordered 22-5-51. Invoice S-1851. CD3 HH-886263.
ALLARD K2 TWO SEATER LHD: Colour red, red leather upholstery.
                          Chassis No. K-2106.
                          Ardun Engine No. 2024-Z.
DAVIES TURNER: ss RAVNESJELL.   Delivered 30-7-51.
                 Freight £145-11-2 Docs recd 13-8-51
                              and K2105

235 AMERICA Lamb Auto   K-2106.

KESKUS AUTO OY.,
Kauppalankatu 39-41,
KOUVOLA.,
FINLAND.   File No. 159.

Ordered 24-4-51.   Invoice S-1918.   CD3 HH-886272. Dlvd 19/9/51.
ALLARD K2 TWO SEATER LHD: Cream, red leather upholstery.
                          Chassis No. K-2153. Engine No.
                                        (Mercury 4375 cc)
LEP TRANSPORT: ss RIGEL..
(Freight & transport forward)   Docs rec'd 15/9/51.

250 FINLAND Keskus.   K-2153.

R/P Imported Motor Car Co.,
147 West 54th Street,
New York 19., New York   File No. 220.

Ordered 30-11-51. Invoice S-2058. CD3 JJ-88660. Dlvd 12-12-51.
ALLARD K2 TWO SEATER LHD: Brewster Green, red leather upholstery.
     Less engine. Cadillac modification.
     CHASSIS NO. K-2154.

DAVIES TURNER.   ss AMERICAN PRESS.   Closing 12-12-51.
Freight £58.-13.-9d.   CA/12/0116   Docs   19-12-51.

Walter S. Glazar, 99-10 Glenwood Road, Brooklyn 36., New York.

288   AMERICA   Seddon/ Glazar/   K-2154.

Denver Imported Motors.,
2610. W. Alameda Avenue,
Denver 19., Colorado.   File No: 305.

Ordered 10-1-52. Invoice S-2083. CD3 JJ-88663. Dlvd 10-1-52.
ALLARD K2 TWO SEATER LHD: Colour Elec.Blue, blue leather upholst.
     ARDUN Engine No: 2036-Z.
     CHASSIS NO: K-2197.

DAVIES TURNER.   ss DEERPOOL.   Closing 10-1-52.
Freight £61-14-10d.   CA/01/0141.   Docs   18-1-52.

James A. Sisler, 3157 44th Place, Sandia Base, Albuquerque,
                                 New Mexico.

314   AMERICA   Denver/ Sisler/   K-2197.

C.W.L. Tatham.,Esq.
41, Ave. Vulliemin,
Lausanne (Vaud).,
SWITZERLAND.   File No. 180.

Ordered 10-7-51. Invoice S-1889. CD3 HH-886270.
ALLARD K2 TWO SEATER LHD: P.O. Red, brown leather.

Chassis No. K-2194.   Engine No. 7259720.

Collection from showroom ... 15th August 1951.
A.A. Customs clearance - client driving from Dunkirk on
Swiss number plates.

(K-2028 sprayed red & allocated new chassis number)

⊕
see chassis K2028

243   SWITZERLAND   Tatham   K-2194.

R/P IMPORTED MOTOR CAR COMPANY,
147 West 54th Street,
NEW YORK 19., N.Y.   File No. 222.   49

Ordered 14-12-51. Invoice S-2074. CD3 JJ-88661. Dlvd 3/1/52.
ALLARD K2 TWO SEATER LHD: Red, black leather.
     Cadillac modification.
     Chassis No. K-2198.

DAVIES TURNER: ss AM. SCIENTIST.   Closing 3/1/52.
Freight £58-16-3.   Docs 10./1/52 CA/12/0131

293   AMERICA   Seddon   K-2198.

Grancor Automotive Specialists.,
5150 North Western Avenue.,
Chicago 25., Illinois.   File No. 208.

Ordered 4-9-51. Invoice S-1967. CD3 JJ-88643. Dlvd 27-9-51.
ALLARD K2 TWO SEATER LHD: Colour Red, black leather upholstery.
     Less engine. Cadillac modification.
     CHASSIS NO. K-2195.

DAVIES TURNER.   ss AM. CLIPPER.   Closing 27-9-51.
Freight £57-6-6d.   Docs   10-10-51.

Edward W. Gaylord., Gaylord Products Inc., 1918-36 Prairie Ave.,
                                 Chicago 16., Illinois.

265   AMERICA   Grancor/ Gaylord/   K-2195.

R/P IMPORTED MOTOR CAR COMPANY.,
147 West 54th Street,
NEW YORK 19., N.Y.   File No. 321.   54

Ordered 25-1-52. Invoice S-2094. CD3 88666. Dlvd 7/2/52.
ALLARD K2 TWO SEATER LHD: Royal blue, red leather.
     (respray - orig. P.green, green)
     Cadillac modification.
     Chassis No. K-2199.

DAVIES TURNER: ss AM. FARMER.   Closing 4-2-52. Reynolds ctn.
Freight £53-6-7   Docs 21-2-52.
                 CA/01/0162

321   AMERICA   Seddon.   K-2199.

NOEL KIRK MOTORS.,
7176 Sunset Boulevard,
HOLLYWOOD 46., CALIF.   File No. 396.

Ordered 5-7-52. Invoice S-2231. CD3 MM-792005. Dlvd 13-9-52.
ALLARD K2 TWO SEATER LHD: Colour Turquoise blue, fawn leather.
                         Less engine; CADILLAC MODIFICATION.

DAVIES TURNER : ss LOCH GARTH. Closing 13-9-52.
Freight £   Docs. ..24-9-52.
                                Nos :

366 AMERICA Noel Kirk Motors   ιK-3125

JUAN RIU - PANAMERICAN IMPORT.,
Transversal 17 No. 25-97.,
Av. Caracas Esquina Calle 26.,
Bogota., Colombia., S. America.   File No. 407.

Ordered 27-8-52. Invoice S-2296. CD3 MM-792024. Dlvd 28-10-52.
ALLARD K2 TWO SEATER LHD: Colour Cream, red leather upholstery.
                         Fitted radio. Tonneau cover.
                         MERCURY ENG. NO: 15869/108.
                         CHASSIS NO. K-3128.

LEP TRANSPORT. ss AM. MILLER. Closing 29-10-52.
Freight (packed) £206-13-4.   Docs .. 17-11-52.

Antonio Izquierdo (Davila), Apartado Nal. 15-74.,
                         Bogota., Colombia., S. America.

387 COLOMBIA Juan Riu/ Izquierdo/   ιK-3128

NOEL KIRK MOTORS.,
7176 Sunset Boulevard,
HOLLYWOOD 46., CALIF.   File No. 397.

Ordered 5-7-52. Invoice S-2232. CD3 MM-792004. Dlvd 10-9-52.
ALLARD K2 TWO SEATER LHD : Bright red, red leather upholstery.
                          Less engine; Cadillac modification.

DAVIES TURNER. ss TARANGER. Closing 19/23-9-52.
Freight £69-11-4   Docs ..8 - 10-52.
                          CA/08/0473

367 AMERICA Noel Kirk Motors   ιK-3126

Riviera Motors (Calif. Sports Car Co.)
160 Sansome Street,
San Francisco 9., California.   File No. 409.

Ordered 21-7-52. Invoice S-2283. CD3 MM-792019. Dlvd 18-10-52.
ALLARD K2 TWO SEATER LHD: Colour Cream, black leather upholstery.
                         Less engine. Cadillac modification.
                         CHASSIS NO. K-3130.

DAVIES TURNER.   ss DURANGO.   Closing 18-10-52.
Freight £58. 0. 0d.   Docs   23-10-52.

Thomas J. Stapleton, 2605 Linda Vista, Napa., California.

384 AMERICA C.S.C. Co./ Stapleton/   ιK-3130.

NOEL KIRK MOTORS.,
7176 Sunset Boulevard,
HOLLYWOOD 46., CALIF.   File No. 405.

Ordered 14-7-52. Invoice S-2234. CD3 MM-792006. Dlvd 10-10-52.
ALLARD K2 TWO SEATER LHD: Pale beige, brown leather upholstery.
                         Less engine; Cadillac modification.
                         CHASSIS NO. K-3127.

DAVIES TURNER : ss POTARO. Closing 10-10-52.
Freight £   Docs ..   -10-52.
                            Nos :

369 AMERICA Noel Kirk Motors   ιK-3127

NOEL KIRK MOTORS.,
7176 Sunset Boulevard,
Hollywood 46., Calif.   File No. 433.

Ordered 26-8-52. Invoice S-2263. CD3 MM-792013. Dlvd 7-11-52.
ALLARD K2 TWO SEATER LHD: Oxford Blue, blue leather upholstery.
                         Less engine: Cadillac Modification.
                         CHASSIS NO. K-3133.

LEP Transport.   ss DRINA.   Closing 7-11-52.
Freight £69-0 -0   Docs M -11-52.

Client :-

378 AMERICA Noel Kirk   ιK-3133

EMELAS & CIA.,
Rincon 661.,
Montevideo.,
URUGUAY.   File No. 86.

Ordered 16-11-49. Invoice S-1137. CD3 FF-720231 Dlvd 2-12-49
ALLARD P1 SALOON LHD: Colour Black, grey leather upholstery.
                ENGINE NO. 7202313. CHASSIS NO. P-1550.

Mr. Irazi Delleon., Cuidad de Calvi 952., Montevideo., Uruguay.

SHIPPERS: Joseph C. Mount.   ss ....
Freight£   Docs ../12/49.   Yb 14/6/54

86 URUGUAY Emelas/ Irazi Delleon/   P-1550

EMELAS & CIA LTDA,
Rincon 661,
MONTEVIDEO., URUGUAY.   S-1137

Ordered 16-11-49   Invoiced 1-12-49   Delivered 17-1-50

4-SEATER SALOON LHD.;   Colour black, brown leather upholstery.

Chassis No. P-1562.   Engine No. 7219814.

90 URUGUAY Salem   P-1562

L. BOCKH & CIA LTDA,
Apartado 3756,
San Isidro A San Julian 11,
CARACAS., VENEZUELA.

Ordered 11-11-49 Invoiced 1-12-49   Delivered 23-1-50

4-SEATER SALOON LHD.; Colour grey, maroon leather upholstery.

Chassis No. P-1560.   Engine No. 7219817.

92 VENEZUELA Bockh   P-1560

SOCIEDAD MERCANTIL INTERNACIONAL S.A.
Ayacusho 266,
LIMA., PERU.   S-1190

Ordered 26-12-49   Invoiced 26-1-50   Delivered 22-2-50.

4-SEATER SALOON LHD.; Colour light blue, blue leather upholstery.

Chassis No. P-1585.   Engine No. 7223833.   C.D.3...............

97 PERU Somerin   P-1585

EMELAS & CIA.,
Rincon 661.,
Montevideo.,
URUGUAY.   File No. 89.

Ordered 16-11-49. Invoice S-1137. CD3 FF-734987. Dlvd 17-1-50
ALLARD P1 SALOON LHD: Colour Black, red leather upholstery.
                ENGINE NO. 7219823.
                CHASSIS NO. P-1561.

Shippers: Joseph C. Mount.   ss ....
Freight £   Docs 27-1-50.   Yb.18/6/54

Atilio Caló., Calle San Antrina 2733., Montevideo., Uruguay.

89 URUGUAY Emelas/ Atilio Caló/   P-1561

G.L. McDermott., Esq.
Second Secretary.,
British Embassy.,
Santiago., Chile.   File No.

Ordered 17-1-50. Invoice S-1192. CD3 DD-352830. Dlvd 22-2-50.
ALLARD P1 SALOON RHD: Colour cream, maroon leather upholstery.
                Engine No. 7223878.
                CHASSIS NO. P-1592.

JOS. C. MOUNT.   ss SAMARCO.   Closing 22-2-50.
Freight £104. 0. 0.   Docs   25-2-50.

98 CHILE McDermott/   P-1592.

Card 1

MOSS MOTORS LTD,
3210, West Olympic Boulevard,
LOS ANGELES 6, CALIFORNIA. U.S.A.
S-1205
Ordered 27-1-50   Invoiced 9-2-50.   Delivered 3-2-50.

ORDER.NO. 5.   2

4-SEATER SALOON LHD.; Colour green, red leather upholstery.

Chassis No. P-1601.   Invoiced 9-2-50.   C.D.3. AA 289080.

SHIPPERS. DAVIES TURNER. Freight. £60.

99   AMERICA   Moss   P-1601

Card 2

Alan Andersson., Esq.
Delsjovagen 11.,
Goteborg 2., Sweden.   File No. 24.

Ordered 28-4-50. Invoice S-1359. CD3 DD-352829. Dlvd 24-8-50.
ALLARD M-TYPE D/HD COUPE RHD: Grey., red leather upholstery.
                               Fitted with Columbia rear axle.
                               Foreshortened grille. Own Mercury
                               block fitted with Ardun ohv kit.
                               Ardun Engine No. 7228240. P.T.O →
                               CHASSIS NO. P-1625.

* Columbia axle necessitated use of P1 chassis although special
  M-type body mounted.

DEALER: Motortillbehor., Wallingsgatan 38., Stockholm., Sweden.
THOMAS MEADOWS: ss MALMO.   Closing 24-8-50. Freight £38. 0. 0.
Ewald Hagstrom., WASA Bilbolag, Marksvardgatan 11., Stockholm.

141 SWEDEN Motortillbehor/ Andersson/ Hagstrom/   P-1625.

Card 3

A/B Motortillbehor.,
Wallingatan 38.,
Stockholm., Sweden.   File No: 7.

Ordered 1-2-50.   Invoice S-1206.   Delivered 13-3-50.
ALLARD 71P SALOON MOTOR CAR RHD: Dove grey, green leather.
                                  Engine No. 7225864.
                                  CHASSIS NO: P-1602.

J.C. MOUNT & CO.   ss MALMO.   Closing 14-3-50
Freight £40. 0. 0d.   Docs   15-3-50.

Douglas Dickson, Box 53., Hovas., Sweden.

                              (CD3 FF-156811)

103   SWEDEN Motortillbehor/ Dickson/   P-1602.

Card 4

R/P IMPORTED MOTOR CAR COMPANY.,   ORDER NO. 67.   22
147 West 54th Street,
NEW YORK 19., N.Y.

Ordered 9-10-50   Invoice S-1554.   CD3 No. HH-537889.

SALOON LHD. Colour silver, red leather upholstery.

Chassis No. P-1860.   Cadillac mod;

SHIPPERS : DAVIES TURNER.   ss AMERICAN CLIPPER.   Delivered 18-1-51.

£71-7-7   Documents received. 26-1-51

170   AMERICA   Seddon.   P-1860

Card 5

Conde de Monte Real.,
Rua de Buenos Aires 39.,
Lisbon., Portugal.   File No.

Ordered 22-3-50. Invoice S-1262. CD3 FF-156817. Dlvd 26-4-50.
ALLARD P1 SALOON LHD: Maroon, maroon leather upholstery.
                       Mercury 4375. ENGINE NO. 5540-28.
                       CHASSIS NO. P-1620.

EVAN COOKS.   ss ANDES.   Closing 27-4-50.
Freight £27. 0. 0d.   Docs   30-4-50.

107 PORTUGAL Cond de Monte Real/   P-1620.

Card 6

Engineering & Industrial Exports (E.A) Ltd.,
Private Bag.,
Nairobi., Kenya.   File No. 65.

Ordered 20-11-50. Invoice S-1549. Delivered 27-1-51.
ALLARD P1 SALOON RHD: Colour Cream, red leather upholstery.
                       Engine No. 7246427.
                       CHASSIS NO. P-1892.

J.H. Carvill., c/o E.I.E. Ltd., Nairobi., Kenya.
             and 5 The Vineyard., Richmond., Surrey.

DAVIES TURNER.   ss DUNNOTAR CASTLE.   Closing 27-1-51.
Freight £70. 10. 0d.   Docs   14-2-51.

161 KENYA E.I.E./ Carvill /   P-1892.

E.I.E. (E.A) LIMITED.,
Private Bag.,
Nairobi., Kenya.   File No. 62.

Ordered 1-12-50. Invoice S-1574. Delivered 25-1-51.
ALLARD P-TYPE SALOON RHD: Colour Grey, grey leather upholstery.
                        Engine No. 7246506.
                        CHASSIS NO. P-1902.

HOULDER BROS.   ss DUNNOTAR CASTLE.   Closing 25-1-51.
* E.I.E. Ltd. arranged own shipment.

Capt. W.F.O. Trench., Molo., Kenya Colony., East Africa.

172 KENYA E.I.E./ Capt. Trench/   P-1902.

2

A.P. & E. SINGER LIMITED.,
Royal London House,
16, Finsbury Square,
LONDON. E.C.2.   Order No. 115.

Ordered 13-2-51.   Invoice S-1702.   CD3 n/a   Delivered 23-3-51.
ALLARD P-1 SALOON: Colour metallic grey, blue leather.
Chassis No. P-1958.   Engine No. 7251628.

LEP TRANSPORT: ss Port Brisbane.   Freight £111-15-10.
                                     Docs received...........

199 NEW ZEALAND Singer.   P-1958.

L.H. Green Pty. Ltd.,
128 Wickham Street,
Brisbane., Queensland.,
Australia.   File No. 104.

Ordered 17-1-51. Invoice S-1668. Delivered 26-2-51.
ALLARD P1 SALOON RHD: Dark Green, grey leather upholstery.
                       600 x 16 tyres. Andre Tele-controls.
                       Engine No. 7249594.
                       CHASSIS NO. P-1937.

DAVIES TURNER.   ss TREVEAN.   Closing 26-2-51.
Freight £127-9-0d.   Docs   3-3-51.

M.J. Grills., Enright Street, Mundingburra., Townsville.,
                       Queensland., Australia.

203 AUSTRALIA Brisbane/ Grills/   P-1937.

SOCIEDAD MERCANTIL INTERNACIONAL S.A.,
Ayacusho 266.,
LIMA., PERU., S. AMERICA.   File No. 102.

ALLARD P1 SALOON LHD: Cream, red leather upholstery.
                       CHASSIS NO. P-1987. REG. NO. MGC 529.
                       MERCURY 4375 cc ENGINE NO. 4G-69244F.

Ordered 15-1-51. Invoice S-1798. CD/3 o.k. Covenant o.k.
HOME DELIVERY (temporary use in U.K.) Delivered 18-6-51.

Client: Mr. Crofton Atkins, Crest Hotel, Crowborough, Sussex.
        & .. Central Railway of Peru, Casilla 301, Lima., Peru.

LEP TRANSPORT: ss SALAVERY. Closing 20-11-51.
Freight £122-10-0.   Docs   3-12-51.

202 PERU Somerin /Crofton Atkins/   P-1987.

1

A.P. & E. SINGER LTD,
Royal London House,
16, Finsbury Square,
LONDON. E.C.2.   Order No.114......

Ordered 13-2-51.   Invoice S-1700.   CD3 n/a.   Dlvd 22-3-51.
ALLARD SALOON P-1: Colour black, maroon leather upholstery.
Chassis No. P-1956.   Engine No. 7250845.

LEP TRANSPORT: ss Port Brisbane.   Freight £111-15-10.
                                     Docs received.........

198 NEW ZEALAND Singer.   P-1956.

---

201 N.ZEALAND   SINGER   P-1960.

3

L.Myxxxxxx.Pty.Ltd.,
A.P. & E. SINGER LTD,
Royal London House,
16, Finsbury Square,
LONDON. E.C.2.   File No. 116.

Ordered 13-2-51. Invoice S-1816. Dlvd Reynolds...8/6/51.
ALLARD P1 SALOON RHD: Grey, grey leather upholstery.
                   Chassis No. P-2094. Eng.No. 7252807.
LEP TRANSPORT: ss RHODESIA STAR. Closing 10-6-51.
               Freight £.143.7.6..   Docs recd..9-7-51.

201 NEW ZEALAND Singer   P-2094.

Card 1 (File No. 119)

A.P. & E. Singer Ltd.,
Royal London House,
16 Finsbury Square.,
London. E.C.1.   File No. 119.

N.Z. DEALER: Tractor Specialties., P.O. Box 2819., Auckland., C.L.

Ordered 13-2-51.   Invoice S-1884.   Delivered 27-7-51.
ALLARD P1 SALOON RHD: Dark Blue., blue leather upholstery.
                     Engine No. 7259275.
                     CHASSIS NO. P-2133.

SHAW SAVILL.   ss SYDNEY STAR.   Delivered (packers) 27-7-51.
Freight £92-2-7.   Docs .... 29-8-51.

J.H. Macdonald., (Helmore, Van Asch & Walton) Solicitors.,
          83 Hereford Street, Christchurch., C.I., N.Z.

239 NEW ZEALAND Tracspecs/ Macdonald/   P-2133.

Card 2 (File No. 139)

A.P. & E. Singer Ltd,
Royal London House,   7
16, Finsbury Square,
LONDON. E.C.2.   File No. 139.

Ordered 13-2-51. Invoice S-1884. CVO sent 25-7-51.
ALLARD P1 SALOON RHD: Battleship Grey, maroon leather.
Chassis No. P-2139.   Engine No. 7259285.

SHAW SAVILL. - ss SYDNEY STAR - Delivered ../7/51 to
                                Reynolds for packing.
Freight £.92.2.7.   Docs received 29/8/51.

242 NEW ZEALAND Singer.   P-2139.

Card 3 (File No. 120)

A.P. & E. Singer Ltd,
Royal London House,   5
16, Finsbury Square,
LONDON. E.C.2.   File No. 120.

Ordered 13-2-51. Invoice S-1884. CVO sent 25-7-51.
ALLARD P1 SALOON RHD: Gunmetal, blue leather.
Chassis No. P-2134.   Engine No. 7259286.

SHAW SAVILL.- ss SYDNEY STAR - Delivered 30/7/51 to
                               Reynolds for packing.
Freight £.92.2.7.   Docs received 29/8/51.

240 NEW ZEALAND Singer.   P-2134.

Card 4 (File No. 141)

A.P. & E. Singer Ltd,
Royal London House,   8
16, Finsbury Square,
LONDON. E.C.2.   File No. 141.

Ordered 30-3-51. Invoice S-1885. CVO sent 25-7-51.
ALLARD P1 SALOON RHD: Grey, grey leather.
Chassis No. P-2140.   Engine No. 7259014.

J.B. WESTRAY - ss RANGITANE - Delivered 11/8/51 for
                              packing to Reynolds.
Freight £.122.3.9.   Docs rec'd 29/8/51.

245 NEW ZEALAND Singer   P-2140.

Card 5 (File No. 121)

A.P. & E. Singer Limited.,
Royal London House,
16 Finsbury Square, E.C.2.   File No. 121.

N.Z. DISTRIBUTOR: Tractor Specialties Ltd., P.O. Box 2514.,
                              Auckland C.I., N.Z.

Ordered 13-2-51. Invoice S-1884. Delivered for packing 31-7-51.
ALLARD P1 SALOON RHD: Colour Black, maroon leather upholstery.
                     Engine No. 7259281.
                     CHASSIS NO: P-2135.

SHAW SAVILL.   ss SYDNEY STAR.   Closing 27-8-51.
Freight £92-2.-7d.   Docs   29-8-51.

Elizabeth Highet., 'Glenview', Kakahu, Geraldine, South Canterbury,
                              New Zealand.

241 NEW ZEALAND Tracspecs/ Highet/   P-2135.

Card 6 (File No. 142)

A.P. & E. Singer Ltd,
Royal London House,   9
16, Finsbury Square,
LONDON. E.C.2.   File No. 142.

Ordered 30-3-51. Invoice S-1885. CVO sent 25-7-51.
ALLARD P1 SALOON RHD: Battleship grey, blue leather.
Chassis No. P-2141.   Engine No. 7259287.

J.B. WESTRAY - ss RANGITANE - Delivered 11/8/51 to
                              Reynolds for packing.
Freight £.122.3.9.   Docs received 29/8/51.

246 NEW ZEALAND Singer   P-2141.

Card 1 (top left):

R/P IMPORTED MOTOR CAR COMPANY.,
147 West 54th Street,
NEW YORK 19., N.Y., U. S. A.   File No. 178.   43

Ordered 29-6-51. Invoice S-1894. CD3 HH-685271.
ALLARD P1 SALOON LHD: Colour green, red leather upholstery.
Chassis No. P-2158; modified to accomodate clients FORD motor.

LEP TRANSPORT : ss ASIA.   Delivered 31-7-51 .
Freight £115.-11.-3)   Docs received 7. /8/51.
          5 and K1981

248   AMERICA   Seddon   P-2158.

Card 2 (top right):

BRISBANE MOTORS PTY LTD.,
128 Wickham Street,
BRISBANE., QUEENSLAND.
AUSTRALIA.   File No. 163.

Ordered 22-5-51. Invoice S-1921. C/O sent 20-8-51.
ALLARD P1 SALOON RHD: Primer, grey leather.
                     Chassis No. P-2166. Engine No.7260707.
DAVIES TURNER : ss Paringa...   Delivered 12/9/51.
FREIGHT £.181.-8.3   Docs received 22/9/51.

258   AUSTRALIA Briscar.   P-2166.

Card 3 (middle left):

BRISBANE MOTORS PTY LTD.,
128 Wickham Street,
BRISBANE., QUEENSLAND.,
AUSTRALIA.   File No. 161.

Ordered 22-5-51. Invoice S-1920. C/O sent 20-8-51.
ALLARD P1 SALOON RHD: Primer, blue leather.
                     Chassis No. P-2163. Engine No. 7260356.

DAVIES TURNER : ss PARINGA Delivered 12/9/51.
Freight £151.-8.-3 Docs received 22/9/51.
          B us N 0. 10.

256   AUSTRALIA Bricar   P-2163.

Card 4 (middle right):

BRISBANE MOTORS PTY LTD.,
128 Wickham Street,
BRISBANE., QUEENSLAND.
AUSTRALIA.   File No. 164.

Ordered 22-5-51. Invoice S-1922. C/O sent 20-8-51.
ALLARD P1 SALOON RHD: Primer, maroon leather.
                     Chassis No. P-2168. Engine No.7260729.

DAVIES TURNER : ss PARINGA.   Delivered 12/9/51.
                     Freight £151-8:3 Docs recd 22/9/51.

259   AUSTRALIA Briscar   P-2168.

Card 5 (bottom left):

Brisbane Motors.,
128 Wickham Street.,
Brisbane., Queensland.   File No. 162.

Ordered 22-5-51. Invoice S-1920. Delivered 20-8-51.
ALLARD P1 SALOON RHD: Primer., maroon leather upholstery.
                     Engine No. 7360377.
                     CHASSIS NO. P-2164.

DAVIES TURNER.   ss PARINGA.   Closing 12-9-51.
Freight £151-8-3d (packed).   Docs   22-9-51.

J.E.F. Abbiss., Carramar Street, Morningside., Brisbane, Queensland.

257   AUSTRALIA Brisbane/ Abbiss/   P-2164.

Card 6 (bottom right):

BRISBANE MOTORS PTY LTD.,
128 Wickham Street,
BRISBANE., QUEENSLAND.
AUSTRALIA.   File No. 165.

Ordered 22-5-51. Invoice S-1923. C/O sent 20-8-51.
ALLARD P1 SALOON RHD: Primer, blue leather.
                     Chassis No. P-2170. Engine No.7260025.

DAVIES TURNER : ss ....   Delivered 12/9/51.
Freight £151.-8.-3   Docs recd 22/9/51.

S.Y. Gresham., Gresham Industries Pty. Ltd,
          141 York Street, Sydney N.S.W., Australia.

260   AUSTRALIA Briscar./Gresham/   P-2170.

Card 1 (261)

Brisbane Motors Pty Ltd.,
128 Wickham Street,
Brisbane., Queensland.   File No. 166.

Ordered 22-5-51. Invoice S-1924. Delivered 20-8-51.
ALLARD P1 SALOON RHD: Primer., grey leather upholstery.
                       Engine No. 7260670.
                       CHASSIS NO. P-2172.

DAVIES TURNER.   ss PARINGA.   Closing 22-9-51.
Freight £151-8-3d.   Docs   22-9-51.

M. Rosenblum., Union Building (3rd Floor)., 8-14 Bond Street,
         Sydney., New South Wales., Australia.

261 AUSTRALIA Brisbane/ Rosenblum/   P-2172.

Card 2 (266)

Keskus Auto Oy.,
Kauppalankatu 39-41.,
KOUVOLA.,
FINLAND.   File No. 203.

Ordered 10-8-51. Invoice S-1958. CD3 JJ-88640. Dlvd 2/10/51.
ALLARD P1 SALOON LHD: Colour grey, red leather.
                       Chassis No. P-2181.
                       Mercury Engine No. WC 16377 F.

LEP TRANSPORT.   ss BALTRADER   Closing 2/10/51.
Freight forward.   Docs received. 9-10-51.

266 FINLAND Keskus   P-2181.

Card 3 (269)

PLANALTO COMERCIO E INDUSTRIA LTDA.,
Av. Pres. Vargas, 446.
RIO DE JANEIRO., BRAZIL.   File No. 197.

Ordered 30-7-51. Invoice S-1968. CD3 JJ-88645. Dlvd 9/10/51.
ALLARD P1 SALOON LHD: Colour dark green, green leather upholstery.
                       Chassis No. P-2176.
                       Engine No. 7261972

LEP TRANSPORT: ss URUGUAY STAR. Closing 9th October 1951.
Freight £130-16-0   Docs received. 16/10/51.

269 BRAZIL Planalto   P-2176.

Card 4 (267)

Keskus Autos Oy.,
Kauppalankatu 39-41.,
KOUVOLA.,
FINLAND.   File No. 206.

Ordered 15-8-51. Invoice S-1959. CD3 JJ-88641. Dlvd 11/10/51.
ALLARD P1 SALOON LHD: Colour maroon, red leather upholstery.
                       Chassis No. P-2182.
                       Mercury Engine No. 36-991168 F

LEP TRANSPORT.   ss Brouwersgracht   Docs received 14/10/51.
Freight forward.

267 FINLAND Keskus   P-2182.

Card 5 (270)

Planalto Comercio e Industria Ltda.,
Av. Pres. Vargas 446.,
Rio de Janeiro., Brazil.   File No. 198.

Ordered 30-7-51. Invoice S-1969. CD3 JJ-88644. Dlvd 9-10-51.
ALLARD P1 SALOON LHD: Colour Black, red leather upholstery.
                       Engine No. 7261966.
                       CHASSIS NO. P-2177.

LEP TRANSPORT.   ss URUGUAY STAR.   Closing 9-10-51.
Freight £130-16-0d.   Docs   16-10-51.

Oswaldo Queiroz Guimaraes., Rua Miguel Lemos 21 - apt 402.,
                      Copacabanca, Rio de Janeiro., Brazil.

270 BRAZIL Planalto/ Guimaraes/   P-2177.

Card 6 (268)

Keskus Autos Oy.,
Kauppalankatu 39-41.,
KOUVOLA.,
FINLAND.   File No. 207.

Ordered 15-8-51. Invoice S-1960. CD3 JJ-88642. Dlvd 23/10/51.
ALLARD P1 SALOON LHD: Colour Blue, blue leather upholstery.
                       Chassis No. P-2183.
                       Mercury Engine No. ....

LEP TRANSPORT.   ss ALDEBARAN   Closing 23/10/51.
Freight forward.   Docs received. 8-11-51

268 FINLAND Keskus   P-2183.

A.P. & E. Singer Ltd,
Royal London House,
16, Finsbury Square,
LONDON. E.C.2.   143.
                          File No. 143.

Ordered 30-3-51. Invoice S-   Delivered 14-11-51.
ALLARD P1 SALOON RHD: Colour grey, blue leather upholstery.
                  Chassis No. P-2239.
                  Engine No. 7264733.
PACKERS: W.J. Reynolds, Barking.
LEP TRANSPORT   ss THISTLEDALE   Closing 14-11-51.
MARKS: T.S.LTD - AUCKLAND - 10. UP.
Freight £812-5-6   Docs received 27/11/51.

273 NEW ZEALAND Singer   P-2239.

10

A.P. & E. Singer Ltd.,
Royal London House,
16, Finsbury Square,
LONDON. E.C.2.

Ordered 30-3-51. Invoice S-2064 Delivered 14-11-51.
ALLARD P1 SALOON RHD : Colour black, tan leather.
                  Chassis No. P-2246.
                  Engine No. 7264596 (7264696) ?
PACKERS: W.J. Reynolds, Barking.
LEP TRANSPORT : ss THISTLEDALE. Closing 14-11-51.
MARKS : T.S.LTD - AUCKLAND - .UP.
Freight £812-5-6   Docks received 27/11/51.

276 NEW ZEALAND Singer   P-2246.

13

A.P. & E. Singer Ltd,
Royal London House,
16, Finsbury Square,
LONDON. E.C.2.   File No. 144.

Ordered 30-3-51.   Invoice S-2064 Delivered 14-11-51.
ALL ARD P1 SALOON RHD: Colour M.grey, blue leather.
                  Chassis No. P-2240.
                  Engine No. 7264594.
PACKERS : W.J. Reynolds, Barking.
LEP TRANSPORT : ss THISTLEDALE. Closing 14-11-51.
MARKS : T.S.LTD - AUCKLAND - .UP.
Freight £812-5-6   Docs received 27/11/51.

275 NEW ZEALAND Singer   P-2240.

12

A.P. & E. Singer Ltd,
Royal London House,
16, Finsbury Square,
LONDON. E.C.2.   File No. 146.

Ordered 30-3-51.   Invoice S-2064 Delivered 14-11-51.
ALLARD P1 SALOON RHD: Colour M.grey, blue leather.
                  Chassis No. P-2247.
                  Engine No. 7264547
PACKERS : W.J. Reynolds, Barking.
LEP TRANSPORT. ss THISTLEDALE. Closing 14-11-51.
MARKS : T.S.LTD - AUCKLAND - .UP.
Freight £812-5-6   Docs received 27/11/51.

277 NEW ZEALAND Singer   P-2247.

14

A.P. & E. Singer Ltd,
Royal London House,
16, Finsbury Square,
LONDON. E.C.2.   File No. 145.

Ordered 30-3-51. Invoice S-   Delivered 14-11-51.
ALLARD P1 SALOON RHD: Colour blue, blue leather.
                  Chassis No. P-2241.
                  Engine No. 7264542.
PACKERS: W.J. Reynolds, Barking.
LEP TRANSPORT: ss THISTLEDALE. Closing 14th November 1951.
MARKS : T.S.LTD - AUCKLAND - .UP.
Freight £812-5-6   Docs received 27/11/51.

274 NEW ZEALAND Singer   P-2241.

11

A.P. & E. Singer Ltd.,
Royal London House,
16, Finsbury Square,
LONDON. E.C.2.   File No. 147.

Ordered 30-3-51.   Invoice S-2064 Delivered 14-11-51.
ALLARD P1 SALOON RHD : Colour black, tan leather.
                  Chassis No. P-2248.
                  Engine No. 7262928
PACKERS : W.J. Reynolds, Barking.
LEP TRANSPORT : ss THISTLEDALE. Closing 14-11-51.
MARKS : T.S.LTD - AUCKLAND - .UP.
Freight £812-5-6   Docs received 27/11/51.
      (6 cars)   B.L No.5.

278 NEW ZEALAND Singer   P-2248.

15

DALTON WATSON FINE BOOKS

COACHBUILDING/DESIGN

Title	Author	Price
Ballot (2-Volume Set) – 2020 Cugnot Award Winner	Daniel Cabart and Gautam Sen	Regular: $350; Leather: $1500
Berlinetta '60s: Exceptional Italian Coupés of the Sixties	Xavier de Nombel and Christian Descombes	$95
The Bertone Collection	Gautam Sen and Michael Robinson	$95
Gaston Grümmer: The Art of Carrosserie (2-Volume Set)	Philippe-Gaston Grümmer and Laurent Friry	Regular: $295
Marcel Pourtout: Carrossier	Jon Pressnell	$150
Marcello Gandini: Maestro of Design (2-Volume Set)	Gautam Sen	Signed/Numbered: $350
Park Ward: The Innovative Coachbuilder 1919-1939 (3-Volume Set)	Malcolm Tucker	Regular: $375; Custom Leather: $1600
The Kellner Affair: Matters of Life and Death (3-Volume Set)	Peter Larsen with Ben Erickson	Regular: $445
Tom Tjaarda: Master of Proportions	Gautam Sen	$150
V. Morel and AJ Grümmer: Builders of Exceptional Carriages	Philippe-Gaston Grümmer	$195

GENERAL AUTOMOTIVE/RACING

Title	Author	Price
Audi RS: History • Models • Technology	Constantin Bergander	$79
Augie Pabst: Behind the Wheel	Robert Birmingham	Regular: $79; Signed/Numbered: $99
Bahamas Speed Weeks	Terry O'Neil	$155
Cobra Pilote: The Ed Hugus Story	Robert D. Walker	$89
Concours d'Elegance: Dream Cars and Lovely Ladies	Patrick Lesueur, Translated by David Burgess-Wise	$69
Cunningham: The Passion, The Cars, The Legacy (2-Volume Set)	Richard Harman	Regular: $350; Leather: $1200
Ferrari 333 SP: A Pictorial History 1993-2003	Terry O'Neil	$150
Fit for a King: The Royal Garage of the Shahs of Iran	Borzou Sepasi	$150
Formula 1	Peter Nygaard	$89
Imagine! Automobile Concept Art from the 1930s to the 1980s	Patrick Kelley	Regular: $90; Signed/Numbered: $135
Lime Rock Park: The Early Years 1955-1975	Terry O'Neil	$225
Meister Bräuser: Harry Heuer's Championship Racing Team	Tom Schultz	Regular: $95; Signed/Numbered: $125
Mid-Atlantic Sports Car Races 1953-1962	Terry O'Neil	Signed/Numbered: $155
Pebble Beach Concours d'Elegance: The Art of the Poster	Robert Devlin, Kandace Hawkinson	Regular: $69; Silk: $295
QPRS: F1 Grand Prix Racing by the Numbers, 1950-2019	Clyde P. Berryman	$95
Shelby Cobras: CSX 2001 - CSX 2125 (2-Volume Set)	Robert D. Walker	$250
Sports Car Racing in the South: Vol. I 1957-1958, Vol. II 1959-1960, Vol. III 1961-1962	Willem Oosthoek	Vol I: $125; Vol II: $155; Vol III (Signed/Numbered): $155
The Golden Days of Thompson Speedway and Raceway 1945-1977	Terry O'Neil	Signed/Numbered: $195
The Straight Eight Engine: Powering Premium Automobiles	Keith Ray	$95
Watkins Glen: The Street Years 1948-1952	Philippe Defechereux	$49

BRITISH CARS

Title	Author	Price
Bentley Motors: On the Road	Bernard L. King	$165
Bentley: Fifty Years of the Marque	Johnnie Green/Hageman, King, Bennett	$92
Making a Marque: Rolls-Royce Motor Car Promotion 1904-1940	Peter Moss and Richard Roberts	$125
Rolls-Royce: Silver Wraith	Martin Bennett	$125
Rolls-Royce: The Classic Elegance	Lawrence Dalton/Bernard L. King	$85
The Goodwood Phantom Drophead Coupe	Malcolm Tucker	$125
The Rolls-Royce Phantom II Continental	André Blaize	Regular: $395; Leather: $1750
The Silver Ghost: A Supernatural Car	Jonathan Harley	$69
Why Not? The Story of The Honourable Charles Stuart Rolls	David Baines	$89
Jaguar E-Type Six-Cylinder Originality Guide	Dr. Thomas F. Haddock & Dr. Michael C. Mueller	$125
Vintage Jaguar Keyrings, 1955-1980	Morrill 'Bud' Marston	Regular: $95; Signed/Numbered: $135

FRENCH CARS

Title	Author	Price
Crossing the Sands: The Sahara Desert Trek to Timbuktu	Ariane Audouin-Debreuil/Ingrid MacGill	$65
Eighty Years of Citroën in the UK	John Reynolds	Regular: $70; Special Edition: $450

GERMAN CARS

Title	Author	Price
Gulf 917	Jay Gillotti	Regular: $150; Leather (2-vol): $1500
Mercedes-Benz 300 SL: The Car of the Century	Hans Kleissl and Harry Niemann	$150
Porsche by Mailander	Karl Ludvigsen	$150
Rudolf Uhlenhaut: Engineer and Gentleman	Wolfgang Scheller and Thomas Pollak	$89

ITALIAN CARS

Title	Author	Price
De Tomaso: From Buenos Aires to Modena	Dr. Daniele Pozzi	$79
Lamborghini: At the Cutting Edge of Design (2-Volume Set)	Gautam Sen	$250
Maserati 300S (Revised, 2-volume set)	Walter Bäumer	Regular: $270
Maserati A6GCS	Walter Bäumer and Jean-François Blachette	$175
Maserati A6G 2000 Frua • Pininfarina • Vignale • Allemano	Walter Bäumer	$125
Maserati Tipo 63, 64, 65: Birdcage to Supercage	Willem Oosthoek	Regular: $140; Special Edition: $550

ICON / GENERAL INTEREST

Title	Author	Price
Steve McQueen: A Tribute to the King of Cool	Marshall Terrill	Special Edition: $95
Steve McQueen: Le Mans in the Rearview Mirror	Don Nunley with Marshall Terrill	$79
Steve McQueen: In His Own Words	Marshall Terrill	$95
Steve McQueen: The Last Mile Revisited	Barbara McQueen and Marshall Terrill	$49

ORDER FROM: Dalton Watson Fine Books / **www.daltonwatson.com** / info@daltonwatson.com / +1 847 945 0568

Tractor Specialties Ltd.,
P.O. Box 2514.,
Auckland C.I., New Zealand.   File No: 148.

Ordered 30-3-51. Invoice S-2064. Dlvd Reynolds 14-12-51.
ALLARD P1 SALOON RHD: Colour Black, brown leather upholstery.
                       Engine No: 18F-7265181.
                       CHASSIS NO: P-2253.

LEP TRANSPORT   ss RANGITANE   Closing 21-12-51.
Freight (4 cars) £555 plus Ins £24 plus packing £112.

W.R. Ashton, 45 Sunbury Street, Andersons Bay, Dunedin, N.Z.

London Agents:

A.P. & E. SINGER LTD., London House, 16 Finsbury Sq, London. E.C.2

                                        YB 10/4/54

289 New Zealand Tracspecs/ Ashton/   P-2253.

A.P. & E. Singer Ltd.,   19
Royal London House,
16, Finsbury Square,
LONDON. E.C.2.   File No. 181.

Ordered 10-7-51. Invoice S-2064. Reynolds dlvd 19-12-51.
ALLARD P1 SALOON RHD : Colour Black, maroon leather.
                       Chassis No. P-2271.
                       Engine No. 7255701 7266542.

LEP TRANSPORT : ss RANGITANE.   Closing 21-12-51.
Freight £ 555 IX C   Docs... 31-12-51.

                                                P.2271
292 NEW ZEALAND Singer   P-2271.

Tractor Specialties Ltd.,
P.O. Box 2514.,
Auckland C.I., New Zealand.   File No: 142

Ordered 30-3-51.   Invoice S-2064. Dlvd Reynolds 14-12-51.
ALLARD P1 SALOON RHD: Colour Black, blue leather upholstery.
                       Engine No. 7264981.
                       CHASSIS NO: P-2265.

A.P. & E. Singer Ltd, Royal London House, 16 Finsbury Sq, E.C.2.

LEP TRANSPORT.   ss RANGITANE.   Closing 21-12-51.
Freight £170. C. Od. (packed)   Docs   31-12-51.

Alexander Maccoll, Kennedy's Bush Rd, Christchurch S.W.2., N.Z.
                                        YB 8/7/54

290 NEW ZEALAND Tracspecs/ Maccoll/   P-2265.

A.P. & E. SINGER LIMITED.,   21
Royal London House,
16, Finsbury Square,
LONDON. E.C.2.   File No. 183.

Ordered 10-7-51.   Invoice S-2076. Delivered 5-1-52.
ALLARD P1 SALOON RHD : Colour grey, maroon leather upholstery.
                       Chassis No. P-2277.
                       Engine No. 7260553.

BECK & POLITZER : ss CONDESA.   Closing 7-1-52.
Freight £309-10-5 (2 cars)   Docs ... -1-52.

Mr. L.H. Kemp, Flat No.3, 51 Windermere Rd, Papanui, Christchurch,
                                                  New Zealand.

295 NEW ZEALAND Singer./Kemp/   P-2277.

A.P. & E. Singer Ltd.,
Royal London House.,
16 Finsbury Square,
London. E.C.2.   File No. 150.

Ordered 30-3-51. Invoice S-2064. Delivered Reynolds 14-12-51.
ALLARD P1 SALOON RHD: Colour Grey, blue leather upholstery.
                       Engine No. 7265169.
                       CHASSIS NO. P-2268.

DEALER: Tractor Specialties., P.O. Box 2819., Auckland C.l., N.Z.

LEP TRANSPORT ss RANGITANE.   Closing 21-12-51.
Freight £555-15-6 (3 cars)   Docs   31-12-51.

E.R. Moore., Moores Road, Walton., North Island, New Zealand.
                                        YB 2/4/54

291 NEW ZEALAND Tracspecs/ Moore/   P-2268.

A.P. & E. SINGER LTD.,   20
Royal London House,
16 Finsbury Square,
LONDON. E.C.2.   File No. 182.

Ordered 10-7-51. Invoice S-2076. Delivered 5-1-52.
ALLARD P1 SALOON RHD : Colour grey, red leather upholstery.
                       Engine No. 7265855.
                       Chassis No. P-2278.

BECK & POLITZER : ss CONDESA.   Closing 7-1-52.
Freight £309-10-5 (2 cars)   Docs II -1-52.

294 NEW ZEALAND Singer   P-2278.

Mr. S. Wilson,
Chief Engineer,
c/o Amalgamated Banket Areas Ltd,
P.O. Box 26, Tarkwa,
GOLD COAST COLONY.   File No. 553.

Ordered 5-2-53. Invoice S-2372. Delivered to ship 13-3-53.
ALLARD P1 SALOON RHD: Black, tan leather upholstery.
                    CHASSIS NO. P-2287. (Formerly P-3100)
                    ENGINE NO. 18F-7268364.

LEP TRANSPORT.   ss CABANO.   Closing 13/3/53.
Freight £111-8-9   Docs   31/3/53.

(Freight & Ins. charges to account of Allard Motor Co,Ltd.)
Mr. L. Knott, 150, Mercatio St., Welldon, O.F.S., S. Africa

416 GOLD COAST /Wilson/Knott/   P-2287.

Mrs. Gettien Thesingh,   Gallop House,
c/o Union Bank of Australia, & 48 Arthur Street,
6 Albemarle St, LONDON. W.1.   Ashfield, SYDNEY., N.S.W.

Ordered 13-3-51. Invoice S-1743. Delivered 10-4-51.
P1 ALLARD SALOON: Colour metallic grey, grey leather. RHD.

Chassis No. P-2023.   Engine No. 7252814.   Reg. No. LKY 14.

DELIVERED FOR TEMPORARY USE IN U.K. PRIOR TO EXPORT.

LEP TRANSPORT: ss TRELEVAN.   Closing 22/24-12-51.
Delivered to Packers - Reynolds - 10-12-51.
Freight £127-16-9   plus packing charges.
                         Docs received 8/1/52.

214 AUSTRALIA Thesingh   P-2023.

Mrs. Jocelyne Hjelme-Lundberg,
Villa Solvik.,
Jönköping., Sweden.   File No. 399.

Ordered 7-7-52. Invoice S-2227. Delivered 23-7-52.
ALLARD P1 SALOON LHD: Dark Blue, red leather upholstery.
                    Registration No. MYM 593. (Home Delivery)
                    Engine No. E1-U-5101.
                    CHASSIS NO. P-3103.

DAVIES TURNER.   ss SVANHOLM.   Closing 23-7-52.
Freight £28. 0. 0d.   Docs   25-7-52.

* A.A. Carnet de Passage issued 30-6-52. No. 85566. ???

356 SWEDEN Lundberg/   P-3103.

L.H. Green Pty. Ltd.,
128 Wickham Street,
Brisbane., Queensland.,
Australia.   File No. 88.

Ordered 12-4-51. Invoice S-1771. Delivered 15-4-51.
ALLARD P1 SALOON RHD: Black, red leather upholstery.
                    Engine No. 7254579.
                    CHASSIS NO. P-2047.

DAVIES TURNER. ss MALOJA.   Closing 17-4-51.
Freight £136. 1. 7d.   Docs   26-5-51.

B.E.G. Admans., Pindorowi., Inverell., N.S.W., Australia.

200 AUSTRALIA Brisbane/ Admans/   P-2047.

Messrs. A.B. Ingvar BERGENGREN.,
Linhagensplan,
STOCKHOLM., SWEDEN.   File No. 365.

Ordered 9-6-52.   Invoice S-2249.   Delivered 1-10-52.
ALLARD P1 SALOON LHD: Colour Black, blue leather.
                    Fitted with clients own Lincoln V8
                    engine & gears imported from U.S.A.
                    CHASSIS NO. P-3107.
                    ENGINE NO. 9424 B (Lincoln).

LEP TRANSPORT.   ss MALMO.   Closing Millwall 1-10-52.
Drawback of Duty & Customs examination required alongside.

Freight £36-4-3   Docs rec'd .6/10/52.

371 Sweden Bergengren   P-3107

L.H. GREEN PTY LTD.,
128 Wickham Street,
Brisbane., Queensland.,
AUSTRALIA.   File No.156.

Ordered 12-4-51. Invoice S-1770. Delivered 15-4-51.
ALLARD P-1 SALOON RHD: Chassis No. P-2047. Engine No. 7254684.
                    Colour cream, red leather.

DAVIES TURNER: ss MALOJA.   Freight £136-1-7..
                         Docs rec'd 26-5-51

206 AUSTRALIA Green.   P-2047

L.H. GREEN PTY LTD,
18 Wickham Street,
Brisbane, Queensland. AUS.   File No. 103.

Ordered 21-4-51. Invoice S-1769. Delivered 15-4-51.
ALLARD P-1 SALOON RHD: Chassis No. P-2052. Engine No. 7256036.
                        Colour grey, maroon leather.

DAVIES TURNER: ss MALOJA.   Freight £.136-17....
                              Docs received.26-5-51.

197   AUSTRALIA   Green   P-2052.

F.G. Wernham.,
c/o Bank of India., Australia & China.,
Colombo., Ceylon.   File No. 170.

Ordered 28-5-51. Invoice S-1837. Delivered 8-6-51.
ALLARD P1 SALOON RHD: Black, brown leather upholstery.
                       Engine No. 7256791.
                       Registration No. MGF 846.
                       CHASSIS NO. P-2078.

U.K.: Craigentore., Elgin., Morayshire., Scotland. (Home address)

LEP TRANSPORT. ss CANNANORE.   Closing 20-12-51.
Freight £136-18-9d.   Docs   24-12-51.

228   CEYLON Wernham/   P-2078.

George Lee Motors.,
George Lee Chambers.,
200 Clemenceau Avenue.,
Singapore., Malaya.   File No. 154.

Ordered 11-4-51. Invoice S-1796. Delivered 21-5-51.
ALLARD P1 SALOON RHD: Gunmetal., blue leather upholstery.
                       Engine No. 7254553.
                       CHASSIS NO. P-2067.

DAVIES TURNER. ss DENBIGHSHIRE.   Closing 21-5-51.
Freight £120-11-9d.   Docs   12-6-51.

A.J. Van der Loo., c/o Interland Ltd., 138 Robinson Road.,
                                        Singapore., Malaya.

220   SINGAPORE George Lee/ VanderLoo/   P-2067.

KESKUS AUTO OY.,
Kauppalankatu 39-41,
KOUVOLA.,
FINLAND.   File No. 159.

Ordered 24-4-51.   Invoice S-1820.   CD3 HH-686257.   Dlvd 26-6-51.

ALLARD P1 SALOON LHD: Grey, red leather.
                       Chassis No. P-2079. Mercury Eng.No..........

DAVIES TURNER: ss BALTRADER.   Docs received.4-7-51.
                Freight £..?..19-9

227   FINLAND   Keskus   P-2079.

KYLE, PALMER & CO. LTD,
Post Box 289,
KUALA LUMPUR.,
MALAYA.   File No. 126.

Ordered 24-2-51. Invoice S-1801. C/o sent. Dlv'd 21-5-51.
ALLARD P-1 SALOON RHD: Colour grey, grey leather.
                        Chassis No. P-2069. Engine No. 7256164.

LEP TRANSPORT: ss Glenroy.   Freight £117-12-9...
                              Docs received.8-6-51.

222   MALAYA Kyle Palmer.   P-2069.

D. A. Coutroubis.,   (BYRON 1181 ext. 54)
54 Herga Court,
Harrow-on-the-Hill, Mx.   File No. 529.

Messrs. A.C. Coutroubis, P.O.Box 212., Athens., Greece.

ALLARD P2 SAFARI MOTOR CAR LHD: Bronze, tan leather.
                             (ex-Show. Worcester w/shlds)
  (extras :-
     HMV radio.   CHASSIS NO. P2-4003.
     Cadillac modfctn.   REGISTRTN.. NLD 412.
     Lucas fog & passlamps.   Cadillac Engine No. 8R-406.
Collected from Works i.e. delivered to client 6th January 1953

Ordered 10-12-52.   Invoice S-2336.   CD3 MM-79 2120.
(temporary use in U.K. - overland delivery to Greece).

NOT EXPORTED - CAR SOLD

Last heard of in Wolverhampton, 1962.
Brian Sharpe, 1985..

403   GREECE   Coutroubis/   P2-4003

JORGE BARRANCO y CIA S.R.L.,
Apartado 21330.,
Niza 35.,
MEXICO D.F., MEXICO.   File No. 482.

Ordered 24-10-52. Invoice S-2415. CD3 JJ-88399. Dlvd 28-3-53.
ALLARD P2 SAFARI LHD: Colour bronze, tan leather upholstery.
                           Less engine. Ford modification kit.
                           Disc wheels. CHASSIS NO. P2-4008.

PALL MALL DEPOSIT: ss AM. HARVESTER.   Closing 30-3-53.
Freight £162-10-7)   Docs 9 -4-53.
) also K 3173.

431   MEXICO   Barranco.   P2-4008.

Dr. D. Reid Tweedie., B.A. B.CH. (Camb).
Sungei Siput N.,
Perak., Malaya.   File No. 404.

Ordered 17-7-52.   Invoice S-2318.   Delivered 15-1-53.
ALLARD P2 MONTE CARLO SALOON RHD: Maroon, pale tan leather uphol.
                            * 1952 Earls Court Show model.
                            1950 CADILLAC NO. 9L-21643.
                            CHASSIS NO. P2-4005.

Brother-in-law: AVM Aitken (ROTTINGDEAN 2220).
                Red Lodge., Saltdean., Sussex.

TOZER KEMSLEY MILBOURNE.   ss CHUSAN.   Closing 16-1-53.
Freight Paid.   Docs direct to client.

* Drawback of Duty on Cadillac engine.
2nd Owner: S.W. Dundas, Chenderoh Power Station, Kuala Kangsar,
                        Perak., Malaya.

393   MALAYA   Dr. Tweedie/Dundas/   * P2-4005.

Mr. L.A. Hart.,
(T.F. Hart Investment Co.)
210, N. Central Expressway,
DALLAS., TEXAS., U.S.A.   File No. 469.

Ordered 4-10-52.   Invoice S-2431.   CD3 JJ-88394.   Dlvd 11-4-53.
ALLARD P2 MONTE CARLO SALOON LHD: Black, red leather upholstery.
                            Less engine. Cadillac modfctn.
                            HMV radio. Fog & spot lamps.
                            Altimeter. Centre gearshift.
                            Red heart crest. Trafficators.
                            CHASSIS NO. P2-4500.

LEP TRANSPORT   ss DEERPOOL.   Closing 10-4-53.
Freight £75-18-1   Docs 17-4-53.
                                  Y/S 15/3/54

394   AMERICA   Custom Auto/ Hart/   P2-4500

Carvill & company,
P.O. Box 5823
Nairobi., Kenya.   File No. 363.

Ordered 3-6-52   Invoice S-2247.   Delivered 28-8-52.
ALLARD P2 SAFARI RHD: Colour Storm grey, grey leather.
                      One extra spare wheel. 7.50 x 16.
                      Lifeguard inner tubes.
                      ENGINE NO: 7277928.
                      CHASSIS NO: P2-4007.

LEP TRANSPORT.   ss DURBAN CASTLE   Closing 28-8-52.
Freight £110-14-5d.   Docs   5-9-52.

Col. F.R.C. Fosdick, P.O.B. 4979, Ngong, Nairobi, Kenya.
(purchased s/hand about November 1954)

363   KENYA   Carvill Co/ Fosdick/   P2-4007.

A.B. Ingvar Bergengren.,
Lindhagensplan.,
Stockholm., Sweden.   File No. 576.

Ordered 1-12-52.   Invoice S-2547.   Delivered 24-9-53.
ALLARD P2 MONTE CARLO SALOON LHD: Electric blue, grey leather.
                            LINCOLN ENG NO. M-821-B.

                            CHASSIS NO. P2-4502.

British Commercial Transport.   ss BELE.   Closing 24-9-53.
Freight forward.   DOCS   5-10-53.

477   SWEDEN   Bergengren.   P-4502

Paul Cousin S.A.,
239 Chaussee de Charleroi.,
Bruxelles., Belgium.   File No. 647

Ordered 28-9-53. Invoice S-2559. CD3 PP-889077. Dlvd 11-11-53.
ALLARD P2 MONTE CARLO SALOON LHD: Royal Blue, dk blue leather.
                                   Cadillac hydramatic.
                                   CADILLAC ENG NO. 516245972.
                                   5 Wire Wheels, hubs & caps.
                                   CHASSIS NO. P2-4503.

PALL MALL. ss CITY OF BRUSSELS.   Closing 11-11-53.
Freight £33. (£30-3-3 actual)   Docs   13-11-53.

Drawback of Duty.

Madame E. Wyckmans, 15 Rue de Ten Bosch., Bruxelles, Belgium.

507 BELGIUM Paul Cousin /Wyckmans/   P2-4503

Mr. William Edward WYATT.,
Box 136 G.P.O.,
Port Moresby.,
Papua., New Guinea.   File No: 686.

Ordered 20-5-55 Invoice S-2641. Exemption PT form. Dlvd 31-5-55.
ALLARD P2 MONTE CARLO SALOON RHD: Light Blue, blue leather upholst.
                                   Whitewall tyres. Air pump.
* Home delivery, temporary   Engine No: B18-7293128.
  use in U.K. pending export   Registration No: OXE 475.
  to New Guinea, September '55.   CHASSIS NO: P2-4508.

Morris Hedstrom Ltd, 73 Cheapside, E.C.2. (agent)

                          Believed the one found in
                          South Australia. June 1986
                          (see A.O.C Magazine April '86)

544 NEW GUINEA Morris Hedstrom /Wyatt/   P2-4508

Denver Imported Motors Inc.
2610, West Alameda Avenue,
Denver 19., Colorado, U.S.A   File No. 640

Ordered 14-8-53. Invoice S-2569. CD3 PP-889082. Dlvd 22-12-53
ALLARD P2 SAFARI MOTOR CAR RHD: Colour Cream, red leather.
                                    Tail gate rear door.
                                    LESS ENGINE. Cadillac modification
                                    CHASSIS NO. P2-4506.

PALL MALL DEPOSIT. ss DALEBY.   Closing 22-12-53.
Freight £ 71-17-0   Docs   29-12-54.

Mrs. Caroline L. Paquin Madison,
       1700 So. Sheridan Blvd, Denver., Colorado., U.S.A.

*Price paid (see warranty) $6529.09.

                 1979 Imported by Lammegel
                 now restored 1986

515 AMERICA Denver Imported /Madison/   S2-4506

Westmount Garage Reg'd,
5402 Sherbrooke Street West,
Montreal, Quebec., Canada.   File No: 664

Ordered 11-3-54 Invoice ASL-5035 CD3 992486 Dlvd 19-1-55
ALLARD P2 MONTE CARLO LHD: Colour Black, grey leather upholstery.
                                    Radio. Lucas Fog & Flamethrower lamps.
                                    4 safety belts. Hydramatic transmissn.
                                    CADILLAC ENGINE NO: AV 6644.
                                    CHASSIS NO: P2-4510.

PALL MALL DEPOSIT   ss ~~ASIA~~   Closing 2-2-55
                           ss MAPLECOVE   Closing 12-2-55.
Freight £   Docs   -2-55.

Dr. Paul Lariviere M.D., 3484 Avenue Laval, Montreal, Quebec.
2nd: Claude Thibodeau, Pres., Laval Ltd, 10210 Rue Lajeunesse St,
                                        Montreal 12., P.Q.

542 CANADA Westmount/ Lariviere/ Thibodeau/   P-4510

E. Whiteaway & Co.,
4-7 Chiswell Street,
London. E.C.1.   File No. 653

Ordered 26-1-54. Invoice ASL-5006 . Delivered 19-4-54.
ALLARD P2 SAFARI RHD: Dark Green, green leather upholstery.
                       Metal panels, backboard & flooring.
                       Engine No.
                       CHASSIS NO. P2- 4001 4507

Client: Thomas Motors., Rhodesia.

* Whiteaway arranging own shipment. ss VANDALIA.   Closing 19/4/

520 RHODESIA Whiteaway/   P2-4507

BELL AUTO PARTS.,   ORDER NO. 4.
3633 East Gage Avenue,
BELL, California. U. S. A.
                          S-1193
Ordered 26-1-50   Invoiced 4-2-50   Delivered 2-3-50

J-TYPE 2 SEATER LHD.;   Colour silver, red leather upholstery.

Chassis No. J-1513.   Engine No. 3953/52.   C.D.3. AA 289078.

SHIPPERS. DAVIES TURNER. LTD.   SS. Loch Avon"

Freight. £60.

100   AMERICA   Bell   J-1513

GRANCOR AUTOMOTIVE SPECIALISTS.,
5652 N. Broadway,
CHICAGO 40., ILLINOIS. U. S. A.

Ordered 4-10-49   Invoiced 1-12-49   Delivered 12-1-50

J-TYPE 2 SEATER LHD.;   Colour silver, red leather.

Chassis No. J-1555.   Engine No. LAK-0107.

88   AMERICA   Grancor   J-1555

Thomas L.H. Cole., Esq.
910 Fifth Avenue,
New York 21., N.Y.   File No.

Ordered 11-8-49. Invoice S-1089. CD3 FF- ...... Dlvd 12-10-49
ALLARD J2 TWO SEATER LHD: Silver, red leather upholstery.
                           Less engine. (Cadillac modification)
                           CHASSIS NO. J-1514.

John Perona, 400 East 52nd Street, New York., N.Y. (Night Club
                                                      prop.)

L.T. & FREIGHT.   QUEEN ELIZABETH.   Closing 13-10-49.
Freight £105.   Docs   15-10-49.

                                     YB 14/6/54

83   AMERICA   Tom Cole/ Perona/   J-1514.

Havell Motors.,
159 South Street,
Morristown., N.J.   File No.

Ordered 10-2-50. Invoice S-1192. CD3 FF-156813. Dlvd 21-3-50.
ALLARD J2 TWO SEATER LHD: Red, red leather upholstery.
                           Wire wheels.
                           Less engine. Cadillac modification.
                           CHASSIS NO. J-1556.

** Supplied specifically for New York Sports Car Exhibition.

A.E. Goldschmidt., 399 Park Avenue, New York 22., N.Y.

(Won Watkins Glen Grand Prix 23/9/50) (225 HP Cadillac D.R.E. Co.)

J.C. MOUNT & CO.   ss AM. IMPORTER.   Closing 21-3-50.
Freight £60.   Docs   24-3-50. B 14/6/54

1988. McCaw.

101   AMERICA   Havell Motors/ Goldschmidt/   J-1556.

Ardun Engine Corporation Inc.,
37 East 28th Street,
New York., N.Y.   File No.

Ordered 17-8-49. Invoice (s.o.r). CD3 FF- ...... Dlvd 10-9-49
ALLARD J2 TYPE 2 SEATER LHD: Silver, red leather upholstery.
                              Less engine. (Ardun modfn) (ex Demo
                              CHASSIS NO. J-1515.   KUC 31

J.C. MOUNT.   AM. MANUFACTURER.   Closing 12-9-49.
Freight £60.   Docs   14-9-49.

Robert J. Wilder, 77 Squirer Street, Palmer., Massachusetts.

                                     YB 14/6/54

81   AMERICA   Ardun/ Wilder/   J-1515.

                                     Order.No.8.
                                              4
MOSS MOTORS LTD, 3210 West Olympic Blvd, LOS ANGELES.

Ordered 4-2-50   Invoiced 9-2-50   Delivered 24-4-50
                        S-1240
Chassis No. J-1571   C.D.3. FF 155809
           L.H.D.   Zessengine
                  Black, green leather

4975cc

104   AMERICA   Moss   J-1571

Card 1 (File No. 19):

Thomas L.H. Cole., Esq.
910 Fifth Avenue,
New York., N.Y.   File No. 19.

Ordered 5-4-50. Invoice S-1336. CD3 FF-891344. Dlvd 8-6-50.
ALLARD J2 TYPE TWO SEATER LHD: Black, red leather upholstery.
                                Less engine. Cadillac modfctn.
                                CHASSIS NO. J-1577.

EVAN COOKS. ss AM. REPORTER.   Closing 8-6-50.
Freight £60. 0. 0d.   Docs 12-6-50.

Fred G. Wacker Jr., Ammco Tools Inc., 2100 Commonwealth Avenue,
                N. Chicago., Illinois.

** Later installed hydramatic/manual transmission (Cadillac).

            THE RENOWNED "8 BALL"-!

115 AMERICA Tom Cole/ Wacker/   J-1577.

Card 2 (File No. 30):

JACK PRY.,
1747 Connecticut Avenue, N.W.
Washington 8., D.C.   File No. 30.

Ordered 19-6-50. Invoice S-1383. CD3 FF-891361. Dlvd 13-9-50
ALLARD J2 TWO SEATER LHD: Metallic blue, blue leather upholstery
                           Less engine. (fitted with K2 wings)
                           Special bumpers. Cadillac modification.
                           CHASSIS NO. J-1733.

1st. Perry Boswell., Largo Rd, R.F.D. 2., Upper Marlboro, Maryland.

2nd. Capt. Jerome Ivor Saubers, Box 340., Bolling AFS.,
                                  Washington 25., D.C.

3rd. G.A. Waldie, Batelle Memorial Institute, 505 King Avenue.,
                                  Columbus., Ohio.

129 AMERICA Pry/ Boswell/ Saubers/ Waldie/   J-1733.

Card 3 (Order No. 51):

R/P IMPORTED MOTOR CAR COMPANY,   ORDER NO. 51
147 West 54th Street,
NEW YORK 19., N.Y.

Ordered 23-8-50   Invoiced S-1428   Delivered 31-8-50

Chassis No. J-1578. Colour British Racing Green., green leather

Original S.H.A. Le Mans car - 1950.

Special £1200.00 Cadillac motor to be fitted by Seddon in the States
car to be entered at WATKINS GLEN race on September 23rd.

SHIPPERS. MESSRS LEP TRANSPORT. LTD.

            FREIGHT £60.

126 AMERICA Seddon. (S.H.A. Le Mans)   J-1578.

Card 4 (File No. 29):

R/P IMPORTED MOTOR CAR CO.,   Query- was this really an X ? No √
147 West 54th Street,
New York 19., N.Y.   File No. 29.

Ordered 13-6-50. Invoiced S-1382. CD3 FF-891352. Dlvd 2/8/50.
ALLARD J2X TWO SEATER LHD: Colour Black, red leather.
                            Less engine. Cadillac modification.
                            CHASSIS NO. J-1732.

THOMAS MEADOWS & CO. ss AM. FARMER. Closing 4-8-50
Freight £60.   Docs 11-8-50

1st owner: Col. Steinmetz, 5524 Tampa Ave, Tarzana., Calif.
2nd owner: Dale Duncan, 2701 W. 71st Street, Kansas City 5., Mo.
3rd owner: John M. Fox Jr., P.O. Box 503., Sausalito, Calif.
4th owner: John W. Williams, 6217-25th Ave N.E., Seattle, Wash.

                                          See Over

122 AMERICA Seddon/Steinmetz/Duncan/Fox/Williams/   J-1732.

Card 5 (File No. 22):

Frederic H. Gibbs.,
Gibbs & Cox Inc.,
1 Broadway,
New York., N.Y.   File No. 22.

Ordered 21-4-50. Invoice S-1304. CD3 DD-352827. Dlvd 27-7-50.
ALLARD J2 TYPE TWO SEATER LHD: Red, red leather upholstery.
                                Mercury. Engine No. 8M-216.
                                CHASSIS NO. J-1696.

EVAN COOKS. ss AMERICAN REPORTER. Closing 28-7-50.
Freight £48. 0. 0d.   Docs 30-7-50.

117 AMERICA Gibbs/   J-1696.

Card 6 (File No. 31):

Jean Davidson., Esq.
Agence-France Presse.,
1416, 'F' Street,
Washington D.C.   File No. 31.

Ordered 19-6-50. Invoice S-1384. CD3 FF-891355. Dlvd 15-8-50.
ALLARD J2 TYPE TWO SEATER LHD: Red, blue leather upholstery.
                                Less engine. Cadillac modification
                                CHASSIS NO. J-1734.

LEP TRANSPORT. ss AM. IMPORTER. Closing 16-8-50.
Freight £71-8-0d.   Docs 19-8-50.

123 AMERICA Davidson/   J-1734.

MOSS MOTORS LTD,
3210 West Olympic Boulevard,
LOS ANGELES 6.

ORDER. NO. 43.   8

Ordered 8-8-50.   Invoice S-1448.   Delivered 24-8-50
                                    C.D.3. FF-891372.

J-TYPE 2 SEATER : Colour vermillion red, red leather.

Chassis No. J-1736 LHD.   Cadillac modification.

ss GRACIA - Liverpool.   LEP Transport.

SHIPPERS. Messrs Lep Transport Ltd. Freight. £60.

146 AMERICA Moss   J-1736

R/P Imported Motor Car Company,
147 West 54th Street,
NEW YORK 19., N.Y. U. S. A.

ORDER NO.38.   5

Ordered 19-7-50   Invoiced S-1422   Delivered 4-9-50 (QUEEN MARY)

Chassis No. J-1780.   C.D.3. FF 891365.   Righthand drive.

J-TYPE 2 SEATER : Colour maroon, blue leather. Cadillac mod. 225/250.

SHIPPERS :- LEP Transport.   CLIENT :- Millionaire enthusiast.
       Freight. £106.   Senator Woods ?
                             Vanderbilt

127 AMERICA Seddon (Senator Woods)   J-1780

Moss Motors Limited.,
3210 W. Olympic Boulevard,
Los Angeles., California.

File No. 36.

Ordered 13-7-50. Invoice S-1386. CD3 FF-891357. Dlvd 25-8-50.
ALLARD J2 TYPE TWO SEATER LHD: V. Red, red leather upholstery.
                                Less engine. ARDUN modification.
                                CHASSIS NO. J-1738.

LEP TRANSPORT. (packed) ss DURANGO.   Closing 25-8-50.
Freight £71. 0. 0d.   Docs   29-8-50.

Col. Steinmetz, 5524 Tampa., Tarzana., California.

125 AMERICA Moss/ Steinmetz/   J-1738.

Bell Autoparts.,
3633 East Gage Avenue.,
Bell., California.

File No. 52.

Ordered 5-9-50. Invoice S-1476. CD3 FF-891381. Dlvd 21-11-50.
ALLARD J2 TWO SEATER LHD: Colour Silver, natural leather upholstery.
                           Wire wheels. Full windshield & top.
                           Less engine. Cadillac modification.
                           CHASSIS NO. J-1787.

THOMAS MEADOWS.   ss AM. MERCHANT. Closing 21-11-50.
Freight £60. 0. 0d.   Docs   23-11-50.

J. Chapman., Chief Engineer, Airsearch Inc.   Y/3 17/6/54
(Home address: 6025 South La Brea Avenue, Los Angeles., Calif.)

143 AMERICA Bell/ Chapman/   J-1787.

R/P Imported Motor Car Company,
147 West 54th Street,
NEW YORK 19, N.Y.

ORDER NO.37.   8

Ordered 17-7-50.   Invoiced S-1388   Delivered 20th September 1950.   9

Chassis No. J-1739.   C.D.3 No. FF 891362.

J-TYPE 2 SEATER : Colour bugatti blue, red leather upholstery.
                  Modified to accomodate Cadillac motor.

Shipped by Thomas Meadows : Ship ss AMERICAN REPORTER.
       Freight. £60.

134 AMERICA Seddon   J-1739

Bell Autoparts.,
3633 East Gage Avenue.,
Bell., California.

File No. 54.

Ordered 5-9-50. Invoice S-1477. CD3 FF-891377. Dlvd 21-11-50.
ALLARD J2 TWO SEATER LHD: Black, red leather upholstery.
                           Wire wheels. Full windshield & top.
                           Less engine. Cadillac modification.
                           CHASSIS NO. J-1788.

THOMAS MEADOWS.   ss DALEBY.   Closing 21-11-50.
Freight £60. 0. 0d.   Docs   23-11-50.

J.G. Armstrong (Test Pilot A-853)   Y/3 17/6/54
Douglas Aircraft Co., Inc. Santa Monica., California.

144 AMERICA Bell / Armstrong/   J-1788.

WOOD MOTORS,
19770 Mack Avenue,
GROSSE POINTE WOODS 30.
MICHIGAN., U.S.A.

ORDER NO. 69.

Ordered 11-10-50.   Invoice S-1520.   C.D.3. HH-537897.
Delivered 7-11-50.

J-TYPE 2 SEATER LHD : Colour bronze, red leather.

Chassis No. J-1789.   Modified to accomodate Cadillac.

Crated - shipped by EVAN COOKS.   *B/L's received 16-11-50*
ss AMERICAN IMPORTER
FREIGHT £71.10.0.

147   AMERICa   Wood   J-1789

R/P IMPORTER MOTOR CAR COMPANY,
147 West 54th Street,
NEW YORK 19., N.Y.   27

Ordered 11-12-50.   Invoice S-1634.   CD3 HH-886390.
ALLARD J2 TWO SEATER : Colour Green, red leather upholstery.
Chassis No. J-1852; cadillac modification;   wire wheels.

DAVIES TURNER;   ss AMERICAN INVENTOR.   Delivered 6-3-51.
Freight £60.   Docs received..........

M. Bradbrook, April 1985 (A.O.C member) letter on file
Jack McGregor   letter on file

Perona/Cole car.

150   AMERICA   Seddon.   J-1852

British Car Sales.,
1325 South Tacoma Way.,
Tacoma 8., Washington.   File No. 79.

Ordered 11-12-50.   Invoice S-1577.   CD3 HH-537387.   Dlvd 23-1-51.
ALLARD J2-TYPE TWO SEATER LHD: Primer, red leather upholstery.
Cadillac mod.   Wire Wheels.
CHASSIS NO. J-1850.

Thos. Carstens., P.O. Box 1636., Tacoma 1., Washington.
(Driver of the fabulous No. 14. - Dave Pollack) Wrecked 17-8-53.

2nd Owner: Fred V. Wellington, 3332 78th Place, N.E.
Bellevue., Washington.

DAVIES TURNER.   ss LOCH RYAN.   Closing 27-1-51.
Freight £60.   Docs   30-1-51.

167   AMERICA   B.C.S./ Carstens/ Wellington/   J-1850

Messrs. BILL CO.,
Grandview Boulevard,
Zelienople., Pennsylvania.
U.S.A.   ORDER NO. 61.

Ordered 5-1-51.   Invoice S-1613.   CD3 No. HH-886395.

J2 TWO SEATER LHD : Colour red, red leather upholstery.

Chassis No. J-1853.   Modified to accomodate Cadillac.

SHIPPERS : DAVIES TURNER.   ss AMERICAN IMPORTER.

Freight £48-8-0   Docs received 10-1-51
Delivered 31-1-51

171   AMERICA   Bill Co.   J-1853

British Cars Sales.,
1325 South Tacoma Way.,
Tacoma 8., Washington.   File No. 64.

Ordered 19-12-50.   Invoice S-1614.   CD3 HH-886394.   Dlvd 30-1-51.
ALLARD J2 TWO SEATER LHD: Colour Black, red leather upholstery.
Wire wheels.   Full windshield & top.
Less engine.   Cadillac modification.
CHASSIS NO. J-1851.

DAVIES TURNER.   ss LOCH RYAN.   Closing 30-1-51.
Crated. (Freight £60. 0. 0d.   Docs   5-2-51.

Dave Fogg., Commonwealth Title Insurance Co.,
W.R. Rust Building, Tacoma 2., Washington.

173   AMERICA   B.C.S. / Fogg /   J-1851.

Mr. Charles Adams,
CUSTOM AUTOMOTIVE.,
2122 N. Pearl Street,
DALLAS., TEXAS.   File No. 118.

Ordered 23-2-51.   Invoice S-1780.   CD3 HH-886246.   Dlv'd 17-5-51.
ALLARD J2 TWO SEATER LHD : Colour black, red leather.
Chassis No. J-1854.   Cadillac mod.

LEP TRANSPORT : ss DEERPOOL.   Freight £42-9-6
Docs received 6-6-51

208   AMERICA   Customs auto.   J-1854.

23

R/P IMPORTED MOTOR CAR COMPANY.,
147 West 54th Street,
NEW YORK 19., N.Y.
U. S. A.

ORDER NO. 90.

Ordered 18-1-51.   Invoice S-1625.   CD3 No. HH-886392.

J2 TWO SEATER LHD : Bronze, brown leather.
                    (National Sportsmen's Exhibition - New York)

Chassis No. J-1857.   Cadillac mod: Delivered.31-1-51...

SHIPPERS : LEP Transport.   ss AMERICAN IMPORTER.
          Freight.£9-15-6   Docs received.7-2-51..

174   AMERICA   Seddon   J-1857

California Sports Car Co.,
1460 Pine Street,
San Francisco., California.   File No. 89.

Ordered 8-1-51. Invoice S-1695. CD3 HH-537880. Dlvd 2-4-51.
ALLARD J2 TWO SEATER LHD: Bugatti Blue, blue leather upholstery.
                         Wire wheels.
                         Less engine. Cadillac modification.
                         CHASSIS NO. J-1974.

LEP TRANSPORT. ss LOCH GARTH.   Closing 24-4-51.
Freight £62-8-3d.   Docs   26-4-51.

George L. Dietz., 757 56th Street, Oakland., California.

191   AMERICA Calif Sports/ Dietz/   J-1974

1

CALIFORNIA SPORTS CAR CO.,
1460 Pine Street,
SAN FRANCISCO 9., CALIF.

Ordered 6-1-51.   Invoice S-1654.   CD3 HH-886389.
                              Delivered for crating 21-2-51.
J2 TWO SEATER LHD : red, red leather.

Chassis No. J-1858.   PACKERS : Reynolds (Dagenham) LTD.

SHIPPERS : LEP Transport.   ss LOCH Garth.
           Freight......... Docs. received.....................

178   CALIFORNIA SPORTS CAR CO.   J-1858.

40

R/P IMPORTED MOTOR CAR COMPANY.,
147 West 54th Street,
NEW YORK 19., N.Y.   File No. 151.

Ordered 2-4-51. Invoice S-1842. CD3 HH-886259. Dlvd 19/7/51.
ALLARD J2 TWO SEATER LHD: Cadillac grey, red leather upholstery.
                         Chassis No. J-1975. Cadillac mod:
LEP TRANSPORT : ss AMERICAN Shipper. Closing 15/7/51.
               Freight £   Docs recd. 26-7-51...

                                   2018
                                   2030   3 cars on same a/c

231   AMERICA   Seddon   J-1975.

38

R/P IMPORTED MOTOR CAR CO.,
147 West 54th Street,
New York 19., N.Y.   File No. 80.

Ordered 11-12-50. Invoice S-1633. CD3 HH-886396. Dlvd 6-3-51.
ALLARD J2 TWO SEATER LHD: Green, brown/biscuit leather upholst:
                            Wire wheels. Full windshield & top.
                            Less engine. Cadillac modification.
                            CHASSIS NO. J-1859.

DAVIES TURNER. ss AM. INVENTOR.   Closing 6-3-51.
Freight £60. 0. 0d.   Docs 11-3-51.

1st Owner: M.E. Abendroth., 231 Walnut Street, Tipton, Indiana.
2nd Owner: Wilfred Gray, 3721 E. 10th St, Indianapolis 1, Indiana.
           (Gray's Truck Service)

177   AMERICA   Seddon/ Abendroth/ Gray/   J-1859.

38

R/P IMPORTED MOTOR CAR COMPANY.,
147 West 54th Street,
NEW YORK 19., N.Y.   Order No. 137.

Ordered 27-3-51. Invoice S-1861. CD3 HH-886264. Dlv'd 11-7-51.
ALLARD J2 TWO SEATER LHD: Red, red leather; wire wheels; two spares
                          on side mounts; undertray etc etc:
Chassis No. J-2018.   Cadillac modification.

LEP TRANSPORT : ss Washington. Loading Southampton.
Freight £   Docs received 21/7/51.   1975
                                                   2030

Client : American millionaire Mr. ....

224   AMERICA   Seddon   J-2018.

R/P IMPORTED MOTOR CAR COMPANY.,
147 West 54th Street,
NEW YORK 19., N.Y. U.S.A.   File No. 152.

Ordered 2-4-51.   Invoice S-1950. CD3 HH-886279.
ALLARD J2 TWO SEATER LHD: Colour blue, red leather.
                          Chassis No. J-2019. Cad. Mod:
                          6 wire wheels.

LEP TRANSPORT.   ss AMERICAN IMPORTER.   Dlvd 19-9-51.
Freight £45-1-0   Docs received 1/10/51.

264 AMERICA Seddon   J-2019

WOOD MOTORS.,
9925, Whittier,
DETROIT 24., MICHIGAN. U.S.A.   File No. 173.

Ordered 5-6-51.   Invoice S-1925. CD3 HH-886276. Dlvd 4/9/51.
ALLARD J2 TWO SEATER LHD: Metalic blue, red leather.
                          Chassis No. J-2123. CADILLAC MOD:

LEP TRANSPORT : ss A.M. Merchant Dlvd to Reynolds 4/9/51.
FREIGHT £.41-7-6   Packing £...... Docs recd 18/9/51.

252 AMERICA Wood Motors   J-2123.

Messrs. Bill Co.,
Grandview Boulevard.,
Zelienople., Penna.   File No. 136.

Ordered 27-3-51. Invoice S-1818. CD3 HH-886255. Dlvd 13-7-51.
ALLARD J2 TWO SEATER LHD: Colour Red, red leather upholstery.
                          Wire wheels. Less engine. Ford modfn.
                          CHASSIS NO. J-2020.

LEP TRANSPORT.   ss WASHINGTON.   Closing 15-7-51.
Freight £43-3-9d.   Docs   21-7-51.

John L. Negley Jr., 429 Reno Street, New Cumberland, Pennsylvania.
** Killed at SOWEGA Road Race, 26-10-'53.

232 AMERICA Bill Co./ Negley */   J-2020.

DENVER IMPORTED MOTORS.,
2610, W. Alameda Avenue,
DENVER., COLORADO.   File No. 224.
                                     (formerly 194 - Keskus)

Ordered 26-12-51. Invoice S-   .   CD3 88662.   Dlvd ../1/52.
ALLARD J2 TWO SEATER LHD: Riviera blue, blue leather.
                          Chassis No. J-2125.
                          ARDUN engine No. 2025-L.
                          Key No. FA 517.

DAVIES TURNER : ss LEERPOOL.   Closing 10/1/52.
Freight £50-5-0   Docs   18/1/52. No. CA/01/0138

254 AMERICA Denver   J-2125.

Fred Wacker., Jr.
Ammco Tools.,
2100 Commonwealth Avenue.,
North Chicago., Illinois.   File No. 153.

Ordered 3-4-51. Invoice S-1768. CD3 HH-537879. Dlvd 21-4-51.
ALLARD J2 TWO SEATER LHD: Colour Red, red leather upholstery.
                          Wire wheels.
                          Less engine. Cadillac modification.
                          CHASSIS NO. J-2086.

DAVIES TURNER.   ss MUNCASTER CASTLE.   Closing 21-4-51.
Freight £46-0-11d.   Docs   1-5-51.

* President., S.C.C.A.

218 AMERICA Fred Wacker Jr./   J-2086.

Sociedad Mercantil International S.A.,
Jiron Antonio Miro Quesada 266,
LIMA., PERU.   File No. 193.

Client: Mr. Santiago Poppe.

Ordered 17-7-51.   Invoice S-1883. CD3 HH-886267.
ALLARD J2 TWO SEATER RHD: (S.H.S. Le Mans car)
Chassis No. J-2137 (originally J-2014.)
Engine No. Cadillac EM-988.   (special extra equipment).
Colour British Racing Green. Green.

LEP TRANSPORT: ss LOBOS. Delivered 25th July 1951.
Freight £24-7-9   Docs rec'd 7/8/51.

237 PERU Poppe   J-2137.

Mr. Reg. Fudge, Jr.
Messrs. REG. FUDGE.,
419 So. La Brea Ave,
LOS ANGELES 36., CALIF.   File No. 200.

Ordered 7-8-51. Invoice S-1898. CD3 HH-886277. Dlvd 4/10/51.
ALLARD J2 TWO SEATER LHD: Black, red leather.
                       Chassis No. J-2156.b CADILLAC MOD:

DAVIES TURNER: ss   Durango   Closing 5./10/51.
Freight £51-3-4..   Docs 24.../10/51.

262 AMERICA Fudge.   J-2156.

Custom Automotive.,
2122 North Pearl.,
Dallas., Texas.   File No. 205.

Ordered 15-8-51. Invoice S-1973. CD3 JJ-88646. Dlvd 18-10-51.
ALLARD J2 TWO SEATER LHD: Colour Black, red leather upholstery.
                          Wire wheels. Full windscreen & hood.
                          Less engine. Mercury modification.
                          CHASSIS NO. J-2179.

DAVIES TURNER.   ss DEERPOOL.   Closing 18-10-51.
Freight £50-4-8d.   Docs   31-10-51.

Fred R. Cook., 7638 Southwestern., Dallas., Texas.

271 AMERICA Custom Auto/ Fred Cook/   J-2179.

ALLARD MOTOR Cº
CLAPHAM
LONDON S.W

ALLARD J2.   RED/RED TRIM.   FIRST PUBLIC APPEARANCE
CHASSIS Nº 888   AT PRESCOTT HILLCLIMB
ENGINE 2007 y ARDUN   JULY 17 1949
REGISTRATION Nº KXC170
PROTOTYPE J.
USED BY S.H. ALLARD IN COMPETION. WITH ALTERNATIVE
ENGINE UNITS i.e ARDUN, O/BORED MERCURY ETC, AND
THE FIRST CADILLAC, INSTALLED FOR THE TARGA FLORIO
[GIRO DE.   ] SICILY 1950
EVENTUALLY SOLD TO: THEN THROUGH SEVERAL OWNERS,
    D.F. ANNABLE   SHIPPED TO U.S.A, AND EVENTUALLY
    MARLOW   BOUGHT BACK TO U.K BY
    BUCKS   R. LARRINAGA.
DELIVERED 23-3-1951   NOW IN RESTORATION.   J888

R. CLARKSON
HALSTEAD

ALLARD J2   SILVER · ? TRIM
CHASSIS 1557
ENGINE 29411 MERC, 4375cc
    DELIVERED 28.2.1950

    EXPORTED U.S.A 1978

REG. Nº CWG 12.   1557

MR CLARK
   NUNEATON

ALLARD J2   NO COLOUR/TRIM RECORDED
CHASSIS 1558
ENGINE 3956/90
   DELIVERED 14-4-1950

                                    1558

T.C. HARRISON

ALLARD J2   BLACK. RED TRIM
CHASSIS 1570
ENGINE 3930-108
   DELIVERED 26-1-1950

                                    1570

A.S. MORT
   WIGTOWN
      SCOTLAND

ALLARD J2   RED. RED TRIM
CHASSIS 1559
ENGINE 3958/60 [THEN CHANGED FOR ARDUN 2034]
   DELIVERED 15-4-1950

CRASHED, REBUILT AND AFTER MANY CHANGES IN OWNERSHIP
NOW OWNED BY CLUB MEMBER M. KNAPMAN (1986)

      REG Nº OS 7525   1559

MR SLEIGHT
   DERBY

ALLARD J2   GREEN - GREEN TRIM
CHASSIS 1572
ENGINE 5341/29
   DELIVERED 4-5-1950

                                    1572

MR HEWITT
     LEEDS

ALLARD J2   GREY - MAROON TRIM - RED WHEELS
CHASSIS 1573   WINDSCREEN & HOOD
ENGINE 5355/40 437scc
     DELIVERED 11-5-1950

          REG Nº NUB 862   1573

MR HYDE
     CHESHIRE

ALLARD J2   POLY-STEEL - GREY TRIM
CHASSIS 1575
ENGINE 5343/31
     DELIVERED 15-6-1950

          REG. Nº BJV 365   1575

MR CURTIS
     NEWCASTLE · ON TYNE

ALLARD J2
CHASSIS 1574
ENGINE 3933/114 (437scc'
     DELIVERED

                                   1574

MR WAY-HOPE
     BOURNEMOUTH

ALLARD J2   GREEN - GREEN TRIM
CHASSIS 1576
ENGINE 5335/23
     DELIVERED 26-5-1950

                                   1576

R. de LARRINAGA
LOUND HOUSE
NORTH MOSSLEY
LIVERPOOL

ALLARD J2   B.R.GREEN - GREEN TRIM

CHASSIS   1693

ENGINE   2005 (ARDUN)

DELIVERED 7-10-1950

   REG No LLP 797

              REG No LLP 787   J 1693

ALLARD MOTOR Cº

ALLARD J2

CHASSIS 1730

ENGINE 2006X

   SOME DOUBT AS TO WHETHER THIS CAR EXISTED.
NO DETAILS QUOTED IN CHASSIS RECORD BOOK, BUT
LIGHT PENCILLING SAYS "DUNTOV/CHASSIS ONLY,
              ALLARD DEMONSTRATOR"

                             J 1730

KEN WATKINS
IVYBRIDGE
  DEVON

  ALLARD J2

  CHASSIS 1695

  ENGINE 7219817

    DELIVERED 22-8-1950

                             1695

ALLARD MOTOR Cº
  CLAPHAM

  ALLARD J2   GREEN - GREEN TRIM

  CHASSIS 1735

  ENGINE 2029 ARDUN
    DELIVERED

ALLARD TEAM CAR
  T.T. RACE, ETC

NOW OWNED BY BRIAN GOLDER sold after decease
      REG Nº LLP 798   1735

 rd Cards

K. WATKINS.
IVYBRIDGE
DEVONSHIRE

ALLARD J2   BLUE - BLUE TRIM.

CHASSIS   1783

ENGINE   2009Y ARDUN

  DELIVERED   6.5.51

EXTRAS
  HOOD
  SCREEN
  CLOSE RATIO
        GEARS
  WIRE WHEELS

        REG Nº NCV 942   1783

A. HITCHINS   1951   LE MANS ENTRY
      WITH
P. REECE

ALLARD J2   GREEN - GREEN TRIM

CHASSIS   1910

ENGINE   CADILLAC 8M 861

  DELIVERED   1-4-1951

      EXTRAS
        RACE FITTINGS.
        I.D LIGHTS
        EXTERNAL FILLERS
          ETC.

* AFTERWARDS TRANSFERRED TO J.R.3409
NOW OWNED BY CLUB MEMBER B. SHARPE. *
(1986)   REG Nº OVT 983   1910

DR. E. MANTON
   LONDON
EX DEMONSTRATION CAR

ALLARD J2   RED - RED TRIM

CHASSIS   1784

ENGINE   2004 ARDUN

   DELIVERED 9-1-1951

EXTRAS
   CLOSE RATIO GEARS
   HOOD + FULL SCREEN
   WIRE WHEELS

                              1784

PETER COLLINS
   KIDDERMINSTER

ALLARD J2   B.R.GREEN - GREEN TRIM

CHASSIS   1911

ENGINE   V8 CADILLAC ? [NOT CONFIRMED] 8M 580

   DELIVERED 29-3-1951

Later Don Farrell
Dismantled + Parts built into special "Farrellac"
1992 Phone call from Tony ?   after re-registering
                                      with any number,

   REG Nº JWP 100 (NOT CONFIRMED) checked   1911

MAURICE WICK.   L X Y 1 < ?
  LONDON

ALLARD J2   PACIFIC GREEN - RED TRIM
CHASSIS 1912
ENGINE 2019 - ARDUN
  DELIVERED 10-4-1951

  EXTRAS
    TWO SPARE WHEELS
    HOOD
    SCREEN
    SIDE - CURTAINS
    CLOSE RATIO GEARS

                                    1912

A. G. IMHOF
  LONDON

ALLARD J2   BLUE - RED TRIM
CHASSIS 1972
ENGINE   CADILLAC SUPPLIED BY CUSTOMER.
DELIVERED 17-3.51

    REG Nº LXT 5

  CONVERTED TO J2X SPECIFICATION
  AT ALLARD SERVICE DEPOT, 12-11-55

                                    1972

ADLARDS   SHA WORKSCAR LXR 749
  BRIXTON   See page 146 in my book
DEMONSTRATION CAR

ALLARD J2   GREEN - TAN TRIM
CHASSIS 1971
ENGINE   CADILLAC
  DELIVERED 7-9-1951

  EXTRAS
    WIRE WHEELS

                                    1971

ALLARD MOTOR Cº   Query over this car loaned
                       - was this Cyrils own
J2 2010   SILVER / TRIM?   car - as shown
                       in photo of Laurence team
SPECIAL LIGHTWEIGHT CAR BUILT FOR SYDNEY ALLARD.
CRASHED (MINOR) ON WAY TO 1951 ALPINE RALLY
INVOLVED IN (MINOR) COLLISION WITH TRUCK ON DELIVERY
TO SCOTLAND FOR MR H.W.
    DRIVEN BY CYRIL WICK, NEW SPORTS CAR RECORD
    AT SHELSLEY, JUNE 1953.
  EVENTUALLY SOLD TO THE CHANNEL ISLANDS WHERE
  SCRAPPED AFTER FATAL CRASH

      REG Nº LYV 366 ?   J2 2010

A G IMHOF
LONDON

ALLARD [SPECIAL] J INCREASED IN W/B FOR CUSTOM BUILT
                                              COUPÉ BODY

CHASSIS 2011   COLOUR RED
ENGINE - MERCURY 4,375 cc   TAN TRIM
  DELIVERED 17·3·51

NOW OWNED BY CLUB MEMBER G AUSEE (1986)
          REG Nº LXN 5   2011

ALLAN GODSAL   original J2 chassis sold to Williams
TWYFORD   reg Nº JFM 780
BERKSHIRE   (page 170)

                        REG Nº GJB 1
ALLARD [SPECIAL] J2   DELIVERED 2-4-1951
CHASSIS 2015 INCREASED IN W/B FOR CUSTOM BUILT SALOON
ENGINE 2017 ARDUN. SPECIFIED BUT NOT USED.   BODY
  DURING THE BUILDING STAGES, MR GODSAL PURCHASED A
  U8 CHRYSLER ENGINE FOR INSTALLATION.
    AFTER USE FOR ABOUT TWO YEARS, A P2 CHASSIS WAS
  BUILT UNDER THE SAME NUMBER, THE BODY TRANSFERRED
  AND THE ENGINE REPLACED BY A U8 CADILLAC.
    THE CAR WAS EVENTUALLY SOLD TO A MR ZIAR, LIVING
  IN PENZANCE BUT FOLLOWING A QUARREL WITH THE
  ALLARD MOTOR Cº THE CAR WAS DRIVEN OUTSIDE AND
  LEFT TO ROT IN 1974.
    WHEN SEEN IN 1980, IT WAS BEYOND RESTORATION AoC 2015
May 1989 Bought by Mark Brett London SE for restoration !! Club member

---

A·J· TATHAM
ORPINGTON
KENT

ALLARD J2   BRONZE - BROWN TRIM.
CHASSIS 2012
ENGINE 2020 ARDUN
DELIVERED 20-6·51
    REG Nº NKT 7.
  EXTRA'S
    WINDSCREEN
    HOOD
    LUGGAGE RACK

                              2012

TATE OF LEEDS   FOR RICHARD PETTY LTD
                   EASTBROOK WORKS
                   BRADFORD

ALLARD J.2.   ROYAL BLUE/ BLUE TRIM / CREAM (WIRE)
                                          WHEELS
CHASSIS Nº 2090
ENGINE 120182
DELIVERED 13-7-1951

    CLOSE RATIO GEARS

                              J 2090

D. TITTERINGTON
    BELFAST

ALLARD J2   RED - RED TRIM - CREAM [WIRE] WHEELS

CHASSIS 2120
ENGINE 2022 ARDUN
    DELIVERED 1-9-1951

SPECIAL FINISH FOR EXHIBITION AT 1951 FESTIVAL OF BRITAIN,
DRIVEN BY MR TITTERINGTON TO WIN THE 1952 LEINSTER
                                TROPHY RACE, ETC.

(1996 For sale (no body) in India) club member Paul Harvey
                        went out for it, but found local
                        restriction and "red tape" too
                        much to overcome.

                                2120

DAGENHAM MOTORS
    LONDON
DEMONSTRATION CAR

ALLARD J2   BRONZE - BROWN TRIM.
CHASSIS 2122
ENGINE 2027. ARDUN.
    DELIVERED 1-5-52

                                2122

DR. A.W. TILLEY   ALSO QUOTED MR B SCOTT-WADE
    HALEBARNS   CHEADLE
    CHESHIRE   CHESHIRE

ALLARD J2. GREY   BLUE TRIM
CHASSIS 2121
ENGINE
    DELIVERED 27.8.51

EXTRAS
    HOOD
    SCREEN
    LUGGAGE GRID

                                2121

DAGENHAM MOTORS
    LONDON

ALLARD J2   RED - RED TRIM
CHASSIS 2155
ENGINE 2131 ARDUN
    DELIVERED 30-4-1952

                                2155

---

rd Cards

Emelas & Cia. Limitada.,
Rincon 661.,
Montevideo., Uruguay.   File No:

Ordered 16-11-49. Invoice S-1135. CD3 JJ-886547. Dlvd 3-2-50.
ALLARD J2 TWO SEATER LHD: Light Blue, blue leather upholstery.
                            Mercury Engine No: D-198.
                            CHASSIS NO: J-1512.

Oscar Mario Gonzalez, Vazquez 1253, Montevideo., Uruguay.

94 URUGUAY Salem/ Gonzalez/   J-1512.

Sociedad Mercantil Internacional S.A.,
Antonio Miro Quesada 266.,
Casilla 651., Lima., Peru.   File No. 16.

Ordered 28-3-50. Invoice S-1330. CD3 FF-891343. Dlvd 24-6-50.
ALLARD J2 TYPE TWO SEATER LHD: Red, red leather upholstery.
                                 Less engine. ARDUN modification.
                                 Full windscreen & top.
                                 CHASSIS NO. J-1691.

Packed. EVAN COOKS.   ss ACONCAGUA.   Closing 24-6-50.
Freight £ 96. 0. 0d.   Docs   30-6-50.

Eduardo 'Chachi' Dibos, c/o The Mayor, Lima., P ru.

* Winner of Miraflres Circuit, Lima - 17-6-51.

113 PERU Somerin/ Dibos/   J-1691.

Salvador Fabregas Bas.,
Cardenal Casenas 8.,
Barcelona., Spain.   File No.

Ordered 23-2-50. Invoice S-1237. CD3 FF-156812. Dlvd 21-4-50.
ALLARD J2 CHASSIS LHD: (Chassis only i.e. less body & engine)
                         * Special 'Pegaso type' body subsequently
                           mounted and fabricated in Spain.
CHASSIS NO. J-1579.   Ardun engine supplied at a later date.
Packed & shipped AIR FREIGHT by Evans Cooks. 21-4-50.
Freight £21-10-6d.

DEALER:- F. On Alfredo Deu., Avenida Generalisimo Franco 339 bis,
                              Barcelona., Spain.

                                              4/6 14/6/54

106 SPAIN Alfredo Deu/ Fabregas Bas/   J-1579.

Palacio Ford de Manoel Alves
             de Freitas & Cia,
165 Avenida dos Aliados 155.,
Porto., Portugal.   File No: 17.

Ordered 29-3-50 Invoice S-1250. CD3 FF-891332. Dlvd 26-5-50
ALLARD J2 TWO SEATER LHD: Colour Red, red leather upholstery.
                            Close ratio gears. Racing tyres.
                            Cotal gear box. Full windscreen & top.
                            Engine No. MERCURY o/b 5556/41
                            CHASSIS NO: J-1692.

EVAN COOKS.   ss DUNNOTAR CASTLE   Closing 27-5-50
Freight £68. 0. 0d.   Docs   5-6-50

Mr. Jose Cabral.,

110 PORTUGAL Palacio/ Cabral/   J-1692.

MOTORTILLBEHOR,   ORDER NO. 15.
Wallingatan 38,
STOCKHOLM,
SWEDEN.

Ordered 28-3-50   Invoiced S-1334   Delivered 5-7-50
Blue, blue.   Engine No.   ?
Chassis No. J-1690 LHD.   C.D.3. FF 891341

SHIPPERS. MESSRS.EVAN COOK'S PACKER LTD.

         FREIGHT £28.4.9.

116 SWEDEN Motortillbehor   J-1690

Palacio Ford de Manoel Alves de Freitas Ltda,
157 Avenida dos Aliados 165.,
Porto., Portugal.   File No. 18.

Ordered 5-4-50. Invoice S-1323. CD3 FF-891340. Dlvd 6-5-50.
ALLARD J2 TWO SEATER LHD: Silver, red leather upholstery.
                            Engine No. (Mercury) 5350/38.
                            CHASSIS NO. J-1694.   LGX 672

Exported to Portugal via Newhaven Ferry 7-6-50.

Casimero Oliveira., Avenida Montevideo 516., Foz-Porto, Portugal.

114 PORTUGAL Palacio Ford/ Oliveira/   J-1694.

·ALLARD·

Robert Nellemann.,
I/S SOFUS NELLEMANN.,
Strommen 27.,
Randers., Denmark.   File No. 28.

Ordered 24-5-50. Invoice S-1381. CD3 FF-891350. Dlvd 27-7-50.
ALLARD J2 TYPE TWO SEATER LHD: Red, red leather upholstery.
                          ARDUN. Engine No. 5348/36.
                          CHASSIS NO. J-1697.

Christened "C'est si bon" - owned and raced by Robert Nellemann.

THOMAS MEADOWS.   ss BIERUM.   Closing 27-7-50.
Freight £22-15-0d.   Docs   29-7-50.

** s.o.r. payment finally completed January '54.

121 DENMARK Nellemann/ Robert Nellemann/   J-1697.

                                      ORDER NO.27.

R.A. Gardiner,
GARDINER'S MOTOR SERVICE,
297/299 Stanmore Road,
PETERSHAM, N.S.W.
AUSTRALIA.

Ordered 18-5-50   Invoiced S-1371   Delivered 8-7-50

Chassis No. J-1731 RHD.
Colour red. red leather .   Eng No. 5338/26

SHIPPERS:Messrs Thomas Meadows & Co Ltd.

        FREIGHT. £54.

120 AUSTRALIA Gardiner   J-1731

Gardiners Motor Service.,
297/299, Stanmore Road.,
Petersham., N.S.W., Australia.   File No. 73.

Ordered 30-10-50. Invoice S-1615. Delivered 25-1-51.
ALLARD J2 TWO SEATER RHD: Colour Red, red leather upholstery.
                          Wire wheels. Full windscreen & hood.
                          Cadillac Engine No. 8M-931. Getz gears.
                          CHASSIS NO. J-1698.

DAVIES TURNER.   ss MOOLTAN.   Closing 25-1-51.
Freight £79-7-0d.   Docs   14-2-51.

Jack E. Murray., 92 Curlewis St, Bondi., Sydney., N.S.W., Australia

176 AUSTRALIA Gardiner/ Murray /   J-1698.

Trident Motors.,
2868, Dufferin Street,
Toronto 10., Ontario.   File No. 40.

Ordered 2-8-50. Invoice p/f 2-8-50. Delivered 15-8-50.
ALLARD J2 TYPE TWO SEATER LHD: Red, red leather upholstery.
                          Mercury Engine No: 5347/35.
                          CHASSIS NO: J-1737.

THOMAS MEADOWS.   ss MAKEFJELL.   Closing 15-8-50
Freight £37.-0.-0d.   Docs   19-8-50

Judge John P. Madden, Court House, Nicholas St, Ottawa, Canada.
                          *** killed XK 120 17-12-53.

Len Frosst, 220 Van Horne Ave, Apt 5, Montreal P.Q., Canada.

140 CANADA Trident/ Madden +/ Frosst/   J-1737

Gardiners Motor Service.,
297/299 Stanmore Road.,
Petersham., N.S.W., Australia.   File No. 74.

Ordered 30-10-50. Invoice S-1570. Delivered 18-1-51.
ALLARD J2 TWO SEATER RHD: Colour Blue, blue leather upholstery.
                          Wire wheels. ARDUN ENG. NO: 2008-X.
                          CHASSIS NO. J-1699.

EVAN COOKS.   ss ARABIA.   Closing 28-1-51.
Freight £73-6-2d.   Docs   2-2-51.

1st Owner: Hastings Dearing,

2nd Owner: Peter H. Martin, 28 Addison Road, Manly., N.S.W.

163 AUSTRALIA Gardiner/ Dearing/ Martin/   J-1699.

Gardiners Motor Services,   Order No. 39
297/299, Stanmore Road,
Petersham, N.S.W.
AUSTRALIA.

Ordered 29-7-50.   Invoiced S-1446.   Delivered 6th October 1950.

Chassis No. J-1781.   Engine (Nil).   C.D.3. (not applicable)

J-TYPE 2 SEATER RHD: Colour bugatti blue, blue leather.

SHIP: ss CHINDWARA   SHIPPERS. LEP TRANSPORT. LTD.

                FREIGHT. £54.

139 AUSTRALIA Gardiner   J-1781.

GARDINERS MOTOR SERVICES,   ORDER NO.71.
297/299 Stanmore Road,
PETERSHAM, N.S.W.
AUSTRALIA.

Ordered 30-10-50.   Invoice S-1508.   Delivered 12-11-50.

J-TYPE 2 SEATER RHD: Colour Bugatti blue, blue leather.

Chassis No. J-1782.   Engine No. 5307/61 (overbored Mercury).

ss PEEBLES - LEP TRANSPORT.   Dec. 29/4/50

     FREIGHT £64.

148   AUSTRALIA   Gardiner   J-1782.

George Wales.,
Garage Excelsior.,
Rue des Eaux Vives 20.,
Geneva., Switzerland.   File No. 128.

Ordered 12-3-51. Invoice S-1777. CD3 HH-886249. Dlvd 17-5-51.
ALLARD J2 TWO SEATER LHD: Br.R. Breen, red leather upholstery.
                            Wire wheels. Aero screen.
                            ARDUN Engine No. 2015-Z.
                            CHASSIS NO. J-1855.

LEP TRANSPORT. (Rail transport to Geneva)
Freight £54-10-6d.   Docs 22-5-51.

Otterino Volonterio., Orselina., Tessin., Switzerland.

210 SWITZERLAND Wales/ Volonterio/   J-1855.

Halim Celaloglu., Esq.
Ensdiye Eronkoy.,
Istanbul., Turkey.   File No. 72.

Ordered 24-10-50. Invoice S-1525. CD3 HH-537896. Dld 23-1-51.
ALLARD J-TYPE 2 SEATER LHD: Colour Red, red leather upholstery.
                            Cadillac Engine No.
                            CHASSIS NO. J-1785.   LXD 516

Father: Abbas Bey.   Dealer: C.G. Norman & Co., Vauxhall.

DAVIES TURNER: ss ANDALUSIAN.   Closing 23-1-51.
Freight £   Docs   7-2-51.

* Turkish Prince.   ** Ex Earls Court Exhibition car.

149 TURKEY   Celaloglu/   J-1785.

Bernardo Wolfenson S.A.,
Defensa 247.,
Buenos Aires., Argentine.   File No. 122.

Ordered 27-4-51. Invoice S-1814. CD3 HH-886245. Dlvd 7-6-51.
ALLARD J2 TWO SEATER LHD: Colour Red, red leather upholstery.
                            Wire wheels. Full windscreen & hood.
                            ARDUN Engine No. 2010-Z.
                            Registration No. MGC 530.
                            CHASSIS NO. J-1973.

1st Owner: J. Ibanez, Obligado 1986, Buenos Aires., Argentine.
2nd Owner: Franco Bruno, Caseros 679, Buenos Aires, Argentine.

RAC clearance Dover/Dunkirk Ferry Boat 22-6-51.

213 ARGENTINE Wolfenson/ Ibanez/ Bruno/   J-1973.

PALACIO FORD De   Order No. 41
Marcel Alves de Freitas & Cia Ltda,
157 avenida Dos Aliados 165,
OPORTO., PORTUGAL.

Ordered 3-8-50.   Delivered 25-9-50.   Invoiced S-1447.

Chassis No. J-1786.   Engine No. 5357/42.   C.D.3. No. FF 891376.

J-TYPE 2 SEATER : Colour bugatti blue, blue leather. LHD.

SHIPPERS. EVANS COOK'S PACKER LTD. FREIGHT. £68.

135 PORTUGAL   Palacio Ford   J-1786.

Oy Suomen Autoteollisuus A/B.,
Flemingsgatan 27.,
Helsinki., Finland.   File No. 133.

Ordered 20-3-51. Invoice S-1763. CD3 HH-886241. Dlvd 20-4-51.
ALLARD J2 TWO SEATER LHD: Cream, red leather upholstery.
                            ARDUN Engine No. 2013-Z.
                            CHASSIS NO. J-2016.

LEP TRANSPORT. ss BALTRAFFIC.   Closing 20-4-51.
Freight £30-11-3d.   Docs   26-4-51.

Client: Mr. Hamstadt ?

216 FINLAND Autoteollisuus   J-2016.

Oy Suomen Autoteollisuus A/B.,
Flemingsgatan 27.,
Helsingfors., Finland.   File No. 132.

Ordered 20-3-51. Invoice S-1764. CD3 HH-886242. Dlvd 25-4-51.
ALLARD J2 TWO SEATER LHD: Colour cream, red leather upholstery.
                    ARDUN Engine NO. 2014-Z.
                    CHASSIS NO. J-2017.

LEP TRANSPORT.   ss RIGEL.   Closing 25-4-51.
Freight £30-11-3.   Docs   28-4-51.

Asser Wallenius., Runeberginkatu 48 A 22., Helsinki., Finland.

215   FINLAND Autoteollisuus/ Wallenius/   J-2017.

Julio C. Iglesias.,
Infanta 16.,
Havana., Cuba.   File No. 196.

also: Cia Petrolera Shell-Mex de Cuba S.A.,
        Ave. Pte Menocal No. 16., Havana., Cuba.

Ordered 21-7-51. Invoice S-1886. CD3 HH-886269. Dlvd 31-7-51.
ALLARD J2 TWO SEATER LHD: Colour Red, red leather upholstery.
                    Wire wheels. Full windshield & top.
                    Mercury Engine No. 12104/154.
                    Registration No. MGT 846.
                    CHASSIS NO. J-2089.

DAVIES TURNER.   ss LAGUNA.   Closing 6-10-51.
Freight £80-14-3d.   Docs   31-10-51.

238   CUBA Iglesias/   J-2089.

Dr. K.P.G. Mears., M.D.
30 Sumner Road.,
Christchurch., New Zealand.   File No. 134.

Ordered 26-4-51. Invoice S-1795. Delivered 4-5-51. (HOME DELIVERY)
ALLARD J2 TWO SEATER RHD: Colour Red, red leather upholstery.
                    Steel wheels. Full windscreen & hood.
                    ARDUN Engine No. 2017-X.
                    Registration No. LYV 364.
                    CHASSIS NO. J-2059.

LEP TRANSPORT.   ss RANGITANE.   Closing 14-8-51. (packed)
Freight £68. 0. 0.   Docs 19-8-51.

2nd Owner: G.L. Horder, Apex Tyre Retreading Co.Ltd.,
                    85 Victoria St, Christchurch, New Zealand.

1989 (April) phoned query ref car on sale at Blauth's auction.
Visited, to confirm authentic - told that
Charles Austin
1989   P.T.O

221   NEW ZEALAND Dr. Mears/ Horder/   J-2059.

KESKUS AUTO OY.,
Kauppalankatu 39-41,
KOUVOLA.,
FINLAND.   File No. 179

Ordered 6-7-51. Invoice S-1916. CD3 HH-886273. Dlvd 10/9/51
ALLARD J2 TWO SEATER LHD: Cream, red leather.
                    Chassis No.J-2124.   20302
                    (Ardun) Engine No. ....

LEP TRANSPORT: ss RIGEL..   FREIGHT FORWARD.
                    Docs recd 14/9/51.

253   FINLAND Keskus   J-2124.

Andrew Donovan.,
217 Second Floor, Victoria Arcade.,
Corner Queen St & Shortland Street,
Auckland C.I., New Zealand.   File No. 111.

Ordered 4-4-51. Invoice S-1776. Delivered (packers) 24-5-51.
ALLARD J2 TWO SEATER RHD: Maroon, maroon leather upholstery.
                    ARDUN Engine No. 2018-Z.
                    CHASSIS NO. J-2088.

GERHARD & HEY LTD.   ss MOOLTAN.   Closing 17-6-51.
(Freight forward)

C.G. Smith., 44 St. Benedict's Street, Auckland C.2., New Zealand.

207   NEW ZEALAND Donovan/ Smith/   J-2088.

GARDINERS MOTOR SERVICES,
297-299 Stanmore Road,
PETERSHAM., N.S.W.
AUSTRALIA.   File No. 160.

Ordered 24-4-51.   Invoice S-1862.   Reynolds 6-7-51.

Chassis No. J-2136.   Engine No. (Ardun) 2003.
J2 ALLARD 1950 EXHIBITION CHASSIS. v RHD.

Packers Reynolds, Barking;
Shippers LEP TRANSPORT LTD.   ss TREVINCE.
                    Freight £74-14-6.   Docs rec'd 4/7/51.

236   AUSTRALIA   Gardiner   J-2136.

L. BOCHI & CIA.,
San Isidro a San Julian 11.,
CARACAS.,
VENEZUELA.   File No. 189.

Ordered 31-7-51. Invoice S-1982. CD3 JJ-88647. Dlvd 12-10-51.
ALLARD J2 TWO SEATER LHD: Colour Ivory, red leather upholstery.
                           Chassis No. J-2157.
                           Engine No. 20332/eben

DAVIES TURNER. ss PARAGUAY. Closing 12-10-51.
Freight £56-12-5.   Docs received... 31-10-51.

272 VENEZUELA Autoboc   J-2157.

Auto Imports.,
415 Chestnut Street,
Rockford., Illinois.   File No. 214.

Ordered 12-11-51. Invoice S-2032. CD3 JJ-88650. Dlvd 21-11-51.
ALLARD J2X TWO SEATER LHD: Pacific Green, red leather upholstery.
                           Wire wheels.
                           Less engine. Cadillac modification.
                           CHASSIS NO. J-2180.

* Earls Court Exhibition model introducing the J2X.

DAVIES TURNER. ss AMERICAN RANGER. Closing 22-11-51.
Freight £53-15-11d.   Docs 28-11-51.

John F. Elwood., 155 North Ocean Shore, Ormand Beach, Florida.

279 AMERICA Auto Imports/ Elwood/   2x J-2180.

Messrs. Jack Pry.,
1507 - 14th Street N.W.,
Washington 5., D.C.   File No. 209.

Ordered 8-10-51. Invoice S-2035. CD3 JJ-88652. Dlvd 28-11-51.
ALLARD J2X TWO SEATER LHD: Elec. Blue, blue leather upholstery.
                           Wire wheels. Full windscreen & hood.
                           Less engine. Cadillac modification.
                           CHASSIS NO. J-2191.

DAVIES TURNER. ss AMERICAN VETERAN. Closing 28-11-51.
Freight £53-11-9d.   Docs   30-11-51.

Jean Davidson., Agence-France Presse, 1416 "F" Street, Washington,
                                                              D.C

123 AMERICA Jack Pry/ Davidson/   2x J-2191.

Wood Motors.,
9925 Whittier.,
Detroit 24., Michigan.   File No. 215.

Ordered 16-11-51. Invoice S-2040. CD3 JJ-88656. Dlvd 31-1-52.
ALLARD J2X TWO SEATER LHD: Primer., red leather upholstery.
                           6 Wire wheels. Extra sidemount.
                           Full size windscreen, wipers, hood.
                           Less engine Cadillac Modification.
                           CHASSIS NO. J-2192.

DAVIES TURNER. ss AMERICAN PRESS. Closing 31-1-52.
Freight £56-6-3d.   Docs   6-2-52.

Fred M. Warner., G.M. Aircraft Operations, Detroit City Airport,
                 Detroit 5., Michigan. (personal pilot G.M. Pres.)
C.E. Wilson, Pres. General Motors Corpn, 3044 W. Grand Blvd,
                                          Detroit 2., Michigan.
                 21/6/54

** Detroit Racing Equipment Co installed & prepared engine.

284 AMERICA Wood Motors/ Warner /   2x J-2192.

Motor Sport Inc.,
5438, Centre Avenue,
PITTSBURGH 32., Pa.   File No. 210.

ALLARD J2X TWO SEATER LHD: Powder blue, red leather.
                            Chassis No. J-2193.
                            CHRYSLER MOD:

DAVIES TURNER: ss AM. PRESS. Closing 12/12/51.
Freight £47-15-0   Docs   24/12/51. CH/11/0075

Ordered 15-10-51. Invoice S-2033. CD3 JJ-88651. Dlvd 14/12/51.

281 AMERICA Motor Sport Inc.   J2X J-2193.

R/P Imported Motor Car Co.,
147 West 54th Street,
New York 19., N.Y.   File No. 213.

Ordered 8-11-51. Invoice S-2082. CD3 JJ-88658. Dlvd 23-1-52.
ALLARD J2X TWO SEATER LHD: Royal Blue, red leather upholstery.
                           Less engine.; Cadillac modification.
                           Wire wheels. Full windshield & top.
                           CHASSIS NO: J- 2222.

EVAN COOKS.   ss AMERICAN PRESS.   Closing 23-1-52.
Freight £50.-8.-5d.   Docs   6-2-52.

P.W. Schwartz., Brookside., Suffield., Connecticut.
(Man. Dir. Colt's Manufacturing Co., Hartford 15., Connecticut.)

266 AMERICA Seddon/ Schwartz/   J2X-2222.

A.E. Goldschmidt.,
80 Maiden Lane.,
New York 38., N.Y.   File No: 211.

Ordered 16-10-51. Invoice S-2077. CD3 JJ-88654. Dlvd 9-1-52.
ALLARD J2X TWO SEATER LHD: Colour scarlet, red leather upholstery.
                           Less engine.; Cadillac modification.
                           Extra sidemount. 7 Wire wheels.
                           Full windshield & top. Numerous extras.
                           CHASSIS NO. J-2219.

* entered for Sebring. Appeared on front cover "LIFE" magazine.

EVAN COOKS.   ss AMERICAN FLYER.   Closing 9-1-52.
Freight £51.-17.-4d.   Docs   21-1-52.

296 AMERICA Goldschmidt/   J2X J-2219.

Messrs. SOMERIN.,
Casilla 2394,
Av. Wilson No. 923.,
LIMA., PERU.   Order No. 216.

Client: Mr. Eduardo 'Chachi' Dibos (son of Mayor - Lima, Peru)

Ordered 8-11-51. Invoice S-2039 CD3 JJ-88655. Dlvd 29/12/51.
ALLARD J2X TWO SEATER LHD: Silver grey. Red.
                           Chassis No. J-2223.
                           CHRYSLER MOD.

DAVIES TURNER: ss Reina del Pacifico. Sailing 10/1/52.
Freight £79-16-6.   Docs recd 16/1/52.
Packing £28-0-0
Packers: W.J. Reynolds. Barking.

283 PERU Somerin   J2X-2223.

R/P Imported Motor Car Co.,
147 West 54th Street,
New York 19., N.Y.   File No. 212.

Ordered 8-11-51. Invoice S-2081. CD3 JJ-88657. Dlvd 23-1-52.
ALLARD J2X TWO SEATER LHD: Red, black leather upholstery.
                           Less engine. Cadillac modification.
                           CHASSIS NO. J-2221.

EVAN COOKS.   ss AMERICAN PRESS.   Closing 23-1-52.
Freight £50.-8.-5d.   Docs   6-2-52.

Frank C. Adams., 48 Evans Avenue., Albertson., N.Y.

285 AMERICA Seddon/ Adams/   J2X-2221.

3037   SEDDON. U.S.A.
       RED / BLACK
              LEATHER

WIRE WHEELS / SPARE WHEEL MOUNTS BOTH SIDES OF
                                        BODY

CHRYSLER MODS. FULL WINDSCREEN

3.78 AXLE   FORD GEARBOX

SHIPPED. 29-1-52

                              J2X 3037

3038   SEDDON   U.SA

SKY BLUE / RED LEATHER / RED TOP.

FULL SIZE WINDSCREEN

CHRYSLER MODS   WIRE WHEELS

3.78 AXLE   FORD GEARBOX

J2x 3038

3041   BILL & CO   PA

IVORY - RED LEATHER, BLACK TOP

CHRYSLER MODS   FORD GEARBOX.
REAR AXLE MODIFIED FOR   PAT WARREN QUICK
                                        CHANGE

SHIPPED 6 - 3 - 52

J2x 3041

3039 DENVER IMPORTED MOTORS
        2610 W. ALAMEDA   DENVER   COLORADO

FRENCH RACING BLUE / RED LEATHER

CADILLAC MODS 3.78 AXLE   FORD G.BOX

FULL SIZE WINDSCREEN   WIRE WHEELS

[DEMONSTRATION CAR FOR NEW DEALER]

SHIPPED 4-2-52
                    J2x 3039

3042   R.P IMPORTED CAR CO   NEW YORK

RED   RED LEATHER

CADILLAC MODS   FORD G.BOX.

FULL SIZE WINDSCREEN, WIPERS, TOP

WIRE WHEELS   3.78 AXLE

SHIPPED 29-2-52

J2x 3042

3040   CALIFORNIA SPORTS CAR CO
        1460 PINE ST   SAN FRANCISCO

BLACK - RED LEATHER,
SIX WIRE WHEELS - TWO SPARE SIDE MOUNTS

CHRYSLER MODS. FORD GEAR BOX, SPECIAL RATIOS ⌠5.75
                              3.27 AXLE   ⌡10·01

FULL SIZE WINDSCREEN
20 GALL TANK
QUICK CHANGE REAR AXLE MODS
SHIPPED 25·2·52
                    J2x 3040

3043   SEDDON   U.SA

BRITISH RACING GREEN / GREEN LEATHER

CADILLAC MODS   FORD G.BOX - GREEN WIRE
                                      WHEELS (5)
FULL SIZE WINDSCREEN, WIPERS, TOP

SHIPPED 29 - 2. 52

J2x 3043

3044 DENVER IMPORTED MOTORS, DENVER COLORADO
RED / RED LEATHER, ~~SILVER~~ WIRE WHEELS

OLDSMOBILE MODS / REAR AXLE MODIFIED FOR PAT WARREN
QUICK CHANGE

FULL WIDTH SCREEN, WIPERS, TOP, TONNEAU COVER.
FRONT WINGS WITH LOUVRES AT BOTTOM.
No PORT HOLES IN BONNET SIDES, BUT ROWS OF
LOUVRES. LEATHER STRAP OVER BONNET.
SPARE WHEEL SIDE MOUNTS WITH LEATHER STRAPS AS
ON LE MANS CARS. HEADLIGHTS WITH WIRE STONE
GUARDS. 40 GALLON TANK. OIL TEMP. GAUGE

SHIPPED 26-3-52   J7x 3044

3045   MOSS MOTORS LOS ANGELES

ROYAL BLUE / BLUE LEATHER

CADILLAC MODS FORD GEAR BOX 3.78 AXLE

WIRE WHEELS

SHIPPED 27-3-52

J7x 3045

3046 CALIFORNIA SPORTS CAR Co SAN FRANCISCO

RED - RED LEATHER

CADILLAC MODS FORD GEAR BOX 3.78 AXLE

SHIPPED 27-3-52

J7x 3046

3047 WALTER A. GREY KANSAS CITY

BRITISH RACING GREEN / RED LEATHER. WHITE WIRE
WHEELS

CADILLAC MODS QUICK CHANGE REAR AXLE

FORD G. BOX

SHIPPED 2-4-52

J7x 3047

3048   SEDDON U.SA

WHITE - BLACK LEATHER   SIX WIRE WHEELS
AND SIDE MOUNT

CHRYSLER MODS FORD GEARBOX
3.78 AXLE

SHIPPED 2-4-52

J7x 3048

3049   1952 LE MAN CAR REG. No
DUNTON/ CURTIS   MXx 974

BOUGHT BY FRANK CURTIS, AFTER RACE SOLD
AND CONVERTED TO SPECIAL KNOWN AS "BUTCH"

BRITISH RACING GREEN

CHRYSLER ENGINE ~~~~ CHR 1.51
4 SPEED GEAR BOX [ALLARD VAN CONVERSION]

QUICK CHANGE REAR AXLE

3049

Card 1 (top left):

3050

HARRY STEELE ARIZONA. (WICKENBURG)

BEIGE - FRONT AND REAR WINGS (FENDERS) ALFA
BODY.   RED LEATHER   (RED)
AND WIRE WHEELS !

LINCOLN MODS   ANDRE SHOCK ABSORBER (ADDIT. TO
7,500 REV COUNTER. OIL TEMP GAUGE.   STANDARD)
DUAL RACING WINDSCREENS. TONNEAU COVER.
OIL RADIATORS, TWO ½ GALL UNITS FITTED
40 GALL TANK WITH RACING TYPE FILLER CAP
STANDARD FORD GEAR BOX. PAT WARREN QUICK CHANGE
AXLE MOD. AXLE RATIO 3·27   J2X 3050

Card 2 (top right):

ALLARD MOTOR COMPANY, INC.
141 West 53rd Street,
NEW YORK 19., N.Y.   File No. 415

Ordered 11-8-52. Invoice S-2421. CD3 JJ-88397. Dlvd 28-3-53.
ALLARD J2X TWO SEATER LHD: Br. R. Green, pigskin leather uphlstry.
                             Cadillac mod. Wire wheels. Power bulge.
                             Windscreen, wipers & hood.
                             CHASSIS NO. J-3142.

PALL MALL DEPOSIT. ss AM. HARVESTER.   Closing 30-3-53.
Freight £46-8-4.   Docs   8-4-53.

Sam Lortz., 625 South Skinker., St. Louis., Missouri.

432 AMERICA AMC INC /Lortz/   J-3142

Card 3 (middle left):

SPEEDCRAFT Enterprises Inc.,
P.O. Box 15.,
Exton., Pennsylvania.   File No. 403.

Ordered 15-7-52. Invoice S-2333. CD3 MM-792116. Dlvd 24/12/52.
ALLARD J2X LE MANS LHD: Colour white, red leather upholstery.
                          9 wire wheels - Competition tyres.
                          Tonneau cover. Quickchange modifctn.
                          Racing mirror. CHRYSLER MODIFICTN.
                          150 mph speedo. 8000 rpm Rev.Counter.
                          CHASSIS NO. J-3140.

LEP TRANSPORT. ss AMERICAN VETERAN. Closing 24-12-52.
Freight £48-13-2.   Docs ...31-12-52.

Freight £48-13-2   31-12-52

396 AMERICA Speedcraft   J-3140

Card 4 (middle right):

Noel Kirk Motors.,
7176 Sunset Boulevard.,
Hollywood 46., California.   File No. 416.

Ordered 11-8-52. Invoice S-2284. CD3 MM-792010. Dlvd 10-10-52.
ALLARD J2X TWO SEATER LHD: Colour Red, black leather upholstry.
                            Less engine. Cadillac modification.
                            Wire wheels. Full windshield & top.
                            CHASSIS NO. J-3143.

DAVIES TURNER.   ss POTARO.   Closing 10-10-52.
Freight £58-0-0d.   Docs   15-10-52.

1st Owner: Dr. Fred Losee,
2nd Owner: Frank Fries., Fall River Mills., California.
3rd Owner: R. Hahn, Hahn Motor Co, POB 382, Yakima., Washington.

385 AMERICA Kirk Motors/ Dr. Losee/ Fries/Hahn/   J-3143.

Card 5 (bottom left):

Allard Motor Company, Inc.
141 West 53rd Street,
New York 19., N.Y.   File No. 414.

Ordered 11-8-52. Invoice S-2331. CD3 MM-792036. Dlvd 7-1-53.
ALLARD J2X LE MANS LHD: Red, pigskin leather upholstery.
                          Less engine. Cadillac modification.
                          5 Wire wheels.
                          CHASSIS NO. J-3141.

John Adler., c/o Nassau Homes, 1 Merrick Ave., Long Island., N.Y.

LEP TRANSPORT.   ss AMERICAN PRODUCER. Closing 7-1-53.
Freight £   Docs ..16-1-53.

398 AMERICA Amc Inc/ Adler/   J-3141

Card 6 (bottom right):

Noel Kirk Motors.,
7176 Sunset Boulevard.,
Hollywood 46, California.   File No. 417.

Ordered 11-8-52. Invoice S-2307. CD3 MM-792027. Dlvd 17-11-52.
ALLARD J2X TWO SEATER LHD: White, red leather upholstery.
                            Less engine. Cadillac modification.
                            Disc wheels. Full windshield & top.
                            CHASSIS NO. J-3144.

LEP TRANSPORT.   ss DEFOE.   Closing 17-11-52.
Freight £61.-5.-7d.   Docs   25-11-52.

Albert T. Zugsmith., President, American Pictures Corporation.,
         846 No. Cahuenga Boulevard, Hollywood, Calif.

374 AMERICA Kirk Motors/ Zugsmith/   J-3144.

Card 1 (File No. 412):

NOEL KIRK MOTORS.,
7176 Sunset Boulevard,
HOLLYWOOD 46., CALIF.   File No. 412.

Ordered 5-8-52. Invoice S-2256. CD3 MM-792007. Dlvd 17-11-52.
ALLARD J2X TWO SEATER LHD: Bright Red, black leather.
                             Cadillac modification.
                             Windscreen, wipers & top.
                             Pressed wheels. (wire ordered, but not
                             supplied.) owing to shortage.
                             CHASSIS NO. J-3145.

DAVIES TURNER: ss DEFOE.   Closing 17-11-52.
Freight £115-8-10   Docs .. 28-11-52. CA/05/0476
    (2 cars - see J3146 also)

Klaus F.J. Bythiner, 4203 Louisiana Street, San Diego 4., Calif.

373 AMERICA Noel Kirk Motors./Bythiner/   J-3145.

Card 2 (File No. 435):

Noel Kirk Motors.,
7176 Sunset Boulevard.,
Hollywood 46., California.   File No. 435.

Ordered 26-8-52. Invoice S-2265. CD3 MM-792028. Dlvd 29-11-52.
ALLARD J2X TWO SEATER LHD: Colour red, black leather upholstery.
                             Less engine. Cadillac modification.
                             6 wire wheels. 2 sidemounts. Oil Cooler.
                             Oil temp. gauge. Full windshield & top.
                             CHASSIS NO. J-3148.

LEP TRANSPORT.   ss SANDANGER.   Closing 29-11-52.
Freight £40-14-1d.   Docs   8-12-52.

Louis Yates, Route 10., Box 181., San Antonio., Texas.

380 AMERICA Kirk Motors/ Yates/   J-3148.

Card 3 (File No. 427):

Noel Kirk Motors.,
7176 Sunset Boulevard.,
Hollywood 46.. California.   File No. 427.

Ordered 14-8-52. Invoice S-2257. CD3 MM-792002. Dlvd 17-11-52.
ALLARD J2X TWO SEATER LHD: Ivory., red leather upholstery.
                             Less engine. Cadillac modification.
                             6 wire wheels. Two sidemounts.
                             Oil cooler. Oil temperature gauge.
                             Luggage grid. Full windshield & top.
                             CHASSIS NO. J-3146.

DAVIES TURNER.   ss DEFOE.   Closing 17-11-52.
Freight £57-9-0d.   Docs   28-11-52. 08/0475.

Roy Cherryhomes, Box 327., Jacksboro'., Texas.

390 AMERICA Kirk Motors/ Cherryhomes/   J-3146.

Card 4 (File No. 434):

NOEL KIRK MOTORS.,
7176 Sunset Boulevard,
HOLLYWOOD 46., CALIF.   File No. 434.

Ordered 26-8-52. Invoice S-2264. CD3 MM-792009. Dlvd 7-1-53
ALLARD J2X LE MANS LHD: Colour pale biscuit, red leather.
                          Le Mans type body. Cadillac modifictn.
                          Windshield, wipers, top, sidecurtains.
                          CHASSIS NO. J-3149.

LEP TRANSPORT: ss LOCH GARTH. Closing 9-1-53.
Freight £52-3-70   Docs .. 20-1-53.

379 AMERICA Noel Kirk   S-J-3149.

Card 5 (File No. 430):

ALLARD MOTOR COMPANY, INC.
141 West 53rd Street,
NEW YORK 19., N.Y.   File No. 430.

Ordered 25-8-52. Invoice S-2401. CD3 MM-792142. Dlvd 18-3-53
ALLARD J2X TWO SEATER LHD: Red, tan pigskin leather upholstery.
                             Less engine. Cadillac modification.
                             (Originally Seddon C/15 order)
                             WIRE WHEELS. Spare in rear deck.
                             No sidemount. CHASSIS NO. J-3147.

LEP TRANSPORT. ss AM. PLANTER. Closing 18-3-53.
Freight £   Docs   -3-53.

422 AMERICA AMC INC   J-3147.

Card 6 (File No. 407):

JUAN RIU.,
Panamerican Import,
Transversal 17. No. 25-97,
(Av. Caracas Esquina Calle 26),
BOGOTA., COLOMBIA., S. AMERICA.   File No. 407.

Ordered 27-8-52. Invoice S-2296. CD3 MM-792024. Dlvd 28-10-52.
ALLARD J2X TWO SEATER LHD: Colour Red, red leather upholstery.
                             CHASSIS NO. J-3150.
                             CADILLAC ENGINE NO.8R-177.
                             Bucket seats, bumpers, radio, fog &
                             spot lamps, wire wheels, fender extns.

LEP TRANSPORT: ss AMERICAN MILLER. closing 29-10-52.
Transhipment New York via Grace Lines to Barranquilla.
Freight £206-13-4   Packing £   Docs 7/11/52.

Sr. Tomas Steuer, c/o Almacenes Tia S.A., Bogota., Colombia.

386 COLOMBIA Jean Riu/ Steuer/   J-3150.

Card 1 (top left):

Noel Kirk Motors,
7176 Sunset Boulevard,
Hollywood 46., Calif.　　　　　　　File No. 466.

Ordered 16-9-52.　Invoice S-2328.　CD3 MM-792033.　Dlvd 6-1-53.
ALLARD J2X TWO SEATER LHD: Colour black, red leather upholstery.
　　　　　　　　　　　　　　Less engine. Cadillac modification.
　　　　　　　　　　　　　　Wire wheels. Extra sidemount.
　　　　　　　　　　　　　　Oil temp. gauge. Full windshield & top
　　　　　　　　　　　　　　CHASSIS NO. J-3151.

PALL MALL DEPOSIT.　　ss LOCH GARTH.　　Closing 9-1-53.
Freight £51-19-5d.　　　　　　　Docs　21-1-53.

Fred M. Aley, 'D' Bty, 1st AAA-AWBA, Camp Pendleton, Oceanside,
　　　　　　　　　　　　　　　　　　　　　　　　California.
(Father, City Attorney, Wichita., Kansas)

400　AMERICA　Kirk Motors/ Aley/　　　　　　　2xJ-3151.

Card 2 (top right):

ALLARD MOTOR COMPANY, INCORPORATED.　　　　　　Atc 2
141 West 52rd Street,
NEW YORK 19., N.Y.　　　　　　　　File No. 477.

Ordered 51-10-52.　Invoice S-2343.　CD3 MM-793119.　Dlvd 8-1-53.
ALLARD J2X TWO SEATER LHD: Colour red, red leather upholstery.
　　　　　　　　　　　　　　Less engine. Cadillac modification.
　　　　　　　　　　　　　　Quickchange mod.
　　　　　　　　　　　　　　Windscreen, wipers & hood.
　　　　　　　　　　　　　　CHASSIS NO. J-3154.

PALL MALL:　　ss AM. PRODUCER.　　Closing 7/8-1-53.
Freight £146-13-6 }seats　　　　　Docs .. 16-1-53.
　　　　　　　　 }K3178/3265

376　AMERICA　AMC INC　　　　　　　2xJ-3154.

Card 3 (middle left):

ALLARD MOTOR COMPANY, INC.　　(Sports Cars Inc.)
147 West 53rd Street,
NEW YORK 19., N.Y.　　　　　　　File No. 365.

Ordered 16-9-52.　Invoice S-2376.　CD3 MM-792130.　Dlvd 23-2-53
ALLARD J2X LE MANS LHD: Br. Racing Green, green leather.
　　　　　　　　　　　　CHRYSLER MODIFICATION.
　　　　　　　　　　　　5 WIRE WHEELS. Oil cooler. O.T.gauge.
　　　　　　　　　　　　CHASSIS NO. J-3152.
　　　　　　　　　　　　(re-allocated from Kirk Motors)

DAVIES TURNER:　ss AISATIA.　Closing 24-2-53.
Freight £ 44-9-9　　　　Docs　6-3-53.　CA/04/0739
ins 10-8-0

413　AMERICA　AMC INC.　　　　　　SJ-3152.

Card 4 (middle right):

Allard Motor Company, Inc.
141 West 53rd Street,
New York 19., N.Y.　　　　　　　File No. 425.

Ordered 12-8-52.　Invoice S-2424.　CD3 JJ-88393.　Dlvd 8-4-53.
Allard J2X Le Mans TWO SEATER LHD: Colour red, red leather.
　　　　　　　　　　　　　　Less engine. Chrysler modfctn.
　　　　　　　　　　　　　　Wire wheels. Le Mans body.
　　　　　　　　　　　　　　CHASSIS NO. J-3155.

LEP TRANSPORT.　　ss AM. MANUFACTURER.　Closing 8-4-53.
Freight £116-16-1 }also　　　　　　Docs　16-4-53.
　　　　　　　　　}K3194
　　　　　　　　　}25014
Edgar S. Dokeych, Pres., Cardec Corpn, 65 Main St, Springfield 5, Mass.
* Bob Wilder wrecked this car at Bridgehampton - killed, May 1953.

434　AMERICA　Amc Inc. /De Mayer/　　　　SJ-3155.

Card 5 (bottom left):

Normand K. Patton., Jr.
Route 2.,
Woodstock, Illinois, U.S.A.　　　　File No. 476.

Ordered 29-10-52.　Invoice S-2409.　CD3 MM-792203.　Dlvd 14-5-53.
DEALER: Grancor Automotive Specialists, 5150 N. Western Ave,
　　　　　　　　　　　　　　　　CHICAGO 25., ILLINOIS.
ALLARD J2X LE MANS LHD:　Colour White, white leather upholstery.
　　　　　　　　　　　　　Chrysler mod. CHRYSLER ENG. NO. S-334.
　　　　　　　　　　　　　Windscreen & hood. Tonneau cover.
　　　　　　　　　　　　　Oil cooler. Quickchange mod. Racing mirror
　　　　　　　　　　　　　Oil temperature gauge.
　　　　　　　　　　　　　CHASSIS NO. J-3153.

LEP TRANSPORT:　ss AMERICAN FLYER.　Closing 14-5-53.
Freight £　　　　　　　　Docs　-5-53.

468　AMERICA　Patton/　　　　　　　2xJ-3153.

Card 6 (bottom right):

A/B Ingvar BERGENGREN.,
Lindhagensplan,
STOCKHOLM., SWEDEN.　　　　　　File No. 479.

Ordered 4-11-52.　Invoice S-2387.　Delivered 4-3-53.
ALLARD J2X TWO SEATER LHD: Colour Red, red leather upholstery.
　　　　　　　　　　　　　　Less engine. U.S. FORD MODIFICATION.
　　　　　　　　　　　　　　Windscreen, wipers & hood.
　　　　　　　　　　　　　　CHASSIS NO. J-3156.

BRITISH COMMERCIAL TRANSPORT.　ss LEO.　Closing 4-3-53.
(Freight & Ins. by consignee).　　　Docs　-3-53.

Thure Mårtenson., Director, Svensk Celluloidindustri A/B.,
　　　　　　　　　　　　　　　Gislaved., Sweden.

20 year old son Björn Mårtenson won the international Stockholm
Skarpnäcksloppet race in 1953.

417　SWEDEN　Bergengren　/Mårtenson/　　　2xJ-3156.

Richard E. Robinson.,
Defense Products Division.,
The Firestone Tire & Rubber Co.,
Akron 17., Ohio.   File No. 490.

Ordered 7-11-52. Invoice S-2313. CD3 MM-792030. Dlvd 10-12-52.
ALLARD J2X TWO SEATER LHD: Colour Red, red leather upholstery.
                           Less engine. Cadillac modification.
                           Wire wheels. Full windshield & top.
                           Luggage carrier.
                           CHASSIS NO. J-3157.

LEP TRANSPORT.   ss AMERICAN REPORTER.   Closing 10-12-52.
Freight £49-4-5d.   Docs   18-12-52.
2nd Owner: D.J. Atkinson, 38 Deaumant Terrace, Kenmore 23, N.Y.

395 AMERICA Firestone (Robinson)/Atkinson/   2xJ-3157.

SHAWNEE MOTOR COMPANY,
616 Quincy Street,
Topeka., Kansas. U.S.A.   File No. 512.

Ordered 21-11-52. Invoice S-2437. CD3 MM-792 195. Dlvd 2-5-53.
ALLARD J2X TWO SEATER LHD: Red, blue leather upholstery.
                           Chrysler modification. Less engine.
* burnt out 8-4-54.,   Windscreen & hood. Extra sidemount.
  new body ordered.   6 wire wheels. Oil temp. gauge.
                           Pat Warren quickchange modification.
                           CHASSIS NO. J-3161.

PALL MALL DEPOSIT. ss DALEBY.   Closing for cargo 3-5-53.
Freight £   Docs -5-53.

Client: Warren B. Turner, 717 Quindaro Blvd, Kansas City 1, Kansas

441 AMERICA Shawnee (Warren B. Turner/   xxJ-3161.

Allard Motor Company, Inc.
141 West 53rd Street,
New York 19., N.Y.   File No. 496.

Ordered 13-11-52. Invoice S-2434. CD3 JJ-88395. Dlvd 22-4-53.
ALLARD J2X TWO SEATER LHD: Red, red leather upholstery.
                           Cadillac modification. Less engine.
                           Windscreen & hood. Extra sidemount.
                           6 steel disc wheels. 160 mph speedo.
                           CHASSIS NO. J-3158.

PALL MALL DEPOSIT. ss AMERICAN BANKER.   Closing 22-4-531
Freight £128-12-2 } also   Docs   28-4-53.
Ins $34.98   } K-3183

439 AMERICA Amc Inc.   2xJ-3158.

Allard Motor Company, Inc.
141 West 53rd Street,
New York 19., New York.   File No: 539.

Ordered 8-1-53. Invoice S-2380. CD3 MM-792127. Dlvd 4-2-53.
ALLARD J2X TWO SEATER LHD: Colour Gunmetal, red leather upholstery.
                           Less engine. Cadillac modification.
                           6 wire wheels. Extra sidemount.
                           Full size windshield & top.
                           CHASSIS NO. J-3162.

Fred B. Asche Jr., Apt 1-N, Gedney, 3 Bryants Crescent, White Plains
                                                          New York.
DEALER:- Bill Frick Motors, 1000 Sunrise Highway, Rockville Center
                                                          N.Y.
DAVIES TURNER.   ss AMERICAN FLYER.   Closing 4-2-53.
Freight £58. 0. 0d.   Docs   8-2-53.
        BOB LYTLE, 1982   3/9/54

411 AMERICA Amc Inc/Frick/Asche/   2xJ-3162.

Not Built

3159
3160

CUSTOM AUTOMOTIVE.,
2122 N. Pearl Street,
DALLAS., TEXAS., U.S.A.   File No. 534.

Ordered 22-12-52. Invoice S-2439. CD3 MM-792197. Dlvd 3-5-53.
ALLARD J2X TWO SEATER LHD: Blue, red leather upholstery.
                           Cadillac modification. Less engine.
                           Quickchange modification. Oil temp gauge
                           5 Wire wheels, hubs & caps.
                           CHASSIS NO. J-3163.

Client: Gary B. Laughlin, 215 Saphire, Balboa Island, California.

PALL MALL DEPOSIT: ss DALEBY.   Closing 5-5-53.
Freight £   Docs   -5-53.

446 AMERICA Custom Autos /Gary B. Laughlin/   xxJ-3163.

Cards

Basil K. Esmond Evans.,
Ewans Shewan Importadora,
Rue Florencio d'Abreu.,
SAO PAULO., BRAZIL.   File No. 593.

Ordered 3-3-53. Invoice S-2497. £2273-10-9. HOME DELIVERY 23-9-53.
ALLARD J2X TWO SEATER RHD: Br.Racing Green, green leather upholst:
                              40 gall tank. 6 Wire wheels. Oil cooler.
Purchase Tax @   Extra sidemount. Oil temperature gauge.
£669-9-8 paid   8000 rpm tachometer. Tonneau cover.
& forfeited   Full windscreen, hood & sidecurtains.
insofar that car   Le Mans headlamps & stoneguards.
is to be retained   CHASSIS NO. J-3164.
permanently in U.K.   CHRYSLER ENGINE NO. 55028. (no drawback

Temporary address:- Brooklands Garth, Dartnell Park, W.Byfleet,
                    "Charters", South Ridge, St. George's Hill,   Surrey.
P/address: (Weybridge 3798)   Weybridge, Surrey.

479 BRAZIL Basil Evans/   (see over)   J-3164.

SHAWNEE MOTOR COMPANY.,
616 Quincy Street,
Topeka., Kansas., U.S.A.   File No. 542.

Ordered 10-1-53. Invoice S-2492. CD3 MM-792244. Dlvd /7/53.
ALLARD J2X LE MANS, RHD: Br. R. Green, red leather upholstery.
                          Wire wheels.(6). 40 gallon tank.
                          Oil pressure gauge. Oil temperature gauge
                          Pat Warren mod. Full windshield & top.
                          8000 rpm tach. Magneto switch. Gal paint.
                          CHASSIS NO. J-3202.

PALL MALL DEPOSIT.   ss DALEBY.   Closing 21-7-53.
Freight £49-2-11   Docs   1-8-53.

462 AMERICA Shawnee   X J-3202.

Allard Motor Company, Inc.
141 West 53rd Street,
New York 19., New York.   File No: 528.

Ordered 5-12-52. Invoice S-2453. CD3 MM-792215. Dlvd 15-7-53.
ALLARD J2X TWO SEATER LHD: Colour Red, red leather upholstery.
                           Wire wheels. Full windshield, & top.
                           Less engine, Cadillac mod. o.t. gauge.
                           CHASSIS NO: J-3200.

PALL MALL DEPOSIT.   ss AMERICAN PRODUCER   Closing 15-7-53
Freight £46. 0. 0d.   Docs   28-7-53

Jack W. Symes Jr, Westwood Cylce Co., 182 Third Ave, Westwood, N.J.
Alan R. Patterson II., 2301 Constitution Blvd, Boston, McKeesport,
                                                          Pennsylvania

459 AMERICA Amc Inc/Symes/ Patterson/   X J-3200.

ALLARD MOTOR COMPANY, INC.
141 West 53rd Street,
New York 19., New York.   File No: 668.

Ordered 19-3-54. Invoice ASL 5016. CD3 889186. Dlvd 16-6-54.
ALLARD J2X TWO SEATER LHD: Red, red leather upholstery.
                           Wire wheels. Full windshield & top.
                           *Dodge Red Ram ENGINE NO: 1013/1554055.
                           CHASSIS NO: J-3205.

PALL MALL DEPOSIT.   s.s. AMERICAN HARVESTER.   Closing 16-6-54
Freight £48-7-9   Docs   23-6-54

*** Dodge Engine subject to DRAWBACK OF DUTY.

524 AMERICA Amc Inc/   X J-3205.

MERRIMACK STREET GARAGES, INC.
52-56, Merrimack Street,
Manchester, New Hampshire.   File No. 643

Ordered 28-8-53. Invoice S-2554. CD3 FF-889072. Dlvd 15-10-53.
ALLARD J2X LE MANS LHD: Red, black leather upholstery.
                        Wire wheels. Oil cooler. 8000 rpm tach.
                        Luggage carrier. Quickchange rearend mod.
                        Windshield & top. Power bulge.
                        Less engine, Oldsmobile (Cad) modification.
                        CHASSIS NO. J-3201.

PALL MALL DEPOSIT.   ss AMERICAN FLYER.   Closing 16-10-53.
Freight £48-17-2   Docs   29-10-53.

1989
Jock Mareyso & man body tub
says car destroyed in slight accident

502 AMERICA Merrimack   X J-3201.

BRITISH MOTOR CAR DISTRIBUTORS LTD.
214, Van Ness Avenue,
San Francisco. Calif. U.S.A.   File No: 554.

Ordered 5-2-53. Invoice S-2522. CD3 MM-792261. Dld 21-8-53

ALLARD MOTOR J2X TYPE: LHD. Colour red, black upholstery.
                        Less engine, Cadillac mod.
                        Wire wheels.
                        CHASSIS NO: J-3208.

PALL MALL DEPOSIT: ss LOCH AVON.   Closing 21-8-53
Freight: £ 49-10-7   Docs. 4-9-53

Don Barnesson., Barnesson Building, 256 Montgomery Street,
                                     San Francisco., Calif.

491 AMERICA BMCD LTD / Barneson/   X J-3208.

All

Messrs. Budd & Dyer Limited.,
5028 Sherbrooke St West,
Montreal, Quebec., Canada.   File No. 586.

Ordered 18-2-53. Invoice S-2457. CD3 MM-792216. Dlvd 15-5-53.
ALLARD J2X TWO SEATER LHD: Colour beige, red leather upholstery.
                           Less engine. Cadillac modification.
                           Set of 5 wire wheels.
                           CHASSIS NO. J-3209.

PALL MALL DEPOSIT. ss EMPRESS of AUSTRALIA. Closing 15-5-53.
Freight £ 43-18-3   Docs   27-5-53.

David Gurd,   Montreal, Canada. (1)
Richard Mauron,   Toronto., Canada. (2)
3rd owner: Frederic J. Hayes, 79 Bideford Street, Toronto 12, Ont.

463 CANADA Budd & Dyer./Gurd/Mauron/Hayes/   ✈ J-3209

Gines Arimany,
Arimany y Cia Ltda.,
8a., C.O.,
10 - 38, Guatemala City,
Guatemala., Central America.   File No. 624.

Ordered 23-5-53. Invoice S-2521. CD3 MM-792260. Dlvd 26-8-53.
ALLARD J2X TWO SEATER LHD: Red, red leather upholstery.
                           Ford V8 3622 cc ENGINE NO. V8-3211.
                           Windshield & top. Tonneau cover.
                           Luggage carrier. 6 wire wheels.
                           Extra sidemount.
                           CHASSIS NO. J-3211. (formerly J-3203)

PALL MALL DEPOSIT.   ss ELECTRO.   Closing 27-8-53.
Freight £   Docs   -9-53.

455 GUATEMALA Arimany/   X J-3211.

Antonio Izquierdo D.,
Apartado Nal 1574.,
Bogota., Colombia.   File No: 657.

Ordered 24-2-54   Invoice ASL-5022   CD3 PP-889193   Dlvd 18/8/54
ALLARD J2X LE MANS LHD: Colour Red, blue leather upholstery.
                         Wire wheels. Tonneau cover. Radio assy.
                         Road Speed Dunlop tyres. Oil cooler.
                         Aircraft type safety belts.
                         CADILLAC ENGINE NO: 9T 136.
                         CHASSIS NO: J-3213.

PALL MALL DEPOSIT.   ss BERESINA.   Closing 20-8-54.
Freight forward.   Docs   -8-54.

(Weight 22 cwt 3 qtrs or 2548 lbs or 1156 Kilos.)

533 COLOMBIA Izquierdo/   X J-3213.

Northwestern Export Co.,
Room 307, Fukoku Bldg,
Tokyo., Japan.   File No: 678.

Ordered 3-6-54   Invoice ASL-5030   CD3 PP-889196   DLVD

ALLARD J2X TWO SEATER LHD: Red, red leather upholstery.
                            Less engine, Chrysler modftn.
                            6 wires. Extras sidemount.
                            Oil cooler. Road Speed tyres.
                            q/c rear end. Oil temp. gauge
                            8000 rpm tach. 150 mph speedo.
                            Airscoop. Full windshield.
                            CHASSIS NO. J-3214.

Paul Whitestine, Box 37, APO 323, c/o P.M. San Francisco.

PALL MALL DEPOSIT   m.v. AIZU MARU Closing 1-12-54
Freight £   Docs   -12-54
538 JAPAN   N.W.Export/Whitestine/   X J-3214.

A.E. GOLDSCHMIDT.?
102, Maiden Lane,
New York 38., N.Y.   File No. 612.

also: 399 Park Avenue, New York, N.Y.

Ordered 24-10-52. Invoice S-2417. CD3 JJ-88398. Dlvd 30-3-53.
ALLARD JR COMPETITION CAR RHD: Red, red leather upholstery.
                                  Less engine. Cadillac modifcctn.
                                  Wire wheels. Olds gearbox.
                                  CHASSIS NO. JR-3401. RHD

PALL MALL DEPOSIT: ss QUEEN ELIZABETH.   Closing 30-3-53.
Freight £94-12-4   Docs   7-4-53.
FOB Southampton sold to US   1976
              1982 Acquired by Peter Bland for
                      restoration (U.S.A)

433 AMERICA Goldschmidt/   JR-3401.

General Curtis E. LeMay., USAF.
Commanding, Strategic Air Force,
Offutt Air Force Base.,
OMAHA., NEBRASKA., U.S.A.   File No. 633.

Ordered 12-6-53. Invoice S-2484. CD3 MM-792240. Dlvd 18-6-53.
ALLARD JR TWO SEATER RHD: Colour blue, blue leather upholstery.
                            Wire wheels. CHASSIS NO. JR-3404.
                            CADILLAC ENGINE NO. 25439.

PALL MALL DEPOSIT.   ss AM. REPORTER.   Closing 18-6-53.
Freight (LeMay/U.S. Lines direct).   Docs .. 22-6-53.

        Some competition use in U.S.A, then "lost"
        for some years until found by Dean Butler
        now (1988) under restoration.

469 AMERICA General LeMay/   JR-3404.

Colonel Dave Schilling., USAF.
Turner AFB,
Turner., Georgia., U.S.A.   File No. 616.

Ordered 21-4-53. Invoice S-2585. CD3 MM-792249. Dlvd 25-7-53.
ALLARD JR COMPETITION RHD: Colour Blue, blue leather upholstery.
                             Cadillac Engine No. 2S-316.

                             CHASSIS NO. JR-3402.

Ordered through Gen. LeMay., Offutt AFB, Omaha, Nebraska.

PALL MALL DEPOSIT.   ss AM. SHIPPER.   Closing 26th July 1953.
Freight U.S. LINES.   Docs 1/7/53.
Le Mans 24 hour race
Driven by SHA/Fotheringham-Parker   Involved in fatal crash in England,
(4 laps only)   rebuilt by Paul Emery, then various
                                     owners; eventually rebuilt by D. Hume
                                     for D March (USA) for 1989 season.

484 AMERICA Col. Schilling/   JR-3402.

JR 3405

Chassis only, ordered by T. Sopwith as basis of a sports car
to be named SPHINX, after the mascot used on Armstrong Siddeley
cars. The Sopwith family were directly concerned with that company.
                                            with the Armstrong Siddeley special
Sopwith had an aer-flowed body fitted, and the car   engine
registered
OLT 101. The car proved underpowered, and Sopwith bowed to
family pressure to stop racing, before any development was
undertaken.
    The car was eventually acquired by B. Groat, and sold around
1985, I understand to France. Further enquiries as to its
present whereabouts have not succeeded. (1988)

Colonel Reade-Tilley., USAF.
Headquarters, Strategic Air Force.,
Offutt Air Force Base,
OMAHA., NEBRASKA., U.S.A.   File No. 636.

Ordered 22-6-53. Invoice S-2483. CD3 MM-792256. Dlvd 4-7-53.
ALLARD JR COMPETITION 2 SEATER RHD: AF Blue, blue leather.
                                      Wire wheels.
                                      CADILLAC ENG. NO. 2S-433.
                                      CHASSIS NO. JR-3403.

No Drawback on motor. General Griswold collection 4-8-53.

FREIGHT FORWARD.   PALL MALL documentation only.
ss AMERICAN HARVESTER.   Closing 7-8-53.   Docs 12/8/53.
Le Mans 24 hour race
Dunton/Merrick   Imported by motor dealer in 1975, floated
                        around various other dealers. Exported again
                        to U.S.A. Purchased by Syd Silverman 1982

485 AMERICA Col. Reade-Tilley/   JR-3403.

JR 3406

Built as touring car, screen, hood etc to the order of
Mr? Moffat, Canada, exported in March 1956

Subsequently found in collapsed shed, and totally stripped and rebuilt
by Du Brul USA (Vermont)
Sold in 1987/8 to - ?

Allard

Card 1 (top left)

TR 3407

James St Clair
8522 Trouville Avenue (Deceased)   EXPORTED SEPT 56
Playa Del Ray
California

~~Before this~~, used by S.H.A and R Larranage during 1956
competition season.

Shown as new car at Earls Court Motor Show, and used for
publicity photograph

Purchased from estate of Mr St Clair by Mr Emmens BS01

Then imported by Mr B Sharpe in 1987

Card 2 (bottom left)

Mr James St Claire
8522, Trouville Avenue,
Playa Del Rey,
California. U.S.A.

Cadillac engined Allard (J2R)
Green, Fitted Borani wheels   INVOICE Nº
4 dual choke Solex
                                     DELIVERED
Shipped to Los Angeles   SEPT 56

STOCK Nº   ENTERED
                ex Larranaga / SHA
VENDOR   Sharpe 1988

43 J. St. Claire.   OVT 983   Rebuilt as ── 3407
                                           (J-1910) (J2R)

Card 3 (top right)

K3 - 3165 - 3284

K3 MODEL CARDS   COVERING K3·3030 TO 3102 LOST,
but details in separate list (compiled by Len Ball) and kept with
chassis record books.

NO CARDS OR LISTED	
3017 no details, except marked Jack Ray	Letter from T Turne April 26 '88
3018 }	gives present owner L ALDEMUS - see v.s.a Letter file
3019 } SEDDON USA	
3020	
3021 } " "	
3022 }	
3023 } " "	
3025	
3026 Curtis Le Mans	
3028 Kirts USA agent	
3029 Seddon	
30 }	
31 }	
32 } 2298 card	

Card 4 (bottom right)

K3 MODEL CARDS, COVERING K3 3030 TO 3102

Not available, but for details
list kept with chassis.

NO CARDS OR LIST	
3017 K USA. 12/2/52 (Jack Ray - both only)	Letter from T Turne 24/4/88 re present owner L ALDEMUS - see USA
3018 } K USA Seddon 6/3/52	
19 }	
20 }	
29 }	
3022 } K USA Seddon 7.5.52	
3023 }	
3025 K USA Seddon 26 5 52	
3026 K Gen Curtis LM 9 5 52	
3028 K USA Kirts 9 7 52	
3024 9 K USA Seddon 17 6 52	

No other details
available for these
numbers.

←   ✓ K

ALLARD MOTOR COMPANY, INC.
141 West 53rd Street,
NEW YORK 19., N.Y.   Order No. 500.   AMC 3

Ordered 17-11-52.   Invoice S-2341.   CD3 MM-792119.   Dlvd 8-1-53.
ALLARD K3 ROADSTER LHD: Colour Opalescent blue, blue leather.
                          Less engine. Cadillac modification.
                          Wire wheels.
                          CHASSIS NO. K-3165.

PALL MALL DEPOSIT: ss AM. PRODUCER.   Closing 12-1-53.
Freight £ (see S3154)   Docs .. 16-1-53.

377   AMERICA Amc INC.   3K-3165.

Allard Motor Company, Inc.
141 West 53rd Street,
New York 19., New York.   File No. 501.

Ordered 17-11-52.   Invoice S-2329.   CD3 MM-792034.   Dlvd 23-12-52.
ALLARD K3 ROADSTER LHD: Colour Cream, black leather upholstery.
                          Less engine. Cadillac modification.
                          Disc wheels (wires out of stock)
                          CHASSIS NO. K-3168.

LEP TRANSPORT.   ss AMERICAN VETERAN.   Closing 24-12-52.
Freight £56.-5.-6d.   Docs   31-12-52.

A. Ciano., Sports Motors Inc, 900 E. Cervantes Street, Pensacola,
                                                              Florida.

401   AMERICA Amc Inc/ Ciano/   K3-3168.

Allard Motor Co., Inc.
147 West 53rd Street,
New York 19., N.Y.   File No. 389.

Ordered 1-7-52.   Invoice S-2384.   CD3 MM-792150.   Dlvd 24-2-53.
ALLARD K3 ROADSTER LHD: Silver Grey, red leather upholstery.
                          Less engine. Chrysler modification.
                          CHASSIS NO. K-3166.

PALL MALL DEPOSIT.   ss ALSATIA.   Closing 24-2-53.
Freight £90-5-11 (2 cars)   Docs   3-3-53.

Frank Pohanka Jr., 1126 20th Street N.W., Washington 6., D.C.

                                        YB 16/9/54

406   AMERICA Amc Inc/ Pohanka /   K-3166.

Noel Kirk Motors.,
7176 Sunset Boulevard,
Hollywood 46., Calif.   File No. 473.

Ordered 20-10-52.   Invoice S-2297.   CD3 MM-792137.   Dlvd 4-3-53.
ALLARD K3 ROADSTER LHD: Cream, red leather upholstery.
                          Less engine: Cadillac modification.
                          CHASSIS NO. K-3169.

* Ordered by client during visit to U.K - discount passed to Kirk.

LEP TRANSPORT.   ss DRINA.   Closing 5-3-53.
Freight £62-2-0.   Docs   14-3-53.

W.W. Valentine., 380 East Green Street, Pasadena 1., California.

418   AMERICA KirkMotors/ Valentine/   K-3169.

OVERSEAS EQUIPMENT CORPORATION.,
350 Fifth Avenue,
NEW YORK 1., N.Y.   Order No.445.

Ordered 7-9-52.   Invoice S-2345.   CD3 MM-792121.   Dlvd ../1/53.
ALLARD K3 ROADSTER LHD: Colour primer, black leather upholstery.
                          Less engine, CHRYSLER MODIFICATION.
                          Pressed steel wheels. (wires required)
                          CHASSIS NO. K-3167.

PALL MALL DEPOSIT: ss AM. PRODUCER. Closing 12-1-53.
Freight £58-15-3   Docs .. 16-1-53.

399   AMERICA O.E. Corpn.   K3-3167

Allard Motor Company, Inc.
141 West 53rd Street,
New York 19., New York.   File No. 595.

Ordered 1-7-52.   Invoice S-2399.   CD3 MM-792140.   Dlvd 18-3-53.
ALLARD K3 ROADSTER LHD: Black, red leather upholstery.
                          Less engine. Cadillac modification.
                          CHASSIS NO. K-3170.

LEP TRANSPORT.   ss AMERICAN PLANTER.   Closing 18-3-53.
Freight £59. 1. 11d.   Docs   21-3-53.

Felippe Arno, c/o Adams House, Harvard University, Cambridge, Mass.

423   AMERICA Amc Inc/ Arno/   K-3170.

E.N. Cole., Esq. Chief Engineer.,
Chevrolet - Central Office.,
Division of General Motors Corporation,
DETROIT 2., MICHIGAN. U.S.A.   File No. 394.

Ordered 7-7-52. Invoices S-2378. CD3 MM-792132. Dlvd ../2/53
ALLARD K3 ROADSTER LHD: Colour Cadillac grey, red leather.
                        CADILLAC ENGINE NO. 1458614.
                        CADILLAC HYDRAMATIC TRANSMISSION.
                        CHASSIS NO. K-3171.

Consignee : General Motors Overseas Operations, 1775 Broadway, N.Y.

DAVIES TURNER : ss AM. ALSATIA   Closing 24/2/53.
Freight £   Docs .. /2/53.

402 AMERICA AMO INC/ E.N. Cole/   K-3171.

ALLARD MOTOR COMPANY, INC.
141 West 53rd Street,
New York 19., N.Y.   File No. 598.

Ordered 26-8-52. Invoice S-2406. CD3 MM-792145 Dlvd /3/53.
ALLARD K3 ROADSTER LHD: Pacific green, green leather upholstery
                        Less engine. Cadillac modification.
                        Steel wheels. CHASSIS NO. K-3174.

PALL MALL DEPOSIT : ss AM. PLANTER   Closing 13/3/53.
Freight £   Docs /3/53.

Dealer :- Motorsports, 9908 Clayton Rd, St. Louis 17, Mo.

425 AMERICA AMC INC (Motorsports)   K-3174.

ALLARD MOTOR COMPANY, INCORPORATED.   AMC 4
141 West 53rd Street,
NEW YORK 19., N.Y.   File No. 533.

Ordered 31-11-52. Invoice S-2330. CD3 MM-792035. Dlvd 24-12-52.
ALLARD K3 ROADSTER LHD: Colour met. blue, red leather.
                        Less engine. Cadillac modification.
  (credit)   Pressed steel wheels. (wires ordered)
                        CHASSIS NO. K-3172.

LEP TRANSPORT. ss AM. VETERAN. Closing 24th December 1952.
Freight £   Docs 16/1/53.

397 AMERICA AMC INC   K-3172.

California Sports Car Co. (British Motor Car Distributors Ltd)
214 Van Ness Avenue,
San Francisco 2., California.   File No. 388.

Ordered 1-7-52. Invoice S-2359. CD3 MM-792124. Dlvd 5-2-53.
ALLARD K3 ROADSTER LHD: Dark Blue, red leather upholstery.
                         Less engine. Chrysler modification.
                         Less gearbox. Disc wheels.
                         CHASSIS NO. K-3175.

PALL MALL DEPOSIT.   ss DURANGO.   Closing 5-2-53.
Freight £66.-1.-5d.   Docs 19-2-53.

W.E. Andrews, 609 Woodland, San Leandro., California.
       also: 848 Acalanes, Lafayette., California.

405 AMERICA C.S.C. Co./ Andrews/   K-3175.

JORGE BARRANCO y CIA S.R.L.
Apartado 21330,
Niza 35.,
MEXICO D.F., MEXICO.   File No. 482.

Ordered 24-10-52. Invoice S-2414. CD3 JJ-88398. Dlvd 28-3-53.
Allard K3 ROADSTER LHD: Colour blue, red leather upholstery.
                         Cadillac modification. (Wires omitted)
                         Pressed steel wheels. (altho' invoiced)
                         CHASSIS NO. K-3173.

PALL MALL DEPOSIT. ss AM. HARVESTER. Closing 30th March 1953.
Freight £ 162-10-7 } Docs 9/4/53.
               } also S-4008.

   Thomas B. Catron, McCormick de Mexico S.A.,
                 Degollado 189, Mexico D.F., Mexico.

430 MEXICO Barranco./Catron/   K-3173.

Npel Kirk Motors.,
7176 Sunset Boulevard,
Hollywood 46., California.   File No. 408.

Ordered 28-8-52. Invoice S-2356. CD3 MM-792122. Dlvd 5-2-53.
ALLARD K3 ROADSTER LHD: Metallic Blue, blue leather upholstery.
                         Less engine. Cadillac modification.
                         Disc wheels.
                         CHASSIS NO. K-3176.

PALL MALL DEPOSIT.   ss DURANGO.   Closing 5-2-53.
Freight £119.-2.-5d.   Docs 19-2-53.

Bill Leyden, 800 Pass Avenue, Burbank., California.
      & K.F.W.B. Radio., Hollywood., California.

408 AMERICA Kirk Motors/ Leyden/   K-3176.

Noel Kirk Motors.,
7176 Sunset Boulevard,
Hollywood 46., California.   File No. 432.

Ordered 26-8-52. Invoice S-2357. . CD3 MM-792123. Dlvd 5-2-53.
ALLARD K3 ROADSTER LHD: Colour Maroon, red leather upholstery.
                          Less engine. Cadillac mod. Disc wheels.
                          CHASSIS NO. K-3177.

PALL MALL DEPOSIT.   ss DURANGO.   Closing 5-2-52.
Freight £119.-2.-5d.   Docs 19-2-52.

Frank Hathaway, 5525 Matilda Avenue, Van Nuys., California.

                                        YB 4/9/54

409 AMERICA Kirk Motors/ Hathaway/   K-3177.

Allard Motor Company, Inc.
141 West 53rd Street,
New York 19., New York.   File No. 521.

Ordered 1-12-52. Invoice S-2363. CD3 MM-792126. Dlvd 4-2-53.
ALLARD K3 ROADSTER LHD: Metallic Blue, red leather upholstery.
                          Less engine. Cadillac modification.
                          CHASSIS NO. K-3180.

DAVIES TURNER.   ss AMERICAN FLYER.   Closing 4-2-53.
Freight £58.-0.-10d.   Docs 9-2-53.

E.O. Roe, c/o Brooks Engineering, 5020 No. Grand River, Lansing,
                                                      Michigan.

                                        YB 16/9/54

410 AMERICA Amc Inc/ Roe/   K-3180.

Allard Motor Company, Inc.
141 West 53rd Street,
New York 19., N.Y.   File No. 428.

Ordered 25-8-52. Invoice S-2342. CD3 MM-792118. Dlvd 8-1-53.
ALLARD K3 ROADSTER LHD: M.G. Red, black leather upholstery.
                          Less engine; Cadillac modification.
                          5 Wire Wheels.
                          CHASSIS NO. K-3178.

1st: L.B. Bartlett., Waterman Ave at Red Bridge, Providence, R.I.

2nd: Col. John G. Fowler, 3601 Connecticutt Ave N.W., Washington,
                                                          D.C.

PALL MALL DEPOSIT.   ss AMERICAN PRODUCER.   Closing 12-1-53.
Freight £   Docs .. 16-1-53

                                        YB 16/9/54

404 AMERICA Amc Inc/ Bartlett/ Fowler/   K-3178

ALLARD MOTOR CO. INC.
141, West 53rd. Street.
New York 19.N.Y.   File No.612.

Ordered 2-9-52. Invoice S-2448. CD3 MM-792207. Dlvd 14-5-53.

ALLARD K3 ROADSTER LHD   Colour Gunmetal,red leather upholstery.
                        Less engine, Cadillac Modification.

                        CHASSIS NO. K-3181.

PALL MALL DEPOSIT   ss AMERICAN FLYER.   Closing 14-5-53
Freight £ 211-4-5 also K-3184   Docs. 27-5-53
mo   8/50. 81   3184
                       3197
                       3179

456 AMERICA AMC INC   K-3181

Allard Motor Company, Inc.
141 West 53rd Street,
New York 19., N.Y.   File No. 390.

Ordered 2-7-52. Invoice S-2471. CD3 MM-792236. Dlvd 14-5-53.
ALLARD K3 ROADSTER LHD: Red, black leather upholstery.
                          Less engine; Chrysler modification.
                          Carburettor airscoop. Disc wheels.
                          CHASSIS NO. K-3179.

DEALER: Knauz Motor Sales Inc., 1060 N. Western Ave, Lake Forest,
                                                        Illinois.

Wayne F. Potter, The Potter Co., 1950 Sheridan Rd, Chicago North,
Fred Woods, 9611 S. Springfield, Evergreen Park, Chic   Illinois.
                                                   -ago 42.
PALL MALL DEPOSIT.   ss AMERICAN FLYER.   Closing 14-5-53.
Freight £211-4-5 (4 cars i.e. K-3181/3184/3197) Docs 27-5-53.

450 AMERICA Amc Inc/ Knauz/ Potter/Woods/   K-3179

NOEL KIRK MOTORS.,
7176, Sunset Boulevard,
Hollywood 46., California.   File No. 447.

Ordered 9-9-52. Invoice S-2455. MM-792212. Dlvd 25-5-53.
ALLARD K3 ROADSTER LHD: Colour Red, black leather upholstery.
                          Less engine. Cadillac modification.
                          Disc wheels.
                          CHASSIS NO. K-3182.

PALL MALL DEPOSIT: ss DRINA LOCH GARTH.... Sailing Closing 3-7-53.
Freight £62-9-8   Docs 9-7-53.

E. Ritter,   El Monte, calif.

451 AMERICA Noel Kirk Motors. (E. Ritter)   K-3182

Allard Motor Company, Inc.
141 West 53rd Street,
New York 19., New York.   File No: 448.

Ordered 9-9-53. Invoice S-2377. CD3 MM-792131. Dlvd 24-2-53.
ALLARD K3 ROADSTER LHD: Cadet Grey, red leather upholstery.
                          Less engine. Cadillac modification.
                     CHASSIS NO: K-3183.

DAVIES TURNER.   ss ALSATIA.   Closing 24-2-53.
Freight £54-17-9d.   Docs   6-3-53. CA/02/0739.

Dr. R.N. Sabourin., Keith-Albee Building, Flushing 54., New York.

414 AMERICA Amc Inc/ Sabourin/   K-3183.

Noel Kirk Motors.,
7176, Sunset Boulevard,
Hollywood 46., California.   File No: 464.

Ordered 9-9-52. Invoice S-2460. CD3 MM-792210. Dlvd 25-5-53.
ALLARD K3 ROADSTER LHD: Turquoise Blue, blue leather upholstery.
                          Less engine. Cadillac modification.
                     CHASSIS NO: K-3186.   (disc wheels)

PALL MALL DEPOSIT.   ss LOCH GARTH.   Closing 25-5-53.
Freight £70. 0. 0.d.   Docs   30-5-53.

J.P. Dallas, 8511 Vicksberg, Los Angeles 45., California.
(Supervisor, Equipment Test Laboratory – Hughes Tool Company,
                                    Culver City, California)

452 AMERICA Kirk Motors/ Dallas/   K-3186.

Allard Motor Company, Inc.
141 West 53rd Street,
New York 19., N.Y.   File No. 620.

Ordered 16-9-52. Invoice S-2450. CD3 MM-792208. Dlvd 14-5-53.
ALLARD K3 ROADSTER LHD: Black, tan leather upholstery.
                          Less engine. Cadillac modification.
                          (* originally Bronze, repainted AMC)
                     CHASSIS NO. K-3184.

Lt. Charles B. Gillett Jr., U.S. Naval Amphibian Base,
                          Little Creek., Virginia.

PALL MALL DEPOSIT. ss AMERICAN FLYER.   Closing 14-5-53
Freight £211-4-5 (K-3181/3197/3179)   Docs   27-5-53.

458 AMERICA Amc Inc / Gillett/   K-3184.

ALLARD MOTOR COMPANY, INC.
141 West 53rd Street,
NEW YORK 19., N.Y.   File No. 599.

Ordered 1-7-52. Invoice S-2407. CD3 MM-792146. Dlvd /3/53.
ALLARD K3 ROADSTER LHD: Cream, black leather upholstery.
                          Less engine. Chrysler modification.
                          CHASSIS NO. K-3187.

PALL MALL DEPOSIT : ss AM. PAINTER   Closing 18/3/53.
Freight £   Docs   /3/53.

Ernie Kovacs, 289 Lantana Avenue, Englewood, N.J.

426 AMERICA AMC INC (E. Kovacs,)   K-3187.

Allard Motor Company, Inc.
141 West 53rd Street,
NEW YORK 19., N.Y.   File No. 492.

Ordered 12-11-52. Invoice S-2435. CD3 MM-792193. Dlvd 22-4-53.
ALLARD K3 MOTOR CAR LHD: Pacific green, brown leather upholstery
                           Cadillac modification. Less engine.
                           Disc wheels. CHASSIS NO. K-3185.

PALL MALL DEPOSIT: AMERICAN BANKER. Closing 22-4-53.
Freight £128-12-2 } also   Docs .. 28-4-53.
ms $34.98   } J-3158

H.T. Chickering, P.O. Box 3423, Daytona Beach, Florida.

438 AMERICA Amc Inc. (H.T. CHICKERING/)   K-3185.

JORGE BARRANCO & CO.,
Niza 35.,
MEXICO D.F., MEXICO.   File No. 600.

Ordered 24-10-52. Invoice S-2408. CD3 MM-792147. Dlvd 14/3/53
ALLARD K3 ROADSTER LHD: Pacific green, tan leather.
                          Less engine. Chrysler modification.
                          Wire wheels. CHASSIS NO. K-3188.

PALL MALL DEPOSIT : ss TRADER. Closing 16-3-53 at Liverpool.
Freight £73-19-2   Docs .. 30-3-53.

427 MEXICO Barranco.   K-3188.

Allard Motor Company, Inc.
141 West 53rd Street,
New York 19., New York.   File No. 481.

Ordered 24-10-52. Invoice S-2379. CD3 MM-792133. Dlvd 18-3-53.
ALLARD K3 ROADSTER LHD: Silver Grey, green leather upholstery.
                          Less engine. Chrysler Modification.
                          CHASSIS NO. K-3189.

LEP TRANSPORT.   ss AMERICAN PLANTER.   Closing 18-3-53.
Freight £58. 0. 0d.   Docs   21-3-53.

Leonard D. Henry, 19 East 72nd Street, New York 21., New York.

415 AMERICA Amc Inc/ Henry/   K-3189.

NOEL KIRK MOTORS.,
7176, Sunset Boulevard,
Hollywood 46., Calif.   File No. 471.

Ordered 10-10-52. Invoice S-2459. CD3 MM-792211. Dlvd 9-7-53.
ALLARD K3 ROADSTER LHD: Colour green, green leather upholstery.
                          Less engine, Cadillac modification.
                          Pressed steel disc wheels.
                          CHASSIS NO. K-3192.

PALL MALL DEPOSIT: ss Dongedyk.   Closing 9-7-53.
Freight £   Docs   -7-53.

          Schacht

Dan Schacht, 736 Cloverdale., Los Angeles., Calif.

453 AMERICA Noel Kirk Motors. (Schacht) Schacht/   K-3192.

Allard Motor Company, Inc.
141 West 53rd Street,
New York 19., New York.   File No: 601.

Ordered 1-7-52. Invoice S-2411. CD3 MM-792142. Dlvd 19-3-53.
ALLARD K3 ROADSTER LHD: Colour Bronze, tan leather upholstery.
                          Less engine. Chrysler modification.
                          Wire wheels. Power bulge.
                          CHASSIS NO: K-3190.

Pall Mall Deposit.   ss QUEEN MARY.   Closing 19-3-53.
Freight £149. 3. 3d.   Docs   23-3-53.
* Required for New York Sportsmans Car Show.

S. Phillips., Gin Lane, Southampton., Long Island., New York.

421 AMERICA Amc Inc/ Phillips/   K-3190.

Noel Kirk Motors.,
7176 Sunset Boulevard,
Hollywood 46., Calif.   File No. 472.

Ordered 10-10-52. Invoice S-2456. CD3 MM-792213. Dlvd 9-7-53.
ALLARD K3 ROADSTER LHD: Crimson, buff leather upholstery.
                          Less engine; Cadillac modification.
                          CHASSIS NO. K-3193.   Disc wheels.

Andre Challé., P.O. Box 241., San Jose., Costa Rica.

PALL MALL DEPOSIT.   ss DONGEDYK.   Closing 9-7-53.
Freight £   Docs   14-7-53.

    Re Imported: at Marqulis, Dec 1973 - very rough.

454 COSTA RICA KirkMotors/ Challé/   K-3193

BRITISH MOTOR CAR DISTRIBUTORS LTD.,
214 Van Ness Avenue,
SAN FRANCISCO 2., CALIFORNIA., U.S.A   File No. 392.

Ordered 2-7-52. Invoice S-2433. CD3 MM-792139. Dlvd 23-4-53.
ALLARD K3 MOTOR CAR LHD: Silver, red leather upholstery.
                           CHRYSLER modification. Less engine.
                           Steel disc wheels.
                           CHASSIS NO. K-3191.

PALL MALL DEPOSIT. ss DARRO. Closing for cargo 24-4-53.
Freight £61-9-6   Docs   6-4-53.

Henry LOFGREN, 662 -5A Beck Street, Oakland, Calif.

Henry Lofgren., 662 -5A Beck Street, Oakland., California.

440 AMERICA BMCD Ltd /Lofgren/   K-3191.

Lawrence W. Richards., Esq.
Allard Motor Co, Inc.
141 West 53rd Street,
NEW YORK 19., N.Y.   File No. 589.

25-2-53. Ordered. Invoice S-2423. CD3 JJ-88392. Dlvd 8-4-53.
ALLARD K3 ROADSTER LHD: Colour Wine, black leather upholstery.
                          Less engine. Cadillac modification.
                          Wire wheels. (chromed type to follow)
                          Alfin drums (to follow). Lincoln gears.
                          CHASSIS NO. K-3194.

LEP TRANSPORT.   ss AM. MANUFACTURER.   Closing 8-4-53.
Freight £116-16-1 } also   Docs   16-4-53.
                  } 2-5074
                  } 5-3155

George Saunders, Thermodyne Corpn, 589 Mountain Avenue,
                                   No. Caldwell, N.J.

435 AMERICA Amc Inc (Richards) (Saunders/.)   K-3194.

Card 1 (top left):

Noel Kirk Motors.,
7176 Sunset Boulevard,
Hollywood 46., Calif.   File No. 639

Ordered 24-7-53. Invoice S-2511. CD3 MM-792252. Dlvd 7-8-53.
ALLARD K3 ROADSTER LHD: Dark Blue, red leather upholstery.
                          5 Wire Wheels. Less engine, Cad modfn.
                          CHASSIS NO. K-3195.

Pall Mall Deposit. ss LOCH AVON. Closing for cargo 22-8-53.
Freight £230-14-7 (4 cars i.e. K-3268/3260/ Z-5137) Docs 9-9-53.

Wm. A. Wallace, P.O. Box 457., Cathedral City., California.
" "   also   P.O. Box 2175, Anchorage., Alaska.

486 AMERICA KirkMotors/ Wallace/   K-3195

Card 2 (top right):

ALLARD MOTOR COMPANY INC.
141 West 53rd Street,
New York. 19.N.Y.   File No. 509

Ordered 14-4-53   Invoice S-2451. CD/3 MM-792204. Dlvd 20-5-53

ALLARD K3 ROADSTER LHD: Colour bronze, red leather upholstery.
                          Less engine, Cadillac modification.
                          Disc wheels.
                          CHASSIS NO. K-3198

PALL MALL DEPOSIT: ss AMERICAN HARVESTER. Closing 20-5-53
Freight £   Docs   5-53

461 AMERICA AMC INC.   K-3198

Card 3 (middle left):

KIRK MOTORS.,
7176 Sunset Boulevard,
Hollywood 46., California.   File No. 473.

Ordered 10-10-52. Invoice S-2440. CD3 MM-792198. Dlvd 27-4-53.
ALLARD K3 ROADSTER LHD: Blue, blue leather upholstery.
                         Less engine. Cadillac modification.
                         Steel disc wheels.
                         CHASSIS NO. K-3196.

PALL MALL DEPOSIT: ss LOCH AVON. Closing 28-4-53.
Freight £   Docs   -5-53.
Robert L. Downey
Client:- Mr Downey, 6032 Ventura Canon Ave, Van Nuys., Calif.

448 AMERICA Kirk Motors. (Downey) Downey/   K-3196

Card 4 (middle right):

ALLARD MOTOR COMPANY, INC.
141 West 53rd Street,
NEW YORK 19., N.Y.   File No. 634

Ordered 19-6-53. Invoice S-2487. CD3 MM-792241. Dlvd 26-6-53.
ALLARD K3 MOTOR CAR LHD: Bronze, tan leather upholstery.
                           Less engine. Chrysler modification.
                           Steel wheels.
                           CHASSIS NO. K-3199.

PALL MALL DEPOSIT.

PALL MALL.   AM. HARVESTER. Closing 26-6-53.
Freight £54. 1. 9 Ins. $12.91.   Docs 30-6-53.

470 AMERICA AMC INC   K-3199

Card 5 (bottom left):

ALLARD MOTOR COMPANY INC.
141, West 53rd Street,
New York. 19.N.Y.   File No.612

Ordered 29-4-53. Invoice S-2442. CD/3 MM-792205. Dlvd. 14/5/53

ALLARD K3 ROADSTER LHD: Colour blue, blue leather upholstery
                          Less engine, Cadillac modification.

                          CHASSIS NO. K-3197.

PALL MALL DEPOSIT: ss AMERICAN FLYER. Closing 14-5-53
Freight £ 24-4-5 } K-3181
Ins $50.81 } K-3184 collectively
            } K-3179

457 AMERICA AMC INC.   K-3197

Card 6 (bottom right):

ALLARD MOTOR COMPANY, INC.
141 West 53rd Street,
NEW YORK 19., N.Y.   File No. 617

Ordered 22-5-53. Invoice S-2446. CD3 MM-792201. Dlvd 28-4-53.
ALLARD K3 ROADSTER LHD: Metallic blue, red leather upholstery.
                          6 Chrome wire wheels & whitewall tyres
                              re Dr. Samuel L. Scher.
                          Cadillac modification. Less engine.
                          CHASSIS NO. K-3250.

PALL MALL DEPOSIT: ss AMERICAN LEADER. Closing 28-4-53.
Freight £53-1-9   Docs 6-5-53.
Ins. $13.45.

Earle A. Wiener (Co), 920/930 Harding Way West, Galion, Ohio.

447 AMERICA AMC INC. (Earle A. Wiener) Wiener/   K-3250

Brigadier General Kern D. Metzger., USAF.
Headquarters,
AIR MATERIAL COMMAND.,
Wright-Patterson Air Force Base,
DAYTON., OHIO., U.S.A.   File No. 527.

Ordered 5-1-53. Invoice S-2444. CD3 MM-792200. Dlvd -5-53.
ALLARD K3 ROADSTER LHD: Colour metallic blue, red leather.
                          Cad mod & installation. Wire wheels.
                          Power bulge. Trafficators & flashers.
                          Tonneau. Spotlamp. Fender mirror.
                          CADILLAC ENGINE NO. 9S 1509. Hydramatic.
                          CHASSIS NO. K-3251.

AMERICAN MANUFACTURER.
USAF Military Vessel ss ....   SHIPPERS: Ruislip AFB.
Freight forward. (payable by USAF)   Docs ...... 5-5-53.

444 AMERICA General Metzger/   K-3251.

MOTORESEARCH COMPANY.,
1600, Junction Avenue,
Racine., Wisconsin, U.S.A.   File No. 540.

Ordered 6-1-53. Invoice S-2473. CD3 MM-792237. Dlvd 25-5-53.
ALLARD K3 TYPE MOTOR CAR LHD: Colour red, grey leather upholstery.
                                Less engine. Lincoln modification.
                                Wire wheels.
                                CHASSIS NO. K-3254.

                          DRINA   Sailed
PALL MALL DEPOSIT. ss LOCH GARTH.   Closing 3-7-53.
Freight £62-9-8   Docs   9-7-53.

Raymond A. Wolff., 2577 No. Teutonia Ave., Milwaukee., Wisconsin.

474 AMERICA Motoresearch. /Wolff/   K-3254.

Major General John P. McConnell.,
Commanding 7th Air Division.,
Ruislip Air Force Base.,
Victoria Park Estate.,
South Ruislip., Middlesex.   File No. 369.

Ordered 11-6-52. Invoice S-2367. CD3 MM-792129. Dlvd 6-2-53.
ALLARD K3 ROADSTER LHD: Colour Biscuit, red leather.
                          Steel wheels.
                          Cadillac Engine No. 8R-394.
                          Registration No. NXC 617.
                          CHASSIS NO. K-3252.

Exported from Southampton – U.S. Military Freighter 21-3-53.

U.S. ADDRESS: Offutt AFB., Omaha., Nebraska. (Strategic Air Force)

407 AMERICA General McConnell/   K-3252.

CUSTOM AUTOMOTIVE.,
2122, North Pearl Street;
DALLAS., TEXAS., U.S.A.   File No. 608.

Ordered 5-3-53. Invoice S-2544. CD3 MM-792271. Dlvd 14-9-53.
ALLARD K3 ROADSTER LHD: Colour red, black leather upholstery.
                          Less engine. NO MODIFICATION although
                          Lincoln engine installation planned.
                          5 WIRE WHEELS. 12 volt Gen & coil.
                          CHASSIS NO. K-3255.

PALL MALL DEPOSIT. ss DEERPOOL. Closing 17-9-53.
Freight £60-4-4   Docs 29 -9-53.

493 AMERICA Custom Auto   K-3255.

Allard Motor Company, Inc.
141 West 53rd Street,
New York 19., N.Y.   File No. 627.

Ordered 6-6-53. Invoice S-2548. CD3 MM-792274. Dlvd 23-9-53.
ALLARD K3 ROADSTER LHD: Pacific Green, green leather upholstery.
                          Less engine. 12 v. generator & coil.
                          No modification.
                          CHASSIS NO. K-3253.

Pall Mall Deposit. ss AM. FLYER. Closing 23-9-53
Freight £117-3-0 also K3277 Docs 5-10-53

501 AMERICA Amc Inc   K-3253

Mrs. Kamalina Sarabhai.,
BAKUBHAI & AMBALAL LTD.,
Baltic Exchange Chambers,
24, St Mary Axe, London. E.C.3.   File No. 538.

Ordered 2-2-53. Invoice S-2370.   HOME DELIVERY 29-5-53.
ALLARD K3 MOTOR CAR RHD: Colour Black, red leather upholstery.
                           CHASSIS NO. K-3256.
                           ENGINE NO. 7797600.
                           REGISTRATION NO. NXC 692.

Shippers: Pall Mall.   ss DONGOLA. Closing 17-9-/53.
Freight forward.   Docs .. 20/9/53.

Gautam Sarabhai., Post Box 28., Ahmedabad., India.

429 INDIA Sarabhai/   3K-3256

Noel Kirk Motors.,
7176 Sunset Boulevard.,
Hollywood 46., Calif.   File No. 545.

Ordered 21-1-53. Invoice S-2400. CD3 MM-792141. Dlvd 2-4-53.
ALLARD K3 ROADSTER LHD: Oatmeal, brown leather upholstery.
                          Wire wheels. Heater. Special Rayon hood.
                          CHRYSLER ENGINE NO. C53-8-1033.
                          CHASSIS NO. K-3257. REGISTRATION NO:
Home Delivery: Temporary use in U.K.   NXC 698

John E. Burrell Jr., 522 San Francisco Ave, Long Beach 12., Calif.

PALL MALL DEPOSIT.   ss DRINA.   Closing 26-6-53.
Freight £62.-9.-8d.   Docs   9-7-53.

2nd Owner: Mr. Jack Whalen, Hotel Carlsbad, Carlsbad., Calif.

424 AMERICA KirkMotors/ Burrell/Whalen/   K-3257

NOEL KIRK MOTORS.,
7176, Sunset Boulevard,
Hollywood 46., California.   File No. 537.

Ordered 1-1-53. Invoice S-2536. CD3 MM-792268. Dlvd 16-9-53.
ALLARD K3 ROADSTER LHD: Colour light Blue, blue leather.
                          Less engine. Cad eng. & hyd. modification
                          5 WIRE WHEELS.
                          CHASSIS NO. K-3261.

PALL MALL DEPOSIT: ss LOCH GARTH.   Closing 22-9-53.
Freight £ 63-2-6   Docs   5-10-53.

David B. Sanderson., NIKE Guided Missile Project, Las Cruces.,
                                                     New Mexico.

499 AMERICA Kirk Motors /Sanderson/   K-3261

Mr. Harry Steele,
P.O. Box 844.,
Wickenburg, Arizona, U.S.A.   File No. 561.

Ordered 9-2-53. Invoice S-2503. CD3 MM-792255. Dlvd 7-8-53.
ALLARD K3 ROADSTER LHD: Primer, beige leather upholstery.
                          Less engine. No modification, although
                          Lincoln installation planned by client.
                          5 wire wheels. 12 volt generator & coil.
                          Less tyres & tubes. Packed in case.

PALL MALL DEPOSIT. ss DALEDYK.   Closing 7-8-53.
Freight & packing £102-0-0   Docs 22-8-53.

* Shipped by Steele direct to Pasadena Lincoln/Mercury dealer.
  Manager Howard Scheib, City Lincoln Mercury, Pasadena, Calif.

476 AMERICA Harry Steele. /Scheib/   K-3259.

ALLARD MOTOR COMPANY, INC.
141 West 53rd Street,
New York 19., N.Y., U.S.A.   File No. 579.

Ordered 19-2-53. Invoice S-2489. CD3 MM-792243. Dlvd /7/53.
ALLARD K3 MOTOR CAR, LHD: Pacific green, green leather.
                            Less engine. Cadillac modification.
                            Steel wheels.
                            CHASSIS NO. K-3262.

PALL MALL DEPOSIT. ss AMERICAN PRODUCER. Closing 8/15-7-53.
Docs 28/7/53.   Freight £ 237-7-11 (5 cars)

Robert J. Wilson, 925 Madison Ave, Painsville, Ohio.

471 AMERICA AMC INC. (Robert J. Wilson) Wilson/   K-3262.

Noel Kirk Motors.,
7176 Sunset Boulevard,
Hollywood 46., Calif.   File No. 635.

Ordered 24-7-53. Invoice S-2528. CD3 MM-792265. Dlvd 21-8-53.
ALLARD K3 ROADSTER LHD: Red, tan leather upholstery.
                          Less engine; Cadillac modification.
                          Wire wheels. Cadillac hydramatic modfn.
                          CHASSIS NO. K-3260.

Pall Mall Deposit. ss LOCH AVON.   Closing 22-8-53.
Freight £230-14-7 (4 cars i.e. K-3268/3195/ Z-5137) Docs 4-9-53.

A.T. Smith., Peninsular Oil & Burner Co., 600 Park Avenue,
                                     San Jose., California.

492 AMERICA KirkMotors/ Smith/   K-3260

ALLARD MOTOR COMPANY, INC.
141 West 53rd Street,
NEW YORK 19., N.Y.   File No. 590.

Ordered 25-2-53. Invoice S-2496. CD3 MM-792245. Dlvd /7/53.
ALLARD K3 MOTOR CAR LHD: White, black leather upholstery.
                           Wire wheels. Less engine. Cad modfctn.
                           CHASSIS NO. K-3266.

PALL MALL DEPOSIT. ss AMERICAN PRODUCER. Closing 8-15/7/53.
Freight £ 237-7-11 (5 cars)   Docs   28 /7/53.

472 AMERICA AMC INC.   K-3266.

rds

Card 1

Allard Motor Company, Inc.
141 West 53rd Street,
New York 19., N.Y.   File No. 591.

Ordered 25-2-53. Invoice S-2508. CD3 MM-792251. Dlvd 5-8-53.
ALLARD K3 ROADSTER LHD: White, black leather upholstery.
                          Less engine: Cadillac modification.
                          5 Wire Wheels, hubs & caps.
                          CHASSIS NO. K-3267.

Pall Mall Deposit. ss AMERICAN HARVESTER. Closing 7-8-53.
£Freight 93-15-2d.   Docs ..13-8-53.
Clinton Lindburg, Forest Cadillac Co.,
                  7733 Forsyth Boulevard, Clayton., Missouri.

Charles M. Huttig, Jr.

                                        St. Louis, Mo.

488 AMERICA Amc Inc / Lindburg/Huttig/   K-3267

Card 2

BARON JEAN du FOUR.,
273 Avenue de Tervueren,
Bruxelles, Belgium.   File No. 410.

Ordered 21-8-52. Invoice S-2479. CD3 MM-792015. Dlvd 30-5-53.
ALLARD K3 MOTOR CAR LHD: Metallic blue, red leather upholstery.
                           Less engine CADILLAC ENG.NO. 2K-23
                           "   "   "   1460088.
                           Wire wheels. H.M.V. Radio.
                           CHASSIS NO. K-3270

PALL MALL DEPOSIT. ss CITY OF BRUSSELS. Closing 30-5-53.
Freight £   Docs   -6-53.

DEALER: Paul E. Cousin S.A., 239 Ch. de Charleroi, Bruxelles.

475 BELGIUM Baron du Four (Cousin)   K-3270

Card 3

Noel Kirk Motors.,
7175 Sunset Boulevard,
Hollywood 46., Calif.   File No. 592.

Ordered 2-3-53. Invoice S-2518. CD3 MM-792257. Dlvd 22-8-53.
ALLARD K3 ROADSTER LHD: Blue, red leather upholstery.
                          Less engine: Cadillac modification.
                          Wire wheels. Carburettor airscoop.
                          CHASSIS NO. K-3268.

Wm. R. Hervey, 458 So. Spring Street, Los Angeles., California.

PALL MALL DEPOSIT.   ss LOCH AVON.   Closing 22-8-53.
Freight £230-14-7 (K-3260/3195/5137) Docs .. 4-9-53.

478 AMERICA KirkMotors / Hervey/   K-3268

Card 4

Colonel Alan Conway,
158 Grunebergweg,
FRANKFURT-Am-Main.,
GERMANY.   File No. 602.

Ordered 19-3-53. Invoice S-2502. CD3 MM-792247. Dlvd 24/7/53.
ALLARD K3 ROADSTER LHD: Larch Green, tan leather upholstery.
                          Wire wheels. Heater. Aluminium heads.
                          Ford V8 3622 cc Engine No. 7284986.
                          CHASSIS NO. K-3275.

PALL MALL DEPOSIT.   ss PINGUIN   Closing 24/7/53.
Freight £29-3-10   Docs 28/7/53.
   Col. Alan Conway, 6806 Meadow Lane, Chevy Chase, Maryland, U.S.A.

481 GERMANY Col. Conway/   K-3275

Card 5

DETROIT RACING EQUIPMENT CO.,
20181 Conant.,
DETROIT 34., MICHIGAN., U.S.A   File No. 596.

Ordered 10-3-53. Invoice S-2504. CD3 MM-792248. Dlvd 20-7-53.
ALLARD K3 ROADSTER LHD: Primer, red leather upholstery.
                          Cadillac modification. Hydramatic mod.
                          5 wire wheels. Heater & defroster.
                          Windscreen washer. Oil temperature gauge.
                          Locks on both doors. Opening ventilators.
                          CHASSIS NO. K-3269.

Client: L.K. Wildberg, Leader Electronics Inc.,
                       5713 Euclid Ave, Cleveland 3., Ohio.

PALL MALL DEPOSIT. ss AM. PRODUCER. Closing 15-7-53.
Freight £237-7-11 (5 cars).   Docs 28-7-53.

483 AMERICA AMC INC (Wildberg) (Detroit)   K-3269

Card 6

SPORTS CARS INC.,
579, Main Street,
Springfield 5., Mass.   File No. 622.

Client:- Frick Motors, 1000 Sunrise Highway, Long Island, N.Y.
Distributor: Allard Motor Co,Inc. 141 West 53rd St, New York, N.Y

Ordered 14-5-53. Invoice S-2546. CD3 MM-792273. Dlvd -9-53.
ALLARD K3 ROADSTER LHD: Colour Red, black leather upholstery.
                          Less engine, gearbox, driveshaft.
                          5 WIRE WHEELS.
                          CHASSIS NO. K-3277.

PALL MALL DEPOSIT.   ss AMERICAN FLYER.   Closing 22-9-53.
Freight £115-3-0 {also K3253   Docs 5-10-53.
J.W. Fisher, 193 Liberty Street, Newburgh., New York.

500 AMERICA Amc Inc / Fisher/   K-3277

Card 1 (File No. 650)

NOEL KIRK MOTORS.,
7176, Sunset Boulevard,
Hollywood 46., Calif.   File No. 650.

Ordered 2-11-53. Invoice S-2562. CD3 PP-889079. Dlvd 14-11-53
ALLARD K3 ROADSTER LHD: Red, black leather upholstery.
                          Cadillac mod. LESS ENGINE.
                          CHASSIS NO. K-3278.   Wire Wheels.

PALL MALL DEPOSIT. ss DRINA.   Closing 14-11-53.
Freight £ 169-2-2 } 3 cars   Docs   28-11-53.

512 AMERICA Noel Kirk Motors   K-3278.

Card 2 (File No. 651)

NOEL KIRK MOTORS.,
7176, Sunset Boulevard,
Hollywood 46., Calif.   File No. 651

Ordered 12-11-53. Invoice S-2561. CD3 PP-889078. Dlvd 14-11-53.
ALLARD K3 ROADSTER LHD: Black, black leather upholstery.
                          LESS ENGINE. Cad mod & hyd mod.
                          5 Wire Wheels.
                          CHASSIS NO. K-3282.

                          ** 1953 Show model.

PALL MALL DEPOSIT. ss DRINA.   Closing 14-11-53.
Freight £ 169-2-2 } 3 cars.   Docs   28-11-53.

511 AMERICA Noel Kirk Motors.   K-3282.

Card 3 (File No. 637)

Messrs. L. Bockh & Cia.,
Apartado 3756.,
San Isido A San Julian 11.,
Caracas., Venezuela.   File No. 637.

Ordered 22-6-53. Invoice S-2587. CD3 PP-889088. Dlvd 18-2-54.
ALLARD K3 ROADSTER LHD: Colour Ivory, red leather upholstery.
                          5 chrome wire wheels. 2 qts cellulose.
                          Cadillac Engine No. 2-S-584.
                          CHASSIS NO. K-3280.

Client: Bernardo R. Casanova., Valutini., Caracas., Venezuela.

PALL MALL DEPOSIT. ss TACOMA STAR. Closing 18-2-54.
Freight £75   Docs   -2-54.

* Drawback Duty on Cadillac engine – re-export.

Consignee (Forwarders): Taurel & Cia., La Guaira., Venezuela.

513 VENEZUELA Bockh /Valutini/   K-3280

Card 4 (File No. 661)

House of Allard.,
7176 Sunset Boulevard.,
Hollywood 46., California.   File No. 661.

Ordered 26-2-54. Invoice S-5002. CD3 PP-889092. Dlvd 5-4-54.
ALLARD K3 ROADSTER LHD: Pacific Green, green leather upholstery.
                          Less engine. Cadillac hydramatic mod.
                          Wire wheels, hubs & caps.
                          CHASSIS NO. K-3283.

PALL MALL DEPOSIT.   ss DESEADO.   Closing 6-4-54.
Freight £   Docs   -4-54.

514 AMERICA H of A/   K-3283

Card 5 (File No. 638)

Westmount Garage Reg'd,
244, Victoria Avenue,
Westmount., PQ., Canada.   File No. 638.

ALLARD K3 ROADSTER LHD: Colour dark Blue, red leather upholstery.
* repainted White.   5 Wire wheels, hubs & caps.
                          CADILLAC ENGINE NO. 2S- 799. (Drawback)
                          CHASSIS NO. K-3281.

PALL MALL DEPOSIT. ss BEAVERBURN. Closing 7-12-53.
Freight £   Docs   -12-53.

** via St John, New Brunswick. (Montreal closed for Season)
Mr. W.T. Leslie, c/o W.T. Lytle, 47 Rosedale Heights Drive,
                                          Toronto.
Order 28-5-53 Invoice S-2566. CD3 PP-889083. Dlvd 7-12-53.

514 CANADA Westmount/Leslie/   K-3281

Card 6 (File No. 671)

Westmount Garage Reg'd,
244, Victoria Avenue,
Westmount., Quebec., Canada.   File No. 671.

Ordered 5-4-54. Invoice ASL 5018. CD3 PP-889187. Dlvd 1?-?-54
ALLARD K3 ROADSTER LHD: Ice Box White, black leather upholstery.
                          Less Engine. Cadillac modification
                          Wire wheels. Lincoln gears. Extra paint.
                          CHASSIS NO: K-3284.

PALL MALL DEPOSIT.   ss BEAVERLODGE.   Closing 12-6-54.
Freight £52.-13.-4d.   Docs   25-6-54.

* originally ordered with Chrysler mod. by Amc Inc.

Duncan M. Hodgson, 523 Argyle Ave, Montreal, Quebec.

523 CANADA Westmount/ Hodgson/   K-3284.

PALM BEACH
29ᵗʰ MARCH 1952   Z5000 - Z5157 8/64

A.O.e member Mr J McLennan, New Zealand
claims ownership of 5158, therefore possibility
that other models exist, but not recorded

Letter to him, June 21ˢᵗ 1980, following request from Roy May.

Letter from Sweden, August 1985 refers to 21Z 5164 (see card)

Allard Motor Company, Inc.
141 West 53rd Street,
New York 19., N.Y.   File No. 470.

Ordered 10-10-52. Invoice S-2452. CD3 MM-792217. Dlvd 15-7-53.
ALLARD 21C PALM BEACH LHD: Cream, red leather upholstery.
                             Curved windshield. Wire wheels.
                             Sleeved down Consul. Bucket seats.
                             Engine No. EOTTA 70545.
                             CHASSIS NO. C-5006.

* Originally intended for Edgar S. DeMeyer, 65 Main Street,
                          Springfield 5., Massachusetts.

** Charles B. Wilson., Anatoak Farm, Milford Center, Ohio.

PALL MALL DEPOSIT.   ss AM. PRODUCER.   Closing 15-7-53.
Freight £237-7-11 (5 cars).   Docs   28-7-53.
*** Harry A. Kito, Joseph Skilken & Co, 383 South Third Street,
                                        Columbus 15., Ohio.

460 AMERICA Amc Inc/ DeMeyer/ Wilson/Kito/   C-5006.

Messrs. Ingvar BERGENGREN A.B.,
Lindhagensplan.,
STOCKHOLM., SWEDEN.   File No. 556.

ALLARD 21C PALM BEACH LHD: Colour red, red leather upholstery.
                             Curved windscreen. Disc wheels.
                             CHASSIS NO. 21C-5017.

Ordered 2-7-52. Invoice S-2472. Delivered 19th May 1953.
British Commercial Transport Co Ltd. ss MALMÖ Closing 15-5-53.
Freight forward.   Docs 18-5-53.

Odd Lundkvist, Gastrikegatan 11,
                 Stockholm Va, Sweden.

449 SWEDEN Bergengren. (Lundkvist)   C-5017.

Major Harry, Grant, Fisher. Jr.
1a., Lansdowne Walk.,
London. W.11.   File No. 395.

Ordered 2-7-52. Invoice S-2306. CD3 PP-889085. Dlvd 8-11-52.
ALLARD 21Z PALM BEACH LHD: Powder Blue, red leather upholstery.
                            Angular flat windshield.
                            Engine No. EOTTA 15807. NGP 971.
                            CHASSIS NO. Z-5025.

(Aide de Camp, General F.H. Griswold, Commanding Third Strategic AF
              Ruislip Air Force Base, Ruislip., Middlesex.)

* Exported to Germany via Dover/Ostend Ferry service 9-12-53.
  Clearance effected through A.A. Port Officer, Dover.

** New Address: Headquarters AMFE., Transportation Directorate.,
                                    Wiesbaden., Germany.

Dr. C.F. MacIntyre, c/o AMEXCO., Wiesbaden., Germany.

389 AMERICA Major Fisher/Dr. MacIntyre/   Z-5025.

Allard Motor Company, Inc.
141 West 53rd Street,
New York 19., N.Y.   File No. 470.
Ordered 10-10-52. Invoice S-2452. CD3 MM-792217. Dlvd 15-7-53.
ALLARD 21C PALM BEACH LHD: Cream, red leather upholstery.
                           Curved windshield. Wire wheels.
                           Sleeved down Consul. Bucket seats.
                           Engine No. EOTTA 70545.
                           CHASSIS NO. C-5006.

* Originally intended for Edgar S. DeMeyer, 65 Main Street,
                          Springfield 5., Massachusetts.

** Charles B. Wilson., Anatoak Farm, Milford Center, Ohio.

PALL MALL DEPOSIT. ss AM. PRODUCER. Closing 15-7-53.
Freight £237-7-11 (5 cars).   Docs   28-7-53.
*** Harry A. Kito, Joseph Skilken & Co, 383 South Third Street,
                                      Columbus 15., Ohio.
460 AMERICA Amc Inc/ DeMeyer/ Wilson/Kito/   C-5006.

Brig. General S.F. Giffin, USAF.
Dep. Dir. for Plans J-3.
HQ US EUCOM., (i.e. Frankfurt, Germany)
APO 128, c/o P.M., New York, N.Y.   File No. 402.

Ordered 14-7-52. Invoice S-2419. CD3 MM-792196. Dlvd 17-4-53.
ALLARD 21Z PALM BEACH LHD: Colour Green, green leather upholstery.
                           Curved windscreen.
                           CHASSIS NO. Z-5026.
                           ENGINE NO. EOTTA 37844.

PALL MALL DEPOSIT: m/v KRAUTSAND. Closing 17-4-53.
Freight £22-7-10.   Docs .. 23-4-53.

Clients tele: FRANKFURT MILITARY 7154. cr FRANKFURT 52221. (Home)

Freight £22-7-10. PM docs 23/4/53.

442 GERMANY General Giffin/   Z-5026.

Messrs. Ingvar BERGENGREN A.B.,
Lindhagensplan.,
STOCKHOLM., SWEDEN.   File No. 556.

ALLARD 21C PALM BEACH LHD: Colour red, red leather upholstery.
                           Curved windscreen. Disc wheels.
                           CHASSIS NO. 21C-5017.

Ordered 2-7-52. Invoice S-2472. Delivered 19th May 1953.
British Commercial Transport Co Ltd. ss MALMO   Closing 15-5-53.
Freight forward.   Docs   18-5-53.

Odd Lundkvist, Gastrikegatan 11,
                Stockholm Va, Sweden.

449 SWEDEN Bergengren. (Lundkvist)   C-5017.

Autohall Servette S.A.
Rue Liotard 48 bis,
Geneva.,
Switzerland.   File No. 517.

Ordered 3-12-52. Invoice S-2390. CD3 MM-792136. 4-3-53.

ALLARD 21Z PALM BEACH LHD: Red, grey leather upholstery.
                           Engine No. EOTTA 33285.
                           CHASSIS NO: 21Z-5027.

R & J. PARKS   ss BREST   Delivered 4-3-53.
                            Docs ... 9-3-53.

420 SWITZERLAND Autohall/   Z-5027.

Major Harry, Grant, Fisher. Jr.
1a., Lansdowne Walk.,
London. W.11.   File No. 395.
Ordered 2-7-52. Invoice S-2306. CD3 PP-889085. Dlvd 8-11-52.
ALLARD 21Z PALM BEACH LHD: Powder Blue, red leather upholstery.
                           Angular flat windshield.
                           Engine No. EOTTA 15807. NGP 971.
                           CHASSIS NO. Z-5025.

(Aide de Camp, General F.H. Griswold, Commanding Third Strategic AF
          Ruislip Air Force Base, Ruislip., Middlesex.)

* Exported to Germany via Dover/Ostend Ferry service 9-12-53.
  Clearance effected through A.A. Port Officer, Dover.

** New Address: Headquarters AMFE., Transportation Directorate.,
                                     Wiesbaden., Germany.

Dr. C.F. MacIntyre, c/o AMEXCO., Wiesbaden., Germany.

389 AMERICA Major Fisher/Dr. MacIntyre/   Z-5025.

ALLARD MOTOR COMPANY, INC.   (Sports Cars Inc.)
147 West 53rd Street,
NEW YORK 19., N.Y.   File No. 588.

Ordered 19-2-53. Invoice S-2385. CD3 MM-792134. Dlvd 23-2-53
ALLARD 21Z PALM BEACH LHD : Colour Bronze, brown leather.
                            CHASSIS NO. Z-5028.
                            ENGINE NO. EOTTA 13954.

PALL MALL DEPOSIT.   ss ALSATIA. Closing 24-2-53.
Freight £90-5-11   Docs .. 3-3-53.
                  2 cars
                  re KG3166

419 AMERICA AMC INC   Z-5028.

Allard Motor Company, Inc.
141 West 53rd Street,
New York 19., New York.   File No: 552.

Ordered 4-2-53. Invoice S-2364. CD3 MM-792128. Dlvd 4-2-53.
ALLARD 21Z PALM BEACH LHD: Peacock Blue, blue leather upholstery.
                           Wire wheels. Curved (new type) w/screen.
                           Engine No. EOTTA 28012.
                           CHASSIS NO: 21Z-5029.

LEP TRANSPORT.   ss AMERICAN FLYER.   Closing 4-2-53.
Freight £36.-8.-10d.   Docs 16-2-53.

Robert C. Edberg, 68 Indian Hill Road, Worcester, Massachusetts.

412 AMERICA Amc Inc/ Edberg/   Z-5029.

NOEL KIRK MOTORS.,
7176, Sunset Boulevard,
HOLLYWOOD 46., CALIF.   File No. 449.

Ordered 24-10-52. Invoice S-2517. CD3 MM-792254. Dlvd 7-8-53.
ALLARD 21Z PALM BEACH LHD: Colour maroon, tan leather upholstery.
                             5 wire wheels.
                             ENGINE NO. EOTTA 51009.
                             CHASSIS NO. Z-5054.

PALL MALL DEPOSIT. ss DALEDYK. Closing 7-8-53.
Freight £ 48-3-8   Docs 21-8-53.

L/Cmdr Patrick C. Doisey, NAMTC, PT MUGU,
Lt/Cmdr Patrick C.Doisey,   Port Hueneme, Calif.
NAMTC., PT MUGU., Port Hueneme., California.

490 AMERICA KIRK MOTORS (Cmdr. Doisey.),   Z-5054.

OVERSEAS EQUIPMENT CORPORATION.,
350 Fifth Avenue,
NEW YORK 1., N.Y.   File No. 446.

Ordered 3-9-52. Invoice S-2325. CD3 MM-792032. Dlvd 23/12/52.
ALLARD 21Z PALM BEACH MODEL LHD : Light blue, red leather.
                                   CHASSIS NO. Z-5038.
                                   ENGINE NO. EOTTA 24657.

LEP TRANSPORT   ss AMERICAN VETERAN. Closing 24-12-52.
Freight £ 38. 2. 1.   Docs ...... 30-12-52.

404 AMERICA O. E. Corpn. (AMC INC)   21Z-5038.

Liberto Pujol Maynou.,
3 Sur # 103.,
Puebla., Pue.,
Mexico.   File No. 491

Ordered 10-11-52. Invoice S-2334. CD3 MM-792202. Dlvd 20-5-53.
ALLARD 21Z PALM BEACH LHD: Light Blue, blue leather upholstery.
                             Curved windscreen. Disc wheels.
                             CHASSIS NO. Z-5061. EOTTA

LEP TRANSPORT. ss HISTORIAN. Closing Liverpool 22-6-53.
Freight £56-16-1d.   Docs .... 11-7-53.

443 MEXICO Liberto Pujol Maynou/   Z-5061

ALLARD MOTOR COMPANY, INC.
141 West 53rd Street,
NEW YORK 19., N.Y., U.S.A.   File No. 614.

Ordered 16-4-53. Invoice S-2426. CD3 MM-792194. Dlvd 22-4-53.
ALLARD 21Z PALM BEACH LHD: Red, red leather upholstery.
                             Curved windscreen.   ENGINE NO.
                             CHASSIS NO. Z-5039.   EOTTA 36423.

PALL MALL DEPOSIT. ss AMERICAN BANKER. Closing 22-4-53.
Freight £   Docs   -4-53.

Albert W. Martin, 45 Ronson Rd, Wilbraham, Mass.

437 AMERICA Amc Inc (A.W.Martin) Martin/   Z-5039.

CLARK SIMPKINS LIMITED.,
(Ford Main Distributors)
1345, West Georgia Street,
Vancouver 5., B.C., CANADA.   File No. 495.

Ordered 13-11-53. Invoice S-2510. CD3 MM-792253. Dlvd 7-8-53.
ALLARD 21Z PALM BEACH LHD: Colour Blue, red leather upholstery.
                             Engine No. Eotta 52035.
                             CHASSIS NO. Z-5064.

PALL MALL DEPOSIT. ss DALEDYK. Closing 7th August 1953.
Freight £46-13-10   Docs 21 August 1953.

489 CANADA Clarke Simpkins.   Z-5064.

Juan Riu., Panamerican Import.,
Edificio Hotel Tequendama.,
Carrera 13 No. 26-12.,
Bogota., Colombia., S. America.   File No. 513.

Ordered 17-10-52. Invoice S-2466. CD3 MM-792233. Dlvd 23-6-53
ALLARD 21Z PALM BEACH LHD: Blue, red leather upholstery.
                          Built in radio. Tonneau cover.
                          Curved windscreen. ENG NO. EOTTA
                          CHASSIS NO. Z-5070 44759

PALL MALL DEPOSIT ss AM. HARVESTER. Closing 23-6-53.
Freight £   Docs .. 30-6-53.

Sr. Jorge Saenz, c/o Obregón y Valenzuela, Edif.AKL.,
            Carrera 7a. con Calle 18., Bogota, Colombia

467 COLOMBIA Juan Riu/ Saenz/   Z-5070

AUTOHALL SERVETTE S.A.,
Rue Liotard 43 bis.,
Geneva., SWITZERLAND.   File No. 516.

Ordered 29-11-52. Invoice S-2405. CD3 MM-792144. Dlvd 17-3-53.
ALLARD 21C PALM BEACH LHD: Dorchester grey, red leather upholstery.
                          CHASSIS NO. C-5075.
                          ENGINE NO. Eotta 81337. (Consul)

R & J PARKS LTD. Allard Motor Co delivery to Newhaven Ferry.
                  ss BREST......
                  Docs 21/3/53.

428 SWITZERLAND Autohall.   C-5075

Noel Kirk Motors.,
7176 Sunset Boulevard,
Hollywood 46., Calif: File No. 441.

Ordered 2-9-52. Invoice S-2555. CD3 PP-889074. Dlvd 20-10-53.
ALLARD 21Z PALM BEACH LHD: Light blue, grey leather upholstery.
                          ENGINE NO. EOTTA 61271.

                          CHASSIS NO. Z-5071.

Client:-

PALL MALL DEPOSIT. ss PACIFIC UNITY. Delivered Manchester 20/10/
Freight £47-0-10.   Docs 3/10/53.   53.

505 AMERICA Kirk Motors   Z-5071.

Mr. Agustin Legoretta., (Director General, Banco Nacional de Mexico
1, La Catolica y V. Carranza.,   S.A.)
MEXICO D.F., MEXICO.   File No. 489.

Ordered 24-10-52. Invoice S-2488. CD3 MM-792242. Dlvd 6-7-53.

ALLARD 21Z PALM BEACH RHD: Red, red leather upholstery.
                              Wire wheels. Tonneau cover.
                              Fog & Spot Lamps. HMV Radio.
                              Lucas windshield washer.
                              CHASSIS NO. Z-5072.

                              ENGINE NO. EOTTA 47126.

Dealer: Jorge Barranco y Cia, Niza 35, Mexico D.F., Mexico.

PALL MALL DEPOSIT. ss HISTORIAN. Closing 6-7-53.
Freight £57-14-9   Docs 20-7-53.

473 MEXICO Legoretta (Barranco)   Z-5072.

Allard Motor Company, Inc.
141 West 53rd Street,
NEW YORK 19., N.Y.   File No. 613.

Ordered 8-4-53. Invoice S-2425. CD3 JJ-88391. Dlvd 8-4-53.
ALLARD 21Z PALM BEACH LHD: Colour grey, red leather upholstery.
                           CHASSIS NO. Z-5074.
                           ENGINE NO. EOTTA 36426.

LEP TRANSPORT   ss AM. MANUFACTURER.   Closing 8-4-53.
Freight £116-16-1 } also 5-3155   Docs 16-4-53.
                    K-3194

436 AMERICA Amc Inc   Z-5074.

Mr. Scott Fuller.,
658 Forest Avenue,
Larchmont., New York.   File No. 560.

Ordered 6-2-53. Invoice S-2432. CD3 MM-792199. Dlvd 14-4-53.
ALLARD 21C PALM BEACH LHD: Light Blue, blue leather upholstery.
                           Curved windscreen. Disc wheels.
                           Registration No. NXD 322.
                           Engine No. EOTA 85180.
                           CHASSIS NO. C-5081.

DEALER: Sports & Utility Motors Inc., 816 E. Boston Post Road,
                           Mamaroneck., New York.

THOMAS MEADOWS: ss AMERICAN MANUFACTURER.   Closing 21-5-53.
Freight (forward).   Docs 27-5-53.

445 AMERICA Brette Hannaway/Scott Fuller/   C-5081

Mr. Schweitzer.,
Petersham Garage Ltd.,
Petersham Mews,
Queensgate Place,
London. S.W.7.   (WESTERN 4107)

ALLARD 21Z PALM BEACH: Black, red leather upholstery.
                         3 carb. manifold. Twin exhausts.
Reg. No. KOK 56   One wing slightly dented, also bonnet.
Registered 11/4/53   Steel soled type of tyres; spare new.
TP525 RSP570   CHASSIS NO: 21Z-5102. *EOTTA 37330*

Original D. K. Scott - Manchester

                                    916 1662

27 Petersham Garage   21Z-5102

Tractor Specialties Limited.,
P.O. Box 2514.,
Auckland C.I., New Zealand.   File No. 642.

Ordered 19-8-53. Invoice S-2543. Delivered Packers
ALLARD 21X PALM BEACH RHD: Colour Bronze, brown leather.
                            ENGINE NO. EOTTA 55382.
                            CHASSIS NO. Z-5106.

PALL MALL DEPOSIT.   ss MATAROA.   Closing 14-9-53.
Freight & Packing £108   Docs 28 -9-53.

    B.F. Harris., Commerce Chambers., Frankton Junction., N.Z.

497 NEW ZEALAND Tracspecs /Harris/   Z-5106

Mr. William J. Hood.,
c/o U.S. Embassy,
Vienna., Austria.   File No. 623.

Ordered 18-5-53. Invoice S-2477. CD3 MM-792246. Dlvd 27/7/53.
ALLARD 21Z PALM BEACH LHD: Black, red leather upholstery.
                              ENGINE NO. Z-226228.
                              CHASSIS NO. 21Z-5103.

DEALER:- Brooklands of Bond St, 103 New Bond St, London. W.1.
PALL MALL DEPOSIT. (*by STARMIGAN*
Freight £33 -10-8.   (*Dover/Calais ferry 29*/7/53)
                              Docs 31/7/53.

480 AUSTRIA Hood/(Brooklands)   Z-5103

Messrs. Ingvar BERGENGREN A.B.,
Lindhagensplan.
STOCKHOLM. SWEDEN.   File No. 555.

ALLARD 21.Z. PALM BEACH. Colour *Oatmeal*, red leather upholstery.
                          Special curved windshield.
                          Engine No. EOTTA 47137.
                          Chassis No. Z-5117.
                          white wall tyres.
    Ordered. 6-2-53. Invoice No. S-2459.   Dlvd. 12-5-53
                                            8-7-53
British Commercial Transport. ss MALMO   Closing 12-5-53.
Freight forward   Docs.   -7-53

465 SWEDEN Bergengren.   Z-5117

PALM BEACH   REG No NYO 66

    N. F. STANDFAST
    10 ROLFE ST
       BRISBANE QLD
          AUSTRALIA

    Letter asking for information received July 9' 1992

                    Z 5104

Westmount Garage Reg'd.,
244 Victoria Avenue.,
Westmount., Quebec.   File No. 665.

Ordered 11-3-54. Invoice S-5007. CD3 PP-889177. Dlvd 5-4-54.
ALLARD 21Z PALM BEACH LHD: Dk Green, green leather upholstery.
                            Engine No. EOTTA 84132.
                            CHASSIS NO. Z-5118.

PALL MALL DEPOSIT.   ss VANDALIA.   Closing 5th April 1954.
Freight £   Docs   /4/54.

519 CANADA Westmount/   Z-5118.

House of Allard.,
7176 Sunset Boulevard.,
Hollywood 46., California.   File No. 658.

Ordered 26-2-54. Invoice S-5000. CD3 PP-889091. Dlvd 5-4-54.
ALLARD 21Z PALM BEACH LHD: Pale Green, green leather upholstery.
                            Engine No. EOTTA 68598. Disc wheels.
                            CHASSIS NO. Z-5119.

PALL MALL DEPOSIT   ss. DESEADO.   Closing 6-4-54.
Freight £   Docs ... -4-54.
Mr. Merwin Fischal, Colombia Broadcasting System, Inc.
                    6121 Sunset Boulevard,
                    Los Angeles 28., California.

515 AMERICA H of A./FISCHAL/   Z-5119

Antonio Izquierdo D.,
Apartado Nal 15-74.,
Bogota., Colombia.   File No. 655.

Ordered 24-2-54. Invoice ASL 5008 CD3 PP-389180 Dlvd 7-5-54.
ALLARD 21Z PALM BEACH LHD: Bronze, blue leather upholstery.
                            Wire wheels. Tonneau cover. Overdrive.
                            3 carb. manifold. Extra elec. fuel pump.
                            CHASSIS NO: Z-5122. (EOTTA 86249)Eng No

PALL MALL DEPOSIT   ss ARABY   Closing 7-5-54.
Freight £   Docs   -5-54.

521 COLOMBIA Izquierdo/   Z-5122.

House of Allard.,
7176 Sunset Boulevard.,
Hollywood 46., California.   File No. 659.

Ordered 26-2-54. Invoice S-5001. CD3 PP-889090. Dlvd 6-4-54.
ALLARD 21Z PALM BEACH LHD: Metallic grey, red leather upholstery.
                            Engine No. EOTTA 68600. Disc wheels.
                            CHASSIS NO. Z-5120.

PALL MALL DEPOSIT.   ss DESEADO.   Closing 6-4-54.
Freight £   Docs   -4-54.

Scotte Gray, 1436 Selby Avenue, Los Angeles 24., California.

(Scotte Gray, Inc. 111 North La Cienega Blvd, Beverly Hills, Calif.

516 AMERICA H of A./Scotte Gray/   Z-5120

Antonio Izquierdo D.,
Apartado Nal 15-74.,
Bogota., Colombia.   File No. 656.

Ordered 24-2-54. Invoice ASL 5009 CD3 PP-389179 Dlvd 7-5-54.
ALLARD 21Z PALM BEACH LHD: Silver grey, red leather upholstery.
                            Wire wheels. Tonneau cover. Radio.
                            Overdrive. 3 carb manifold. Extra pump
                            Engine No. EOTTA 87198.
                            CHASSIS NO: Z-5123.

PALL MALL DEPOSIT.   ss ARABY   Closing 7-5-54.
Freight £   Docs   -5-54.

522 COLOMBIA Izquierdo/   Z-5123.

Mr. N. Willoughby,
c/o Mene Grane Oil Co.,
Apartado 79.,
Barcelona, Anzoategui.,
VENEZUELA.   File No. 648

Ordered 2-11-53. Invoice S-2563. CD3 PP-889080. Dlvd 16-11-53.
ALLARD 21Z PALM BEACH LHD: Black, red leather upholstery.
                            Disc wheels.
                            ENGINE NO. EOTTA 65636.

                            CHASSIS NO. Z-5121.

PALL MALL DEPOSIT. ss GASCONY. Closing 16-11-53. (La Guaira)
Freight £60-19-9   Docs 14-12-53.

510 VENEZUELA Willoughby/   Z-5121

Tractor Specialties Limited.,
P.O. Box 2514.,
Auckland C.I., New Zealand.   File No. 662.

Ordered 2-3-54.   Invoice ASL-5011. CD3 n/a.   Dlvd 21-5-54.
ALLARD 21Z PALM BEACH RHD: Colour Red, grey leather upholstery.
                            Disc wheels. Standard specification.
                            Engine No. EOTTA 90976.
                            CHASSIS NO. 21Z- 5124.

PALL MALL DEPOSIT.   ss RHODESIA STAR.   Closing 21-5-54
Freight £79.-1.-10d.   Docs   -5-54

525 NEW ZEALAND Tracspecs/   Z-5124.

Card 1:

Tractor Specialties Limited.,
P.O. Box 2514.,
Auckland C.I., New Zealand.   File No. 663.

Ordered 2-3-54.   Invoice ASL-5012.   CD3 n/a.   Dlvd 21-5-54.
ALLARD 21Z PALM BEACH R.H.D.:   Red, grey leather upholstery.
                                Disc wheels. Standard specification
                                Engine No. EOTTA 91995.
                                CHASSIS NO. 21Z-5125.

PALL MALL DEPOSIT.   ss RHODESIA STAR.   Closing 21-5-54.
Freight £79.-1.-10d.   Docs   -5-54.

526 NEW ZEALAND Tracspecs/   Z-5125.

Card 2:

Tractor Specialties Ltd.,
P.O. Box 2514.,
Auckland C.I.,
New Zealand.   File No. 669.

Ordered 29-3-54.   ASL 5014.   CD3 n/a.   Delivered 4-6-54.
ALLARD 21Z PALM BEACH RHD: Dark Green, brown leather upholstery.
                             Disc wheels. Standard specification.
                             Engine No. EOTTA 93835.
                             CHASSIS NO: 21Z-5128.

PALL MALL DEPOSIT.   ss PIPIRIKI.   Closing 8-6-54.
Freight £73-6-9   Docs 25-6-54.

527 NEW ZEALAND Tracspecs/   Z-5128.

Card 3:

Mr. D.F. Sidnell.,
Cia. Shell de Venezuela.,
Apartado 19., Maracaibo.,
Venezuela.   File No. 673.

Ordered 4-5-54.   Invoice S-2636.   CD3 PP-889188.   Dlvd 17-6-54.
ALLARD 21Z PALM BEACH RHD: Off-White, red leather upholstery.
                             Wire wheels. 3 Zenith carb. manifold.
                             Overdrive. Radio. Le Mans headlamps.
                             Engine No. EOTTA 94306.
Pall Mall Deposit   REGISTRATION NO. OUL 641
American Reporter   CHASSIS NO: 21Z-5126.
Closing 30/4/54
Docs 12/5/54
HOME DELIVERY 17-6-54.   *Freight £84-8-0*

HOME ADDRESS: 48 New Street, Salisbury., Wilts.

also c/o B.C. Sidnell, 34 Meadowcroft Close, Horley., Surrey.
also c/o Miss E.A. Rossiter, 1 Hyde Park Gate Mews, London. S.W.7.

528 VENEZUELA Sidnell/   Z-5126.

Card 4:

Westmount Garage Reg'd.,
244, Victoria Avenue,
Westmount, P.Q., Canada.   File No: 666.

Ordered 11-3-54.   Invoice ASL-5020.   CD3 PP-889191.   Dlvd 21-7-54.
ALLARD 21Z PALM BEACH LHD: Colour Beige, tan leather upholstery.
                             Fitted with overdrive.
                             Engine No: EOTTA 96047.
                             CHASSIS NO: 21Z-5129.

PALL MALL DEPOSIT.   ss ADOLPH GLEUE.   Closing 22-7-54.
Freight £   Docs   -7-54.

Mr. Eugène Jousse, 3435 Broadway, Lachine., P.Q.

530 CANADA Westmount/Jousse/   Z-5129.

Card 5:

Antonio Izquierdo D.,
Apartado Nal 1574.,
Bogota., Colombia., S.A.   File No: 672.

Ordered 20-4-54.   Invoice ASL-5023.   CD3 PP-889192.   Dlvd 6-8-54
ALLARD 21Z PALM BEACH LHD: Colour pale-Green, green leather.
                             Fitted radio. Tonneau cover.
                             Elec. pump. 3 carburettor manifold.
                             Engine No: EOTTA 98324.
                             CHASSIS NO: 21Z-5127.

PALL MALL DEPOSIT.   ss ARABY   Closing 6-8-54
Freight £   Docs   -8-54

531 COLOMBIA Izquierdo/   Z-5127.

Card 6:

Edwin Mayer & Co., Limited.
Boite Postale No. 170.,
Tananarive., Madagascar.   File No. 683.

Ordered 12-8-54   Invoice ASL 5031.   CD3 PP-889197.   Dlvd 11-10-54.
ALLARD 21Z PALM BEACH RHD: Colour Dk Blue, red leather upholstery.
                             Tonneau cover. Overdrive. Wire wheels.
                             3 Carburettor Manifold.
                             ENGINE NO: EOTTA 105816.
                             CHASSIS NO: 21Z-5130.

PALL MALL DEPOSIT   (Bricklayers Arms to Dover/Dunkirk) 11-10-54
Freight £26-1-11.   Docs   -10-54

chassis number changed — see Z 5154.

535 MADAGASCAR Mayer   Z-5130.

Herbert N. Berge.,
7416 Harwood Avenue,
Milwaukee 13., Wisconsin.   File No: 679.

Ordered 29-6-54. Invoice ASL 5025. CD3 PP-889194. Dlvd 11-8-54
ALLARD 21Z PALM BEACH LHD: Grey, red leather upholstery.
                             6 Branch Exhaust Manifold.
                             3 Carburettor Manifold. Overdrive.
                             Lucas 'Flamethrower' road lamp.
                             Body 'underseal'. Electric clock.
                             Centre arm rest. Wing mirror. Tonneau.
                             ENGINE NO. EOTTA 97184.
                             CHASSIS NO: 21Z-5131.

PALL MALL DEPOSIT.   ss VESLEFJELL.   Closing 11-8-54
Freight £   Docs   -8-54

532 AMERICA Berge/   Z-5131.

L.H. PALACIOS N.V. (Inc)
P.O. Box 59., Curacao.,
Netherlands West Indies.   File No: 682.

Order 3-8-54 Inv.ASL 5033   CD3 PP-889199 Dlvd 24/11/54
ALLARD 21Z PALM BEACH LHD: Grey, maroon leather upholst.
                             Wire wheels. Radio. Tonneau.
                             Overdrive. 3 carb Manifold.
                             Eng.No: EOTTA 106970.
                             CHASSIS NO: 21Z-5136.

PALL MALL DEPOSIT   ss AM. FLYER.   Closing 24-11-54
Freight £84-10-0   Docs   2-12-54

539 CURACAO PALACIOS   Z-5136.

Antonio Izquierdo D.,
Apartado Nal 1574.,
Bogota., Colombia., S.A.   File No: 680.

Ordered 27-7-54. Invoice ASL-5028. CD3 PP-889198. Dlvd /10/54
ALLARD 21Z PALM BEACH LHD: Colour Ivory, red leather upholstery.
                             Wire wheels. RAYMOND MAYS CONVERSION.
                             Tonneau cover. Radio. extra Fuel pump.
                             ENGINE NO: EOTTA 103929.
                             CHASSIS NO: 21Z-5134.

IMPORT LICENCE NO: 070026.

PALL MALL DEPOSIT.   ss AM. FLYER   Closing 24/10/54
Freight £   Docs   -10-54

537 COLOMBIA Izquierdo/   Z-5134.

NOEL KIRK MOTORS
7176, Sunset Boulevard.
Hollywood 46. Calif. U.S.A.   File No: 442.

Ordered 2-8-52. Invoice S-2527. CD3 MM-792264. Dld 21-8-53

ALLARD 21Z TYPE MOTOR CAR: LHD.Colour ivory,black leather
                             Complete with engine. Tonneau
                             cover.
                             CHASSIS NO: Z-5137

PALL MALL DEPOSIT. ss LOCH AVON   Closing 21-8-53
Freight: 230-14-7(1(3268   Docs: 4-9-53
                    3260
              3195

                                  (SEE INSIDE)

494 AMERICA NOEL KIRK MOTORS.   Z-5137.

L.H. Palacios N.V. (Inc).,
P.O. Box 59., Curacao.,
Netherlands West Indies.   File No: 681.

Ordered 3-8-54. Invoice ASL 5026, CD3 PP-889195. Dlvd 21-9-54

ALLARD 21Z PALM BEACH LHD: Colour Ivory, red leather upholstery,
                             Wire wheels. Radio. Tonneau cover.
                             Overdrive. 3 Carburettor Manifold.
                             Engine No: EOTTA 101665.
                             CHASSIS NO: 21Z-5135.

PALL MALL DEPOSIT.   ss FALCON.   Closing 21-9-54.
Freight £84-10-0   Docs   2-9-54.

536 CURACAO Palacios/   Z-5135.

RAY'S INCORPORATED   Noel Kirk
4222 LATONA N.E.   Ivory, Black trim
SEATTLE, WASHINGTON   20 8 53

Allard Motor Co., Ltd.
57 Upper Richmond Rd.
S.W. 15 London, England

Dear Sirs:
   The facsimile below is of the nameplate of an
Allard sports car which we have contracted to
restore. The chassis identification number is
213 5137.
   Can you provide us with the shop manual, or advise
where one is available? Any data on Allard maintenance and restoration would be greatly appreciated.
                              Sincerely yours

Tractor Specialties Ltd.,
P.O. Box 2514.,
Auckland C.I., New Zealand.   File No. 597.

Ordered 13-3-53.   Invoice S-2462.   Delivered 26-5-53.
ALLARD 21Z PALM BEACH RHD: Colour Grey, red leather upholstery.
                            Curved windscreen.   Disc wheels.
                            Engine No. Eotta 42899.
                            CHASSIS NO. Z-5138.
LONDON AGENTS
A.P. & E. Singer Ltd, 16 Finsbury Square, London. E.C.2.

R.C. McDonald, Laura No. 2. R.D., Winton., New Zealand.

PALL MALL DEPOSIT.   ss KARAMEA.   Closing 26-5-53.
Freight £   Docs   3-6-53.

464 NEW ZEALAND Tracspecs/ McDonald/   Z-5138

Major General E.H. Underhill., USAF
DEPARTMENT OF THE AIR FORCE.,
JOINT TACTICAL AIR SUPPORT BOARD
Office of the Director,
FORT BRAGG., NORTH CAROLINA., U.S.A.   File No. 626

Ordered 4-6-53.   Invoice S-2512. CD3 MM-792226. Dlvd 27-8-53
ALLARD 21Z PALM BEACH LHD: Dark Blue, red leather upholstery.
                            Engine No: EOTTA 53258.
                            CHASSIS NO: 21Z-5143/3.

PALL MALL DEPOSIT.   ss BENWYVIS   Closing 27-8-53
Freight £75. 0. 0d.   Docs   2-10-53

482 JAPAN Maj. Gen. Underhill/   Z-5143/3

ALLARD MOTOR COMPANY, INC.
141 West 53rd Street,
NEW YORK 19., N.Y.   File No. 615.

Ordered 17-4-53. Invoice S-2509. CD3 MM-792250. Dlvd 5-8-53.
ALLARD 21Z PALM BEACH LHD: Colour white, blue leather upholstery.
                            Engine No. Eotta 52046.
                            CHASSIS NO. Z-5139.

PALL MALL DEPOSIT.   ss AM. HARVESTER.   Closing 5-8-53.
Freight £ 93-15-2 } also K5267   Docs 13-8-53.
          $23.07 }

H. Parker Mason, 525 Granville Street,
                               Newark, Ohio.
H. Parker Mason., 525 Granville Street, Newark., Ohio.

487 AMERICA AMC INC /Parker Mason/   Z-5139.

A.B. Ingvar BERGENGREN.,
Lindhagensplan.,
Stockholm., Sweden.   File No. 644.

Ordered 3-9-53. Invoice S-2541. Delivered 9th September 1953.

ALLARD 21Z PALM BEACH LHD: Colour Red, red leather upholstery.
                            ENGINE NO. EOTTA 55564.
                            CHASSIS NO. Z-5144.

BRITISH COMMERCIAL TRANSPORT CO.   ss FREJA. Closing 9-9-53.
Freight forward.   Docs   -9-53.

493 SWEDEN Bergengren.   Z-5144

TRACTOR SPECIALTIES LTD.,
P.O. Box 2514.,
Auckland C.I.,
NEW ZEALAND.   File No. 641.

Ordered 19-8-53. Invoice S-2542. Delivered Packers 2-9-53.

ALLARD 21Z PALM BEACH RHD: Colour Blue, grey leather upholstery.
                            Engine No. EOTTA 54624.
                            CHASSIS NO. Z-5142.

PALL MALL DEPOSIT: ss MATAROA.   Closing 14th September 1953.
Freight & Packing £ 103   Docs .. 28 September 1953.

496 NEW ZEALAND Tracspecs   Z-5142

Ingvar BERGENGREN A/B.,
Lindhagensplan.,
Stockholm.,
Sweden   File No. 645.

Ordered 3-9-53. Invoice S-2550. CD3 (nil). Delivered 24-9-53.
ALLARD 21Z PALM BEACH LHD: Red, black leather upholstery.
                            Wire wheels. Eng No. EOTTA 58513.
                            CHASSIS NO. 21Z-5145.

British Commercial Transport. ss BELE. Closing 24-9-53.
Freight forward.   Docs   30-9-53.

503 SWEDEN Bergengren.   Z-5145.

Noel Kirk Motors.,
7176, Sunset Boulevard,
Hollywood 46., Calif.   File No. 439.

Ordered 2-9-52. Invoice S-2557. CD3 PP-889076. Dlvd 2-11-53.
ALLARD 21Z PALM BEACH LHD: Ming (light) blue, blue leather.
                           Disc wheels.
                           Zephyr ENGINE NO. EOTTA 62299.
                           CHASSIS NO. Z-5146.

PALL MALL DEPOSIT. ss DONGEDYK. Closing 2-11-53.
Freight £ 45-4-6   Docs 14-11-53.

506 AMERICA Kirk Motors   Z-5146.

House of Allard.,
7176 Sunset Boulevard.,
Hollywood 46., California.   File No. 660.

Ordered 26-2-54. Invoice S-5003. CD3 PP-889089. Dlvd 5-4-54.
ALLARD 21Z PALM BEACH LHD: Cream, red leather upholstery.
                            Engine No. EOTTA 80788. Disc wheels.
                            CHASSIS NO. Z-5149.

PALL MALL DEPOSIT.   ss DESEADO.   Closing 6-4-54.
Freight £   Docs   -4-54.

517 AMERICA H of A./   Z-5149

Noel Kirk Motors.,
7176 Sunset Boulevard,
Hollywood 46., Calif.   File No. 440.

Ordered 2-9-52. Invoice S-2558. CD3 PP-889075. Dlvd 14-11-53.
ALLARD 21Z PALM BEACH LHD: Black, brown leather upholstery.
                           Disc wheels.
                           ENGINE NO. EOTTA 63589.
                           CHASSIS NO. Z-5147.

PALL MALL DEPOSIT. ss DRINA. Closing 14-11-53.
Freight £ 169-2-2 §3cars   Docs   28-11-53.

H.Richard Alexander., 1355 Westwood Blvd, Los Angeles 24, Calif.
(West Coast Manager, STRATOS Division-Fairchild Engine & Airplane
                     Bay Shore, L.I., New York.   Corpn.)

508 AMERICA Noel Kirk Motors./Alexander/   Z-5147.

Messrs. FACEL.,   (Tele: BALZAC 07-42)
19, Avenue George V.,   (Cable: FACEL-PARIS)
Paris 8., France.   File No. 646.

Ordered 6/7/53. Invoice 11605 AM. CD3 MM-792272. Dlvd 15-9-53.

ALLARD 21H PALMBEACH LHD: Chassis frame, front suspension,
                              rear axle, steering assembly, all
                              instruments, wheels. LESS TYRES,
                              Horn, BATTERIES.
                              (experimental chassis for the instal-
                              ation of Hotchkiss engine & French
                              produced bodywork.)
                              CHASSIS NO. 21H-5150.

General Transport, 13 Coopers Row, London. E.C.3. (Shippers)
Shipped Air Cargo - Flight No. 126., 16th September 1953.
                              Docs 17/9/53

425 FRANCE Facel-Metallon et Cie.   21H-5150

British Motor Car Distributors Ltd.,
214 Van Ness Avenue.,
SAN FRANCISCO 2., CALIFORNIA.   File No. 374.

Ordered 1st July 1952. Invoice S-2556. CD3 PP-889073.
ALLARD 21Z PALM BEACH LHD: Ivory, red leather upholstery.
                           ENGINE NO. EOTTA 61179.
                           CHASSIS NO. Z-5148.

Client:-
PALL MALL DEPOSIT. ss PACIFIC UNITY. Closing 23-10-53.
                              Dlvd Manchester 20-10-53.
Freight £ 47-11-10   Docs 3 -10-53.

        Tom Turner
          1988

504 AMERICA BMCD LTD   Z-5148

Bernardo Wolfenson S.A.   THE RED RAM
Bolivar 330/32.,
Buenos Aires., Argentine.   File No. 667.

Ordered 16-3-54. Invoice ASL-5005 CD3 PP-889178. Dlvd 7/4/54.
ALLARD 21D PALM BEACH LHD: Colour Red, red leather upholstery.
                           3.27 Salisbury rear axle. Wire wheels.
                           12" Lockheed brakes. Reinforced chassis.
                           "5000 mile Works experimental car.
        "RED RAM Dodge Engine No. 044-83879.
                           Registration No. OGY 456.
                           CHASSIS NO. 21D-5151.

* Home Delivery: José, Ismael, Wolfenson.
  P.T. Exemption signed ../4/54. P.T. Indemnity. R.A.C. Docs.

PALL MALL DEPOSIT   ss   Closing 7/4/54.
Freight £ (via Dover/Bologne Ferry) Docs 10/4/54.

518 ARGENTINE Wolfenson/   HD.(* D-5151.

NOEL KIRK MOTORS.,
7176 Sunset Boulevard,
HOLLYWOOD 46., CALIF.   File No. 443.

Ordered 2-9-53. Invoice S-2564. CD3 PP-889081. Dlvd 20-11-53
ALLARD 21Z PALM BEACH LHD: Ming (light) Blue, red leather.
                          Disc wheels.
                          ENGINE NO. EOTTA   .
                          CHASSIS NO. Z-5152.

PALL MALL DEPOSIT. ss PILCOMAYO. Closing 20-11-53.
Freight £ 47-5-0   Docs   10-11-53.

 * Charles Conn.,   Toluca Lake., Calif.

509 AMERICA Noel Kirk Motors / Conn/   Z-5152.

Alexander Tarpinian,
LONDON MOTORS LIMITED,
3801 Beach Channel Drive,
Edgemere, L.I., New York.   File No: 685.

Brokers: John J. Coates Co, 40 Exchange Place, New York.

Ordered 31-12-54. Invoice ASL-5034. CD3 SS-70056.
ALLARD 21Z PALM BEACH LHD: Red, red leather upholstery.
                          Wire wheels, hubs & caps.
                          (ex-Earls Court Show car.)
                          ENGINE NO: EOTTA 108596.
                          CHASSIS NO: 21Z-5156.

PALL MALL DEPOSIT.   ss AMERICAN BANKER   Closing 12-1-55
Freight £   Docs   -1-55

541 AMERICA Tarpinian/   Z-5156

Tractor Specialties Limited.,
P.O. Box 2514.,
Auckland C.I., New Zealand.   File No. 684.

Ordered 16-8-54.   Invoice ASL-5027. Delivered 28th August '54.
ALLARD 21Z PALM BEACH RHD: (* formerly Z-5130 Madagascar) XX
                          Colour Blue, red leather upholstery.
                          Steel wheels. Zephyr Engine.
                          Engine No. EOTTA 96029.
                          CHASSIS NO. 21Z-5154.

Pall Mall Deposit.   ss DEVON.   Closing 28-8-54
Freight £   Docs   -9-54

534 NEW ZEALAND Tracspecs   Z-5154.

Regulr says 5157 was shipped to New York on 5-8-55 ...?

5157

Alexander Tarpinian,
LONDON MOTORS LIMITED.,
3801, Beach Channel Drive,
Edgemere, Long Island., N.Y.   File No. 685.

Ordered 1-1-55. Invoice S-5036. CD3 RR-992487. Dlvd 16-4-55
ALLARD 21Z PALM BEACH LHD: Colour Red, blue leather upholstery.
                          Disc wheels. 3 carburettor manifold.
                          Engine No: EOTTA 137335.
                          CHASSIS NO: 21Z-5155.

FLEXHILL SHIPPING CO.   ss AMERICAN HARVESTER. Closing 16-4-55
Freight £37-3-5d.   Docs   23-4-55

Mr. Albert Oettinger, 238 Rock Creek Lane, Scarsdale, New York.

543 AMERICA Tarpinian/ Oettinger/   Z-5155.

Sgt. CA Wells,
605 Sqdn,
RAF Honiley,
Warwicks

£285.00

*Now for re sale
late '50s*

1947 Allard Tourer

54 Sgt. C.A. Wells.   JIM 3   L-314

Coupe - now owned by
Chubb Hales of Worthing
(1962)

64 E.P. Alexander.   IL 4287   M-530.

S. F. Jones,
95, Blenheim Gardens, & 103, Green Lane,
London, S.W.2   Morden, Surrey.

£185··0·0   1948, Allard   *Now for re sale
                                    late '50s*
STOCK N° U-386

47 S.F. Jones.,   DFR 376   M-472.

Catford Car Mart LTD.,
9-13, Catford Hill,   (see over)
London. S E 6

£175/0/0   1948, Black Allard Tourer   INVOICE NO
                BO   J 4568

VENDOR   DELIVERED
DAGG   12/3/56

STOCK NO U227   ENTERED 26/1/56

21 Catford Car Mart   JYK 120   L-538

---

*now in Allard stock
for re sale,
date late '50s*

63 A.D. Freeman.   JKD 874   K-485.

Mr. C.M. Newton.
Coton Hall,
Sudbury, Derby.   (TUTBURY 6116)

ALLARD L-TYPE TOURER: First registered 26-10-48.
                        Recent respray, Tyres as new, Hood and
                        sidecurtains unused, Recon engine 8000,
                        Chrome perfect, Leather good, Batteries
         £350   good, New plugs, Marchall lamps, Good
                        brakes, Electrical equipment etc.
                        CHASSIS NO. 71L-560.   UML 128

26 C.M. Newton.   L-560.

Card 1

Forbes - Falke
2, Glendower Place,
S.W7

£220/0/0   Grey

INVOICE Nº
C136

VENDOR
B. JOHNSON

DELIVERED
4/5/56

STOCK Nº U311

ENTERED
4/5/56

32 Forbes & Falke   FWM 453   M-563

Card 2

Mr E.S Shields
42 Woodcote Close
Epsom
Surrey

M Type Black/ Grey Trim
mileage 42,000

delivered 11.1.49

Price £260

See reverse of envelope for M 874

M. 857

Card 3

Mr P.S Nicholson,
215-219, High Street,
Elgin,
Scotland.

£ 280/0/0   Allard Drophead Coupé
Grey

INVOICE Nº
J4567

DELIVERED 9/3/56

VENDOR
SHEPHERD

ENTERED 22/12/55

STOCK Nº U190

23 P.S. Nicholson   FDW 92   M-756

Card 4

Mr. E.S. Shields,
42, Woodcote Close,
Epsom., Surrey.   (Epsom 2947)

ALLARD M-TYPE D/HD COUPE: Colour Black, grey leather upholstery.
Tyres, hood, leather .... Fair.
Offered £260.   Mileage 42,500. Orig Engine No. 7204742.
Delivered 11-1-49.
CHASSIS NO: M-857.

Interested later in change over or trade in for a P1 saloon

23 Mr. Shields   M857
1949 M-type

Card 5

Mr A.I. MacGregor
The Farm,
Lydart,
NR, Monmouth.

£300 0 0   Grey Allard 81M Drophead Coupé
75 0 0

INVOICE Nº
2 -

DELIVERED
23/3/56

STOCK Nº
SBR

ENTERED
12/2/56

VENDOR BROOKS

26 A.I. MacGregor   KLL 138   M-853

Card 4

A.J. Van Kempen.,
Anglo Dutch Gold & Silver Co,
Dix, Blott & Van Kempen Ltd.,
59, Shaftesbury Avenue, W.1.

STOCK U—

FILE NO: 4.

Ordered 14-6-55. Invoice No. * 43 Acre. Delivered 7-7-55

ALLARD DROPHEAD COUPE: Colour Black, red leather upholstery.
First registered 28th January, 1949.
COST £275
Gross 58
Completely overhauled & resprayed.
CHASSIS NO: M-874. REG. NO. KLK 657

* Purchased from Farquharson, Invercauld, Braemar, Scotland.

4 A.J. Van Kempen   KLK 657   M-857   M-874

Card 35

G. R. Hays

Black, M-1058

INVOICE NO C-141

STOCK NO U—

DELIVERED 10.5.56

ENTERED 9.4.56

VENDOR CRAIG

35 G.R. Hays   UMC 938   M-1058

Card 44

F/Lt. M.W. Kendrick,
R.A.F. Sandtoft,
Nr Doncaster,
Yorks.

H.P. Agreement No 393867

1949, Allard D/H Coupé

INVOICE No C101

£310-0-0

44 F/Lt M.W. Kendrick.   JVF 14   M-877.

Card 33

L. Reis,
103, Woodland Drive,
Watford, Herts

Green

£260/0/0

VENDOR Barber

STOCK No S.O.R

INVOICE No C137

DELIVERED 7/5/56

ENTERED 16/3/56

33 Ludwig Reis   JOP 851   M-1070

Card 1

Major B.H. Roberts,
9, Mount Beacon.,
Bath., Somerset.

File No. 1.

Ordered 9-5-55. Invoice No. 6492. Delivered. 9-5-55.
ALLARD DROPHEAD COUPE: First registered 11-2-49.
Colour Maroon, maroon leather.
Repainted Grey.
CHASSIS NO: M-890. REG. NO. KLL 577

S.O.R. £260
S.P. £350
Gross £90
STOCK NO. n/a.

1 B.H. Roberts   KLL 577   M-890

Card (Brian King)

Mr Brian King,
Robin Hill,
Hutton Mount,
Essex.

Allard 81M Drophead Coupé
First registered 30.8.49

£200
20/0/0

GYS 513
M.1102

Mr Brian King
Robin Hill
Hutton Mount.
Essex

Coupe M 1102   First registered
GYZ 513   30ᵗʰ August 1949
      Price £200

⁷/ₜ October, 1955   M 1102

K.C. Kennett,

£240 ·· 0 ·· 0

57 K.C. Kennett.   LGP 1   P-1647

Mr. Bailey,   for re-sale - November 1955
Milford House,   late 50s, (PTO)
Chobham,
nr Woking, Surrey.   Gunmetal grey, red leather upholstery.
                       31,000. Mercury engine. (spare engine)+
ALLARD J2 TWO SEATER: ¾ race cam. Full windscreen & hood.
                       Body shows signs of repair - hood needs
S.O.R.   recovering. 6 disc wheels complete with
                       ....res. 3 spare wheels also available.
                       CHASSIS J-1573. REGISTRATION NUB 862

                                            (PTO)

34 Mr. Bailey.   (NUB 862) J-1573

---

2 G. Slater
   The Willows
  Darrington,
  Pontefract.
   York

   P. Saloon 1662

   Reg No   LGP. 258

£260
                                              P 1662

Mr T Prewett,
35, Cissbury Rd,
   Worthing, Sussex

£310 ·· 0 ·· 0   Allard 91P Saloon

                      INVOICE C196

51 T. Prewett.   KLV 880   P-1582

P. D. Woodman.

                              INVOICE Nº
                                 C 130
                              DELIVERED
                               3/4/56
STOCK Nº   ENTERED
   SOR   4/4/56
VENDOR
  SMITH

29 P.D. Woodman   P-1715

Card 1:

Mr. G. Renson Smith, Re-Sale.
Sangers (Chemists) Ltd,
<u>258 Euston Rd, N.W.1.</u> (EUSton 4343)

<u>ALLARD 1950 J2 TWO SEATER:</u> Br. R. Green, green leather upholstery
                                  Steel dis wheels.
£450 less 10% comm.   Full windscreen & hood.
                                  Ardun/Mercury engine.
                                  CHASSIS NO. J-1735.   LLP 798

                                  REG P 2270

32 G. Renson Smith   (LLP 798)   J-1735

Card 2:

W. A Morris,
Electrical Instrument Co LTD,
Hillington,
Glasgow, S W 2.
Scotland

£465   Allard 9IP Saloon
            REG Nº WMF877

    Subsequent Trade in of M Type Cc re REG Nº GYS513
    against above

9 W.A. Morris   WMF 837   P-1929

Card 3:

Messrs J A Laidlaw (Airdrie) LTD,
Ford Main Dealers,
South Biggar Road
Airdrie, Scotland.

                                INVOICE Nº
                                   C-215
£280·00   Allard Saloon

                                DELIVERED
                                 18/10/56

61 J.A. Laidlaw Ltd.   KNX 847   P-1799.

Card 4:

MR A F Samuels
E Norman - Bailey. Partners,
Cattennie House,
25/27, Cattennia Place,
London. S W 1
                    Allard 9P (1993) (HYS853)   INVOICE Nº
£903/12/0   against purchase of New Ford   2B126
                    Zephyr (Green)   DELIVERED
                                                    29/3/56
STOCK Nº   ENTERED
   B70S   15/3/56

                                                    P 1943

24 A.F. Samuels   SLX 975   FORD ZEPHYR 11

Card 5:

Mr. George Rice,   STOCK B-665
133/135, Euston Road,
London. N.W.1.   FILE NO. 2.

Ordered 3-5-55. Invoice No. * 43 Acre. Delivered 16-6-55
<u>FORD ZODIAC SALOON:</u> Colour Grey/Fawn, with fawn leather.
                          To manufacturers specification.
COST £487.   Fitted with Heater & Radio.
GROSS 113.   EOTTA 147353. REGISTRATION NO: RGY 802
Trade-in Allard P-1929.   REG. NO. WMF 837. Allowance £300.

                                         P. 1929

2 G. Rice   RGY 802   FORD ZODIAC

Card 6:

Mr A E Holland,
 85, South Hill Rd,
   Shortlands, Kent.

739/9/0   Trade in Allard K2, 1951, HMR162
 - STOCK Nº395B against New Consul (£400)
300/0/0

                                         K2 1951

13 E.A. Holland   HMR...   FORD CONSUL

Card 1 (top left):

P.1976 ?

INVOICE

DELIVERED
31/3/56
ENTERED
2/2/56

STOCK Nº
U-

VENDOR
Armstrong

1976 was K2
shipped to U.S.A.

see next
card

P1976

27 Partridge (Adl.3K)   HWS 896   P-1976 S161

Card 2 (top right):

T.P. Tunnard Moore,
The Quarries,
Chagford, Devon.   STOCK U-

                                          FILE NO. 3.

Also:- Moore & Tucker Ltd, 118 Cromwell Rd, S.W.7.

Ordered 14-6-55. Invoice No. # 43 Acre Delivered 24-6-55

ALLARD 91P SALOON: Colour Black, brown leather upholstery.
                     First registered 1st June, 1951.
COST £357   New tyres. Heater. Windscreen washer.
Gross 128   CHASSIS NO: P-2076. REG. NO. LOH 800

* Purchased from Dunlop Rubber Co., Birmingham.

** Subsequently traded in car against new Ford Zephyr.

3 T.P. Tunnard-Moore   LOH 800   P-2076

Card 3 (middle left):

Mr. A.J. Price,
98, Three Shires Oak Rd,   RE-Sale
Bearwood, Birmingham.

1950 J2 TWO SEATER: Colour
                      Clean condition; good mechanically; good tyre:
                      Ardun/Mercury engine.
                      Cus tomer wants £360. RSP £410.
                      First registered 25/12/50.
                      CHASSIS NO: J-2004 ?
                              2014 ?

                              See chassis list - shown
                              as blank #2. almost certainly
                              J-2004 ?

31 A.J. Price   J-2004 ?

Card 4 (middle right):

A/c Richard Klarchek,
AF 16420114,
20 Operation Sqdn,
Weathersfield RAF Station,
Nr Braintree, Essex.

                    Grey Allard K2   INVOICE Nº C115

                                            DELIVERED 5/3/56

                                            ENTERED 5/3/56

VENDOR
HOLLAND

19 R. Klarchek   HMR 162   K2-2091

Card 5 (bottom left):

Mr. Alan Godsal,
Haines Hill,
Twyford., Berks.

1952 Allard J2X Chassis: Special 112" LWB (12" longer than usual)
         2015   Wide P2 type De Dion rear axle.(4" wider)
                           Small mileage. No instruments. 5000 mls.
* advertised AUTOSPORT   Alfin Drums. Steel wheels. Andre Tele.
25/11/55   Competition type shockabsorbers.
@ £350.   Two (2) brake master cylinders. Good tyre
                           Chrysler 180 BHP engine. "Firepower"
                           Ford (Lincoln) gears.

Sold to John William
& Swansea, re registered
as JFM 736 and disposed of
with partially completed
GRP bodywork

see page 170   PTO M 1102
30 A. Godsal.   my Book   2015   * J2X Chassis.

Card 6 (bottom right):

Mr. R. Woodward,   * 2nd owner.
55 Woodstock Road,
Golders Green,
London. N.W.11.   * Purchased 10/11/55 @ £370 AMC cheque.

ALLARD 91P SALOON: Black, blue leather upholstery.
                     Bodywork, cellulose, leather above average.
                     Interior woodwork, linings, perfect.
PP370   4 good tyres & 1 poor. Tubeless tyres on rear.
                     Recon engine 6000 mls. New batteries Oct.
RSP465   1st class mech. cond. "A" type radiator grille
                     EXTRAS: Heater, Spotlamp, Wing mirrors, wide
                             view int. mirror, Windscreen washer.
                     CHASSIS NO: P-2270. REG. NO. KGA 165.

                              PTO P1929
29 ALLARD MOTOR CO.   (KGA 165)   P-2270

R R Rogers,
Heatherbank,
Wellington Rd,
Crowthorne, Berks

£400 . 0 - 0   1952. P1 Saloon   INVOICE C167
15 . 0 - 0   DELIVERED
STOCK N°   2/8/56

45 R.R. Rogers.   JFY 499   P-2272.

Mr. Michael Court,
42, McIntosh Street,
Gordon,
Sydney N.S.W

£ 378/0/0   Black, 1952 H2X Allard.   INVOICE N°
                                                C-175
                                  PURCHASE C180
                                                DELIVERED
                                                14/8/56

49 M. Court.   YMD 692   M2X-3119.

Mr A Pitts
The Garage,
Streets Brook Rd,
Shirley, Birmingham

£435.00   Allard 91P Saloon

                                INVOICE N°
                                C-226
STOCK N°
UR 468

* formerly HUJ 760 Viscount Boyne. P-3084.

66 Pitts/Merrick.   KBC 148   P-2279

Dr DM Armstrong,
6, Craigweil Place,
Ayr,
Scotland

                         surely greg (G. Allard) £1. . 00
                              enquires by John Allard.

£ 640/0/0   Green Allard "Monte Carlo" Saloon   INVOICE N°
                 P/exchang P1 Saloon.
                                                          DELIVERED
STOCK N°   17/2/56
B 617
                                                          ENTERERED
VENDOR   2/2/56
Sheddon
                                        Ex 1 ton Mr faun
                                        las Brooks, NSW
18 Dr. D.M. Armstrong   MDG 160   scrapped   P2-4504

Mr C A V Johnson,
49, Gore Rd,
London, S.W.20

480/0/0   Grey Allard M2X   INVOICE N° CS100
                                       DELIVERED 6/1/56
                                       STOCK N° J174
                                       VENDOR.
                                       Escott
                                       Entered
                                       17/11/55

                                       M2X-2205

ALLARD
WARRANTY BOOK

The order of entry is as indicated in this inside cover starting with Adlards, and gives a good insight into the volume of Allards that were sold and the tailing off in the later years.

ADLARDS MOTORS LTD.

Chassis No.	Engine No.	Dealers Name + Address	Customers Name	Address	Date Delivered		Warranty Received
K-488	7198987	E.O. Abbott Ltd., Farnham, Surrey.	J.A. Birnie, Westbrook,	Oxshead, Surrey.	6. 8. 48		16. 8. 48.
M-615	7200061		F.N. Turner, Ramsey,	Woodcote Rd., Purley.	19. 8. 48		19. 8. 48
M-618	7200071		S. Compton, Red Knob,	Downside Rd., Guildford	1. 9. 48		1. 9. 48
M-625	7200168		T.O. Wacher, Earley	House, Petham, Kent	6. 9. 48		6. 9. 48
M-614	7200014		G.O. Field, Green Gates	Walton-on-Thames	9. 9. 48		9. 9. 48
M-709	7202469		B.O. Rapps, Bridge	Esher, Surrey.	2. 10. 48	✓	2. 10. 48
M-725	7202444				6. 10. 48		NOT REC'D
M-730	7202464	Barkers Garage, Three Bridges, Surrey.	G.S. Mundell, Wraysbury	Crawley Enfield Rd.,	14. 10. 48		29.9. 48
M-726	7202971				14. 10. 48		NOT REC'D
M-747	7202978		Bernard Seddon, 282,	Wigan Wigan Lane,	26. 10. 48		5. 11. 48
M-760	7203768	This car has been resold. Warranty is void			18. 11. 48	Trophy Garage, E.St., Farnham) H.C. Lucas, 156, Weybourne Rd., Farnham	15. 11. 48
L-688	7200693		Hubert L. Vickery, Maple	wood, Beech Drive, Surrey.	24. 11. 48		23. 11. 48
M-720	7202506	Pentiles Service Garage, Guildford	C.S. Bell, Lower Fairbrook	Oxshead, Surrey.	24. 11. 48		27. 11. 48
M-731	7202491	F.H. Peacock Ltd., Folkstone.	J. Pearlman, Seaview	Folkstone, Kent. Jones St,	1. 12. 48		2. 12. 48
M-836	7204587	Wilbert Motors Eng. Co. Ltd., S.W.1.	F.A. Medley, Lent	Hall Farm, Northumberland;	17. 12. 48		26. 3. 49
L-890	7204159		P.Q. Greene, Heath Hill	Surrey, Coldharbour	17. 12. 48		17. 12. 48.
M-857	7204742	O. Rowe Co. Ltd., Chichester.	R. Clifford-Brown, Tang	mere, Nr. Chichester	11. 1. 49		14. 1. 49
M-875	7204934	F.H. Peacock Ltd., S.W.17.	K.C. Derigpole, Uveerhurst	Nr. Birmingham	25. 1. 49		23. 3. 49.
M-873	7206589		E.R. Midgley, Hartley. Mist	High Rd., by, 90/92, Heston	27. 1. 49.		19. 1. 49.
M-826	7204737	F.H. Peacock, 219-221, Heston	R. Peacock, Director, F.H.	Peacock Ltd., Huddersfield.	31. 1. 49.		7. 2. 49
M-818	7204333		H.R. Sykes, Nook, Sharp	Lane, Almondbury,	9. 2. 49		9. 2. 49
M-889	7206771		J.C. Wild, Woodcroft,	Surrey.	21. 2. 49		2. 3. 49
M-1005	7207734	L.Q. Mitchell Ltd., S.W.12	O.E. Godfrey, Upalong,	Haslemere, Surrey. Shepherds Hill	2. 3. 49		2. 3. 49
M-1007	7207733				5. 3. 49		NOT REC'D
M-1006	7207750				7. 3. 49.		NOT REC'D
M-1003	7207144		R. Shaker, W. Shaker Ltd., Nr. Pulborough, Sussex	13/23, Shroton St., S.E.1.	9. 3. 49.		9. 3. 49.
M-852	7206928		Mrs. Pamela May,	Cottage, Surreygate,	17. 3. 49	Maroon/Beige (phone call 11/3/96)	17. 3. 49
M-1030	7209291				18. 3. 49		NOT REC'D
M-1022	7209287	Hartley, Midgley, 90/92, Heston Rd., Bignor	R.Q. Jenner, 18, Dean	Gardens, Brighton	23. 3. 49		31. 3. 49
M-1030	7207815				29. 3. 49		NOT REC'D
M-1016	7209251 290		B.G. Clark, 239, Baker St.	N.W.1.	29. 3. 49		29. 5. 49
M-1032	7207281	Meares Motors Ltd., East Sheen.	W.G. Broom, 143, Haz	wood Rd., S.W.15.	1. 4. 49		8. 4. 49
M-1047	7209749	Hungerford Motors, Putney	J.R. Garland, Secretary	W. Harbrow, Big Horley.	14. 4. 49		19. 4. 49
M-1062	7210565		Capt. C. Treon, Bond	Services, Nr. Chichester	4. 5. 49		4. 5. 49
M-1056	7210650	O. Rowe Co. Ltd., Chichester.	P.J. Sainsbury, Little Court	Farm, Huntington, Chichester	14. 5. 49		16. 5. 49
M-1069	7210821	O. Rowe Co. Ltd., Chichester.	W.A. Jarvis, Green Bank	Stortford, Surrey.	16. 5. 49		16. 5. 49
M-1075	7210984	Coombe Service Station, Guildford	Elsie Lucas-Scudamore,	York.	18. 5. 49		20. 5. 49
M-1071	7210988		J. Walton, 54, Belgrave Rd.,	Reigate	19. 5. 49		19. 5. 49
K-439	7200952				20. 5. 49		NOT REC'D
M-108	7210810	Coombe Service Station, Guildford	C. Jenkinson, Doone Cottage		14. 6. 49		14. 6. 49

ADLARDS MOTORS LTD.

Chassis No.	Engine No.	Dealers Name - Address	Customers Name - Address	Date Delivered 19		Warranty Received
M-1074	7210937	Phillips Garages, E. Grinstead	P.C. Chorley, Retford, London	..., E. Grinstead	16. 6. 49.	18. 6. 49
M-1072	7210925	Demonstration Vehicle Used by Allards			30. 6. 49.	NOT REC'D
M-1051	7209892	F.H. Peacock.	B.S. Gordon, 75 Alexandra	Road, St. Austell	7. 7. 49.	11. 7. 49
K-696	7200475		H.E. Quennell 115/117, Conw.	Road S.E.18.	20. 7. 49.	20. 7. 49
L-867	7207204	Soans & Dunn, Bromley, Kent.	A.B. de Boxar 16 Great Thrift	Petts Wood Kent	24. 6. 49.	29. 6. 49
M-1532	7212357	Phillips Garages, East Grinstead	F.T. Moore, Charlett, Holtye Road	East Grinstead	23. 9. 49.	1. 10. 49
M-1524	7215392		Gardiner Ltd 13 Donegall Sq.	East Belfast	20. 9. 49.	15. 11. 49
M-1100	7212112		Oscar King Hardy, Kandelnor, Barnes	SW 13	28. 9. 49	28. 9. 49
M-1523	7215400	Cooper Auto Service, 1043 Newlands Park SE26	Lords Novel Laundry Ltd 23A Sydenham	Road SE22	28. 9. 49.	1. 10. 48
~~P-1506~~	~~7212116~~					
M-1522	7210892	Cooper Automobile Services Ltd SE.26.	Harry Wm. Maxwell Telling 30 Elstree Rose, West Hill	SW15	7. 10. 49	8. 10. 49
P-1514	7217522		The Bullerley Co. Ltd, Bullerley Park	Repley Nr Derby	9. 11. 49	11. 11. 1.49
~~P-1548~~	7215392		GARDINERS. LTD. 13 DONEGALL	WEST. BELFAST.	25. 11. 49	30. 11. 51.
P-627	7200186		J. O'Kill 14 Norfolk St	W.C.2n.	8. 11. 49	8. 12. 49
P-1548	7219361	A. Mitchell Motors, Balham	Godfrey (Balham) Ltd, Moyser Rd. Balham	23. 12. 49	24. 12. 49
P-1587	7223852		J.W.H. Eastwood 2, Priesland	...Rd. Sidcup KENT	9. 2. 50.	10. 2. 50.
P-1591	7223879	Baynes Bros. Ltd Maidstone Kent	T.H. Dobson, 4 Penbury Gdns.	Maidstone	16. 2. 50	21. 2. 50.
M-529	7198916				17. 2. 50	NOT REC'D
P-1597	7224156	D. Rowe & Co Ltd. Chichester.	R. Clifford-Brown, Tangmere Cottage, Tangmere	21. 2. 50	22. 1. 50
L-905	7207822		T.O. Adkin, Ravenshell, Su...	...nroeshill,	24. 2. 50	25. 2. 50.
P-1595	7188852		S.A. Rolli, Little Barwick, Bonkton	King Lynn NFK.	31. 3. 50	14. 4. 50
P-1630	7228510	Naylor & Root Ltd, Clapham Junc'n	L.J. Drew, 23 Glamborne Rd.	...D. Wickham	19. 4. 50	19. 4. 50.
P-1632	7228907				28. 4. 50	NOT REC'D
P-1635	7228918	A. Owen Ltd, Clapham	Portenay & Co Ltd "Kent House" Barbican	..., Oxford Circus W.1.	26. 4. 50.	26. 4. 50
P-1640	7228509				4. 5. 50	NOT REC'D
P-1650	7229903		R. Langston-Jones & Co Ltd.	Weddington, Middx	19. 5. 50	20. 5. 50
P-1652	7229726		N.L. Cowling 35 Chatsworth Ave.	Bromley Kent	25. 5. 50	26. 5. 50
P-1657	7231838		J.W. Salmond, Lyminster House	Littlehampton, Sx.	2. 6. 50	2. 6. 50
P-1658	7231852		F.A. Norton, Byron House, Gatley	Wood, Chelmsford	2. 6. 50	3. 6. 50
P-1672	7232488		F.J. Wymer, Sundridge Park Hotel	Bromley, KENT	1. 7. 50	1. 7. 50
P-1678	7238560		H.D. Greenwood, 177 Kirkwood Rd, Peckham SE15	1. 7. 50	1. 7. 50
P-1688	7233678		R.G. Swiss, 93 West Way	Pinner Middx	19. 7. 50	19. 7. 50
P-1723	7235795	Masons Garage Ltd. Chichester	M.R. Hamilton, The Tithe Barn, Oving. Nr. Chichester	3. 8. 50	3. 8. 50.
P-1727	7233878	Hare & Sons Ltd, Littlehampton	J.W.D.L. Godfray, "Fernsdown" Greville Rd. LITTLE'N	17. 8. 50	18. 8. 50
P-1749	7237913	Eastbourne Motor Ltd, Eastbourne	S.A. Oades, 7, Beachlands, Pevensey Bay Sussex	29. 8. 50	29. 8. 50
P-1751	7226140	Drift Bridge Garage Epsom	W.D. Jerome, Stapely, Hartley ...	Harrogate Co Hire	30. 8. 50.	8. 9. 50
P-1754	7238756		D. Gordon, 6 Coburgh Mews	W.C.	2. 9. 50	2. 9. 50
P-1761	7238761		P.J. Winstone, Walton Manor, Holland Rd. Epsom	8. 9. 50	9. 9. 50
P-1770	7240741	L.F. Pritchard Ltd, Wimbourne	H.F. Root, Sydney House, St John's Rd, Southcliffe	18. 9. 50	5. 10. 50
P-1792	7240023		S.O. Carter 57 Petworth Ave	Harbury S.W.16	9. 10. 50	8. 10. 50

ADLARDS MOTORS LTD.

Chassis No	Engine No	Dealers Name + Address	Customers Name +	Address	Date Delivered		Warranty Rec'd
J-1693	2005		R.O.R. de Larrinaga, Laund Hu	North Mossley Hill Rd. Liverpool 18	7-10-50	Green (B.R.) / Green Trim	7-10-50
P-1820	7242158	Caffyns Ltd, Worthing	Alderman R. Johnson, 2 Lans-	down Rd. Worthing	11-10-50		14-10-50
P-1813	7240933		H.K. Marcel, Little Stacey,	Sandhurst, Kent	14-10-50		14-10-50
P-1823	7242408	E.G. Pritchard Ltd, Sittingbourne	J.R. Weaver, Ivanhoe, Harplesh	Lane Detling Kent	16-10-50		18-10-50
P-1824	7242135	Caffyns Ltd. Worthing	Mr. R.E. Jacques, 1 Grand Ave	Lancing Sussex	19-10-50		1-11-50
P-1831	7242157		John Lees, Newlands Bald	RINE. ISLE OF MAN	31-10-50		21-2-51
P-1873	7244484	CAFFYNS LTD. WORTHING.	A.J. Farie, Willow Cott. W. R.Tring Rd. STORRINGTON.		27-11-50		9-4-51
P-1881	7244920 Putney		C.L. Tyson, Royal Kent Hotel.	Sandgate	1-12-50		1-12-50
P-1880	7244929	E.C. Pritchard Ltd Sittingbourne Kent	Kenwood Timber Co. Haselwood House Bishopsgate W. Elvy Aspley House, Nottinghamshire Kent. E.C.2.		1-12-50		20-3-51
P-1884	7244934	CENTRAL GARAGE BIRCHINGTON.	R. WARREN KINGSHEAD HOTEL L. MARGATE		4-1-51	fired.	16-2-51
P-1901	7246494		LLEWELLYN SON STATION GARAGE ROSS/ON/WYE		12-1-51		14-2-51
P-1887	7244998		EASTES LOUD L.D ASHFORD KENT. (SEED GROWERS).		24-1-51		29-1-51
P-1920	7246931		E. TYLER. CANNON LANE.	TONBRIDGE. KENT.	24-1-51.		29-1-51.
P-1914	7246916		Mrs B. Frayling. 11.Preston Rd	S.W-20	26-1-51.		8-2-51
P-1918	7246844		BARBARA AGNEW. Thornden Boundstone. Surrey		27-1-51		29-1-51.
P-1926	7246913				9-1-51	RED - RED TRIM	?
J-1784	2004X				3-2-51.	(Demonstration Model)	NO WARRANTY
P-1816	7240726						24-2-51
K-1925	9088/144		T.N. BLOCKLEY BAYSWATER COURT ST. STEPHENS GARD W.2.		19-2-51		NO WARRANTY
P-1989	CHASSIS ONLY				28-2-51		13-3-51
P-1954	7250834	PHILLIPS GARAGE. E. GRINSTEAD.	P.C. CHORLEY BARCLAYS BANK. E. GRINSTEAD		5-3-51.		NO WARRANTY
P-1964	7250979		MR McDOWELL		10-3-51.		14-3-51
P-1963	7250977	J. Hollingsworth, Ltd. Hastings	H.G. Powell "Brockhurst" East Grinstead.		12-3-51.		NO WARRANTY
J-1972	OWN ENG. FITTED		MR IMHOF.		17-3-51		6-4-51
J-888	2004		D.F. ANNABLE. "Blounts"	MARLOW. BUCKS	23-3-51	RED - RED TRIM	6-4-51.
P-2126	7252806				6-4-51.		
P-1922	7246971		J.B. Guinness 133 Dorset Rd 137	MERTON PARK. S.W.19	4-4-51.		9-4-51.
P-2024	7254310	F. Watson (Croydon) Thornton Heath.	L.F. Feldmar "Darent. H" Ulm Shoreham Sevenoaks.		9-4-51		12-4-51.
P-2040	7252988				10-4-51.		
K-2028	7240391				10-4-51.		SEE L.H.S.
J-1912	2019-Z		MAURICE WICK. ESQ.		10-4-51.		SEE L.H.S.
J-2015	2017-Z		ALAN GODSAL ESQ.		24-4-51		30-4-51
P-2045	7254572		C.H. JENKINS VINEHALL FARM ROBERTSBRIDGE		25-4-51		
P-2061	7256225	RICE BROS LTD BILLINGSHURST SX	J.L. BREEDS CHICORY COTT. UCKFIELD SX		15-5-51.		21-5-51
P-2076	7256766		DUNLOP RUBBER CO. LTD. FORT DUNLOP ERDINGTON B'HAM 24		6-6-51		6-6-51
J-2012	2020-Z	ROOTES LTD. LEN ENGINEERING WORKS MAIDSTONE.	A.J. TATHAM (BUILDERS) 204 HIGH ST. ORPINGTON CROSS MOOR GARDENS. Kent.		20-6-51		5-7-51.
P-2040	7258985		RUBBAGLAS LTD, 3 GROSVENOR GDS. S.W.1		13-7-51	(Ex DEMO)	13-7-51.
P-2117	7258542		R.O. WHITE. "SUFFIELD GREEN" PUTTENHAM GUILDFORD Sy.		18-7-51		18-7-51
P-2126	7258720	PHILLIPS GARAGE LTD E. GRINSTEAD.	M. CROOKSHANK. CHERRY HAY. 19 HILL. FOREST ROW SX.		2-8-51		28-8-51
J-2138	2028-Z	MGT 850	O.P.L.C. SHEA SIMONDS ROSE HOUSE	FIGHELDEAN, SALISBURY. WILTS.	4-9-51.		7-9-51
J-1941	1456291.				4-9-51.	(Ex DEMO)	

ADLARD'S MOTORS LTD.

Chassis. No.	Engine No.	Dealers Name & Address	Customers Name and Address	Date Delivered		Warranty Reg.
P-2175	7261983		Maj. Faulkner Amberley Farm. Godalming. Surrey	1-10-51.		1-10-51 ✓
P-2173	7261749		R. Simon. 9 & 10. 68/70 Mark Lane. London. E.C.3.	16-10-51.		16-10-51. ✓
P-2256	7265164		Miss. G. Garton 28, Belvedere. Court, Upper. Richmond Rd.,	23-11-07	Putney S.W.15.	23-11-51. ✓
M-2295	7265176		Mabel M. Escott, 7, Hares Gdns. Cheyne Walk S.W.3	28-11-51		28-11-51. ✓
P-2252	7263584		I.C. Trafford Grafton House, Warlingham. Surrey.	1-12-51		1-12-51. ✓
P-2263	7264876		L.W. Elliott 13, Victoria Sq. London. S.W.1.	15-12-51.		15-12-51. ✓
P-2269	7265037		C.J.M. Abbott. 12, London. Road. Chelmsford.	8/1/52.		8/1/52. ✓
P-2281	7264458		Clarke. Blanch & Co. Ltd. 79, Leadenhall St. E.C.3.	2-2-52		2-2-52. ✓
M-3092	7269430		Westinghouse Brake & Signal Co. Ltd. 83, York Road Way	14-2-52.	London. N.1.	14-2-52. ✓
P-2286	E.409.		Mrs Allard. "Kabibu" Blackhills, Esher.	13-3-52.	No Warranty Required.	
P-3082	7269840	C.E. Jenkins Ti	C.E. Jenkins Oldbury Grange Lower. Broadheath Worc.	26.3.52.		26.3.52 ✓
P-3080	7269839	Site Caterers Ltd. 4	Grosvendr. Gardens Mews. North Victoria. S.W.1.	3.4.52		3.4.52 ✓
M-2203	7269801	A & B. Garages Ltd. Grange Rd. Ramsgate Kent.	Martin Thompson Dettyn Broadstairs. Kent.	21.3.52.		2.4.52 ✓
M-3097	7271488	H.E. Tudor Thompson Motor Pressings. Sealon Works Wolverhampton	Staffordshire	26.4.52	Staffordshire	26.4.52 ✓
P-3088	7273164		Z.N. Gyerey 56/8 Whitcomb St. London W.C.2	16.5.52		16.5.52 ✓
M-3098	484 H426		D. Cussen, 16, Goodwood Court. Devonshire St. W.1.	4-6-52	W.1.	4.6.52 ✓
M-3122	484 H428		C.E. Smith Dominions Export. Co. Ltd Sterling House, 8, Heddon St. London W.1.	4.6.52		4.6.52 ✓
P2-4003	4259/80	Worcester. Windfields. Ltd.		15.11.52		
J2X-3164	55028 Jiydee Allard			24.9.53.		
P2-4501	7287263	Allied Colloids (Manufact) Co. Ltd. Bradford.	Allied Colloids (Manufact) Co. Ltd. Bradford	23.12.53.		
212-5110	Kotta-71016	E.D. Abbott Ltd Farnham Surrey		6.1.54		
K-3286	7290334		J.P. Lawstais Mulberry Cottage	8.10.54	Netheravon Rd Chiswick W.4	13.10.54

DAGENHAM. MOTORS.

CHASSIS no.	Engine. no.	DEALERS. Name. & add:	CUSTOMERS & ADDRESS	DATE. DELIVERED	WARRANTY. Received
K- 581	7199148	Not Delivered Yet		11. 8. 48	
M- 631	7200208	Car Mart Ltd., Euston Rd.,	C. E. Marshall, Thatch End., E. Horsley, Surrey	27. 8. 48	1. 9. 48
K- 600	7199671	Offord - Sons Ltd., 154, Gloucester Rd	O.J. Poise, Sarborne Rd., Croydon	31. 8. 48	9. 9. 48
K- 607	7200060	Blue Star Garage, Sloane Ave. S.W.3	E.F. Richardson, Castle Hills, Bucking	31. 8. 48	31. 8. 48
M- 674	7200770		H. Hodgson, Haring-	son, Hertfordshire	9. 9. 48	15. 9. 48
M- 656	7200774		R.E. Fowler, 81, Western Rd., Southall	16. 9. 48	25. 9. 48
L- 689	7200755	Chinerys Garage, Harpenden, Herts	W. Q. Alderton, 7. West field Ave., Herts	30. 9. 48	30. 9. 48
M- 735	7202950	H. C. Nelson (1942) Ltd. 6/11, Appletree Yard	L. E. De Rome, 2, Christon Gar. Studio, Surrey	15. 10. 48	26. 10. 48
L- 695	7202236	University Motors Ltd., W.1.	J. McNally, Mineola, Hare Field Pl., Uxbridge	8. 11. 48	9. 11. 48
M- 751	7202168		Capt. R.H. Carpenter, Ogbourne, Monmouth, Herts.	24. 11. 48	24. 11. 48
M- 762	7203590	Car Mart Ltd., Euston Rd., N.W.1	Q. L. Forward, Red House, Wauchan Cross,	17. 11. 48	1. 1. 49
M- 754	7203657			17. 11. 48	NOT REC'D
M- 793	7204088	H.M. Bartley. Partners, W.1.	I.7. Stamp, Woodlands Causeway Ave. N.6	7. 12. 48	8. 1. 49
M- 853	7204657	Russell Motors (Knightsbridge) Ltd.	7. H.W. Clarke, 19, Knightsbridge Rd., S.W.3.	5. 1. 49	22. 1. 49
M- 871	7204805		G. E. R. Osbourne, 25, Pink Ridge Rd., Herts.	19. 1. 49	20. 1. 49
M- 876	7204973		Aberdeen	28. 1. 49	NOT REC'D
M- 874	7206612	Mann Egerton, W.1.	F.S.L. Compton, Inverness Gerald House,	28. 1. 49	5. 2. 49
M- 881	7206811		E. de Valve, Bolton, 23, Church Road, Mews, W.3.	2. 2. 49	7. 2. 49
M- 802	7204091	John W. Whalley, Bishops Stortford	E.M. Griffith, Little Hallingbury, Park, Essex.	4. 2. 49	16. 2. 49
M- 890	7206864	Gollys Garage, 111a, Earls Court Rd	P. W. Nachar (Dr.) 43, Earls Court Sq. S.W.5	11. 2. 49	27. 2. 49 X
M- 899	7207148	University Motors, 80, Piccadilly, how	I.W. Glegg, Crofton, Nuthurst Hill, Horsham	22. 2. 49	21. 2. 49 X
M- 1001	7207231	H.C. Paul Ltd., 32 Brixton Place, W.1.	J. Greenhalgh, 1. Eaton Sq., S.W.1.	5. 3. 49	10. 3. 49
M- 1017	7209271		Stanley Baker, 3, Bentinck Mansions, W.1. x	15. 3. 49	18. 3. 49
M- 1021	7209281	Offord - Sons Ltd., 67, George St., W.	P. Smith, 32, Greville Pl. N.W.6	18. 3. 49.	18. 3. 49
M- 1013	7207757		I.P. Jenkin, 25, Perrine Wlest, N.W.3	23. 3. 49	14. 4. 49
M- 1050	7209894	Wembley Court Motors, Wembley	H.S. Lindsay, 38, Brook Street, W.1. W.8.	13. 4. 49	13. 4. 49
M- 1055	7209941	Car Mart, 150, Park Lane, W.1	Major Q. Graham, 70. 24, Edithgate Sq., Stratford, Herts	25. 4. 49.	16. 6. 49
M- 1058	7210579		W. Young Craig, Little L.order, Bishops	28. 4. 49	28. 4. 49
K- 8811	7204491		Solax Ltd., 223/331, Marylebone Rd, N.W.1	3. 5. 49	4. 5. 49
K- 653	7200754	Chaseside Motor Co. Enfield.	U.J. Painter, 39, Gordon Hill, Enfield	6. 5. 49	10. 5. 49
L- 822	7204734	Wembley Court Motors, Wembley.	E.T. Crane, 579, Whitton Ave. West, Middx	10. 5. 49	19. 5. 49
M- 1066	7210708		Eric Coates, 39, Hill St., W.1.	23. 5. 49.	26. 5. 49
M- 1084	7212070	Offord - Sons Ltd., 154, Gloucester Rd., S.W.7.	O.J. Poise, Hanbeis, Salterns Rd, Croydon	30. 5. 49.	3. 6. 49
M- 1068	7210744		H.F. Robinson, 9, The Green, Banovfield, Herts.	1. 6. 49	3. 6. 49
M- 1089	7212094		R.B. Walpole, 87, New Road, St. Wales	10. 6. 49	15. 6. 49
M- 1088	7210924		K.A. Pearce, 12 Castlebar Rd Ealing W.5	16. 6. 49	30. 7. 49
M- 1078	7210935	Of Pereira	Q. L. Pereira, 37, Devon St., Princes Place, W.1.	21. 6. 49	22. 6. 49
M- 1096	7212352		Rev. Sir Q.P. Ferguson Davis B.T.	19. 7. 49.	25. 7. 49
M- 1093	7212113.		Mjr. W.H.P. Puryeat, M.B.E.	22. 7. 49.	22. 7. 49
M- 1521	7209742	Dunhams Haines, 46 Castle St., Luton, Beds.	M. Guerin, Bracken Knoll, Country Ave., London N.6	30. 6. 49.	14. 10. 49
L- 860	7206963	Car Mart, 150 Park Lane, W.1.	A. McDougal, 5a Thorney Ct., Hyde Pk. Gate, W.8.	3. 9. 49.	3. 9. 49

DAGENHAM MOTORS.

CHASSIS No.	ENGINE No.	DEALERS NAME + ADDRESS	CUSTOMERS NAME	+ ADDRESS.	DATE DELIVERED		WARRANTY REC'D
1528-M	7215512		b.E. Birdsall 94. Portland	Place W.1.	12 · 9 · 49		12 - 9 · 49. ✓
1506-P	7212146		Mrs C. M. Gleadows, "Water-	-bullock", The Drive, Northwood Middx	4 10 49		22 11 49
1531-M	7215523		D.P.F. Embleton, 12 Grove Road	Northwood Middx	17 10 48		22 10 49. ✓
1534 P	7217523		D McCampbell, The Drive	Horley Surrey	29 10. 49.		8 · 11 47 ✓
903-L	7204826	Kevill-Davies March Ltd, 41, Hays Mews, W.1	E.D. Graham, Ewelme Down Hse.	Ewelme, Oxon	14 11 49		1 - 6 - 50
815 L	7263384		Dagenham Motor Wholesale Dept.	Essex	11. 11. 49.		28 11 49 ✓
647 K	7200763		C.L Devereux, 9 Glenhurst	Rd. Prittlewell	14 11 49		15 · 2 - 50 ✓
1538 P	7217638		W.G. Broomfield, 43. Hazelwell	Rd, S.W 15.	2 · 12 49		5 12 49. ✓
832 L	7204735		C.J. Titterton, 53 Marple	Rd, Offerton, Stockport	16 12 49		22 4 - 50
558-K	9198905		W.J Gunter 21 Lipson La.	ne. Harlington Woking HAYES, MIDDX	16. 12. 49.		14 · 2 · 50
1551 P	7219563	Nash Concessionaires, Park St. W1	P.A. Gibb. Woodbury The	Drive Hook Hth	19 12 49		5 · 1 · 50 ✓
772-L	7202171	Rod Ric's Automobiles.	W.A. Watson, The Belmont Hotel	Kenton, Harrow	22 12 49.		14 - 6 - 50 ✓
P-1552	7219818	The Car Mart Ltd. 150 Park Lane W.1.	H.R. Chapman, 9. Bracondale	Norwich Norfolk	10 1 50		23. 1. 50.
P-1590	7223880		S Torey, 12 The Avenue	Colchester, Essex GLOS.	13 · 2 · 50 ✱		10 3 50
P-1586	7222488		P. Barrett, Bourton on the Hill	Moreton-in-Marsh	3 2 50		11 · 2 · 50 ✓
P-1600	7224155	H.C. Nelson Ltd., 6/11 Applebee Yard S.W.	Sir. Theo. Brinkman, Neuvaide	Inverness-shire House, Neuvaide	8 3 50		1 - 5 - 50 ✓
P-1603	7225837	Car Mart Ltd. 150 Park Lane W.1.	A.W. Arthur "Aldgate House" 46-56	Monsell St. E.1.	9 3 50		21 - 3 - 50 ✓
P-1606	7225896	Dagenham Motors, Ealing Rd, Alperton	O. Owen, "Kolagiri, Davenham Ave	Northwood MIDDX.	13 - 3 - 5		29 - 3 - 50
P-1637	7228905	Car Mart Ltd. Euston Rd, N.W.1.	Lt. Col. J.B.S. Lewin, Old Farm	Wisborough Green SUSSEX	1 - 5 - 50		12 - 5 - 50 ✓
P-1647	7229759	Warwick Wright & Co Ltd. New Bond St.	Standard Range & Foundry Co Ltd.	WATFORD, HERTS.	16 - 5 - 50		17 - 5 - 50 ✓
P-1649	7229739		C.L Mardall, 2 Hyde Park	Place W.2.	18 - 5 - 50		24 - 5 - 50 ✓
P-1590	7223880		H.Q. Clayman Ltd, 1/2 Cynthia St	London, N.1.	13 - 2 - 50 ✱		5 - 5 - 50
P-1686	7233689	Brooklands of Bond St. Ltd. W.1.	D.H. Leicester Esq, 21, Bloomsbury Sq., W.1.	SUSSEX	11 - 7 - 50		14 - 7 - 50.
P-1712	7235796		A.L. Sinclair, "Woodpeckers", Kings Lane, Coldwaltham		20 - 7 - 50		25 - 7 - 50. ✓
P-1715	7233880	Procton Motors Ltd, 122 High St. Uxbridge	T. Parker & Sons Ltd, 114 B'dway	West Ealing W.13	27 - 7 - 50		2 - 8 - 50 ✓
P-1724	7235799	Kevill-Davies March Ltd, 41/42 Hays Mews. W.1.	G.R.S. Whitelaw, Knockando Hse.	Knockando, Moray.	1 - 8 - 50		3 - 8 - 50 ✓
P-1756	7238759	W.H. Arthur & Co Ltd, Station Gar	Rev M. N. Foster, Stock Rectory	Stock, ESSEX	4 - 9 - 50		5 - 9 - 50 ✓
P-1752	7238744	Arthur Gibb, 6 St. Peters, Bedford	Laxton Bros, Bedford	High St Bedford	4 - 9 - 50		4 - 9 - 50 ✓
P-1757	7238770	Brooklands of Bond St, 103 New Bond St.	G.D. Peters & Ltd, Windsor Dks	Slough, Bucks	6 - 9 - 50		13 - 9 - 50 ✓
P-1763	7238779	W.H. Arthur & Co Ltd, Station Gar, Billericay	Miss M.C. Watson, Church Green	Cottage, STOCK	14 - 9 - 50		17 - 9 - 50 ✓
P-1794	7238766	Procton Motors Ltd, 122 High St Uxbridge	J.E. Chapman, 22, The Broadway	West Ealing W.13	27 - 9 - 50		6 - 10 - 50 ✓
P-1809	7239414	Eleali Ltd, Saffron Walden	J.R.D. Haylock, Farm Hampton	Saffron Walden	27 - 10 - 50		4 - 11 - 50 ✓
P-1815	7240943		P. Day, Esq, 123 Spilsby Rd.	Boston Lincs.	10 - 10 - 50		3 - 11 - 50 ✓
P-1833	7240728	Brooklands of Bond St, 103 New Bond St. W.1.	C.V.A. Jigs Tools Moulds Ltd, 7, B	Buckingham Rd, B'ham	3 - 11 - 50		20 - 11 - 50. ✓
P-1838	7242992	W.H. Arthur, Nation Garage, Billericay Essex	S. Earnshaw, Kings Road Cottages	Stock, Essex	13 - 11 - 50		18 - 11 - 50. ✓
P-1874	7244501		The Motor Reg Co. Ltd., Beeh-	Ashers Radish, 9	24 - 11 - 50		6 - 1 - 51 ✓
P-1890	7244999	Roundabout Garages St. Western Ave, Greenford	English Metal Power Co. Ltd. West	Drayton, Middx	14 - 12 - 50		20 - 12 - 50 ✓
P-1883	7244972	Henlys Ltd, 385 Euston Rd, N.W.1.	H.F. Cooper 27 Connaught St.	London W.2.	11 - 12 - 50		20 - 12 - 50
P-1896	7246469	Roundabout Garages, Western Ave, Greenford	English Metal Powder Co. Ltd	West Drayton Middx	31 - 12 - 50		6 - 1 - 51 ✓
P-1904	7246817	G. Davis Ltd, Neasdon Lane N.W.10	Lilley & Skinner, Pentonville	Rd. W.1.	8 - 1 - 51		11 - 1 - 51 ✓
P-1915	7246818	BROOKLANDS OF BOND ST.	GOODALL ENG. Co. 144 PERRIVALE	SE 23	18 3 - 51		27. 3. 51 ✓

DAGENHAM MOTORS

Chassis No	Engine No	Dealers Name & Address	Customers Name & Address	Received	Date Delivered	To Customer	Warranty Recd
P.1929	7249342		A. FALL. MESSRS TECHNIFON LTD. 133/136 EUSTON RD. LONDON NW1.	29.1.51			15.2.51
P.1932	7249699	SANDERS GARAGE, RICHMOND RD. TWICKENHAM	MR SEEAR. QUEENSBURY ENG. Co. STANMORE	15.2.51			1.3.51
P.1940	7249601	THE SERVICE GARAGE, EAST HILL COLCHESTER ESSEX	E. G. NASH. 95, MALDON RD. COLCHESTER. ESSEX	19.2.51			6.3.51
K.1924	7249344		MR. ACLAND GEDDES. 31, BIRKELEY COURT BAKER STREET N.W.	21.2.51			20.3.51
P.1945	7250054		BRITISH HEAT RESISTING GLASS Co. BILSTON PHOENIX WKS	21.2.51			5.3.51
P.1951	7250065	ROUNDABOUT GARAGES. GREENFORD	THOMPSON & NORRIS BRENTFORD. MIDDX	26.2.51			6.3.51
P.1994	7252465		THE OILCAKES & OILSEEDS TRADING Co. Ltd. 180A CANNON	29.3.51			4.4.51
P.2022	7252810	W. J. BROWN LTD. 339, FINCHLEY RD.	MESSES. LILLEY & SKINNER. 192, PENTONVILLE RD. KINGS X.	9.4.51			3.5.51
P.2026	7252744	E. C. STEARNS & Co. LTD. 250/262 BROMPTON RD.	W.G. GOODA HURST DOWN ILB WAY GORING BY SEA	9.4.51			19.4.51
P.2044	7256464	E. C. STEARNS & Co. LTD. 250/262 BROMPTON RD.	BARRANQUILLA SECURITIES LTD LITTLEWICK HOUSE	4.6.51		LITTLEWICK GH. NR. MAIDENHEAD BERKS	9.7.51
K.2034	7249391		A. GOULANDRIS 44 GROSVENOR SQ. W.1.	4.6.51			12.6.51
P.2103	7258084	W. H. ARTHUR & Co. LTD. STATION GARAGE	C. A. W. HARDING. 16, TAUNTON DRIVE WESTCLIFF-ON-SEA	29.6.51			2.7.51
K.2109	7259626		W. H. GOLMINGS & ASSOCIATES LTD. 21 HERTFORD STREET W1	26.7.51			3.8.51 ✓
P.2161	7260376		RAYNER & KEELER LTD. NEW BOND ST. LONDON W.1.	30.8.51			10.11.51 ✓
P.2147	7259727		D. M. LEAPMAN 7, BURLINGTON ARCADE LONDON W.1	11.9.51			9.11.51 ✓
P.2187	7261354		MAJOR. S A RAMI LITTLE BARNILY STANHOE, KINGS LYNN NORFOLK	4.10.51		NORFOLK	30.10.51 ✓
P.2232	7262934		PILCHER HERSHAM & PARTNERS, 74, BROOK STREET. W.1.	6.11.51			17.11.51 ✓
K.2202	7264732		A. L. SINCLAIR, 8 RUTLAND MEWS, S.W.7.	20.11.51			25.7.52 ✓
P.2258	7265700		P. CLARKE 17, WESTBOURNE HOUSE, RICHMOND RD. TWICKENHAM	3.12.51		MIDDX.	7.12.51 ✓
P.2260	7265761	A. W. WATKINS. LTD. 14, SHORTMEAD ST. BIGGLESWADE	FORDS. (FINSBURY) LTD. CHANTRY AVE. KEMPSTON. BEDS	5.12.51			7.12.52 ✓
P.2263	7265777	H. G. GREASEY & SONS LTD KNEBWORTH	W.H. DAVIES & SONS (WAGONS) LTD. LANGWITH JUNCTION	5.12.51			15.3.52 ✓
P.2264	7263696	RUSSELL MOTORS. W1. SLOANE ST. S.W.1.	RT. HON. EARL OF WIMBERLEY WYMONDHAM NORFOLK	15.12.51			26.3.52 ✓
MX.2299	7265691		F. G. B. WADDELL. 41, WESTERN RD. ROMFORD ESSEX	21.12.51			3.1.52 ✓
P.2274	7265854		C & E. RUSSELL. 66. STATION ROAD CHINGFORD E.4	31.12.51			19.2.52 ✓
M.3014	7266545	BROOKLANDS OF BOND ST. W.1	H. M. PALIN. THE TOWERS WARWICK RD COVENTRY	1.1.52			5.2.53 ✓
M.3016	7268373	H. M. BENTLEY & PARTNERS LTD. 9, ALBEMARLE ST. W.1.	IAN TEMPERLEY STAMP. 26, HENDON AVE., N.3.	25.1.52			1.2.52 ✓
M.3015	7268025	TANKARD & SMITH 194/198, KINGS RD. S.W.3	H. A. GAMMRIDGE 4, MANOR COURT NEMIUS PLACE S.W.3	25.1.52			26.1.52 ✓
P.2284	7268369		P. Z. HENDERSON. 133, WIDMORE RD. BROMLEY. KENT.	19.2.52			27.2.52 ✓
M.3013	7266582		WIMBLEDON SPEEDWAY LTD. PLOUGH LANE	22.2.52		S.W.17 STILL IN STOCK	28.8.52 ✓
P.2294	7269434		F. C. GRIFFITHS BONNYBRIDGE SILICON & FIRECLAY Co. Ltd	26.2.52		BONNYBRIDGE, STIRLINGSHIRE	14.5.52 ✓
J.2155	2131 Z			30.4.52			
J.2122	2027 Z		see also Bristol St Motor entries	1.5.52			
P.2.4006	7274425	BROOKLANDS 103. OF BOND STREET.	IAIN. A. CAMPBELL TRAIGH A RAINE. ARDNAINE ARGYLL SCOTLAND.	6.8.52			14.8.52 ✓
M.3119	F. 1280348		JACKSON & CURTISS (BUILDERS) LTD 15, HANOVER SQUARE W1.	2.9.52			22.9.52 ✓
P.2249	7262954	TRANSFERRED FROM RATCLIFF MOTORS LTD.	J. C. SMITH. "PLASHES" LONDON RD.			BUNTINGFORD, HERTS.	5.3.53 ✓
J12.5070	KOTTA 4587		J. P. CARSTAIRS. MULBERRY COTTAGE	14.7.53		NETHERAVON RD. CHISWICK. W4	1.9.53
J12.5141	KOTTA 5036			6.8.53			
J12.5108	KOTTA 4047	PETERSHAM GARAGE LTD.	MAJOR A SCHWEIZER FIELDHEAD	8.1.54		ARTHUR ROAD S.W.19	8.1.54

Chassis No.	Engine No.	Dealers name and address	Customers name	and	Address	Date Delivered.		Warranty.
21Z-5111	KOTTA.81368		MISS.W.B.KNIGHT.	LITTLE REDHATCH. SELSRY BILL		1. 4. 54	SUSSEX.	1. 4. 54
P2-4509	7289179		BARTON RADIO,	RUTNEY,		30. 6. 54		

A. E. GOULD. LIMITED.

CHASSIS no	ENGINE no	DEALERS. NAME & ADDRESS.	CUSTOMERS. NAME	ADDRESS	DATE	DELIVERED	WARRANTY RECIEVED
M-619	7200161		Major. G. Whitehead, Whitebrook, M. Chep-	Chep.	24. 8. 48		1. 9. 48
K-708	7200402		J. H. Gotch, Eastacre.	Saffron Walden	14. 9. 48		14. 9. 48
M-698	7200782		M. J. Miles, 34, Gt. Queen St., W.C.2	W.C.2	27. 9. 48		1. 10. 48
L-690	7202223	Wells & Le Voi, Tottenham, N.15.	O. P. Prestwick, 82, Crediton Hill, Hampstead	ton Hill,	15. 10. 48		16. 10. 48
M-753	7202593		Gates Hyslop, 6, Eardleigh Pl, W.C.1	leigh Pl. W.C.1	19. 11. 48		30. 11. 48.
M-804	7204233	Motourists (Lond) Ltd. N.2.	Paul Zetter, 20, Lyttleton Rd, N.2.	Rd, N.2.	23. 12. 48		1. 1. 49.
M-879	7206667	H.W. Perry Ltd Invicta Works, N. Finchley	Betty Box Film Services Ltd, 32	Charing X. Rd. W.C.2	27. 1. 49		8. 9. 49.
M-1092	7212020	Wag Bennett & Sons, Rainham, Essex.	Dr. Stephens, 125, Wennington Rd, Rainham.	ington Rd, Rainham.	7. 7. 49		9. 7. 49.
M-1091	7212 613	Wag. Bennett & Sons, Rainham Essex.	B. Wyers, "Raydens" Upminster Rd, Essex.	minster Rd, Essex.	11. 7. 49		14. 7. 49.
P-1516	7193088	Cleale Ltd, Saffron Walden	J. G. Craig, Stonards Farm, Stokeby Clare, Suffolk	Stokeby Clare, Suffolk	10. 11. 49		20. 2. 50.
P-1541	7206 959		Greaves Thomas Ltd, Gt. Missenden	Clapton London, Bucks	10. 12. 49		6. 1. 50
P-1567	7222084		G. L. Mellington, Humble Farm, Green Lane	Farm, Green Lane	19. 1. 49		1. 2. 50
P-1593	7223889		Dr. C. Keighley, 44 Devonshire St. W.1	shire St. W.1	17. 2. 49		23. 2. 50
P-1614	7226077		Dr. R. J. Talbot, 51 Queens Gate	Queens Gate	25. 3. 50		6. 4. 50.
P-1662	7229911		O. H. Hunter, Langholme, Marylebone, Wigan	Marylebone, Wigan	7. 6. 50		15. 6. 50.
P-1723	7235359	Bonallack & Sons Ltd, Nursery Lane, E.7.	J. L. Kaufman, 17 Portman Sq, W.1.	Sq, W.1.	2. 8. 50		1. 8. 50.
P-1790	7240048		D. Stone T/A Fashion Fabrics, 157 Gt. Portland St. W.1	Gt. Portland St. W.1	30. 9. 50		30. 10. 50
P-1871	7244329		Mrs. E. Hunter Langholme, Marylebone Wigan	Marylebone Wigan	20. 11. 50		23. 10. 50
P-1878	7244504		E. b. Freedman Esq., 33 Bruton St., W.1.	Bruton St., W.1.	1. 12. 50		16. 12. 50
P-1953	7260069		G. WHITEHEAD TRAFALGAEL WHITEBROOK, CHEPSTOW.	WHITEBROOK	28. 2. 51		31. 3. 51
P-1964	7252461.		MISS P. M. READ CHALTON CROSS LUTON.	CROSS LUTON.	9. 3. 51.		15. 3. 51.
P-2041.	7253956.		F. FISCHEL, 135. SUSSEX GDNS. W.2	GDNS. W. 2	19. 4. 51.		30. 4. 51.
P-2043	7256444		MRS. C. D. SCOTT. DEERING GOOD DAUNE PERTH	GOOD DAUNE PERTH	4. 6. 51		15. 6. 51
P-2127	7258764		REG. LEATHER, 20, GREENWAY CLOSE. TOTTERIDGE	CLOSE. TOTTERIDGE	17. 7. 51.	WHETSTONE N. 20.	18. 7. 51.
P-2207	7262343		A. H. CARTER. R. HOLLEY HOUSE, HAGGMARNE. KINGS	HAGGMARNE. KINGS	17. 10. 51	LYNN NORFOLK.	31. 10. 51.
P-2261	7262955		R. D. CARTER. CRABBS ABBEY, GASTON BRIDGE.	GASTON BRIDGE.	21. 11. 51	KINGS LYNN NORFOLK.	22. 11. 51.
M-3089	7268377		D. P. PRESTWICH. 32, CREDITION HILL, LONDON N.V.	HILL, LONDON N.V.	31. 1. 52.		2. 2. 52.
P-2288	7268379.				9. 2. 52	STILL IN STOCK	allocated 20/2/52

F. ENGLISH. LIMITED.

Chassis no.	Engine no.	Dealers. Names. Address	Customer's Name and Address	Date	Delivered	Warranty Recd
K-592	7199720	Boizot · Caine. Fareham.	W.H. Waing, Everslie House, Gower End,	17. 8. 48		5. 8. 48
M-603	7199755	Westover Garage, Bournemouth	B.W. Parkes, 1, Cotham Pk., Ntd., Bristol.	19. 8. 48		4. 9. 48
K-599	7199688	G. Hartwell, Holdenhurst Rd.	C.F.S. Brooks, 8, Park Lane, Kirkfield, Cheshire.	1. 9. 48		4. 9. 48
M-646	7200672	Westover Garage. Bournemouth	J. Ward. Sqrs. Moyster, Pk. Spalding. Lincs.	1. 9. 48		22. 9. 48
K-591	7199664	Westover Garage, Bournemouth	E. Martin, Sturbridge, Dorset.	8. 9. 48		14. 9. 48
M-683	7200769	Lee Motors (Bournemouth) Ltd.	P.H. Fagahole, Blandford. Dorset	13. 9. 48		11. 10. 48
L-671	7200778		G. Mason, Travaleois Club Pall Mall, S.W.1	7. 10. 48		28. 10. 48
M-722	7202949	E. Childs Sons, Sherborne, Dorset	K.S.D. Digby. House of Commons, S., S.W.1	12. 10. 48		1. 11. 48
L-652	7200762	G.A. Cox, Redbridge Causeway, Southampton	A.J.Q. Hamsworth, High Coxbeer, Lyndhurst, Hants.	18. 10. 48		30. 10. 48
M-739	7202951	G.W. Cox, Redbridge Causeway, Southampton	A.J.A. Hamsworth, High Coxbeer,	1. 11. 48		9. 11. 48
M-795	7203944	Erskine Motors. Wilts.	R.M. Everett Avonturn, Amesbury, Wilts.	8. 11. 48		16. 11. 49
M-750	7202560	Andrew Sloane, Amesbury	Dr. J.L.O. Lewis, Orestbrook, Stonehenge Rd.	16. 11. 48		17. 11. 48
M-783	7203734	Vine · Son Ltd, 733 Wimborne Rd. Winton, Bournemouth	T.H. Haydon, Branksome, Tower Hotel	17. 11. 48		1. 12. 48
M-789	7203953			17. 12. 48		NOT RECD
K-644	7200970	Knott Bros. Ltd, Bournemouth	E.E. Longmead, 171A, Queens Pk. Ave. B'mouth Dorset	23. 12. 48		3. 1. 49
M-813	7204368	Knott Bros. Ltd, Bournemouth	E. Gayton, Middle Bere Farm, Arne, Wareham	4. 1. 49		20. 1. 49
M-768	7203625			25. 1. 49		NOT RECD
M-860	7204819	G.W. Cox, Redbridge Causeway, Southampton	Dr. W.L. Milligan, 41, Rothall Rd, Couplan, Hants.	25. 1. 49		10. 2. 49
M-883	7206521	Andrew Sloan, Amesbury	G.P. Shea Simmonds, Melrose Cottage, Salisbury, Wilts.	2. 2. 49		4. 2. 49
M-880	7206627	G.W. Cox, Redbridge Causeway, Southampton	Charles St John, St Cloud, S. Hotel, Brockenhurst	7. 2. 49		28. 2. 49
M-832	7204556	G.W. Cox, Redbridge Causeway,	A.H. Saunders, Carlton, Cadnam, Hants.	22. 2. 49		22. 2. 49
M-859	7207238	Lee Motors (Bournemouth) Ltd	H.R. Paul, Whitcombe, Dorch.	23. 2. 49		15. 8. 49
M-1004	7207582	South Hants Motor Co.	O.J. Philipson, Mallards, Bucklers Hard, Southpton	7. 3. 49		5. 4. 49
M-1002	7207111	E.W. Cox & Co. Ltd., Southampton	Dr. H.O. White, 144a, Wm. Michell Rd.	11. 3. 49		12. 3. 49
M-1012	7207297	Wadham Bros. 108/114, Palmista, Portsmouth	B.L. Williams, 1, Helene Rd. Southsea.	21. 3. 49		7. 4. 49
M-1019	7209286	Dorchester, West St. Wimborne	G.H. Richardson, Chilbridge Farm, Dorset.	21. 3. 49		9. 4. 49
M-1015	7206832	Lee Motors, 674/680, Wimborne Rd.	S.A. Savel, 434, Boscombe, Bournemouth	23. 3. 49		25. 6. 49
M-1038	7209747	Geo. Hartwell Ltd., Bournemouth	R. Cole, Broomsgrove, Milton, Marlborough, Wilts.	4. 4. 49		5. 4. 49
M-1042	7209744		J. Woolford, 26 Clwg	Swanage Dorset	5. 4. 49		16. 4. 49
M-1039	7209762		Present, Lymington, Hants	13. 4. 49		27. 12. 48
M-1057	7210568	Pennington Cross Garage, Lymington.	Dr. B.M. Thornton Wisteria, St. Thomas St, Dorset	6. 5. 49		11. 5. 49
P-1502	7212115	La Motor Works (Bournemouth) Dunbone Dorset	Mrs. R.M. Copley, Roselliey · Bryan Place Farm, Mappowder,	16. 9. 49		2. 2. 50
P-1537	7255637	T. Dibben & Sons, West St.	Mrs. A. Toomer, Merrylands, Liddington, Swindon.	7. 11. 49		22. 11. 49
L-757	7202218	G.W. Cox & Co, Redbridge Causeway, S'hta.	K.R.Q. Allwon-Bennett, "Clouds" Longham Dorset	26. 11. 49		22. 3. 50
K-643	7200816		J. Schneedler, 12 Haskells Flats, Lyndhurst Hants	26. 11. 48		2. 12. 49
P-1549	7219357		H.J. Adeney, "Purbeck View" Sandbourne Rd. B'mouth	30. 12. 49		26. 1. 50
P-1588	7223857	G.W. Cox & Co, Redbridge Causeway, Southampton	P.M. Coombes Ltd., Eastleigh, Hants.	13. 2. 49		7. 3. 50
P-1613	7226135		South Somerset Glove Co. Ltd., Stoke under Ham, Somerset	20. 3. 50		31. 3. 50
P-1615	7226085	Geo. Hartwell Ltd., 199 Charminster Rd.	R.L. Cole, Broomsgrove, Milton, Marlborough, Wilts	30. 3. 50		4. 5. 50
P-1651	7229920		P.W. Moore, Regina Court, Bournemouth	19. 5. 50		3. 6. 50
J-1576	5335/23		J.E.A. Way-Hope, Seagull House, Poole, Dorset	26. 5. 50		27. 5. 50

4/

F. ENGLISH LTD.

CHASSIS No	ENGINE No.	DEALERS NAME + ADDRESS	CUSTOMERS	NAME + ADDRESS	DATE	DELIVERED	WARRANTY REC'D
P-1664	7232476	Cox Co. Ltd., Redbridge, South'ton	H.P. White, c/o Camper +	Nicholsons, Norlam, So'ton	10-6-50		16-6-50 ✓
P-1680	7231846	Stevens Bros. (Fleet) Ltd.	Sir Paul Pechell,	Brackley, Dinorben Ave, Hants	4-7-50		1-8-50
P-1689	7235793	G.W. Cox Co Ltd, Redbridge Cswy Bo'ton	P.R. Stephen Bassett	House, Chalmford Rd, Bo'ton	1-8-50		2-9-50 ✓
P-1728	7233903		V.G. Boyle, 8, Ovington	Court, Kensington, S.W.3.	21-8-50		22-8-50 ✓
P-1758	7238779	Ward Motors, New Park St Devizes	? D Chester, Hartmoor	House, Devizes, Wilts	6-9-50		16-9-50 ✓
K-622	7200193				6-9-50		NOT REC'D
P-1765	7238783		J.H. Joyce, Church	Farm, Rode nr. Bath, SOMERSET.	22-9-50		2-10-50 ✓
P-1810	7240732	The Carbury Gar Carbery Nr B'mth	C. Lord Ltd., 30	Wellington Place, Belfast	3-10-50		8-10-50 ✓
P-1836	7242413	Lee Motor Works (B'mouth) Ltd.	J.C. Bugg, Tarrant	Monkton, Nr Blandford, DORSET	6-11-50		14-11-50 ✓
P-1867	7244328	Carr's Cars, The Border Gar Corsley	J. Holloway + Sons	Ltd, Upper Eden Vale, Westbury WILTS	16-11-50		11-12-50 ✓
P-18701	7244323	G.W. COX LTD REDBRIDGE HANTS	A.A. Thompson "The Haven"	GARDEN CLOSE, N. MILTON, Branksome Bournemouth	22-11-50		31-1-51 ✓
P-1876	7244482	" "	P.G. Bankart, Bran-	-ksome Manor Avenue Rd.,	99-11-50		2-1-51 ✓
P-1893	7246430		G.R. Read, Messrs Re-	-ad & Lord (Salisbury) Ltd	18-12-50		12-1-51 ✓
P-1908	7246896	LEE MOTOR WORKS LTD	M.A. Pitt-Rivers	HINTON ST MARY DORSET	15-1-51		24-2-51 ✓
P-1961	7250980	G.W. Cox and Co. Ltd.,	BOSHERS	CHOL-SEY BERKS	12-3-51		12-4-51 ✓
P-1993	7252459	"	H. CARRUTHERS	MURCOTT, CRUDWELL WILTS	29-3-51		4-4-51 ✓
P-2055.	7256184		LORD WARDINGTON.	WARDINGTON MANOR, BANBURY	6-5-51		11-5-51
K-2091.	7258545	CARR'S CARS CORSLEY. N'WARMINSTER	G. SMITH-BOSANQUET,	NORTON. BAVANT MANOR WINCHMOORE HILL	26-6-51	WARMINSTER. WILTS.	9-7-51.
P-2148	726-0148		DAVID. W.D.R. ABERDEEN,	20, GREEN MOORE LINK LONDON	13-9-51	N.21.	26-9-51 ✓
K-2200	7262943		C.F.S. STREET, HOTEL	GROSVENOR, SWANAGE, DORSET.	19-10-51.		20-10-51 ✓
P-2208	7262561 ABOVE		J.W.F. COLES, 4,	STANDHILL STREET. OTTERY	23-10-51.	ST. STREET. MARY DEVON.	24-1-52. ✓
P-3099	7291156	COX CO. LTD, REDBRIDGE CAUSEWAY, SOTON.	CAMPER + NICHOLSONS	LTD, WILLIAM STREET,	9-5-52.	NORTHAM, SOUTHAMPTON	12-5-52. ✓

5. HUGHES of EXETER

CHASSIS no.	ENGINE no.	DEALERS NAME & ADDRESS	CUSTOMERS NAME	& ADDRESS	DATE	DELIVERED	WARRANTY. Received
K-553	7198514		J.H. Lockyer, Wingcroft	...ston, N. Devon.	16. 8. 48		26. 7. 48
M-636	7200409	Midsomer Norton, Somerset.	7. Garg, Simpsons, Hoop	...in Ave., Exeter.	3. 9. 48		7. 9. 48
M-630	7200147	Midsomer Norton Motor Co.,	G.B. Beauchamp, Nortn	Hall, N. Bath, Som	9. 9. 48		14. 10. 48
M-658	7200939	Brown's Garage, Montpelier Garage, Bath	L. Sawyer, The Rest	House, Westbury. Wilts	15. 9. 48		9. 9. 48
M-785	7203735		O. Scarborough, Wool	Lane, Crese, Falmouth	25. 11. 48		28. 11. 48
M-820	7204413	Not yet Sold			17. 1. 49		NOT REC'D
K-742	7203408	Elliott & Sons, Kingsley Ave. Bideford	J. Foden, "May Grove",	Cleavehouses, Bideford	21. 1. 49.		24. 1. 49
L-792	7204183	Hug...	S.D. Chapple, Oakleigh,	Torrington Devon	18. 8. 49.		19. 8. 49.
M-1525	7215388	New Central Garage, Cornwall			13. 12. 49.		✗ NOT REC'D
P-1553	7219819		A.J. Perry, 9. Tremena	Rd., St Austell, Cnwll	10. 1. 50.		8. 1. 50.

HARTWELLS LIMITED.

CHASSIS no.	ENGINE no.	DEALERS NAMES & ADDRESS	CUSTOMERS NAME & ADDRESS		DATE	DELIVERED.	WARRANTY Rec'vd
M-692	7200736	Q.Q. Clark Ltd, Windsor.	H.K. Marsden, M.A, The	Priory, Eton College.	22. 9. 48		1. 3. 49.
M-711	7202488		Philippa. M. Lamb, Silver-	stone House, Montacute.	1. 10. 48		1. 10. 48
M-734	7202999		J. B. Powell, Aldbourne,	Marlborough, Wilts.	16. 10. 48.		21. 10. 48
M-799	7203959				9. 11. 48		NOT REC'D
M-779	7203784				18. 11. 48		
M-786	720733		J. Hywood Jones, Manor	Maisey, Marlborough. Stables, Ogbourne	30. 11. 48		26. 3. 49.
L-845	7204736				28. 2. 49		NOT REC'D
M-1033	7209682		F.C. Hancock, 22, Queens	Park, Aylesbury, Bucks.	21. 3. 49		12. 4. 49.
M-1052	7209991		D. Emmet, Amberley Castle	Amberley, Sussex	21. 4. 49		7. 5. 49.
M-1064	7210700	Stevensons (Auto) Sales, Newbury Berks	J.S Pauy. Texton, Eype Bid	part, Dorset	26. 5. 49		4. 6. 49.
M-1073	7210931	Wheeler (Newbury) Ltd, 7 the Broadway	F.J. Reynolds Ltd, Bath Rd.	Thatcham Berks	11. 6. 49.		27. 12. 48.
P-1869	7244333		E. WORTH. THE GARAGE.	ENSTONE. OXON.	20-11-50		12. 2.51.
P-2046	7254682	NORTH OXFORD GARAGE Ltd OXFORD.	J.W. WATTS NEW ESTATE	BLACK BOURTON OXON	30-4-51.		3-5-51.
P-2185	7260728	LODDON BRIDGE MOTORS. EARLEY READING	Betty Culpin "Pine Tor" Leice ster Rd BRANKSOME PARK		26-9-51.	BOURNEMOUTH.	10-12-51.
P-2257	7265763	LODDON BRIDGE MOTORS EARLEY READING.	H.M. PRICE. 106, LONDON RD.	READING.	4-12-51.		8-12-51.
P-2267	7266394		W.J. HOPPER. 48 HEATH	DRIVE. GIDEA PARK	18-12-51	ESSEX	6. 10. 52

TAYLORS (GLOUCESTER) Limited.

CHASSIS no	ENGINE no	DEALERS NAME & address	CUSTOMERS NAME	& ADDRESS	DATE	DELIVERED	WARRENTY Recvd
M- 667	7200722		E. N. Dicking, 82, High St,	Stourbridge.	12. 8. 48		2. 10. 48
M- 582	7199374		J. P. Round, 60, Oakham	Rd, Dudley. Worcs.	12. 8. 48		13. 8. 48
M- 666	7200748	Edwards Marshall Ltd, Glos.	C. G. P. Martin, Radcliff, Wellington Rd	Wallasey	24. 8. 48		2. 8. 49
L- 672	7200765				1. 9. 48		NOT REC'D
M- 651	7200951		H. J. Burton, 25, Soverk	gate St, Glos,	8. 9. 48		16. 9. 48
M- 673	7200943	E. Wilkins Ltd. Worcester. Bach Rd, Worcester	T. P. Baneby, Saltmarie	Eello, Scompid, Herei	17. 9. 48		14. 7. 49
M- 738	7202979	T. J. Daniel Ltd, Motor Horse,	F. Probert, 193, Bideford Rd,	Worcester.	20. 10. 48.		25. 10. 48
M- 765	7203605	Apex Motor Ltd, Stourbridge.	H. S. Bayley, 146, Jesson	Rd, Walsall.	5. 11. 48		10. 11. 48.
M- 723	7202946	Road Factor	P. & J. Parkes, 1. Cotham	Pk, Nd, Bristol 1.	12. 11. 48		14. 11. 48
M- 764	7203614	Whitehouse Garage, Stourbridge	Dr. K. W. Vardy. Dunkirk	House, Devizes	3. 12. 48		2. 12. 48.
M- 861	7204641	Apex Motors Ltd Hagley Rd			18. 1. 49		17. 1. 49
P- 1747	7237911		A. J. Tommi, 854 Walsall Rd,	Gt. Barr. Birmingham	24- 8- 50		25- 8- 50
P- 1266	7238789	Stow Valley Motor Co Ltd, Hagley Rd, STOURBRIDGE	H. Birmingham Sound Reproducers Ltd	Claremont M, Old Hill, Staffs	20- 9- 50		
P- 1882	7240159		Cecil Collin Evans, Westacres,	Brentry, Bristol	19- 10- 50		4- 11- 50
P- 1835	7242421	STEELS CIRENCESTER Ltd CIRENCESTER DYER ST.	HON: MRS J PAINE, HOME FARM,	STOWELL PK. GLOS	5. 4. 51.		20. 4. 51.
P 1999	7252812	KIDDERMINSTER MOTORS LTD. KIDDERMINSTER	MRS. E. COLLINS SHATTERFORD GRANGE MR KIDDERMINSTER		9. 4. 51		12. 4. 51. 9. 4. 53
P 2021	7252811						
P 4504	7283424	IMPERIAL MOTOR MART CHELTENHAM	HON. MRS PAINE HOME	FARM.	16. 6. 53.	1. STOWELLS PARK NORTHLEACH GLOS.	16. 6. 53

A.E. HARRIS LIMITED.

CHASSIS no.	ENGINE no.	DEALERS NAME & ADDRESS	CUSTOMERS NAME & ADDRESS		DATE	DELIVERED	WARRANTY RECD.
M-610	7199789	Geog Rees Sons, Crosshands, Llanelly	Dr. L.C. Edwards,	Pencaster, Llanelly	18. 8. 48		20. 8. 48
M-651	7200946	Gibbs Bros, Garages, Mon.,	D. Spectar Dr., West cott,	Tyntyla, Llynypia	9. 9. 48		5. 10. 48
M-756	7203506	Gibbs Bros. Garages, Mon.	H. Shephard, Lynwood,	Sto Park Cndle, Newport	8. 11. 48		11. 7. 48
M-769	7203789	W. Hicks, Madocks Garage, Hay-on-Wye.	S. Southall, Lower	Court, Clifford, Herts.	23. 11. 48		5. 11. 48
M-743	7202527	J.W. Leason, Central Garage.	W.S. Gordon Rees, 7. S. Wales	Gelli, Bryn, Carms.	3. 12. 48		2. 12. 48
M-781	7203884	Edwards, Caernarvon.	J. Rhys Davies, "Four Pembs.	Cndle, Haverfordwest	11. 12. 48		18. 12. 48
M-1080	7210823				27. 5. 49		X NOT REC'D
P-1520	7217520		L. Robinson 65 St.	Michaels Rd., Llanclaff Cardiff.	26. 11. 48		30. 11. 49
P-1549	7202519		Gibbs Bros Garages,	Pontllanfraith, MON.	8. 12. 49		8. 12. 49
P-1580	7222111	W. Edwards Son (Carmarthen)	D. Evans Lammas St	Carmarthen.	27. 1. 50.		X 4. 2. 50
P-1584	7202313				3. 2. 50		X NOT REC'D
P-1624	7228241	(LLANELLY)	L. D. Jones, 5 Park Rd,	Barry, Glam.	14. 4. -50		27. -6. -50
P-1663	7229772	G. Rees Son, THE GARAGE CROSSHANDS	A.P. Davies, PAXTON HOUSE.	Cross Hands, Llanelly	13. 6. -50		31. 1. 51.
P-1670	7233210	W.H. Baker, Merthyr Tydfil	S. Williams Glynbargoed Hse,	Treharris, Glam.	17. 6. -50		20. -7. -50
P-1711	7235798	"	Y. Davies Esq, 33	Windsor Ple. Cardiff	21. 7. -50		20. -7. -50
P-1753	7238767	"	Dr. W. Hughes, 1. Park Rd	BARRY, GLAM.	2. -9. -50		31. 1. 51.
P-1822	7242159				19. 10. 50		SEE:- TAYLORS OF GLOS
P-1837	7242988		D.A. Low, THE ORCHARDS	LISUANE N. CARDIFF.	6. -11. -50		19. 2. 51
P-1865	7244325	W.H. Baker, Merthyr Tydfil	Mrs. L. Davies, Dolserdd,	Caeracca Villas, Pont. Deulais	17. -11. -50		30. -11. -50
P-1898	7846514	GLANFIELD LAWRENCE LD	LIONETTE SPECIALISTS	14 COWING DEAN RD CARDIFF	29. -12. -50	SALOON TRANSFERRED TO P.B. WALKER-JONES 13 CALVERT TCE SWANSEA 4/5/51	14. 2. 51.
P-1919	7246894	HANDEL DAVIES. 230 OXFORD ST SWANSEA.	L. THOMAS, 1 LON MAFON	TYCOCH SWANSEA.	20-1-51.		20. 1. 51.
P-1924	7249402		PRINCIPALITY FURNISHERS. 30/	CASTLE ARCADE	29. 1. 51.		10. 3. 51
P-1644.	7242409.		E. LIGHT & SON LIMITED	2 WEMBLEY RD. CARDIFF	3. 2. 51.		19. 2. 51.
P-1948	7250056.		BURLINGTON GLOVES LD TREFOREST TRADING EST. GLAM		22. 2. 51.		26. 2. 51.
P-1938.	7249652		W.R. GRAVES, THE GRANGE	LLANTWIT MAJOR. GLAM.	1. 3. 51.		2. 3. 51.
P-1997	7252805.		A.G. TEXTILES LD WREMO HOUSE REGENT ST.		3. 4. 51.		24. 4. 51.
P-2071	7254760	HANDEL DAVIES LTD. 230 OXFORD ST. SWANSEA	F.E. BARRON. CLYND MOOR	MAY A L S. SWANSEA	29. 5. 51		3. 10. 51.
P-2072	7256764		P. SALAWAN. 22. CRIGHTON ST. CARDIFF.		24. 5. 51.		29. 5. 10. 51.
P-2100	7258089.	GEORGE REES & SONS. THE GARAGE CROSS HANDS	THE WELSH TINPLATE & METAL STAMPING CO LD LLANELLY		25. 6. 51.		25. 6. 51.
P-3083.	7270578.	MORTON GARAGE NARBERTH, PEMBS	W. BEY. EVANS. SODSTON HOUSE NARBERTH. PEMBS.		19. 3. 52.		19. 3. 52.

9 FURROWS LIMITED

CHASSIS. NO	ENGINE no.	DEALERS NAME & ADD	CUSTOMERS NAME	ADDRESS	DATE	DELIVERED	WARRANTY. REC'D
M-609	7199780		E.M. Houghton, Cressage	Nr Shrewsbury	16.8.48		18.8.48
K-554	7198835	Braid Bros. Colwyn Bay.	K.T. Wild, Green Roads,	Stoke on Trent.	23.8.48		24.9.48
L-642	7200863		J.E. Stevens, Chatwynd,	Grove, Nr Wrexham Liverpool	7.9.48		7.9.48 / 8.10.48
M-693	7200698	Braid Bros. Colwyn Bay.	Dr. J.B. Hargreaves. 114,	Gigburgh Drive, Wrexham	24.9.48		24.9.48
M-741	7203195	Wrexham Motor Co. Chester Rd., The Cop.	Mr Brown, J.F.A. Brown, Sons,	89, Hope St,	30.9.48		1.10.48
M-715	7204486	Wales. Edwards, Shrewsbury	C.L. Dennis, Coed Hill	Wem, Salop,	12.10.48		18.10.48
M-714	7203750	H.R. Williams, Valley Garage.	Dr E.R. Hughes, Holyhead, Anglesey.		15.11.48		22.11.48
M-791	7203882		J.L. Sleep, The Gables,	Whitchurch	16.11.48		18.2.49
M-687	7200743		S. Coster-Baker, 46, Walker St	Wellington.	25.11.48		30.11.48
M-853	7204436	LONDON - PEKIN RALLY			21.12.48		NOT REC'D
M-882	7206581	Salop.	L. Hemingway, Holly Cottage	Kinton, Nr Kidderminster.	2.2.49	9.2.49	
M-814	7203464	A. & J. Hemmings Ltd, Bishops Castle	W.B. Cragg, 16 Church St.,	Bishops Castle, Salop	23.2.49		15.3.49
M-831	7206817	Braid Bros. Abergele Rd, Colwyn Bay.	Lady O. Grey Edwards,	Bistreya, Criccieth	10.3.49		9.6.49
M-1011	7207362	Wrexham Motor Co. Denbigh	G.T. McIntyre, Bolton,	Kennoxtown Stirling	17.3.49		29.3.49
M-844	7204847		N.W.A. Sotheby, Bourton	Garage, Llanymynech	23.3.49		8.6.49
M-1101	7209082	Body not yet Completed			25.6.49		NOT REC'D
P-1503	7212114		Fred Leferre, Furnace Hill, Wyre Forest,	Nr Kidderminster.	21.9.49		22.9.49
P-1517	7217525	Bettws-y-Coed Motor Services Ltd	J.B. Smith, Esq., 1-3 Stanley	St Liverpool	26.11.48		26.11.49
K-691	7202186		J.B. Carr, Abbey House Builders	Salop.	26.12.50	del 17.12.49	
P-1563	7221934		Francis Garage Ltd., Colwyn	Bay. Nth Wales	26.12.50		1.2.50.
P-1604	7225843		R.L. Sanderson, 6 Preston	Rd, Southport, Lancs	10-3-50		10.3.50
P-1611	7226136	Bromfields Motors Ltd, Mold.	W.H. Caldie, The Chase,	Hendy Rd, Mold.	21-3-50		25-3-50
P-1631	7228548	Hutchison & Wilde	Dr W.H. Owles, 4 Whitehall Rd	Rhos-on-Sea, Colwyn Bay.	21-4-50		24.4.50
P-1679	7233167		Mr N.J. Kirk, Somerford Grange,	Brewood, Staffs	4-7-50		3-7-50
P-1746	7237910		S.R.B. Greensmith, Petch—	ford Nr Condover, Salop	24-8-50		24-8-50
P-1839	7248985	Francis Garage Ltd Colwyn Bay.	G.C. Gibbs, Whiteoaks Vincent	Close, Esher, Surrey	8-11-50		10-11-50
K2092	7258541		J.P. DENNIS. PARK HOUSE	OAKLEY SALOP	27.6.51.		29.6.51
P 2162	7261353		G.E.S. PLEAVIN. STANFORD,	HALFWAY HOUSE (SALOP	13-9-51		14-9-51
P-2284	7268026	THE STATION GARAGE. MARSHBROOK. CHURCH STRETTON SALOP.	VERE, NATHANIEL FABER Survey, THE RT. HON.	ACTON SCOTT HALL	5-2-52.	CHURCH STRETTON.	23.2.52
P.3084	7240583	CROWN MOTOR CO. BRIDGNORTH	V. BOYNE BURWARTON House	BRIDGNORTH SALOP	4.4.52.		4.4.52
P.3049	4269838		J. HOWARD HILL, 238, SOHO ROAD. HANDSWORTH		16.9.52.	BIRMINGHAM 19.	

MANN EGERTON & COMPANY

CHASSIS. no.	ENGINE. no.	DEALERS NAMES & ADDRESS	CUSTOMERS NAME	ADDRESS	DATE	DELIVERED	WARRANTY REGIS.
K-685	7200746	Mr. W. H. King, Southgates, Kings Lynn.	Munro Transport, Monaghan	Dinealor, Cornwall	15.11.48		15.11.48
M-761	7203589	Wm. H. King, Kings Lynn.	M. Rex Carter, West Lodge,	Aylsham, Norwich	17.11.48		17.11.48
M-843	7204598	Wm. H. King, Kings Lynn.	Bramley F. Burrell, 49, Butter market, Ipswich, Suffolk	3.1.49		3.1.49
M-877	7206613	W.O. Chitty Ltd. Diss, Norfolk	B.C. Bisset Pearce, The Grove Gardon, Diss, Norfolk	27.1.49		27.1.49
M-896	7207274	W. H. King, Kings Lynn	D.R. Grey, White Horse, Colby, Aylsham, Norwich	14.2.49		14.2.49
M-1024	7209269	Mann Egerton, Ipswich.	A.K. Mann, Grove Farm, Wroxton, Suffolk.	23.3.49		23.3.49
P-1539	7212149		W. Burroughes, Rockland Manor	Attleborough, Nfk.	2.12.49		7.12.49
P-1598	7224198		E.O. Benton, Kempton Hall Fm.	Sth. Heveringham, NFK.	24.2.50		25.2.50
P-1618	7228018	Creswells Garage, High St, Newm'kt.	Dr. Barber, Alton House, High	St. Newmarket	3.4.50		4.4.50
P-1623	7228242		D.E. Layton Esq., Tudor Hse., Poplar	Ave., Eaton, Norwich	13.4.50		18.5.50
P-1669	7233207	W.H. King. Kings Lynn	Davis & Co. Ltd. 22 Lynn Road,	Wisbech. CAMBS.	22.6.50		22.6.50
P-1719	7235354		G.F. Andrews, The Croft,	Horning NFK.	31.7.50		1.9.50
P-1814	7240735	Marshalls Cambridge, Austin House, Jesus Lane, Cambs.	Ilford Ltd., Roden St., Ilford,	Essex	7.10.50		26.10.50
P-1872	7244485		W.C. Saunders, Billingford Hall,	Diss Norfolk	24.11.50		29.11.50
P-2038	7252989		P.C. GRAY, 29, St. Andrews Street,	CAMBRIDGE.	10.4.51		19.4.51
P-2097	7258770	Botwoods Ltd. Majors Cr. Ipswich.	F.R. Fisher 113, Valley. Rd.	Ipswich. Suffolk.	9.7.51		31.10.57
M-3096	7240599.		F.S. Clayton. 134. Churchill Rd.	Norwich. Norfolk.	1.5.52.		31.5.52

BRISTOL. STREET. MOTORS LIMITED.

CHASSIS no.	ENGINE no.	DEALERS NAME & ADDRESS	CUSTOMERS NAME & ADDRESS	DATE	DELIVERED	WARRANTY REC
M-583	7199387		Wilmott Taylor Ltd, Tyseley, Birm.	10. 8. 48		20. 8. 48
M-635	7200149	Mists Garage, Handsworth, B'ham.	H. Tipper, Davidson, Little Aston Rd, Streetly, Birm.	31. 8. 48		15. 9. 48
K-611	7200184		P. Mould, Tamworth, Shirley.	16. 9. 48		20. 7. 48
M-682	7300766		L. K. Greene, 35, Moor Green Lane, B'ds.	17. 9. 48		20. 9. 48
K-612	7199989		J. Mansfield, Old Rec. Fay, Bretce,	22. 9. 48		24. 9. 48
M-736	7029144	"	Hughes Motor, Pitman St, 59 Parade, Birm. 1.	22. 9. 48		20. 3. 49
M-732	7202447			23. 9. 48		NOT REC'D
M-705	7200726		J. E. Keightley, White Lion, Bidford-on-Avon.	29. 9. 48		5. 10. 48
M-766	7203774	Body Builders 13th Nov.		21. 10. 48		NOT REC'D
M-800	7204091	Cancelled 24. 11. 48		10. 11. 48		NOT REC'D
M-784	7203883	Central Motors, 41, London Rd., Leicester	L. R. Curtis, 5, Guildford Rd, Leicester.	17. 11. 48		25. 11. 48
K-633	7200466	Frank Greet Ltd, 377, High St, W. Brom.	R. Lilleshope, Palech anges Ltd, Tipton	26. 11. 48		30. 11. 48
K-655	7200783		S. T. Smith, 7/A, Wychall San Mill Rd.	3. 12. 48		10. 1. 49
K-773	7206408	Frank Greet Ltd. 377, High St. West Bromwich	G. L. Sedwick, 108, Bescot Rd, Walsall, Coventry.	1. 12. 48		4. 12. 48
M-808	7204186		D. C. Shepherd, 68, Amprey Close, Rocky Hwy	14. 12. 48		16. 12. 48
M-843	7204589		J. W. Tomkinson Ltd., Fort Terrace, Birm.	10. 1. 49		10. 1. 49
M-839	7204586		J. L. Collis, 15, Highfield Rd, Birmingham, 15.	18. 1. 49		20. 1. 49
M-870	7204841	Central Motor Co. Leicester.	W. C. Smith, 548, Welford Rd., Leicester	27. 1. 49		3. 2. 49
M-884	7206791	Overdale Motors, 15, Bing Rd, B'ham.	M. Stone, 275, Kings Rd, Kingstanding	2. 2. 49		11. 2. 49.
M-847	7206593	Central Motor Co, Leicester.	Dr. B. C. Jennings, 2, Wes Haigh Rd, Leic.,	16. 2. 49		11. 3. 49
M-846	7206530	Bagshaw Cars, Hannan Court, Leic	W. Rowan Co. Wharf St, Leicester.	16. 2. 49		23. 2. 49
M-801	7204090	Central Motor Co. Leicester.	C. Binns, 39, Hallwood Rd, Kettering, Northant	23. 2. 49.		2. 4. 49
M-895	7207122		Lilian Clark, Lincoln of Wales Inn, Wanstead, Birm.	25. 2. 49.		26. 2. 49
K-648	7200817	Central Motor, 41, London Rd, Leicester	Fosse Knitwear Ltd, 124, Church Gate, Leic.	22. 2. 49		22. 2. 49.
M-1023	7209393		M. S. Keeley, Dooley & Co. Ltd, 1, George St., Birm. 12.	31. 3. 49		31. 3. 49
M-1025	7209387		J. W. Bond & Co. Ltd, 39, 42, Cox St., West Walsall Heath, Birm.	22. 3. 49		2. 4. 49.
M-1034	7209609	Chambers of Sutton, Sutton Coldfield	J. Wickes, Marsh Farm, Benson, Wolcm.	2. 4. 49		7. 4. 49
M-1041	7209743		B. N. Pulleen (miss) Bayhall House, Kempley, Worcester.	9. 4. 49		7. 6. 49
M-1036	7209611	Central Motor Co. 41, London Rd. Glos.	Lord Allerton, Loddington Hall, Leics.	11. 4. 49		5. 8. 49
K-755	7202175		R. A. Langley, 25, Heaton Rd., Solihull, Warks.	21. 4. 49		30. 5. 49
M-1065	7210747		P. B. Hudson, Son Ltd., Livery St, Birm.	29. 4. 49		29. 4. 49.
M-1059	7210551		J. C. McWhirter, 83, Wake Green Rd, Moseley, Birm.	4. 5. 49		14. 6. 49
M-1067	7210710		C. Mould, 1659, Stratford Rd, Hall Green, Birm.	9. 5. 49		31. 5. 49
M-1070	7210933		Dr. C. Egar, Bigger, 35, Warwick Rd., Birm. 11.	22. 6. 49		5. 7. 49
M-1090	7210930		J. Godrich, 22, Bennetts Hill, Birmingham	8. 7. 49		3. 12. 49
P-1505	7200691		W. H. Short & Co. Wrenham St. Birmingham 5.	11. 10. 49.		21. 10. 49.
P-1509	7200761	P. B.	J. H. Pagett, Motha Dennis, Dunsley, N. Stourbridge	26. 10. 49.	1 del'd	1. 11. 49
P-1542	7214705	Central Motor Co Ltd, Leicester	L. E. Rudkin, Rudkin Laundon St. Saffron Rd, Leicester	13. 12. 49		1. 1. 50
P-1554	7221926	Central Motor Co. Leicester	S. R. Curtis, 5, Guildford Rd, Leicester	16. 1. 50		15. 2. 50
P-1569	7222083	Central Motor Co. Leicester	Dr. J. L. Freer, White Lodge, Knighton Rd, Leics.	26. 1. 50		14. 12. 50

BRISTOL ST. MOTORS LTD.

11/

Chassis No	Engine No	Dealers Name + Address	Customers Name	+ Address	Date	Delivered	Warranty Rec'd
P-1594	7223836		M.E. Miles, 231 Jockey	Rd. Sutton Coldf.	20. 2. 50		8 - 3 - 50
P-1609	7226083		Lt.Col. H.J. Tedder, C.O. Hoo	SE. Budbrook	14 - 3 - 50		16 - 3 - 50 ✓
K-796	7204739		D. St Clair L. Henderson	31 Woodlea, Hocking.	31 - 3 - 50		25 - 4 - 50 ✓
J-1558	3956/90/F263		S.C. Clarke, 1160 Long Shoal	Nuneaton Worc.	7 ? - 50		? - 4 - 50 ✓
P-1626	7228238		J.B. Thornton, Bennington Hse	Tenbury Wells	12 - 4 - 50		12 - 4 - 50 ✓
P-1628	7228590		The Repetition Wood Turning Co.	Helens St. B'm'l	19 - 4 - 50		20 - 4 - 50 ✓
P-1633	7228924	Reeve + Stockford Ltd., Birmingham	N. Hartell, c/o J. Potts + Co Ltd., Old	Hill. Staffs Nr Rugby	25 - 4 - 50		26 - 4 - 50 ✓
P-1634	7228904	Central Motor Co. Ltd., 41, London Rd., Leicester	E. M. Groocock, Red Roofs,	Bruntingthorpe	28 - 4 - 50		5 - 4 - 50 ✓
P-1648	7229713		H.E. Whitehouse, 268 Heely Rd.	Selly Oak, B'm	16 - 5 - 50		19 - 5 - 50 ✓
K-681	7200476		Dr. C.E. Bigger, 524 impola Rd	Colchester Essex	26 - 11 - 49		11 - 5 - 50 ✓
P-1655	7231831	Central Motor Co. Leicester.	T.L. White, 10, Fosse Rd.	Central, Leics.	31 - 5 - 50		16 - 7 - 50 ✓
P-1671	7228340	Frank Guest Ltd., 377 High St., W. Bromwich	N.J. Vaughan, Heathlands,	Kinver, Nr. Stourbridge	21 - 6 - 50		31 - 7 - 50 ✓
P-1685	7233193		G.M. Appleton, The Gap,	Solway, No. Staffs	10 - 7 - 50		20 - 7 - 50 ✓
P-1713	7235794	Old Hill Motor Ltd., Old Hill STAFFS	D. Dunn, B.S.R. Ltd. Old Hill	Staffs	25 - 7 - 50		14 - 8 - 50 ✓
P-1721	7233877	Central Motor Co Ltd, Leicester	Lord Allerton, Saddington	Hall, LEICS	1 - 8 - 50		14 - 8 - 50 ✓
P-1729	7233156		Sm. Appleton Ltd, 41 Chamber	New St., B'm Jom. Bldgs	18 - 8 - 50		19 - 8 - 50 ✓
P-1675	7233183		D.W. Rees, Delnco, 43	Reservoir Rd, Old Hill STAFF	25 - 8 - 50		29 - 8 - 50 ✓
P-1676	7233217		J.H. Beard, 337 Hales—	Owen Rd. LEICESTER	25 - 8 - 50	1951	10 - 9 - 50 ✓
P-1759	7235763	Central Motor Co Leicester.	Mr N. Taylor The Corner	Mouse Westhorp	7 - 9 - 50		11 - 9 - 50 ✓
P-1763	7238800		P.V. Walker, 21 Coventry Rd.	Coleshill.	13 - 9 - 50		22 - 9 - 50 ✓
P-1769	7240030	Central Motor Co Ltd, Leicester	J.A. Harden + Co, Pump Sq.	Boston Lincs	20 - 9 - 50		16 - 10 - 50 ✓
P-1799	7240739	Abbey Garage, Sutton Rd., Birmingham 23	L. Goode, Hill Hook House, Clare	nce Rd. Sutton	27 - 9 - 50		24 - 10 - 50 ✓
P-1818	7240936		H. H. Morris, 15 South	Gate, Sleaford	13 - 10 - 50		7 - 11 - 50 ✓
P-1861	7242991	Central Motor (Leicester)Ltd, 41 London Rd	J.B. Groocock & Sons Ltd, Church	St. Earl Shilton	10 - 11 - 50		4 - 1 - 51 ✓
K-1803	7240932		L.H. Newton + Co Ltd. Nechells	Birmingham 7.	10 - 11 - 50		9 - 11 - 50 ✓
P-1863	7242987	Meteor Gar. (Moseley) Ltd. Birmingham 3, Sutton Rd	Messrs Ewert Ltd. Burnt Tree	Dudley	14 - 11 - 50		17 - 11 - 50 ✓
P-1875	7244481	ABBEY GARAGE. SUTTON ROAD. BIRMINGHAM 23	W. Bennett, 31 Corbridge	Coldfield.	28 - 11 - 50		27 - 3 - 51 ✓
P-1889	7246359	Central Motors (Leicester)Ltd 41 London Rd. Leicester	Lieut. W. L. Glazebrook, Heath Cottage	Sunningdale Berks	13 - 12 - 50		24 - 1 - 51 ✓
P-1885	7244956	ABBEY GARAGE, 31 SUTTON RD, BIRMINGHAM	Mr W.E. Guy, Pendennis, 85 Kl	Lenhall Rd. W. Lotus	13 - 12 - 50		1 - ? - 51 ✓
P-1905	7246895		J.H. Hill, 226 Soho Rd. HANDSWORTH	B'HAM. WKS	5 - 1 - 51		29 - 1 - 51 ✓
P+1921	7246915		H.J. Liggins "Sark" Coleshill	Rd. B'ham	22 - 1 - 51		19 - 2 - 51 ✓
P-1933	7249376	Central Motor Co. Ltd. 41, London Rd. Leicester	H. Christian & Co. Ltd. 62, NG	Walk Leicester	9 - 2 - 51		7 - 3 - 51 ✓
P-1944	7250067	Central Motor Co Ltd. 41, London Rd. Leics	E.M. Sowter — Walter Mountene	Co. 33, Ashby	20 - 2 - 51	Loughborough. Laics.	21 - 9 - 51 ✓
K-1923	7244921				19 - 2 - 51		18 - 4 - 51 ✓
P-1952	7250062		P.R. Arthur. 207, Hilton R	Cambridge.	28 - 2 - 51		6 - 4 - 51 ✓
P-1960	7250831		C.M. Armstrong. 9 Ascot Rd	Moseley Bham.	9 - 3 - 51		5 - 5 - 51 ✓
P-1992	7252460		G.W. Borley. 18 Castle Gte.	Nottingham	28 - 3 - 51		12 - 5 - 51 ✓
P-2053	7256036	ABBEY GARAGE. 31 SUTTON RD ERDINGTON	W. Hampton. 10 Halesowen	Rd. Netherton H. Erdington	6 - 51		11 - 5 - 51 ✓
P-2060	7256022	BEACON MOTORS Ltd. ASTON RD BHAM 6.	H.S. Beon. Merrishall, 3A	Ward Bridge Wks.	9 - 5 - 51		letter sent 27/9/51
P-2063	7256161				16 5 51	Still in stock (Beacon Motors)	8.1.52

·ALLARD·

BRISTOL STREET MOTORS LTD

CHASSIS Nº	ENGINE Nº	DEALERS NAME & ADDRESS	CUSTOMERS NAME AND ADDRESS	DATE DELIVERED		WARRANTY REC'D.
K 1923	7244921		K. A. H. LAWRENCE 99 VYSE ST. B'HAM. 8.	19.2.51		21.5.51 ✓
K 2035	7246933		A. B. VIALL. 9 EDGECOMBE RD HALL GREEN	4.6.51		8.6.51 ✓
P 2075	7256465	ABBEY GARAGE. 37 SUTTON RD. B'HAM	J. F. TIPPER 24, HILL V. HAGLEY RD. FOUR	15.6.51	OAKS. WARKS	9.7.51 ✓
P 2116	7258171		G. BENNETT. BRIARS. HOTEL HAGLEY RD	13.7.51	B'HAM. 16.	8.8.51 ✓
P 2114	7259220		W. H. BEDDON. 898, COVENTRY RD. B'HAM. 10.	11.7.51		06.7.51 ✓
P 2128	7259272	ABBEY GARAGE. 37 SUTTON RD. B'HAM.	W. G BEACH. CORFTON EST. OFF. CRAVEN ARMS.	20.7.51		14.8.51 ✓
K 2149	7260352		R. H. BAILEY 'GREY GABLES' BROADWAY WORKS	2.8.51		16.8.51 ✓
P 2142	7259282	RUGBY HOTCAR Cº Lº HINCKLEY RD. NUNEATON	GEO. ROBERTS. MAIN ST. STOKE GOLDING	16.8.51	NR. NUNEATON.	10.10.51 ✓
P 2146	7259418			21.8.51		
K 2122	2024-Z			7.9.51	Car Returned	
P 2184	7260369	ASHMORES Lº. WEST. BROMWICH	BRAITHWAITE & Cº. CROWN BRIDGE WORKS	26.9.51	WEST BROMWICH. STAFF.	4.10.51 ✓
K 2196	7261789		JOHN GURST (NOTS & BOLT LTD) Nº, FACTORY	29.9.51	CENTER BIRMINGHAM. 30	1.10.51 ✓
K 2242	7262014		W. H. DREW Esq. T/A CONTACT PLATING Cº	3.10.51	BELL STREET. TIPTON.	13.12.51 ✓
P. 2206	7262392	FLEWITT. Lº. 120-122 ALMA ST. BIRMINGHAM. 6.	P. St. V. TABBERNER 30 CROSE IE RD. B'HAM. 17	15.10.51		18.10.51 ✓
P. 2226	7262937	ASHMORES GARAGE. WEST. BROMWICH	BRAITHWAITE ENGINEERS Cº Lº. THE NOORINGS	27.10.51	CHURCH RD. GT. BARKHAM.	8.11.51 ✓
P 2229	7262335			29.10.51		
P. 2230	7262468		G. H. GRAHAM 10, MEADOW LANE TRENTHAM,	3.11.51	STOKE-ON-TRENT	13.11.51 ✓
P. 2228	7261992	ASHMOORS GARAGE WEST BROMWICH	BRAITHWAIT & Cº ENGINEERING LTD. THE NOORINGS	29.10.51	CHURCH ROAD. GT. BARKHAM.	1.11.51 ✓
P 2235	7262462	COLMALS DEPOT LT. ROCHORCH LANE WEST BROMWICH	E. L. FIRMIN 86, HIGH STREET. WEST BROMWICH	7.11.51	STAFFS	29.11.51 ✓
P. 2237	7262374	ASHMORES GARAGE. WEST BROMWICH	BRAITHWAIT & Cº. STRUCTURAL Lº. CROWN BRIDGE	7.11.51	WORKS. WEST BROMWICH.	15.11.51 ✓
P. 2238	7263582			13.11.51	Abbey Garage Stock LETTER SENT. 8.8.52	
P. 2255	7265163	ASHMORES GARAGE Lº. WEST BROMWICH.	BIRMINGHAM STOPPER AND CYCLE COMPONENTS Cº.	30.11.51	LTD. 205. MELCHETT. ROAD. KINGS NORTON BIRMINGHAM	1.3.52 ✓
MX. 2297	7265766		P. JOHN LEIGH-COLLINS. 15, HIGHFIE ROAD. EDGBASTON	11.12.51	BIRMINGHAM.	29.1.52
P. 2273	7265701		E. W. STONE 32, CHAPEL ST. TIPTON,	21.12.51	STAFFS.	22.12.51
P. 2276	7265770	MISTS GARAGE HAMPSTEAD ROAD, HANDSWORTH B'HAM	W. HILL 153, WOLVERHAMPTON ROAD. SOUTH	3.1.52	QUINTON BIRMINGHAM 33.	10.3.52 ✓
M. 3091	7268855	HEWITTS GARAGE LT. AMBLECOTE STOURBRIDGE	A. GURREVITCH, FLAT 3. 317 HAGLEY ROAD	9.2.52	EDGBASTON. BIRMINGHAM.	26.2.52
P 2291	7268850		ARTHUR ROWE & SONS 51, LONDON ROAD	28.2.52	CHATTERIS CAMBRIDGE	3.3.52 ✓
P. 3077	7269838		STILL	5.9.52		
P. 3101	18/F. 7260981		JAMES WESLEY. THOMPSON OAK GRANGE	1.10.52	HERMITAGE ROAD. RDG BASTON BIRMINGHAM	20.10.52 ✓
P2 4003	7269758	WORCESTER WINDSHIELDS LTD.		15.11.52 5.3.52		
P. 3049	7269838		J. HOWARD HILL 238 SOHO ROAD	5.3.52	HANDSWORTH. BIRMINGHAM. 19.	16.9.52 ✓
P2 4009	7287541	MR. PHILLIPS. The Central Garage	Mary dyce 9, Hartopp Rd	28.1.54	Sutton Coldfield	19.2.54
	7287431		Mary dyce 9, Hartopp Rd.		Sutton Coldfield	19.2.54
2LR-5153	EOTTA-852N		JOHN BULLOCK. ST. ELM	4.4.54	PORTLAND RD. ALDRIDGE. STAFFS.	15.4.54

12 UNIVERSAL CAR Co: (DERBY) LTD:

CHASSIS no.	ENGINE no.	DEALERS NAME & ADDRESS	CUSTOMERS NAME & ADDRESS		DATE	DELIVERED	WARRANTY RE
M-623	7300158		P.P. Ayre, Westwood	Aughfield, Derby	27.8.48		30.8.48 ✓
M-697	7200697	Brooks Motor Co (Newark) Ltd, Newark 23.25, Castle Gate.	W. Sanders, 17, Hare Wood	Ave, Newark, Notts	14.9.48		20.10.48 ✓
M-731	7202466	Body Builder 10th 1151		re Ripley	24.9.48		NOT REC'D
M-745	7202936		Butterley Co. Ltd, Civil Butterley Park	Engineering Dept	22.10.48		29.10.48 ✓
M-805	7204248	Standhill Garage, 123/5, Carlton Hill, Notts.	Bradbury & Sons, Dane	Agnes St, Notts.	8.12.48		10.1.49
M-828	7204074		E.M. Porteous, Ivy Cott	age, Long Jane, Derby	13.1.49	re-sered at ST 16-4-52 in name of Barbara Goalen. (model girl)	14.1.49
M-858	7204635		Butterley Co Butterley Park	K. Ripley, Nr Derby	28.1.49		31.1.49
M-677	7202507	Bennetts (Nottm) Ltd, Shakespeare Rd.	R.W. Jackson, 20, Valley	Rd. W.Bridgford, Notts	4.2.49		NOT REC'D
M-878	7206526	Lincs Motor Co. Ltd, Grimsby, Lincs.	J.W Ellmore, 23, Brighow	ate, Grimsby, Lincs	9.2.49		25.2.49
M-821	7204461		E. Hammond, Ockmanton	Old Farm, Derby	18.2.49	letter rec. from W. Allan, California USA on July 31 59 now owns car (with 1955 Chevrolet engine)!	22.2.49 ✓
M-851	7206589	Standhill Garage, Carlton Hill, Notts	R.J. Glaister, Lagoon, Garage Notts.	ge Rd, Edwalton	2.3.49		2.5.49 ✓
M-1021	7209272	Standhill Garage, Carlton Hill, Notts	Midland Model Dairy	Farm, Notts	28.3.49		10.4.49
M-1035	7209616	Austin Munks Boston Lincs	Noel Jaques Bee, Drayly	Boston Lincs	30.3.49		14.7.49 ✓
M-1046	7209760	Standhill Garage, Carlton Hill, Notts	Midland Model Dairy Fa	m, Notts	13.4.49		10.4.49 ✓
M-1054	7209897	Standhill Gar. Carlton Hill Notts	L.W. Bott, A.L. Bott Ltd, Newark	St, Grimsby, Notts	19.5.49		1.7.49 ✓
M-1085	7212103	Lincs Motor Co, Wellowgate, Lincs	M. Phillips, Phillips Travel products, King Edward St		30.5.49		25.5.49 ✓
L-670	7300768	Standhill Garage	Mr Sniffin		21.6.49	Ex Demo.	NOT REC'D
K-713	6943346				15.7.49		NOT REC'D
M-1087	7212145				15.7.49		NOT REC'D
M-1529	7215524		J. Derner Hill, B. Clarence	Street Belfast	20.9.49		28.11.48
K-681	7200476	PP	" "		28.11.49	Transferred to Bristol St Motors ✗	
P-1549	7219362	Standhill Gar, Nottingham.	E. Hobson, 441, Affreton	Rd., Nottingham	30.12.49		12.1.50 ✓
P-1564	7221924	" " "	W. Gray "Woodlands" Forest Lane	Papplewick, Notts	19.1.49		11-2-50 ✓
P-1589	7223823	Grantham Motors, Grantham.	J. Johnston, 5, St. Catherine	Road, Grantham	13.2.50		6-6-50 ✓
P-1599	7224197	Standhill Garage, Nottingham.	J. Burnside, Tudor Cottage,	Bramcote Lane, Notts	25.2.50		23-2-50 ✓
P-1610	7226141	" " "	D.J. Whitaker, 37, Highbury	Rd., Bulwell, Notts	16-3-50		8-4-50 ✓
P-1621	7228247	Standhill Gar, Carlton Hill, Notts	Midland Model Dairy Co Ltd	Carlton Hill, Notts	13-4-50		21-4-50 ✓
S-1572	5341/29	Lincs. Motor Co Ltd, Wellowgate, Grimsby	G.J. Sleight Jnr Hillside	Grimsby, Farm, Brigsley	4-5-50		5-5-50 ✓
P-1642	7229762	Standhill Garage, Nottingham.	J. Smee, Midland Model Dairy	Carlton Hill, Notts.	11-5-50		15-6-50 ✓
P-1646	7229718	Lt. Col. Sir P. Brocklehurst, Macclesfield. →			23-5-50		16-5-50 ✓
P-1656	7231834				26-5-50.		NOT REC'D
P-1667	7232479		L.N. Bakewell, Bridge Hill,	Belper, Derbyshire	16-6-50		19-6-50 ✓
P-1683	7229913				11-7-50		NOT REC'D
P-1710	7235800		A.E.J. Thrupp, 172, Harrington	Street, Derby	18-7-50		21-7-50 ✓
P-1718	7235801		J.W. Hampshire & Co Ltd, Simfin	Lane, Derby	31-7-50		15-8-50 ✓
P-1638	7228239	STANDHILL GARAGE, NOTTINGHAM	KING OF M Ford AARROW King No.18	HOLLOW STONE	21-8-50	✗	14.2.51
P-1755	7238965		J. Hibbert, Hill Croft, Hilt	Derbyshire	4-9-50		12-7-50 ✓
P-1768	7240041	Cramers Gar. Derbyturn, Burton-on-Trent	M. Gosh, "Mayfield" Ashby	Rd, Burton on Tent	20-9-50		14-10-50 ✓
P-1811	7240727	Standhill Gar, Carlton Hill Nottm	O.J. Bradbury & Sons Ltd, Dane	Agnes St, Nottm	3-10-50		16-10-50 ✓
P-1828	7242419		J. Ward, The Grange, Carrington	Nr Boston Lincs	8-11-50		9-11-50 ✓

UNIVERSAL CAR CO. (DERBY) LTD.

Chassis No	Engine No	Dealers Name & Address	Customers Name +	Address	Date Delivered		Warranty Received
P-1834	7242146		V.M.O Withington, 74 Gassey Lane	Cannock, Staffs	13-11-50		17-11-50
P-1886	7233877	Standhill Gar. Carlton Hill, Sherwood	J. Topping, 24 Hampden	St. Giltbrook Notts	11-12-50		10-1-51
P-1897	7246479	Standhill Gar. 123 Carlton Hill. Nottm	R. Harwood, 38, Valmont Rd.	Hucknall Rd. Nor.	28-12-50		1-3-51
P-1909	7246880	Standhill Ga. Carlton Hill Nottm	W.R. Hart, Flat 2, 73 Portland Place	London W.1.	12-1-51		12-1-51
P-1934	7249410	Links Motors Ltd. Grimsby	John Robinson "The Hall"	Ravendale.	12.2.51.		19.2.51
P1990	7250738	Whites Garage Ltd. Grimsby. Lincs	Rowland A. Smith. The Old Rectory	Swinhope Lincs	22.3.51		29-3-51.
P 2130	7259721		Ken. Sumner 16, Ferrers W.	ay. Allestree.	24-7-51.	Derby.	28-7-51
P 2132	7259013	Central Garage (Worksop) Ltd.	Godley & Goulding. Work	sop. Notts.	31.7.51		8.8.61
P-2145	7259628	Standhill Garage (Nottm)	H. Goodman 1, Fletcher St.	Heanor Derby.	1-9-51.		3-9-51
P 2174	7261367		Herb. K. Bower, 52 Cromford Rd.	Wilksworth	25-9-51.		21.3.52
P-2279	7266039	Central Motor Co Ltd. Leicester. London Rd.	F.P. Faulkner. 113A London Rd.	Waterlooville.	28-1-52.	A. Portsmouth.	14.5.53
P-3086	7241455				24-4-52.		

·ALLARD·

13

H.E. NUNN & COMPANY LTD.

CHASSIS no	ENGINE no	DEALERS NAME & ADDRESS	CUSTOMERS NAME & ADDRESS	DATE	DELIVERED	WARRANTY REC.
M-641	7200665	G.E. Chatfield, Hightown, Crewe	F. Lea, Wheelock, Mi..., Sandbach	10.8.48		20.10.48
K-680	7200776	Body Builder 19th Oct		27.8.48		NOT REC'D
M-737	7202953	"		24.9.48		NOT REC'D
M-701	7200671		J. Brown, (Bradley Fold... Bradley Fold, Nr Bolton	30.9.48		6.10.48
M-703	7189889	F. Ellison (Warrington) Ltd.	J. Tennant, Hawthorne, St. Warrington	9.10.48		13.10.48
M-710	7202162		J.B. Shaw, Warrington, Works, St. Stephens	15.10.48		22.10.48
L-694	7200490	Pilkingtons, Garside St. Bridgegate, Warrington	Managing Dir. W. Haynes, Ltd, Chiswick St.	25.10.48		21.10.48
M-744	7202987	F. Ellison (Warr), Manchester Rd., Bolton	H.L. Gee, % The Gee Manning Co. Ltd., Fazakerley Ltd.	28.10.48		3.11.48
M-759	7203491	Wistaston Garage, Crewe	W.M. White, Kingscliffe, Willaston, Nantwich Cheshire	10.11.48		4.11.48
M-797	7204034	Burrows, Seed Ltd., Brynley Rd., Lancs	J.R. Sutherland, Ald, View Cottage, hanse	3.12.48		6.12.48
M-778	7203643	A.W. Webb Ltd, 27/31, Berry St.	M.S.H. Lomax, Co. 83, Bridge St., Manchester	7.12.48		26.11.48
M-776	7203614	Seaview Motors, 88, Seaview Rd. Liverpool	R. Parkes Davis, 3, Fenw... rsey St., Liverpool	7.12.48		14.12.48
M-809	7204312	A.W. Webb, Ltd. 27/31, Berry St.	E.W. Taylor, 303, Part La... d Court, N. Brighton	16.12.48		14.1.49
M-827	7204466	T.B. Anderson Co. 7, Little Carlune...	Dr. D. Boulton, 47, Roda... rey St., Liverpool	23.12.48		18.12.48
K-724	7200557		C.F. Simon, Didsbury, Court, Manchester 20	17.1.49		24.1.49
M-854	7204769			21.1.49		NOT REC'D
M-863	7204650			21.1.49		NOT REC'D
M-833	7204527	Jas. S. Leaver, Eanam, Blackburn	J.D. Greenwood, Sunny...ad, Clitheroe, Lancs	31.1.49		31.1.49
M-825	7204525	Jas. S. Leaver, Eanam, Blackburn	L. Greenwood, Westbo... ve, Mains Rd., Black...	17.2.49		18.2.49
M-1026	7209399	Jas. S. Leaver, Eanam, Blackburn	J. Bardsley & Sons Ltd., 26, Cross St., Manc.	22.3.49		22.3.49
M-1031	7206840		R.E. Hat, Red Thorn. Manchester.	9.4.49		6.4.49
M-1098	7212297	Seymore Motors Ltd, Bury Old Rd. Man.		2.8.49		29.7.49
M-1094	7212331	Cliff Holden (Motors) Ltd Bury Lancs	Ashworths Ltd. Allison Mills, Elton, Bury	8.7.49		14.7.49
M-1527	7215393	Union Garage Co Ltd Harcholme Rossendale	Ed Gaskell Esq, border Bros, Newchurch in Rossendale Lancs	8.9.49		6.9.49
P-1504	7212336	Didsbury Garage Ltd, 8/2 Barlow Moor Rd, Manch 20	J. M. Salenstons, 14 Sep St., Manchester	23.9.49		27.10.49
L-869	7207804		Leadbeaters Co, Grotton, Brickworks Oldham	17.10.49		21.10.49
M-1530	7215521			7.10.49		NOT REC'D
P-1535	7217529	A. Webb Ltd 27/31 Berry St. Liverpool	Dr. J. M. McCurdy, 161 Wigan Rd, Ashton-in-Makerfield Lancs.	16.11.49		9.12.49
K-654	7200957		T. Hope & Sankey Hudson Ltd. Chapel St. Man. 1.	28.12.49		29.12.49
P-1565	7221923	A.W. Webb & Co 27/31 Berry St Liverpool	E.E. Smallwood, 19, Prim... nore Rd. Liverpool 18	23.1.50		18.1.50
P-1582	7222493	A.W. Webb & Co 27/31 Berry St. Liverpool Manchester	H.G. Goldrich, 'Enslin' Church Rd. Liverpool 15	2.2.50		3.2.42
P-1605	7225839	Munn Didsbury, Barlow Moor Road	J.G. Hope, Upton Hall Macclesfield	9.3.50		10.3.50
P-1607	7225886	A.W. Webb & Co. Ltd. Berry St. Liverpool	J. Hemmings Ltd., Hale, Nr. Liverpool	14-3-50		16-3-50
P-1612	7226082	A.W. Webb & Co Ltd, Berry St., Liverpool	J. Hemmings Ltd, Hale, Nr. Liverpool	21-3-50		22-3-50
P-1627	7228017		H. Catterall Ltd, Whitefield Mill Nelson. Lancs.	14-4-50		19-4-50
P-1636	7228517	A.W. Webb Ltd, Berry St., Liverpool	T.J. Milbourne, 58 Princes Rd, Liverpool.	4-5-50		27-4-50
P-1660	5342/30	A.W. Webb Ltd, 27/31 Berry St.	A.W. Webb Ltd. Liverpool	8-6-50		6-6-50
P-1661	7229853		Pooles Central Warehouse Ltd 2/40 Station Rd. Wigan	6-6-50		8-6-50
J-1575	5343-31	Wm Arnold Ltd., Upper Brook St., Man.13	E. Hyde, Craigmore, Colne.	15-6-50		12-6-50
P-1644	7229765	A. Webb Ltd., Berry St. Liverpool	B. Rotheram, 9B Manor H... Alexander Drive Liverpool	19-5-50		11-5-50

13

H.E. NUNN + Co LTD

Chassis No	Engine No	Dealers Name + Address	Customers Name	+ Address	Date Delivered		Warranty Reg
1684-P	7235353	Holland Motors Ltd, Southport.	M.J. Wright, 26 Marsh	-side Rd, South'p	11-7-50		6-7-50 ✓
P-1687	7233680	Paramount Gar. Ltd. Cheetham Hill	R.A. Hey Willson Ltd. 2 Black-	London Rd. SALE.	13-7-50		13-7-50 ✓
P-1714	7233679	A.W. Webb. Ltd, Berry St. Liverpool	J. Lunn + Co Ltd, Violet St.,	Widnes, LANCS.	29-7-50		24-7-50 ✓
P-1725	7235-797	A.W. Webb. Ltd, Berry St. Liverpool	J. Shepherd, The Bungalow	Gar. Queens Drive LIVERPOOL	21-8-50		25-8-50 ✓
P-1726	7233903	A.W. Webb, Berry St. Liverpool	R.W. Dickson Ltd, 41	North John St.	21-8-50		25-8-50 ✓
P-1760	7238764	Trustrams Ltd, City Road, Chester	L.G.J. Johnson Esq. Ashton	Hayes, CHESTER	11-9-50		6-9-50 ✓
P-1793	7240038	PARAMOUNT GARAGES Ltd. CHEETHAM	M. HARDY (MOSS SIDE) 16. ALEXANDER RD M/C 11		21-9-50		20.2.51 ✓
P-1795	5359-44	Lorns Ltd, Knowsley St., Bury	Messrs J. Hunt (Bolton) Ltd.	Alma Works, Radcliffe Rd	2-10-50		3-10-50 ✓
P-1798	7238801	J. Timmins Sons Ltd. Leigh Lancs.	Saxton, Metals Ltd. Kaye Lodge	Pocket Nook Lane, Linton	1-10-50		5-10-50 ✓
P-1821	7242134	Parkers Ltd., Bradshawgate, Bolton	M. Isherwood & Co Ltd,	Folds, Bolton	18-10-50		19-10-50 ✓
P-1826	7242427		M. Dinuger Ltd, Carnarvon	St, Manchester 3	20-10-50		17-10-50 ✓
P-1827	7242415	J. Timmins + Co. Leigh, LANCS.	J.W. Wilde Ltd, Wallgate,	Wigan	27-10-50		31-10-50 ✓
P-1832	7242160	A.W. Webb. Ltd, Berry St. Liverpool	Mr P. Williams, Floral Hall,	Elliot St. Liverpool 1.	31-10-50		27-10-50 ✓
P-1830	7242449	The Bank Top Motor House Ltd, Railway St. Burnley	W. Brown, 61, Briercliff Rd,	Burnley	31-10-50		27-10-50 ✓
P-1868	7244326	PARAMOUNT GARAGE CHEETHAM HILL RD M/C	J.A. WILKINSON SCRAMWAY BRAMHALL	L. CHESHIRE.	22-11-50		12.2.51 ✓
P-1879	7244958	The Bank Top Motor House Ltd, Railway St. Burnley	H. Walton & Sons Ltd., Bishop	House Mill, Burnley	30-11-50	31	30-11-50 ✓
P-1894	7246428	The Bank Top Motor House Ltd., Railway St. Burnley	J.E. Metcalf Ltd., Argyle Works	Accrington Lancashire	21-12-50		1-1-51 ✓
P-1888	7246360	A.W. WEBB 27/31. BERRY St. L'POOL.	A.R. WILSON. LONGACRE.	Haymard Ave. Bromboro'	1-1-51		31.1.51. ✓
P-1903	7246519		JAYUC. DAVIES. DITTON RD.	WIDNES. LANCS.	13-1-51		2-2-51 ✓
P-1916	7246930	LOXHAMS GARAGES WHITEGATE DVE. BLACKPOOL	H.S. DAVIES, 58, CLEVELETON DRIVE GLASGOW W2		18-1-51		3.2.51 13-
P-1931	7249408		A.K. THORNTON. M/ESSRS CLUFF PICKERING. ARDWICK		4.2.01		20.2.51 ✓
P-1933	7249351	H.J. QUICK L'º 221 DEANSGATE (M/C) LANCS	RUTH BARTON. NORTHWICH RD. WEAVERHAM.		10.2.51		21.2.51 ✓
P-1941	7249594		B. FORSTER & Co. LTD. MARIT. WORKS DERBY ST. MANCHESTER		20.2.51		2-3-51 ✓
P-1950	7250049	Paramount Garages Ltd. Cheetham Hill	BRADBURY (KINGSWAY) Ltd. H. Central Buildings KINGSWAY MANCHE.		26.2.51		28-2-51 ✓
P-1956	7250060	Paramount Garages Ltd Cheetham Hill Rd.	R.H. HARRIS Fernsham Cottage Dean Row WILMSLOW Cheshire		4.3.51		8-3-51 ✓
P-1959	7250851	Autocars (St. Annes) St. Annes-on-Sea Ltd.	Photo Finishers (M/C) Recy M/C Morecambe		13.3.51		27.4.51 ✓
P-1996	7252439		MR. T.S. HARTLEY 420 DALE ROAD BLACKLEY MANCHESTER. 9		30.3.51		17-4-51 ✓
P-1995	7252743	A.W. WEBB Ltd 27/31 LIVERPOOL BERRY ST.	Mr T. SANDERS 'RAVENSCRO' ST. ORIENT DRIVE GT. ACRE		2.4.51		23.4.51 ✓
P-2024	7252815	WILLIAMS & Co Lᵗᵈ WALLGATE WIGAN	R.O. LACE 53 STANDISH GATE LANCS		3.4.51	(CHASSIS ONLY)	2-5-51 ✓
P-2043	7254552		B.J. MOON. GLENWOOD Park Road HALE CHESHIRE		20.4.51		30-4-51 ✓
P-2042	7252881	LUND Vco PRESTON RD GARAGE COPPULL	LEONARD FAIRCLOUGH. 'ADLINGTON' CHAPEL STREET. NEAR CHORLEY		20.4.51		25-4-51 ✓
P-2054	7254454	A.W. WEBB Lᵗᵈ 27A BERRY ST L'POOL	E.H. COATES. ESQ. 33 MERSEY RD. LIVERPOOL LANCS.		8/5/51		8/5/51 ✓
P-2056	7256026	LOXHAMS GARAGE (BLACKPOOL)	S.D. KARUM. V SONS, 29 MINSHULL ST. M/C 1.		9.5.51		12/5/51 ✓
P-2057	7256176	H & J QUICK. N.P. 221 DEANSGATE. MANCHESTER	MET-VICKERS. ELECTRICAL, TRAFFORD PARK M/C 17		11.5.51		15/5/51 ✓
P-2048	7254712	THE DAVENPORT GARAGE BUXTON RD STOCKPORT	G.G. MELLOR Nº 6 FLAT. PARKWOOD COURT E. DIDSBURY M/C		15.5.51		25/5/51 ✓
P-2065	7252955	A.W. WEBB Lᵗᵈ 27/31. BERRY St L'POOL	Rᵗ J. GOULD 114, LIVERPOOL ROAD HUYTON		24-5-51		1-6-51 ✓
P-2095	7258538.		G.V.H. BAERLIN, 12 BLACKFRIARS ST. M/C 3.		19.6.51		20.6.51 ✓
S-1910	8M. 861.	Le Man Car	A.P. HITCHINGS (C. ATKINSON) MORLEY ST. HANLEY STAFFS.		1.4.51		(SEE L.H.S)
P-2110	7258054		H. NISBET. 28 GROSVENOR, BIRKDALE SOUTHPORT.		2.7.51		3/7/51 ✓
P-2112	7259012		J. FLETCHER. 'FAIRWAYS' CLAYTON GN. Nr CHORLEY LANCS		2.7.51		6/7/51 ✓

134

H.E. NUNN & Co LTD.

CHASSIS No	ENGINE No	DEALERS NAME AND ADDRESS	CUSTOMERS NAME & ADDRESS	DATE DELIVERED		WARRANTY RECEIVED
P 2116	7259227	BANK TOP MOTOR HOUSE LTD RAILWAY ST. BURNLEY	W. PLATT. RIBBLESDALE. OSBALDESTON NR BLACKBURN	17-7-51		30·8·51 ✓
P 2118	7258711		J.H. MILNES. WALKER. NEWFIELD HALL. MINSHULL VERNON	19-7-51.	MIDDLEWICH CHESHIRE.	20/7/51 ✓
P 2129	7259717		D. W. ASTLEY-BIRTWISTLE. HOGHTON HSE. HOGHTON PRESTON	31-7-51		5/8/51 ✓
K 2151	7260116	BANK TOP MOTORS HOUSE. RAILWAY ST. BURNLEY	J. CUNLIFFE. JACKSON. SUNNYSIDE. HOUSE. CRAWSHAWBOOTH	·8-51	LANCS.	A·8·51 ✓
K 2150	7260147		S.G.M. FORRESTER THE COTTAGE WATFORD ROAD	8-8-51	RADLETT.	21·9·51 ✓
P 2159	7260137		G.H. CLEGG LONG RIDGE, DELAMERE, NORTHWICH,	31·8·51	CHESHIRE.	4·9·51 ✓
J. 2121	20262		O. SCOTT-WADE SUNSHINE HOUSE BOLSHAW ROAD	27·8·51	CHEADLE CHESHIRE.	25·3·52
K 2080	7260024	BANK TOP MOTORS HOUSE LTD RAILWAY ST. BURNLEY	J.R. BRIERLEY, 39. GLEN VIEW ROAD BURNLEY LANCS	29-8-51		31·8·51 ✓
P 2167	7261710	H & J. QUICK. LTD. CHESTER RD OLD TRAFFORD M.16	THE HON MARK A. RATHBONE ~ CAYSER, SEDGEWICK PARK	18·9·51	HORSHAM SUSSEX.	16-11-51
P 2169	7261750	BOYLES CO LTD CHILDWALL FIVEWAYS L.pool	THOS. JONES CHESHIRE HOUSE DELAMAH RD.	20·9·51	CHEADLE. CHESHIRE. 3. CHILDWALL ABBEY Rd, L.pool. 16.	28·3·52
P 2186	7261360	BANK TOP MOTOR HOUSE LTD RAILWAY ST. BURNLEY	DON BURKE, 108, ACCRINGTON ROAD BURNLEY LANCS	1-10-51		15-2-52
P·2205	7262460		M. LAWRANCE GRAFTON ETTE WORKS, POLLARD ST, ANCOATS	23-10-51	MANCHESTER	24-10-51 ✓
P-2209	7262957	PARAMOUNT GARAGES. CHEETHAM HILL RD MANCH.	H. HILL, 1, MORCOMBE & DOVE. STAYA ROAD GATLEY.	24·10·51	CHESHIRE.	12-2-52
P·2227	7262952	BANK TOP MOTOR HOUSE LTD. RAILWAY ST. BURN	H.H. LANE, T/A, LANCS CELLULOSES, MOSS LANE,	1-11-51	WALKDEN MANCHESTER	15·2·52.
P·2190	7261709	BANK TOP MOTOR HOUSE LTD. RAILWAY ST. BURNLEY	H·O·DOLE. THE POULTRY FARM HOLME. NR. BURNLEY LANCS.	·8-11-51		1·3·52
P·3239	7262385 7262969		MRS. HILARY HIGGINS MARLAND GRANGE CASTLETON	27-11-51	ROCHDALE LANCS	15.6.52 ✓
P·2250		H & J. QUICK LTD. CHESTER RD OLD TRAFFORD M.16	THE WILLEY KEY. CO. LTD BATH ST. LONDON E.C.1. TRAFFORD GRAFTON HOUSE, WARLINGHAM S.4	1-12-51		1·12·51 ✓
P·2272	7266396	MIDDLETON GARAGE, MIDDLETON, NORFOLK KINGS LYNN	W. FELL, ROYDON HALL KINGS LYNN. NORFOLK.	28-1-52		30·4·53 ✓
P·2282	7266389.	Warranty not necessary owe of date		13·3·52	PARAMOUNT GARAGES still in STOCK. LETTER SENT 8.8.52	
P·3078	7269845	BANK TOP MOTOR HOUSE LTD. BURNLEY	ALEX. PICKLES RIDGE END. HALL NELSON	14·3·52		24·3·52 ✓
M.3120	7271486	A.W. WEBB LTD. 24-31 BERRY ST. L.pool	IAN DOUGLAS, RIVACRE HOUSE. HOOTON. WIRRAL	8·5·52		9·5·52 ✓
P2-4002	7275054	A.N. WEBB LTD, 27-31 BERRY ST., LIVERPOOL 1, OLD TRAFFORD	M.W. WILSON, LANE END, WILLASTON, WIRRAL	14·7·52		15·7·52 ✓
21Z-5102	KOTTA-37860	H & J QUICK. LTD. CHESTER RD. MANCHESTER 16	D. E. SCOTT. LOCKSHEAD HOUSE.	11·4·53	PRESTBURY, CHESHIRE.	22·4·53 ✓
21Z-5100	KOTTA-49587	Ardwick		16·7·53		
21C-5140	EOTA.100359			31·7·53		
21C-5143 100359	KOTA·100347			1·7·54		

+ Curtis
Brewery Lane
Felling 82308

Brewery Lane
Felling 82308

14

TATE of LEEDS LTD.

CHASSIS no.	Engine no.	DEALERS NAME & ADD.	CUSTOMERS NAMES & ADDRESS	DATE	DELIVERED	WARRANTY REG.
M-604	7199762		O.C. Hall, Oxford Rd. Guiseley, N. Leeds	12.8.48		1.9.48
L-616	7200000	J.R. Graham Co. Ltd., Dewsbury	J.W. France, Albert Mills, Dewsbury	13.9.48		15.9.48
M-704	7200772		L.H. Hobday, 26. Kensgrove Lane, Huddersfield	13.9.48		10.9.48
M-684	7200771		F. Broadbent, Central Ironworks	17.9.48		24.9.48
M-678	7200982	B. Waterhouse, 82, Manningham	H. Mosley, Guiseley, Leeds	21.9.48		28.9.48
M-702	7202468		L. Chappell, 101, Roundhay Rd, Leeds 11	27.9.48		6.10.48
M-749	7203591		A.W. Hole, The New House, Shiplate Rise	15.10.48		19.10.48
M-746	7203157		S. Emmott, 3, The Drive, Crossgates, Leeds	29.10.48		22.11.48
K-608	7200052	T.C. Harrison, 58/61, London Rd, Sheffield	H.A. McCrum, 211, Bellevue Rd, Leeds 2.	17.11.48		5.11.48
M-787	7203885		A.F. Easton, 61, Norfolk St, Sheffield	23.11.48		15.4.49
M-790	7203594		F. Tate, Director, Tate of Leeds	2.12.48		3.1.49
M-849	7204665	Fred Sims (Keighley) Sth Street	Sam Wells, Ingrabhan, Ltd, Greengate Works	23.12.48		23.12.48
M-840	7204658	Central Motors, West St. Sheffield	Robert Older, 44, B..	19.1.49	Ice, New Sampson	6.5.49
M-869	7204812	Jameson (Hull) Motor Co. Hull	Bowes Booch, H. Broadbent, 1 Vice, the Cat, Hull, Yorks	21.1.49	resold to: J.W. Cook Co. Ltd, Hull	17.1.49
M-864	7204615		J. Dixon, The Firs, Whitley Bridge, Yorks	25.1.49		9.2.49
E-638	7200767		E.N. Riddiough, Harden, Greengate House, Bradford	9.2.49		3.2.49
M-885	7206656		H. Kinross, Gaychons, Maytor Lane, Rawdon	10.2.49		17.2.49
M-892	7207010		H. Walker, England, c/o. W.H.T. Ltd, N. Halifax	10.2.49		15.2.49
M-829	7204526		H.G. Johnson, 44, Regent Sq, Doncaster	11.2.49		16.2.49
M-891	7206790	Brown White Roundhay Rd, Leeds	H. White, 93, Roundhay Rd, Leeds 7.	15.2.49		15.2.49
M-897	7207123	Ernest Davis Ltd, Bradford	H.W.H. Price, Oakdale, Hud, Fairfax Rd, Bury, Huddersfield	25.2.49		26.2.49
M-716	7202454		H.L. Mosley, Fred Bros, (Shipley) Ltd.	28.2.49		28.2.49
M-901	7207207	Brown White (Leeds) Ltd, Leeds	G. Ramsden, The Cottage, Westway, Yorks	7.3.49		12.5.49
M-1000	7207230		P.M.J. Thorpe, Spring Gdns, W. Teater, Yorks.	7.3.49		8.3.49
M-817	7204415	Ripleys Ltd, Hamilton Rd, Birthington	J.G. Shaw, Murton Hall, Murton, Frey, Yorks	7.3.49		8.3.49
M-900	7207110			8.3.49		NOT REG'D
M-1009	7207938	T. Claybourn Co. Ltd, Doncaster	D.H. Gowley, The Grange, Torksey, Lincoln	11.3.49		20.3.49
M-1048	7209933	E. Davis Ltd, Bradford Rd,	J.T. Marriott Co. Ltd, Hol, one St, Liversedge	20.4.49		11.7.49
M-1048	7209933			21.4.49		
L-860	7206932	M/s Bantry Motors S. Yorks.	E.J. Taylor, Scaft Ward, Hall, Bantry, Nr Doncaster	6.5.49		5.5.49
K-775	7200477		W.P. Anelay, 54, Hob, gate, Acomb Rd, York	15.7.49	Remain with John Postell, July 50	15.7.49
M-1049	7209852		W. Wood, G. Ellis Sons Ltd, Saville Mills, Dewsbury	19.7.49		5.8.49
M-1095	7812354		P. Warrington, 12, Wentworth Terrace, Wakefield	4.8.49		5.8.49
M-1099	7812353	Delivered through Furrows	E.S. Walley Co. Ltd, 135, Sankey St, Warrington	9.8.49		2.1.49
P-1508	7212076	Reynolds Ltd, Peel St, Barnsley	G.B. Creighton, 91, Dodworth Rd. Barnsley	18.10.49		18.2.50
K-807	7204738		E.J.G. Waymon, 'Ormiston', 2, Park Ave, Harrogate	5.11.49		1.4.50
K-717	7200764		Transferred to Alex. anders, Edinburgh	5.11.49		NOT REG'D
P-1568	7922086		R. Pettigrew, 2, Oliver Hill, Horsforth, Nr Leeds, Outwood Lane	26.1.50		23.3.50
P-1608	7226137	Reynolds Ltd (Barnsley)	Walter Frank Sons Ltd, Peel St, Barnsley	17.3.50		17.3.50
P-1616	7226076		N. Ward, 17, Church Lane, Pudsey, YORKS.	28.3.50		31.3.50
P-1617	7888009		Brown Ogden Co Ltd, Dean, Triangle, Nr Halifax, YORKS	31.3.50		25.4.50
P-1619	7828015	Reynolds Ltd (Barnsley)	Mr G. Royston, The Grange, Barnsley, 40, Broadway	5.4.50		5.4.50

·ALLARD·

TATE OF LEED LTD

CHASSIS NO	ENGINE NO	DEALERS NAME + ADDRESS	CUSTOMERS NAME + ADDRESS		DATE DELIVERED		WARRANTY RECEIVED
P-1629	7228525		W. A. Hogg Ltd., 19 Queen St.,	Leeds 1.	21-4-50.		11-5-50 ✓
J-1570	3930/108	T. C. Harrison Ltd., Sheffield.	M. Webb Eq. Stainland,	Halifax.	26-4-50		26-4-50 ✓
P-1643	7229764	W. Parkinson & Son, Bradford	L. Auty? Ha Ltd. West End Mills Rushn	Rd Bradfor	9-5-50		12-5-50 ✓
J-1573	53/5540.		E. N. R. Hewitt, Greengates House,	Greengates, Bradford	11-5-50		11-5-50 ✓
P-1653	7229916		W. D. Lane Cardigan Court,	Leeds 6.	25-5-50		6-6-50 ✓
P-1673	7233173		B. D. S. Porter, Middleton Lodge,	Harrogate.	27-6-50		29-6-50 ✓
P-1674	7233157		J. M. P. Clark, 29 Park Sq.	Leeds 1.	29-6-50		6-7-50 ✓
P-1717	7233681		John Hartley & Sons Ltd., Gillroyd	Mills, Morley	29-7-50		18-8-50
P-1764	7238768		O. Thornton, Tate of Leeds, Ltd		15-9-50		26-9-50 ✓
P-1767	7240049	E S Myers Ltd, 52/62 Newington	C. Vere Way, 3 Wilmar Drive Heaton	Bradford Lane, Bradford.	19-9-50		2-10-50 ✓
P-1791	7238824	Station Garages Ltd, Scarborough	W. Broadly & Son, English St. Hull	E YORKS	27-9-50		11-10-50 ✓
P-1812	7240730		O. Mills Eq. 11 Roslyn Rd., Harrow	-Gate.	5-10-50		6-10-50
P-1825	7242436		Mark Day Ltd, Savelletown. Dew	-sbury YORKS	20-10-50		8-12-50
P-1864	7242990		Messrs Hurst Mills, 26. York Place	Leeds 1.	14-11-50		1-1-51 ✓
P-1895	7246470		Simpsons of Kirkgate Ltd, 73 Kirk	-gate, LEEDS	22-12-50		12-1-51
P-1928	7249341.		Dr CROWE BEECH HOUSE 10 OTLEY RD LEEDS		6.2.51		5-2.51
P-1942	7250064		H. G. GRAHAM & SONS LTD., 19, DONN-	-INGTON ST, LEEDS	9 2.51.		1-3-51
P-1963	7250948		CATTON & CO. LTD. 29 CHADWICK	ST LEEDS, 101.	14.3.51		21-3-51
P-1998.	7252813		STEPHEN EMMOTT. 3 THE DRIVE	CROSSGATES. YORKS	6.4.51		9-4.51
P-2044.	7254581.		H. S. SHARP. 149 HARLEY ST.	W1.	25.4.51.		25-51
P-2064	7256029	BROWN & WHITE LEEDS	N. SHUTE 29 STREET LANE	LEEDS 8	18-5-51		25-5-51
P-2098.	7258540.		CATTON & Co. 29. CHADWICK ST.	LEEDS. 10.	21.6.51		12-7-51
P-2104.	7258446.		Mrs. H. A. McCRUM. 58. CARDIGAN RD	LEEDS 6.	23.6.51		20-9-51
P-2101.	7258040	W. Parkinson & Sons, Bowlands Bradford	ALLIED COLLOIDS Lo Ltd. 18A. N. PARK	de BRADFORD Yd	27-6-51.		6-7-51. ✓
J-2090	12018/Z		RICHARD PETTY. Lo EASTBROOK WORKS.	DIAMOND ST. BRADFORD	3-7-51		13-7-51.
P-2119	7259636		J. G. HAILAND. BOWLING PARK LAUN-	DRI. Lo. BOWLING	20-7-51	HALL ROAD, BRADFORD,	25-7-51. ✓
P-2144.	7259632		P. NAGELE. EEQ. 14 PRIMLEY	PARK. LEEDS	17-8-51		18-8-51 ✓
P-2160	7260146.		Mrs. B. Todd. 19, HAREHILLS. ROAD.	LEEDS 8.	8-9-51		20-9-51
P-2189	7262013	BROWN & WHITE Lo. ROUNDHAY Rd LEEDS	THE FARM SHOPS, 48. KIRKGATE.	OTLEY. YORKS	10-10-51		15-10-51. ✓
P-2225	7262939	FRED BINNS. SOUTH ST. KEIGHLEY	JOHN WEBB. Rd, GREENGATE	WORKS KEIGHLEY.	29-10-51		1-11-51. ✓
P-2231	7262389		Cns. LANE & SONS Lo. LEEDS	WORKS ATHINSON	8-11-51	STREET LEEDS.	23-1-52.
M-13-2296	7262377		TATE OF LEEDS Lo. NEW YORK ROAD	LEED. 2.	8-11-51.		1-12-51
P-2234	7264457		SCHOFIELDS (LEEDS) THE HEADROW	LEEDS 1.	8-11-51.		3-1-52.
P-2233	7262479		W. M. SHAW. & SON Lo. GEORGE STREET	MIRRSBRIDGE LEEDS	8-11-51.	HUDDERSFIELD. YORKS.	22-11-51 ✓
P-2236	7264506.		Woods Bacon Factory. Lo. MIRFIELD	YRKS.	13-11-51		22-11-51
P-2283	7268037		W. A. CHURCH 17, SOUTHGATE, WAKE	-FIELD, YORKS.	2-2-52		4-2-52
M-3690	7268859	ALBERT. FARNELL. LTD, BRADFORD.	F. A. WHITAKER, 7. LONGLANDS AVE., DEN	-E, BRADFORD, YORKS	1-2-52		10-7-52
P-2290	726641		Warranty not necessary		6-3-52.	see Tate's letter 10.7.53.	

TOTAL 79 (Sept. 1948 July 1952)

R.H. PATTERSON & COMPANY LTD

CHASSIS no.	ENGINE. no.	DEALERS NAMES & ADDRESS	CUSTOMERS no.	NAME & ADDRESS	DATE	DELIVERED.	WARRANTY. REC'D
M- 640	7200374		A. J. Hogg, 15, Clare -	Newcastle on Tyne, mont Place,	30. 8. 48		6. 9. 48
M- 734	7202999				16 · 10 · 48		
M- 733	7202998	Z. Crabtree, Co. Kirkland, Kendal, Westmorland,	S.W. Wood, 52, Stram	ongate Kendal, Westmorland,	15. 10. 48		1. 11. 48.
M- 777	7203623	Stoutt's Garage, 2, Lowther St., Cumb,	Harry Ingham, Cleve	How Duke Mere, Bowness Club, New	28. 11. 48		26. 11. 48
M- 824	7204450	E. Dugdale Harris St.		castle-on-tyne, John, Northern	10. 12. 48		23. 12. 48 A
M- 794	7204089		County Garage, N. Gillig	Articles, on, Lowther St.,	7. 1. 49		7. 1. 49
M- 82	7206520	S.M.T. Sales & Service, Viaduct Garage, Carlisle.	Margaret E. Jagger	Rochdale, Cumb, son, Hall Croft, Cumb,	12. 2. 49		26. 4. 49
L- 830	7204740	County Garage Co., Carlisle.	A.G. Abraham,	Cockermouth	17. 6. 49		7. 6. 49
M- 1533	7202305				13 10 49		NOT REC'D
P- 1501	7212295				21 10·49		NOT REC'D
P 1536	7217643.		W & A Swan 2 Win	Newcastle on Tyne sor Terrace	22 11 48		25 11 48
P 1581	7222487	Not yet completed 4/3/50			11 1 50	x	NOT REC'D
P- 1566	7222123	Young Motor Ltd, Chester - le Street Co. Durham	G. Thompson Vicarage	Co. Durham form, Eaglesworth,	25. 1. 50		1. 2. 50
P- 1641	7229717		F. H. Newrick, 2, Pearith.	Co. Durham, Grove, Roker, Sunderland	14 - 5 - 50		11 - 5 - 50 √
P- 1654	7229904	Wm. Duno, 37 Monkseaton Drive, Whitley Bay	7		22 - 5 - 50		13 - 6 - 50 √
J- 1574	3933/114		F. J. Curtis, c/o 33 Groat	Market, Newcastle	25 - 5 - 50		25 - 5 - 50 √
P- 1682	7233192	H. Young (Motors) Ltd, Chester-le-Street Co. Durham	Dr. A. Charlton, Grove	Co. Durham Lodge Tow Law,	10 - 7 - 50		14 - 7 - 50 √
P- 1750	7237914		E.E. Shafto, 230 West	gate Rd, Newcastle	31 - 8 - 50		5 - 9 - 50 √
P- 1906	7246816		G. M. Carrick, Acton Hse,	Felton, Morpeth, Northld	8 - 1 - 50		17 - 1 - 51 √
P- 1930.	7249401	COUNTY GARAGE CO. LOWTHER ST. CARLISLE.	ALLEN. W. CARRICK. KIR	KBY THORE. Hall Gateshead	9. 2. 51		18 - 4 - 51. √
P- 1940	7249400.		W. H. Skinner (Dr) 15	Whitehall Rd Co. Durham	22. 2. 51		3 - 3 - 51
P. 2051.	7256025.	Normobiles Co. Ltd. Dinsdale Road	Wm. Latimer, Co. Ltd, 10	Armstrong Ter. N/T.	1. 5. 51.		11 - 6 - 51. √
P 2143	7259221.	COUNTY GARAGE Co. LOWTHER St CARLISLE.	A. L. WALLIS. THE GREEN	GREEN DALSTON. CARLISLE.	11. 8. 51.		11. 8. 51 √
P. 2293	7269443.	FEWSTERS (STOCKSFIELD) PRUDHOE-ON-TYNE	W. M. HUMPHREY	WESTBANK.	22. 2. 52	NEW RIDLEY. STOCKSFIELD. N/humberland	10. 4. 52 √
M. 3093.	7269429.		Corrugated Packing & Sheet Metal	Wensley Sk Yorkshire Co. Witham	29. 3. 52		29. 3. 52
P. 3087	7271089.		G.F. CLAY. 2 H.	DENHILL PARK	9. 5. 52	NEWCASTLE. J.	23. 9. 53.
212-5102	ROTTA37380				11. 4. 53		

GEORGE & JOBLING

CHASSIS no	ENGINE no	DEALERS NAME & ADDRESS	CUSTOMERS NAME	& ADDRESS	DATE	DELIVERED	RECIEVED WARRANTY
M-624	7200148	J. M. Miller Ltd., Geor.den Rd. Falkirk	J. D. Ross, 27, Glen Broa	Falkirk.	27. 8. 48		14. 9. 48
L-632	7200470	Rusby Motor Co. 86, Causeyside St. Paisley	Dr. R. Allan, 86, Mello House	Love St, Paisley.	1. 9. 48		3. 9. 48
M-712	7202514		J. L. Stevenson, 1, Wilsock	ton Rd, Troon.	11. 10. 48		20. 10. 48
M-748	7203194	Body Builders			22. 10. 48		NOT REC'D
M-727	7202988		Dr. J. Scott Glover, Pickering	Co. Ltd, Wishaw	14. 10. 48		8. 10. 48
M-782	7203893	Body Builders			15. 11. 48.		NOT REC'D
M-780	7203766	J. R. Alexander Co Ltd, Gt Western Rd Glasgow	A. Hamilton, 511, Duke St,	Glasgow, E.4.	17. 11. 48		27. 11. 48
M-788	7203948	Cameron. Campbell, Glasgow, C.3.	J. Johnston, 325, Dumbarton	Rd, W.4 Cargil	3. 12. 48		1. 1. 49
M-838	7204597	J. R. Alexander Co Ltd, Gt Western Rd, Glasgow	J. C. Blair, Dalchenna Home	Farm, Inveraray.	23. 12. 48		21. 1. 49
M-865	7204624	J. Martin Ltd. Kelvin Valley Works, Kirkintilloch	J. Oc. Mackay, 30, Mansield Rd	Glasgow, S.3	19. 1. 49		5. 2. 49
M-894	7207143	J. Martin Ltd, Kelvin Valley Works	J. G. Craig, 64, Turrebo	Ave, Glasgow, S.1.	14. 2. 49		19. 2. 49
M-855	7206586		R. L. Laurie, 1, Tanter Bank Ho	M. Doncaster, Old Wich no St, Glasgow, n	18. 2. 49		19. 3. 49
M-1040	7209403		C. D. Moodie, Moodie Co, 1	57/29, Colston Rd, Glasgow	8. 4. 49		14. 4. 49
M-1060	7210523	Cameron. Campbell, Glasgow, C.3	J. O. K. Stewart, 148, Glencairn	Drive, Pollokshields, St, Glasgow n.	27. 4. 49		26. 5. 49
M-1061	7210555	J. Martin Ltd. Dumbartonshire	North British Locomotive	Co. 110, Flemming Co.	9. 5. 49		14. 5. 49
M-1083	7212029	Cameron & Campbell, 172, Bothwell St, Glas.	J. R. Anderson, The Woodlands, Manse	Motherwell	1. 6. 49		21. 9. 49
M-1082	7212057	Park Autos Co. 69, Dumbreck Rd,	W. Burns (Glasgow) Ltd, 21	Bothinas St, Glasgow 11.	6. 49		11. 6. 49
M-1102	7212148	Queens Garage, 640, Pollokshaw Rd, Glasgow	J. S. Gardiner 31, Queen Mary	Ave, Glasgow.	19. 8. 49		30. 8. 49
P-1500	7207588		James Anderson 15, Bothwell St	Glasgow C.2.	24-10-49		27. 10. 49
P-1504	7217107	Cameron & Campbell 151, Bothwell St, Glasgow	J. Findlay, Foxbar House	Paisley by Glasgow	5. 12. 49		5. 12. 49
M-1526	7215399	James Martin, Kelvin Valley Wks. Dumbarton	Mr. N. K. Gordon, Dunluce Pioneer use Trallatus Wigtownshire.	3. 12. 49		4. 12. 49
P-1544	7219356		Mrs. M. H. Wilson, Kildonnan,	Stoneykirk, Renfrewshire	5. 1. 50		13. 1. 50
P-1596	7224160	Cameron & Campbell, Bothwell St., Glasgow	J. Park, 53, Fermant St., Greenock	Renfrewshire	23. 2. 50		22-5-50
J-1559	3958/60	J. McHarrie Ltd, County Gar, Stranraer Wigtown	H. S. Mort Sescroft Stranraer		15-4-50		148-4-50
P-1622	7224205	McKnight Motor Ltd, York Place, Dumfries	Dr. J. McPherson, Drumlanrig St,	Thornhill, Dumfries	11-4-50		21-4-50
P-1645	7229693	Stobcross Co. Ltd, Glasgow			13-5-50		18-6-50
P-1668	7233186	A. C. Penman Ltd, Castle Douglas, Kirkcud bright	J. M. Donald, Chapel Place, Castle-	Douglas, Kirkcudbright	16-6-50		19-6-50
P-1666	7232462	Grosvenor Motor Works, Glasgow.	Mr W. Blyth, M.D. 3101 London Rd	Glasgow E.2	13-6-50		12-6-50
P-1681	7232480		Prof. L. J. Davis, 79, Oakfield Ave	Glasgow W.2.	19-7-50		10-8-50
P-1716	7233677	Cameron & Campbell, Bothwell St. Glasgow	W. R. Ralley, 17, Montgomery	St, Kirkaldy	31-7-50		31-8-50
P-1796	7238822	Callander Gar., Hughenden Rd, Glasgow W.2	Dr. J. L. Armstrong, 6, Craigweil Pl	Ayr.	28-9-50		7-10-50
P-1866	7244327	Cameron & Campbell Bothwell St, Glasgow	Clayton Star Hosiery Co. 25-27 Ma	Street, Irvine	17-11-50		28-11-50
P-1888	7244981	Gas. Martin Ltd, Kelvin Valley Wks. Kirkintilloch	Dr. A. G. Blair, 8, Bungalow, Se.	Burnside Ave, Rutherglen, Stirling	1-12-50		1-1-51
P-1899	7246503	Callanders Gar. Hughenden Rd. Glasgow W2	R. L. Carswell, The Hill, Alphington	Rd, Whitecraigs	27-12-50		23-1-51
P-1907	7246914	Cameron & Campbell, 171, Bothwell St. Glasgow	J. H. Capel, 16, Albert Dr. Burnside,	erglen	10-1-51		15-1-51
P-1914	M246826	DAVID INGLIS, 167 2, SHETTLESTON, GLASGOW.	JAS. MORTON, MILLERFIELD RD	GLASGOW. S.E.	16-1-51		31. 1. 51
P-1939	7249440	GROSVENOR MOTOR WORKS, 380, SHIELDS RD GLASGOW	Dr. J. W. BURKE, 39, WINTON	AVE. GLASGOW. W.2	22. 2. 51		26. 2. 51
P-1966	7252809	CALLANDERS GARAGE 60, HUGHENDEN RD GLASGOW	6. Q.C. WADDILOVE, 58, C....	DEN DRIVE, GLASGOW	21. 3. 51		28. 3. 51
K-2033	9615-86	" "	J. WATT, 119, SAUCHIEHALL S.	GLASGOW. C.2.	10. 4. 51		24/4/51
P-2062	7256177	CAMERON & CAMPBELL, 181, BOTHWELL ST. GLASGOW. C2.	Dr. W. YOUNG-LAIDLAW, FAIRSI	LD BONESS.	16/5/51		19. 6. 51
P-2070	7256171		JAMES C. MITCHELL, 16, Hun	bloss, GLASGOW W.2	28. 5. 51		1-6-51.

George and Jobling.

Chassis No.	Engine No.	Dealers Name and Address	Customers	Name and Address	Date Delivered		Warranty Recd
P-2111	7258765	Wylie's Ltd. 370, Pollokshaws Rd. Glasgow	H.M. Roemele & Co. Ltd.	65, W. Regent St. Glasgow 2	5/7/51		8-7-51
P-2113	7258766	Dalblair Motors Ltd. Dalblair Rd. Ayr	G. Greenlees, Dinwoodie	Hollybush Ayr	18-7-51		20-8-51
P-2204	7261753	Cameron and Campbell 171-181, Bothwell St.	John McKenna, 6, Hope Street	St. Andrews, Fife	11-10-51		26-11-51
P-2262	7264737	Callanders. Garage Hughenden Rd. Glasgow	Watt. Bros. Ltd. 121,	Sauchiehall St. Glasgow 6-12-51		C-2	1-1-52
P-2266	7264738		Paterson Scott Mackay	Ltd. 203, Hope St. Glasgow 18-12-51			18-12-51
P-2270	7266551	Cameron & Campbell 171-181, Bothwell St.	Mrs M. Turner. 228,	Glenlora Drive Craigbank 2-1-52		Glasgow	7-3-52
P-3085	7270581	T. Prosser & Sons. Glasgow 2.	Bartholomew Gross.	"Clevedon" Manse Rd. 18-4-52		Wishaw, Lanarkshire	26-4-52

ALEXANDERS of EDINBURGH LTD.

CHASSIS. no.	Engine. no.	DEALERS. NAMES. ADD.	CUSTOMERS NAME & ADD.		DATE	DELIVERED	WARRANTY REG.
M-650	7200941		Lt. P.G. Guest Howard,	3, Kilmaurs Terr. Edinburgh.	3.9.48		13.9.48
K-621	7200192	Milligan. Bell, Hawick	C. Bell, Bellevue,	Hawick.	29.9.48		28.9.48
M-707	7200727		J.H. Stoney, Preston	field House, Edinburgh. 9.	30.9.48		6.10.48
M-798	7204087		L. Jackson, Norwood,	Lymington.	13.12.48		16.12.48
M-850	7204756		E.B. Murray, 356, Morningside Rd, Edin.		30.12.48		31.12.48
M-834	7204486		R. Manson, 116, Charlotte Sq, Edinburgh		27.1.49		31.1.49
M-816	7204414	J. Brown, 6, Lochrin Pl, Edinburgh	O.G. Clark, "Gbanor", mister, Mussel.		7.3.49		7.3.49
M-1014	7207258		H.E. Gould, 101, High St, Dalkeith		17.3.49		16.3.49
M-1029	7209396	H.C. Hutchison, Almillan Motor Wks Edin.	W. Black, Holton,	Milnathort	29.3.49		29.3.49
M-1079	7210811	O. Harrison, 69, Devon Place, Edin.	P. Laing, 2, Craigleith View, Edin. 4		24.5.49		23.5.49
K-717	7200764	W.B. Turnbull Ltd, Sheddon Pk. Rd, Kelso.	R.W.B. Boswell Haining, Coldstream, Berwick		17-4-50		17-4-50
P-1814	7240930		V.C.E. Harrington 2 Orchard Rd, Lth		13-10-50		18-10-50
P-1877	7244506	G. Mac Andrews Co. 86 Lothian Rd, Edinburgh	R.L. Scott, Breaside, Loanhead Midlothian		30-11-50		30-11-50
P-1943	7250061	D. Harrison. Esq 78 Haymarket Tce EDINBURGH.	R. Gairn. 46. Craigmillar Pk. Edinburgh		19.2.51		15.3.51
P-1965	7252602		J. Graham Woyka. Standingstone, Scotland, Haddington		19.3.51		9.4.51
P2039	7254520	DAVID ROSE. HADDINGTON.	J.G.D. CLARK. 89 LUGGATE.		10.4.51		25.4.51
P2096	7258085.		J.B.T. LOUDON. 47. Gt. KING St. EDINBURGH		10.6.51		6-7-51

FREW & COMPANY LIMITED.

CHASSIS no	Engine no	DEALERS NAME & ADD:	CUSTOMERS NAME	& ADD:	DATE	DELIVERED	WARRANTY REC
M-645	7189886	Grassick's Garage. Blairgowrie	J.R.Scott, 14. Windsor	St. Dundee.	6.9.48		1.10.48.
M-706	7200128		W.H.Lomas, Royal	George Hotel	1.10.48		23.10.48
L-718	7200471		J.L.Fraser, Ins Co. Ltd.,		1.11.48.		1.11.48.
M-752	7203450	Harper Motor Co. Aberdeen	Major Cab Marsden, Kink ey Aberdeen		9.11.48		30.12.48
M-758	7203705		W.F.Barbar, March House, Carlton-on-Lind		8.12.48		20.11.48
L-729	7202815		Dr.W.E.Robinson, Ascog.	Pitlochry.	13.12.48		11.12.48.
M-848	7204668	Elgin Garage, Elgin.	Geo. M.Gray Sunnyside, W.	Cathcart St, Buckie	23.12.48		8.9.48.
M-893	7206838		Alice Hay Davidson, Croc. An. Thistle, Angus		14.2.49		9.3.49.
M-898	7207288		Dr Jessie R. Robinson, Ascog. Pitlochry Errol, Perks.		28.2.49.		13.4.49.
M-1008	7207021	O. McIntosh, Erol.	W.Lindsay Gillies, East Inchmichael, Perthshire		11.3.49		8.4.49.
M-1037	7209615	Elgin Motors Ltd, Elgin. Macyshire	R.V.Christie, Braes of Enzie, Aochan,		5.4.49.		21.4.49.
M-1063	7210570		Mrs G.H.Cook. The Crofts, Glenmuick Aberdeenshire		4.49.		6.9.49.
M-1055	7209955	P.S.Nicholson (Forres) Ltd	W.Scott, White Row, Forres, Moray		6.5.49		13.5.49.
M-565	7199664	Sold as chassis May 1948.	J.L.Fraser, Fair Hill	Perth	29.6.49	Body Fitted by Hiltons	9.8.49. ✓
P-1583	7222477	Robb's Garage, Kirkcaldy.	J.M.Lockhart, 41, Abbotshall Rd. Kirkcaldy, Fife		1.2.50.	x	6-5-50 ✓
P-1639	7228917		Capt. E. Jackson, Keppock, Strathpeffer		4-5-50		12-5-50. ✓
P-1659	7231829	Messrs Grassick's Commercial St. Blairgowrie	Dr. W. Shaw, High St, Blair- Sourie. Perth		7-6-50		6-6-50. ✓
P-1797	7238786	W.H.Harris Ltd. Leven, Fife	H.Paterson Esq. Commercial Rd Leven Fife		29-9-50		5-10-50 ✓
P-1891	7246358	MUTCH MOTORS. 366. KING ST. ABERDEEN	HR.SPENCE. 81 GORDON ST. HUNTLY.		4-12-50		2.2.51 ✓
P-1913	M246897	ROBB'S GARAGE. KIRKCALDY.	T.MENZIES. TOWNSEND Pl. KIRKCALDY.		15-1-51		7.2.51. ✓
P-1954	7249596	MESSRS GEORGE McLEAN - DUNDEE	I.S.SMILLIE. BALCARRAES. ALBANY RD BROUGHTY FERRY		1.3.51		13.3.51 ✓
P-1988	7252436	MUTCH MOTORS (LTD) ABERDEEN.	J. BARRON ESQ. DARRAHILL UDNY STATION ABERDEEN		20.3.51		10.4.51 ✓
P-2065	7252890	P.S.NICHOLSON. HIGH ST. ELGIN	G.C.SHEPHERD. 111 TENNSON RD CAMBRIDGE		24-5-51		21.6.51. ✓
P-2099	7254941	WM.ROBB BROS. KIRKCALDY.	MAXWELL C. DICK. 125 CONSTITUTION ST. LEITH.		21.6.51	EDINBURGH.	27-4-51 ✓
P-2131	7259634	J.G.MUTCH MOTORS LTD ABERDEEN	E.C.EDWARDS. CLINTON. PETERCULTER.		25-7-51.		17.8.51 ✓
P-2171	7261748	J.G.MUTCH. MOTORS LTD. ABERDEEN.	R.M.LEDINGHAM Esq. 11, FOREST ROAD ABERDEEN		22-9-51		29-9-51 ✓
P-2249	7262954	Transferred from Mutch & Co Ltd. to Dag. Motors,			30-11-51	LETTER Sent 7.2.52 Sold to Dag. Motors	

19   R.E. HAMILTON & COMPANY.

CHASSIS no	Engine no.	DEALERS. NAMES ADD:	CUSTOMERS	NAMES ADD:	DATE	DELIVERED.	WARRANTY REC
M-835	7204573	Dudys Garage, Omagh, Tyrone.	D. H. Watson, Main	St. Favagh, Tyrone	7.1.49.		7.1.49.
P-1543	7217634		J. F. McCandless & Sons	3/5 Oxford St. Belfast	19 12 49	X	3-1-50
P-1665	7232436	L. Porter Ltd, 20/36 Gt. Victoria St., Belfast.	R. W. Lightbody, 38 Adelaide	Park, Belfast.	13-6-50		23-6-50
P-2066	7254685		John Scott Ltd 10. Church St. Belfast		24-5-51.		29-6-51
J-2120	2022/2		J. D. Titterington 130, M	alone Rd. Belfast.	1-9-51.		1-9-51
P-2261	7265860	John Patterson Ltd. Belfast	A. T. Marshall 144,	Dun Creggan Road	10-12-51	Londonderry	1.1.52 X
21C-5109	K3TA-122656	Wrights Deliveries R. E. Hamilton			6.2.54		
P2-4505	9.T.163. Cad.	Mr.	Mr. Scott.		24.8.54		

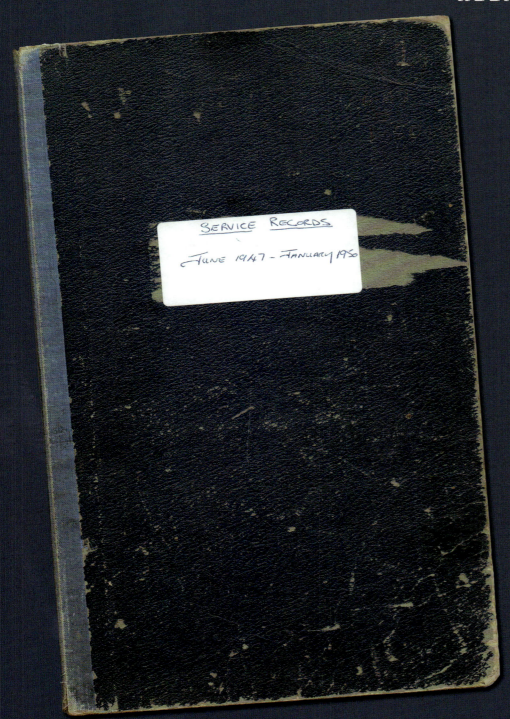

SERVICE RECORDS

June 1947 – January 1950

ALLARD
SERVICE RECORDS

JUNE 1947 – JANUARY 1950

The reader requires a good eye to decipher some of these service notes, but it should be well worth the effort. Look out for entries with Sydney's competition cars and those of his close friends, Goff Imhof (page 443), the Wick brothers, Ken Hutchison (pages 418, 588 and 589) and many others who had repeated visits.

From June 1947

to Jan, 1950

8/6/47	3019	214 71M.	Make runner. Check over fit grilles etc. Weld radius
10/6/47	3020	217M.	Make runner. Check chassis Fit grilles etc. Weld radius
11/6/47	3021	133G	Front spring. Weld radius Front tray and blanking plate.
12/6/47	3022 Richards	116 GL	Mud flaps. change grille - tray - blanking plate tighten gear change Shock absorbers hauling New bonnet handle Vent in pet tank Repair wing bracket.
12/6/47	3023	236. 71K.	Make runner. Weld radius arms.
16/6/47	3024	249 71K.	Make runner. Chassis
17/6/47	3025	150 71K	Chassis with body. Completed car. Fit blanking plate and tray Weld radius. Check over.
17/6/47	3026	246. 71L	Make runner - chassis only

Date	No.	Reg.	Work
8/6/47	3027	228 71M	Make runner.
18/6/47	3028	141.7M	Finished car. from White. Weld radius arm. Brakes. Fit Blanking plate and mud flaps.
20/6/47	3029	154 71K	Finished car at White. Change rad. 6 Blade fan. Cut grille. Fit S.U. pet pump. Change rear axle " gear box. (Rally Car)
26/6/47	3030	205 71K.	Change over to L.H. drive.
28/6/47	3031	252 K	Make runner.
30/6/47	3032	164 L	Finished car. Check
1/7/47	3033	248 K.	Make runner.
1/7/47	3034	251 K.	Change rear axle. Repair damage to rear tank. Make runner.
1/7/47	3035	160 K.	Finished car. Mud flaps. cowl plate and tray. Chrome pipe.
4/7/47	3036.	234 K	Make runner. Chassis with body.
1/7/47	3037	165 K. Finished car.	Remove axle. change prop. Fit coppered heads and Chrome parts.
7/7/47	3038	158 K	Finished car. Coppered heads. Chrome parts.
8/7/47	3039	128 L S.M.C. 649 McGladstone.	Change front grille.
9/7/47	3040	251.	Runner chassis Replace 1 engine valve.
9/7/47	3041	256 K 144 K McCanio Inspection	Tighten front wings. Tighten U Bolts. Rectify wiring New grille
14/7/47	3042	147 K	Change front spring. Finished car. Mud flaps. Cowl tray. Check over.
14/7/47	3043	259 K	Inspection Rectify fan.
14/7/47	3044	256 L	Inspection.
14/7/47	3045	260 K	Inspection
14/7/47	3046	258 K	Inspection.
14/7/47	3047	209 L	Finished car. Brakes. Mud flaps. Trays.
16/7/47	3048	140 L	Finished car. Chrome parts on engine. 6 Bladed fan. Adjust brakes. Fit cowl tray etc.
18/7/47	3049	148 Asbury.	Change front spring " Rad. Rectify wiring Adjust brakes.

18/7/47	3050	240.K	Inspection of chassis.
21/7/47	3051	151 K	Finished car. Change front spring. Mud Flap. Cowl tray - blanking plate. Handbrake faulty. Washer on fan.
22/7/47	3052	164 L	Gearbox - jumps out of Top and noisy.
22/7/47	3053	200 L	Finished car. Check over.
22/7/47	3054	224 L	Finished car. Change fan 12V. Dynamo. New lead to C.B. to coil. Check over.
23/7/47	3055	261 K	Chassis inspection.
23/7/47	3056	262 K	Chassis inspection.
24/7/47	3057	162 K	Finished car. Alter pedals. fit mud flaps. Adjust brakes.
5/8/47	3058	143 K	Finished car. Alter pedals. Cowl tray etc. Fan assem.
6/8/47	3059	222 K	Finished car. Weld radius. Cowl tray.

7/8/47	3060	203 L	Finished car. Chrome parts. Weld radius. Cowl tray etc.	
11/8/47	3061	161 K	Finished car. Inane pipe. Mud Flap. Blanking shield. Battery tray. Weld radius. Brakes.	
13/8/47	3062	NH.X 798 16 L	Tighten universal housing.	
14/8/47	3063	213 71 KL	Finished car. L.H. Drive. Change heads. Chrome parts. Rad.	
15/8/47	3064	163. 71 K.	Finished car. Change grille. Fit Cowl tray - mud flaps. Chrome pipes.	
18/8/47	3065	221 71 K.	Finished car. Water pump change. Steering heavy. Battery tray. Fit end. bullet.	
20/8/47	3066	2 71 M.	Make runners.	Group Capt Hose. Saltwell Green. Parton Herts
1/9/47	3067.	71 K.	Service distributor. Adjust brakes.	
2/9/47	3068	71 G 128	Change rad and fan.	Mr Gladstone Pad 5314

6/10/47	250 71K	3087	Mud flaps. Wheel doors. batten trays Adjust brakes. Track.	12/11/47	Adlards. Aeroplane. 127. J.G.V.108	3096	Change front spring.	
7/10/47	Imperial 217 M. JGU 5	3088	Prop shaft trouble.	17/11/47	121 M. J.LF575. Spedo 3-794.	3097	Change front spring and rad.	
7/10/47	230 71K	3089	New spedo cable. Throttle sticking Tighten steering wheel clamps	19/11/47	Imperial J.GU.5	3098	Change front spring. Brake judder. Change rad. Lower steering column Lubricator (no pulley) Check brown. Fan pulley out of alignment	
9/10/47	243C	3090	Adjust brakes. A. Body. Pulley cover Track.					
9/10/47	241K	3091	Fit Bumpers - cowl trays - mud flaps. Adjust brakes.					
9/10/47	253C	3092	Fit Bumpers.					
20/10/47	159 K	3093	Exchange o/s water pump. Bonoulak. Mr. Cook.					
22/10/47	151K Bradshaw		New grille oil leak on engine fit bumper. Damage rear of cowl to Service.					
28/10/47	J.A.L465. 138C Tongue.	3094	Remove axle for repair.					
1/11/47	Mrs Dubois 214.	3095	New races in fan. Change grille Steering bracket.					

			Dec '47.	
3099	# Robouts 147 K FHH 211	12/12/47	Cracked chassis frame.	Mil 5198.
309 3100	DBX939 200	15/12/47	Wheel hump over 80. Cracked paint on bonnet. Water coming in between screen and hood. Chrome grilles loose	
3101	309 C A.S. Loces Barnes Pk 2575	16/12/47	Remove axle change torque tube and prop shaft. Mil 176.	
3102	208 M. Stourmont Eng	22/12/47	Change grille Weld radius rods.	
3103.	121 M. Hill. 2LF575.	30/12/47	Steering wobble New ball joint Play in steering box.	mil 5266.

			Jan '48	
3103A	239 K CUD918 Hartwells Oxford.	6/1/48	Repair gearbox Adjust brakes. Starting handle. Spedo - wrong ratio	Mil 1400
3104	213 M. 2LM245. Dagenham Motor	8/1/48.	Faulty batts.	Mil 344
3105	Frews. BGS.1. 263 M.	14/1/48	Rectify front spring. Change radius rods.	Mil 1974
3106	226 L E.A.W163	28/1/48.	Change torque tube Spedo gear. Bodywork.	Mil 2101.

Feb. 48.

Date	Name/Reg	No.	Work
16/2/48	Daniels. 9 LU 676. 216 M Mil 396	3107	Change torque tube Change oil in gear box Adjust Brakes. Check track Starting handle guide.
17/2/48	Imhof. 9 G.U.5. Mil 4913. 217 M.	3108	Repair gearbox Examine brakes Change torque tube and prop shaft.
18/2/48	Stonimont Eng 208 M. 1225.	3109	
25/2/48	Burgess. M. KHW 100.	3110.	Change torque tube " prop Shaft.

Date	Name/Reg	No.	Work
			Mar.
2/3/48	Roberts. F. EH.211 147 K.	3111	Change Front spring. Mil 5711 Torque tube Examine wheels and brake drums.
23/3/48	Millward 231	3112.	Change torque tube and prop. Mil 2611

April.

Date	Name	No.	Work	Notes
1/4/48	Roberts. 147	3113	Change shock absorbers.	
5/4/48	Bamber. 373M.	3114.	Adjust Timer / " Brakes. / " Fan belt.	
12/4/48	L.V.K 160 N.C. Road C286.	3115	Remove axle for tongue tube / and prop. / Spedo cable. / Adjust neg. / Tune engine. / Crankshaft at Timson.	
14/4/48	JLK 832	3116	Recon engine.	mil 8924
19/4/48	717 208 Adolphin	3117.	Change road / " grille / " Front spring / Adjust brakes. / Chrome pipes.	mil 5618. / Eng 18F 7199886
30/4/48	JLX 978 Mr Hale	3118	Change front spring / Adjust Brakes.	

May.

Date	Name	No.	Work	Notes
5/5/48	JLC 681 Hale. 325M.	3119.	Change front spring / " " down. / " Tongue tube / Prop shaft.	Mil 655.
10/5/48	Magd Lawson CRK222	3120	Blown or gasket washer. / Adjust brakes. / Change spedo gear. / O/S Door stick.	Mil 558
11/5/48	FOD 793. Western Garage Newbridge	3121.	Change tongue tube / Spedo. / Change grille	
21/5/48	Hale. 325M.	3122.		
21/5/48	Millwort JLM 345.	3123.	Rev axle shaft.	
26/5/48	JUC 310. Stroud (Dick Bratty) 510K.	3124.	Repair gearbox. / Jumps out of second.	mil 2089.
26/5/48.	Armstrong Siddeley M.P.D 142	3125	Rectify safety catch. / " Wiper bracket. / Hood worn. Hand brake. / Throttle.	

June.

2/6/48	Thursin Blackford	3126	Change to R.H. Drive
11/6/48	A.M.C. Gearbox	3127	Repair gearbox
11/6/48	Rear Axle A.M.C.	3128	Repair new axle (noisy)
14/6/48	Lucas. 309	3129	Rear steered in prop shaft
			Fit electric clock.
16/6/48	Dagenham Motors.	3130	Rectify paintwork.
16/6/48	Mordaunt 9.P.G 329.	3131	
23/6/48	austin motor M.P.D 28	3131	Gearbox jump out of 2nd. Mil 1271
			Paintwork
			Hand pass batten trim out.

July.

7/7/48	Godfery EAW163	3132	Respray
8/7/48	A.M.C ? 9.GY 119.	3133	Adjust Points ½ pink R.K. adjust clutch Etc.
14/7/48	Swan. 9.LX689. 325M.	3134	Change front spring Adjust brakes. Nutscer
27/7/48	Maud Lacorr	3135	Alter castor angle
28/7/48	Dagenham Motors	3136	Change fan.
29/7/48	Col Dolphin LSH 856	3137	Steering wobble Mil 11 929.

August.

9/8/48	Mills 454 M. 9.Y.M 273	3138.	Change Fan.
6/8/48	Dixon T.M.H. 6.09	3139.	Change Sol switch
6/8/48.	Capt Hess 162 K SMC 665.	3139A.	Change O/S Wheel bearing
7/8/48.	Franklin	3140	Change front spring Mil 10000 South brake Brake Gearbox Fan belt. Bodywork.
10/8/48	Miller 9.Y.K639 354 M.	3141	
11/8/48	Thompson 9UC 301 509/712 Extra Canvas Gilbert	3142	Repair gearbox Rear drums rubbing on canvas. Windscreen rubber Mil 3903
13/8/48.	Hale 7IM.	3143.	Pack rear spring.
14/8/48	Reiss CUMI.	3144	Change rear spring Wiper motor Fan cleaner blander to left.
19/8/48	9.A.K.599	3145	Change own headlight. New bonnet handle

19/8/48	Mcdonald.	3146	Change front Brakes.
24/8/48	Du Sellon ENT 295	3147.	Respray.
26/8/48	Jefferys S.M. X 835 517 M	3148.	Brakes. 5363 Mls. Pet Gauge. Speedo. Clock.
30/8/48	Clark No 631	3149	Fit New Locking levers Etc
31/8/48	EBX 49 Chas 410.	3150	Chassis No 410 Fit New Clock and Speedo Head
1/9/48	EBX 761 Du Edwards. 610 M	3151	Fit New Speedo Head inner and outer cable Bulb in Head lamp '' warning lamp Change Traffic indicator Adjust Brakes.
1/9/48	GFH 27 P. Pound. 582 M.	3152	Fit New Clock Miles 940 Fit New Handbrake lever
1/9/48	JYT 849	3153	Fit new longer tube Dyno not charge Petrol gauge fit tie Rod on front Brakes

2/9/48	S.Compton JYT 943	3154	Repair Hood Not Change offside door adjust lamps change Swing strims adjust gears and Brakes weld Bumbers
2/9/48	ARC 319 Boulthosterns	3155	Bonnet rattles Rattle in near boat Vent windows loose on catches
7/9/48	AFb 798 Jackson. 392L mil 3485.	3156	New near spring Check plugs and ignition Handbrake flys off Back seat squab lifts at speed N/S Bonnet side loose Noise in O/S rear wheel O/S door rattles.
11/9/48	B.CF206 3731C	3157	Change rear axle (noisy)
13/9/48	G.B.H 856 Dolphin 206.M.	3158	New chassis frame
16/9/48	OUL 427.	3159	Bodywork Gear lever. Windscreen wiper Back axle filler plug Engine tune.

(After this page, blank up to paper-clip at 64)
first entry 20.9.48

Pages blank from date 16-9-48, up to this paper slip

Job N°.	Customer's Name & Address	Chassis N°.	Reg N°.	Date In	
1.	H.N. Bentley. A.M.C. Accounts	257. Y1.C.	MPB- 118.	30.9.48.	Renew Rear Axle, Change Propshaft.
2.	M/s. J. Rea.	257. Y1.M.	MBB- 802.	..	Remove Rear axle rectify chatter. Change Rad Grille.
3.	Gate of Leeds Ltd.	279. Y1.C.H.	LUB- 265.	E. 10046.	Convert to R/H steering. Examine for heat inside Car.
5.	J. Preston & Wife de Col Dolphin.	280. M	Col.E. 856.	R. 10053.	New Chassis Frame including removing and refitting Body.
6.	C.R. Abbott.	367.Q Y1.K.	THX- 533.	E. 9962/A	Tune Engine, 1 New Front Bumper Bar Check for oil leaks, New Driving Mirror Transfers on Bulkhead.
7.	Railway Passenger Assurance Co	457.Q Y1.M.	2UM- 89	R. 1004/4	Repairs after Crash. Already Estimated.
8.	M/s. Imhof	58 Y1.M.	JSA- 4		Fit New Hand- Brake Cable. Cancelled.
9.	M/s. Richardson.	607. Y1.K.		E. 9618/A 30.9.48.	Fit New Bonnet Handle.
10.	Universal Coachworks (Spalding) Ltd.	575. Y1.M.	SLY- 687.	E. 10066.	Estimate for Repairs after Crash.
12.	Mayor. E. Hempsall.	585. Y1.M.	JYU- 371.	E. 10031. 25.9.48	Repair Bonnet Sides, Repairs to Paintwork on Rear of Body. Rattles on Screen, Engine Vibration, Etc.
13.	Thomas Motor Blackpool.	L/P. A. Y1.M.	N.F.R- 376.	E. 10055.	Convert to R/Hand Drive, Fit Air Filter. Tune Engine, Rectify Rattles (R. 10046.)
14.	A.L. Woodman Esq.	464. A Y1.M.	N-B-F- 343.	E. 10040 27.9.48	Repair cracks in Rear Paint Panel, Headlamp glass, Rim. Repair Front Lt wing. Repair
15.	M/s. Imhof	J.S.D.L. Coupe		E. 9919/51.	Adjust Brakes, Grease, Pressure.
19.	M/s. Phillips	J.Y.A. 671.	536 Y1M	E. 10004/A	Tune Engine, Handbrake Rattles on Lamp, Rectify Fault in reverse unit. Attend (Rt/H) Brake. Throttle control Knob Loose, Door have dropped Rattle on Rear of Body.
20.	Mr. Hinstein	J.Y.I. 949.	364. Y1.M.	E. 10002/A	Fit Frame, Air cleaner on Carb, Change oils & Grease, Adjust Brakes, Fit 2 Exchange
21.	Allard Motor Co.	146. Y1.K.	Demo. Rep.	..	Prepare Car for Sale.
	Doris Roots	Coupe Y1.M.		E. 9980/A	Clean Carb and Adjust, Adjust Hand- Brake

Job Nº	Customers Names + Address	Chassis Nº	Reg Nº	Date In	Invoice Nº	Instructions for Repairs
23	Decca Records.	400. 71M.	JUC-503.	29·9·48.	E-10030	Supply and Fit L62.A. Junior Complete With Leads, 1 Fan Belt.
24.	D. Compton	6189. 71.M.	JXT. 943.	30. 9. 48	E-10014	New Battery. Attend to Steering Wheel 8.10.48. Fit New Distributor.
26.	Thing Car. Hire.	163. 71.M.	SMC 655 / LOW-391	,,		Respray, New bodies on Screen, Reline Brakes, Check Dist., Plugs, Change Engine oil, Check Levels.
27.	Mr. Ashbury.	139. 71L.	JRR-360.	5-10-48.	E-10032 / E-10014	Attend to Steering Box, Back Axle, Weld Radius Rods Same Engine, attend to o/s door.
28.	51, Upper Richmond Road.	Clock.				Recondition and Complete With Fittings.
29.	Mr. Swan.	517. 71M.	JVO-585	,,	E-10086	Change Steering Wheel Nut for Latest Type.
30.	Mr. Millward.	231. 71M.	JXM. 345.		E-1003?	Reline Brakes, Change Front axle Beam for 3° Castor, Lower Steering 1" from Rim of Wheel.
31.	Dagenham Motors.	314. 71.M.	S.M.V. 579.	10-10-48.		Return to Farnham.
33.	Mr. Tapper.	419. 61M.	HGC-893	,,	E-10035	General Service, Change oils, Grease Chass. 2/Screen Wipe. Same Engine.
33.	Mr. Nick.		NAS-198	13-10-48.	E-10058 / E-10043	Decarbonise Engine, Check Timer, Adjust Brakes, Change Front Spring.
38.	Mr. Saw	336. M.	BSS-835	,,	E-10066	Supply + Fit Columbia 3, Speed Axle. Change Front Spring, Check Pinch Bolts, Check Spacers.
39.	W. J. Hopper.	568. M.	NWL-138.	13-10-48.		Check Petrol Gauge, Rest Valor, Check Charging, Steering Pulls slightly to n/s Adjust Brakes
40.	Mr. Clifford Hindle	71. K. 435	JNT)-955	,,		Rear Axle Beam to 3° Castor Hand Brake Check Gear Lever Rattle
42	Sales Department (C/o BDS GINN (car now for sale?)	71. K. 510	JUC-310.	19-10-48.		Change all oils + Grease, Replace Gear Lever Knob, Headlamp Rim, Number Plate Glass.
43.	Mr. Frist.	415. 79-5.		,,	E-10014	New Hand-Brake, Fit Badge on Cowl.
44.	Mr. Phillips	JVR-671	—	,,	E-10050	Change oil Service, Adjust Brakes, Rattle on Bonnet, General Check over Car
45.	Mr. S. Pyman.	JVU-371.				Wash + Polish, Garage Car.

No.	Name	Reg.		Date	Job No.	Work
46	Mr. Imhof		H.L.P. 5.		E. 10019	Adjust Brakes, Adjust Ignition, Change over Lamps, Attend to Clutch.
47.	E. F. G. Hanebeck		L.B.H. 691.	443. A.	21. 10. 48	E. 10064. Remove Cylinder Heads. Trace Water Loss.
48.	Mr. Imhof		J.S.U - 5.	317 Y.M.	23. 10. 48.	Repair to Hand-Brake, Adjust Brakes, Repair Exhaust, Change over Headlamps, Dash Repairs Fixing, Check Luggage Boot, Repair Radiator.
49.	N. Ashe		J.A.W. 490.	3/0.	23. 10. 48.	1. Front Bumper, Change over Rear lights.
50.	J. Compton.		JVT. 943.	6186. Y.M.	26. 10. 48.	E. 10063. Change oils, Repairs to Piping on string Shield. Fit Vokes Economiser.
51.	Mr. H. J. Udll.		J.7.W - 750.			E. 10070 General Service, Change oils, Rattle on steering column. / E. 10069
52.	J. A. Gray.		MWL - 380.	A/203		10103. Change Brakes, Adjust Wiper, Supply starting Handle & Jack.
53.	J/r. Wick		LMG - 173.			Fit Cost Rings.
54.	J/r. Imhof		H.L.P. 5.		31. 10. 48.	2. Front Wings & Side Lamps, Refit Rear Plate. New Steering Wheel, Double Line etc.
55.	Layton		298.			Change Crank, Scope Side Propshaft, Attend to Brake Wires, Front Spring Bumper.
56.	The Allard Mfrg. Co.				28. 10. 48.	Rebuild to Stub Axles.
57.	A. M. C. Sales		Allard	JYM - 3/3	29. 10. 48.	Replace Shackle Brake (Front) Tighten Engine Bolts.
58.	Sears Bros.		7147354			E. 10018. Fit oil Filler, Replace Temp Gauge.
59.	Mr. Gollborg					Collect Car Temp Seymour Place.
60.	J/r. Sidnal.		NPC - 357		29. 10. 48	Change Safety cup Plug, Stop light Tighten Fan Belt.
61.	Col. Corbutt		ENT. 701		29. 10. 48	Convert to R/h. Drive.
62.	Mr. Napper.		NSC - 693.	719. Sim.	30. 10. 48	E. 10096. General Service, Change all oils, Check Rudders etc.

No.	Name	Reg. No.	Chassis No.		Work
63.	Dr. Parker	HRV - 201	6039 · YM	10084	Dash Light, Exhaust Blows, Washer Bottle, Squeak in Rear.
64.	Mr. Houston	JYO - 634	561	10083	Hard Starting, Check Lights, Charging Rate, Spray in Rear Wing
65.	M/s. Imhoff	386 - H		10084	Service, Change oil, Fit new Starter Tube.
66.	Mr. Hopper.	NUH - 138	658	E 10087	Supply and Fit Columbia 2-Speed Axle.
67.	Mr. Silsthorpe	T.H.X 323.	367.2 · YM		Estimate for Crash Work.
68.	Messrs Holland Motors. Ref. Mr. Hall.	FMW - 458.	563. YM.		Convert to R/H Drive, Fit Bolts in Rear Floor, and Lower Seat Pan (give Estimate) Fit Extra Ashtray etc.
69.	Dr. Compton	JYT - 943.	618. S.		Fit Air Cleaner, Repairs to Carndure, supply 1 Gaiter
70.	Messrs Universal Car Co. Derby.	TMH - 616	M 745.		Repairs to Indicator not Working, Change Fan Fit 3/4 Axle Ream.
71.	Mr. Phillips	JYR - 641.			Complete Service. 3, Rennick Road.
72.	G.H.S. Hempe-Roberts.	KHM - 477.	3052 YM.	E 10694	Balance Wheels.
73.	Dr. Eadie.	JJF - 339.	584 Q YM.		Attend to Steering, Paint Work, Ignition Switch broken. Check Lens Headlamp. Attend d/Handle.
74.	Messrs. Velvet Paper Co. Ltd.	SMX - 535.	57. YM.		Electric Clock (Bad Earth) Attend to Passenger Seat, f/s Door Sticks Fit oil Bath, Check Dynamos.
75.	Messrs. Belk Service Garage.	N-E-U - 86.	397/A.	K 10101	Fit 2 Extra Silencers, Check Dynamo output, Check Electric Clock. Attend to n/s Bonnet Handle
76.	Mr. Dawson.	TMH - 809			Send to Enтом for Body Work. Thermometer n/s.
77.	Decca Records.	Allard Coupe.	Reg No. YM.	Feb 1st 52	
78.	Mr. De Voet	YOW - 749.	435. SYM.		Change Brake Back Plate Assembly. Bleed & adjust Brakes
79.	Mr. Reid.	JFJ - 356.	549. YM.		Fan Vibration, Windscreen support standard, Check Ignition, adjust Brakes, Check s/s.

		Chassis Nº.	Reg Nº.	Date.	Customer's Instructions
80.	Sydenham Road Garage	71M. 6089		15·11·48.	Repair. Front axle 7/20 type.
81.	E. Crompton	71M. 618·S.	341—948.		Change Front Axle Beams. Fit Columbia Rear Axle, Adjust Brakes, Change oil in B/box, Grease, Spray Springs. Check Toffeeler, Fit Fog Lamp, Repair o/s Front Bumper, Angle Nipples on Steering.
82.	Car Sales Account	EBK-238.			500 Mile Free Service.
83.	Messr. Vernon Richardson (Bentley.)	JLM—3.	71·?·848.		Change Front Axle Beams, Remove Lamp, Rectify oil surge, New relief valve
84.	Mr. V. G. Davis	N.H.N. 461.	Ch. 356. Reg 3915.	✓	Fit Strengthening Plate To Hand Brake, Adjust Brakes.
85.	ATLAS INSURANCE (P.MOULD):- OWNER	71K 67G JOE 884	JOE 884	22·11·48	Remove rear axle. Examine S/S axle shaft & brake drum for damage. Remove petrol tank, Rear spring. for repair, & body repairs.
86.	Mr. Wick	A.M. 8.	LMG 192	22·11·48	Change Engine Oil (5" from top of dipstick). Supply 10g fuses. Change Diff. Saddletank 8 plugs. Examine ~~Battery~~ brake linings. Wash car.
87.	Mr. Daniels	7117. 216	JLO 676	23·11·48.	Examine B/linings, Bolts missing from both front wings to wing arches S/Fit Barnacle mirror.
88.	Mr. Elliot Cole (Guarantee)	71M 188P	JLW 562	23·11·48	Rectify Handbrake. Lever
89.	Jan. G. Brown	71M 556	GFO 97H	24·11·48	Crankcock etc
90.	Mr. S. Eastmead	71K 685G	KLF 147.	25·11·48.	1st 500 mile service. Body rattle. steering felt. tune up
91.	Mrs. Johnston. (R.P. Garage)	N.V.1. 7117. 322	JFO 194	25·11·48	Rectify c/s. Speedo Trip. Investigate binding of brake pedal ½ pint Redex in gearbox. Change gills.
92.	Dr. Whitehurst, Manby Lodge, Weybridge Surrey	71K. 252	MPH 429	28·11·48	
93.	Mr. Stephens & Smethurst	71M 618	EBK 338	30·11·48	Bad starting. Check ignition, check charging rate 1,000 mile service
94.	Major Rhodes	71K 400	JUC 302	1·12·48	Front Shackle Bushes b/s.
95.	Kirby ... Bournemouth	71M 341	HLJ 161.	1·12·48	Redex in steering box. Oxendon
96.	~~Mr. Compton~~	~~71M 685~~	~~JFT 948~~	~~1·12·48~~	~~Fit de niesta~~
97.	Gold Garage	71K 510	JUC 310	2·12·48	Oils & grease, check jets
98.		71M 618G	JYT 949	1·12·48	Fit de niesta. Brake drum

JOB NO.	CUSTOMER'S NAME.	THE. CHA. NO.	MILEAGE REG. NO.	DATE IN.	CUSTOMER'S PARTICULARS OF WORK.
A23.	Lt. P. Howard, Edinburgh.	71M 650G	2950 GSC 374	16.12.48	Rectify faulty tank gauge, Replace headlamp rim, carpet fasteners.
A24.	Parkhill. (Chassis only.)	81M 546	23 Chass.	18.12.48	Fit rear spring bracket.
A25.	H.L. Vickery. Esq.	71L 688G	466 KLD 758	18.12.48	Fit spring radius in gearbox. Adjust clutch & gear lever.
A26	AMC. Parkhill.	71M 627G	1455 Chass.	20.12.48	Change Head Gaskets.
A27.	Dr. Whitehurst.	71K 252	557 MPH 429	20.12.48	Fit 2 degree axle beams, 3.78 C.W.&P. Check rear shockers, & exhaust system. Fit new throttle spring & longer handbrake lever.
A29.	A.M.C. (H.M. Bentley.)	81M 793	12 Chass.	21.12.48	Change Rear spring bracket.
A30.	Dr. Compton.	71M 618G	JYT 943	21.12.48	S/F spot lamp.
A31.	Mr. Haydon.	81M 783	1169 HRU 789	22.12.48	Fit rear spring bracket. Fit 2 degree axle beams.
A32	A.M.C.	71K 572	126 Chass.	22.12.48	Fit 2 degree axle beams, new copper tie bars. change G/Box for I.P.S. type.
A33	Armitage Motor Co.			23.12.48	Repair gear box & fit new clutch. thrust assembly.
A34	G.H. Cooke - Yarborough	61L 122	12126 JLY 51	24.12.48	Tune-up, Andre's on rear, set up rear springs. S/F bumpers & clean chassis, new belt discs, 2 mirrors. & plugs. Service & touch.
A35	Peter Elliott - Cohen,	71M 433P	3735 JLM 582	28.12.48	Service & tune. Repair accident damage. Fit Kitty plates
A36.	A. Imhof - Esq		KLD 5	28.12.48	Rectify noisy rear axle. Attend to starting. Rewire
37)	Mrs. Imhof.	71M 214	5661 JGU 4	29.12.48	Fit spring, N/S/R brake shoes.
38	Armitage Motors			29.12.48	Rectification of twisted axle beams & radius rod.
	.... & etc	71M 326	1800 JYT 958	31.12.48	Change gear box, rear spring & Radius bar.

JOB	NAME	TYPE. CH.NO	MILEAGE REG. NO	DATE	CUSTOMER'S INSTRUCTIONS
A40.	A.M.C.	71K 559.	thing.	31.12.48	Change over beams, gear box to front spring
A41.	4 Point Garage. Feltham.			31.12.48	Converting Columbia axle casing to E62A axle casing to J type.
A42.	Mr. Graham.	71M 217	16893 JGV5	1.1.49.	Check brakes, decoke, pt A/c leads, change over headlamps. Service. S/f larger meter, headlamps change types & fuel pump.
A43.	Armitage Motors Ltd.	71M 268	5575 MPD 27	3.1.49	Convert to RH drive.
A44.	A.M.C. (Dunblery.)	71M 331	19625 JLK 957	4.1.44.	Renew engine, check traffs, clock, headlights, grease up, brakes, Coachwork (Hood, rear window handle etc.).
A45.	Mr. Herriot. Anti	81M 725	311 MPH 147	4.1.49.	S/F Oil bath air cleaner, fuel filter, 2 demisters, 500 mile service. Front number plate rattles. O.S.R. bonnet squeaks.
A46.	Mr. Gordon.	71L 411	6800 THX 875	5.1.49.	Investigate noisy rear axle.
A47.	Mr. Brown (A. Turner Riley & Co.).	71M 241	85 MPJ 219	5.1.49	Rectify charging rate.
A48	Mr. Sherman.	71M 446Q	7244 JGY 719	5.1.49	S/f bumpers. Tune up. Charge batteries. B + A brakes, check lights + H/s traffs, steering knock. Noisy clutch. 2½ beams.
A49	Rangers Motors				
A50.	Mr. Harvey.	71SF 148	3114 HPR 472	8.1.49.	Jumping out of second gear.
A52	Mr. Godsal.	71M 527	6647 NFC 189	8.1.49	2½ beams, s/f spotlamps, defroster, inspection lamp. B + A brakes. S/f galley heater. Rectify traffs.
A53	Mr. H. Hart:	71M 592A	10550 NEV 26	8.1.49	Adjusting brakes. S/f bumpers air cleaner & Dyn charging rate needs adjusting.
A54	Mr. Daniels	71M 216	6864 JLL 676	8.1.49.	S/F bumpers air cleaner. Adjust brakes.
A55	Lewis Records	71M 400	14733 JUC 302	10.1.49	Detune brakes. H/G 9th S/f spotlamps. Check ignition. Rectify traffs. Renew complete silencing system. 2 three beams.
A56	Mr. Soles	81M 740	2938 KGC 896	10.1.49	2 three beams, service.

JOB.	CUSTOMER'S NAME	CHASSIS TYPE	REG.NO MILEAGE	DATE	CUSTOMER'S INSTRUCTIONS
A57.	A.M.C. (Mr. S. Allard)	81M 745	MKB441 1845	10.1.49.	Decoke. Fit S.U Pump, heater, defroster, spotlamps. Tune up, check all bolts. Oil speedo. Change P. Box & R. axle oils. Charge H. Lights
A58.	Mr. Napper	81M 719	KGC893 2669	11.1.49.	Rectify quill damage? Horn, staff & wipers O/S
A59.	Mr. Compton	71M 618G	JYT943	11.1.49.	Fit new Columbia casing
A60.	Mr. H.L. Vickery	71L 688G	RLD758 804	12.1.49.	2nd gear difficult to obtain, Clock U/S. Hard riding at rear, Adjust brakes. Service.
A61.	Dagenham Motors	71M 656G	TMH616 1352	13.1.49.	Water leaks into glove box from N/S bonnet hinge. Difficulty in engaging gears when cold. Vibration. O/S Handbrake Ratchet.
A62.	Mr. Shepherd	81M 756	FJW92 2700	15.1.49.	B.& R. brakes, bonnet rattle, check steering. Repair & respray bonnet.
A63.	Mr. Hardman	71L 281.	DFR118 10710	17.1.49.	Rebore when servicing. Tune up. Fit S.U C.W.& P. grease coming from front bearings. Felt in steering column. O/S Traff. sticks.
A64.	Mr. Macdowell	71M 470A	STE359. 2435	17.1.49	Change power valve for one from Park hill.
A65.	Mr. Eversmier	71M 550	TMH812 3800	17.1.49	Service, Adjust brakes. S/F Dampers, Air cleaner.
A66.	Hughes, Exeter. Mr. Fitz	71M 537.	JFJ293 3517	18.1.49.	Handbrake ratchet. Body work (Samantha).
A67	Bentleys Ltd.	81M 793	TME3 269	18.6.49.	Joins headlamps, Bodywork.
A68	Mr. Symondson.	71K 248.	KKX672 4700	28.1.49.	2 degree beams. Brakes. Change front spring, new Kingpins & bushes.
A50.	Mr. Parloff		V.8. Engine.		Strip, clean & offset grind con. rods.
A70.	Maintenance				
A71	Moss & Lesson	71M 297.	GPK222 6649.	19.1.49	Oil leak from steering box. Clock U/S.
A72	Mr. Compton	71M 618G.	JYT943	19.1.49.	Fit 2 Sun Visors

JOB.	CUSTOMER'S NAME.	CHA.	MILEAGE. REG. NO.	DATE.	CUSTOMER'S INSTRUCTIONS.
A73	Mr. Brinton	71L672	160 Chisag.	19.1.49.	Change gearbox & change mechanism to steering column type
A74	Mr. Robert Howell	71M447P	62 KLF681	19.1.49.	Fit handbrake mechanism
A75	Mr. Bryant.	SALOON	1822 HOH507	20.1.49.	Change stator tube
A76	Count A.M.C	71M67Xr	12 Chisag.	20.1.49	Conversion to R.H. drive
A77	R. Dimbleby	71M331.	500 JLK 957	21.1.49.	Change engine with, o/s track shock u/S.
A78	Mr. V. Saunders	71M267.	1168. EDR121	21.1.49.	Check all lighting & processing, steering wheel rattle.
A79	Mr. Potter	71M5746	314 272	21.1.49.	Fit radio, check track & balance wheels, tighten belts.
A80	de Rouet	81M735	JWW 769	22.1.49.	Adjust brakes.
A81	D. Vernon Pain	71K240	4335. DRW525	24.1.49	Change torque tube, propshaft & speedo drive.
A82	Burgess	Y.B. Express.		25.1.49	Grind crank, fit rings.
A83	Mr. Hold.	71M317	4532 JKO 585	25.1.49	Change batteries & check for duff cells. S/F Bungees 8 & 6a brakes. S/F bonnet handle, Tune-up.
A84	Mr. S. Eastmead.	71K6856	KLF161	25.1.49	S/F foam filter, clean carbs pump.
A85	Mr. Butcher.	71M472H	1950 DFR 376	26.1.49.	Examine engine for oiling up of plugs.
A86	Sales Account.	81M 818	10 Chisag.	26.1.49.	Fit wireless & theftproof device.
A87	Mr. Hold.	Tower.		26.1.49.	Adjust brakes.
A88	Sales Records.	71M 400	18554 JUC 302	26.1.49.	Clean out, adjust brakes. S/F S.U. Pump, Grease all.

No.	Name	Chassis	Reg.	Date	Work
489	Dr. Whitehurst	81K252	MPH429 (A110)	26.1.49	Check timing, Check all exhaust system. Fit speedo drive & bonnet spring.
490	A.O. Pollard	81M762	KTH505 (776)	2.2.49	Rectify n/s bonnet handle, S/F frame, adjust brakes, window rattles. Sticky throttle pedal.
491	Mrs. Imhof	71M214	JGW44 (9013)	27.1.49	Reline brakes, rectify handbrake ratchet, attend to rear light, Charge batteries, adjust clutch.
492	Sales A/c	81M874	(") thing.	27.1.49	Fit Radio & aerial, & foglamp.
493	S. Bingfield Digby 12P	81M722	CTK330 (1911)	27.1.49	S/F Bumpers + 2 defrosters. Stiff throttle, Paintwork on o/s Rear wing.
494	Offord & Lees	71K600	SYW64 (5500)	27.1.49	Charge oils, Rest & respray wings, S/F headlamp glass & rad. caps. Trafs o/s, dipping u/s.
495	Rev. Sargent		SALOON (38.)	28.1.49	Charging generator & control for steering column type.
496	Universal coachworks	81M724	PRD505 (330)	28.1.49	Change exhaust system. Rectify rear lighting.
497	Mr. Daniels	71M216	JL4676	31.1.49	Repaired n/s accident damage, S/F n/f/f bumper over-rider.
498	Mr. Johnston	71M322	YO184 (550)	31.1.49	S/F Bumpers, o/s stuff.
499	Mr. Osborne	81M871	TMK8 (557)	31.1.49	Change pull break from front of body.
500	Mr. P.Q. Green	71L800	KLD755 (1000)	31.1.49	Speedo cable broken, replace stop lamp switch, 1000 mile service.
501	Dr. Compton	71M686	JYT943	3.2.49	Fit interior light, grease, check hubs.
502	Motomart Ltd.	81M804	TMX198 (670)	3.2.49	Check o/s, 1st 500 mile service, driver seat slips back. Rpt. Rider in gearbox.
503	Mrs. Imhof		Ford Anglia	3.2.49	Some reason plugs, clean out car, wash & polish car.
504	Mr. Layton	71L298	CVG428 (4540.)	4.2.49	Fit Columbia, extra leaf in rear spring, noisy universal, noisy clutch thrust.

No.	Name	No.	Reg.	Date	Work
B6	S. Allard Esq.	81M745	5628 MRB441	4.2.49	Fit wiper blade, wash & polish, fit standard nut to steering column. Coachwork. Exhaust blows.
B7	Car Sales a/c	71K 826	cheng	5.2.49	Fit petrol filler lock, remove distributor & check points
B8	Mr. Pinkey	71M217	4500 JGW5	5.2.49	Broken spring & perch bolt; change headlamps.
B9	J.P. Davis	71K4848	3640 THX560	5.2.49	Fit bonnet check strap; adjust brakes.
B10	Mr. Eastwood	7K 6855	3185 KLF147	7.2.49	Decoke, balance wheels, steering felt; steering wheel bolt fouling gear lever bracket.
B11	Mr. Brown	71M 241	774 MRS219	7.2.49	Fit hingers & drain B&A brakes; stronger throttle spring. 1st 500 mile service.
B12	Mr. Godsal	71M 527	10450 NFC139	7.2.49	Consider gearbox motor / check brakes, tighten bolts, repair o/s wing damage, check starter lead. Change tyres.
B13	Mr. Stephens	71M613	4144 ERK388	8.2.49	Rectify faulty exhaust wiper. Replace fan & steer.
B14	Mr. Hole (AMC)	81M704	638 DRD578	8.2.49	Rectify clutch judder, change stop/switch.
B15	Car Sales Alpine 2 Str.	81M 740	JYK438 KG6896	9.2.49	Remove speedo. head, rectify, & refit, deliver car to showrooms, Clapham. Repair Puncture
B16	Mr. Mills	71K 3842	3894 LHU836	9.2.49	2 o broken r'r spring; wipers arms not keeping pressure on screen. Handbrake ratchet u/s.
B17	Clapham Motors	71M 6746	2927 JMC 3	10.2.49	Rectify handbrake & steam valve.
B18	Mr. Happer	81M 919	3048 KGC893	11.2.49	Sticky throttle, u/s steering felt. n/p/f shocker o/s.
B19	Mr. Hole	81M704	700 DRD505	11.2.49	Fit extra leaf in rear spring, grease chassis pin H/B
B20	Mr. Wirth	71M 326	4000 FYT950	11.2.49	Rectify gearbox, handbrake, fuel gauge & speedo, steering wanders over 40 m.p.h. Coachwork
B22	Miss Gowell	71M 407	633 KLA151	14.2.49	Rectify clutch & handbrake, 500 mile service, check for body rattles

B23	H.M. Bentley & Co.	7M.327	327 KLF 633.	14-2-49	2 degree beams, check noisy rear axle, check speedo, adjust brakes
B24	Mr. Hole	7M 325	6952 JLY 687	15-2-49	Decoke.
B25	R. Dombleby	7M 331	20800 JLK 957	15-2-49	S/F two wing mirrors, change all oils, wash car, check engine for pinking.
B26	Imhof Esq.		KLJ5.	15-2-49	Rectify electrical short, noisy s/f, ignition switch & handbrake, fit new head gaskets.
B27	F. English	7M 451P	5443 HLS 636	15-2-49	Modify doors to late type windows, repair panel cracked at corners, repair damaged rear wing, check oil consumption, test steering for fit new tank & units.
B29	Sales dept.	8M 116	33. Unreg	18-2-49	
B30	Mr. Richardson	7K 607	7586. JYT881.	18-2-49	Columbia, decoke. Puncture. Trap. Handbrake.
B31	Mr. Bowman	7M 353A	188 Unreg	17-2-49	Change crankshaft.
B32	Central Motor Co.	8M 878.	520 PRY 449	17-2-49	Wheels out of true, wheel wobble, check petrol consumption.
B33	Mr. Herriot	8M 725.	1300 MPH 147	18-2-49	Check all levels, frame, springy springs, tighten nuts.
B34	Epps Bros.	7M 354A6	4494 JYK 439	21-2-49	Examine front end. 2° beams.
B35	Mr. Potter	7M 594G	10000 JYM 272	21-2-49	Service. Wash & Polish. Check over generally.
B36	Mr. Knot	7M 577.	3370 MPF 576.	22-2-49	Check front end. Handbrake u/s.
B37	Mr. Carey	7M 268	5952 MFD 27	22-2-49	Handbrake u/s.
B38	Mr.	7M 613.	4743 EBR 338		Tune up.
B39	Mr. Hole	8M 704.	1148 DRD 505	24-2-49	Check perch bolts, gaiter bars, reverse gear, fuel tank & vent, engine tray rattles, sticky throttle, warning light u/s. Change for tappet oil & temp gauge.

No.	Customer	Reg.		Date	Work
B40	Sales Dept	7LL 852	18 thou	24-2-49	Fit petrol filler lock.
B41	24 H.P. V/8 Engine 4 Cylinder.		EPX761 28-2-49		Stock Engine. Overhaul.
B42	Dr. Edwards	7LM610G	5420 miles EDX761	28-2-49	2° service & adjust brakes
B43	Stock Engine V/8 22 H.P.				Overhaul
B44	Mr. Raun...	71M5824G	8376 GFH27	28-2-49	Bodywork, tune, grease up, spray springs.
B45	D. Layton	7LL 288	5280 CVG428	8-3-49	Change gearbox. banjo casing.
B46	Mr. Clark	81M853	1142 B4138	1-3-49	Service 1000 miles, adjust brakes, check "U" Bolts.
B47	AMC (Universal Coachworks)	81M799	62 Unreg.	1-3-49	Fit bracket to rear spring, rectify handbrake. Burgess
B48	Dr. Vardy	81M764	3459 LHW5	23-2-49	Rectify handbrake, electric clock, atmospheric valve. Hood cover. Chrome front number plate mounting.
B49	Park Garage	7LL 440	8183 SGY720	2-3-49	Fit recovery engine, check chassis, O/S silencers, fit S.S C.W.&P.
B51	Mrs. Imhoff	7LM 214	9428 JGS44	2-3-49	Transmission clock, steering patter.
B52	Mr. Watkins	7LK433A	10009 JYE356	2-3-49	Fit front spring, check clutch judder.
B53	Velvet Crepe Paper Co	7LM517	9788 SMX836	2-3-49	S/F New Ignition switch, fit new fuel gauge & unit, check battery. Will demist through ignition.
B54	Mr. Knox	7LM597	3537 MPF570	3-3-49	Test car for steering, check track.
B55	Mr. Fowler	7LM656G	1876 TMH616	4-3-49	Engine vibration, water comes in on passenger feet, rattle from hood. Change super flywheel & clutch, ...
B56	Mr. Kelly	7LL432G	5020 LHW29	4-3-49	S/F Burgess air cleaner, new carb, fit ...

B57.	Mr. Gosnell.	71M606	189 KLM9.	4-3-49	Fit two thermostats, fit Burgess air cleaner.
B58.	Mr. Compton.	71M618G	JYT343	4-3-49	Fit side grille, adjust brakes. Repair puncture.
B59.	de Rouet.	81M735.	5WW749	5-3-49	Adjust brakes. Check & top up G/Box & R/Axle.
B60.	Mr. Hopper.	81M919	3497 KSC593	7-3-49	Check R/axle & g/box. Check for play in front hubs, rectify O/S door squeak, check oil levels in shockers
B61.	Mr. Rotley.	71L432Q	LHW29	7-3-49	Fit 62A distributor, 3.5 C.W.&P., decoke, check silencer at rear, check for sinking, fit bonnet safety catch
B62.	Dr. Parkes.	71M603G	6825 HRU201	7-3-49	Remove petrol box & straps, check judder bars. Service.
B63.	Roberts.	81M882	1812 EUX808.	8-3-49	Check for steering wander.
B64.	Mr. Godfrey.	81M1005	215 KUU756	8-3-49	Check for clutch judder, rectify sticky throttle. Test car.
B65	Moss & Lawson.	71M297	7055. GRK222	9-3-49	Check front brakes & spring for hard riding.
B66	Mr. Brown (B. Turner, Riley & Co)	71M241	1754. HRJ219	9-3-49	Fit & wire switch for headlamps to O/S Dash, grease & spray springs.
B67	Mr. Donald Shacklum.	71M295	8656 MPD142	9-3-49	Remove engine, strip & examine.
B68	Mr. Wick	71M326	1000 JYT950	9-3-49	Change speedo, rectify hand throttle.
B69	Sales A/C.	71M594G	JYT272	11-3-49	Fit latest type André telecontrols front & rear.
B71.	Sales A/c	71L670	5850 KGC855	11-3-49	Fit bonnet catch
B72	Mr. Daniels	71M216	8066 JLU676	14-3-49	Adjust carbs & brakes, rectify steering rubbing on full lock, hand throttle, check fuel reserve.
B73	Dr. Pearce	81M877	2455 JVF14	14-3-49	S/F. Lucas 700 lamp. 3.5 C.W.&P. + one extra rear lamp, check slow running, change gearbox oil, check U/S bolts etc.

B74	Mr. S. Allard		8117719	329 KLO130	15-3-49	Fit Radio & straps, check slow-running, track, brakes etc. charge batteries.
B75	S. Millward		71M231	19078 JLM245	15-3-49	Fit owner's 32 H.P. Mercury engine, lap in valves, fit 2 extra silencers, fit N/S bonnet catch.
B76	Sales A/C		71K510	9778 JUC310	16-3-49	Check for water leak & rectify
B77	L. Millward		71L 478A	1519 LHH107	16-3-49	Tune-up, fit 2 thermostats & bonnet catch
B78	Pentiles Garage		8117720	4197 HPS200	16-3-49	L.H. to R.H. Conversion. Coachwork
B79	Sales dept.		8117010B	22 Unreg	16-3-49	Fit locking type petrol caps. Fit 2 bonnet locks.
B80	Sales dept.		8117806	114 Unreg	17-3-49	Fit spotlamp & 2 reverse lights.
B81	Decca Records.		7117400	17542 JVC302	17-3-49	Rectify clutch judder, flooding of carb. check speedo & drive, change if necessary
B82	Mr. Sargent		71M593	71L164	17-3-49	Rectify panel lights not working, sticky fuel gauge & unit fit ~~both~~ air cleaner, rectify sticky throttle
B83	Mr. Hole		8117749	304 DRI)73	18-3-49	Service, adjust brakes, check for fuel consumption, fit Bonnacle trim.
B84	E. Harris-St. John		8117824	5188 MTN575	19-3-49	Tow car from Berkeley, Horace garage, Repair all accident damage. Oil consumption.
B85	Buyers		V8 ENGINE.		21-3-49	Strip and examine
B86	Mr. Dimbleby		71M331	22020 JLK857	21-3-49	Service & Polish, trafficators sticking, fit on steering column, handbrake flies off, rectify pinking. Accident damage
B87	Sales A/C		91M1511	91M1511 HXX210	21-3-49	Check car over generally.
B88	L. Chappell		8117702	4876 MWW149	22-3-49	Conversion to coil springing & telescopic shockers, rectify flat spot & pinking, tune-up. Change speedo.
B89	O.H. Sandell. Esq.		71M-666.	598 KLN-9.	23-3-49	500. After first Service Change Gear Control Parts, Throttle Spring. Check for Body Rattles, Check 1st Gear Stiff Change. Clean Carb, & Pump.

No.	Name				Date	Work
B90.	Mr. Stephens		7147613	5882 EBR338	22-3-49	Drain & refill R/axle & G/Box. top up shockers & brake fluid
B91.	J.C. Charlesworth		7L313	1840 NFC 965	22-3-49	Hood & side screen modifications, move seat forward. Make up & fit rail for spot lamp. Seat modifications. S/F Hood.
B92.	Chas. Gardner		7K467A	GRK84	23-3-49	
B93.	Mr. S. Onstead		7K6836	KLF147	23-3-49	Fit chrome bar to front. Repair accident damage. Adjust brakes.
B94.	Mr. D.R. Plunkett		8147806	388 KLP818	23-3-49	500 mile service, check, pink up, taffs, oil pressure & panel lights. S/F 2 wing mirrors & Romac Radio. Remove gearbox.
B95.	Mr. Prowd		614164	DPM158	23-3-49	
B96.	S.W. Wood		8147733	7709 MTV123	23-3-49	Rectify front wheel wobble, electric clock U/S. Petrol reserve U/S, also brake stop light. Bonnet catch broken 2 bars Change front spring.
B97.	Oakley's Garage		7147515	8611 249515 EO54	23-3-49	
B98.	Mr. S.H. Allard		V/8	Sydney Allard	24-3-49	Fit main & big end bearings
B99.	Salles ATC		8147029	13	24-3-49	Fit windscreen washing equipment (stores)
B100.	Mr. Knox		7147577	4273 MFF570	25-3-49	Front suspension
C1.	Mr. Imhof		KLD5		26-3-49	Rectify O/S & head blow, Repair O/S/R puncture
C2	George & Jobling		7L300	H81 GGD594	28-3-49	Repair accident damage
C3	G.B. Craddock		7L201	9237 SMH107	28-3-49	Tune-up. Check brakes, rad valve, charging rate, U bolts etc.
4	Mr. Featherstonehaugh		8147088	172 KLP82	28-3-49	Check oil pressure, engine knocks. Rectify oil leaks, in gearbox, rectify panel lights not working, change C/gas flush & refill rings, adjust brakes, fit new filter cartridge. Fit new speedo head. Set front bumper
5	Swain Records		7147400	JUC302	29-3-49	

C 6.	Mr. Stephens.	71M 338	613 ETK 338	29-3-49	✓

Check clutch operation, specific gravity of batteries + charging rate.

C 7.	Lt. Col. Bagley.	71M542	4770 GOR 827	30-3-49	✓

Check steering + track. Petrol filler. (Ref Mr. Tyler)
Fit Hood Clamp + screws.

C 8.	Mr. Godfrey.	81M1005	556 KLL736	30-3-49	✓

1st. 500 mile service, drop sump, check frame

C 9.	Mr. Compton.	81M874	3182 KLK 657	30-3-49	✓

Service change oils, fit small G.B. Plate. fit frame
Tune engine, change headlamps to English lighting.

C 10.	Mr. Barton.	81M827	2385 KKA32	30-3-49	✓

Repair damage at rear of car.

C 11	Mr. Sargent.	71M583	588 TML164	1-4-49	✓

1st. 500 service.

C 12	Mr. Black.	81M 1029	550 KLP820	2-4-49	✓

1st. 500 service.

C 13	Sales A/c	71L 670	6077 KGC898	4-4-49	✓

Rectify grease throwing out of o/s/f whel.
Check level of hydraulic fluid.

C 14	Mr. Powell.	71M447	1632 KLF681	4-4-49	✓

2° beams. Tighten wings. Modify o/s/R axle shafts to take latest type hub caps. Check oil levels, grease.

C 16	J. Shaw	81M 710	4861 DRS120	4-4-49	✓

Wheel wobble. felt bush u/s. Windows Rattle, engine motor rattles, air intake whistle, steering check.

C 17	Mr. Marshall.	71M 536	500 JYR671	4-4-49	✓

Repair accident damage, tune up + service

C 18	Mr. Mac Millan.	71M 319.	1513 340 365	5-4-49	✓

Check Speedo, fuel reserve. clutch + handbrake.

C 19	Sales	71M 1031018	33 Stores	5-4-49	✓

Fit S.U. Petrol Pump.

C 21	Mr. Fryers	71L 455	10117 KKX 146	6-4-49	✓

Brake Reline, Coachwork, new rear number plate.
Service.

C 22.	Mr. Vardy.	81M 764	LHW523	6-4-49	✓

Fit Hood cover, chrome facing for front number plate, change speedo. clock.

C 23.	Brig Calre. Greenhalgh.	81M 1001	500 KLL 999.	6-4-49	✓

Check plugs + time, check brake linings; fit petrol lock, check fuel reserve + fuel blockage, fit lock + boot lock.

· **ALLARD** ·

C24	G. O'Kill		71M614G	709 JY6272	7-4-49	Service, Oil bath air cleaner, Rectify N/S Rattle.
C25	Mr. T. Hartstein		71M264	2620 JYT949	7-4-49	fit air cleaner, O/S/F wheel creaks on lock + is warped. N/S/F wheel wobble, fit 40W bulbs to Headlamps.
C26	Mr. Gladstone		71L128	10627 SMC649	7-4-49	S/F 3.5 C.W.&P. Reline brakes if necessary. tighten up front wings; change grille
C27	Mr. S. Allard		81M719	KLO130	7-4-49	Supress Radio, wash & polish
C29	Mr. de Ronet		81M735	5767 JYN749	9-4-49	Check ignition + judder bars.
C30	Mr. Dimbleby		71M331	22883 JLK957	11-4-49	steering wobble, fit extra silencers, rectify exhaust blow, check N/S trafic, safety catch, N/S pilot bulb, oil throwing out of fan.
C31	Mr. Frost		Gearbox.		12-4-49	Strip & rebuild with new parts as necessary.
C32	Mr. Turner		71M615G	3414 JYR13	13-4-49	Check front axle assembly, Spray springs etc, slacken tail fit 20 beams pipes approx. 2". Remove small O/S grille & refit.
C33	Mr. Stone		71M613	6720 EBK338	13-4-49	check Batteries.
C34	S. Eastwood		71R655G	KLF147	14-4-49	Check over brakes, & adjust.
C35	Mr. Baynent		71M593	1220 TM2164	19-4-49	1,000 mile service,
C36	Mr. S. Pilliard		71M231	JSO245	19-4-49	Change fuel pump, check system; fit new flexipipe.
C37	Dr. Hart		71M3G713	NEV26	19-4-49	Adjust brakes.
C38	Mr. + Lewson		71M297	8427 GMX222	20-4-49	Paintwork.
C39	Mr. Ronet		81M735	JY607749	20-4-49	Starter U/S. Replace H.T. lead, adjust brakes, service
	Vacuum Records		71M600	VUC302	20-4-49	brake, extra silencers, Handbrake U/S. Machine clutch judder, jumps out of 2nd gear.

C42	Mr. Reardon		7194267	4849. EDK121	20·4·49
C44	Mr. Frost		81M1007B	2884. EPM96	20·4·49
C45	Mr. Lindsay		81M1805oB	402 TML804	20·4·49
C46	J.D. Keightley		81M705	4686 JoF189	21·4·49
C47	Mr. Broomfield		81M1032B	480 NPR871	21·4·49
C48	Mr. Jervin		81M1013B	475 UMC924	21·4·49
C49	Mr. Symondson		71K248	9100 KKX672	21·4·49
C51	W. Turner-Riley		71M421	2713 PMD219	22·4·49
C52	P.A. Clark Ltd., (H.K. Marsden)		71L845	2810 ERX946	22·4·49
C53	Mr. J. Eastmead		71K685G	6605 KGC147	23·4·49
C54	Mr. Pepper		81M709	4554 KGC893	25·4·49
C55	Doon & Porter			Gearbox	25·4·49
C56	Car Mart Ltd		81M754	280. KLO300	25·4·49
C57	Crawford		71M565	32 Trade	25·4·49
	Sales A/c		71L670	0868 KGC895	26·4·49
			71M217	JGW5	26·4·49

2° brns, rectify hand throttle, petrol reserve, starter, tighten plugs change wheels around for wear, check track.

Rectify wheel wobble & clutch judder. Fit boot key clip.

S/F fan, 2 Wing Mirrors, modify drivers seat to suit owner, set throttle pedal 1" nearer brake pedal. Service.

noisy rear axle, exhaust blow o/s. Coachwork rectification.

Replace faulty starter solenoid + dynamo belt, Rectify sticking throttle, shake up hood cover.

500 mile service, squeak on O/S Pillar, sticking throttle

Check rear shockers, drag link fouls on full lock, check track.

Rectify faulty windscreen wiper, grease + spray springs, fit new wiper knob.

Tune-up, fit new windscreen, fit new glasses to rear lamps, 'Ignition warning' light u/s.

Check chassis alignment. S/F 3.5 C.W. & P. Adjust brakes.

decoke, adjust brakes, flood cover, grease, change engine oil, leaking water pumps, check shock-absorbers. Service.

Fit extra leaf in rear spring, focusing front lamps, change engine oil, fit oil bath air cleaner, rectify handbrake.

Tow chassis from St. Pancras. Fit extra silencer + steering column control gearbox.

Change n/s battery, check tie bars.

Fit customer's special engine.

C60	Mr. Goldthorpe	71K 367	3756 THX323	27-4-49	✓	S/F 3.75 C.W. + Pinion.
C61	Mr. Powell	711W6069	1296 KLM9.	27-4-49		S/F 3.5 C.W.+P./Pinion, 1000 miles service. fit front mud flaps, lighter throttle spring.
C62	Dr. Shepherd	811M756	6284 FDW92	27-4-49	✓	Handbrake U/S, one horn U/S, N/S headlamp flickers, starting handle bent, poor fuel consumption, tune engine.
C63	Dr. Pearce	811M877	4342 JVF14	27-4-49	✓	S/F Hood + tonneau cover.
C64	Countess Mory	711L 852	991 KLO128	27-4-49	✓	1,000 mile service
C65	Lt. Howard	711M65×9	6908 GSC314	28-4-49	✓	S/F 3.5 C.W.+P. Service.
C66	Mr. Bennett	711W 464A	12103 NPF343	28-4-49		Focus headlamps, rectify loose O/S bonnet handle, tighten judder bars, fit bonnet lock flaps
C67	Sales A/C	711M627G	6577 KLO123	30-4-49	✓	Rattles from body, exhaust vibration.
C68	Decca Records	711M400	JUC302	2-5-49	✓	Coachwork.
C69	Mr. Broomfield	811M10328	722 NPA871	2-5-49	✓	Charge Batteries
C71	Mr. Plunkett	811M806	2224 KLPS18	2-5-49	✓	Paintwork O/S/F Wing. Handbrake too tight, N/S traff U/S. Wiper blade missing.
C72	Mr. Inglis	711L 4558	11087 LKX146	2-5-49	✓	Coachwork, spray springs, grease up, adjust brakes.
C73	Mr. Broomfield	811M10328	722 NPA871	3-5-49	✓	Fit windscreen washer, leaking fuel cap, + chrome spotlamp bar.
C74	Dr. Williams	711K 404	9838 LUB906	4-5-49	✓	Rear spring bottoming. S/F 3.5 Crown wheel & pinion, check car over periodically.
C75	Mr. Southall	811M768	3000 FVJ941	5-5-49	✓	Brakes (need bleeding). Pinking. Front suspension.
	Mr. Craig	811M1058B	290 OMC938	6-5-49	✓	1st 500 mile service

C77	Sales.	71K 510	10370 JUC310	7-5-49	✓	Reline brakes, grease, check levels, lights etc.
C78	Dr. Janvrin	81M1033B	1370 UMC924	9-5-49	✓	1,000 mile service. S/F pinion. Fit secret switch. Brakes squeak.
C79	T. Rhys Davis	81M781	3721 KDE794	9-5-49	✓	Fit Reversing lamps, rheostat to dash lights, Coachwork, rattles etc, rear spring bottoms. 2° beams.
C80	b/ Bruce Hare.	71K 162	9445 SMC665	9-5-49	✓	Check front suspension & steering for hard riding, o/s wing bracket broken, under tray broken, grease, check S/Box & R/axle levels.
C81	S. H. Allard.	81M719	4287 KLO130	10-5-49		Fit new engine.
C82	Mr. Riddell.	71K 639	113 KLX dams 473	10-5-49	✓	Fit special engine & gearbox 83.5 C.W. &P.
C83	Mr. Cyprian.	71L 388	12183 SMX278.	10-5-49	✓	Wheel wobble, screen support, brakes, speedo cable, accident damage. Decoke.
C84	Sales A/c.	71L 670	7000 KGC373	10-5-49		Track steering, check gear lever mounting bracket
C86.	Dr. Hart.	71M397A.	NEV26	10-5-49	✓	Service car.
C87	Mr. Fowler.	71M656G	2867 TMH616	12-5-49	✓	Tune up.
C88	Paul Emery	61K104	18040 541664	12-5-49	✓	Fit new regulator unit, new front spring & bushes.
C89.	Mr. Golsthorpe.	71K 362Q	4980 THX 823	16-5-49	✓	Decoke. rectify fuel tank leak, rev. counter o/s. N/S/F hub throwing oil.
C90.	Mr. R. Strakes	81M1003B.	1391 KLO127	16-5-49	✓	1,000 mile service, N/S/F wheel not true.
C91	Godfrey Ltd	81M1005	1966 KLL736	16-5-49.		3.5 C.W. &P. Tune up, grease chassis, change engine oil.
C92	R.P. Turner.	81M1022D	1200 JUF620	16-5-49	✓	Windows Rattle, dropped doors.
	J.P. Jones	81M857 L.H.	985 KLY 15	16-5-49.	✓	1,000 mile service, adjust brakes, drain & flush off heater, adjust clutch, rectify stop lamps.

No.	Name			Date	Work
C94	H. M. Bentley	81M793	2011 TA1E 3	16-5-49 ✓	S/F 3.5. Check brakes, door handle + bonnet handle loose o/s vent catch faulty.
C95	Sales A/c Mr. Ryan	71K 580	10385 JUR 310	16-5-49	S/F 6 new tyres, rectify steering wobble. Decoke. machine cyl. heads. Petrie 4991 brakes.
C96	G/Cmdr Greenhalgh	81M 10013	1429 KLL 999	16-5-49 ✓	Fit Tonneau cover, Service, check voltage control, gear change, loss of water, adjust brakes, + modify.
C97	Mr. Hewitt	71K 628	1640 MNW 624	16-5-49	Fit 91A gear box, S.U. fuel pump under bonnet, new set pipes. Remove old exhaust pipes, adjust handbrake.
C100	Mr. Knox	71M 597	5418 17PF 570	17-5-49 ✓	Lower grille bracket, wing stays bracket.
D1	Mr. Lindsay	81M 1050	1018 TML 804	17-5-49 ✓	1,000 mile service. adjust brakes, wiper blades fowl studs on screen.
D2	Mr. Brown	71M 421	3485 17PS 219	17-5-49 ✓	Oil + grease, wash + Polish. Extra silencers.
D4	Dr. Marshall	71M 536	4595 SYR 671	18-5-49 ✓	Grease, spray springs. Fit 2 Wing mirrors.
D3	Mr. Stevens	71M 613	8271 ERK 118	18-5-49	Sticky throttle, steering wobble.
D5	Decca Records	71M 400	JUC 302	18-5-49 ✓	Make up rear seat with Hairlock springs.
D6	Mr. A.R. Plunkett	81M 506	2787 KLP 818	18-5-49	Engine misfiring. N/S window Rattle.
D7	Harwoods Garage	71M 459A	1454 RPO 564	18-5-49	Steering vibration + poor fuel consumption 2° beams.
D8	Dr. Pearce	81M 877	JVF 14	18-5-49	Paintwork under guarantee.
D9	Mr. R. Johannssen	71M 463A	2828 3287	20 -5-49 ✓	Tune-up, check oils & lights etc. adjust brakes, grease, Spray springs. charge batteries.
D10	Dr. Compton	71M 618G	JTT 943	20 -5-49 ✓	Fit new glass + letter "T" to rear number plate.
		71M 217	JGO 5	21-5-49	Change to continental lighting, rectify wipers.

D12	Mr. Griffin	71L 4550	LKX146	23.5.49 ✓	Grease, charge engine oil, rectify 2nd jumping out on overdrive. Play in steering box.
D13	Mr. Sitcomb	81M 1020	3053 KLR294	3.5.49	Guarantee coachwork, tune-up, adjust brakes
D14.15	R. Carter	81M 761	7204 JNG878	23.5.49	Bottoming at rear, steering wheel down + lock, peeling paint; sticky throttle. Bulb o/s in rear.
D16	Mr. J. Forbes	81M 887	KLY15	23.5.49 ✓	Tune-up, fit defroster, wash & polish, faulty wiper motor, oil leak under dash, unscrew hood cover + place in boot. N/S/R brake grabbing.
D17	Gross & Lawson	71M 297	8740 GRK222	24.5.49 ✓	
D18	Cox Road	81M 754	603 KL0300	24.5.49 ✓	Check over car generally. Grease, spray springs.
D19	Dr. Vardy	81M 764	6193 LHH523	24.5.49 ✓	Front end shudder, loss of water.
D20	Mr. Plunkett	81M 806	3301 KLF818	24.5.49 ✓	Service, adjust brakes.
D21	Tate of Leeds	71M 293	1465 LUS502	26.5.49	Conversion to R/H. drive.
D21	Dr. Marshal	71M 536	4725 JYR671	30.5.49 ✓	3.78 C.W. & P. Air cleaner. Panel bulb. Tighten steering wheel.
D22	Mr. Griffin	71L 4550	LKX146	30.5.49	O/S/F wing (coachwork)
D23	Park Garage	71L 140	9020 JGY720	30.5.49	Wheel wobble. Fit 2° beam.
D24	A.M.C.	71K 535	595 8276 JYK438	30.5.49 ✓	Remove engine, fit all heads, 2 carburettors, 3 branch manifolds, change gearbox, 3.5 axle, fuel gauge u/s.
D25	Dr. Shepherd	81M 756	FDW92	30.5.49	Weld + fit G.B. plate bracket.
D26	Mr. Compton	71M 6158	JYT943	31.5.49	Fit new half shell casing, fit machined heads
	Mr. Regent	71M 593	TMH643	31.5.49	Fit vents in side of scuttle. Wash & Polish. rubber around pedals.

D29	Blue Star Garages	8M876	754 KLK535	31/5/49	Attend to brakes & exhaust blows.
D30	Gross & Lawson	7M299	8763 GRK222	31/5/49	Brakes.
D31	R.J. Tellam	7IK488Q	840 MPF647	31-5-49 ✓	S/F from 3.5 C.W.&P. 1000 mile service. Paint crack on bonnet. Adjust brakes. Paint bumper brackets.
D32	Mr. O'Kill	7M614G	9348 JYV272	1-6-49	Decoke, oil & grease, adjust brakes, wheel wobble.
D33	Decca	7M400	JUC302	31.5.49	Leaky head gasket, Gear shift mounting loose.
D34	Hartwells of Oxford	8M786	3755 NTO335	31.5.49	Front end & steering.
D35	Mr. Craig	8M1058	249 UMC938	1.6.49	1,000 mile service, window rattles, hood rattles, N/S dash leaks, rear window leaks. O/S door dropped. Repair O/S/R wing. 3.5 C.W.&P.
D36	Sales A/c	7IK670	8230 KSC895	2-6-49	Faulty coil H.T. lead. Starter button does not always work.
D37	Mr. Riddell	7IK633	627 KLX493	2-6-49	Check for "clonk" in rear axle.
D38	Mr. Knot	7M597	5562 MPF570	3-6-49	Rectify wheel wobble
D39	Mr. Kirkby	7IK432Q	LHW29	4-6-49	Repair N/S/R bumper bracket. Adjust brakes.
D40	Mr. Stevens	7M613	9000 EBR338	7-6-49	Remove axle beams, change front spring & axle beams.
D41	Blue Star Garage	8M876	1300 KLK535	7-6-49	N/S door dropped. check brakes, N/S/R grabbing.
D42	J. Ross	7IK387	5305 LUM12	7-6-49	Decoke. Bonnet handles rattle. Wiper blades need synchronising. 3.5 C.W.&P. Handbrake flies off.
D43	L. Marshall	7M534	JYR671	8-6-49 ✓	Repair accident damage.
	L. Dick	7M326	1971 JYT950	8-6-49 ✓	Check steering. Transmission drumming. Scuttle Rattle. Change Fan & belts.

No.	Name			Date	Work
D45	P. L. Lawrie	879 855	1753 GSG196	9/6/49	Rough Running engine, adjust brakes, windows rattle, hood torn.
D46	P. Eliot-Cohen	7147433P	7185 JLK582	9/6/49	S/F Air cleaner, new F&R bumpers, decoke, repair rear damage. S/F sun visors.
D47	~~Sales~~ A/C / R. Brindley	7147331 / 7146670	24625 8298 / KGC895 JLK857	10-6-49	Tune-up, change oils, grease, spray springs, repair o/s/f windshield.
D48	Continental Cars		Columbia Axle		Build up customers axle.
D49	Mr. Goldthorpe	71K 367Q	THX323	11-6-49	Repair petrol tank leak.
D50	Mr. Lindsay	8171050	1500 TML804	13-6-49	Wheel wobble, sticky throttle, Adjust brakes.
D51	De Tawin	8171030	414C924	13-6-49	Service, fit secret switch, fit chrome beading.
D52	Mr. Fitzroy Robinson	8171065B	410 UMJ198	13-6-49	S/F 2 Lucas F.T.700 Spotlamps. 500 mile service.
D53	A/C	71K146	Money	13-6-49	Change engine.
D54	Lt. Col. Bagley	7147542	5543 GOR82	14-6-49	Examine front suspension, adjust brakes, Service. Check fuel lines.
D55	W/Cmdr. Greenhalgh	8171001B	2287 KLC993	14-6-49	Repair w/s/f spring, difficulty in engaging gears, spongy brakes, fuel starvation.
D56	Sales A/C	71K 647	104 Money	15-6-49	Rectify water leak into sump.
D57	Mrs Johnston	7147322	1743 J40194	15-6-49	Fit new door locks & hinges, Service.
D58	Mr. Barclay Inglis	71C4559	1347 LHX147	17-6-49	Service, Adjust clutch, check rad. valve, clean fuel pump filter. Rectify noise from n/s/f brake drum.
D59	Lucas Records	7147400	SUC302	20-6-49	Check brakes, tie-rods, & steering. Service. New h/plate.
D60	Goldthorpe	71K 367Q	6052 THX323	21-6-49	Fit 2 new front brake pipes.

1761.	A.M.C. (T. Broadbent)		7LM6846	MNW149	21-6-49
1762.	Offord & Sons		8LM0840	KLU7	23-6-49
1763.	J. Frey		712203	MWL180	24-6-49
1764.	Mr. Tatler (Motorist) / Mr. Capstan		814804 / 712388	TMX198 / SMX278	25-6-49
1765.	Mr. Cyprian		712388	SMX278	25-6-49
1766.	Mr. Broomfield		8LM1032B	NPA871	27-6-49
1767.	Mr. W. A. Jervis		8LM1067	KPX	27-6-49
1768.	Mr. Cook		7LM7414	LWB27	27-6-49
1769.	Mr. S. Eastmead		7LK688	KLP147	28-6-49
1770.	P. L. Walker (Ready.) (28.7.49.)		7LK489	MF789	28-6-49
1771.	Rowe		8LM1056G	KPX11	28-6-49
1772.	Southern Counties Garage		8LM730	KBP866	28-6-49
1773.	Smith		8LM870	FRY999	28-6-49
1774.	Mr. Lemesurier		7LM50	TMH812	29-6-49
1775.	Mr. Godfrey		8LM1005	KLL36	29-6-49
	Sales		7LK622	KUW66	30-6-49

2° beams. Repair grille; o/s door dropped. Boot corners.

1,000 mile service. Adjust brakes.

Decoke, service, adjust brakes, repair exhaust flex.

Decoke, service, loud rattles, sticky traps.

Fit screen rubber, deliver car.

Decoke, service, new fan element, adjust brakes.

S/F 2 wing mirrors.

Remove rear axle, check drive shaft & pin.

Cracked body, front axle busters, service, machine heads, tune-up.

Repair accident damage.

Engine stalls, check carburation.

Doors dropped, poor paint, tune-up, adjust brakes. Roof leaks.

N S F & N S R wings damaged.

Service, check c/b points.

Adjust brakes, check fuel consumption & repair lighter.

Service, brakes u/s. Windscreen rattles.

No.	Name			Date	Work
777	Dr. Shepherd	81M756	8172 FD492	30-6-49.	Paintwork, side shield missing. Windscreen w/s
778	Dr. Marshall	71M534	5278 JYR91	30-6-49.	Grease, tune-up.
779	Mr. Wick	71M326	2552 JYP950	30-6-49.	Wheel wobble, sticky throttle, car does not pull away smoothly in 2nd gear. Adjust brakes
780	Mr. Lindsay	81M050	TML804	30-6-49	
782	Mr. Cyprian	71L388	10539 SMX278	30-6-49.	Change main jets, adjust tuners & belts.
783	Mr. O'Kiel	71M614G	10539 JYV272	1-7-49.	Fit new gear change bracket on cyl. head.
784	Mr. Sykes	81M818	6500 QB1446	1-7-49	Loss of water, service. Tune-up. Brakes
785	Mr. J.C.A. Janks	71M514	2228 JYE351	1-7-49	Service, tune-up.
786	Dr. Compton	71M618G	JYT943	1-7-49	Exhaust blows, fit G.B. letters, check track.
087	Barclay Foplin	71L455Q	14461 LKX146	1-7-49	Grease, change engine oil, spray springs, locate & rectify creak on N.S.R.
088	J.M. Lockyer	71K553	KTA3082	2-7-49.	Decoke, 2 beams, brake reline if necessary
089	Dr. Herriot. AJ	81M725	MPH147	4-7-49.	Fit 2 wing mirrors, Rectify traffic. Tune up. adjust brakes.
090	Mr. Hopper	81M708	6737 KGC893	4-7-48	Service. Alter from return pipe, repair exhaust bracket. Fan belt too tight. Tune-up.
091	Mr. Michelin	71K154	10000 JGP474	4-7-49	Change engine, adjust brakes, fuel gauge c/s. Make up new hood & side curtains
093	Mr. Dugent	71M593	TML164	4-7-49	Clutch judder when hot. Car interior overheating.
095	Mr. Janks	71M514	JYE351	4-7-49.	Repair hood & accident damage.
096	Peters Ivory	71L852	2427 KLO128	4-7-49.	S/F O/S wing mirror, fit luggage grid. Service.

D97	Sales Alex	81M1051	27 Unreg	4-7-49	S/F 3.5 C & 4P
D100	Mr. Twentyman	71K713	117 Unreg	4-7-49	S/F 3.5 C & 4P
E1	Bell Garage	81M1062B	3776 KLY 14	5-7-49	Poor brakes, sticky throttle, clock & cigar lighter u/s. front end vibration, bake up hood cover.
E2	D.D. Swithenbank	81M720	7877 MFJ200	5-7-49	Repair all accident damage.
E3	Velvet Crepe Paper Co.	71M517	11629 SMX835	6-7-49	Reline brakes, 2° beams. Tune up.
E4	Stoneycroft Chicks Cook's Garage	71136Q	3543 HA0717	6-7-49	Repair accident damage.
E5	De. Compton	71M618G	1325 JYT9S3	8-7-49	Renew shackle bushes, clean plugs, adjust brakes. Check N/S road light.
E6	George + Jobling	8M788	QGD210	8-7-49	Noisy rear axle, no clearance between front beam & spring bushes. Penking.
E7	O.Kill Esq.	71M614	10947 JN272	9/7/49	Change gear operating lever, check clutch toe bars, adjust clutch. Repair front + rear wings.
E8	Mr. H. Riddell	71K639	1456 KLX473	11/7/49	Elliminate clonk in rear axle, car bottoms when cornering, Service + tune, supply + fit aluminium cyl heads + twin carbs. attend to petrol gauge, starter sticks. Stiff steering, fit trans. Service
E9	Mr. Boonell	71M606	2154 KLM9	11/7/49	Speedo not working, Oil leaking from N/S rear hub, N/S battery leaking, check over front wings, fit sorbo rubber round gear- change, replace N/S front spring bushes.
E10	Mr. Dent	71L314	JLM3 71L314	12/7/49	Attend to headlamp wiring + throttle return spring
E05	Mr. Rapper	81M709	HGC893 6949	12/7/49	Tow car from Esher, fit distributor cap + base, fit fan belt.
E12	Mr. Millward	71M231	JLM245 22800	13/7/49	Fit distributor cap + tune engine.
	Mr. Owens	71K145	CHM316 5617	14/7/49	change all oils, spray, springs, check carburettor.

E/15	Dagenham Motors Ltd	81M 1096B	22 Unreg	14/7/49	Fit H.M.V. Radio.
E/16	Mr. de Rouet	81M 735	3788 JYW749	18/7/49	make wood cover, repair holes in wood, fit bench seat in front. Decoke Engine, check brakes, batteries, trafficators, horn, judder bars, track, fit fram, oil bath air cleaner, 2 tyres
E/17	Lt/Cmdr. Greenhalgh	81M 1001B	3401 KLL 999	18/7/49	Remove clutch & examine decoke engine
E/18	Mr J. S. Perry	81M 1064	B 1299 FBL 687	18/7/49	Wheel tramp, Engine overheating, Engine knocks, attend to o/s. trafficator, o/s R/Wing beading + o/s hood straps
E/19	Messrs Hartwells of Oxford	81M 786	4654 NJO 335	18/7/49	Engine overheating, fit N/S. Bonnet
E/20	Dr. Price	81M 897	6671 HWW222	18/7/49	Change rear spring, remove fan & examine, replace front shackle bushes, fit restrictor washer, holes in wood change oils & service, wash & polish, adjust hood, fit mirror, check o/s front & rear tyres (scrubbing) adjust brakes, check ignition & carb. plugs, clutch tie bars, rubber bands for air filter
E/21	Mrs Portons	81M 828	7835 NNU 8	19/7/49	n/s door paint bumper drainage rattles on screen fit Tricco washers knock out n/s wing & body dents
E/22	Mr Gill	71K 236	8986 BGS 825	19/8/49	Reline brakes, take-up play in steering, check front shackles. check ignition, strengthen floor boards, drain gearbox oil.
E/23	Mr Baigent	71M 593	3411 TML 164	19/7/49	check fan + horn
E/24	Dr. Clarke	81M 853	6194 KLL 138	20/7/49	General service adjust brakes etc change all oils replace rear bulb, fit G.B. plate o/s door catches loose.
E/25	Capt Tween	81M 1062B	4030 KLY 14	20/7/49	Remove front axle & check remove front spring, remove brake drums & check linings
E/26	Turner Riley	71M 421	6050 MPV 219	21/7/49	Grease & spray springs top-up batteries, all oil levels & shock absorbers
E/27	~~Carr~~ W. H. P. Barngeat	81M 1093	25 Un reg	21/7/49	Fit Fram.
E/28 (31)	Mr Roy	71M 329	HWE 38 2613	21/7/49	Change front spring & front shock absorbers, adjust brakes, sticky throttle
E/29	Mr J. D. Leigh	71M 324	UMV 5 57	21/7/49	add ½ point ledex to rear axle
E/30	Mr Jenks	71M 514	12376 JYE 302	21/7/49	poor performance
	Decca	71M 400	302 JUC 816	22/7/49	Service change oil check engine tune

E33.	J. Binns Ltd.	3768 HUT814	81M849	25-7-49.	Examine front end for wheel tramp etc.
E34.	Mr. Fairchild	5320 JYO365	71M319	25-7-49	Gearbox & clutch service, adjust brakes? Handbrake does not hold.
E35.	Cecornwall Ltd. (Mr. Jacobs)	5000 JOC63	71429.0	25-7-49.	Decoke, front suspension, cabin overheating, check fuel gauge, reserve unit & speedo. Fit rear bumper
E36	Mr. Rexford	CLR5		25-7-49.	Check & examine rear axle, check prop end.
E37.	Dr. O. Scarborough	8031 JRS621 81M785		26-7-49.	Peeling paint, wheel wobble, door dropped. Sticking brakes, loose rear hubs.
E38.	Mr. Robinson	1313 UMJJ98 81M488		26-7-49.	Remove rear axle
E39.	Velvet Crepe Paper.	12345 71M517 STX85		26-7-49	Adjust brakes
E40.	Dr. Matthews	12490 71M5798 GGA282		26-7-49	Change oil & water gauge. Adjust brakes
E41.	Barclay Inglis.	1848 71L455Q LKX146		26-7-49.	Take play from steering box, check rear hubs & brakes, grease, check oils. Tune. Change starter
E42.	Mr. Broomfield	6000 81M105A NPA871		26-7-49	
E43.	Mr. J.R. Scott	10008 71M6455 CES146		28-7-49.	Decoke, 3.5. C & P. Machine heads. Cracked boot corners.
E44.	~~Mr. Godfrey.~~				
E44/5.	Austin Gauge.				Conversion of pedal assembly,
E44.	Mr. Godfrey.	5000 81M1005 KU756		28-7-49.	Decoke, trim hood.
E46.	Mr. Holley.	71L432Q HW29		29-7-49.	Fit new headlamp rim. Repack front hubs with grease.
E47.	L. Potter.	13342 71K595 JYK438		29-7-49.	Examine front end.
E48.	B. Howard.	10085 71M606 GSC314		2-8-49.	2 beams. Fit bonnet handles.

E49	Mr Lanesure		7117550	8211 TPH1812	2-8-49
E50	Mr Pill		71K216	BG8528	2-8-49
E51	Mr Nash		81M10076	2538 EP1796	2-8-49
E52	Pars Mr Mr Gee		RGC224	6638 81M698	2-8-49
E53	Mr Fitzg—		JFJ293	5954 7117537	2-8-49
E54	Mr Goodwin		8117704	4728 DRD505	3-8-49
E55	Harwells Ltd		8114786	4928 NTO335	3-8-49
E56	Mr Bunning		71K206	4581 JLR618	3-8-49
E57	Mr Cookston		71K452A	752 KUW556	5-8-49
E58	Imhof		71M217	JGU5	5-8-49
E59	E.Bolton Esq—		8117651	1228 7117744	5-8-49
E60	Mr Imhof		71M214	12441 JGU4	5-8-49
E61	L Beardon		7117267	9033 KDR121	5-8-49
E62	Mr Jannvin		8114086	411C924	5-8-49
E63	W/Cdr Hare		71K162	511C665	8-8-49
	Sapenham Motors		81411093	277 417D465	8-8-49

Clutch judder, Trim hood, Grease, check oil levels, check front brakes. Fit new fan belt. Change spare.

Fit battery carrier brackets, 2 bolts missing from screen, windscreen rubbers.

Trim hood. Clutch judder.

O/S traff sticking. Tune up. Service. Clutch judder. Holes in hood. Adjust brakes. Fit late type bumpers.

Tune up. Service. Fit late type bumper to front.

Fit 2 extra silencers, cabin & engine overheats.

Brakes, check for front end rattle, make up sidescreens.

500 mile service. Check tank unit. Throttle knob. Rectify dynamo output. Rear squeak. Clutch slip, check ignition. Condenser tank. Bottom up at rear.

Fit return? throttle spring.

Brakes. Repair n/s/f wing. Exhaust leak. Fit vents in scuttle.

Fit new coil, check & set timer points.

Change engine oils, check levels. Tune up.

New King pins & brushes. Check steering.

Fit new dash. Paintwork on —

No.	Name			Date	Work
E65	Peacock, Balham	71K826	3002 KLW45	9-8-49	Fit 3.5 C.W. +P.
E66	Mr. Oldthorpe	71K367Q	THX323	9-8-49	Tune up. Fit bonnet handle. Balance wheels
E67	Mr. Craig	81M1058B	2484 UMC938	9-8-49	Fit new torque tube
E68	Mrs. M. M. Lee	81M698	6744 KGC224	9-8-49	Inspect gearbox
E69	Mr. Wick	71M326	JYY950	11-8-49	Brakes, flush Rad. Fit 6 bladed fan. Change to continental lighting. Service
E71	Mr. W. Stevens	71M613	RBK338	12-8-49	
E72	Mr. W. Stevens	71K391	9284 LYK765	15-8-49	Tune up, brakes, foam. Air cleaner, focus lights
E73	Mr. Tapper	81M709	KGC893	16-8-49	Service & wash. Replace w/s/f shocker link
E74	W/Cmdr Greenhalgh	81M100B	KLL999	16-8-49	Change gearbox & rear axle oil, grease up. Spray springs.
E75	Mr. G. O'Kill	71M6146	JYV272	16-8-49	Tune-up. Service. Adjust clutch & brakes
E76	Mr. Dembleby	71M331	26000 YXK957	17-8-49	Balance wheels. Noise under front. Ham - Spedo. - N/S front light. Engine time. Service (all oils) Throttle sticks - dark.
E77	Mr. White	81M759	2819 LMB595	17-8-49	Adjust brakes, cracked dash, bottoming & rear engine noise.
E78	Sales A/c	71M699	328 trees	18-8-49	Fit 3.78 C.W. +P. Fit Heater
E79	Wilkins Bros	71K239	12948 CWD818	18-8-49	Fit new o/s punch bolt & bushes. Tune-up
E83	Mr. Twentymans	71K713	2033 GOK660	22-8-49	Fit competition manifolds, adjust clutch & brakes. Fit telecontrols to front.
E84	Mr. Broomfield	81M1022B	5880 NPA871	22-8-49	3.78 C.W. +P.

E84	Miss B.N. Prelen.	81M2041 B	1441. HUY 140	22-8-49	Fit 6 bladed fan. Remove front spring.
E85.	Holl Parke	613E(1)	4161. HYW331.	22-8-49	Fit rev counter drive, check track, adjust brakes, S/F new shackle pins on front springs.
E86	G.S. Lundell.	81M730.	5717. RBP466	22-8-49	Wheel wobble, peeling paint. leaking hood.
E87	Mr. J. Kastmead	71K685G	12285 KLF147	22-8-49	Check brakes.
E88	Mr. Rumford.	CLK5		23-8-49.	Remove rear axle & gearbox.
E89.	L.C. Edwards.	71M610G	12097 EBX761	23-8-49.	Decoke. Steering wobble, touch up paintwork. Machine heads. Adjust brakes.
E90	Mr. Hart	71M397A	NEV26	23-8-49	Adjust brakes.
E92	Mr. Turner.	71M6156	7257 NYR13	24-8-49	Decoke. Adjust brakes. Machine heads. S/F KK2A distributor.
E93	Rectification Job E43				
E95	Mr. Michelin	71K154	UGP4)4	24-8-49	Fit late type grille. Fit new o/d peneck belt. S/F front shackle bushes.
E96	Mr. Simmons	81M883	5602 FMW416	24-8-49	Accident damage. Decoke.
E97	D.H. Solling	71L393.	2226 JLT913	25-8-49	Tune up. Service. Rectify wheel wobble.
E98	Ramon de Larrinaga	71K480A	JKD874	26-8-49	Fit 4½ litre engine. 91A gearbox + 3.78 C.W.P. S.U. pump, comp. manifolds + ali. heads.
E99	Mr. O'Kill	71M614G	FRV272	27-8-49	Fit new belts, check lamps.
E1	Peacocks.	71K826	3000 KLN45	27-8-49	Check braking system.
	Cocketown	71M482A	1363 KVW556	29-8-49	Modify diesel (remove clock), set clutch, check handbrake, service.

F 6	Mr. Byrne.		71L-388.	SMX-878.	31.8.49.	Jam. sticking rod. Take up play in steering, missing when hot. To fit King Pins & Bushes.
F 7	Mr. Simpson.		71M-818.S.	575-943.	30.8.49.	H.S. dead. Adjust Timing. Remove boot. and clean & adjust, Ladder belts. Adjust belts.
F 8	Cash Sale.		61L123	CRS-818.	30.8.49.	Modify Pedal assembly as per instructions.
F 9	Sales.		71L866	55 Unreg.	30.8.49.	Change front Spring, Rectify Rev Counter Spring
F 10	Hall Park.		645-117.	HYW-351.	30.8.49.	Fit New Stud in Wing, Peg in n/s of Screen. Tighten Spare wheel bracket.
F 11	Mr. Baigenti.		71L336	10644 HLS.070.	31.8.49.	Rectify poor brakes
F 12	Mr. Lindsay.		81M1050	2429 TML804	31-8-49.	Fit special V/8 engine.
F 13	Sales A/C (L.Johnson.)		91M1524	12 Unreg.	31-8-49.	Service car
F 14	Mr. Craig.		81M10580	938 UML	31-8-49	Repair damage, deliver car
F 15	P. Eliot Cohen		71M1433P	JLW582	31-8-49.	Fit heating system, check brakes. 2° beams.
F 16	Furious Ltd. (C.H. Dennis.)		81M715	13765 EW999	1-9-49.	Service, Sticky throttle. S/F wing mirror.
F 17	A. Pereira		81M1038B	2541 UMJ680	1-9-49	Decoke, service. André's all round, two carbs & all leads. Adjust brakes.
F 18	Dr. Pearce.		81M577.	10118 JYF14	1-9-49	Repairs to rear of car. Repair of fuel tank.
F 19	L. Potter,		71K595	JYK438	1-9-49	André on front only. 2° beams.
F 20	S. Eastwood.		71K686	KLF147	5-9-49	Decoke, new pistons, check speedo.
	Park Garage.		71K140	11172 JGY720	5-8-49.	

F22	Polly's Garage.	71M890.	6019. KLL577	5-9-49.	Peeling paint, corroded battery box, bumpers fall off.
F23	Rectification E88.				
F24	J. Bold (T.C. Harrison Ltd.)	71M554.	10025 LWA19.	5-9-49.	Rattling bonnet, cowl, valances etc, change spring & beams. Tune-up.
F26	Harkstein.	71M264.	6468. JYT949	6-9-49.	Decoke, machine heads. Adjust brakes. Service
F27	Austin Hunts (Sir N.J. Bee)	81M1035B.	2500 CJL795	6-9-49.	3.78. C.W. & P. Tune up. Check brakes
F28	Sir. Compton.	71M6156	JYT943	6-9-49.	Adjust brakes.
F29	Jenkinson	81M 1081	2040. N.P.D.482	7-9-49	Balance all Wheels. Adjust Brakes & Gear Change. Check overflow Valve, Check O/S Valance Screws.
F30	Carey-Evans	81M 831	2458. FUN649	7-9-49	Check Shock Absorbers. Adjust Brakes. Sticky throttle. Check hand throttle. 1st Gear Stiff. Fit Saloon Head Spring if time permits.
F31	Manfield	71K 612	5275. JOE972	7-9-49	Double Swing Arm Suspension, 2° Axle Beams, Front Spring Change. Adjust Brakes.
F32	Le Mesurier	71M 550	TMH812	7-9-49	Top up all Oils, Grease, Spray Springs, Check Carb., & Timer
F33	Haydon. Esq.	81M783.	9549 HR9759.	8-9-49.	Decoke, Gr/Heads. Service, Check brakes & new tyres.
F34	Jenkins	71K586.	5531 FBL14.	8-9-49	2° beams.
F35	McDougall.	71L866.	458. KXH502	12-9-49	Check wipers, fit new master cylinder & battery.
F36	Dubost.	81M1020	8037 KLR294.	8-9-4	Check all wiring. Service. Tune-up.
F38	R.B. Walpole	81M1089B.	1788 OMH876	9-9-	Service, Tune-up. 3.78 C.W.&P. Check fuel consumption
	Mr Keppan	81M709.	10728 KGC893.	12-9-49	Check & locate click from under car.

			25195		
F40	S. Milward		717231.	JLM245	12-9-49.
F41	Mr. Sorrell.		71M606	KLM9.	12-9-49.
F42	Mr. Smitherbank.		81M720.	MPJ200	12-9-49.
F43	Dr. Clarke		11080 / 81M883	KLL138	13-9-49.
F44	Mr. Caddock		12097 / 71L201	JMH107	13-9-49.
F45	Rolls-Royce.		AGC496		13-9-49.
F46	Russell.		KXC162	1700od. 71696.	14-9-49.
F47	Mr. Symondson		71K248	KKX692	15-9-49.
F48	Wags Bennet Ltd	Dr. Stevens 234	81M10928	2165. OVW625	17-9-49.
F49	Dr. Crompton		71M618G	2097. JYT943	17-9-49.
F50	H. K. Marsden.		71L845	8234. ORX946	19-9-49.
F51	Park Garage		71L140	11201. JG4720	19-9-49.
F52	Mr. Rodney.		81M1065	6718. KLL736	19-9-49.
F54	Poolaston-Mills		71L351Q	11334. LHU836.	20-9-49.
F55	Mr. Austin.		71L695	5382. TML183	20-9-49.
F56	L. Johnson (S.B. Ltd.)		71M	26839. JM7271	20-9-49.

Take up play in Steering Box. Fit then Cylindroid head
fit new acc. pump washer. clean carbs. Tune up
Check brakes. Fit 3½° beams & new front spring.
Rectify speedo. Clean plugs, adjust brakes.

Repair scrapes to rear wings.

Adjust brakes, tune up, service.

Check for rear spring bottoming, 2° axle beams &
sticky throttle.
Rectify steering gear noise.

Check "U" bolts, change tyre.

Fit new centre bolt & packing piece to rear spring.

Overheating badly.

Rectify noisy gearbox.

Tune up, adjust brakes, refit safety catch and o/s bonnet
handle.
Repair cracked n/s/r axle casing.

Change front spring, check all brakes.

Decoke, reline if nec. rectify clutch judder, check
pawl & ratchet.
Service, tune up, check brakes, rad. valve, tie bars,
rear "U" bolts & engine beam bolts.
Service, chrome beading coming adrift.
Clean down engine.

57	Mr. Skewes.		LVK765	71L391.	21-9-49	Check steering, noisy tyres when cornering. Suspension. check stator tube.
58	Mr. Harbrow		KLR872	7315. 81M1047B	21-9-49	Tune-up. Service. Fit Radio.
59	Mr. Gill.		BGS825	13444 71K 236	21-9-49	Service, repair o/s/f wing & grille, check brakes, fit new perch bolt, screen glass & rubber.
60	Decca Records.		JUCJ02	7277 1M400	22-9-49	Adjust brakes. Tune up.
61	Sales dept.		Unreg.	19. 91M152	22-9-49	S/f Reversing lamps.
62	Murray Coutts.		KLO300	3152 81M754	22-9-49	J.78. 1.8d Gearbox. Convert rad, adjust brakes, repair rear of body, clutch judder.
63	Bearden		KDR121	71M267	23/9/4	Clutch judder. Wheel catching drop arm on lock. Check petrol consumption, Check Back axle & Gearbox oils, change sump oil. Grease shackle springs. Top up Shock absorbers. Check Bonnet catch. Fit Water Hose
64	Mr. De-Rovet		JYW.749	81M 735	24/9/49	Adjust Brakes. Rectify Exhaust Blow. Rectify Speedometer. Fit Dash Bulb.
65	Mr. Bromfield		NPA.871.	81M-1032.B	26.9.49	Complete Service. Change oils. Spray Springs. Tune up.
66	c/o Earls Greenhalgh		KLR999	81M1001B	26-9-49	Change Dynamo. Stop Belts.
67	Dent.		JMJ	22968. 71L314	27-9-49	Tune carb. Separate switch. SU Pumps. Adjust brakes. Balance front wheels.
68	Decker.		WD248	3546 41M104	29-9-49	Brakes.
69	Rigby.		CTK930.	8442. 8LL 722	29-9-49	Water loss and oil con. Service. Fit Frame - wobble - Bodywork. Check + top up Batteries. Adjust Accelerator. (Stocks)
	A.M.C.		New Car.	71K647.	29-9-49	Oil leak from sump - fit 2 head gaskets.
	Mr. J. Richmond.	Iver 583	H.J.F-843.	1M-353.A.	29.9.49	Fit Extra Silencers. Rectify Pinping Rattle in Exhaust. Fit Footwell for Drivers Feet.
	Eastwood.		KLF-147.	71K-685-2	30-9-49	Fit Twin Carburettors.

F.73.	Knaltey			1/10/49.	Fit twin carbs.	
F.74.	Michelin	J.G.P.474	12577. 154 71K	6/10/49.	Respray - fit old type bumpers. (Sent Encon 71K front and O/S Rear bumper in car.)	
F.75	Bolton	TMX747	2078 81M891	6/10/49.	Engine tune - complete service change oils regrind head.	
F.76.	Broomfield	NPA871	81M10303	6/10/49	Reline brakes	
F/77	Stevens			4/10/49.	Tighten. Oil filter. Supply 1 rear spring R H Bushes (Davies)	
F/78	Cyprian	SMX278	71K 388	6/10/49	Mag & Zc.78 Crown Wheel & Pinion attach loose. taking play in steering. Supply 2 screws for O/S door lock, Adjust brakes, rally lamps lead.	
F/79	Riddell					
F/80	Cunnell	KXC162	71K 695	6/10/49	Fit twin Manifold	
F/81	Janvrin	81M 10138	81M 10138	6/10/49	Check & Adjust Brakes. Change Engine oil & Frame cartridge	
F/82.	Riddell	71KB KLX473	71K639 2443.	8/10/49.	Fit 2° beams - damage O/S front wing	
F/83	Myhill.	71K152	71K699	8/10/49.	Accident damage coachwork. tune engine	
F/84	Dellamy Knight	JPX504.	4704 JPX504	11/10/49	3.78 Brakes - service.	
F/45,	Hughes of Exeter	KUW239	2951 81M10511	11/10/49.	Engine - Remove send to Pk Hill.	
F/86	Irvine	KXD 423	81M 767	11/10/49.	3.78 Ratio, Decoke Fit Scintilla. Adjust Brakes. out battery Check wisk gaytian Head engine for blown silver left.	
F/87	Balfour	DMU59.	4714 71M 309	12/10/49.	Latest type bumper FT700 lamp.	
F/98	Mrs Pierce	4MO460	2131 71M 1048	13/10/49	Chipped paint - adjust brakes.	

No.	Name	Reg.		Date	Work
F/189	Block.				New Stand and curtains
F/191	Maxwell-Telling	KXK865	91M 1522	17/10/49	Charge and loan Batt.
F/192	Dr Henriet	MPH144	9448 81M 72C	17/10/49	Tune - service
F/193	Turner Riley	MPJ219	8928 71M 44	17/10/49	Service adjust brakes.
F/194	Dr Vandy	C.H.W 523	14475 81M 964	17/10/49	3.78, 2 Carb. manifold. brakes, shackle bushes.
F/195	De Rouet	JY W749	7751 81M 735	18/10/49	Pinking plugs fog lamp Trico washer. check levels.
F/197	P. O'Declar	NPD 52	3017 81M 726	18/10/49	3.78. Axle leak Tune engine adjust brakes.
F/199	O.K Hardy	KXF 819	629 81M 1100	18/10/49	Tappet noisy
F/200	H. Penny & Co	UMK 735	214 81M 879	18/10/49	Check axle beam change front spring.
G1.	Les. Johnson	KXF 815	91M 1524	19/10/49	Accident damage to rear. engine vibration - steering.
G2.	Dagenham Motors Owner. Evan Cook	UMC 538	2699 81M 1066	19/10/49	Fit 3.78.
G3.	Quennell (charge AMC)	KXC 162	71K 695	20/10/49	Fit E62A Distributor.
G4	Mrs Johnson	9 YO 199	4189 81M 322	24/10/49	Change engine oil, Fram element, changed M/S disc. trim - grease etc,
G5.	Gill	9 YO 194 BGS 825	3589 71K 236	24/10/49	Fit Tele shocker. change head (1 7/32")
G6.	Rumford	CLK5		24/10/49	Weld. section rod.

		R. No.	Mil.			
97	Ross	SV 1655	5763	81M 10868	24/10/49	Examine N/S Stub bearing - service - tune - adjust brakes. change oil.
98	Car Sales Clapham	MNU 326	9214	81M 868	24/10/49	Service - adjust brakes - starting handle loose - check over for sale.
99	Widd	KLO 126	9764	81M 869	26/10/49	Examine brakes. Water loss and oil. Batt charge.
G 10	Dagenham Motors	NHX 898	12250	116 712	26/10/49	Replace carb with Chandler Grove. rectify gearbox jumping out of 2nd. New glass in windscreen.
G 11	O. Kelly	SVV 272	15561	81M 614	28/10/49	Change beams, spring bushes, reline brakes - antifreeze.
S 13	Miss Pullin	HOY 141	2059. 81110418	81M 2091	30.10.49	Check front suspension, loss of water. Wash. Sparking Plugs.
S 13	Dr. Henriot	MPH 147	9771	81M 726	31/10/49	Change front axle beams and spring.
S 14	Major Waring	RD 1606	22728	71M 355	1/10/49	Axle - gearbox - suspension - electrical - grille
S 15	Allen	KLY 24	2693	81M 1071	1/11/49	Head leaking, accelerator sticks - change oils - brakes - distributor
S 16	Myhill	QLB 2105	5423	71K 699	1/11/49	Parking N/S F wing tighten - check shockers. air cushion punctured - Stitch gaiter change oil etc.
S 17	White	MNW 414	8319	71M 566	1/11/49	Service - change oils Tune engine antifreeze.
S 18	Elliot Cohen	GLW 452	10054	71M 433	2/11/49	Jump out at 2nd. Handbrake flies off. Brakes. Head rattles.
S 20	Mrs. Pamela May	KLO 128		71L 852	2/11/49	Bad paintwork - service.
S 21	Dr. Clarke	KLL 138	13269	81M 853	2/11/49	Decoke fit machined heads. Decarbonize & machined heads.
S 22	Stonecliffe Close Garage	HAM 138. KLO 96	81M 853 81M 10218	13269 345	4.11.49 7.11.49	Fit 3.78.
S 23	Car Sales	JKK 438	14651	71M 695	7.11.49	Service etc.
S 24	Barclay Ingles	LKK 146	20014	71L 453	7.11.49	Service etc.

G 25.	Galathorpe	THX 323	100 72	71K367Q	8/11/49	Crankcase. Pet gauge - may switch.
G 26.	D.A. Jones.	FWN 659	94 11	81M 1080	9/11/49	Bad road holding. Engine vibration. check brakes & oil
G 27.	A.L Pereira	UMD 681	6247	81M 1078	9/11/49.	Decoke - machine heads - straighten rear bumper. - service.
G 28.	Den Hartog.	NEV 26	18624	71M 397A	11/11/49.	Front spring - King pins and bushes. Tune. check brakes.
G 29.	Patterson - Newcastle	LVK 766	5123	71M413A	14/11/49.	Wheel wabble 35. 40. M.P.H.
G 30.	Forelen.	TMH 616	7143	71M 659	14/11/49.	2° Beams - change front spring.
G 31.	Thompson	MPF 342	20918	71M 669	14/11/49.	Clutch judder
G 32.	Bristol St. Motors.	JOK 114	11097	81M 839	16/11/49.	Reline brakes.
G 33.	Napper	KGC 993	12827	71M 709	16/11/49.	Change engine oil. service
G 34.	Car Sales.	KLO 122	10154	71M 5299	17/11/49.	Service - check levels. fit steering handle tube. - ready for sale.
G 35.	Car Sales.	MRB 441	16973.	81M 745.	17/11/49.	Service - ready for sale.
G 36	O'Kill	JYE 272	16420	81M 614	18/11/49.	Fit 2 Lucas FT. 100 Lamps - demister (own) - adjust brakes
G 37.	Car Sales.	KUW 565	2958	71K 622.	19/11/49	Service change engine oil check car for sale.
G 38.	Owen.	CHM 316.	10260.	71K 145.	21/11/49.	Front & rear spring 2° Beams. check brakes.
G 39.	Bellamy Knight.	JPX 507	5640	71M 532	21/11/49.	Service - rad muff - antifreeze - clean plugs etc.
G 40.	Car Sales.	KXF 620	652	71M 5525	21/11/49	Service - change engine oil.

Job No.	Names	Reg. No.	Mileage	Chassis No.	Date	Customers Instructions For Repairs
S/41.	B/ Sleuens	EBK333		71M613	24/11/49	Fit blocks to rear spring.
S/42.	Balfour	MMU59.	2467.	71M307.	24/11/49.	Fit 2° beams. FT700. Service coachwork.
S/43.	Richards.	J.LJ.6.	6190.	71M228	24/11/49.	2° beams. front spring. 2 extra ex. silencers trim again repair grille
S/45.	Piereira	MMD671		81M1077.	24/11/49.	Supply and fit. sal. switch.
S/46.	Hartstein	Q.YJ.969.	9016	71M269	25/11/49	Hood. clutch judder.
S/47.	Car Sales (S.H.A.)	KLO.130	8249.	81M719	28/11/49.	Change gearbox & engine - check res. dash lamps. - exten fuel line.
S/48.	Jarvis.	MMC924	10326	81M1013	24/11/49.	Change engine oil - service - tim engine - new plugs - antifreeze
S/49.	Miles	HRU800.	11375.	81M489.	30/11/49.	2° beams. - indicators - wiper - temp gauge. brakes.
S/50.	Farrows. New car.	—	—	71K691	30/11/49.	Fit. H.M.V Radio.
S/51.	Maxwell Telling	KXK965.	1798.	81M9522.	30/11/49.	1000 Ml Service.
S/52.	H/r Walker.	HLY.24.		81M.171.	30.11.49.	Repairs to Accident Damage.
S/53	O'Keith	Q.Y.E727	16500.	81M614.	30.11.49.	Battery. 2 new.
S/54	Dick	32 bhp engine			1.12.49.	32 Engine convert to 4.4 litre.
S/55.	Blllat Cohen.	Q.LW5R2.			1.12.49.	Attend to transmission
	Docra Records.	J.YC.302	9337.	71M400.	2.12.49	Fit. Voltmeter
	Dr Crompton	J.YK69R		R555		Loan 6V Batt.

Ref	Name	Reg			Date	Notes
G57.	Blackley	9YK438			3/12/49	Antifreeze exhaust blow - horns - headlight.
G58.	Northern Organisation	940585	14707	71M.319.	5/12/49	2° beam - spring - service change oils tune.
G59.	Bertram Smith	KKG752	503.	91P 1517	6/12/49	600 Service 2 FT 700.
G60	Dr Hobson	KXM943	703	91M 1530	6/12/49	500 Service - O/S indicator.
G61.	Car Sales	KLO123.	71M 6079 5765	Photo Saloon	6/12/49	service for sale.
G62.	O'Kell	↑	↑		↑	Fit 2 FT 700 Lamps.
G63.	Tormen Rdg.	MPJ 219	71M 421 10265		9/12/49.	Wash - service - change oils, 2° Beams spring time engine.
G64	Bramfield	UMX450	91P 1538 13		9/12/49.	Frame - 2 mirrors - D.A. Overdrive. Fit Lamps.
G65.	Dr Roberts	H.R.U.2.	71M 542. 23116		9/12/49.	2° Beams.
G66	De Ronel.	9YW749.	81M 749. 10000		10/12/49	Check back axle and gearbox bevels.
G67.	Sales.	New car.	71L 772		12/12/49	Check for sale.
G68	Sales.	"	71L 837		12/12/49.	check for sale.
G69.	J.B. Manufacturing	KXF 814	5061 91M 1524		12/12/49.	2 Thermostats. Coachwork.
G69A.	A.M.C.	"	"		"	Modify centre steering.
70.	Messrs Gifford & Sons Ltd.		M. 1084.		12.12.49.	Check cooling system, overheat. Adjust Brakes. Rectify Parking.
71.	Cavendish Mill House Sidlesham Chichester	1147P Malta.	3434 71K 154		12·12·49.	Respray (white) Decoke service.
72.						

G.72.	Gypriam	SMX278	20138	71L388	12/12/49	Decoke machine heads. caml ring		88
G.73.	Sales	Maxey	—	71K558	13/12/49	Check for sale		
G.74	Mr. Letter	SMX-198	7098	81M-804	.. 11	Repairs to Gear Box. Tune Engine. & demister. Check Brakes. Luggage Boot &/Cover Replace		
G.75.	Phillips	BEE277	9916	81M1085	13/12/49	O/S front wing damage change beams		180
G.76.	T. Clark. Prince of Wales. Woodstock Nr. Bicester	JOL85	5204	81M895	13/12/49	Brakes tune engine		
G.77	Walpole	HMR816	3120	81M1087½	14/12/49	Coachwork. Tune engine		
G.78	Maxwell Tilling	KXK865	2115	91M1522	14/12/49	Coachwork — Change fulcrum bracket		
G.79	Imhof	JCM5			14/12/49	Check rear brakes. wipe		
G.80.	Sales R.K. Macmillan & Co. 33, Linen Hall St. Belfast. N. Irelan	Maxey	—	91P1573	14/12/49	Fit heaters. 4 overriders		
G.81.	Sir Philip Brocklehurst Swythamley Park Macclesfield				15/12/49	Supply and fit front bumper		
G.82	George Newman	EDL14	6500	71K586	16/12/49	Brakes		
G.83	McDarrell	JYE359	13676	71M470A	17/12/49	Feb 3.78. Decoke fit set brake shoes		
G.84	Craig	MMC938	5806	81M1053B	19/12/49	Service work		
G.85	Owen	CHM316	10641	71K145	19/12/49	91A gearbox — 3.78		
G.86	Millward	JLM295	27943	71M231	19/12/49	Repair Columbia axle -44		
G.87	White	MNV474	8499	71M566	20/12/49	2 Sun vizors 2 demisters		

G.88.	Dr Hanson	UMC 29	11097	4M1043K	21/12/49	Twice weekly O/S indicator.	
G.89.	Godfrey	U.Car.	—	9M1548	22/12/49	Fit Heater - radio - overriders - 2 FT700 lamps.	
G.90	Sales	—	—	TMK654	23/12/49.	Remove Fram - check for sale.	
G.91.	Decca	JU.C 302	—	7IM400	23/12/49.	Fit 91A gearbox.	
G.92.	Ray	KUE 28	10000	7IM329	29/12/49.	Change front spring.	
G.93.	Imhof	I.GM5		7IM217	29/12/49.	Overhaul engine 18E6050	
G.94	Imhof	NNU198			29/12/49	Fit G.93's engine - gearbox 91A. new head - change O/S front wing. change rear wing. fit own spotlights. Rally car.	
G.95	Handly	KXF819	2019	1100B	29/12/49	Fit 1 demister check brakes.	
G.96	Du Hant	NEV27	18957	7IM397M	29/12/49	Fit new O/S silencers.	
G.97	O'Kill	KLO123.	6931.	7IM627M	30/12/49.	32hp Mercury engine.	
G.98	Bromfield	UMX450	268	91P1538	30/12/49	Heater - number plate holder - change belts.	
G.99	Dagenham Motors	—	—	9IP1551	2/1/50	Fit Heater - bonnet leaks-	
G.100	Car Sales	KLO122	11531	7IM529.	3/1/50	Service - brakes - tune.	(Remarks. P.H. 11 brakes Tub shockers.
H.1.	Potter	9KM272	15318	7IM594	3/1/50	Decoke - machine heads - 91A centralising gearbox - mod exhaust.	
H.2.	Greenhalgh	KMM999	8864	9IM1001s	3/1/50	Fit saloon type heater. check levels and serviced	
H.3.	Mr Dollar	KLR872	91800	8IM104PB H800	3.1.50.	Decoke, fit heads, Poor fuel consumption (14m.pg.) Adjust brakes, change all oils, check Radio Suppression.	

H.4	Dimbleby	2LK957	71M331	30822	4/1/50	Reline brakes - king pins - exchange front spring.
H.5	Bellamy Knight	9PX609	71M532	6889	4/1/50	Fit 2. FT100 lamp. Service change. change oils.
H.6	Mrs Constantanen	SMT946	71L924	10410	4/1/50	Check one car - road test - service as required
H.7	Mr. Tapper	KGC449	71M709		4.1.50	Check brake shoes - adjust, adjust belt
H.8	Mr. Cyprian	SMX278	71L388		5.1.50	Fit new dynamo bearing. Tighten Heads. fit dash bulb. 500 ml service
H.9	Godfrey	KYM669	9P1548	545	9/1/50	
H.10	Symondson	KKXB72	71K248	19156	9/1/50	Fit 2 panel bolts temp. gauge - felt in column.
H.11	Mr Godfrey	KLL736	81M1005	7419	11/1/50	Change oils. Reune tune engine - check leaks
H.12	Mrs Imhof	9GU4	71M214	16395	12/1/50	Decoke - new plugs. - brakes adjusted. fit types
H.13	Mr Millar	JYOX5	71M319	8655	17/1/50	Decoke - change oils - service. machined heads
H.14	O'Kill	KLO123	71M6278	-	16-1-50	
H.15	De Rouet	9YW449	10441	81M735	18-1-50	Service - adjust brakes - exhaust blow -
H.16	Gormley	GDT523	81M1009	4732	18-1-50	Fit saloon type heater.
H.17	Ca Janvrin	UMC24	81M1043		19-1-50	
H.18	Quennell	KXC162			19-1-50	Decoke.
H.19	De Pearlman	LKG780	10291	81M721	19-1-50	Remove front suspension for examination.

20.	R. Sweet. Moorland Crowden. Bedford.	NPB-811.	SIM-1130.8	19.1.50		Fit & Supply Lucas. Headlamp. SFT 700
H.21.	A.M.C. Ford 10 Van.	FGH 370		20.1.50		Dynamo not charging — change belt. repair starter.
H.22	Knaltey	LHW29	7L432Q	25.1.50	19342.	Fit 2 SFT 700 lamps. Recore. radiator heads.
H.23.	Greenhalgh	KLL999				Kit of spares. fit D.F. holder in O/S headlamp.
H.24.	Capt Treen.	KLY14	SIM1062B	23.1.50	160.12	General check over — bodywork etc.
H.25.	Duboff — Croydon.	KLR294	SIM1020B	24.1.50	15798. 6086	General check over - service. — change oils.
H.26.	Oakland Metal Co Ltd.	KCC896	SIM.740.	26.1.50	·11	General check over.
H.27.	Turner Riley	MPJ219	7LM421.			Rectify dynamo. not charging.
H.28.	Dr Compton	2XT943	7LM618G	27.1.50		Fit service gearbox.
H.29.	Dent.	JM3	7L314.	27.1.50		Fit new stay bar for front wing brackets.
H.30	O'Kell	KLO123	7LM627G	30.1.50		Straighten front bumper - spray wheels - front wing.
H.31.	Dr Robinson	EUH926	91P1520	30.1.50	1319.	Fit Saloon heater.
H.32	Leigh Lee	GWP777	7L310	30.1.50		2° Beam - new otherwise.
H.33.	Lee Dr Gamley	U.MX875	91P1506	31.1.50	3098.	Convert to single arm steering — service.
H.34.	Dr Habson.	KXM943	91M1530	31.1.50	2459	Convert to single arm steering — service.
H.35	Mr. Stevens.	7L-391.	2VH-765	31.1.50	12859.	Exchange Steering Column.

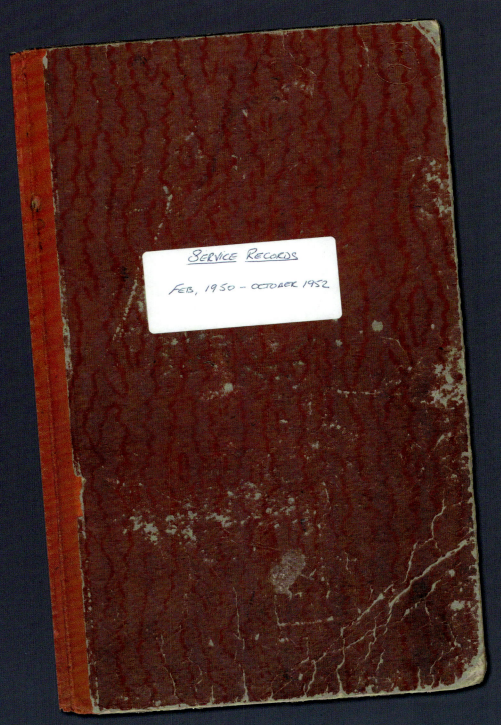

Service Records

Feb, 1950 – October 1952

ALLARD
SERVICE RECORDS

FEBRUARY 1950 – OCTOBER 1952

Job Nos.		Reg. No.	Chassis No.	Date	Mileage	
36.	Emmet. 3 Grosvenor Cottages. SW1.	NJO504	81M1052B	1.2.50.	5913	Check gear change - engine tune - retraction period
37.	Mr. Quinnell.	KXC-160.	41K-695.	2.2.50.		
38.	De Rouet.	JSW749	41M735	2-2-50		Fit Trico 3 note horn.
39.	Mrs. Campbell.	UMX720	91M1534	6/2-50	1904	One demisti (Berkshire) 2 snow tyres.
40.	Offords.	KLU7	41M1084	6-2-50	12981	Decoke. check car over.
41.	Napper.	KGC893	81M709	6-2-50	15900	Play in diff. 15000 ml service. Play in steering.
42.	Barclay Ingles.	C.KX146	7IL455Q	6-2-50.		Repair to front of car after accident.
43.	Car Sales. Mr S.H.A. Co.	KVLL69		6-2-50.		Fit new dynamo. and fan belts.
44.	Goswell.	KLM9	91M606	8/2/50	4387	2 Beams.
45.	Handy.	KXF819	81M1100	8/2/50		Repair O/S Front wing.
47.	Champ.			8/2/50		Adjust Brakes, Check Rear Axle & Gearbox levels.
48.	Craig	UMC938	41M1058B	10/2/50	7197	Decoke - machined heads - Twin Solex bodywork.
49.	Richards	9LT6	71M228	10/2/50	8068	Packing in rear spring
50.	Godfrey	KYMC69	41P1548	10/2/50	1200	Fit 2 pedal rubbers - 1 chrome hub disc
51.	O'Kell	KLO12B	71M627G	13/2/50	1577	Decoke - machined heads.
52.	Leicester Garage Ltd	EPM96	81M1007B	13/2/50	11143	Decoke machined heads - twin "Solex" 3.78
53.	Car Mart. Oh MS5113.	DVG440	91P1552.	13/2/50	599	Fit Galley heater
54.	Le Mesurier.	SMH812	71M550	13/2/50	1438	Service.
55.	Barber. Coll &/ Slick & Rose Mewin Ltd. Keyworth Works	VAL317	81M758	14/2/50	1357	Decoke - convert to central gear change
56.	Adlards - Brixton.	JYV272	71M272	14/2/50	17193	Fit Solex type heater.

#		Regn.	Chassis	Date	Mil.	
57	Dimbleby	DLK 957	71M 331	15/2/50	32600	Check beam - charge over headlamp charge lips.
58	Mr Rumford	KLP5		15/2/50		New Falcon bracket.
59	Davis	KLF651	71M449P	16/2/50	3746	Change spring - service - check car over.
60	Richardson	"Kaxle with Columbia"		16/2/50		Repair Columbia axle.
61	Lindsay	TML804	51M1050B	17/2/50	3486	Service change oils modified 1st rev beam. Work.
62	Layton	CVG428	71L298	17/2/50	20820	Fit 3·78 - Remove Columbia - extra leaf rear spring.
63	Broomfield	JMX450	91P1538	17/2/50	970	1000 ml service. Faulty Sol. switch.
64	Godsal	NFC139	71M527	20/2/50	23123	3·78 - Twin carbs. chassis check.
65	White	MNW474	71M566	20/2/50		New HT Lead.
66	Park Garage	JGY 720	71L140	20/2/50		Tune
67	Mr Rom Greenhalgh	KLL999	91M1001B	21/2/50		3·78 Ratio axle. Service - pantwork.
68	Velvet Cheque Paper	SMX835		21/2/50		Supply & fit interior light
69	Arthur Gadsel	New Car	91P1593	21/2/50		Supply and fit heater.
70	Rumford	KLD5	619	22/2/50		Supply & fit 6" Beam.
71	Imhof	NNY326	91M858	22/2/50	14060	Replace car in original condition after Rally.
72	Dr Edwards	EBX 761	71M610	23/2/50	15629	Recalb. temp gauge check indicators - wing
73	A.P. Noble	DRD923	61M749	24/2/50	6430	Change axle beam 2° check front end & shackers.
74	Rees	GVW69	71K600	25/2/50	13931	Bracket in rear spring.
75	Deacon	JUC302	71M400	25/2/50	13109	Service change oils.
76	D.P. Johnson	MZ1201	71M401	25/2/50	1453	Cracked bowl corners - 91A gearbox.

77	Tanner Riley	MPJ 219	71M421	27/2/50		New Silencer
78	De Ranet	9YW949	71M735	27/2/50	12394	Petrol pump 2° Beans
79	Bellamy Knight	9PX509	71M532	28/2/50	8188	Service Fit foam adjust brakes tune engine
80	Mrs Campbell	11M720 UMX720	91M1534	28/2/50	4309	Check car over - remove heads examine block service etc
81	Dimbleby	91K957	71M331	28/2/50	33190	Collect car from Kingston rectify engine fault
	March					
82	Stevens	ENT184	71M509	1/3/50	2849	Change axle beam 2°
83	Adkin	KYP636	71L905B	1/3/50		5000 service Fit foam Repair N/S wearing
84	Sykes	KLM661	91M818	2/3/50	13174	Decoke tune Salon 1 Type - front spring - check rear shockers
85	Evan	4TH 50	91P 1580	2/3/50	1381	Bodywork - front suspension battery - electrical
86	De Eaton Garage	FPY 621	81M984	3/3/50	7742	Convert to centre change
87	Symondson	KKX672	71K248	6/3/50	21013	Engine - play in steering - mudflaps front wings
88	Riddell	KLX493	71K639	6/3/50	3269	Extra fuel line SU pump check plugs
89	De Jannin	UMC24	81M1043B	6/3/50		Service - change engine oil
90	De Haer	NEV26	71M399	6/3/50		Repair bracket
91	AMC Car Sales	KUW465	71K622	7/3/50	4813	Check tank - check axle nuts - fit rubber on bonnet
92	Barclay Inglis	LKX196	71L455Q	7/3/50		Fit new ex. silencer
93	Goldthorpe	THX323	91K367	7/3/50	11423	Repair N/S Silencer
94	Forrow Shrenberry	—	P1604	8/3/50	N/C	Heater avenders wing mirrors
95	Austin	THH383	71L695	8/3/50	7530	Service tune
96	Anthony Gould	KYO650	91P1593	9/3/50	—	5000 Service

H.						
97	O'Kell.	71M6279	KCO123	9/3/50	2747	Repair gearbox.
98	Car Sales A.M.C.	81M 745	MRB991	9/3/50	6358	Change engine. Fit decline gearbox - with c/s clutch
99	White	71M566	MNW474	11/3/50		Clean carb - new float.
100	Rapper	81M 709	KGC893	13/3/50	17681	
In						
1.	Owen.	71K	CHM316	13/3/50		Adjust brakes. — New pet float unit.
2.	Craddock.	71L201	SMH107	13/3/50	15555	Decoke. adjust brakes. check levels. S.C. felt.
3.	Tate of Leeds	P1608	—	13/3/50	—	Fit Radiomobile and Heater.
4.	Patten.	71M594	9.Y.M272	13/3/50	20834	Blown gasket. adjust brakes. bodywork.
5.	Stevens.	71M613	EBK338	14/3/50	16073	Grease spray — retard ignition
6.	Quennell.	71K 696	KXC162	14/3/50	5399	Supply & Fit Scintilla.
7.	White	71M566	MNW474	14/3/50	10326	Fit Radiomobile - Service change oils tuned (9/13/11926)
8.	Graham.	81M1053	QB7202	16/3/50	10134	Personal cap road. 6 blade fan. bodywork.
9.	Mrs. Copley.	P1502		16/3/50		Brake squeak. Rough on tick. Clock not working.
10.	Crump.	81M730	KDP466	17/3/50	102686	Decoke. Supply type and wheel.
11.	Lockyer.	71K 553	KTA309	18/3/50	15611	Face up on flange. Kingpins - brake linings - repair screen.
12.	Greenhalgh.	81M1001K	KLL999	20/3/50	11058	Repair O/S front wing
13.	Foran.	71M6589	AGL377	20/3/50	5133	Service — change oil
14.	Fowler.	71M656	TMH616	20/3/50	5996	Decoke — machined heads.
15.	Lyndsay.	81M 1050	TML 804	21/3/50	3663	Change belts. Repair damage on rear wings
16.	Dr. Hobson.	91M1530	KXM943	21/3/50	4090	Service change oils repair rear bumper.

I

17	O. Kell.	71M627	KLO 123	21/3/50	3201	Remove pistons.
18.	Blockley.	71K 595	9VK438	23/3/50	16389	Service - rear panel repair. check car for Ireland Rally.
19	Shen Simond	81M883	FMW416	22/3/50	8695	2 Solex carbs. drop sump for cleaning
20.	Bellamy Knight.	71M532	9PX507	22/3/50	9234	Twin carb manifold. change front spring
21.	Steven.	71L391	LVK765	22/3/50	14142	Repair puncture.
22	Imhof.	71M217	9G45	23/3/50	5422	Fit engine and gearbox.
23	Waller.	KLY29	41M1071	23/3/50	3605	Service change oil line.
24.	Adkin.	RYP636	71L905B	23/3/50	1206	1000 mile service D.I.H. chipper.
25.	Furness.	—	P.1611	23/3/50	—	Fit Radiomobile and Heater.
26	Lavenuga.	71K455A	9KD574	24/3/50	1724	Fit 2 Solex carbs. time engine. 2 Goodyear tyre & tubes.
27	Le Renart.	81M735	9VW749	27/3/50	13252	Decoke. Coil wings.
28.	Bromfield.	P.1538	41MX450	27/3/50	1660	Twin carb - heads (alt).
29	D W Price.	89M1097	KUC40	27/3/50	10213	Reality miss in engine steering wander.
30	Powiggn	6K 123	CRJ218	27/3/50		Steering Petrol gauge Tune engine.
31	Dent.	71L314	9LM3	27/3/50	28363	Exchange engine R586345P. — old engine 7190989
32	Barclay Ingles.	71L453	L.KX146	28/3/50	24341	Service
33	Gallings	71L393	9LT913	28/3/50	4869	Decoke - check brakes.
34	Lt Col Bailey	71M 542	GOR 827	28/3/50	9343	Replace wheel kingpin service
35	Forrest Riley	71M 421	M.PJ 219	29/3/50		Service. Slip in clutch. adjust hand throttle. Clean Reg. club
36	Emmet.	81M1052	NJ0509	29/3/50		Blown gaskets - set of plugs

No.	Name			Date		Work
37	Evans	6L 102	HLB624	29/3/50	6461	Sped cabl leakdway leak.
38	Dr McCarthy	7LM614	9YV272	29/3/50	18906	Tune carb. adjust broke - service.
39	Rumpett	—	—	29/3/50	—	Build 1.P.U. Gearbox.
41	Wyatt	7LM618	9YT.943	3/4/50	26421	General check over.
42	Griffith	8LM802	KNK24	4/4/50	15315	Decoke.
43	Dr Vardy	9LM769	CHW523	4/4/50	19372	Change axle beam for 2° - Pressure cup used.
44	Emett	8LM1052	MJO604	4/4/50	6501	3.78
45	Stone	9YM277	7LM594	4/4/50	21129	Noise on front suspension.
46	Dr Beggen	M1070	90P851	9/4/50	4696	Clutch judder - general check - bodywork.
47	Dr Sireman	M1059	90N971	9/4/50	5223	Steering tramp.
48	Dr Tanvnir	M1013	UMC924	5/4/50	15364	Service change oil - tune
49	Godfrey	9LP1548	KYM669	11/4/50	2885	Decoke, Machined heads. Tune carbs. Adjust brakes. fit new front springs. Check shock absorbers. General check over
50	Sales Dept, Acre Lane.	9LP1595	KYP630	11/4/50	885	S/f Machine. Change engine oil. Check top up all levels. Adjust brakes. Advance ignition. Check for rattles. Rectify non light
51	Quennell	7LK696	KXC162	12/4/50	·	3.78 Ratio.
52	Nattey	7LL932	CHW69	13/4/50	21932	Salex twin carb manifold - Scintilla Vertex.
53	Anstham Gerolds	9LP1593	KYO669	13/4/50	969	1000 mls service - door switch - change dyn. pulley.
54	Dagenham	8LM870	FRY999	14/4/50	10718	Fit saloon type heater.
55	Dr Carter	EPM96	8LM1007	14/4/50	12417	Shackle bushes. 2 air cleaners.
56	Mr White	7LM566	MNW474	17/4/50	157/11264	Decoke - machined heads.
57	Millwood	7LM231	9LM245	17/4/50	29218	2 Silencers 10" deep own - Fram cartridge
58	Housby	7LM328	9YO646	17/4/50		Decoke - 2° beam. 3.78.

I

59	Shea Simonds	81M853	FMW416	19/4/50	8977	Engine vibration
60.	I R Thompson	ML309	BUC301	19/4/50	6210	Accident damage.
61	I B Mann Co.	—	—	—		Wings and bumper
62	Gosnell	7IM606	KLM9	19/4/50	6068	Decoke — change front spring
63.	McDonell	7IM440	DYE359	20/4/50	17096	Cowl wings.
64.	Larenaga	7IK485	JKD877	20/4/50		Rectify carb settings.
65.	R.S. Busuego 33 Han Place S.W.1.	Mercury	AXO692	21/4/50		Decoke
66	Dessa	7IM400	JHC302	21/4/50	13314	Adjust brakes — slow running
67	Du Haut	7IM397	NEV26	21/4/50		1. Silencer.
68	Du Jannin	M1013	UMC924	21/4 21/4/50		Coachwork.
69	Maxwell Tulling	KXK865	91M322	24/4/50	5231.	Coachwork. Service time.
70	McDonell	KUC36	Fixed Prefect	24/4/50		Fit Philco car Radio — Check over car.
71	Davis	KLF681	7IM447	24/4/50	4888	Decoke. Rear spring.
72	Anathan Charlels	KVL949	91A1567	24/4/50	1420	Service. Adjust heater control
73	Barthenbank	MPJ200	81M720	24/4/50	10982.	Decoke. front spring - coachwork.
74	Dagenham Motor	DMC538	81M1066	27/4/50	6867.	Fit air duct.
75	Kenning Ltd Sheffield Zest.	Chassis Frame & front susp		26/4/50		Chassis frame repair with front suspension only
76	Car Mart Ch. PL3835.	7IL866	KXH502	27/4/50	3630.	3.78 Ratio
77	Walker	7IM506	DBA631.	27/4/50	12565.	Service. Tune.
78	Earl Farquharson	81M874	KUK657	27/4/50	14119	Change front spring. bodywork.

79	Atkin	KYP 636	71C905	1/5/50	3272	Tonneau cover - service
80	Bromfield	UMX 450	91P1538	1/5/50	2172	Service - fit high pressure SU Pump
81	Bloakley	94K850	71K595	2/5/50	18184	Front bumpers. Prepare for Alpine Rally
82	Major Rolli	91P1595	94P630	2/5/50	1443	Service
83	Evans	HLB924	61C102	2/5/50		Change front spring and peack bolts
84	Greenhalgh	KLL 999	31M1001	2/5/50		Exchange E62A Dis
85	Twentyman	GUK 660	71K 713	3/5/50	5913	Low oil pressure
86	Cramp	KBP466	81M730	3/5/50	11736	Bonnet handle
87	Wish	9VT 950	71M326	3/5/50	16579	Noise from 54 prop & dynamo pulley
88	Wild	NRO 126	81M 889	4/5/50	13983	Replace starter
89	Napper	KGC 893	81M709	8/5/50	19348	Service - change steering box
90	Car Sales	K.U.W. 565	71K62	8/5/50	5902	Jumping out of 2nd gear - Service
91	A.M.C	KYP 640	91P1362	8/5/50	740	Replace rear shocker
92	Gibbs	KYM 774	91P1551	9/5/50	6856	Brakes noisy. Demister not working
93	Charley	EPM 890	71M1014	10/5/50	8900	Decarbs - service wheel bump bodywork
94	Natty	CHW 29	71C482	10/5/50		Fit 3.78 in exchange for 3.6
95	Maxwell Telling	KXK865 KX	91M1522	10/5/50		Coachwork
96	Godsal	NFC 139	71M527	11/5/50		Bodywork
97	Barber	CCF 915	P1618	11/5/50	1242	Change front shockers. Brakes
98	Dermer	GRT 218	61C 123	11/5/50	19892	Rot - fan assembly
99	Richardson	OYT 847	71K609	12/5/50	24250	2° Axle beam

I

100	Bell.	Daimler 15	AXA 102	12/5/50	12240	Decoke.
H 1	Stone	71M599	PMM 271	15/5/50	22212	2 Solex carbs
H 2	Bramfield	P1535	UMY450	15/5/50	2365	Scintilla Vertex
H 3	O'Kill	71M679	KLO123	15/5/50	5536	Service - change engine oil
4	Mrs Johannesson	71M463	QB2119	16/5/50	7032	Check on own.
5	J R Knowles	71M330	PKH996	15/5/50	7811	Rectify wiring
6	Rummell	71K696	KXC162	16/5/50		Fit aluminium 30hp heads
7	Greenhalgh	71M1001	KPP999	16/5/50		Fan belt
8	Faulkner	91P1532	DUG 440	16/5/50	4825	Tune
9	Walker	71M506	DPA 651	16/5/50	12685	2° Beam. Front spring
10	Kennings Ltd	Chom Frame		16/5/50		Repair and enamel
11	Decca	71M400	JYC 302	16/5/50		Grease check also running
12	Kelvin Ct Garage	WOM Gearbox		17/5/50		Convert to Blocker ring
13	Nipper	71M709	KGC 893	18/5/50	19673	
14	Cranwell Manns 8		CG 9975	18/5/50		Crank wing - decoke
15	Car Mart	71M781	KDK799	22/5/50	12363	Check over for sale
16	Fram	71M658	AGL377	22/5/50	8527	Service fit banks air cleaner
17	Dr Darwin	71M1013B	UMC924	22/5/50	17028	Service - change engine oil
18	Mrs Egerton	91M 1524	UMU 360	23/5/50	13493	Convert to single arm steering
19	Car Sale		KYP640	23/5/50		Repair wiper resistor, adjust brakes

J

No.	Name			Date		Description
20.	Godfrey.	91P 1548	KYM669	23/5/50	—	Indicator.
21.	Evans.	71C 360.	LHT839.	23/5/50.	12297	Decoke.
22	Skinne.	81M 767.	KLD423	24/5/50	11598.	Twin Solex carbs & manifold
23.	Major Constandares	71C224	SMT946	24/5/50	12620.	Service.
24	Evans	61C 102.	HLB 929.	24/5/50	13540	Repair to near hubs
25.	Pratt.	91P 1649.		25/5/50.	282	New stop switch. from head lamp.
26.	Dagenham Motors.		LUM956	25/5/50.		
27	Emmett.	81M 1052	NJO504	30/5/50	7051	Decoke - reversing lights, brake.
28	Le Messurier	71M550.	TMH 812	30/5/50.	13355	Decoke - coachwork
29	Car Mart.	71M503.	JPJ60	30/5/50	13900	Prepare for sale
30	Standard Range Steam Co.	91P 1697	CGP1.	30/5/50	462	500 service
31	Clark	81M816	SYJ088	30/5/50	17575	Snap on road.
32	Grundy.	91P 1650	KYP638	31/5/50	461	500 service — change prop shaft
33	Rev. Greenhalgh.	81M 1001	KLC 999.	1/6/50	13900	Master cylinder Service.
34	Crump.	81M730	KBP466	1/6/50.	14287	Service repair indicator switch
35	Rev — Chichester.	91P 1597	CPO247	1/6/50	9952	Quarantee work.
36	Col Dailey	71M 542	GOR527	1/6/50.	11918	Service.
37	Dr. Clark.		KLC135	1/6/50		Service.
38	Pearson.	71C449A	TMH 809.	1/6/50	20139	General overhaul - bodywork
39	Cam Bell	71C 351	JCJ522	1/6/50.	13928	99 Torque convert from 32 hp

J						
40.	Porteous.	81M 828	NN48	2/6/50	18516	Check timing.
41.	De Raad.	81M 735.	9YW749.	2/6/50.		Service.
42.	Millward.	71M 231.	9 LM 245.	5/6/50.	30526.	Brakes.
43	Bellamy Knight.	71M 532.	9PX 507.	5/6/50.	12967.	Tune – brakes.
44	Stone.	71R 599	9YM 272.	6/6/50.	22855.	Clutch slip.
45.	Leslie Millward.	71L 478A	LHW478	6/6/50.	13156.	Decoke etc.
46.	QK Hardy.	81M 1100B.	KXF819.	6/6/50.	4213	Service
47.	Messrs Sumer Riley Co.	71M- 481.	MP5. 219.	6. 6. 50.		Complete Service
48.	Bertram Smith.	91P.		6. 6. 50		Tune carb. adjust brakes. check batt.
49.	Gallins	71L 393.	JLT 913	6. 6. 50.	5900.	Screen – service.
50.	De Hope Scott.	81M 793.	TME3.	7.6.50	13342	Decoke – brakes.
51	O'Kill	71M 627.	KLO123	7.6.50		Fit saloon type rad 6 Blade fan.
52	Steven.	71L 391.	LVK765	7.6.50	15062	Service.
53.	Broomfield	4MX 950.		7.6.50.		Replace standard manifold.
54	Nelson Garage.	91P 1600	LGO133	7.6.50	914	Change front shockers.
55.	British & Colonial Motors.	71K 755.	9GN 710	8.6.50.		Change on the beams 2°.
56	Adkin	71L 905.	KYP636	8.6.50.	1665	Rectify switch.
57	Bromfield	91P 1538.	4MX450	8.6.50.	2688.	Replace standard manifold.
58.	Standhill Garage.	91P 1549.	CHL437.	9.6.50.	2281.	Change 3.78 ratio (noisy) engine bin.
59.	De Vandz.	81M 769.	LHW523.	9.6.50		New silencer.
60.	Mann Egerton Norwich	91P 1623.	DVG 779	10.6.50.	520	Change engine & Crown&pinion

J						
61.	Penny.	81M1064	FBL687	10/6/50	13886	Adjust brakes.
62.	Stewart.	7LL484R	THX560.	12/6/50.	9562.	Ali head linin. manifold Solex 3.78.
63.	Owen.	91K145	CHM316	12/6/50		Repair grille service
64.	Maxwell Telling	91M1522	KXK865.	13/6/50.		New dynamo pulley adjust brakes.
65.	Dueren	91P1630	LGK100	14/6/50	2144	Service Dynamo work
66.	Standard Rang	91P1649	LGP1.	14/6/50	1000	Service.
67.	De Banken.	91P1670	CCF915.	14/6/50	2644	Sleef on gymbers
68.	Chesterfield Garden Garage	81M1021	KLO196	14/6/50	5350	Noise on front suspension brakes.
69.	Hollingsworth.	91P1640	CDY177	14/6/50	1673	Change front shockers
70.	Horsley.	71M328	940676	14/6/50	—	Check rear shockers
71.	Fitzhenry Robinson.	91M1068	UMD798	14/6/50	9592	Tune service
72.	Imhof.		HLP5.	15/6/50		Fit coil adjust brakes.
73.	Alzatt.		9XT.943.	15/6/50.		Check brakes.
74.	Arthur	71L405B	KYP636	16/6/50	1947	Alter grille Tune Solex
75.	White	71M56C.	MHW474	17/6/50		Service
76.	De Dickson.	71L429R	CHY474	19/6/50	5606	Suspension
77.	W.H. King	P1669	N/car	19/6/50	N/car	Fit Heater
78.	Grundy	P1650.	KYP633	20/6/50	1453.	1000 mil service.
J.79	Goldthorp.	71K367R	THK333.	20/6/50	14599	Tank strip brakes service brakes.
J.80	Cyprien.	71L388.	SMX278.	20/6/50.	26422.	Reline brakes.

J.

81.	Stewart.	7IL484	THX560	21/6/50	9654	Decoke.
82.	J. Reise	7IL387	LYM1	21/6/50.	16159.	Decoke. Check shacker.
83.	Dr Keighley	P1593	KYO689	21/6/50	2536 7378	Charge drag arm – bodywork.
84	Car Sales.	7IK622.	KUW565	21/6/50	7378.	Service.
85.	Mudell	P1649	VHX560	21/6/50.	963.	1000 Service
86.	George Hartwells Bournemouth.	P1615.	KEL821.	24/6/50	2875.	Water leak on body – steering.
87.	Harris Cardiff Dr Robinson.	P1620	EIH726.	24/6/50.	4952.	Agama. – bodywork.
88.	H. Young Motors Ltd.	P1566.	KUP904	24/6/50	6206.	Steering – bodywork.
89.	Hansley.	7IM328	9YO646.	26/6/50.	8636.	P. Type rear spring conversion.
90.	Salmond.	P1657.	KYP635.	26/6/50	1735.	1000ml service.
91.	Blockley.	7IK595.	9YK438	26/6/50.	18876.	Repair bonnet sides – silencer & top temp – cooler.
92	Walker.	7IM506	DBA631.	26/6/50.	12075.	Silencer – spedo.
93	Paulden.	7IM7265	QB7315	26/6/50.		Rear Hand. steering.
94	Cramp	8IM730	KBP466.	26/6/50		Repair petrol tank.
95	Maxwell Telling	7IM1522	KXR865	26/6/50.		Replace window in hood.
96	Davis	7IM447	KLC81	28/6/50.	5884	Repair gearbox.
97.	Fredrick.	7IL201	SMH107.	28/6/50	18842	Service.
98	Cam Bell.	7IL351	JLT522	28/6/50.		Replace thermo – repair gear lever.
99	Emmet.	8IM1052	NJO509	28/6/50.		Bulb in lamp.
100.						

1.	Stewart	71C489	THX560	30/6/50	9886.	2.Tyres. SU pump.
2	Car Sales.	71K622	KHW565	30/6/50	7435.	Change for 2° beams.
3	Dr Wiseman.	81M1059.	90N971	1/7/50.	9744.	Decoke. service.
4	Car Mart.	71M503.	9F960.	1/7/50		Balance wheels.
5	Cyprien	71C388.	SMX278	1/7/50.	—	Balance wheels adjust brakes. clutch bear
6	McMason - Repetition Dead Turning Co.	P1628.	NOJ343.	3/7/50.	4399.	Decoke. Twin solex. Guarantee Work.
7	Mrs Johnson.	71M322.	9YO194	4/7/50	7687.	Repair to rear axle.
8	Farm.	71M658.	AGL377.	4/7/50.	11013.	Decoke. Clutch judder.
9	Thompson	71M265.	QB7315.	4/7/50	13776.	Coachwork Hood. steering column
10	C H Brewer.	81M760.	OPE237	5/7/50	500.	Rear spring - 500 service
11	Bellamy Knight	71M532	JPX507.	5/7/50.		2° Beams - Rattles in front.
12	Dr McCarthy.	9YV272	71M614	6/7/50	25665.	Mercury engine - brakes - bodywork.
13	Wallis.	71K639.	KLX473. 40TT	6/7/50	4871.	Extra head gaskets. Service.
14	Godfrey.	91P1548.	KTM669	10/7/50.	7251.	Change shockers. Parking plate. Tune engine.
15	Wyatt.	71M618.	9YT943	10/7/50.	28827.	Decoke.
16	Mrs Campbell.	91M1534	UMX720	10/7/50	8249	Front suspension - throttle slack. Service
17	Bramfield.	P1538.	UMX650	10/7/50.	3320	Service
18	Hardy.	81M1100.	KXF819.	11/7/50.	6657.	Decoke. Service - bodywork.
19	Godfrey	81M1005.	KLL736	11/7/50.	12549.	Rattles shockers.
20	Major Constandros	71C229	SMT946.	11/7/50	14980.	Change front spring.

K.

No.	Name			Date	Job No.	Work
21.	H.M.C. Moore.	P 1651.	KLJ 90	11/7/50	2242.	Shocker 5½" drop arm. Badly peark.
22	Da Costa.	61M 1004	GPM 96	11/7/50	15678.	Check brakes - line service.
23	Messrs. Hewitt Davis & Marsh Ltd.	71L. 903.	281. 7/5.	13.7.50.		Repairs to Accident Damage.
24	Mr. Evans.		HLB 424.	13.7.50.		
25	Messrs. Car Mart Ltd.	71M. 681.	HLO. 133.	13.7.50.		
26.	D.R. Clark	81M 953	KLL 138	17.7.50	22367	Decoke. Pressurised Radiator. Exam, Grease & change oils.
27.	J. Frey	71L 203	MWL 380	17.7.50	15571	Pressurised Radiator. Service. Adjust Brakes. 6 Bladed fan
28	Edmunds Morris 8.	-	CG 9925	17.7.50		Check Brakes. Clean Brake linings. fit cable.
29	Mr. Wallis	71K 639	KLX 473	18/7/50	5895	Twin SUs. Twin Manifold. New Rear Tyres. Check Brakes. Check Under Cylinders. Decoke if required. 6 Bladed fan. Pressurised radiator. 2nd Gear jumps out. Tune Engine.
30.	British & Colonial Motors Ltd	71K 755	JON 710	18/7/50		
31	Mr. Godfrey	91P 1548	KVM 669	18/7/50	71565	Check Shockers, Track. Balance Wheels.
32	Mr. De Lent			18/7/50		Send fitter to Foxes Garage, Brights Lane. fit Gear change bracket
33	Klayehart	71M 327	KLF 639	18/7/50	22613	Check Brakes, Transmission. Replace tyres if necessary. Balance wheels. Check Electrical system steel wobble.
34	Mr. Champ	81M 730	KBP 466	19/7/50	15927	Check Brakes. Check for Water Leak. Tune Engine.
35	K.C. Clarke Baton	71M 613	FBK 338	20/7/50	16465	Fit Roloflow front shockers. Bonnet spring. Change Engine oil
36	Mr. Goldstein	91P 1635	LGK 36	20/7/50	2392	Check Track & Shocker 5½ Drop Arm. Change Engine oil. Check Petrol Pipe. Check Hub nuts. Adjust Brakes
37	Davies	71M 478	KLF 681	21/7/50	6332	Fit Modified Gear box. Bend in Steering.
38	W.A. Howell	81M 799	NUX 630	24/7/50	15094	2° Beam.
39	Car Sales	71K 622 86116	KUW 365	24/7/50	4616	Brakes ... ... Clean
40	N.C. Cemley (Charlton) Ltd.	P 1652	KYP 654	25/7/50	2372.	Brakes - dynamo. bodywork.

K

No.	Name			Date		Notes
41.	Stewart.	71L484	THX560	26/7/50		Check carbs. – fit 6 Blade fan.
42.	Drew	91P.1630	CGK100	26/7/50	4342.	Service – fit 9D plate
43.	Cyprien.					Transfered to K5
44.	Da Costa	8P1007	EPM96	26/7/50		New reflector assembly
45.	Mr. Esotto	81M1066	UMC538	26/7/50	7602.	Service. 4 Tyres. Tune
46.	Dr. Habson.	91M1530.	KXW963	27/7/50	9378	Brake.
47.	County Garage Ltd.	P1501.	DHH556	28/7/50	18000	Check brakes change rear shockers.
50.	Car Sales	91P1633	KYP690	28/7/50	4959.	Adjust brakes fit 9B plate
51.	Swiss	91P1688	LCC40.	28/7/50	400.	500 Service
52.	Stonecliffe Close Garage	81M1104.	KLO196.	28/7/50	5537.	Front spring discontact – axle noise.
53.	Wyatt.	71M618.	9XT443	28/7/50.		
54.	Leister	91P1686	CFM1	31/7/50	729	Repair gearbox.
55.	Vincent. Morris Minor 1950	51MM/31501.	KLV23	31/7/50	8382.	Brake service.
56.	Beamish	81M764	UMK807	1/8/50	14392	Fit air scoop.
57.	Nunton	91P1654	CGX671	1/8/50	2554	Brakes bleed, grease bolts
58.	Gibb	P1551	KYM779	1/8/50	10.669	Wheel wobble
59.	White	71L312	9X0634	3/8/50.	15099	Service Tune engine.
60.	Salmond	P1657	KYP635	3/8/50	4213.	Accident damage service
61.	Sutcliffe	P1643	9KW155	3/8/50.	4932.	Wheel wobble.
62.	King of Kings Egan	P1669.	BJE990	3/8/50	2275	Accident damage.

63.	Car Sales.	71K622	KUW565	3/8/50.		Service. Rectify brake gear.
64	Car Sales.	81M858	NNU326	4/8/50.		Service.
65	Cyprien.	71L388	SMX278	4/8/50.		Triplex rear seal.
66	Gadsal.	71M527	NFC139	4/8/50.		Check tune.
67	Dr Habson	B.S.1.22956.	9TC.763.	4/8/50.	16196.	Decoke — broken piston
68	Mill Garage.	Gearbox.		4/8/50.		W041 content to I.P.U.
69	Sir Patrick Ferguson	51M1096	LTA300	8/8/50	14336.	Decoke.
70	Carruthers	71M526	HDF396	8/8/50	30962.	32bp Mercury engine.
71	Steven	71L391.	LVK765	8/8/50	14752.	Service.
72	Da Costa.	81M1007.	EPM96	8/8/50		New silencer.
73	Ray	71M329	KWE28	9/8/50.	14898.	Steering wander.
74	Parker.	91P1915.	WME227	9/8/50.	519.	Clutch cover leak - check steering.
75.	Bellamy Knight	71M532	9PX507	11/8/50.	16017.	Service. Adjust brakes
76.	Cable.	P1611		11/8/50.		Heater tap — Change front silencer.
77	Perry. Daimler	EL24 45·619.	ELK136.	14/8/50.	66564	Decoke.
78	P.B. Bettinson & Co.	81M781.	KDE799	14/8/50.	15287.	Accident damage.
79	Dr Marshall The Stable Cottage St Cottage House Guildford	71M536.	9YP.671.	14/8/50.	14098.	New silencer.
80	Watson Lincoln Zep.		PRT566	14/8/50.	27410.	Check steering.
81	Craig.	81M1058.	UMC939	14/8/50	18405.	Service. Fit steering.
82.	Thornley Taylor	71L860.	KPR118	14/8/50	11114.	Brakes.

K.						
83	Broomfield.	P1538.	9MX450.	15/8/50.		Service 5½" drop arm.
84	Denyfield Digby	81M422.	CTK900.	15/8/50.	11373	Decoke. Service
85	Guildthorpe Gn 5572.	71K367.	THX323.		17706	Decoke silencer.
86	Frews.	81M706.	CES575.	16/8/50.	14069	Accident repair.
87	Regster — Payman Bromley	P1614.		16/8/50		Backgeanh steering.
88	Johnson .	M322	9YO194	17/8/50.		Service backworks.
89	A.M.C.	P1632	KYP640	19/8/50	6533	Decoke
90	Greenwood.	P1678.	LGX679.	22/8/50	1254.	Service
91	A.M.C.	P1681	HUS202	22/8/50.	900.	Genneten work.
92	Wyman.	P-1672		22/8/50.	2000	Shockers.
93	Munch.	71M413.	LVK766	22/8/50.	7503.	Service — engine tune.
94	Dr Hobson.	91M1530.	KXM943	22/8/50	10951	Check shockers. Throttle spring — service.
95	A&P.V. Rolls. 25		AGC496.	22/8/50.		Check clutch.
96	Twentyman.	71K713.	GUK660	23/8/50	10613	Brakes.
97	A.M.C.	P1619	DHL-34	28/8/50.	3094.	5½" drop arm
98	Dr Jannin	81M1013B	UMC924	29/8/50		Accident damage to N/S rear wing. Tune Engine New set of Plugs.
99	Dr Thornton — AMC.	P1626		24/8/50.		
100	Bowman.	9148	HRR692	24/8/50.	7531.	Tune engine.

No.	Name				Date	Work
1	Barnell	M606	"KLM9"		25/8/50	Coachwork.
2	Fram.	M658	AGL377	14445	25/8/50	Service - change all oils. From element.
3	Com Everall.	M795	HOR595	5077	25/8/50	Decoke.
4	H.R. Owen Ltd.	91P1552	DXG440	11967	26/8/50	replace shockers. tune cards. sticky throttle
5	K.J. Allen	81M879	UMK735	9615	28/8/50	Decoke & off heads. O/S brake pulls. Replace exchange bracket Clutch juddered N/S wiper blade & arm. Fan dynamo belts if required
6	M. Godfrey	81M1005B	KLL736		28/8/50	Decoke. Sticky throttle. Check Benders. Balance wheel. Punchcovered wiper blade, Speedo Clock & Check Heater clock
7	Mr McGregor	71K554	JFM780	6904	26/8/60	Check levers. Sticky throttle. Bargene Air Cleaned.
8	Car Sales	91P1750		31	28/8/50	heated + de-misted. Over-riders. From oil filler.
9	Hutchinson & Ariel (Le Cooler)	91P1631	GCA866	6856	28/8/50	Change front Shockbarbers. Fit 5½" Drop Arm. attend to wobble.
10	Dobrah	91P1591	MKM109	3772	28/8/50	Change front Shock Absorbers. Fit 5½ Drop Arm. Check Radiator for loss of Water.
11	C.H. Brown	81M760	OPE237	679	29/8/50	Remove blasted Cylinder, fit new rubber. 1000 Mile service
12	Reynolds	81M1073	FMO333	17416	29/8/50	Check front Suspension. Check for over heating. Fit New oil & Dated gauge
13	M. Maysed				30/8/50	Fit New Fan & Dynamo Belts
14	V.G. Boyle	91P1728	KLT3714	581	30/8/50	Tighten rear axle nuts. Check for metallise rattle. Electric on switch Check tyre pressures. Fit heat switch. Squeak back seat 500 Mile Service
15	Charles-Bathon	71M613	FBK338	1.7991	30/8/50	Check Gearbox & rear axle oil. Check Brakes. Steering Column fault
16	Dr. Thornton	91P1626	KOH761	7438	30/8/50	Rectify Steering box leak.
17	M. De Ruet				29/8/50	Collect Car, Deliver to Newlingham Coachworks.
18	Miss Peake	81M881	TMX744	8150	1/9/50	Exhaust Blow. Repair to bring apart.
19	White	81M759	LMB595	13023	4/9/50	2° Beam.
20	Beauman.	71J148	HRR472	8.051	4/9/50	Twin Sales.

21	Imhof.	71M 219	JG445	6772.	4/9/50	Check ignition.
22	Turner Riley	M 421.	MPJ 219	20258.	4/9/50	Decoke – brakes.
23	Adkins.	71L 905	KYPG3C	–	4/9/50	Check brakes. – rear axle leak.
24	Carey Evans.	M 831.	FUM 649	9684.	5/9/50	Decoke. Hum in axle. Fit vents.
25	Lord Latymer.	M 754	K10300	8236.	5/9/50	Check ignition - front shackle.
26	De Rouet.		9KW749		5/9/50	New hood.
27	Parker.	P 1715	WME 227	1609	5/9/50	Guarantee work.
28	Dr Thornton.	P 1626.	KOH 761.		6/9/50	New Sol and stop switch.
29	~~Faskett~~ Bushell.	M 820.	KFJ 599.	6000.	6/9/50	Change Fram – tune – service.
30	~~Millwall~~ Millward.	M 231.	9LM 245.	33305.	6/9/50	Repair gearbox
31	Maxwell Telling.	M 1522	KXK 865.	9368.	7/9/50	Accident damage
32	Goldstein	P 1635.	LGK 36.	3571.	7/9/50	Service .
33	Bell.	Daimler 15.				Engine Tune.
34	Rumbly Motors.		QUE 648.		7/9/50.	Change front spring.
35	Major Constantaras	L 224	SMT 946	16571.	7/9/50	2 Beams.
36	Car Sales.	KYP 640.		7900.	9/9/50	Adjust brakes.
37	Swim .	P 1648.	LLC 40.	1768.	11/9/50	1000 service.
38	Munin .	K 162.	SMC 665	5990.	11/9/50	New radius rod.
39	Dunstan. 13 Bruton St W1.	P 1761.	CLM 565.	300.	12/9/50.	Service .
40.	Caamp.	M 730.	KBP 466.	17513.	11/9/50	Repair to gearbox.

41	Rumfitt.		9FH.613	7954.	12/9/50.	Fit new front and rear spring.
42	White.	M566.	MYW474		12/9/50.	Accident damage — service.
43	Dr Keighley	P1593.	KYO689	4562	12/9/50.	Guarantee work — Hilton
44	Wingfield Digby	M722.	CTK930	13401.	13/9/50	3.78. Twin Solex.
45	H. A. Clayman.	P1590.	VHX883	5497.	13/9/50	Guarantee work. Replace front bumper.
46	Smith	P1517.	KKF752.	7452.	14/9/50	Service. etc.
47	Dick.	M326	9FT950		14/9/50	King pins tight.
48	Gosnell.	M606	KLM9.		14/9/50	Flat spot in carb.
49	Beauman.	9148.	HRR472	8648.	14/9/50	Decoke. New rings on piston.
50	Miles	P1594	KOH43	9019	15/9/50	Accident damage.
51	Decosa.		74C302.	18857.	15/9/50	Bonnet handle - mirror - speedo adjust brakes.
52	Broomfield.	P1538	QKK450.	5926.	18/9/50	Service.
53	Dr Morris.	7LC127.	OGX708	6436.	18/9/50	Service - brakes.
54	Dr Vernon White	M1002B.	HHA478	14654	18/9/50	Front suspension.
55	Atkins.	L905.	KYP636	6624.	19/9/50	Service etc.
56	Black.	M1029B.	KLP820	14534	19/9/50	Noise from rear axle. service - bodywork.
57	Pallard.		KJH505		19/9/50	Fit rear spring shackle.
58	Frey.		MWL380	18664	20/9/50	Brakes & service
59	Mrs Johnson.	M463.	OB2119.	10000.	23/9/50	Set up rear spring.
60	GST Johnson.	P1760	NLG38.	1024	23/9/50	Check ignition

61	D. McDonald Bromington Sewed Reproducen	P4713	KOP52	2677	23/9/50	service. Guarantee work
62	Lf Cyprian	L388	SMX278	32446	25/9/50	Decoke. service
63	Farquharson	14874	KLK657	18946	25/9/50	Service
64	L.H. Newton	M1078	HMD680	19394	25/9/50	Twin Solex. 3·78
65	Sid Millward	M231	9LM243	34301	25/9/50	3·78
66	Mrs Escott	M1066	UMC538	12793	26/9/50	Service – bodywork
67	Raltey Mercury Special	9L9585	L77	924	28/9/50	Decoke
68	A.M.C. Bagle	P1728	KLJ374	1342	29/9/50	Guarantee work
69	Rumfitt		9YH613	8126	29/9/50	4·1 Ratio
70	Dr Charlton A.M.C.	P1782	CPT809	4000	29/9/50	Wheel wobble
71	Smee	P1621		7402	29/9/50	Wiper
72	Dr Habson	91M1530	KXM943	12749	29/9/50	Balance front wheels. service
73	Galling		9LT913	1036	29/9/50	Wheel wobble check Balance. Tune
74			UMC924		29/9/50	
75	Bagle	P1728	KLJ374		2/10/50	Accident damage N/S front wing
76	Lord Allerton	91P1921	9J4514	1152	2/10/50	Clutch judder – noisy axle
77	Major S. Ralli	P1595	KTP630	6519	2/10/50	Wheel wobble. tune engine
78	Turner	M615G	9YR13	15045	2/10/50	Decoke
79	Marshall	91P1649	VHX560	2964	3/10/50	Service. Rear modification
80	Mr Armstrong	M1072B	KWW567	15742	3/10/50	Remove play from steering column. front shackles

81	Tenner Riley.	M421	MPJ 219		3/10/50	New H.T Leads. escheat blew.
82	Craddock.		SMH 107		3/10/50	Fitting 4 tyre
83	Gardner.		NEV 26		3/10/50	917 drop arm.
84	Stracker.	M1003B	KLO 127	18858.	3/10/50	Repair accident damage. Resake.
85	Weck.		L.M.G.		3/10/50	Reset tank.
86	Imhof.	M214.	9.G.U.6.	7728.	4/10/50	Decake etc.
87	✗					
88	Imhof.					
89	Blockley.	K595.	9YK438.	23304	5/10/50	Decake.
90	Richards.	M224	9LT6.	16176	6/10/50	King pin and brake.
91	Car Mart.	M6829.	9OE820.	7521.	6/10/50	Check over for sale.
92	Steeles Garage.	M603.	HRU201		6/10/30	Report on car.
93	Dick.	AM8.	CMG.192.		9/10/50	New valves etc. Fit Fram.
94	Dr Clark.	M853.	KLL 138		9/10/50	Sealing filter to rectify oil starvation.
95	Godfrey.	P1548.	KYM669	10700.	9/10/50	Decake. clutch check gearbox
96	Whiteton	P1724	CLH951	5371	9/10/50	Bodywork checked.
97	Cpt Treen.	KLY14	M1062.	30553	9/10/50	Bodywork - service
98	Central Motor Co.	GBC845.	P1542.	11750	9/10/50	Decoke.
99	Mandell 2 Hyde Pk Place Amb 2451 W2	P1849.	VHX 560		9/10/50	Accident damage to door.
100	Dzett.	M618.	9YT443		9/10/50	Adjust brakes.

M.

No.	Name				Date	Work
1.	Carruthers.	M526.	HDF396	24466.	10/10/50	Tune.
2.	Maxwell Telling.	M1522	KXK865		11/10/50	Window winder. etc
3.	Smith, Chesterfield Gdns Garage.	M1021.	KLO196.		11/10/50	Recoke ½ of head. Twin Solex
4.	Napper.	M709	KGC893		13/10/50	Axle oil leak. adjust brakes.
5.	Winston	PM61.	LLM565	1000	13/10/50	Guarantee — 1000 mls service.
6.	Richmond.	M1525.	KXF820	12801.	13/10/50	3.78. Twin Solex decoke. refit heads. check steering.
7.	Gibbs Fox ... Kingsgate Rve N3.	M1050.	TML804		16/10/50	Service. tune engine
8.	Gibbs Bros	P1540.	JAX234.	6164	14/10/50	Wheel wobble. slack in transmission
9.	Lord Latimer.	M754	KLO300	8987	16/10/50	Decoke
10	Grundy.	M1650.	KYP638	8207	16/10/50	Wobble. adjust brakes.
11	A.J. Perry.	P1553.	KFJ599	6452.	16/10/50	Bodywork. — service engine etc
12	Salmond.	P1657.	KYP635.	7803.	17/10/50	Tune engine Fit lamp & dynamo service
13	Decca.	M400	MUC302	20653	17/10/50	Exchange V830 engine
14	Johnston.	M322.	JYO194	11833.	17/10/50	Service. O/S door.
15	Turner.	615G	JYR13.		17/10/50	Wheel wobble.
16	Cramp.	M730	KBP466.	18998	20/10/50	Fit head Front shocker change polyquops
17	Cyprien.	71C368	SMX278		20/10/50	Rad. hoses. Repair gearbox.
18	Fram,	M658.	AGL377	17490	23/10/50	Service. etc.
19	Gardner.	M397.	NEV26	15910	23/10/50	Repair gearbox. adjust steering column
20.	Mrs Ingatestone	M1087.	SRE801.	12241.	25/10/50	Repair struts. steering wander.

M.

21.	Canven.	K440	DFK62	11091.	26/10/50	Decoke.
22	Farquharson.	KLK657			26/10/50	Check track & brakes.
23	Owe.	P1630	LGK100	9432.	26/10/50	Shackles screws.
24	Dr Hope Scott		TMG3.		26/10/50	Change front shackles – repair wiper drive.
25.	Sgt Holtrout Dr Wiseman.	M1059.	90N971.	16393.	30/10/50	Turn ½" off heads brakes etc.
26.	J. A Thompson.	M265.	QB 7315.	23352	30/10/50	Bodywork – front spring.
27	Danziger	P1826	ERJ220	684	30/10/50	Bad cornering.
28	Parker	P1715.	WME224	2334	30/10/50	Set radius rods.
29	Da Costa.	M1007	EPM96	1614?	30/10/50	Turn service.
30	Owen	P1630	LGK100	9000.	30/10/50	Armstrong shackles – N/S king pin.
31	Dr Clark.	M853.	KLL134		30/10/50	Reline brakes check clutch.
32	Wymer.	P1672.		4000.	30/10/50	Set radius rods – shackles.
33	Gyrien.	7LL388	SMX378		30/10/50	Weld radius rod bracket – pinch bolt.
34	White Central Motor Co Leicester	P1655.	GJF110	4807	30/10/50	Guarantee work.
35	Dr Garvin	M1013		26225	1/11/50	Service
36	Lanevaga.	995 1693	LLP797	3077	2/11/50	Fit high comp gaskets and raise 3.5.
37	Adkin.	7LL905	K4P636	—	2/11/50	Antifreeze – controls.
38	Dr Hope Scott.		TME3.		2/11/50	Rectify wheel wobble repair wiper drive.
39	Winston	P1761.	LLM565.	1615.	2/11/50	Thermostats.
40	Bearman	J148.	HRH472		2/11/50	Service. sold thro' Unwood, Derby – see charms line

M						
41	Fashion Fabrics	P1790.	LXB561	110.	3/11/50	Change starter drive.
42	Parker	P1794	WMC39.	5500	3/11/50	500 service
43	Dagenham Motors.		L.G.P.1.		3/11/50	Fit Armstrong shockers.
44	Col. Crabbe	M782.	GGD769.	13065.	3/11/50	Spring bracket & shock absorber.
45	T. Whittle & Sons	M1046B	KNN919		7/11/50	Wheel tramp.
46	Universal Car Co	P18.34.	New Car.	—	7/11/50	Fit Heater.
47	Emmett.	M1052.	NJ0504	14526	7/11/50	Recon engine — convert to coolie gearchange.
48	Standhill Garage	P1811	MTV953	812	8/11/50	Repair gearbox.
49	Bristol St Motors	P1863	—	—	8/11/50	Fit Heater.
50	Stroker	M1003	KLO127.	19901	9/11/50	Decoke.
51	O.K. Hanily.	M1100B	KXF819		9/11/50	Check U Bolts.
52	Mrs Wright	GWM309.	P1684	7000	9/11/50	Engine tune etc
53	Dagobut Decca	M400	JUC302		9/11/50	New H.T. leads.
54	Turner.	M615.	94R13		10/11/50	Check front suspension.
55	Beauman.	9148.			10/11/50	2. 16×750 Goodyear.
56	Dr Jarvis	M1013	UMC924		11/11/50	Bodywork — front shackle bonder.
57	Mrs Campbell	M1534	MMX720.	13149.	13/11/50.	Set radius rods
58	Shawcliffe Garage.	M1021	KLO196.		13/11/50	Fit Zenith filter - hand throttle - air cleaner.
59	Fashion Fabrics	P1790.	LXB561	899	14/11/50.	
60.	Clapham.	P1690	VHX883.	7299.	14/11/50	Front bumper. Tune etc

M

No.	Name				Date	Work
60	Mrs Inskip	M214	JGU4	17142	15/11/50	Adjust brakes. Change oils service
62	Cravens Garage	P1765	AFA166	1564	15/11/50	Harsh suspension. Fit Heater.
63	Goldstein	P1635	CGK36	5537	15/11/50	Repair gearbox
64	Bushell	M820	KFJ549	9698	16/11/50	Decoke.
65	De Wilmes	L429	CHY474	8714	16/11/50	New rear spring
66	Weck	AM8	LMG192		16/11/50	Estimate for accident repairs
67	Car Mart	M749	DRD723	12225	16/11/50	Check over car etc.
68	Cawling	P1652	KYP637	6000	16/11/50	Fit stop & top switch.
69	Jacques	P1829	MPB216	1800	16/11/50	Fit stop switch.
70	Haydon	M753	HRV739	23435	16/11/50	Decoke relive brakes bodywork.
71	Dagenham Motors		JLF575			Short on wiring
72	Loxton	71L298	CVG428	34000	17/11/50	Exchange engine leak on road play in steering.
73	Le Meaurier	M550	TMH812	20000	17/11/50	Check over car.
74	De Rouel	M735	JFW749	22800	18/11/50	Water Pump
75	Car Mart	M6274	KLO123	10870	18/11/50	Oil consumption and pressure — judder on suspension
76	Maxwell Telling	M522	KXK865		21/11/50	Repair headlamp.
77	Walker	71M506	NBA631	6032	21/11/50	New silencer service
~~78~~	~~Parker~~		~~Ealing~~			
79	Ramfitt	Gearbox Repair			21/11/50	Repair gearbox (only)
80	Mrs Escott	M1066	GMG538	14543	21/11/50	Fit Heater Service

M.

81	Cheetham.	M1523.	KXK714	15197	22/11/50	Check valves change seals. Tune carb.
82	Garnell.	M606	KLM9.	11435.	23/11/50	Repair gearbox
83	Godfrey.	M1005.	KLL736	1530.	24/11/50	Repair engine.
84	Turner Riley.	M421	MPJ219	—	24/11/50	Adjust brakes.
85	Critchley.		FXL657		25/11/50	Tune engine
86	Beacon Jn.	P1728.	KLJ374	2401	25/11/50	Accident damage.
87	Wallis.	K639	KLXF73	12938	27/11/50	Check valves — repair ex manifold.
88	Reynolds Garage Barnsley	P1508.	CHE940	11355	27/11/50	Wheel wobble
89	Dr McCarthy.	M614	9VV272	32603	27/11/50	Single carb manifold.
90	Mrs Stonhoe.	M1087	SRE801	13316	27/11/50	Recake.
91	Stonehill Garage.	P1638.	LRR587	6805.	28/11/50	Accident damage - convert to R/Hdrive
92	Godfrey.		KYM669.		1/12/50	Front coil spring.
93	Parker.	P1715.	WME227	2889.	1/12/50	Pull to left brakes sway bracket.
94	Barker.	M354	JYK439	27295	1/12/50	Ex recon engine - brakes
95	McFram.	M658	AGC377	15841	2/12/50	Noisy tappet
96	Snowdon.	P1863	KOX744	844.	4/12/50	500 Service.
97	Broomfield	P1538	UMX450	17268	4/12/50	Service.
98	Stone.	P1613.	LYD165	5959.	5/12/50	Accident damage - beaten. set radius rods
99	Adkins.	C905.	KYP636	9580	6/12/50	Service
100	Cyprien.	M388.	SMX246.		6/12/50	New king pin and brakes.

N.						
1	Hindle	M1027	KNN897	25994	6/12/50	Check oil pressure and steering
2	De Klee	M445	MRB441	14863	6/12/50	King pins and bushes
3	Balfam	M309	UMV59	8448	8/12/50	Accident damage
4	Major Graham	M1053B	5172BZ	21314	8/12/50	General service
5	Beauman	JL48	ARR472	11719	11/12/50	Change engine sleeves N/S bore
6	Sutterbank	M720	MPJ200	C2314	11/12/50	Accident damage
7	Gaulds	P1875	CXF445	46	12/12/50	Fit Heater
8	Algones		LGX675	5000	13/12/50	Service
9	Rumfitt	J.1.			13/12/50	Tighten engine bolts check leak
10	Dr Gleadow	91P	UMX875		13/12/50	Repair wiring on panel
11	Harold Radford	P1609	KOH233	9689	14/12/50	Set radius rods
12	Evans		HLB424		14/12/50	Repair near axle
13	Gadsal	M524	NFC139	45279	14/12/50	Replace front spring
14	Craig	M1058	UMC938	19639	14/12/50	Decoke 2 clemistor
15	Kemble Davis	P1724	LLH951	6028	14/12/50	Sway bar bracket - leaking dis cap
16	Mazam Constandavos	C224	SMT946	19288	18/12/50	Tune service
17	Mr Gordon Davies from P.H.	P1711	FBO945	9154	19/12/50	Tune + wiper - brakes
18	A.A. Cameron	K250	HOL846	14201	19/12/50	Clutch tie bar service
19	F.Gron	P1881	LXD516	794	19/12/50	Change dis - brakes
20	Laxton	P1752	9AM636	3734	19/12/50	Decoke. steering

N

No.	Name				Date	Work
21.	Stock 4375 Engine	—	—	—	19/12/50	Build 4375cc engine.
N22.	Imhof.	M217	JGU5.		20/12/50	Chain repairs.
23	Quinnell.	K696.	KXC162.		20/12/50	Check for rear axle noise. service
24.		P1645.	HOP392	3752.	21/12/50	Convert to L.H. drive - set under rods.
25	De Janviez.	M1013.	UMC924		21/12/40	Service - plugs.
26	Cyprien.	L388	SYX278		21/12/50	Ex. pet. pump.
27	Wallis.	K639.	KLX473	13674	21/12/50	Ex seat pump. 2 Ali heads.
28	Caniger.	ERJ220	P1826	2625	21/12/50	Repair wing.
29	Waller.	M1071.	KLY24.	6319	27/12/50	Steering wander. Engine tune.
30	Graham.	P1669.	BJE490.	3190.	27/12/50	Fit radio.
31.	Gibbs.	P1839.	GUN606	669	28/12/50	Service 500 ml.
32	Dexon.	M400	JUC302		28/12/50	Service tune.
33	Waller	K639	KLX473		28/12/50.	Repair gearbox.
34	Gardner.	M397	NEV26.	19900	28/12/50	Repair ex.
35	Grail Kard Ltd	P1810	KRU38	4407	28/12/50.	Repair O/S front wing.
36.	Richards		JLT6.	18123.	1/1/51.	Change torque tube. Decoke
37.	De Habron.				1/1/51.	Repair wings.
38.	Lord Latimer	M754	KLO300	11163	2/1/51.	Silencer - service
39.	Dagenham Motors.	P1874.	Mary.	34.	2/1/51.	Fit Heater.
40.	Fashion Fabrics	P1790.	LYB561.	1797	2/1/51.	Service 1000 ml. Fit Heater

No.	Name				Date	Work
N41	Dr Hobson	91M1530	KXM943	17095	4/1/51	Service tune.
42	Adkins	L905	KYR636	10000	4/1/51	Service repair speedo.
43	Rapper	M709	KGC893	51101	4/1/51	Water pump service.
44	Maxwell Telling	M1522	KXK865	13078	9/1/51	Service tune.
45	McDowell	M470	9YE359	28316	10/1/51	Brakes.
46	Rymer		LGX678		10/1/51	Fit Armstrong shockers
47	Notley	LHW29	L432Q	24144	10/1/51	Fit (own) tun manifold
48	Pontious		RNU8		10/1/51	Accident damage — king pin
49	Gibb	P1551	KYM774	17400	10/1/51	Service tune.
50	Mrs Sapperson	M1044B	KLR872	17269	12/1/51	Accident damage
51	Godfrey	M1005	KLL736		12/1/51	
52	Bankins Garage Three Bridges	Front Suspension			15/1/51	Overhaul front suspension
53	Bromfield	P1538	UMX850	7826	15/1/51	Decoke
54	Blackley	K595	94K438	23975	17/1/51	Engine work.
55	Con Mount	627	KLO123	12650	18/1/51	Rear main bearing — Steering
56	Midgett	M618	9ST443	33845	18/1/51	Adjust brakes etc.
57	Clarkson	19T1551	CWQ12	1532	19/1/51	Body repair — steering repair
58	Evans		HLB829	3083	19/1/51	Accident repair
59	Graham	BTK470	91F1669	3706	22/1/51	Check shockers, charging rate, Check brakes tie rods
60	Dr Barrett	M1013	4MC924			Dir. service silencer

61	De Klee	MRD 441	M445	16876	22/1/51	Service Bodywork
62	Automobile Eng.	KYP 640	P1652	15849	22/1/51	Accident repair
63	Beaumon	HRR 672	J35148	13883	22/1/51	Reset Casting? Remove play from S/Column
64	Aitken	KYP 636	L905	10582	23/1/51	Repair O/S front wing
65	Gill	QQS 825	K236		24/1/51	Repair O/S front suspension bodywork
66	Mc Talbot	KYX 642	91P1603	14850	25/1/51	Wheel Wobble, Change radius arms, Check shockers
67	Mr Eprien	SMX 278	C388	36695	25/1/51	Silencer
68	Tall of Leads	NUB 361	P1629	6682	25/1/51	Set radius rods
69	Fran PH Hill	MKJ 631	P1823	2695	23/1/51	Flat spot
70	Major Ralli	KYP 630	P1595	10383	29/1/51	Service, change radius rods
71	Mc Callin	KLX 493	K639		30/1/51	Accident repair
72	Tippetts	LYD 525	91K1603	3548	31/1/51	Guarantee and service
73	Clayman	VHX 883	P1590	9515	1/2/51	Accident damage
74	Oxychem Motors	—	P1929	—	1/2/51	Fit Heater & Radio
75	A.M.C	HGA 833	P1507	14041	1/2/51	Set radius rods
76	Royal Exchange In.	A 8055	M392	10744	1/2/51	Accident damage
77	Went	Green	366		1/2/51	Test etc
78	Runnabout Garage	WMF 906	P1896	941	1/2/51	Guarantee Bodywork
79	Hare & Sans	LPX 719	P1727	1746	5/2/51	Adherence Bodywork G.
80	Gibbs	P1839	GUM 606	1124	6/2/51	1000 Service

81	Kunns.	P1931	—	—	3/2/51	Fit radio and Heater.
82	Daniger	P1826	GRJ220	3905	6/2/51	Accident damage.
83	Dr Clark.	M853	KLL138	31530	6/2/51	Service.
84	Deena	M400	OUC302	29699	6/2/51	Service
85	Bennett.	M751	UMV207		6/2/51	Accident damage.
86	Dr Critchley				6/2/51	Check touch — cable
87	Sanders Garage	P1932	—	—	7/2/51	From FT 700 etc
88	Langston Tunes & Co	P1650	KYP638	13715	7/2/51	2 Thermostats and gauge
89	Godfrey.	P1548	KYM667	14427	7/2/51	Service bracket table
90	Davies	P1903.	GRJ521	957	9/2/51	From . Guarantee work.
91	Gallings	L393.	PLT913	2411	9/2/51	Body work.
92	M. Ott — Lilly & S Bruce	P1909	WMD350	992	12/2/51	Radio Heater Guarantee work
93	Winfield Digby	M722	CTK930	15701	12/2/51	Service work
94	Turner.	M615	PYR13	16657	12/2/51	Gt silencer blowing
95	Mrs Frayling					
96	Dr Winston	P1761	LLM505	3877	15/2/51	Accident damage
97	Edward.	P1652	KYP65	13131	19/2/51	Repair.
98	Research Rd	Rolls			16/2/51	Adjusting clutch
99	A.M.C. Head Office	M719	KLO130	30006	19/2/51	Change dynamo
100	Morris	P1818	KOX292	5214	19/2/51	Service - change oils. Dash

1	Mr Haverith.	K440	2D 8610	2/2/51	23741	Check over repair a. necessary.
2	Arnold Gauld.	P1878	LXF 445	22/2/51	1240	Heater not working.
3	Dr Glendon.		UMX875	21/2/51	10000	Set radius rods rear lights
4	Evans.	P1835	NHC930	21/2/51	2573	Axle noise — (heater and radio supply, not fit)
5	Welch.	M366	TY50	22/2/51	24614	Repair gearbox
6	Barker.	M354	JYK437	22/2/51	29372	Change rear spring — beam bush
7	Mr Dean	P1823	NKJ631	23/2/51	3654	Change radius rods
8	Car Mart.	M749	DRD723	27/2/51	13281	Axle noise
9	Mrs Escott	M1086	UMC538	27/2/51	16173	Brake service
10	Mr Talbot	K374	SMV519	27/2/51	3663	3.78
11	V.E Ryland.	K489	HDG105	28/2/51	12638	Brake — springs
12	Balsom.	M405	JYM271	1/3/51		2° Beam
13	F.A. Thompson	P1926	LX0502	2/3/51	1580	Steering wander.
14	Dr Jarvis	M1013	UMC924	2/3/51		Relieve Brakes
15	Adkin.	905L	KYP636	5/3/51	12303	Service.
16	Dr Hope Scott.	M793	FME3	5/3/51	26700	2° Beam — rear axle repair
17	Godfrey.	M1005	KLL736	5/3/51	3197?	Sticking throttle.
18	Decca.	M400	94C302	5/3/51	26401	Silence.
19	Craig.	M1058	UMC938	5/3/51	23737	Service.
20	Saunders Garage	P1932	WHXR3	6/3/51	546	500 Service gearbox noisy.

O						
21	Turner Riley	MPJ 219		7/3/51		Service — adjust brakes.
22	Brooklands Motors	K654	KVM713	8/3/51	2241	Front suspension.
23	Le Mesurier	MM550	TMH 812	12/3/51	20000	Silencers, Change oil in Lamps. New Hub caps. Brakes. Tyres.
24	Mr Fraepling.	P1918	LTM906	12/3/51	1246	1000 mil Service.
25	Walters.			12/3/51		O/S front wing — repair bonnet side.
26	Gadsal.	M527.	NFC139	12/3/51		Head gasket.
27	Winston	P1761	LCM565	12/3/51	4360	Twin Solex
28	Cheetham.	M1523	KXK714	13/3/51	18673.	King pin and bush.
29	Price.	L548	CCB110	13/3/51	15090	Fit extra silencer.
30	White.	M735	OYW749	13/3/51	16522	Check over.
31	Cameron & Co.	L310	CWP777	14/3/51	4383	3.78 Ali heads.
32	Blackley.	K1925	LXT335	14/3/51	500	500 Service
33	Balfour.	M309	UMV59	14/3/51	9234	Recake and badgework.
34	Reiss.	L387.	LUMI.	14/3/51	28520	Change engine 2nd gear jumping out.
35	Evans.		HLB424	14/3/51		Accident damage.
36	Graham.	P1669	BJC490	19/3/51	4339	Gearbox repair.
37	Ginn.	K510	J4C310	19/3/51	22354	Exchange column.
38	Standhill Garage.	P1811	MTV953	19/3/51	5320.	Set Radius arms.
39	Lt Cooper.		KPX11.	20/3/51		Bodywork.
40	Broomfield.	P1538	UMX450	21/3/51.	8000	Service.

41.	Arthur Gould	P1953	LXV301	68	9/3/51	Fit Radio & Heater.
42	Goodhale	P1915	LX4597	289	21/3/51	Service work
43	Turner Riley	MH21	MPJ219		22/3/51	Replace flywheel belt — check dis
44.	H.R. Owen	P1552	DVG440	21517	22/3/51	Brakes.
45	Mr Cable	P1611	GAW569	6370	24/3/51	Set radius rods.
46	White	L312	940634	24230	27/3/51	Recon engine 784172P.
47	Gardner	M397A	NEV26	23542	27/3/51	Accident damage.
48	Lee	P1837	KTG652	1703	27/3/51	Accident damage.
49	Hollingworth	P1640	GPY177	8662	28/3/51	Reset castor angle.
50	Freedman	P1848	LXF445	2130	28/3/51	1000 ml service
51	Sir Philip Brocklehurst	P1646	TRF692	6495	28/3/51	Replace steering bracket.
52	Penny	P1816	LXD575	4860	28/3/51	Service
53	Acme Lane	P	LLC44		28/3/51	Fit Heater.
54	Maxwell Telling	M1522	KXK865	15493	29/3/51	Recon engine 774097P
55	Freebody	M1088	UMP460	16605	29/3/51	Check brakes
56	Cyprian	SM4278	C388	—	29/3/51	Adjust brakes.
57	Miss Dwight	P1684	GWM309	15625	29/3/51	Accident repair.
58	H.C. Nelson	P1600	LGO133	3885	30/3/51	Steering wander.
59	Osmer	P1672	CGX678	7433	2/4/51	Service
60	La Marris	L127	JGY708	9654	2/4/51	Front axle beams. 2°

61	Major Ralli.	P1595.	KYP630.	12478	2/4/51	Beam bushes.
62	Dr Hope Scott.	M793	TME 3	28122	4/4/51	Decoke. Twin ...
63	Quennell.	M696	KAC162	15000	4/4/51	Reline brakes.
64	Bashell.	M820.	KFJ549	12698	4/4/51	3·78 - Service
65.	~~Harris~~ Dr Clark.	M853.	KLL138	33857	4/4/51	Silencers.
66	Dr Mann.	P.1586	VMG577	12343.	4/4/51	Set valve rods
67	Saunders Garage.	P1932	WHX123	1477	5/4/51	1000 ml service
68	Dr Hobson.	M1530.	KXM943	17281	5/4/51	Service.
69	Champion	Pilot	LLN566	3471	5/4/51	Fit Chandler Groves ...
70	Wyatt.	M618			5/4/51	Fit washer in Columbia cylinder
71	Leaca.	M400	JUC302		5/4/51	New PLC switch
72	Le Messurier	M650	TMH812		5/4/51	Adjust foot belt.
73	From PH.	PM52	JBM636	6285.	9/4/51	Tune
74	Hart.	P1909	LXM903		9/4/51	Check steering.
75	Godfrey.	P1548	KYM669		9/4/51	Marshal reflector.
76	Tankard & Smith.	M564	MPF392	36835	10/4/51	Convert to RH Steering.
77	Brown Bros.	K260	MPH823	11323.	10/4/51	Recon 30. IPU. 3·78. Brake line
78	Major Spence.	P1591	GSA99	2686	10/4/51	Performance - steering.
79	Car Mart.	91M1524	KXF814	13589.	10/4/51	Check steering
80.	Gassell.	M606	KLM9.	15278	13/4/51	Check front suspension.

0						
81	Browne Clements Publication	M737	GBU78	4823	14/4/51	2° Beam.
82	Sutcliffe *Telephone No. Bradford 23357*	P1643	GKW153	13720	16/4/51	Accident damage.
83	Bar Putney Autos.	M709	KGC893		16/4/51	Water Pump.
84	Dick.	M326	947950	26369	16/4/51	Change engine for cont. over.
85	Osborne.	M571	TMX5	50552	16/4/51	Recon engine. 3.78.
86	Annable	89J888	KXC170		17/4/51	Service work.
87	Hill & Phillips.	M1051	KYW239	16613	17/4/51	Accident repairs.
88	Mc Cyprien.	L388	SMX278	39935	17/4/51	Brake.
89	Hopkins	P1874	WMF831	2409	17/4/51	Service.
90	Allen.	K488	MPF647	13963	18/4/51	Service. Check over.
91	Salmond.				19/4/51	Service etc.
92	Mr Tilley	M546	FFH927	19919	20/4/51	Nail in new wheel.
93	Heatley	91P1999	FAH190	500	20/4/51	500 ml service.
94	Knifton.	M870	FRY999	18914	20/4/51	Ex blow.
95	A R Wilson	P1888	LLV559	1998	23/4/51	Brake lubricants
96	Lord Latimer.	M759	KLO300	12166	23/4/51	Bodywork.
97	Mrs Escott.	M1066	UMC538	17716	24/4/51	Service.
98	Griffiths.	M802	KNK26	34249	24/4/51	Brake.
99	Da Costa.	M1007	EPM96	4610	25/4/51	Service.
100	Major Leyton.	P1623	DVG479	2092	25/4/51	Service work

P.	Name				Date	Work
1	Mr Godfrey	P1548	KYK669	17343	26/4/51	Brakes – slacken
2	Cheetham	M1523	KYK714		26/4/51	Set castor – coil springs
3	Henley	P1997	FYH490	1143	27/4/51	1000 Service
4	Tunnell	M593	TMK164	18359	27/4/51	Front susp.
5	Haydon	M753	HRU739	28079	30/4/51	Decoke etc
6	Winston	P1761	LLM565	6105	30/4/51	Change to single carb and service
7	Godsal	M527	NFC139	48353	30/4/51	Oversteering
8	Payne	M530	IL4287	10659	30/4/51	Solex carbs
9	Farquharson	M879	KLK657	23643	30/4/51	Check steering
10	Champ	M730	KBP666	27712	30/4/51	Check rear tyre
11	Mrs Moss	L852	KLO128	20365	30/4/51	Recon engine NEW805960
12	Mr Gve	M546	FFH927		30/4/51	Brakes
13	Allen		UMK735		1/5/51	Brakes
14	Capt Lucas	M307	9LY958		1/5/51	New N/S front wing
15	Blackley	K1925	CXT335	2.68	3/5/51	Service work
16	Davies	M444	KLF681	11164	2/5/51	Plug in gen change
17	Barclay Inglis	7L455	LKX146		2/5/51	Accident repairs
18	Mjr Constanduros	L224	SMT966	23400	3/5/51	Engine tune etc
19	Acland Geddes	K1929	WHX777	1500	7/5/51	Change rear spring
20	Nalley	L4320	LHW29		7/5/51	Change over manifold etc

21	Friedman.	P1878	CXF445	3062	7/5/51	Service work.
22.	Mrs Goulden.	M858	NNY326	7753	7/5/51	Tune - service.
23	Warren	P1901	FFN539	1500.	7/5/51	
24	Adlards Motor Brixton	P1792	LLC44	2162	7/5/51	Radiomobile Ali heads - twin carbs.
25	Fidel.	P2041	LNY399	300	8/5/51	500 service.
26	Dr Hobson (12923) (12924)	M1530	KXM943	23206	8/5/51	Accident repair
27	Wiggins	M1091	OVW450		8/5/51	Brake. Engine tune.
28	Le Measurer				8/5/51	
29	Mrs Campbell.	M1079			8/5/51	Check steering.
30	Dr Sharp.	P2044	OUB294	342	9/5/51	500 Service Foam. Eng No. 7254581.
31	Allen.					
32	Hentzay	P1997	FHH190	2000	10/5/51	Sub-outlet.
33	Frey.	L203	MWL380	22499	11/5/51	Tune - service
34	Imhof.	91972	CXT5.		11/5/51	Gearbox
35.	Paramount Garage (12973)	P1793	LND503	5524	15/5/51	Radius rods. — gearbox repair
36	Graham.	P1569	BJE490		15/5/51	Steering brackets — speedo
37.	Benning	K206	9LK618	14800	15/5/51	Service work.
38.	Decca.	M400	9UC302	29587	16/5/51	Nois in engine.
39	Cheetham	M1523	KXR714	21760	16/5/51	Decoke.
40	Chevin Garage - Columbia	~~M603~~ Rear Axle	~~KXE~~	~~2~~	16/5/51	Build up axle with new Columbia

P						
41	Dr Grant.	M1014	SYY099	29981	16/5/51	Front spring Tune.
42	Mr Johnston.	M322	970194	17074	18/5/51	Service work.
43	Hopkins		WMF831		18/5/51	Service Foam.
44	Mrs Freyling				18/5/51	Service.
45	Annable.	9888	KXC170	3026	18/5/51	Decoke
46	Lt Cooper.	M1056	KPX11	19810	19/5/51	Bodywork — water pump.
47	M. Allen	P1927	FKG873		21/5/51	Road test etc.
48	Coffyn. (13016 E)	P1824	MBP216	5880	21/5/51	Clutch slip.
49	Dr Wiseman	M1059	90N971	26196	21/5/51	Change over cowl etc.
50	Le Messurier.	M550	TMH812	20000	21/5/51	Head — change engine TIA8195666P.
51	Wigmore		LGX678		21/5/51	Antiroar, handbrake.
52	From P. H. Mc Carothers.	P1993	LFL317	2659	22/5/51	Steering.
53	Samuel	M1032	NPA871	12176	22/5/51	Accident repair
54	Dr Darwin	M1013	UMC924		23/5/51	6 Bladed fan.
55	Mrs Gzalen	Spare wheel.			23/5/51	Remove tyre and repair wheel.
56	Cypier 1	C384	SMX278 26		26/5/51	Adjust brake.
57	Allen.	M593	TML169	19712	28/5/51	Brakes.
58	Russell	M693	HAU404	21019	28/5/51	Accident repairs NEW ENGINE NO. R770631P.
59	Fisher.	P2041	LYY399	936	28/5/51	1000 ml service.
60	Dr Sharp	P2044	040299	1379	28/5/51	Wheel balance etc.

P

No.	Name	Code	Reg.	Mileage	Date	Notes
61	The Trustees of K E Page (E 13005)	L905.	KYP636	15200	28/5/51	Front spring - lever.
62	Arthur.				28/5/51	Remove U Bolts .
63	Allen	P			25/5/51	
64	Mr S.H.A.	Sleeve engine			27/5/51	
65	Mr Eve	M546	FFH926	20919	29/5/51	
66	Allan .	M879	VMK735	20027	30/5/51	Tune do .
67	Harmer & Simonds	M434.	NNO990	13153.	30/5/51	Accident repairs .
68	Mr Roy	M329.	KWE28	31125	31/5/51	Mercury engine .
69	Maxwell Telling .	M1522	KXK865		1/6/51	Backspark .
70	Dr Michael Transferred	Kenneth Rd .			1/6/51	
71	Mr Harris .	P1955.	CVR314	8500	1/6/51	Wobble
72	Quennell .	K696 .	KXC162	17569	4/6/51	Decoke .
73	Thrush .	P2050	NRL837	710	4/6/51	500
74	Turner Riley	M421	MPJ219	31757	4/6/51	Ex engine — old No. 7196931 — New No. R820395P.
75	Land Warrington	P2055	LLL696	1113	5/6/51	1000
76	Deacon .				5/6/51	Change engine oil and filter .
77	Major Rollit	P1595.	KYP630	15160	5/6/51	Brake relined
78	O. K. Handy	M1100	KXF819	14285	6/6/51	Pressured cap 6 Bleed free
79	Talbot .	K374.	SMU519	16146	6/6/51	Big end knock .
80	Capt Barnett		HDF793		6/6/51	Accident repairs .

P						
87	Dalton	M.	DSA631		6/6/51	Service
82	Fram Park Hull.	P1943	HWS853	2403	6/6/51	Springs hitting
83	Mr Beamish.	M751	UMV207	1621	6/6/51	Service
64	Car Mart.		DRD723		5/6/51	Tune.
85	Blackley					
86	Godsal.	M327	NPC139	50143	12/6/51	Mercury engine — king pins
87	3 Keswick Rd. Camberwell 15.		AXH342	74392	12/6/51	Overhaul engine
88	Randall Arthur.	P1952	LOG822	3096	12/6/51	Fit Heater
89	Henley	P1883	LXF746	2692	12/6/51	Noise gearbox
90	Mr Craggigge	M873.	JYF870	14275	13/6/51	Service.
91	Natley.	L432	LHW29	28593	13/6/51	Ex blau.
92	Gardner.		NGV26		13/6/51	Slab axle.
93	Mr Freyling		CXM906		13/6/51	Indication.
94	Ingram	M271LH.	DSA772	29668	13/6/51	Service work.
95	Mrs Gee	M698.	KGC824	21028	13/6/51	H.T leads.
96	Le Mesurier	M550	TMH812	20000	13/6/51	Adjust brakes etc.
97	Change H.O.	J1973LH	MGC530	395	13/6/51	500 Service
98	117 Viall	91K2035	LOJ211	795	14/6/51	Service 500 miles...
99	P R Stephen.	P1689	XCG99	11021	14/6/51	Steering.
100	Cooke — Hawle	M717	JM7942	25145	14/6/51	Suspension.

Q

#	Name				Date	Description
1	Major Cantonturos	7L 224	SMT 986	25196	19/6/51	Decoke.
2	Parry	P 1816	LXD 375		18/6/51	Service. Repair rear bumper.
3	Mr Winston	91P 1761	LLM 565	8154	9/6/51	Reline brakes. Change front radius rods.
4	Mr Blockley	19K 1925	LXT 335	2878	20/6/51	Repairs & Maintenance
5	Mr McDermott	91P 1592		7,097	20/6/51	Bodywork, check car over, Change all oils, grease service
6	P. R. Stephens	P 1689	JCQ99	11021	20/6/51	Steering wanders, Sway bar bracket, Paintwork - Hiltons
7	Cash Sale. Head Office	J2 1973	MGC530	1000	21/6/51	Service. 1000.
8	Escott	M 1066	LMC338	22771	21/6/51	Service
9	Capt Farquason	M 574	MLK657	27537	21/6/51	Same
10	Mr Mitchell	P 2070	9CD876	1148	22/6/51	Hann.
11	Freedman		LXF 445		22/6/51	Service
12	Gardner	71M 397	NEV 26	2630	23/6/51	Change O/S Axle Beam.
13	Wallis	K 639	MLX 473	19296	23/6/51	Fit Drag link & Ball ends if required.
14	Lord Alston	91 1994	WHX635	767	25/6/51	Brakes Tune
15	Annable	J 888	KXC170	6158	25/6/51	Decoke, Change Shockers, Adjust Brakes, Check shock, Clutch
16	Magot		7UH190		26/6/51	Brakes. glass in headlamps. Engine miss.
17	Bucketson	91P 1948	KTX 337	2314	26/6/51	Render Damage, Check Steering, Check car
18	Hann in Cardiff	71M 434	MPE 343	38454	26/6/51	Fit 2 Brake shoes, Clutch judder, Tune if possible.
19	Woodall	P 1649	VHX560		26/6/51	Tune, Service, wheel wobble.
20			KTX 393		28/6/51	Accident damage. Transferred to 9/51
21		71L 771	MPK 36	7925	28/6/51	Replace front brake back

Q						
22	Cyprian		L388	SMX278		30/6/51	Check Brakes. 17 Gallons Petrol
23	White					30/6/51	Fit Radio. Check Gearbox & Rear Axle Brakes. Adjust
24	Champs		M730	KBPN66		27/6/51	Check front Suspension. Tune Engine.
25	Membridge		M10549	LTV218	10193	3/7/51	Pressure cap rad. New oil seals to Petrol Pump
26	Michael	Malan Ltd	K439	JHE356	14359	3/7/51	2° beam.
27	Fischel		P2041	CTY399		3/7/51	Tune Ten service.
28	Snell		P1621	CNN415	20818	4/7/51	Brakes. E+Clear.
29	Watson		P1726	LKD39	9062	4/7/51	Shocks. — radius rods.
30	Fram		176569	AGC377	23970	9/7/51	Bodywork & gearing
31	Talbot		P1603	KYN642	18484	9/7/51	Decoke.
32	McDowell		Prefect	K4036	17000	9/7/51	Decoke rings.
33	Bloomfield		P1538	UMX450	11149	9/7/51	Columbia decoke NEW ENG. No 71A8259 56
34	McQun		P1654	ODB604	15910	9/7/51	Set radius rods.
35	Derick		M725	NPD82	10176	9/7/51	2° Beam.
Q36	Myr Merryweat		M1093	UMD465	7895	9/7/51	Twin carbs air heads. decoke
Q37	Mr Dennis		P2092	HAW917	1441	10/7/51	Service.
Q38	Techrofan Ltd.		P1929	WMF837	7258	10/7/51	Bodywork service
Q39	Gadsel		19527	NFC139		10/7/51	Bodywork.
40	Parker		P1715	WME227	10560	10/7/51	Radius rods.

Q

41.	Godsal	M527	NFC139		10/7/51	Bodywork
42.	Bushell	M820	KFJ549		18/7/51	U Bolts
43.	Col Hazlehurst		KLF639		14/7/51	Front suspension
44.	Austin	L695	TMH383	22199	17/7/51	Check over
45.	F. A Gluck	K519	HLJ575	11485	17/7/51	C & clean brake
46.	Brown	M760	OPE237	4753	17/7/51	service live
47.	Mrs Thesingh	P2023	CXY14	10308	14/7/51	Steering - axle - clutch
48.	Fernley	M603	HRU201	37000	19/7/51	Engine tie rods
49	De Shenp	9IP2044	OUB294		19/7/51	Check leaks
50	Dr Gluck Frau Hiller	P1768	AFA166		4/7/51	Anti sway bracket
51	Allen	M879	UMK735	23249	23/7/51	Decoke
52	Chesterfield Gdns Garage	M1021	KLO196	7855	23/7/51	
53.	Mrs Frayling	P1918	CXM906	5354	23/7/51	Service
54	Cam Chawley	P1957	FPN300	6073	24/7/51	Service etc
55	Mrs Lamb	M411	NWL355	31238	25/7/51	Recon engine - head No No 8243b0P
56	Michael Mutin	K439A	9YE356	14754	25/7/51	C & clean
57	Mrs Escott	M1066	UMC538	23648	25/7/51	Overhaul front susp
58.	Graves	P1938	KTX393	5013	25/7/51	Accident bodywork - decoke
59	Caddeleak	C201	SMH107	27196	26/7/51	brake - live
60	Kelly				26/7/51	Adjust brakes

Q

No.	Name				Date	Work
61	Mr Thrush	P 2050	NRK 857	2896	27·7·51 / 27-7-51	Brakes - Sticking Throttle - Stop Light Switch - Leak on rear Brake pipe
62	Gearbox Gardner	M 397	NEV 26	27530	28 7 51	Gearbox
63	Mr Cheetham	M 1523	KXK 714	26145	31/7/51	Repair gearbox
64	Scott-Macaad	K 654	KVM 713	4383	31/7/51	Fan
65	Dr Morris	L 127	9 GY 708	11254	31/7/51	Decoke
66	Friedman	P 1878	LXP 945	3103	1/8/51	Service
67	W. J. March	M 413	CVK 766	11	1/8/51	Bodywork. Tune - service
68	Hudson	P 1814	JCG 911	6236	1/8/51	Stub axle
69	Hill	LX 420	M 2000	6146	2/8/51	Service want kit
70	Craggigs	M 873	24 F 470	16133	3/8/51	Repair on system
71	Alimbash	M 507	ENT 184	17945	3/8/51	Tax service bill
72	Ulgen	P 1672	LGX 678	11025	4/4/51	Decoke
73	Feldman	P 2027	DRK 321	3640	9/8/51	Accident repair
74	Dr Vandy	Cab			9/8/51	Overhaul carb
75						
76						
77	Aldridge	L 125	BES 495	29622	9/8/51	Decoke
78	Dugmore	M 211	DBA 772	33471	9/8/51	Service work
79	West	J 2-1912	LXX 15	6954	9/8/51	Transmission
80						

Q

81	Godfrey	P1548	KYM669	21130	9/8/51	Accident repair
83	~~Dick~~ White	P2114	MGK909	968	9/8/51	500 Service
84						
85	Leather	P2127	MGK470	1347	9/8/51	
86	Snowden	P1863	KOX799	10107	9/8/51	Decoke etc
87						
88	Hallamworth	P1963	CDX615	9682	9/8/51	Bodywork etc ENG. NO. B18F 7250977
89						
90	Stone	P1613	LYD165	14265	9/8/51	Steering
91	Venity	K653	UMC561	1491	10/8/51	Overheating
92	Broomfield	P1538	UMX850	12222	13/8/51	Service
93	Mrs Gee	M698	KGC224	22693	13/8/51	New hood
94	Riess	C387	CUM1	40810	13/8/51	Check shocks etc
95	Humphrey Evans		HLB431	39623	14/8/51	Brakes, change pump Diaphram, change Battery
96	Gollings	K2109	XMC365		13/8/51	500 Miles Service
97	De Latham	EM890	HLL577	21027	15/8/51	Tune Engine Check Wipers, & Indicators etc
98	Winston	P1761	LLM565	9271	15/8/51	Wheel wobble
99	Fisher				15/8/51	Steering Box oil leak
	McGlashe	P1506	OMX875	12801	15/8/51	Remove Axle Beams, fit shocks

"R"

1.	Appleton		P1685	NON359	24119	15/8/51	Steering
2.	Decca			JUC 302		15/8/51	Fit Cylinder Head Gasket. Service
3.	Brown		7IM 421	MPJ 219	33679	16/8/51	Exhaust Blow.
4.	Boyle					16/8/51	Check for noise on transmission
5.	Sharp		P2044	OUB 297		16/8/51	Service. Change Blow. Eng No. 7254581
6.	Cragnigge		M873	94F 470	16434	17/8/51	Bodywork
7.	BLUCKLEY		K21925	LYT 335	1925	18/8/51	
8.	Cyprien			SMX278		20/8/51	Brakes
9.	Peters		91P 1757	LLX 801	12291	17/8/51	Exhaust Blow. Change Tyres Round. Sticking throttle
10.	Friedman		P1878	LYF 445	3864	21/8/51	General service. Set Radius rods.
11.	Leather		P2127	MGK 470	1500	21/8/51	Change crank. Eng No. 7258764
12.	Rice Bros		P1637	LGP 36	11775	21/8/51	Radius rods. exhaust clamp arm.
13.	Dr. Curd			FRX 999		20/8/51	Change oils. Service.
14.	Dr. Janvrin						Fit Battery lead. Adjust Brakes.
15.	Peter						Exhaust. Change Brakes
15.	Du Cooke					20/8/51	Check Distributor. Change leads. Exhaust Gasket.
16.	Waller			KLY 24		20/8/51	Service. Check Brakes.
17.	Hugot	moved to ...@1160	91P 1997	FUM 190	74919	23/8/51	Tuned Engine. Service. Spring fitting. Chains.
18.	Sanby		91P 1683	MTV 257	12878	22/8/51	Change Radius rods. Check brakes. Plays steering ...
19.							

R

No.	Name				Date	Work
20.	Overall	M 891	MYA 241	31293	28/8/51	Handbrake cable — service.
21	Annable	92888	KYC170		28/8/51	Repair gearbox. and axle.
22.	Major Craig	K145	CHM316	29308	28/8/51	Repaint.
23	Mrs Agnew	P1926	LYO502	9776	28/8/51	5000 Service
24	Afton	P1994	WHX535	2621	28/8/51	Max speed 70.
25	Diggins		OVW750		28/8/51	Check trouble
26	Murch	M413	LVK766	11994	29/8/51	Balance spare wheel.
27						
28	Dr Gould	P2065	MKC37	—	31/8/51	5000 service
29	Gardner	M394	NEV26	28809	31/8/51	Fitting customers own 32 hp engine
30	Richardson		Columbia Axle		31/8/51	Repair
31	Miss Wright	P1657	GWM309	30000	31/8/51	Decoke etc
32	Reynolds	7MK595	JYK 438	20322	1/9/51	Fit small Dynamo Pulley. Fit Shock absorbers spigot
33	Graykigg	8M 873	JUF 470	16799	1/9/51	Fit New Radiator Hoses
34	Staples	K 439	JYK 356	16045	3/9/51	Exhaust Blow. Fiddle Box. Air Cleaner.
35	Maxwell Tilling	9M 1522	KXK 865	19037	4/9/51	Service. Tune Engine New Ignition Switch (3 hrs)
36	Mc Bean James Riley	7M 431	MPJ219	34503	4/9/51	Check Distributor
37	Mc Leather	9M 2127	NGK 470	1175	4/9/51	Adjust Brakes
38	Major R.H.D. Riggall	7M 547	GER 966	18745	4/9/51	2 Axle Beams. Exhaust Blow.
39	Byatt	7M 618	JYT 943	38151	4/9/51	Adjust Brakes
40	A G Walker		DBA 631		5/9/51	King Pins & Bushes. Wing Mirror.

R

41	Mc Dent	ML 3144	JLM 3	22914	5/9/51	Check Steering. New rear shockers. Check Axle Beam N/S. Etc.
42	Bradford	FEA 3644	91P		5/9/51	Fit Speedo Cable.
43.	Dr. Janovin	81M 1013	VMC 924	39057	5/9/51	Tec Service Change oil. Loan Battery.
44	Mr Champ	81M 730	KBP 466	34185	5/9/51	Convert to single carb. Tune engine. Check 1st Gear
45	Mc Godfrey	91P 1548	KVM 669	21750	5/9/51	Adjust Brakes & Clutch
46	E.E. Walters	81M 1074	EPM 890	25449	6/9/51	Wheel Balance. Buzz in steering. Temperature gauge
47	Dr Houghton	81M 8146	FJF 84	24869	6/9/51	General check over. Tune engine. etc.
48	T.B. Walker Jones	91P 1919	HCV 1	6345	6/9/51	Jumping out of 1st Gear 2nd & Top Stiff. Tune up. Etc
49	Mc Boarlin	91P 2095	ERJ 966	4388	7/9/51	Accident damage.
50	Dr Coate Amb. 5604.	71M 517	SMX 835	33707	10/9/51	Tune Engine. Service. Seat Broken. etc.
51	Wiggin	M1091	OUW 750	14932	10/9/51	Tune service.
52	W. Greenwood Sans Ltd.	P1678	LGX 679	12418	10/9/51	Self Radius seal
53	Corn Charley	P1957	FPN 300	7425	11/9/51	Clutch judder.
54	Jakobi Mc	71M 536	JVR 671	26982	11/9/51	Clutch judder. Check Gears. Exhaust Blow.
55	Aldridge Jnr	L 125	BES 495	32423	11/9/51	Wheel balance
56.	Freyling	P1918	LTM 906	7009	12/9/51	Service.
57	Aldridge	L 125	BES 495	32423	12/9/51	2° Beams.
58	Dr Michael	M343	KWE 24	28808	13/9/51	Service mark.
59	Gaslon	M858	NNU 326	12556	14/9/51	Wheel balance etc
60.	Bloove	M844	TML 209	12160	14/9/51	2° Beams. decoke

R.

61	Mc Cyprian	71L 388	SMX278	46083	17/9/51	Repaired Gearbox. Check brake linings. New Brushes
62	Mc Roosnage Mills	71L 361 9	LHV 836	A2297	17/9/51	Recondition Engine. Check Steering Column... R836028P
63	Decca	71M 400	JUC 302	37059	17/9/51	Tune up. Exhaust Blows.
64	W.L. Butler	K 1924	WHX777	5281	17/9/51	Wobble. Tune Engine. O/S Cylinder Head Gasket blown
65	A.C. Geel	71K 595	JYK A38	24707	17/9/51	Seak filter for Klaxe. S.H.B. to repair tool
66	Wallis	K639	KLY473		17/9/51	2° Beam.
67	Bentham Smith	P1517	KKF752	12167	18/9/51	Check steering.
68	Winstan	P1761	CCM565	11529	18/9/51	Check steering etc.
69	White	P2117	MGK409	1657	18/9/51	1000 ml service.
70	Friedman	P1878	LXF445	6788	18/9/51	Service etc.
71	Nottey	L432	LHW29	32744	19/9/51	Accident damage.
72	F. Smith & Son Grimsby	P1990	CEE494	11197	19/9/51	2 Tie rods. excessive tyre wear.
73	A.C. Geel	71K595	JYK A38	24798	20/9/51	Fit Temperature Guage. Check brakes
74	Tilling	M546	FFH927	23167	21/9/51	Front spring.
75	Bayle	P1926 1728	KCJ374	10119	21/9/51	Noise on transmission
76	Davis	P1903	ERJ521	15028	21/9/51	Set radius rods.
77	Burlington Glass	P1948	KTY33	6096	21/9/51	Accident repair
78	Dr Gt. Cann	M870	FRY999	20670	21/9/51	Rings - decoke. Front spring
79	Dr Vandy	M764	LHW523	27891	24/9/51	Low oil pressure.
80	Dr Blair	P1589	GTC231	15835	24/9/51	Repair gearbox.

R

No.	Name				Date	Work
81.	A. Grogan	M898.	LGS99	17199	25/9/51	Decoke etc
82.	Da Costa	M1007	EPM96	9339	25/9/51	Decoke etc
83.	Searle.	P1819.	HCV79	8000.	25/9/51	Reset castor angle.
84.	Godfrey	P1548	KYM669	–	25/9/51	Fit new indicator.
85.	Mrs J Paine	P1999.	KDG586	7957	26/9/51	Service.
86.	Mrs Freyling	P1918	CXM906		26/9/51	Service.
87.	Hindle	K681	KOJ888	6964	27/9/51	Clutch.
88.	Cox.	M1030	LKT659 35542		27/9/51	Brakes Shackle bushes.
89.	Wyatt.	M618.	GAT943	18519.	27/9/51	Brakes.
90.	Lavenaya.	91693.	LLP797	6241	28/9/51	Rear axle.
91.	Craddock.	L201	SMH107		28/9/51	Adjust brakes and track.
92.	Broomfield.	P1538	UMX450	13231	28/9/51	Service demister.
93.	Dr W.M. Levitt.	P1932	WHV123.	6399.	1/10/51	Service – steering.
94.	Stamp.	? 91M.	GM4416	9645.	1/10/51	Steering.
95.	Dr Janvrin	M1013	UMC929	40017	2/10/51	Bodywork.
96.	Graham.	91669.	BJE490	8877	1/10/51	Ex Oliver.
97.	Capt. Griffith	M802	KNK29	39238	2/10/51	Recar engine etc. has eng 71A861N85A
98.	Jakabar.	M536	GYR671	27661	2/10/51	Service etc
99.	Roy Wilson Dickson Ltd	P1926	LKD39	12001	2/10/51	Service etc.
100.	White.	M566.			2/10/51	Service.

5						
1	Waddell.	M1091	OVW750	15572	3/10/51	Check steering + rear spring.
2	Geers.		94K438	29819.	3/10/51	Ex road.
3	Gardner.	M397	NEV26	18726	4/10/51	Service.
4	O.K Handy.	M1100	KXF819	18726	4/10/51	Service.
5	Richard Afton.	P1994	MHX535	3661	4/10/51	Service
6	Bank Top Motor Co.	K2080.	BCW14	1549	4/10/51	Change crank.
7	Adler.	M265.	LXK44	17606	4/10/51	Repair gearbox
8	Harris of Cardiff.	M464	MPF343	40720	4/10/51	Steering.
9	E.P Fernley	M603.	HRU201	42197	5/10/51	gearbox. etc.
10	Carey Evans.	M831	FUM649	20073	5/10/51	Brake etc.
11.	Aberdeen.	P2148.	LLJ888	718	9/10/51	Spring bolts, chassis
12.	Lord Latimer.	M789	KLO300	15573	9/10/51	4375cc engine. check steering etc.
13	Fashion Fabrics.	P1790.	LXB561	1705	9/10/51	Accident repair.
14.	Stamp.	P1792	LLC44	8061	9/10/51	Set radius rods. Key points.
15	Johnston.	M322	JYO194	22548	9/10/51	Service. line brakes.
16.	Michie	M821.	NNU519	30733	10/10/51	steering
17	Mr Goalen.	M858.	NNU326.		12/10/51	Brake.
18	Sinclair	P1712	WME816.	15435.	15/10/51	Brake etc.
19	Champion.	L611	GBL844.	8298.	15/10/51	New rings.
20.	Da Costa.	M1007.	EPM96	9418	15/10/51	Rear axle gearbox.

S

No.	Name		Chassis	Reg.	Mileage	Date	Work
21	(Thrush)	Century In Co.	P2060	NRL 837	3952	15/10/51	Accident repairs
22	Richard Afton	(13147) (13146)	P1999	WHX 535	9191	16/10/51	Accident repairs
23.	Taylor		P1959	NTB 268	1066	16/10/51	Tune
24	Clifford Braven		P1994	LPO 251	34009	17/10/51	New engine etc.
25.	Godfrey Graham (General Accident)		BK669	BJE 490	—	17/10/51	Front bumper.
26	Faulkner		P2175	MPJ 460	1206	17/10/51	Service
27	Tomkinson		K458	KWJ 770	23009	18/10/51	Accident repairs etc.
28.	Crofton Atkins	(12933) (12934)	P1987	MGC 529	14525	18/10/51	Undue etc, etc.
29.	Quidnell		K696	KYC 162		18/10/51	Pet. Gauge.
30	Turner Riley		M421	MPJ 219		18/10/51	Check carb.
31.	Godfrey		M1005B	KLL 736	8471	18/10/51	Brakes, reline
32	Munro		91P1540	JAX 234	84171	23/10/51	Steering & anchors, Bodywork.
33	Grogan		81M898	CGS 99	17950	23/10/51	Tune Engine. Repair Window winder
34	Gibbs	(12970)	91P1839	GUN 606	4875	23/10/51	Clean armature, Rectify Speedo & Bonnet
35	Friedman		91P1878	LXF 445	7977	23/10/51	Service, Decoke.
36	Imhof	(12300)	92J1972	LXF5	9550	23/10/51	Prepare for Rally.
37	Gavin		81M1013	UMC 924	40209	23/10/51	Check wheel bearings.
38	P.C. Ford		61M121	JLF 575	21014	24/10/51	Fit 2 Beavers.
39	Graham		91P1869	BJE 490	9594	24/10/51	Tune Engine. Renew front bumper.
40	Cheetham		91M1623	KXK 714	29425	24/10/51	Check for oil leaks, timing
41	Godfrey		81M1005B	KLL 736	8855	24/10/51	Remove Engine & Check

5

42	Mr Parry	91P 1816	LXD 515	10871	24/10/51	Service, Fit Reflectors. etc
43	Decca Records	71M 400	JUC 302	38780	24/10/51	Decoke. Exhaust Blows.
44	Mr Gollings	91K 2109	XMC 365	4531	25/10/51	Tune Engine. Service. Etc.
45	Mr Hartley	91P 1996	ERJ 701	6329	25/10/51	Wheel Wobble. Adjust Brakes.
46	Mr Doniger	91P 1826	ERJ 220	15728	25/10/51	Check Steering. Tune Engine. Etc.
47	Mr Cramps	81M 730	KBP 466	36847	25/10/51	Check Clutch. Decoke. Etc
48	Mr Gardner	71M 357A	NEV 26		25/10/51	Check Big Ends. Adjust Brakes. Etc
49	Miss Read	P 1967	LYU 119	6317	30/10/51	Set radius arms etc
50	White	M566	MNW 474		30/10/51	
51	Andrews Garage	P 1747	HFH 544	28000	30/10/51	Accident repairs - decoke - etc
52	C E Walters	M1074	EPM 890	27874	30/10/51	Decoke etc
53	Waller	M1071	KLY 24	9294	31/10/51	Change engine and service etc
54	Cranshaw	M561	CFH 70	25416	31/10/51	Front suspension.
55	Chesterfield Glass Garage	M1021	KLO 196	11580	31/10/51	4375cc Engine. 3.27 axle. wire wheels.
56	Mrs Escott	M1066	UMC 578	26208	31/10/51	Service.
57	Royal Insurance (Dr Shepperd)	P 2068	SO 9724	6368	31/10/51	Accident repairs.
58	Adler	M265	LXK 44	18398	1/11/51	Reline brakes.
59	Mr Hertzog	91P 1997	FUH 190	1911	5/11/51	Accident Repairs.
60	Dr Ward	91P 1586	VMG 577	18369	5/11/51	Check Steering
61	Mr McDonald	91P 1713	HOP 62	9709	5/11/51	Check Steering
62	Mr Bishop	71M 214	JGU 4	22058	5/11/51	Fit 4:1 rear axle etc

5.

63	Mc...an Lewis Riley	9JM 421	MPJ259	3769...	5/11/51	Check Ignition, Batteries, Grease. Adjust track ...
64	Maxwell Gilling	9JM 1522	KXK 865	21025	6/11/51	Service & Check Brakes. Accident Damage. New Hood.
65	Le Nurwier?	7JM 550	TMH812	1447?	9/11/51	Adjust Brakes check steering. ... Bodywork.
66	Elliott Cohen	M433	SLW582	31760	12/11/51	Recon 30 engine
67	Paine	M530	1L4287	19435	12/11/51	Wheel wobble. Play in steering.
68	Geen (12902)	K595	JYK438	28402	12/11/51	Ali heads and twin carbs.
69	G.W. Motors	P1794	WMC39	6250	12/11/51	Reset caster angle.
70	Dunstan	P1761	LLM565	~~1559~~	12/11/51	Repair ignition.
71	Godfrey (12928)	30hp engine			12/11/51	Overhaul.
72	Jacobar	M536	JYP671		14/11/51	Service etc.
73	Capt Farquharson	M874	KLK657	31000	14/11/51	Decoke etc.
74	Hopkins	P1874	WMF831	7630	14/11/51	SLR and SFT Lamp. Service.
75	Rawse	K419	DFR259	28632	16/11/51	Suspension - king pin - hub bearings.
76	Frain	M658	AGL377	28843	16/11/51	Service
77	Irving Swift	M270	9LW490	460cc	19/11/51	New Hood.
78	Hudson Ilford Ltd	P1874	9CE911	12008	20/11/51	Reset caster
79	Barclay Ingles	LXK146	L455		20/11/51	Ignition.
80	Galdthorp	K367	THX323	25891	20/11/51	Rear spring centre bolt.
81	Birdseye	P2228	GEA322	739	20/11/51	500 Service.

S

82	Lilley & Skinner	P1904	WMD350	7954	20/11/51	Reset castor angle.
83.	R. Simon	P2173	MJJ959	627	20/11/51	500 service.
84	Tien Thesingh	P2023	CAY19	16195	20/11/51	Check steering etc.
85	Simpson	S21559	OSY525	727	20/11/51	After Sales Service.
86	Jakabar	M536	9YR671	29191	22/11/51	Accident repairs.
87	Elgin Motors (13295)(13310)	M1037	SE6994	30319	22/11/51	Accident repair.
88	Ingram	M271 LH	DBA772	39738	22/11/51	service etc.
89	Crappige	M573	JUF470	18236	23/11/51	Tune and service.
90	Cyprien	C388	SMY278	48298	24/11/51	Accident repair.
91	Mr Cooke	8IM1072	KJN567	24958	24/11/51	Service. Adjust Brakes. Etc.
92	Irwin Swift	M270	JAWA90	16310	26/11/51	Fit S.U. Pump. Tune Engine. Fit Static tube Assy.
93.	F.G Wornham	P2074	M.G.846	9920	26/11/51	Tune. wobble
94.	Mrs Paine	P1999	KPG586	10783	27/11/51	service etc.
95	Hopkins	P1874	WMF831	7563	29/11/51	Accident repair.
~~96~~	~~~~		~~~~			
97	Car Sales H.O.	P2260	—	—	29/11/51	Fit radio.
98	Cook Hussle	M777	9M7942	28875	29/11/51	New front spring - accident repair.
99	Patten	K826	KLN45	08862	29/11/51	Fit silencer.
100.	Gaudds	P2207	MLO312	858	30/11/51	Fit Heater etc.

Job No	Name & Address	Chassis No	Reg No	Mileage	Date	Work to be carried out
1	Cheetham	M.1523	KXK714	?	30-11-51	Fitting Reflectors. (Marchal.) Optique.
2	Dr McCarthy #29 (12895)	M.614g	JYV.272	49402.	30-11-51	Fitting S/Abs. Rear Spring & Bushes.
3	Dr Morris		J9Y 705	?	30-11-51	Fitting Head Gasket.
4	Mr Simpson	J2.1559.	CS 7525	10439.	30-11-51.	1000 mile service
5	Rowse.	K419.	DFR259	28843	3/12/51	Regrind crank.
6	Stourcliff. Close Garage.	P1020	KCR294	12770	4/12/51	Brakes - steering service.
7	Mrs Pregging	P1918	LYM906	9577	4/12/51	Service.
8	Major Ranni.	P2187	XMF656	1287	4-12-51.	1,000 Mile Service Check Springs Steering Lengthened Generally Check over.
9	Goldstein.	P1635.	LGK36	14795.	5/12/51	Steering.
10	Freedman.	P1878	LYF445	9304	5/12/51	Service.
11	Graham	P1669	BJE 490		5/12/51	Repair H/S Rear wing accident ewin
12	D. Leapman.	P2149	XMY999	563.	5/12/51	500 service
13	Phillips (128914)	P1595.	KYP630	22296	6/12/51	Check steering — decoke — all beads.
14	Johnson	471M	ARC319	32674	7/12/51	2° Beam
15	Overall.	P2891	MWA241	23359.	7/12/51	Small dynamo pulley.
16	Galliers	K2109	XYC365	4945.	7/12/51	Decoke.
17	George & Gabling	P2266	—	—	10/12/51	Fit roof aerial only.
18	Elliot Cohen (12972)	M.433	JLW 582	32185	10/12/51.	
19	Richard Felton (12939)	P1994	WHX535	5134	10/12/51.	Fit Over-riders. Check Hi-Throttle. 2nd gear, Steering wheel, Radiator Radio etc.
20	Mr Carter Snr	P2257	NAH 2	3838	11/12/51	Convert to Centre Gear Change. Check choke control, Heater & Demister. Coil Spring O/S Indicator. Water leak Radiator.

Job No. T	Name	Chassis No	Reg No	Mileage	Date	Work to be carried out.
21	Rossin.	M.1066 B	UMC 538	9375	17-12-51	Change Radiator & Fill with Antifreeze
22	Mr Taylee. c/o Tate of Leeds.	M.669.	JDD 702	22645	11-12-51.	Inspect Car. Estimate to make same Br. Roadworthy.
23	Inner		LXT 5		11-12-51.	Collect Car, Removing Starter & Freeing Bendix
24	Mr Wexson. (12991) (12992)	K 510	JUC 310	29838.	11-12-51.	Accident Repairs.
25	Dr Javrir	M.1013	UMC 924		11-12-51.	Check M Drain Tap Leak. Check Hose Joints. Top up with Bancol.
26	Clarke Taylor	P 1645	HGE 895	9060	12-12-51.	Clutch Judder, Steering, Stop Light, N/S Door Inte Light Switch Focus H/lights Fit 2 Marchal Lamps. Check Rear U Bolts & Anti Sway Bar
27	Mrs Ercatt.	M2X 2295	MLX 155	518	12-12-51.	500 Mile Service 2 Way Mirror H/S Wiper sticks.
28	Leader	M3K 620	P2127		11-12-51.	Fit Special adaptors.
29	Broomfield (12913)	P 1538	UMX 450	14400	14-12-51	Service
30.	Perris Miss.	K 2092.	HAW 717	5939	17-12-51	Tune engine Adjust reset
31	D. Leapman.	P.2149	XMX 977		14-12-51.	Fit Door Handle & adjust Clutch.
32	D. Aberdeen. Holbert 2800	P.2148	LLS 488	1659	18-12-51.	1,000 Mile Service, Change Oils. Grease, Tune Eng (Whistle)
33	Mr Davis	M.447 P.	KXF 681	17113	18-12-51.	Check Eng & renew Parts as necessary. From Fitted, Adjust Brakes. Check Tracks. Shockers. Petrol Pump.
34	Miss G. Garton.	P 2257			18-12-51	Removing Starter & Freeing off Bendix Drive.
35	Cheetham.	M1523	KXK 716		18-12-51	Remove Road Wheels. Adjust Bkes. Tighten Anti Sway Bar. Fit New Strap on o/s Axle Beam.
36	Cennicott.	L 423	JNE 133	38303	18-12-51	Front sus - decoke
37	Ragnar.	P 2161.	MLT 909	1045.	19-12-51	Heater and Screen washer.
38	O.K. Hardy.	M1100.	KXF 819.	20669.	19-12-51.	Repair ex.
39	Simpson. ex Mort	J2659	OS 4525	2398.	20-12-51.	Tenno Spare wheel cover Torven cover
40.	Munroe,	P 1540	JAX. 234		20-12-51	Fit o/s Boot Quadrant.

	NAME	Chassis Nº	Reg Nº	Mileage	Date	Work to be carried out.
41	POTTER.	L 800	KLD 759.	19,652	21-12-51.	
42	Fishel		Lx Y 399		21-12-51	Tune Eng.
43	Walters.	M1074	EPM890.	29469	24-12-51	Marshal ref - service
44	Lord Latimer. (12914)	M 754.	KLO300	16486	24-12-51	Fit Bar.
45.	P Hughes.	M1102.	GYS513	22428	26-12-51.	Rings Heated.
46	M⁰ heatten	P 2127.	MGK. 470	6399	31-12-51	Wecoke.
47	M⁰ Bourke.	K. 248	KKK 672	6600	31-12-51.	Fit 2 Aluminium Cyl Heads.
48	Decca. (12971)	M400	JVC 302.		31-12-51.	Repair o/s Rear wing Stay & facing, adjust Brks.
49	W.S.Soons. (12901)		LYT. 602.		31-12-51	Check Cancelling of End. Check 2ⁿᵈ Gear. O/S Rear-wing. Hub cap missing. using water. Service.
50	Brann. (12903)	M760	OPE237	7513	1/1/52	Service etc.
51	Cannicott.	L. 423	JME. 133	38750	1-1-52.	Check 5 dines, adjust Brks. Check wiring, Tighten Alu Heads Grease all round. Fit Smaller Dynamo Pulley.
52	IRVING SWIFT. (12512)	M 270	JLW 490		28-12-51.	Rectifying N/S. Frt wheel Brke Cylinder Leaking.
53	Mr Wymer. (12930)	P 1672	LGX678	16364	28-12-51.	Accident Repairs.
54	S H ALLARD. (12904)	P 1964	LXR 946	16509.	31-12-51.	Change C.W & Pinion to 4.1
55	Chambers	M. 1523	KAK. 714.		1-1-52	Fit 2 Shock Absorbers.
56	Miss Durrant. (12966)(12967)	M. 597	MPE. 570	19999.	1-1-52.	Accident Repairs. Prov. 3310. Mon
57	Maxwell Telling. (12920)	KXK865.	M1522		1-1-52	Fit Brkt to Steering & rectify Trafficators
58	Mr Wise (13068) Bitton Servo Reproducers (13060)	P1822.	J4Y89	14299	1-1-52.	Accident Repairs.
59	D Loweman (12921)	P. 2149.	AMX 977.		2-1-52.	Complete Service. Exhaust Blow.
60	Col Hazlehurst (12896)	M 327	KLF639	40368.	2-1-52	Check ignition

	NAME	CHASSIS NO	REG. NO	MILEAGE	DATE	WORK TO BE CARRIED OUT.
61	Mr Chapel. (12906)	M.719	KLO 130	4480	2-2-52.	Check Shock Abs. Weld Rebound Bkts. Shorten check Straps. Floor Boards.
62	Mr Harris (12893) (12925) (13976)	P.2250	MLW.873	363	4-1-52	Service, Clutch Slipping, Pinking & Shuddering Cig Lighter not working. Rubber on Driver's Door. Handle Loose. Not Starting.
63.	Godfrey (12952) (13069)	P1548.	KYM669.	26245.	4.1.52	Change engine etc.
64.	Graham.	P.1669	BJE 490	—	3-1-52	Adjust Dkes + Clutch, attend to Speedo. Fix Mud Flap
65	Wenston. (12915)	P1761.	LLM565.	14367.	7-1-52	Clutch judder - adjust brakes. etc.
66	Gallisp. (12969)	K2-2109	XMC 365.	5794	7-1-52	Bray water heater.
67.	Mrs B Culpin. (12931) (12987) (12988) (12989)	P2188,	GMO999	6454.	7-1-52	Repair damaged wings and service.
68	Ford. (12917)	P.2260	KNN.626	1520	7-1-52	Front coil spring.
69	Cony Evans. (12943) Cen 3486	M931.	FUU649	23863	4-1-52.	Service etc.
70.	Inshap (12905)	M 217	9GU5.	12504	8-1-52.	Front spring Grblow.
71	Hon Miss Joan Paine (12918)	P1999,	KDG 586.	12337	8-1-52	Fit heater + Wefrater. Lubricate Glass Broken n/s Rear Light Reversing Light Faulty Door Lock Faulty
72	Richard Afton (12932)	P199#	WHX535	5654	9-1-52	Tune etc
73	LATIMER.	M754	KLO300		9	
74	Swift. (12974)	P2101.	HKU80	4599.	13-1-52	Engine rain badgeconb, Short Bille.
75	Ingram.		DGA 772			
76	Mr Hudson Ilford Ltd. (12944)	P.1816	JGE 911	13584.	14-1-52	Fit heater, Noise on Prop Car, pronounced when turning Left. Speedo Noisy & Hand Jumping. Reversing Light Fit Wg Belt. Oil Filler.
77.	Green 12946.	K595.	GYK 438	31726.	14-1-52.	Back axle noise
78	White. (12942)	M566.	MNW474	25092	14-1-52.	Weld bracket.
79	Dr Manns (12965)	L127	9G8908	14492	15-1-52	Repair gearbox.
80	Bindrege (12941)	P2228	GFA322	2544	16-1-52	Service

	NAME	CHASSIS NO	REG Nº	MILEAGE	DATE	WORK TO BE CARRIED OUT
81	Mr A. Godsal (12938)	M.527	NFC. 139	61100	17-1-52.	Adjust Brks. Check Track.
82	Mr Fredman (2936)	P. 1878	LXF. 445	10440	17-1-52.	Service. Check n/s. Tube (running L.513. on night) Check Trafficator.
83	M. Innes.?	Mon 2803			17-1-52.	Repair Road wheel.
84	Mr (Dr) Sharpe (12964)	P. 2044	OuO 297	10248	17-1-52.	Complete Service. Change G.Box & Axle Oils & Grease.
85.	Bank Top Water House. (12997)	P 2115.	BCW10.	5757	17-1-52	Noise in engine.
86.	Lockyer. (12961)	K553.	KTA309	29838	19-1-52	Axle gearbox repair.
87	Mr Barron.	P. 2091	HCY 863	7021	21-1-52.	Check Steering, Clutch Judder, Brake Squeak. Easy Gear change. n/s Door Noise. [NEW ENGINE WORK 864-955 P.]
88	H.R. Owen LTD. (12962)	6646.	LWB. 773.		21-1-52.	Heavy oil Consumption, Loss of Power to Engine. Rattle to Gear Lever. Occasional Jamming of Starter Motor.
89.	Mr Godfery. (13066)	Engine			19-1-52	Overhaul
90	Mr Winston. (12937)	P 1761	LLM 565		19-1-52.	Clean Carb. etc. Fit Petrol Pump.
91.	Mr Drew. (12996) & (12999 Mr Drew) PARK H.	K. 2242.	LOU 600	1092.	19-1-52.	Remove Eng. & stripping weld Rebound Brkts. Shorten check Straps.
92	Mr Forster.				19-1-52.	Fit Overriders, Check & Clean Petrol Pump.
93	Major Rani (12939)	2.189	XMF 656		21-1-52.	Adjust Brks Steering Wheel, & Clutch. Retard Advance Ignition.
94	Connicott. (12935)	L.423.	JNE 133.		21-1-52.	Clutch. Intermittent fault on Side Lights. Wipers fuse blowing.
95	Stewart & Gray (12940)	L. 867	LKR 963.	14723	22-1-52.	Replacement Rear Spring check S/ABS & replace if Nec.
96	Mr Walker (12943)		OBA 631.		22-1-52.	Service Check all Levels.
97	Sales Dept H/Office.	M2A 3015	New Car		22-1-52.	Supply & Fit H.M.V. Radio & Side Aerial.
98	Hartwells of Oxford.	91P. 2055.			22-1-52.	Check Chassis Frame & restore to correct Specification.
99	Bristol Street Motors. (13022)(13025)	P. 1952.	LOE 822	2147.	24-1-52.	Line to n/s. o/s Rear Wing close to Body. Starting handle does not fit. Inlide Grille out of Position. o/s Fr Door rubbing. [complete Respray]
100.	R. Stanmer. (13081)(13080)	M 10038	RLO 127	34441	24-1-52.	Accident Damage. Fit Radio

U.

Job No.	Name	Chassis No	Reg. No.	Mileage	Date	Work to be carried out
1.	A.R. Goода. (12981)	P. 1915	LXU. 597	10893	25.1.52	Check Car thoroughly, Tune Ignition & Carb. Wing Chisel Wobble @ 20 mph new Cigar Lighter. Change oil, add Collordol Graphite. Smiths Heater w/Screen Washer. Bkes. Element.
2.	Broomfield (12984)	P. 1538	UMX 450	14971	28.1.52	Reline Bkes, Check K.Pins & Fit Hub Bearings, Weld on Bkts for Buffers.
3.	Smith. Chesterfield Garage (13009)	M. 1020	KLR 294		28.1.52	Exchange Petrol Pumps & Gaskets. (2 Cars).
4.	Mr Smith Chesterfield Garage (13010) (13011)	M. 1021 B.	KLO 196	3203	28.1.52	Decoke, Examine Piston, Pull down Heads, Check Ignition Timing, Con. Clutch, & Clunk Radiator. Refill Sump w/undershield Damper, Wood Screws, Plug for Heater, New Plugs, Wiper Arms, H/grounds Bolt 1 on Cartridge, Petrol filter.
5.	Mr Irwin (12975) (12976)	M 628	Sou. 758	74771	28.1.52	Recon Engine, Ali Heads. 3.78 Ratio - Check w/pens
6.	Mr Caake. (13106)	M 1072	KUW 567	27709	29.1.52	Service. Tune.
7.	Mr Gzen. (12998)	K 595	JYK 438		29.1.52	Check Carburettors & Clean Plugs.
8.	Cheedham (13062)	M 1523	KKK 714		30.1.52	Fit new window winder.
9.	H/Office new car. (12982)	P 2281			31.1.52	Fit H.M.V. Radio.
10.	Lealden (12983)	P 2127	MGK 670		31.1.52	Remove dim clean & adjust Contacts.
11.	Godfrey, C. Billen. (13047)	P 1548	KYM 669		1.2.51	Change Cyl Heads. Adjust Bkes. Fit Grille Muff. Wing Mirror, Fan Belt. & Retard Ignition.
12.	Irwin Swift. (12999)	M 270.	JCW 490	42614	5.2.52	Repair gearbox.
13.	Mr Richardson (8593) (12995)	K. 607	JYT. 881	50169	5.2.52	Repair Rear Axle.
14.	Mr Clappel. (12990)	M. 719	KLO 130.		5.2.52	Andre Shock Absorbers.
15.	Hon Mrs Joan Paine (13064)	P. 1999	KDG 586	14015	5.2.52	Collect Car from Camridges Hotel. Rattle in m/s. Leak in R/H Bottom corner of Screen, Reversing Light Still Faulty, Upholstery L/H Seat Oil.
16.	R. Clews. (13049)	L. 426	HAJ 576	44398	5.2.52	Collect Car from Cobham, Remove Electric Gear Box, Fit Customers own Gear Box, Fit new S/Absorber. To Car.
17.	Burnyeat (13025)	M 1093	UMD 465	10263	8.2.52	Marchal ref service etc
18.	Imhofs. (13190)	99J 1972	LXT5.	11725.	8.2.52	Pocoke — Overhaul rear axle.
19.	Sempren. (13309)	J2 1559.	OSY 525.		8.2.52	Tow in check gear change.
20.	Mrs Escott. (13067) (13066)	M2K 2295	MKK 155	1560	8.2.52	Fit 2 Spot Lamps (yellow bulbs). Check Gear Change (2nd). Service. Change all Oils. Check Radio. Dent o/s Mudguard. Rev Gauge

U.

Job No	Name	Chassis No	Reg. No	Mileage	Date	Work to be carrying out
21	Mr Broomfield (12994)	P.1538	UMN 450		9.2.52	Clean & adjust Distributor.
22	Mr Geer (12998)	K.695	JYK 438	33073	11.2.52	Towing from Gt West Road. Fit new Canadian Gear.
23	Innes (13166)	993.204	LXN 5	5.710.	11.2.52	Change Engine, Steering Light, Petrol Starvation - correct Pumps. Rubber mount Rear Axle.
24	Leagman (13018)	P2149	XMX977	2524	12.2.52	Accident repair - service - line.
25	Technifau (13008)	P1929	WMF 837	12773	12.2.52	Mercury engine, Brake service.
26	Mr T.C. Wowell (13050)	P.1964	LXN 946		12.2.52	Recon Engine, Repair Gear Box. Check for play in Steering Box. Check King Pins & Bushes & report. Fit new W/Screen Glass.
27	Gollings & Associates (13020)	K.2109	XMC 365	6193	12.2.52	Drain Sump & re-fill, Adjust Bkes, Grease & check all levels H/S Indicator. Re-fix Pegs on Side Screens, Report Rev Counter, Check W/S. Wiper.
28	Dr McCarthy (13162)	M.5449	JYV 272	50822	12.2.52	Repair Boot, Stop Rattles on Fr Cowl & Bumper, Replace Fr Spring check King Pins & Bushes. Check Steering for Play, Fit Twin Carbs, Pedal Rubbers Check Bkes & Correct Wobble adjust Brakes. Rad Cap, Check Track, wash, Body Work, Tin of Paint.
29	Hertzog (13056)	P.1997	FUM 190	12854	14.2.52	
30	Godfrey (13103)	P.1548	KYM 669		14.2.52	Fit Fr Drum, Fit Steering Column Bolt. Retard Ignition Fit Check Straps.
31	Dr Morris (13110)	K127	JGY 708		14.2.52	Check W/Smburton. Rectify defective Ignition & Rear Light.
32	H.R. Owen (13021)	6649	LWB 773			Fit Petrol Filter & check Petrol System.
33	Mr Smee (13006)(13007)	P.1621	LNN 415	33470	18.2.52	Exchange Eng. (check Bkes & Timer) new 882225
34	Mr Bland (13012)(13013)	P.2281	MXA.546	354	18.2.52	Engine Stalls Tighten Steering Wheel in Worn position, Rattle under Bonnet, Throttle Sticks, Hand Throttle Knob, W/S Rattles Complete Service Check Pass Seat
35	Destinghouse (13015)(13032)(13033)	M273092	MX 551	450	19.2.52	500 Service.
36	Coundley (13051)	M1511	NPG 827	18603	19.2.52	Weld on bracket.
37	Irwin (13045)	M628	GOU 758	212	20.2.52	Silencer.
38	Stamp (13048)	M273016	XME222	196	20.2.52	Spray wheels, etc.
39	Mr Wood (13054)	P.2236	OUM 876	3844	20.2.52	Fit Alli Heads, Check Rear 'U' Bolts & Ant. Sway Bar. Tyre Pressures. 30 Rear 25 Fr Service.
40	Turner Riley (13211)	M421	MPJ 219	42197	21.2.52	Bkes. Check Fr Suspension. Engine cuts out. Short on Ignition Smell of neat Petrol. Charge Batteries Service Top up oils wash.

• U,

Job No	Name	Chassis No	Reg No	Mileage	Date	Description of work to be carried out.
41	R. Simon. (13014)	P. 2173	MJJ 659	1828	21·2·52	Service.
42	Mr Ingram (13044)	71L·271A.	DBA·772.	43352.	21·2·52.	Check, Carb, Flooding & Poor Feed, Clutch Judder. Check + Clean Plugs. Steering Column Squeaks. & Grease, Check Bkes, Bleed System. Ratchet on
43	Terlinjen	P.1929.	WMF.837.	12817	21·2·52.	Stoplight Frosty. Check Eng. Check + Clean Plugs. Re-set Carb. New Cotter Pin in Stub Axle. Cut Bolts on Fan Cleaner
44	Mr Waddell (13168)	M2A2299			21·2·52	O/S Fr Spring Fouling Chassis.
45	Mr Broomfield. (13046)	P.1538	UTA·450		21·2·52.	Check Plugs. Fit new Set Plugs.
46	Mr Frew (13052)	M·658	AGL 377	30·464	22·2·52.	Fit new Silencer. Clean Plugs
47	Mr Wallis. (13053)	K·639	KLX 473	27720	22·2·52.	Check Gear Box. & 1st Gear. Check Clutch. Top up Andre. Shock Absorbers.
48	Mr Simpson (13309)	993·1559	OS. 7525	4067	22·2·52.	Change all Oils. Refill with Castrol R. Grease.
49	Hopkins. (13024)	P1874	WMF831	9431	25·2·52	Service.
50	Mr Davis (13017)	K895			22·2·52.	Change Eng Oil. Fit new Fram Cartridge. Adjust Fan Belt.
51	Mr Adler	cancelled	see Job No 54.		25·2·52.	Check + Top up Master Cyl.
52	Mr Harrison (13019)	M·1007D	EBN 96	11592.	25·2·52	Recon Engine. No R8830799. Old 318F7207753.
53	Dr Ker. (13054)	P.1880.	PPA 830.	14061.	26·2·52.	Play in steering. Wobble. Brakes. Tune service etc.
54	Adler (13055)	M265.	CYK44.	23551	26·2·52.	Check + Top up Master Cyl.
55	Miss Wman	M 647	MPF 570.		25·2·52	Welding Bumper Bar.
56	Mr Leather (13191)	P 2121	NGK 470		26·2·52.	Adjust Bkes. Free off Footbrake Pedal.
57	Mr Gibbs. (13056)				26·2·52.	Welding Seat Bkt. strengthen Runner + Bolts.
58	J.D Simon	P 1920	LXA. 908	17967	26·2·52.	Fit 12L Dynamo.
59	Le M Simpson (13072)	M. 550	TNW. 812.	4369.	27·2·52.	Clutch Judder, Noise under Bonnet, Check Transmission Noise Gear Lever + Idler. Fit swan neck pins. Service S/Abs Andre. Fan Pulley.
60	Mrs Wynne (13059)	P. 1672	LGA 678	14716.	28·2·52	Adjust Bkes. Reamer out Jacking Bkts.

U

Job Nº	Name	Chassis Nº	Reg. Nº	Mileage	Date	Description of work to be carried out.
61	M. Harris. (13087)	P 2250.	MLW 873	990.	28-2-52	1000 ml service.
62	Quinell (13078)	K.696	KXC 162	26974	29.2.52.	
63	Bridge Garage.	P 1688	LLC 40	12071	29.2.52.	Modify Panard Rod.
64	M. Godfery (13126)	P.1548	KYM 669.	28250	29.2.52	2 OMW. Exhaust Blow, Exhaust Rattle, Adjust Bres. Check Rear 'U' Bolts. + Anti Sway Bar.
65	Regents Park Garage (13027)	M 517	SMY 835.	38311	29-2-52	Mercury Engine.
66	Sprakie. (13043)	P 1901.	F.F.N 539	4989.	1-3-52	Decoke service Heater SFT900
67	Bramfield.	P 1538.	UMY 450.	15494	3-3-52.	Service.
68	Craig. (13077)	M 1058.	UMC 938.	36179.	3-3-52	Mercury engine
69	Clifford Brown. (13088)	P 1547.	LPO 251	40595.	4-3-52	Bodywork service.
70	Geer. (13041)	K 595.	HAW 717 JY 5438	34883.	5-3-52.	Play in rear axle.
71	Miss Dennis. (13076)	K2/2092.	HAW 717	6902.	5-3-52	Leak in tank.
72	Aberdeen. (13083)	P 2148.	I.L.J. 488.	3144	5-3-52	Service Heater.
73	Westinghouse. (13210)(13073)	M2 x 3092	MXA 551	1758.	5-3-52	1000 ml service. Screen washer.
74	Car Sales (2-28 ?) (13093)	91R 1552	OXG 440	4328.	7-3-52.	Grease all Points. Check all levels. Change Engine Oil. Adjust Brakes. Check Steering (Very Stiff)
75	P. Rushton. (13108)	K 439 A	JYE 356.	22065.	10-3-52.	Cord ring and decoke.
76	Barran Metal Spin Co. (13110) midland	P 2071.	HCY 863.	9749.	10-3-52	Accident repairs.
77	Cradlock. (13084)	K 201.	SMH 107.	33326.	10-3-52	Recon engine.
78	Walters. (13085)	M 1074.	EPM 890.	31944	10-3-52	Bodywork. Tune.
79	G. Smith Bosanquet (13107)	K 2091.	HMR 162.	2784.	10-3-52	Service Notek lamp.
80	Max Faulkner. (13192)	P 2175.	MJJ 460.	5371	10-3-52	Service - bodywork.

#	Name				Date	Work
81	Dunston.		P1761.	CCM565		10-3-52	Weld Shocker Brackets.
82	Dec. Sharp.	(13063)	P2044.	OUB 297		10-3-52	New throttle assembly.
83	R. Aften.	(13094)	P1994.	WHX535.		10-3-52	Noise in rear axle.
84	AGOMBAR.	(13093)	P.1815.	WMC WHX 515.	14548	11-3-52	Fit Badge. Bot. Waterproof Distributor. Attend to Screen. Catch. Tune. Engine. Check Brakes. Map Reading. Note K. long range.
85	Irving Swift.	(13109)	M 270	9LW490.	437600	11-3-52	Replacement Mercury engine.
86	Rosen.	(13086)	M1066.	UMC538	30128	11-3-52	Brakes. Tune.
87	Waddell.	(13168)	XMY 237	M2X2299	1943	12-3-52	1000 Service.
88	O. K. Hardy.	(13089)	KXF 819.	M1100.		12-3-52.	Service. Check steering.
89	Roy.	(13093)	M1329.	KWE 28.	42826	13-3-52	Front suspension — gearbox.
90.	Stock Engine.		32 hp. Mercury.			13-3-52	Recon 32 hp. engine.
91.	Mrs Fregley.	(13099)	P1918.	CXM906	11262	17-3-52.	Kingpin — Service.
92	Mrs Lamb.	(13130)	M 211	NKW 355	41007	18/3/52.	Gears. Fit. Tune. Eng. Adjust Bkes. H/light. Fuse. Bearing.
93	H. A. Stranson.	(13082)	L. 521	UMC 363	17630	18/3/52.	Check Rear Spring. Fulcrum Bkts. Check Fr. Spring. Fit 2° axle Beams.
94	Mr Talbot.	(13097) Royal. 7210	P 1603	KYV 642.	24060	18/3/52.	Check Carb. Fit new Bonnet Rubber. repair Bonnet Spring.
95	Irwin	(13096)	M 628	JOU 756		18/3/52.	Oil. Change.
96	Elliar Colin	(13095)	M. 433	JUU 582	34735	18/3/52.	Fit Alli Heads.
97.	C.R.O. Russell.		P 2274	XME.696	877	18/3/52.	Damaged Steering Wheel & Gear Lever Knob. Paint Chippings round door Shuts.
98.	S. Wingfield-Digby.	(13155)	M 722	CTK.930	20357	18/3/52.	Oil & Change. New Hood. Car Heater. Weld Split in ½ Bonnet. Check Suspension. Adjust Bkes. Tacting of acc. Tighten up Doors. Rear window fit.
99.	F. A. Jones.	(13112) Reliance 2406	M. 519	HLJ. 575	18531	18/3/52.	Fit new Tyres. Realign Camber 10° of Fr. Wheels. Recheck track. Tighten Members on Steering Checks. adjust Steering box. Check Bkes. adjust Reed. Check S/ABS. Sun. Gromley. Tune up Eng. Check wing. Bar.
100	Winston	(13165)	P 1761	LLM. 565	16571	18/3/52.	Adjust Bkes. Radius Vibrates. Springs Camp. R. S/ABS. W/Screen. Rattles. Fit. Spare Tyres. worn Rear Side. Fit Fan Belt. Adjust. Clutch Wire. Joint Break.

Job No	Name	Chassis No	Reg No	Mileage	Date	Work to be carried out
1	Car Sales Head Office (13104)	M 901	SKY 832	10419	19-2-52	S/Fit new Front Spring Oil & grease Cal Points
2	Dr Garrin (13102)	M1013.	UMC 924	45567	19-3-52	Shackle bushes – ignition leads.
3	Mr Green.	K595	JYK 438		19-3-52	Rectification
4	Harwells of Oxford (13105)	P 2102.	Units only		20-3-52	Check. Front Axle & Independent Fr Wheel Suspension Units.
5	Mr Sandner. (13090)		NEV. 26.		(E131570) 20-3-52	Fit new H/Bke Cable.
6	Technifon	P. 1929	WMF 832	13872	20-3-52	Wheel Rubs on right Lock. Fit oil Coil. Replace Filter. New Batteries Flat Spot. Cut out Lags. Change Eng Oil M/s Battery Terminal Sulphated.
7	Dr. Sharp. (13091)	91P-2044	OUB-297	12,910	20-3-52	Hums Engine.
8	Gowers. (13113)	P 1751	OPH 518.	18483	24-3-52	Clutch judder. filling numn.
9	A.M.C. Park Hill (E13351)	J.2.	B 81370.	4493 K.	24-3-52	Remake. check Calet box for slip.
10	Mr Fowler (13151)	656g.	TMH 616	18812.	24-3-52	Car Wanders & corners badly. Adjust Bkes Eng Pinks. Service Wrought entering Car Passenger Seat requires attention. Clean Refix Over. Riders
11	Mr Rosen. (13127)	M. 1066	4MC 538		22-3-52	Test. Check Steering. Tighten Rear 'U' Bolts. Check King Pins & Bushes.
12	Mr Whitehead. (13114)	P. 1953	LAV. 301	9859	25-3-52	Fr Suspension Rear Torque Bar. Ignition (Oil Coil Overheating) Rough Eng Period. Pack w/Screen. HandBrake.
13	Westinghouse Bke & Signal (E13357)	M2K 3092	MXA 557	2922	19-3-52	Fit replacement Speedo Head. New Con-Rod & Big End Bearing.
14	Mr Cramp. (13161)	M. 730	KBP 611	44032.	25-3-52	Eng. Wreck. Tune. (report Wear Tear). Shudder Bars. Clutch adjusted. Shock Abs. Back Axle. ¼. Shift. Grease & Spray Spring Wheel Wobble.
15	Mr Tynan (13101)	P. 1881	LXO. 516	5029?	25-3-52	
16	Godfrey (13201)	M. 10050	KLL. 736	750	25-3-52	Check for Eng Noise Intermitten cut out on Ignition Circuit L.T.
17	Mr Fredman. (13129)	P. 1879	LXF. 645	12186	25-3-52	Service Change all Oils. Check Eng. Tune. Rattle on Front End of Car.
18	Mr Cox. (13141)	81M 10303	LKT 645	44790.	26-3-52	Fit Mercury Eng. 2 Boss Handles.
19	Mrs Gee. (13154)	M. 698	KGC 224	29300	26-3-52	Recon Eng. Check Bkes Bdr Shield Lock fully W/g Rear Bumper to clean. number Plate Screws & plate chipped. Doors not closing properly.
20	Mr. Smith.					

W

Job Nº	Name	Chassis No	Reg Nº	Mileage	Date	Work to be carried out.
21	Dr Michael £13319 (13409)	M.343A	KWB27	32688	26.3.52	Traffication Weld, Boot Cylr. Accident Repairs, Wing Mirrors, Exhaust Blow, 2 Headlamps, King Pins & Bushes Bkts on Wind, Wrangle Noise, Recon Eng Bkts. Service
22	(E.13316-) (E.13317) (E.13316) 778 (W.Burke) Strange, Strange × Japoner.	P.2186	BCW.276	657	26.3.52	Accident Repairs
23	Irving Smart. (13160)	M.270	JLW 440		28.3.52.	Rev light.
24	Cheatham (13128)	M1523	KXKY19	34399	31-3-52	Exhaust silencer.
25	Decca Smartz (13164)	M400	JUC302	44458	31-3-52	Supply & fit Mercury Eng.
26	Rosen. (13127)	M1066	UMC538		31-3-52	King pins and bushes.
27	Richard Afton (13226)	P1994.	WHX535	7713	31-3-52	Service.
28	Gamero. (13168)	P1751	OPH518	18315	1-4-52.	Refit bonnet.
29	Lord Latimer (13149)	M754	KLO300	18035	1-4-52	Service, bodywork.
30	Miss Wilkes (E13256) (E13257)	K239	CHP818	86095	1-4-52	Accident repairs
31	Miss Yapp. (13140)	P1662.	LGP258	23157	1-4-52	Clutch, Service Tune 714TT 2× test with tester
32	Slaap (13163) (13179)	M243016	XMG222	721.	1-4-52.	Master cyl. sol switch.
33	Mr Crowderdam (13170) (13169)	P2126.	GAP269	16521.	2-4-52	Accident repair.
34	Mr Fausset. (13139)		LBH 856		2.4.52.	Check Bkes
35	Mr Birdseye. (13152)		9EA 322		2-4-52.	
36	Furnar. (13138)	P3084	—	—	2-4.52	Fit roof aerial.
37	Zadsal. (13146)		NFC139.		2-4-52	Check distributor.
38	Whitehead (13159)	M619	9XR690	35206	3-4-52	Recon engine – repair gearbox OLD 18F7200161 NEW R403797P.
39	Mr Hopkins (13167)	P.1874	WMF 831		5-4-52.	Faulty Clock. N/s Traffica sticking Bonnet Squeak. Top up Batteries check Bke Fluid Grease all Points adjust Bkes.
40	Cheevey. (13158)	L.357	MPG 118	22350	7.4.52.	2° Beams. Check M Cyl. adjust Bkes. adjust Carb. Tighten Tudda Bar for Noise

W.

Job No	Name	Chassis No	Reg. No	Mileage	Date	Work to be carried out
41	Mr Ingram (E.13302)		DBA.772		7.4.52	Clutch, Steering Judder, Carb & Petrol Pump. New lead wire to coil. Glass Rear No Plate & lights (wash & Polish Repair Rain)
42	Mr Gardner (13157)	M.392 A.	NEU.26	36641	7.4.52	Fit new Silencer
43	Mr Leapman (13197)(13299)(13200)	P.2147	XMY 9770	4117	7.4.52	Accident Damage.
44	Capt Farquarson (13153)	T.874	KHC.667	3292	7.4.52	Check Steering for Wander. Check Track, Rear U'Bolts. Tune Eng. Difficult to Start when hot. Nut on Battery Bolt Missing Tried = ask... Patch on Hood
45	Mrs Escott (13150)	M272295.	MCX855.		8-4-52	Service
46	Johnson.	M491	ARC 319	38551	8-4-52	Repair gearbox
47	Turner Riley (13155)	M421	MPX219.		7-4-52	Fit new Bonnet Handle
48	Cook Yarborough (13193)	L.122	JLy 81	46210.	7.4.52	Repair Front Cross Member.
49	Technicon (13156)	P1929	WMF 837.		7.4.52	Fit new Wire Cap & Lead.
50	I—L.P. (E.13325)	92-1972.	CYT5.	15276	8.4.52	Fit cyl heads. noise on turn. clutch plate.
51	Seymore Harrison.		EPM.96.		7.4.52	Exhaust Bearings Noisy. Tappets Noisy check Oil Seals (Smell of Oil in car over 50mph. Body Rattles.
52	E. F. Evans.		LXR.942.		8.4.52	Change Battery
53	Car Mart Ltd. (13177)	P1829	RYX 333	9728	8.4.52	Check & Rectify faulty Gear Box.
54	C. E. Walters (E13380)(E13606)	M 1074	EMP 890		8.4.52	Accident Damage. Remove Damaged Rear Bumper Straighten Rear Cross Fit new Bumper.
55	Dyster (13194)	P 1692	LGX 678	15624	8.4.52	Service Fit Silencer Cabin Stay
13524 E 56	Terminus Gge M Pegrie (E13372) Westinghouse Bke Sigs	M2X3092	MXR.551	12627	8.4.53	Check Bearings
57	Mr Culpin (13172)	P2185	gno.999	10166	15.4.52	Steering Wandering @ Speed. Bkes. Tune Eng Indicators out of adjustment. Bonnet Rattles & Doors. Fit Eng Shields WASH & POLISH
58	Mr Bugg. (13195)		KRU 364	14738	15.4.52	Wanders @ Speed. Adjust Brakes & Tune Carbs. New Bonnet Handle. Refix Licence.
59	Mr Taylor. (13196)		ExH 455	43978	15.4.52	Clean & check Fuel System. Tune Eng. Plugs. Charge Eng. Oil. Oil Filler Cap. Air Cleaner & Carb. water tox, Bkes, Plugs Steering Heat filter Wander cng. ETC
60	Mr Carr (13173)	M.870	FRY 999		15.4.52	Fit H/Bke Cable.

W

Job No	Name	Chassis No	Reg No	Mileage	Date	Work to be carried out.
61	R. Haggard. Washington. 2689	P. 1792	LLC 44.	11874	16-4-52	Clutch Judder. Steering Wander. Play in wheels & Steering wheel. Check Bkes. Service. Check 2nd Gear. Ft new Pedal Rubbers. Check Carb.
62	Elliot Cohen. (13202)	M. 433 P.	JAW 582	35743	16-4-52	Gear Box. Bumper Loose. Spot Light not working. Mirror N/S.
63	J. P. Davis. (13205)	M. 447 P.	KLF 681	19299	16-4-52	Convert to Centre Change. Bottom Gears. o/s Rear Bumper Bkt. Wrain oil & check Points. Rices Spot about 30 in 2nd. Fit Leather Fringe Pull or top of Steering column. Examine for Bearing Metal. Refill KL or XXL. Adjust Bkes. Top up S/ABS. Check Track & Steng
64	Mr Fredman. (13204)	P. 1879	LLF 446		16-4-52	Windscreen Wiper not working.
65	J. R. Cheetham (13145)	M. 1523	KXK. 714.		(9-4-52) 16-4-52	Fit new Hood. Black. Re. cellulose Bonnet.
66	Clark Branch (13206)	P 2281	TXA 546	1248	17-4-52	Down on o/s 1,000 Mile Service. Wheels Foul on Lock. Fit Fire Extinguisher. G.B. Plate.
67	Hugh Clapp. (13208)	P. 1607	LCA. 491	25782	19-4-52	Car Rattled. Rebound Rubbers & check Straps Steering S/ABS. Armstrong. Reline Bkes. Throttle Sticking Brake Light Support foul floor. Fit Centre G. Change. Wing Mirror. Wanders. Check over Service Tune up Ft
68	Turner Riley (13212)	M 421	MPJ 219	45137	21-4-52	Check Batteries. change Rear Tyres to Fr. Check S/ABS
69	Mr Cherry (13198)	L. 257	MPJ 118	22699	21-4-52	Replace. Eng. Condenser & Points & reg. H/Bke Lever. Loose. Renew H/B Cable. Fit Engine Shell SAE 30 or 60. Oil — G. Box & R. Axle. Check Fr. S/ABS. Sorbo round G. Box. Check Fr. Wheel
70	H. Williamson. (13207)	M. 6789	FKU. 916	20769	21-4-52	Central remote Control Gear change. check over car. report on what is required to make car A1.
71	Mr Forster. (13174)	P 1941	ERJ. 600	20851	19-4-52	Fit 2 New S/ABS. Fit Eng Tie Bar.
72	H. L. Vickery. (13215)	L. 6883	KLD. 758	6705	21-4-52	Beat out & respray N/S Rear Wing. Adjust Bkes. Repair Speedo. Tune Eng. Service Generally.
73	Mr Henderson. 13211	P 2289	XMY 540	1088	21-4-52	1,000 Mile Service. Standing Check Bonnet Spring. Fit new Safety Catch. Fit SFT 700 Spot Lamp. Tighten Steering wheel. Fit Radio Roof Aerial
74	Maxwell Telling (13213)	M. 1522	KYK 865	25083	21-4-52	
75	Mr Fawcett (13233)		LBH 856		18-4-52	Refitting Baterias. Fit new Throttle & accelerator Pedals. Fit new Bell. Check over Steering. Rectify wheel Rubbing
76	Mr Cramp. (13175)	M 430	KBP 666		21-4-52	Reline Bke Shoes.
77	R. W. Lowe (13116)	M 326	JYT 950	43748	21-4-52	Check Fr Wheels. Engine Tune. Steering check Track. Rattles around Dash.
78	R. Afton. (13214)	P 1994.	WHX 535.	8500.	22-4-52	Flat Spot Stalls. Noise on n/s Ft. Eng. Change round Wheels. o/s Fr & Rear Wings n/s Quarter Panel. Rattle on n/s Arm Rest
79	Mr Butcher (13228)	P 3080	MXM 420	611	22-4-52	n/s Window Catch. Focus H/Lamps. Prime on Wheels. 500 Service. Wiper. Water Leak. Ft Badges.
80	Gregan. (13216)	M 894	CYS 99	23521.	23-4-52	Engine recon. brakes. service.

W

Job No	Name	Chassis No	Reg No	Mileage	Date	Work To Be Carried Out
81	Mr Geer. (13418-9)(13420)	K 595	JYK 438	35785	22/4/52	Accident Repairs.
82	Siman. (13225)	P 2173	N33 459	3034	26-4-52	Clutch Judder, Check Boot.
83	C. M. Armstrong (13218)	P. 1960			26-4-52	Wheel Wobble. Boot Handle. Conversion Plate.
84	Decca. (13219)	M 400	JUC 302		24-4-52	New Exhaust Flex. Tighten down Cyl Heads. Eng Oil
85	Stourbridge Cross Garage (13220)	M 1021B	KLO196	4477	28-4-52	King Pins & Bushes. Ball Ends. Noise on Eng. Eng dies @ 60 m.p.h. on 2nd. ½ gal ErroRacer. Check Ignition.
86	McNish. (13223)	P. 1612	LKA. 492	9339.	25-4-52	Steering Wobble & Pulling on Lock. Check S/Abs. Gear Change Stiff. Indicator Safty bult in bonnet. Rattle in Scuttle. Greasing + Oil Change.
87	Mr Gardner (13221)	M 3978	NEV 26		26-4-52	Fit new King Pins & Bushes. Check Track.
88	P. A. Jessen. (13222)	P. 1840	WMC. 579	21392	28-4-52	Rectify Clutch Judder, Decarbonise Tune Eng. Throttle Sticks Check W/Screen wper Motor. Rectify Boot Lock. Refit Panelling L/H H/S Rear any new.
89	Elliot Cohen (13203)	M 4338	JLW.582	35961	28-4-52	New Hood (Black Leather). Spare Wheel c/w Tyre & Tube.
90	Sinclair (13224)	P 1712	WME 816	20805	28-4-52	Repair Exhaust Blow. Check & adjust Bkes.
91	F. A. H. Fazy (13234)	L 203	MWL. 380	6002	28-4-52	Recon Eng. Clutch away. Check Bkes re-line if nec. Check Gear Box. Will not stay in 2nd gear.
92	Mr Newport (13227)	10148	DFX 826	28157	29-4-52	Adjust Steering Column, Gear Change Mech. Mod. Lever. Check Bkes. Tighten Rear U Bolts. Check Track. Squeak o/s Rear wheel
93	Childs (13229)(13230)	K 565	JFJ 356	26322.	3-5-52	Bodywork.
94	Technifor (13231)	P. 1929	WMF 831	15585	5-5-52	Pulling on Right Lock. 2 wiper arms & Blades Squeaks unsteady. Panel Light Ball. adjust H/Bk. Change Wheel. Indicator
95	Irving Swift (E13274)	M 270	JLW 490		1-5-52	Adjust Bkes. Change Petrol Pump.
96	Mr Hopkins (13235)	P 1874	WMF 831		1-5-52	Change Eng. Oil.
97	Mr Godfrey (E13275)	M. 1005B	KLL 736		2-5-52	Adjust Bkes.
98	Mr Butler (13236)	K 1924	WFX 777	13985	2-5-52	Weasabe. Check Steering check Rear S/Abs. Remove Rear Spring & Shorter Master Leaf by 3"
99	Mr Frame. (E13260)	M. 658	AGC. 377.		3-5-52	Fit Gear Change Bkt.
100	Braincliffe Close Garage (E.13329).	M. 1020B	KLR 294	14419	5/5/52.	Steering very Bad box. must be recon. adjust Bkes H/Bk Stiff Check Rear Spring inplace of nuts Renew any bad Water hose.

X

Job No	Name	Chassis No	Reg No	Mileage	Date	Work to be carried out
1	R. Stanton (E13270)	P. 2235	GEA. 372	3766	5·5·52	Check Steering (?Stocked). C.P. Bad. Check Heater, Panel Light, Cigar Light, Roof Light, Printsarth N/S Door, Boot Lid. N Wing, Edges Sticking
2	R. Haggard	P. 1792	LLC 44	12217	5·5·52	Bad vibration Fr End. Doors jam!! Check King Pins & Bushes. Check Fr Wheel Balance. Adjust Brakes. Gear change Stiff
3	R. Afton (E13260)	P. 1994	WHN 635		5·5·52	Body work.
4	Gilletts Garage (13238)	P 1886	LVO 895	10480	6·5·52	Attend to Steering, Slight Wheel Wobble D 30 PH. Fit new Hinges to Rear Locker.
5	C. K. Hard (13239)	M 1100	KXF 819	23636	6·5·52	Decoke. Cord. Rings
6	James (13240)	P 1751	OPH. 518	19249	6·5·52	Decoke
7	~~J.F.~~ Gluck (E13229)	K 519	HLJ. 575	20305	7·5·52	Repairs N/S Fr Wing.
8	S. Cliff. (E.13327).	M 217	JGU 5	13158	7·5·52	Eng Change. Steering Overhaul.
9	M's Escott (E13272)	M2A 2295	MLR 155	6354	7·5·52	Clutch Shudder, Check Wire & Tyres. Steering Column Clamp Bolt Seu. winter. Rad. Fully Seat Lamp Sun Visor. Seats. Indicators. Accident
10	Maxwell Talling (E13269)	M. 1522	KXK865	25625	7·5·52	Fit Premium Radiator. Poor sparks from Ignition
11	Mr Louis. (13254)	M 704	DRD 505	27809	8·5·52	Rad Leak. Repair Rad Grille Supply Grille Gate. Service. Tune Eng. 1st 2nd Gear Stiff Check Acc. Pedd. Choke Stiff Chassis Lits Body etc.
12	Mr Broomfield	P. 1538	HMA 450	16774	8/5/52	Complete Service, Fix Foam Filler.
13	Mr Sharp (13241)	P 2044	OUB 297	16519	8/5/52	Grease. Check all Levels.
14	Mr Garden (13242)	M 391 A	NGU 26		8/5/52	Hub Bearing N/S. Front.
15	Decca. (13253)	M 400	JUC 302		10/5/52	Service. Fix Supers.
16	Craddock (13252)	L 201	SMH 407		10/5/52	Fit H/me Cable.
17	Cyprian (E13273)	L 388	SMK 278	52774.	10/5/52	Decoke Plenum Gasket, Check Judder Bars. Ex Blow Service
18	Banks - Collis (13232)		JGG. 820		10/5/52	Exhaust Blow.
19	Ford (13339) (13255)	M 121.	9KF 575.	(Credit No E.13339)	12/5/52	As Per Sheet attached to Job Card
20	Griffith (13209) (13251)	P1583	HSP. 757	13318	12/5/52	Steering wander. Noise at Rear. Gear change Stiff

X

Job No	Name	Chassis No	Reg No	Mileage	Date	Work To Be Carried Out.
21	Overall (E.13306)	M 891	MUA 241	26319	12/5/52	Repair Gear Box.
22	O.B Walters (E13381)	M. 1074	EPM 890		12/5/52	Repairs as per Estimate plus Accident Damage.
23	Billy	P 1943	HWS 353	12384	12/5/52	Fit Mercury Eng. Supply & fit 3-27 Rear Axle Ratio.
24	Clark-Taylor (13250)	P 1645	HGE 895	16011	12/5/52	Check Steering
25	Mr Wyatt. (E13202)	M 6189	JYF 943	41540	13/5/52	Check Reg. Fit Lowrens Washer. Rewire HT. Check Coil Repairing Elec Set Pumps Ex Customer AC Pump. Check Springs 35/0015 Check Steering etc
26	Mrs Lamb (E13266)	M 711	NWL 355	44098	13/5/52	Engine Tune. Fit Pressurized Radiator. Check for Vibration Period.
27	Leapman (13249)	P 2147	XMX 977	4485	13/5/52	Fit Electric Horn.
28	Mrs Frayling (13248)	P 1928	LXM 906	14173	14/5/52	Change Oils, Grease. Check Speedo. Fit Balance Weight Check Steering wobble (King Pins) Adjust Bks. 2 Bumper Stop Bolts
29	George Fitt Motors	P 1720	NKJ 73	10295	14/5/52	Fit 2 New Coil Springs, fit new Armstrong S/Absorbers Reline Rubber Bks. Check Clutch Slips 1st Check 2nd Gear
30	Dr Carr. (E.13298)		FRY 999		14/5/52	Accident Repairs.
31	Car Mart (13247)	993-2155	Not Registered	176	14/5/52	
32	Mr Gregor. (13333)	M. 895	CGS 99	24769	17/5/52	Rectify door in Bracket. Nearside. Petrol Filler, Doors Rattles. Mud Flaps Bonnet Sides Exhaust Tighten Gl Adj. Ignition Child Fiddler
33	Dr Carmicot (13245)		JNG 133	40973	17/5/52	Service. 2 Batteries
34	Crayman. (E13259) (13474)	P 1590	VHX 883	26466	17/5/52	Check Steering. Estimate for Accident Damage Rear Panel N/S.
35	Dr Shepherd. (13416)	P 2068	SO 9724	10406	17/5/52	Accident Damage O/S.
36	Simonize LTD. (E13261)	M 6589	AGL 377	33510	17/5/52	Decoke. Ammeter Faulty Batteries Top up & Charge. Check Water Pump. S/ABS Service Adjust Bks. Reline if nec New HT Leads
37	Dr Janssen (13244)	M. 1013	UNC 924		17/5/52	Change Plugs & fit Points to Distributor
38	Mr Weston (13246)	P 1761	LLN 565		17/5/52	Change Petrol Pump.
39	Henry Swift (E13274)	M 270	JCW 490		17/5/52	Remove fuel Pump fitting new Coil
40	Godfrey (E13276)	P 1548	KYM 669		17/5/52	Change Drums & adjust Bks.

Job No	NAME	CHASSIS No	Reg No	MILEAGE		DATE	WORK TO BE CARRIED OUT
41	Mr McLeod (E13319)	M 343	KWE 277	33611		19/5/52	Engine Overheating. Check Tudder for Petrol Pump. Steering. Fr Wheel Bearings. Tune Engine. Flush Rad.
42	Enochs Equipment (13243)	P 1589	ETL 231	12912		20/5/52	Check Steering. Fit Armstrong's S/ABS Gut Rear Rods
43	Blockway (E13284)		ORT 335			20/5/52	Fit 2 wells in Fr Wings to carry Spare wheels.
44	Maxwell Telling (E13362)	M 1522	KWE 865			20/5/52	Fr Bumper. N/S Fr Wing Touch Body work. Rattling O/S Door. Hood Strap. Park Light. Union Seat Speed Clock. Clutch. Bke Linings. Steering Lecks. Punct
45	Leather (E13277)	P 2127	MGK 670	16975		20/5/52	Fit Push Rod to Columbia Control. Remove Rear O/S Bracelet & free off. Bleed Brakes. Gear Box.
46	Burke-Collis (E13324)		Jee 820			20/5/52	Check Carburetor.
47	Bailey (E13323)	P 1963	HWS 853			20/5/52	Fit Speedo block. Rectify wipers.
48	Cyprian (E13278)	L 388	SXX 278	53076		21/5/52	Fit new C/Shaft & Bearings.
49	A J C Roy (E13390)	M 329	KWE 28	46240		21/5/52	N/S front Shocker. Gear Box Noise.
50	Le Mesurier (E13361)	M 550	TMH 812	7119		21/5/52	Tighten front Spring. Change Shackle Bush. Check King Pin & Fr Hub. Bkes. Snip Oil Tight Wipers. Fan Belt
51	J.P Davis (E13264)	M 467p	KLF 681	19523		22/5/52	Check Distributor. Change Engine Oil. Top up S/Abs Adjust Bkes. Speedo Cable.
52	Mrs Frayling (13243)	P 1918	LXM 906	14319		22/5/52	Low Speed wheel wobble. Change front Shock Absorbers. (Armstrong).
53	Mr Ross	M 231	JLN 245	13589		22/5/52	Flat Spot.
54	Miss Barton	P 2256	MLO 469	14218		22/5/52	Check Indicator.
55	Mr Henderson (E13392)(E13263)	P 2289	XMY 590	2045		23/5/52	Complete Service. Wash & Polish. Change wheel. Check Radio. Cellbore splitting on Boot. Towel in O/S Door.
56	White 13263	MNW	MNW 474	—		24/5/52	Service.
57	Toomer (E13334)	P 1537	OPR 650	16245		24/5/52	Decoke or Tune. Steering. Service. W/Screen Rattle. Bke Anti Roll Bar. Clutch Judder. Check Exhaust. Demisters. Gear Box. Wears.
58	D.A. Parry (E13330)	P 1816	LXD 515	15277		26-5-52	Decoke. General Service. Clutch Judder. Sticking Throttle.
59	Leapman (E13265)	P 2147	XMX 977	15299		26/5/52	Grease Body Rattles. Align H/Lamps. Acc Pedal. O/S Fr Side Light. Vibration @ 20 mph in Top. Wash & Polish. O/S Indicator Sticks.
60	Gardner (E13283)	M 391A	Neu 26			26/5/52	Check Clutch. Change Eng oil

ID No	Name	Chassis No	Reg No	Mileage	Date	Work to be carried out
61	Lilly & Skinner (E.13279)	P 1904	WMO 350	?	24/5/52	Fit new Cork Pump assy.
62	Samet R.L (E.13268)	M 1032	NPA 871	?	16/5/52	Fit Fan Belt check Steering. Body work
63	Mrs Wynn (E.13280)	P 1672	KYX 675	16454	26/5/52	Repair Gear Box.
64	Mr Winston (E.13281)	P 1761	LLM 565	18978	28/5/52	Repair Exhaust. Weld. S/Abs. Brkt.
65	Imhof (E.13328)	J2. 1972	LAT.5	19697	28/5/52	Remove Engine & Gear Box for overhaul
66	Mr Hopkins (E.13282)	P 1876	WMF 831		28/5/52	Service, top up Batteries. Adjust Brks. Check over Points. Tighten Prop & Bolts. Centre Swing Bar. Relock Friction. Check over Car.
67	Mr Strange (13331)				28/5/52	Bring out fit Suspension Blocks & adjust Brks.
68	C.K. Hardy (13332)	M 1166	KKF 819		28/5/52	Tune Eng. Oil & Grease. Steering adjust Brks. Check w/screen wiper Mechanism. Examine Speedo & Calib. c/s Trafficator
69	Necca (E.13335)	M 400	JUC 302	M 47104	29/5/52	Noise on Fr. End. Fit new Shackle & Panel. Bolt. Check Thermostat.
70	Newbury (E.13336)	M 317.	PY0585	4281	3/6/52	Check over for Rally.
71	Pecca (E.13373)	M 400	JUC 302	47278	3/6/52	Change Engine Oil. Service change from Filter
72	Ingram (E.13387)	M 271'A.	DBA 772.	48804	4/6/52	Accident Repairs. Beat out & Respray Rear wing. Check Tow in fr wheels. Carb slide (1/16" open).
73	S.W. Wells (E.13364)	P 2325	KWY 558	4721	4/6/51	Steering wander.
74	Viscount Payne (E.13413)	P 3084	HUS 760	4095	4/6/52	Accident Repairs.
75	Winston (E.13345)	P 1761	LLM 565	19380	5/6/52	Check for Rattles. Spring on Accelerator Pedal Sticks. w/Screen wiper Sticks. Check fr Seat L/H side.
76	Max Garage 2246 (E.13326)	M 795	HLR 595	25388	5/6/52	Fit Anchor Conversion Kit
77	Moons Motors.	P 2167	MMB 905	5764	5/6/52	Supply fr 2 Fr S/Abs. Eng Tune. Check fr Wheel Alignment. Check Steering
78	Dr Morris (E.13384)	M 127	JGY 708	17691	7-6-52	Eng Tune, Service change all Oils Exhaust Blow. Play in Steering. Throttle Sticking. Jump out of 2nd gear
79	Le Mesurer (E.13361)	M 550	TMH 812		7-6-52	Remove Induction Manifold & Cyl heads. Check No 2 Valves.
80	Mr Rosen (E.13346)	M. 1066	UMC 538		7-6-52	Fit Exhaust Silencer.

X

Job No	Name	Chassis No	Reg No	Mileage	Date	Work to be carried out
81	Mr Mann (13420)(19)(13337)	P.158b	VMG 577	21688	9-6-52	Convert Gear Box to Centre Change.
82	T.N. Bleakley (13342)(13343)(E.13347)	K.1925	MAT 335	13357	9-6-52	Ft. Spring Bkts. Shock Absorbers. Reline Bkes U995. Fit new Ammeter. O/S Rear Wing binds on R/H Bonnet Top
83	Maxwell Telling	M.1522	KAM 865		10-6-52	Rectification work.
84	Peacocks Bauman (E13320)					Check Brakes & Linings M/S Track Rod. Adjust Track.
85	Woosnam Mills (E.13348)	L 301	LHU 836	6209b	10-6-52	Repair Gear Box.
86	W.S. Morland (E.13369)	M.721	LKE 780	25908	11-6-52	Engine Tune. Ft End Judder. M/S Exhaust Pipe set down Hot air passed column.
87	K.G. Cramp (E.13349)	M 730	KBP 466	47496	11-6-52	Engine runs very erratically especially when hot. Engine Tune. Check Ft Spring Shackles. replace when new water Thermostat 45
88	Mrs Escott (13350 E)	M2X.2295	MXX 155	7295	11-6-52	Service
89	S. Rosen (E13363)	M.1000 b.	UMC 538	33275	11-6-52	Exhaust Blow. Marlin Cyl Rollers.
90	Mr Wills (E.13320)	M.560	MNW 47A	27227	11-6-52	Reline Brakes.
91	Gallings (E 13358)	K.2109	XMC 365	8143	11-6-52	Check Engine. Fix Rev. Counter.
92	M. Wick (E13364)	SS-1912	LXY 15	8713	11-6-52	Rev Counter Wire. Track Steering
93	C.G. Newbury (E13359)	M 317	JYO 585	269	12-6-52	Fix 2 New 6.25x16 Avon Tyres. Fix one New Battery
94	Mr Thrush (E.13443)(E13365)	P 2050	NRA 837	10530	13-6-52	Engine Tune.
95	Mr Costard (E13371)	M.634	HAB 319	26032	16-6-52	Overhaul Ft Suspension fit Late Type Ft System Check Bkes & Clutch Ammeter Steering Check Speedo. Bonnet. Fog Lamps, 3 Hub Caps. Check Eng. O/S Vent Pipe
96	Clark Branch (13440)(13411)(E13324)	P 2281	MXA 546	4188	16-6-52	Service. Bkes, Clutch. Steering Binds. Wander 30 mph. Reset Ft Bumper. Water. Steering Column. Body Bolts Loose. Doors. Eng Fast. Fylter Slem Wind etc
97	Mr Walker (E13366)		PBA 631		16-6-52	Adjust Bkes.
98	Colonel HAZELHURST (E.13472)-1		KLF 639		17-6-52	Accident Repairs.
99	Armitage (E13374)	P.2102	NTH 244	17854	18-6-52	WHEEL WOBBLE, WHEEL TRAMP @ SPEED. CHECK CHASSIS ALIGNMENT OILING & GREASING SERVICE. STOP LAMP. N/S DOOR DROPPED. TUNE ENGINE. INTERIOR MIRROR.
100	Frey (E13370)	L 203	MWL 380	6590	17-6-52	Service. Change Eng OD. Change Ft Bke Hoses. adjust Brake. Deliver car to Lincoln.

Y

JOB No	INV. No	NAME	CHASSIS No	Reg. No	MILEAGE	DATE	WORK TO BE CARRIED OUT
1	E13368	MARDEN. (E13368)	P.1649	VHX 560	16603	18-6-52	Decoke. Ex. Blow. Check Indicators
2	E13402	Miss Yarrow.	P.1662	LGP.258	30573	18-6-52	Decoke. Check Spec. Grav. of Batteries. Reg. Cut out. Starter. & Handle. Ex. Blow. Stop Light. Boot Hinge. Fit No Plate. Rubon Drag Link. Parking Light o/s. O/S Ind.
3	E13408	J. S. W. Robinson Junr.	P.1934	CEE 308	25520	21-6-52 NEW Q15552 P OLD B18F7249410	Coil Springs. Fr S/Abs. Replacement Eng. Check Bkes. Service Change all Oils. 15 y/n not charging. General Checkover. Tighten Bonnet Sides.
4		G. Hicks	K.554	JFM 780	27405	23-6-52	Exhaust Blow
5	13444	Dr Nathan.	M.890	KLL 577	28039	23-6-52	Ring Gear on Flywheel. Ex. Blow. Check Charging. New Hood. Maroon (Mallachide Leather). 6 Bladed Fan. H/Bke. Flies Off. Tune Engine
6	E13386	Mr Graves.	M.10223	JUF620	20263	23-6-52	Reline Bkes. Service change all Oils. Check Steering (Pulls to left) Check w/s King Pin. 2 Rubber Door Stops.
7	E13356	F. Smickstern (E13356)	P.1948	KTX 337	10929	23-6-52	Check Steering
8	E13393	G. E. Sims.	P.1839	Sun 606	9211	23-6-52	Check Brakes. Damage o/s Fr Wing.
9	E13377	Park Garage.	M.795	HLR. 595	25481	23-6-52	Check Bkes. Water Pump leak. N/s. Check Engine heat. Distributor.
10		Norvell.		KKE 59	15519	21-6-52	Tune. Engine.
11	E13375	Barclay Inglis.		LKX 146		21-6-52	Replace Track Rod End.
12	E13376	Fram. Simonye	M.6589	AGL. 377		21-6-52	Exhaust Blow.
13	E13385	Mrs Culpin	P.2185	9MO 999	17063	23-6-52	Fit 2 Wing Mirrors. Fit Bkes. Rally Plates. Check Bkes. Fit new Door Handle. Eng Tune. adjust Clutch. Bonnet Sides. Respray Fr Wing. Indicators & Screen Opener. Rubber on Boot. Door Screws
14	E13521	Tarbunt.	993.3012	MKT 17	4554	23-6-52	Fit Mercury Eng. & Build up as Ardun.
15	E13388	Reh	M.1531	UMX 874	14786	24-6-52	Low speed wheel wobble.
16	E13383	St John	M.880	HAA.325	62941	24-6-52	Wheel Tramp. Service. Change all Oils. Screws in Door Locks.
17	E13389	Cyprian	L.388	SMX 278	54723	26-6-52	Clean & adjust Plugs. Adjust Bkes. Clean Carb. Fit Economiser valve.
18	E13395	Martin Thomson.	K2203	OKM. 728	2155	26-6-52	Check Tuning, adjust Bkes. Check focus of H/Lamps. Check fitting of Curtain o/s. Centralise Indicator Switch.
19	E13394	Dr C. Hagenbach	M.1534	UMX 720	34845	27-6-52	Balance 5 Wheels.
20	E13391	Dr S. Ray		DUD 297		26-6-52	Service.

Y

Job No	Inv No	Name	Chassis No	Reg No	Mileage	Date	Work To Be Carried Out
21	13454	Enoch's Equipment	P 1589	ETL 231	14217	30-6-52	Change King Pins & Bushes. Play in Steering Box. Check Engine.
22	13455	G. H. Brown.	M. 760	OPE 237	9497	30·6·52	Decoke, Change Eng Oil. Service, Top up S/ABS. Check Bkes - very uneven. Sticking Throttle. Repair Bonnet Sides
23	E 13456	B. Jackober.	M. 536.	JYR. 671.	30941	30·6·52	Gear Box. Tappets. Engine Tune Repair. O/S. Trafficator Rehang. O/S Door. S/ABS. Checked & Topped up. Etc.
24	E 13397	Gollings.	K. 2109.	XMC. 365	8143.	11·6·52	Change Ammeter. Fit Spring to Throttle Cotrol Adjust Brakes.
25	E 13457	FE. Barron Esq.	P. 2017	HCY 863	16184	30·6·52	Set Radius. Rod. Fit Large Armstrong S/ABS Check Brks Check Adjusting Screws Check Brke Pipes Ft. Check Clutch for Judder
26		Clark-Blanch.	P. 2281	MXA 546	4898	1-7-52	Clutch Judder, Rubbing on Right Lock. W/Screen Rattles.
27	{13547} {13548} {13456}	Miss Garton.	P 2256	MLO. 469	5190	1-7-52	Handbrake Cable. Exhaust Blow.
28	E 13396	W. Craig	M. 1058	UMC. 938		30·6·52	Fit Petrol Pump.
29	13439	D. K.W. Vandy	M. 764	LHW 523		1-7-52	Faulty Ignition Re-wire
30	E 13469	Imhof.	J. 1972	LXT 5		1-7-52	Overhaul Steering Overhaul Rear Brakes.
31	13440	P. Elliot-Colon.	M. 433p	JLW. 582		1-7-52	Fit 6 Bladed Fan Flush our Radiator.
32	E 13407	Wilkins Ingram	Fr Axle.	—	—	2·7·52	Overhaul Front Axle.
33	E 13445	~~Mrs Pat~~ Ingram	M 271m	DBA 772	49616	3-7-52	Balance Road Wheels & Check Toe-in
34	E 13456	Mrs Paine.	P 1999	KOG 586	17468	3·7·52	L/H Small Window Loose. Big Window Stuck. Drain Anti Freeze Flush Rad. Engine Tune. Check Bkes. Noise on Rear.
35	E 13459	T. Ellis.	M. 405	JYM 271	13935	4-7-52	Fit new Shackle Bushes, Change Fr Tyres to Rear.
36	E 13441	Dr Marr.	P 1986	VMG 577		5·7·52	
37	13446-E	C. J. M. Abbott	P 2269	MUC 169	5497	4-7-52	Convert Gear Box. Noisy in Neutral. Big End or Piston Rattle when cold. Fit Spare wheel in M/S F-wing
38		Samet	M. 1032	NPA 871	22534	7-7-52	Adjust Bkes. Fit new Silencer & Rod Hose
39		D.V. Pain	M 530	IL-4287	28285	7-7-52	Adjust Carb. Fit S.U. Pump.
40		Bailey	P 1943	HWS 853	1369	7-7-52	Rectification Rear Axle.

Job No	Inv No	Name	Chassis No	Reg No	Mileage		Work to be Carried Out
41	E13475	V. G. Boyle.	P 1728	KLJ 376	19578	7-7-52	Noisy Rear Axle. A Low Speed. Exhaust Blow. Car Wanders.
42	E13449	Cramp.	M 730	KBP 466	48592	7-7-52	Decoke.
43	E13476	G. W. S. Broome.	M 6749	TML 209	17268	7-7-52	Decoke, New N/S Exhaust pipe. Acc. Spring Sticks. Adjust Bkes. Dynamo Check S/Abs. Top up. Service change all oils. Check Rad. Flush out. H/Blue Spring. Mod' Rectification
44	E13445	Leather	P 2127	MGK 470	13208	8-7-52	Reline Bkes. Fit new Plugs. Change Fram Filter. Road Test Car.
45	E-13468	Fredman.	P 1878	LXF 445	15497	8-7-52	Engine Tune. Service Change All Oils.
46	E13498	Steele.	P 1763	KOV 223	28054	8-7-52	As Per Letter.
47	E.13566 R / E.13585	Swithenbank.	M. 720 LH	MPJ 200	40132	7-7-52	Accident Damage.
48		Gardner.	M 397	NEV 26	39364	7-7-52	Accident Damage.
49	E13490.	F. A. Snuck.		HLJ. 575		10-7-52	Check Brake Bulb N/S H/Lamp. Check Dist. 2 ⁿᵈ Gear. Play N/S Fr Wheel Change Oils. Fill Eng Mobiloil Grade A. Service. Adjust o/s Door Lock & Peg in Side Curtain
50		Hopkins	P. 1874	WOE 831	15280	10-7-52	Steering Wander N/S Tyre. Flex pipe on Pump leaks. Throttle Sticks. Service change Eng Oil. Air Filter Cleaned. Side Light Bulb o/s.
51	E-13455	Mrs Paine	P 1999	KPG 586	18013	10-7-52	Replace T Bar on Rear Axle. R/H Door Dropped. Not Pulling Well. Noise on Rear. Starting Handle unusable. Play in Steering.
52	E-13470	Westinghouse	M2X 3092	MXA 551	6975	11-7-52	Clutch Judder. Dropped. Doors.
53	E. 13450	Leapman.	P 2147	XMX 977	17176	11-7-52	Check Axle. Fit 2 Spot Lights. Service, change all oils. Top up S/Abs. Body Bolts. Check Fr Wheel Alignment. Suspension. Tune Eng. Check Acc. Simonize Car. Worm N/S Fr Wing. Straighten Bumper.
54	E13454	Harrison	M. 10078.	EPM 96	16242	15-7-52	Service check levels. Check & adjust Bkes & Steering. Replace Broken Arm on S/Abs. Wheel Wobble. Check toe-in. Check Trafficator. Tune Eng & Carb. Tighten all Bolts.
55	E.13526 / E.13527	Clifford Brown.	P. 1597.	LPO 251	49066	15-7-52	Accident Repairs. Bonnet Sides Loose. Bonnet Rubber. Rattles on Woods. Ft S/A 700 & Marchal Reflectors. Paint Grille Plate. Echo Radio. Cool. o/Screen catches rear locker. Straighten Fr Rear Bumpers. Focus Lamps. H/3700
56	E13499	Decca	M 400	JUC 302	49693	15-7-52	Adjust Brakes.
57	E13483	J. B. Sons.	P. 2223	PUA 74	7812	15-7-52	Flat Spot. Dropped Doors. Sundry Squeaks.
58	E13478	Countess Moy	K 1085	LXR 525	12120	16-7-52	Change Eng Oil. Adjust Bkes. Check Choke.
59	E-13454	J. L. Cooke.	M 1072 B	KUW 567	35843	16-7-52	Exhaust Blow. Tune Eng. Service change all oils. check & top up S/Abs.
60	E13484	Wⁿ Caae.		FRY 999		16-7-52	Service - check all levels. Clean Plugs. Adjust Bkes. Repair puncture & replace on Rear. Check Steering for Play.

Job No	Inv No	NAME	CHASSIS No	Reg No	Mileage	DATE	WORK TO BE CARRIED OUT.
61	E.13488	Mr Adler	M.265	LKK.44	30528	16-7-52	Remove Cyl Hds Decoke if nec. Service - Tune Carb Petrol Pump & Dist. Flush out Rad. Check Water Pump Fit new Fan Belts. Repair Exhaust. Rectify water leak on w/screen Scuttle ETC.
62	E.13486	Mr Parker	P.1794	UMC.33	13197	16-7-52	Fit new Flywheel Ring Gear. Weld S/Abs Mountings on Rear X. Member.
63	E13586 / E13500	Mr Cherry	L.257	MOG 118	25623	16-7-52	Change Front Spring. Check Fr Shock Absorbers.
64		Mr Parsons.	L.866	KXH 502	14418	21-7-52	Replace Fr V Bolts. adjust Bkes. Slight Play in Steering.
65	E.13479	Fram Simonig.	M.658y	AGL.377		14-7-52	Fit c/shaft Pulley.
66	E.13550	Mr Smith	M.10210	KLO 196	10406	21-7-52	As per Letter
67	E.13616 / E.13607	R. Afton.	P.1794	WHX 535	11369	21-7-52	Accident Repairs
68	E.13522	Mr Wallis	K.639	KLX 478	28989	21-7-52	New Big End Bearings.
69	E.13480	Mr Grogan	M.898	CGS 99	26097	22-7-52	Replace Fr Shackles. Clutch Judder (Rectification)
70		H.W. WHYTE	99J-2010	LYV 366	830	22-7-52	Accident Repairs
71	E.13481	Dr. Janvain.	M.1013	UMC-924	50362	22-7-52	Water Pump. Adjust Brakes. Tune Engine. Trafficators. Stop Switch.
72	E.13449	Richards & Cath.	P.2045	LYV-363	17938	23-7-52	Decoke. Service Change all oils O/S. WATER IMPELLOR (PUMP) ON ENG. LEAKING. NEW REAR GLASS LIGHT N/S. NEW TRAFFICITOR. O/S. NEAR Door HANDLE N/S. NEW BOOT HANDLE
73		Dr. Gannicott.	L-423Q	JNE-133	41999	24-7-52	CHECK HORNS. CHECK PETROL SYSTEM FIT BONNET HANDLE.
74	E.13482	MR. ABERDEEN	91P-2148	LLJ 48%	07647	25.7.52	TUNE ENGINE. SERVICE. CHANGE ALL OILS. CHECK ALL BOLTS
75	E.13485	Mr Winston	P1761	LLM 565	20923	24-7-52	Fit Ex Petrol Pump Adjust Bkes adjust Clutch.
76		Mr Newbury	M317	JYO685	2630	24-7-52	Accident Repairs.
77	E.13523	Mrs Tickell	P2041	LXV 399	12120	28/7/52	Check Brakes. Tune Engine Etc.
78		MR. BENADO	K-374Q	SMV-519	5822	28/4/52	Engine Tune. Service. Check King Pins. Adjust Brakes. Adjust Clutch. CHECK STEERING "FOR "PLAY"
79	E13501	MRS STANACK.	M-1087.B	SRE-801	27229	28/4/52	FRONT SUSPENSION.
80	E.13502	ELLIOT-COHEN.	M-433 P.	JLW.582	40052	28/4/52	FIT PRESSURISED RADIATOR.

Y

Job Nº	Inv Nº	Name	Chassis Nº	Reg Nº	Mileage	Date	Work to be carried out
81	E13503	K.J. Annan.	M879	UMK 735	36615	28.7.52	Repair Gear Box. Fit Customer's own Cyl Hds. New Shackle Bushes on Front Suspension.
82	E13504	Henderson. Meredith & Drew.	P.2289	XMY 590	4821	30.7.52	Service Change all Oils. C/work. Throttle Rod Loose. Press on Radio Loose. Change round all wheels. Repair damaged o/s wheel. Adjust Bkes Check Dist & Plugs. Polish car.
X 83	E13637	Lt. Com. Leach.	L.351Q	JHT. 522	30890	30.7.52	1,000 Mile Service. Check Bkes Tune Eng. Check Oil & Temp Gauge. Connect H.Throttle Faulty Trafficators. Short on Batteries R.Nº Plate new. Body work. Touching HT Leads. Lower Seats. Body work.
84	E13505	B. Peake.	M.881	TMX 744	18943	30.7.52	Oil & Grease all round. Check Batteries Check all Oils. Adjust Bkes. Fr Bke faulty. Repair or Renew Leaking Exhaust Pipe. Frwing Mud Flaps Adjust Points & Check Plugs ETC.
85	E13506	S. Rosen.	10660.	UMC 538	35109	31.7.52	Overheating Tighten Belts. Fit new Ignition Switch Service Change Eng Oil.
86	E.13552	Brown.	M-760.	OPE- 237.	9738	1.8.52	REDUCE CASTOR. FIT CUSTOMERS TYRES (TWO) BALANCE WHEELS
87	E13508	Broomfield.	P.1538.	UMX- 450	16774	5.8.52	Welding Shock Absorber Bracket
88	E13509	Darwin.	M1013	UMC924		2.8.52	Tighten bent brackets.
89	E13510	Parlanti.	P1720.	NKJ 73	15969.	2.8.52	Reset radius rods service car.
90	E13511	Simonius — Fram	M6587	AGC 377	36389	7/8/52.	Front shackles.
91	E13622	Com Chorley.	P1957.	FPN 300	15503	7/8/52	Check Bkes Tune - Check Coil Cover for Sidelight. Check Indication & means tight 1 Horn faulty. Repair Fr Seats. O/S Front.
92	E13512	Rosen	M1066.	UMC538	35572	7/8/52	Service Change all Oils Tune Indicators
93	E13513	Cheetham.	M1523	KXK 714	39328	7/8/52	Play in Steering Column. New Hub Bearing O/S Front.
94	E13514	Regents Pk Garage.	M1514.	SMX875	43325	7/8/52	Service Wire. Check Coil
95	E13515	Bailey	P1943	HWS 853	2893	8/8/52.	Repair Gear Box
96	E13624	Owens.	M6649	LWB473	91916	8/8/52.	Overhaul Gear Change Steering Pillar to O/S. Noise from rear Hub?
97	E13548	J. Duff.	K248	KKX672	15648	8/8/52.	Service Change all Oils. Check Bkes. Check Eng. Rails. Tune. Eng jumps out of 2nd Change from Spring to 6IL. Check Steering
78	E13516	Birdseye	P2228	GEA 322	10989.	8/8/52	Replace N/S water Pump. Replace shields
79	E13510	Mr Doyle.	L391	LXK. 765	22623	11/8/52	Tune Engine. Brakes. Front Suspension.
100	E13497	Little.	J1575	BTV365	27770	11/8/52	Repair Gearbox. or Todham Hydl

Z

Job No	Inv No	Name	Chassis No	Reg. No	Mileage	Date	Work to be carried out
1	E 13553	Mr Thrush	91P-2060	NRL 837	12194	11/8/52	Decoke. Exhaust Blow. Clutch Juddal. Check why tyre wears quickly o near side. Deal
2	E 13518	Mr Gibbs	M 705	JOF 189	44376	11/8/52	Decoke. Cord rings. Refuted Way. Petrol Unit. Dent in Wing.
3	E 13619 E 13654	Mr Mathews	M 1080	FWN 689	37983	11/8/52	Accident Damage.
4	E 13517	Countess May	K 1080	LXD 525		12/8/52	Attend to ignition & fit new Wire Cap.
5	E 13526	Crissop Brown	P 1597	LPO 251		11 8 52	Fit Echo Radio
6	E 13519	Mrs Tallan		HCQ 626	53074	12 8 52	2nd Gear Jumps out. Clutch Slating. Bonnet Rear wing. Hinges Connom Foot Pedals adjust Brakes Faulty Lights, etc
7	E 13542	Richard & Cam	L 478 M	LHW 107	27380	12 8 52	Adjust Bues Grease & Spring Steering
8	E 13507	Mrs Gill	M 602 y	NFC 811	42669	14 8 52	Fit Exchange Engine & Clutch
9		Geo & Jobling	M 579	99 A 202		14 8 52	Fit Aluminium Cyl Hd. Adjust Brakes.
10	E 13583 E 13584	Mr Salmond	P 1657	KYP 635	38514	14 8 52	Recon Eng Bodywork adjust o/s door near Stretch Stranghen Rear Bumper Lights, new Paull (Accident damage)
11	E 13551	D Morris	L 127	JSY 708	19133	15 8 52	Service Brakes Body Check Gear Box Lever Vibration Decoke Coil
12		Mr Amey	Saloon			18 8 52	Wheel Wobble
13	13543 E	Mr Ingram	M 271 A	DDA 172		19 8 52	Supply & Fit 2 new 6-25 x 16 Goodyear Tyres Tubes
14	13528 13 13521 13541 E	Mr Sparke	P 1901	FCN 539	9113	19 8 52	Clutch Alignment & Fr wheels Fit Bonnit Rubber Clean Dist Points grease Cabin Heater Faulty
15	E 13555	Mr Green	L 388	SMX 278	56586	20 8 52	Gear box Brakes Check Carburretor & Pipe Stop Light Faulty.
16	F 13554	Mr KS Allen	M 879	HNK 735		20 8 52	Fit new Rubbers in all Wheels Cylinders
17	E 13609	Mr Stocker	M 802	KLO 127	38880	21 8 52	Fuel ...
18	E 13544	Westinghouse	MAX 3092	MAA 551	8916	21 8 52	Decoke.
19		Mr Jones	K 595	JY 60380	36766	25 8 52	Rectify ...
20	E 13576	AA & Fly Co	L 302	990 574	41518	25 8 52	Excessive Tyre Wear o/s/r & o/s Fr wheels Wander & Wobble at Deck Greasing

Z

Job.	Invoice Nº	Name	Chassis Nº	Reg Nº	Mileage	Date	Work to be carried out.
21		M. Gould	P 1830	Aug 484	23411	25-8-52	Check tyre pressures. Clutch slip. Starter. Throttle. Check ignition timing. Service. Change all oils.
22	E. 13573	H.R. Owen.	664g	LWD 773	42129	25.8.52	Rectification.
23	E.13588	Mr Sinclair	K 2202	YRC 693	1022	25.8.52	Service. Tune coil (Slow Running). Petrol Gauge.
24		Mr Ingram.	M 2711a.	DSA 772	52389	25.8.52	Carburetter.
25	E. 13549	Loapman	P 2147	XMX 977	8508	26-8-52	Service. Fit GB Plate. Clutch adjusted tighter. Judder Bar
26	E. 13550	Mrs Tatham		HLB 424	53376	26-8-52	Accelerator Squeak. Fr Shackles. Bad Rattle n/s front.
27	E. 13546	Mr Walters.	1074 D	EPM 90	38390	26-8-52	Tighten Fr Wheel Bearings. Judder Bars. Service. Adjust Brakes. Clean and adjust points. Check wiring. Check own car. Tighten Rear U Bolts.
28	E.13587	Sinclair	P 1712	WME 810	25969	26-8-52	Silencer. Flush out Rad. Decoke. Change oils. Grease Hubs. w/Screen wiper. Tick over. Check Brakes. Clutch. Gear change & s/Abs.
29	E.13545	Decca	M400.	JUC 302		26-8-52	Change Foam Cartridge. Change Engine Oil.
30	E. 13577	Friedman	P. 1828	LXF 445	17799	27-8-52	Renew Hose Top n/s Rad. Check o/s Water Pump. Check all levels & Service incl. Batteries.
31	C/54 2756	Huggenbach	M. 1534	UMX 726	33755	27-8-52	Fit Replacement Rear Spring & Front S/Absorbers. Fit Rebound Rubbers.
32		Mr Cherry	L 257	MPG 118		27-8-52	Change Front Springs
33	C/54 2757	Chatteris Rowe.	91P 2291	MOK 962	95228	28-8-52	New Dynamo Belt. Engine Tune. Check Track. Slip. Lights not working. Adjust Brakes. Road Test & check generally.
34	E. 13578	Parlante	P. 1720	HMJ 73	17232	28/8/52	Wheel wobble
35	E. 13579	Galling	2109	XMC 365	10311	29/8/52	Clutch Squeaks. Remove Cyl Hds. Tune Eng. Starter for cleaning. Also repair o/s/f wing. Felt n/s seal. Check over.
36	E. 13580.	March.	MG13.	LVR 766	17418	1/9/52	Tune etc.
37	C/5 2768/9	Doyle.	C 391	CVK 765.	23461	1/9/52	
38	E. 13581	Gibbs.	P 1839	GUN 606.	10105.	1/9/52	Reset castor.
39	E.13666	Marland.	14721	LKF 780.	28402	2/9/52	Decoke - clutch.
40	E. 13682	Viscount Boyle.	P 3084	H.U.J. 760	7560	2.9.52.	Check Brakes.

Z

Job	Invoice No	Name	Chassis No	Reg. No	Mileage	Date	Work to be carried out
41	E 13564	Logan	M 719	KLO 130		3·9·52	
42	E. 13578	Butcher	P 3080	MXN 420	5781	5·9·52	Tune
43	E. 13651	D. Allard	P2.3000	MXA 554	7579	5·9·52	Replace clutch pedal
44	E. 13565	Mendellsson	P 2062	JGG 2062	15039	5·9·52	Wander
45	E. 13571	Mr Doyle	L 391	LVK 761	23630	8·9·52	Repair Gear Box
46	E 13633 E 13634	Goldie	M 1068	UMD 798	10000 2	8·9·52	Recon engine · repair gearbox · service work
47	13545 E	Hilton Bros	M2+3122	MXT 990		8·9·52	Complete Service change from oil filter
48	E 13614	Backworth - Young	M 751	UMV 204	10460	9·9·52	Decoke
49	E 13625	Cheetham	M 1523	KTK 714	H0462	9·9·52	Remove Beams & fit Bushes. Fit S/ABS Bkrs
50	E 13631	Adlards Brixton	M2x 3098	MYL 773	4994	10·9·52	Steering Noise from Wrag links Slack bearing Pin on clevis Ex. Pipe touching Battery Boxes. Water Leaks. Water Pump H. Pulleys U/S. Engine racing Bke Drums
51	E. 13574	3 Keswick Rd	—	—	—	5·9·52	Face up 8 Valves
52	E 13621	Stewart & Gray	L 867	LKR 963	7491	11·9·52	Clutch Clock Track
53		Graham	71L 903	L9T 175	38580	11·9·52	Peach balls - Belts · renew
54	E. 13653	S.C. Ingram	M. 271a	DBA 772		13·9·52	Supply & fit 2 new Batteries, Supply 1 Jack
55	E 13626	F. A. Gluck	K 519	HNJ 575		13·9·52	Supply & fit new wheel
56	E 13627	Hogedam Motors	P 1583	HSP 757	14998	13·9·52	Check g why ear bottoms on Rear
57	E 13630	N. Bailly	P. 1943	HWS 850	4598	15·9·52	Noise on Engine · check Tuning · Clutch Judder Wheel Wobble. Radio Silencer Rattle Seat Spring New Spare Tyre goodyear M/S Tightly run
58	E 13632	P. Barlow	M 777	JM 7942	23972	15·9·52	Recon Eng. Doors Wrapped Tampo over ob Ltd. Anglebbelind Bumper fit AA Badge. Boot Lock cover change Tyres x Dash Board. Plug hole
59		Jardan	993·2012	NKT·17	4654	15·9·52	Check Tappets. Eng Oil & Plugs Fit Special Sleeves 2 Dents in Body Work. Fit Mats & Driving Mirror
60	E. 13652	Clark-Bland	P 2281	MXA·546	7989	16·9·52	Service - change all Oils, attend to H/Bke Cables & Wipers Fix Screen, Clutch Judder, Replace clutch Straps, Replace Bleeder Screws in M/S Rear Bke Rattles Front & Rear

Z

Job No	Inv. No	Name	Chassis No	Reg. No	Mileage	Date	Work to be carried out.
61	E.13643	Leather	P.2127	MGK.470	17005	16-9-52	Reno Clutch, Oil Fumes, Decoke, grind valves Fit Pleasol Gaskets & Speedo cable. Valve Springs Fit new Water Hose. Adjust Bkes & H/Bke. Top up M/Cyl Fill Steering Box
62		Miss B. Goalen	M 858	NNV.321	22434	16-9-52	Accident Repairs.
63	E.13646	Hagenbach. W.	M.1534	UMX 720		18-9-52	Wheel Wobble.
64	E.13629	Allard Motor Co.	Engine.			18-9-52	Grinding & fitting Valves in Heads of Ardun Engine.
65	E.13628	Cheetham	M.1523	KXK 714	40099	18-9-52	Change Fr Spring. Check Track.
66	E.13620	Broomfield.	P.1538	UMX 450		20-9-52	Fit Remould Tyres.
67		Goulandris	K2034	XMC.673	4980	22-9-52	Change Rear Spring check Steering
68	E.13667	Grogan.	M. 898	CGS 99	28189	22-9-52	Decoke. Oil Pipes on Cleaner. Clutch Judder. Hood Bad fit. o/s w/winder faulty. check Bkes & Report. Warninglight Service. Repair Puncture. Rattles.
69	E.13644 GRO.9000. E.13645	J.C. KLAFFENBACH. EXT 492.	K.3033.	MXY 9.	1203.	23-9-52	Petrol Gauge Sticks. N/S Indicator Sticky Rattle (Rear) strong Ex. Vibration in Wind Tunnel. Panelling. Check Clutch & Adjust Water Leaking from R/Hd. & escaping
70	E.13687.	Leapman.	P 2147	XMY 977	8727	23-9-52	Accident Damage.
71	E.13667	Escott.	M2X. 2295	MLX 153	10502	24-9-52	Service Change all Oils Lighting Circuit Faulty Braking Lights Faulty Doors Squeak. Check Batteries N/S Sun Visor Faulty.
72	E.13648	W. Russell.	P.1920	LXN.908	23641	24-9-52	Service - Change all oils Top up M/Cyl. Check Fr Wheel Alignment. Horn Button Faulty. Oil Dynamo.
73	E.13649	Clifford Brown	P.1597	LPO.251.	51772	24-9-52	W/Screen Wipers
74	E.13666	Marland.	M 721	LKE 780	29380	24-9-52	Engine overheating. New Gaiters around Pedals M/Bke.
75	E.13668	Goldstein.	P.1635	LGK 36	19998	25-9-52	Service - change all Oils. Flush Rad fill with Anti Freeze. Adjust H/Bke Tune Engine Squeak. 2nd Gear Stiff. Grease Springs.
76	E.13650	Doyle.	L.391	LVK		25-9-52	Check & Adjust Bkes.
77		Perens.	P.1757	LNK. 801.	26908	24-9-52	Decoke. Silencer o/s. check Transmission. check Fr Wheel Track. Balance Wheels Wander. Heater & Demister & Washer. Rattles on W/Screen)
78	E.13669	Fischel	P2061	LXY 399		24-9-52	Strata
79	E.13670	Newbury.	M 317	JYO 585.	2444.	1-10-52	Service gearbox noise.
80	E.13675	Clifford Brown.	P1597	LPO251	52289	1-10-52	Adjust Bake.

Lib.	Z/In	Name	Chas.No	Reg.N.	Mil.	Date	
81	E.13560	H. Rourke	7IM-217	JGU-5	17927	1.10.52	Remove Gearbox & Check. Checking. Engine
82	E.13665	Doniger	P.1826	ERJ.220	31264	3.10.52	Ex.Brake Eng Tune. Clutch Judder. Check Bkes. N/S King Pin Check Anti Sway Bar. Check G.B. Report only Window winder. Horns. Lights. Service. Speedo Cigar Lighter.
83	E.13685	Griffiths	M.802	KMK.28	50506	3.10.52	Reline Bkes. check M/cyl. Water Temp Gauge. Check water leaks in Rad Valve. Cigar Lighter Shorts. Radio not working
84	E.13601	Gibbs	M.705	JOF 189	46419	2.10.52	Repairs to Gear Box.
85	E.13663	Fredman	P.1878	LTF 445.		3.10.52	Solsnilch, dynamo. Belt.
86	E.13664	Barclay Inglis	L.455	LXK.146	—	4.10.52	Repair Fr. Bumper Iron.
87	B676.	V. Pain	M.530	IL-4287	32930	4.10.52	Gear Box, Recon Engine Rear Axle Leaking Check Steering Shockers.
88	E.13685	Harris-St John.	M.880	HAA.325	70856	6.10.52	Service, Change all oils. Bkes. Fr S/Abs Bushes in Radius Rods. Balance wheels Rad. Hoses. Fill Rad with Blucol. Free o/s Door. Screws o/s Door Plate. Rear window H/s Fixing
89		Gardner.	M.347A	NGV-26	39780	6.10.52	Repair Gear Box,
90	13700	E.B.Richards	P.1872	LVF. 363	20209	7.10.52	Steering. Fit Heater. Check wiring + Ignition Service Change all Oils. Straighten N/s Fixing Acorn Nut on H/s window seat. Spot Lamp.
91	96H 2814	Barren	M.777	JM 9962		7.10.52	500 mile Service.
92	13672.	Craig	M.1058	UMC938	44624	7.10.52	Decoke. Re-set Ignition. Service change all oils. O/s Door Handle. H/Bke Sticks
93	13674.	W. Russell	P.1920	LXM.908		6.10.52	Fit 2 S/Abs. Fit 1 inner Tube.
94	E.13686	Goldie	M.1068	UMD798	704.	9.10.52	4 Gearbox lips
95	13670.	Exotic Trade Ltd.	L.300	GGD599	43635.	9.10.52	Service adjust brake.
96		Dr. Nathan	M.890	KLL577	29371	9.10.52	Remove Eng. fit new Flywheel. Ring Gear & check clutch.
97	13684	R.O. White	P.2117	NGK409	12002	9.10.52	Check. Eng Tune.
98	13689	A.L. Sinclair	K.2202	YTC.693	3495	9.10.52	Check Petrol Gauge. Fan Bearing Bkes. check H/Bke. Service change Oils.
99		W. Carr.	M.810	FYY 999		9.10.52	Service change all oils. check Ignition S/Abs. Safe. Trafficator faulty. Gearie Spring
100	13673	Winslow	P.1701	LLM.505		9.10.52	check for missing @ Low Speeds.

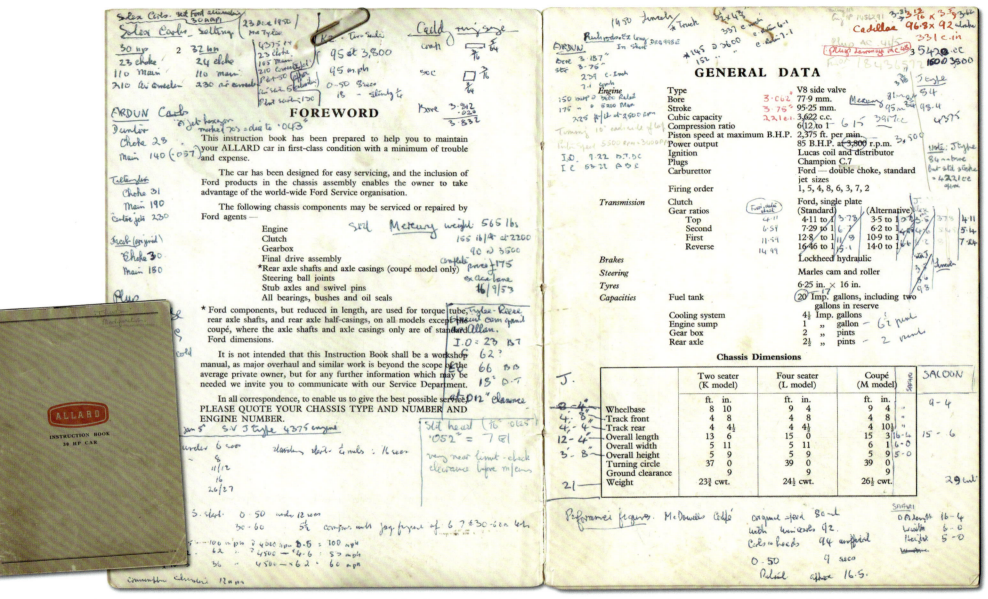

·ALLARD·

FOREWORD

This instruction book has been prepared to help you to maintain your ALLARD car in first-class condition with a minimum of trouble and expense.

The car has been designed for easy servicing, and the inclusion of Ford products in the chassis assembly enables the owner to take advantage of the world-wide Ford Service organisation.

The following chassis components may be serviced or repaired by Ford agents —

Engine
Clutch
Gearbox
Final drive assembly
*Rear axle shafts and axle casings (coupé model only)
Steering ball joints
Stub axles and swivel pins
All bearings, bushes and oil seals

* Ford components, but reduced in length, are used for torque tube, rear axle shafts, and rear axle half-casings, on all models except the coupé, where the axle shafts and axle casings only are of standard Ford dimensions.

It is not intended that this Instruction Book shall be a workshop manual, as major overhaul and similar work is beyond the scope of the average private owner, but for any further information which may be needed we invite you to communicate with our Service Department.

In all correspondence, to enable us to give the best possible service, PLEASE QUOTE YOUR CHASSIS TYPE AND NUMBER AND ENGINE NUMBER.

GENERAL DATA

Engine	Type	V8 side valve
	Bore	77·9 mm.
	Stroke	95·25 mm.
	Cubic capacity	3,622 c.c.
	Compression ratio	6(12) to 1
	Piston speed at maximum B.H.P.	2,375 ft. per min.
	Power output	85 B.H.P. at 3,800 r.p.m.
	Ignition	Lucas coil and distributor
	Plugs	Champion C.7
	Carburettor	Ford — double choke, standard jet sizes
	Firing order	1, 5, 4, 8, 6, 3, 7, 2
Transmission	Clutch	Ford, single plate
	Gear ratios	(Standard) (Alternative)
	Top	4·11 to 1 3·5 to 1
	Second	7·29 to 1 6·2 to 1
	First	12·8 to 1 10·9 to 1
	Reverse	16·46 to 1 14·0 to 1
Brakes		Lockheed hydraulic
Steering		Marles cam and roller
Tyres		6·25 in. × 16 in.
Capacities	Fuel tank	20 Imp. gallons, including two gallons in reserve
	Cooling system	4½ Imp. gallons
	Engine sump	1 ″ gallon
	Gear box	2 ″ pints
	Rear axle	2½ ″ pints

Chassis Dimensions

	Two seater (K model)		Four seater (L model)		Coupé (M model)	
	ft.	in.	ft.	in.	ft.	in.
Wheelbase	8	10	9	4	9	4
Track front	4	8	4	8	4	8
Track rear	4	4½	4	4½	4	10½
Overall length	13	6	15	0	15	3
Overall width	5	11	5	11	6	1
Overall height	5	9	5	9	5	9
Turning circle	37	0	39	0	39	0
Ground clearance						
Weight	23¾ cwt.		24½ cwt.		26½ cwt.	

Allard produced an instruction book for their Ford V8-engined cars giving the owners facts, figures and advice on car maintenance. Here, Sydney's right-hand man, Tom Lush, had his own copy at the factory and the reader can see he heavily modified it. The Foreword and General Data sheets are revealed.

Beyond home maintenance, scheduled servicing and repairs were undertaken by Allard.

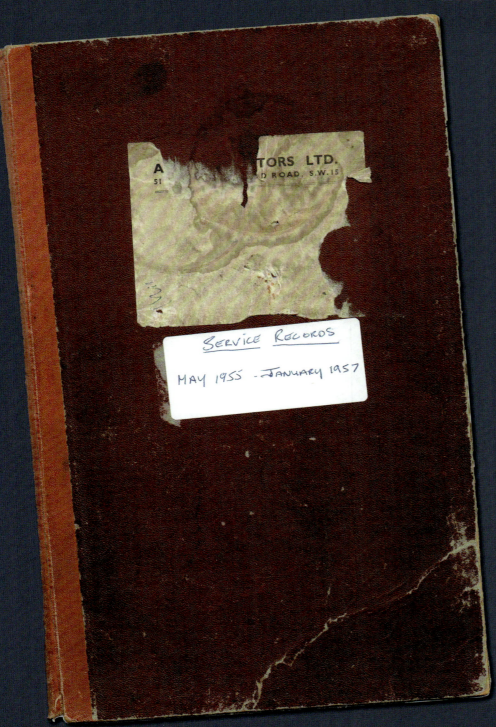

ALLARD
SERVICE RECORDS

MAY 1955 – JANUARY 1957

It will become apparent that work was tailing off somewhat on Allards with these entries, indeed Fords are seen sporadically, and even non-Ford based cars. However, it was also true that Allard service was offered at least until the early 1970s, as the photograph from the late 1960s of the Keswick Road site on page 630 shows a backlit ALLARD SERVICE sign.

No	No. P.	Name	Type No	Reg No	Mileage	Date	
E.16008	P.47	Goldie.	P 296/	U.4777	1000	31.5.55	Fit fume pipe. Special distributor. Adjust brakes. Flat spot
C/SH.408	P.48	W. A. G. Bennett.	91P 647.	LEP 1.	4,203	31.5.55	Check vibration and cure. 65 m.p.h.
	P.49	Head Office				27.5.55	Loan of mechanic.
E.16009	P.50	Alexander Arthur	J. 2 X.		6035	27.5.55	Building up Diff.
E.16010	P.51	Green.	M.2130.2	VMD 668		27.5.55	Adjust brakes.
E.16014	P.52	Scott Miller.	P 24008	AKC 461		27.5.55	Adjust distributor.
E.15453	P.53	Woodford	K 696.	KXC 162	18931.	1.6.55	Repair exhaust.
E.15920	P.54	Gibb.	P 1754.	LLC 46.	31758.	1.6.55	Recon. check steering. king pins etc. Service. Speedo noisy.
E.16006	P.55	Newbury	M. 317.	J.4.0.585.	29388.	1.6.55	New front tyres and balance. New hose on petrol tank filler. Adjust brakes. Check shockers. Service.
E.16048	P.56	Bailey	91P 1854	CCH 597		3.6.55	Reline brakes. Fit new springs. Fit ex indicators. Fit thrust washers. Tune engine. Service.
	P.57	Hyde	81M.73A.	CFK 765	33701.	4.6.55	Oil pressure. Brakes.
E.15933	P.58	Drury & Drury	P.2205.	MXA 555		6.6.55	Recon engine. New joint. Bumper. Fit fram filter.
	P.59	Bassett.	Ford Popular.		9402.	6.6.55	Fit new parts. Collect car from H.O. Fit engine & axle.
	P.60	Picture Post	Ford V8.				
E.15988	P.61	Storkey	91P.2257	NHH 2.	16,824.	7.6.55	Rear axle noise. Change axle ratios. Check for rich carburation. Check distributor. Fit fram.
	P.62	Brian Peake.		UWW 940	3H 829	7.6.55	Change oil. Batteries. Adjust brakes. Check wiper motor. Fit tyres.
	P.63	Barbour.		KKR 59	31 578	10.6.55	Check exhaust leak.

P.

Invoice	Job No	NAME	TYPE	Reg No.	Mileage	DATE	
E.16012	P64	D? MORRIS	7IL.127.	S.G.Y.708	13,511.	10.6.55.	SERVICE - CHANGE OILS. TUNE ENGINE, CHECK BRAKES, CHECK STEERING ETC.
E.16013	65	HAGGARD	91P.1792	LLC.44	673	13.6.55	WHEEL WOBBLE. NEW BONNET SAFETY CATCH.
F.15989	66	SHAW.	P1X.2275	M.L.X.381	1914.	13.6.55	TUNE ENGINE. CLUTCH, CHECK BRAKES.
	67	CROWD.	7IM.40528.	J.I.M.371.	19299	13.6.55	TRANSMISSION FAULT.
E.15952	68	ALLAN.	8IM.879.	U.M.K.735	3812.	14.6.55.	FITTING NEW CYLINDER HEAD GASKET.
E.16121	69	GRAHAM	P.1504	K.M.F.599.	33,996.	14.6.55	REPAIR O/S + N/S DOORS. TUNE ENGINE, SERVICE - CHANGE OILS, CHECK H.B CABLE. CHECK FIRST SPEED. STEERING STIFF.
E.16129	70	Geoffrey Transport.	Dodge Engine	151	19293	14.6.55	Dodge Engine Work for overhaul.
E.16131	71	HURLINGHAM CAR SALES.	91P.2193	S.I.X.165	33,996	16.6.55	ENGINE MISSING. WHEEL BALANCE.
E.16038 E.16039	72	CAMERON.	M.664.	L.W.877.	59959.	15.6.55	ACCIDENT DAMAGE.
E.15961	73	SAKER.	K.685.	K.L.F.149.	5885.	15.6.55	BUSH ON STEERING COLUMN. ADJUST BRAKES, SERVICE C/OILS. TUNE. REPAIR N/S FRONT WING.
E.16057 440.90	74	FLETCHER.	7IM.267.	E.D.R.191.	3787.	16.6.55	ACCIDENT DAMAGE.
E.16050	75.	Searle.	P.1618.	C.C.F.915	55101.	20.6.55	CHECK ENGINE. TUNE. SERVICE. ADJUST BRAKES. CHECK WIPERS. CHECK RADIO. CHECK KING PINS. PETROL LEAK ON TANK.
E.15999 E.16000	76	Walker.	M506.	OBA 631.	49240.	20.6.55	Decoke - accident repairs.
E.16016	77.	CAR SALES.	M.874.	KLK.657	25167	21.6.55	COACHWORK. REPAIRS. CLUTCH JUDDER. CHECK BRAKES.
E/?	78	CHOOLE.	P.697.	K.L.O.123.	42226.	21.6.55	SERVICE CHANGE ALL OILS, ADJUST BRAKES. CLEAN CARBURETTER. TUNE. REPORT ON ENGINE NOISE.
15960 E.15962	79	DEVEY + DEVEY.	P.2205	M.X.A.555		21.6.55	BRAKES, KING PINS, SERVICE. WASH.
E.1453	80	SMITHS GARAGE.	M.853	K.L.L.133		22.6.55	FRONT BRAKING SYSTEM.

Invoice No	Job No	Name	Type	Reg No	Mileage
E.15963	81	Blank	71C 288	LUU.468.	25637
	82	Picture Post		STOCK CAR	
	83	Penton			
E16120	84	RICHARDSON	91P 1629	NUB. 861	47279
E.16020	85	CAR SALES	91P 2076	L.O.H 800	32298
E16152	86	MUIR	M. 1087	SRE.801	—
F.16061	87	BRAITHWAITE	91P 2237	CEA 444	37418
E.16022	88	HEWBURY	71M.317	JYO.585	31512
E16159	89	SMITH + HEWPORT	M.80H	T.M.X.198	86834
F.16041	90	CAR SALES. Mr WYATT	P2.4508	OXE.175	01399
F.16051	91	RICHARD + CARR	M2X 3089	NUV.186	25821
F.16066	92	LEVEY	M.2X.3119	YMD 690	26854
E.16021	93	CAR SALES	91P 2269	MUC 189	30340
	94	PARSONS	71M.6146	JYV.372	16915
	95	GIBBS	91P.1954	LLC.46	816
16140	96	WHEEL RILEY	71M.421	MPJ.219	89903
	97	WYLIE	91P.1672	LCX 618	37061

Repair Gearbox.

Fit Engine & Axle.

SERVICE CHANGE GEAR BOX & AXLE. REPORT ON MESH CONDITION.

Replace o/s side light bulb. Install wireless. Repair older or install new aerial. Adjust choke lead so that knob returns flush to dash board. Usual maintenance on oils etc.
TUNE ENGINE, RELINE BRAKES. FIT NEW BEAMS.

ENGINE TUNE. FRONT WHEELS BALANCE.

EXHAUST BLOW. LOW SPEED MISS, SQUEAK ON REAR.

SERVICE - CHANGE ENGINE OIL. TOP UP LEVELS. GEARBOX. BUMPER. HOSE ON FILLER.
WINDOW WIPER. ADJUST CLUTCH.
ADJUST BRAKES. FRONT SHACKLES.

GEAR LEVER, DOOR LOCKS, BONNET GRILLE, REHANG DROPPED DOOR, CHECK RATTLE ETC.

Fit reconditioned engine transferring high compression head from present engine. New things fan and fan belt. filler, Relay brakes. Rear gearbox - one shaft standing fixed away, not tight out of alignment, left rear shock absorber. Attend rear and anti sway. Exhaust anti mounted out fit new silencer or silencer or renew. Adjust - attempt to tow shield on front. Attend to a dent at rear of near side door. Repair or renew windscreen or trafficators as required. Touch in bodywork generally where chipped.
BRAKES TUNE ENGINE. SERVICE CHECK LEVELS.

ADJUST BRAKES, CHECK CLUTCH, CHECK FAN BELT, CLEAN & ADJUST TIMER, PLUGS, FILL SCREEN WIPER WASHER, OIL & GREASE, REPLACE S/ABSORBERS. ETC.
ADJUST BRAKES, TUNE ENGINE.

Service.

Check Ignition. Check Petrol Pump. Adjust Brakes. Check Front Suspension. Check Near side Indicator. Tighten linch and grease around. Check Exhaust Blow.
ADJUST BRAKES. CHECK STEERING. CHECK CLUTCH, C/IGNITION, SERVICE, EXHAUST BLOW ETC.

No		Name	Type No	Reg. No	Mileage		
98	E16234	Lynhurst	91P 1790	L.K.B. 561	40374	6.7.55	Accident Repairs.
99	E 15992	Luton	71L 449	T.M.H. 809	39522	6.7.55	Fit New Cord Rings. Service-Change Oils. Fit New King Pins & Bushes. Gear Box Checked 2nd Gear if Necessary Tune Carburettor. Adjust Brakes
100	E 15990	Back:	71LH 2714	DBH 718	1937	7.7.55	Tow Car: Tune Engine: Fan Belt: Fuel Stoppage: Front S/H:
Q.1.	E16015	Phillips.	P. 1588	H.O.T. 631	69034	8.7.55	Steering etc: King Pins & Bushes.
Q.2.	E16127	Prudence.	91P 1506	U.M.X. 875	37401	11.7.55	Steering. Adjust Brakes. Radio. Bootwork. O/S Indicator.
Q.3.	E.16060	Richards.	P. 1872	L.L.F. 363	—	11.7.55	Bootwork.
Q.4.	E16238	Samuels	91P 1943	H.W. 5853	—	11.7.55	Bootwork.
Q.5		Adlards Car Sales.	91P 1929	W.M.F. 837	44075	12.7.55	Touch Up Paintwork. Check over Car. Front Bumper. Straighten Rear
Q.6	E.15997	Hudson.	71L 520	D.Y.D. 561	37025	13.7.55	Decoke. New Spring under Steering Wheel.
Q.7	E.16018	Allan.	81M 899	U.M.K 725	3821	13.7.55	Fitting New Cylinder Head Gaskets.
Q.8	E.16017	Sinclair.	91P 1712	U.M.X 816	58757	14.7.55	Recon Engine Steering Etc.
Q.9	E.16019	Escott.	M24. 2295	M.L.X. 158	16855	15.7.55	New Water Pump. Tune. Check Clutch.
Q.10	E.16049	Elliot.	71H 433P	J.L.W. 582	1674	15.7.55	Fit Centre Steering Arm Bush.
Q.11	E16214	Goldie.	P. 2261	U.L 4777	00555	18.7.55	Fit Twin Carbs. Oil Leak. Water Leak. Check Steering. Front Springs. Indicator etc S/H
Q.12	E.16054	Aberdeen.	P. 2148	L.L.J. 488	28095	19.7.55	Tune. Service. 2 New Tyres.
Q.13	E.16056	Richards & Carr.	91P 1723	D.S.D. 345	38196	19.7.55	Fit Cord Rings.
Q.14	E.16002	Whaley.	71K 510	J.U.C. 310	58516	20.7.55	Change Cylinder Heads. Adjust Clutch. Adjust Ignition.

No	Name	Type	Reg. No.	Mileage		
Q15	E.16007 Drury & Drury	P.2205	M.X.A.555.	05509.	19.7.55	Torque Tube, Thrust Washers.
Q16	E.16064 Samuels.	91P.1943.	H.W.S.853	44981	25.7.55	Gear Box.
Q17	E.16063 Le Measurer.	P.1635	L.G.K.36	49004	26.7.55	Check Horns. Clean flaps from rod. Mud flaps, Adjust brakes. Tighten side panels. Check radio push buttons. Tighten belts. Tail light. Indicator. Service - Brakes, Exhaust Blow, Check Alignment.
Q18	E.16062 Braithwaites	P.9237	GEA.334.	38387.		
Q19	E16118 Weaver.	P.1823.	N.K.J.631.	37406	27.7.56	Accident Repairs.
Q20	E16011 Shaw.	P/X.2275.	M.L.X.381.	64174	28.7.55	Clutch & Gearbox.
Q21	E16161 Frey	71L.203	M.W.L.380.	29202.	28.7.55	Change all oils. Exhaust Blow. Check Brakes. Fit new terminals.
Q22	E.16055 Richards & Carr.	/	K.H.W.100.	13819.	28.7.55	Check Brakes. & Clutch Judder.
Q23	E.16180 W/C. Hyde	M.738	C.K.M.765.		2.8.55	Fit new Spring & Perch bolts bushes. Adjusting Brakes. Flushing out Rod.
Q24	E16155 Mr. Smith (Smith & Newbt)	81M.804	T.M.X.198	58223.	3.8.55	Recon Engine. Check Gear Change Linkage. Shock Absorber Links. Kingpins & bushes. Drag Link, Straighten Front Bumper. Tighten Stator Tube ass; O/S door rattle. Tighten Bolts.
Q25	H.4073 Mr. S.S. Demeza	P.2252	M.L.W.872.	38096	4.8.55	Torque Tube cracked at rear end. Brakes pulling to Left and low pedal Handbrake. Front leaf Springs weak. Play in steering Boxe.
Q26	E16610 Mr. Graham.	91P.1504.	K.N.F.599	27007	4.8.55	Flat Spot. Starter jamming.
Q27	E16128 Mr. Graham Taylor.	212.5141	2.B.M.L	13179	4.8.55	Side screens altered. Restray met. Bronze. Exc. rattle. Fasteners on bonnet. Heaters hose cut. Safety catch. Accident Repairs. Insulator round fuse. from check short.
Q28	E16148 Mr. Richards	P.1872	L.Y.F.363.		4.8.55	Tune Engine. Exc. Blow. Fit rubber to seat. Adjust Brake. Tighten door Strike. 2.9.B.Numbers. Change Tyres F to B. Fit foot mats. handle on bonnet.
Q29	Mr. Churchill	P.1652	K.Y.P.637	59791	5.8.55	Repair accident damage off side front wing. New bumper.
Q30	H.4076 Mr. Marshall.	71L.659.	M.M.B.874	04543.	6.8.55	Hand Brake cable. Joint Broken - check most cylinders. Check low speed miss on engine. leak on WP of rod. Service - change all oils.
Q31	E16128 Mr. Paxton	91P.1952.	L.O.F.822.	45768.	9.8.55	Play in steering - column. Check brakes. Service - Change all oils. Bumper bolt loose (rear) squeaking from springs?

No.	Invoice No.	Name	Type	Reg. No.	Mileage	Date	Work
Q32	E.16181	Mr. Leather	P.2127	MGH.470		8.8.55	Reline Brakes. New shackles & New Spring. Let Customer own engine
Q33	E16084	Mr. Sofer	K685	M.L.F.149			Repair Accident Damage. Hand Brake held.
Q34	E16206	Sangers Ltd (Penson Smith)	995.1735	LWP.798	12625	9.8.55	Check for Play in transmission. Adjust torroll Clearance. Check for noise - exhaust Blow? ...
Q35	E16146	Mr. Barlow (Atlas Insurance)		LXN.5	16940	10.8.55	Accident repair to rear...
Q36	E16139	Mr. May	P.2165	NTA.582	13523	10.8.55	Repair Master Cylinder. Connect Trans filter.
Q37	E16173	Mr. Turner Riley	71M.421	MPJ.219	90924	11.8.55	Repair Gearbox.
Q38	E.16046	Chesterfield Garage Ltd	ZEPHYR	NYL.629		11.8.55	Check Steering for Alignment.
Q39		Dr. Keighley	91P.1593	KY.0669			Rectification. Bodywork
Q40	H4052	Mr. Wicks		MPF.647		12.8.55	Tighten front "U" Bolts. Check Front Shock Absorbers. Adjust Brakes. Balance Wheels.
Q41	H4084	Demeza	P.2252	MHW872	455	15.8.55	Foot Springs. Play in Steering Box. Brakes pulling to near side...
Q42	E16141	Stamp	M2X.3016	XME 222	32956	15.8.55	Play in rear axle. N/S rear Shocker broken.
Q43	E16142	Dr. Morris	71MY127	IGY 708	183405	15.8.55	Engine miss...
Q44	H4087	Mr. Drummond	81M.1057	SF.6997	65326	15.8.55	Tune Engine.
Q45		STOCK ENGINE				16.8.55	OVERHAUL ENGINE
Q46	E16132	PERKSON LTD	FORD PILOT	LRL265		17.8.55	BRAKING SYSTEM. TUNE ENGINE.
Q47	E16244	CAR SALES	91P.1929	WMF.834	44058	17.8.55	TORQUE TUBE. FOOT BRAKES
Q48	E16281	Car Sales, Clapham High St.	PI.2269	MUC.189	35678	18.8.55	Adjust Brakes & reline if necessary. Check Ignition. Check...
Q49	E16281	Mr. Mills	H.1089	SRF801	0	18.8.55	CHECKING OVER CAR

No	Invoice	Name	Type	Reg No	Mileage	Date	
Q50	E16144	Newport	SIM.1019 B	DFX 826	—	19.8.55	Adjust Brakes.
Q51	E16086	Mr Mills	M.1087	SRE 801	49464	19.8.55	Recon - Dynamo, Brakes. Service. Leak on Petrol Pump. Wheel Brace. Shaft.
Q52	H4695 (91)	Mr Marshall	K HR874	71 LS9	5089	23.8.55	Check Shockers.
Q53	E16088	Col Morrison	91P.1959	HTB 268	16505	24.8.55	Check Steering. Straighten Front Bumper. Check Heater. Brakes Fluid Leak. Service. Clutch. Clean Plugs. Cigar Lighter. Seat Springs.
Q54		Scott-Miller	P.24006	AKC 461	08406	26.8.55	Hand Brake. Adjust Brakes. Check Clutch.
Q55	E16166	Aberdeen	91P.2142	LLJ A82	29085	24.8.55	Change Fan + Dynamo Belts. Change Stop Light Switch.
Q56	C/SH4097	Major Tice	71M.629	GOU 758	36883	24.8.55	Bad Oil Consumption.
Q57	C/HH099	Mr Meads	M.533	CYG.609	60199	24.8.55	Tune Engine. Hand Pump. Pressure Gauge. Jack. Overheating Etc.
Q58	E16085	Whaley	J.U.C.310	YIK.510	89031	25.8.55	Steering Box, Front Suspension.
Q59	E16170	Turner Riley	71M.421	MPJ 219	90924	26.8.55	Gearbox. Exhaust. Door Locks. Grease. Bodywork.
Q60		Shiers	P.1548	KYM 669	28547	29.8.55	Tune engine. Change all oils. Service. Check camber. Check front wheel alignment.
Q61	E16153	Graeme Muir	M2X 3034	MUU.186	26840	24.8.55	Repair gearbox. Change oil for 2.5500. Pull down heads.
Q62	E16133	Fischel	91P 2041	LXY 399	—	29.8.55	Fit New Cylinder Head Gaskets.
Q63	E16134	Woodward	91P.2230	KGA.165	—	29.8.55	Rec Distributor.
Q64	E16154	Richards + Carr	—	KHU 100	13819	30.8.55	Replacement Clutch.
Q65		Hardman + Collis	91P.1839	GUH 606	21811	31.8.55	Re-align Castor + Camber on H/S.
Q66	E16135	Richards + Carr	SIM 824	MTA 595	44050	31.8.55	Change Crankshaft

No	Invoice	Name	Type	Reg. No.	Mileage	Date	
Q.67	E16282	Adlards. Car Sales. (C.H).		MXA.554	47363	2.9.55	Engine Overhaul. Gearbox. Clutch. Grease. Etc.
Q.68	E16136	Stourcliffe Close. Garage	81M.1020.	K.L.R.294.	32522.	2.9.55	Gear Change. Check for Popping Back. Wiper.
Q.69	C/S4420	Demitza.	P.2252.	M.L.W.873.	1331.	5.9.55	Steering Column. Fit Heater Tap. Check King Pins. Brakes. Flat Spot. Etc.
Q.70	E16114	Tallis.		HWA.916.	84791.	6.9.55	Fit Recon Mercury Engine.
Q.71		Ballatine	7K.519.	HLJ.575.	13636.	7.9.55	Engine Tune.
Q.72	E16209	Searle.	P.1618.	C.C.F.915.	58875.	9.9.55	Service. Check Levels. 2. Screen Jets. Hand Brake. Check Brakes. Ect.
Q.73	C/S4420	Barker.	81M.1070.	J.P.O.851.	20312	12.9.55.	Charge Axle Beams.
Q.74	E16608	Graham.	P.1504.	K.A.F.899.	27549	12.9.55	Replace Flywheel Ring Gear.
Q.75	E16213	Goldie.	P.2261.	V.14777.	05613.	12.9.55	Adjust Brakes. Clutch. Fit 2. New Covers.
Q.76	E16143	Shaw.	PIX.2276.	M.L.X.381.	66110.	12.9.55	Check Steering. Adjust Brakes. Fit New Carb. Tune.
Q.77	E16149	Peabody.	Pilot.	L.X.L.265.	80317	12.9.55	Exhaust Blow.
Q.78	E16114	Willson.		L.P.O.251.		12.9.55	Distributor.
Q.79	E16164	Barron.	91P.204	H.C.Y.863.	21461	13.9.55	Service. Brakes. Tune. Check Steering. Fit Thrust Washers.
Q.80	E16227	Tinedale Ltd.	91P.2145.	M.J.J.400	18015	13.9.55	Steering. Shock Absorbers. Front Springs.
Q.81	E16262	Samuels.	91P.1943.	H.D.S.853	51440	14.9.55	Repair Gearbox.
Q.82	E16145	Allen.	81M.849	U.M.K.788.		14.9.55	Fit 2. Gear Rods.
Q.83	E16130	Riggs & Hens	P.1869.	EUD.740.	32880	19.9.55	King pin – wheel tramp.

No	Invoice No	Name	Type	Reg. No	Mileage	Date	
Q84		Brockwell	81M. 10688.	U.M.D 798.	23855	17.9.55	Change Rear Spring.
Q85		Stock Engine.	—			19.9.55	Stock Engine Overhaul.
Q86	E16167	Ames.	91P 1606	V.H.X.885.	27420	19.9.55	Recon Engine.
Q87	d.SK 414	D. Lewis.	J2X.	M.G.F 850.		20.9.55	Adjust Brakes. Clean Plugs, Points.
Q88	E16211	Braithwaite	P.2234.	GEA334	40206		Service. Change Engine Oil, Check Instrument Light. o/s Exhaust Blow. Straighten Tail Pipe.
Q89	E16207	Aberdeen	P.2148.	LLJ488	30461.	23.9.55.	Brakes. gear change. auto sway bracket — weld.
Q90	E16174	Turner Riley.	71M. 421	M.P.J 219	61887.	23.9.55	Exhaust blow. Rear Shocker. Diff.
Q91	E16198	Cameron.	M.664	L.W.B.743	62884	23.9.55	Clutch Not Dis-engaging.
Q92	E16334	Goldie.	P.2261.	U.I 4777.	06034	26.9.55	Fit Lincoln Gears. Complete Respray.
Q93	E16197	Ward.	81M. 898	G.G.S.99.	54227	26.9.55	Doors Dropped. Repair R.S. Doors. New Piping on Spats. etc.
Q94	E16183	Walker.	71M. 506.	O.BA.631.	52565.	26.9.55	Remove Rear Axle. Check U.J.
Q95	E16196	Mr Van Kempen	81M.874	K.L.K.657	28686	26.9.55	Recon Engine. Fit New Carb. Rectify Radio. Temp Gauge. Brakes. Fit New Shock Absorbers. Check Steering etc.
Q96	E16195	Richardson.	91P.1629.	N.U.B.861.	49214	26.9.55	Tuning Knob. Rivet in Mudflap. Headlamp. Check Ignition.
Q97	E16193	Simon	91P 2143.	M.J.J.459	04021	26.9.55	Steering. Service Headlamp Bulbs. G.C. Plate. o/s Trunk. Seat Squeak. Adjust Brakes.
Q98	E16224	Godfrey.	T181 - 4725C. Dodge			27.9.55	Overhaul Engine.
Q99	E16182	Drummond.	81M. 10378	SE. 699.	64779.	27.9.55	Flat Spot. 2. New Tyres.

No	Invoice	Name	Type	Reg. No	Mileage	Date	
P.100	4/5 H4136	Demeza	91P.2252	M.L.W.872	2654	29.9.55	Change Beams.
R1	E16286	Renson Smith	99S.1753	L.L.P.798	10456	28.9.55	Examine for noise in rear axle.
R.2	E16212	Fischel	91P.2041	L.X.Y.359	49614	28.9.55	Check Brakes.
R.3	E16168	Handman & Collis	91P.1839	G.U.L.606		28.9.55	Changing F. Shockers.
R4	E16210	Corfield	91P.1815	W.M.C.515	18899	29.9.55	Flat spot in carb.
R5	E16185	Lawman	P.2228	C.E.A.322	49179	3.10.55	Check steering. King pins. etc. Balance wheels. Tune. Exhaust blows. Rear light glass. Aerial. Flush radiator. Service. etc.
R.6		Stock Engine	17047B			3.10.55	Overhaul. Engine.
R.7	E16199	Langrick	91P.2259	H.R.O.351	64483	5.10.55	Brakes. Noise on rear axle.
R.8	E16205	Mardell	91P.1649	V.X.H.560	40767	5.10.55	Service - Change oils. Check brakes. Check clutch.
R.9	E16200	Jefferson	71L360	L.H.T.839	62109	6.10.55	Ft universal joint.
R.10	E16220	Leather	P.2127	M.G.K.470	64982	6.10.55	Accident Repairs.
R.11	4/5 H4139	Barker	71M.329	K.W.E.28	35456	7.10.55	Repair Exhaust System.
R.12	4/5 H4148	Murphy	71L.378.Q	L.U.B.901	54285	7.10.55	Steering, Head lamp, Service. Tune, Door hinges indicators.
R.13	E16204	Scott	T.Z.300		OX103	8.10.55	3-27. Crown Wheel Pinion. Rootroad Badges New Water pump check. A/s Rear Lamp. Engine idling
R14	E16219	Allen	81.M.844	U.M.K.435	0746	10.10.55	Accident Repairs.
R.15	E16223	Godfrey Balham	T.81	47780		10.10.55	Overhaul Dodge Engine.
R16	4/5 H4149	Mr Barbour	Q	KKE.59	32460	14.10.55	Change engine gearbox oils. Service Take up platters. Oil filters are missing. Check speedometer - not working. N/s indicator. Antifreeze.

No.	Invoice	Name	Type	Reg. No.	Mileage	Date	
R.17	E16202	Winston	91P.1761	LLM.565	40806	11·10·55	Tune Engine. Check Exhaust. Adjust Brakes & Clutch. Fit Chrome Ends to Exhaust Pipes. Disc heaters to rear windows.
R.18	E16201	Col. Ladew	P.1646	T.R.F.692.	41509	12·10·55	Exhaust Blow. Check Batteries, Service Tune. Ignition Light etc.
R.19	E16222	Hyde.	81M 738	C.F.K.765	42318.	12·10·55	Noise Rear Axle. n/h Headlamp. New Front Bumper. Brakes etc.
R.20	E16194	Richardson.	91P.1629	H.U.R.861.	50139	12·10·55	Test Fuel Pump. o/s Rear Brake.
R.21	E16221	Luton.	91K.4494	T.M.H.809	43439.	12·10·55	Check Front Suspension.
R.22.		Monte Carlo.	4375.			12·10·55	Rebuild Engine.
R.23.		Monte Carlo.	91P.1823	A.K.J.831.	—	12·10·55	Strip & Dismantling Car for Rebuilding.
24.	E16227	Newbury.	M.314.	J.Y.O.585	34302.	14·10·55	Charge Batteries. Service. Fit Missing Bolt n/s Water Pump etc.
25.	E16285	Muir.	M2X.3084	H.U.O.186.	—	14·10·55	Changing Fan Belt. Adjusting Brakes.
26.	E16192 o/s 4153	Dagg.	71K 538	J.Y.K.120.	52991.	17·10·55	Towing Car. Brake Failure.
27.	E16296.	Car Sales.	81M	G.Y.S 513.	20684	18·10·55	Check Steering.
28.	E16244	Allard Car Sales.	J.2.	—		19·10·55	Delivering Car to Show.
29.	E16245 E16246	Drury & Drury.	P.2205	M.X.A.555.	05699	20·10·55	Accident Repairs.
30.	E16258	Stamp.	M2X.3018	X.M.E.222.	74436.	20·10·55	Overhaul Steering.
31.	E16225	Drummond.	81M.10376	S.E.6999	70812.	21·10·55	Engine Miss. Near Side Exhaust Leak. Adjust Brakes
32.	E16259	Peabody Ltd.	A10025150	K.X.L.180.		23·10·55	Accident Repairs. Clutch. Brakes. Two Tyres. Speedo Cable etc.
33.	E16226	Scott Miller	P.24002	A.K.C.461		24·10·55	Tune Engine

R.

No	Invoice no.	Name	Type	Reg. No	Mileage	Date	
34	E16218	Cordoor.	—	T.H.X.875.	56094	25.10.55	PERCH BOLTS. SHACKLE BUSHES.
35.	E16255	BARKER	91P2145.	M.J.J.460.	20532	25.10.55	CHANGE AXLE BEAM. FIT THRUST WASHERS
36.	E16265.	Viscount Boyne.	P.3084	QE9888.	19686.	28.10.55	REPLACE SHOCK ABSORBER MOUNTINGS. CHECK SPRINGS. NEAR SIDE EXHAUST
37	E16260	Newbury.	M.317.	J.Y.O.525.	34883.	28.10.55	O/S WATER PUMP. FIT SPARE TIRE.
38	E16582.	LEATHER	P.2127.	M.G.K.470.	67982.	28.10.55	STRIP. CAR.
39		BALLANTINE	41K519.	H.L.J.545.	5586	28.10.55	OIL & GREASE. BLUCOL. ADJUST BRAKES, LIGHTS.
40.	O/S H4156	BURGESS.	81M1087B	K.H.H.879.	82255	28.10.55	FRONT SHACKLES. OIL & TEMP GAUGE. STEERING. CARB. SHACKLES
41	E16263	GREEN	M2K3013	Y.M.J.688	55361.	31.10.55	CHECK INDICATORS. BRAKES. CHECK SHOCK ABSORBERS. BLUCOL.
42	E16264	W/C. Hyde.	M.738.	C.F.K.765.	—	31.10.55	N/S REFLECTOR. O/S DOOR RATTLES. O/S LAMP RIM. BACK SEAT.
43	E16242	Mr. Cordoor	71L.	THX.875.	56188.	31.10.55	GEARBOX. CHANGE ENGINE OIL. BLUCOL
44	E16258	PEABODY LTD.	ROVER.	G.R.F.970	12643	31.10.55	ENGINE OIL. BLUCOL. THERMOSTAT. CHECK BRAKE.
45	E16294	ALLARD CAR SALES	81M1102.	G.Y.8513.	20981.	31.10.55	FIT 30 HP V8. ENGINE.
46	E16266	RICHARDS.	91P1872	L.Y.J.363	52102.	4.11.55	DECOKE, BIG ENDS, LIGHTS, CHANGE OILS, BRAKES.
47	E16241	MAJOR WARING.		Q.D.1606	6113.	4.11.55	RECON, WIPERS, CHECK GEARBOX. NEW PETROL TANK. STEERING, HAND BRAKE ETC.
48	E16249	SIMON	91P2173	M.J.J.459	29153.	6.11.55	ACCIDENT DAMAGE ETC.
49		SAMUELS.	91P.1943	H.W.S.853	54323	9.11.55	STEERING.
50	E16264	GRAHAM TAYLOR	21Z.5141	J.R.M.L.		10.11.55	CHECK CLUTCH.

R.	INVOICE	NAME	TYPE	REG. No	MILEAGE	DATE	
51	E16433	IMHOF	J.2	L.X.T.5.	06418	10.11.55	CONVERT FRONT END TO J.2X.
52	E16328	De KEIGHLEY	91P. 1593	K.Y.O. 689.	42626	11.11.55	REPAIR EXHAUST, TUNE UP ENGINE.
53	E16261	LANGRICK	P. 2259	A.P.O.381.	—	14.11.55	REMOVE DYNAMO, FIT NEW BEARING.
54	E16391	GODFREY BALHAM.	T11. 87615C.			15.11.55	OVERHAUL ENGINE.
55	E16334	Bracknell.	M.1068.	U.M.D.798.	26919	16.11.55	STRAIGHTED P. PLATE FRONT BUMPER. BLOW IN PAINT.
56	E16306	WILLCOCKS.	GEARBOX			16.11.55	OVERHAUL GEARBOX, SUPPLY. 21Z FRONT AXLE.
57	E16284	BARLOW.	—	L.X.T. 5	19246	16.11.55	FIT RADIATOR BLIND. PETROL LINE. PUSH ROD. KING PINS.
58	E16251	GRAHAM.	P.1504.	K.H.F. 599	—	17.11.55	ACCIDENT REPAIRS.
59	E16243	SMITH & HEWPORT.	81M. 804	T.M.X. 198.	64939	17.11.55	BRAKES. GREASE. W/S WIPERS.
60	E16242	RICHARDS & CARR	91P 2118	F.B.A.50	86930	17.11.55	BRAKES.
61	E16447-4	CAR SALES.	91P. 2270.	K.G.A 165.	40796	17.11.55	SPEEDOMETER. HAND BRAKE, STEERING. BUSH. FLAT SPOT. SERVICE. ETC.
62	E16280 H478	UPTON.	4LL 601	K.K.P. 816	53104	21.11.55	PETROL GAUGE.
63	E16324	LEATHER.	P.2252.	M.L.W.842.	05623.	22.11.55	CYLINDER HEAD GASKET.
64	E16499	CAR SALES.	M3X 2295	M.L.X. 155	20979	22.11.55	OVERHAUL FRONT SUSPENSION & STEERING.
65		FISCHEL	91P 2041	L.X.Y. 399	51336	22.11.55	SUPPLY & FIT MERCURY ENGINE. REPAIR GEARBOX.
66	E16340	BARLOW.	—	L.X.T. 5	19399	24.11.55	REPLACE. BROKEN DRIVE SHAFT.
67	E16321	SMITH & HEWPORT.	81M. 1019B	D.F.X 826	66721	24.11.55	RECON ENGINE.

No	Invoice	Name	Type	Reg No	Mileage		
268.	E16320	Turner Riley.	TMA 21	MPS 219	84321	24.11.55	Ignition. Exhaust.
R.69	E16288	Peabody Ltd.	Austin A40	O.YE.825.	13439	25.11.55	Reline Brakes.
R.70.		Stock Gearbox.	—	—	—	25.11.55	Strip & Clean
R.71	E16535	Clay.		S.V.K. 519.	33965	25.11.55	Accident Repairs.
R.72	E16394	Goudie.	Chrysler.	D.L.H. 986.	74584	25.11.55	Overhaul Engine. Check Speedo. Steering. Wipers. Cigar Lighter etc.
R.73	E16325	White.	M.566.	M.A.W. 474	—	28.11.55	Steering Motor.
R.74		Stock Engine.	1900/10	—	—	28.11.55	Overhaul Engine.
R.75	E16331	Richardson.	91P. 1629.	H.U.B. 861	50790	29.11.55	Service. Recell.
R.76		Hardy.	T12X 3091.	WRF. 529.	33221	29.11.55	Fit N/S. Water Pump.
R.77	E16329	Mr. White.	91P. 2117	M.G.K. 409	37462	29.11.55	Repair Gearbox.
R.78	E16327	Peabody Burners.	Austin A.70.	O.YF. 825.	13492	29.11.55	Broken Half Shaft.
R.79	E16471-70	Car Sales.	9117. 664	L.H.B. 793	63430.	1.12.55	Bodywork.
R.80	E16517	Tatham.	71K 146	H.U.B. 381	61897.	2.12.55	Towing Car. Report on Car.
R.81	E16230	Ward.	S1M 898	G.G.S. 99	—	3.12.55	Fit Rear Blind. Change Speedo Head.
R.82	E16213	Dr. Morris.	71K 124	I.G.Y.708.	19436	5.12.55	Service. Change oils. Speedo Short on lights o/s Water Pump.
R.83	E16333	Green.	M9X 3013	Y.M.D. 688.	56344	6.12.55	Change Coil Springs.
R.84	E16226	Peabody.	Rover	G.R.F. 940	13462	6.12.55	New Thrust Race.

No.	Invoice	Name	Type No.	Reg. No.	Mileage	Date	
R.85	E16624	Muir	M2X 3089	M.U.U.186	28906	9.12.55	Gearbox.
R.86	E16419	Fischel	91P 2041	L.X.Y 399	51336	12.12.55	Check water leak. Change engine oil.
R.87	E16319	Kaye	91P 1836	K.R.U.344	3485	14.12.55	Check steering. Check king pins. Service remould tyres. Engine tune.
R.88	E16336	Jefferson	41L 260	L.H.T 839	63808	14.12.55	Brake cable. Gasket. Fitting bulbs.
R.89	E16225	Green	M2X 3013	Y.M.D.688	—	14.12.55	Fitting fan belt.
R.90	E16455	Peabodys	Zodiac	527.D.T.U.	—	14.12.55	Service - change engine oil - adjust brakes.
R.91		Condon	41L 411	T.H.X.875	06235	16.12.55	New hoses. H/C rear bracestor. Fix plate on scuttle.
R.92	E16353	Peabodys	Pilot	L.X.C 644	—	19.12.55	Fan house on heater. ~~14.12.55~~ ~~Accident~~ ~~Repairs.~~
R.93	E16504	Barker	81M 1040B	J.O.P.851	91742	19.12.55	Accident repairs.
R.94	E16500	Car Sales. (SA)	P2 3000	M.X.A.554	47987	19.12.55	Gearbox.
R.95		Morpeth	41M 664	L.W.B 773	63430	23.12.55	Check levels. New wing mirror. Two new tyres.
R.96		Car Sales	Austin			24.12.55	Deliver car to Malden.
R.97		Van (51)				24.12.55	Tune & grease.
R.98		Wooldridge	N. 665G	L.W.B. 664	50884	28.12.55	Front spring. Check steering. Rear spring and body clearances.
R.99		Curran	MK 622	K.U.W.565	12441	24.12.55	Ignition. Carburetters.
R.100		Reece	81M 813	K.R.U.994	53852	29.12.55	Brakes.
S.1	E16524	Goldie	P.2261	U.1.4444		2.1.56	Paint damage. O/S front wing. Tent gauge. Flat spot.

No	Invoice	Name	Type No.	Reg No	Mileage	Date	
S.2	E16464	Allards Car Sales	81M. 456.	F.D.W.92.	30955.	8.1.56.	Tune Engine. Service check levers steering rear v roller brake
S.3	E16368	Newbury.	41M. 314.	J.40.585	36385	3.1.56.	Bleed. Charge Batteries. Adjust Brakes + Hand Brake. Tune.
S.4	E16606-05	Bradford.	91P.543.	M.Z.7880.	43100.	4.1.56.	Accident Repairs.
S.5		Morpeth.	41M.664	L.W.8.477	64470.	5.1.56.	Adjust Gear Change Water Leaks. Steering Wheel Balance.
S.6	E16376	Col. Loader.	P.1649.	T.R.F.693.	42952.	6.1.56.	Perise Tune. Fit Badge Heater Control. Brakes.
S.7		Stock Gearbox.	—	—	—	6.1.56.	Strip + Clean.
S.8	E16370	White.	91P.3114	M.G.K.409	—	7.1.56.	Hand Brake Cable.
S.9	E16766	Drury + Drury.	P.51058 (chassis plate)	M.X.A.555	—	7.1.56.	Rectify Rev Drive. Interior Lights.
S.10		Richards + Carr	Gearbox.	—	—	9.1.56.	Repair Gearbox.
S.11	E16502	Car Sales	K.2.2041.	H.M.R.163.	—	9.1.56.	Wash + Polish.
S.12	E16518.	Car. Sales.	Chassis.	—	—	9.1.56.	Strip. Chassis.
S.13	E16414	Turner Riley.	41M.431	M.P.J.319.	95624.	9.1.56.	R. Shock Absorber Change.
S.14	E16412	Miles.	M.1533.	E.P.H.603.	29302.	10.1.56.	Accident Repairs.
S.15	E16450	Newport.	81M.1019B	D.F.X.826	64043.	10.1.56.	New Timing Wheels o under Warranty.
S.16	E16374	Leather.	P.2253.	M.L.U.842.	—	10.1.56.	Oil + Temp Gauge.
S.17	E16166	Peabody Buences.	Zodiac.	527.D.T.W.		12.1.56.	Accident Repairs.
S.18		Sampson.	K.2.2022.	M.L.P.114.	28040.	14.1.56.	O/S Front Bumper. N/S R. Bumper Brakes Reline Tune Service Etc.

no	Invoice	Name	Type	Reg No	Mileage	Date	
S.14	E16381	Prudeall	P.150b	O.M.X.875	43771	10.1.56	Steering box leaks. Grease steering. Drivers window. Noise on engine.
S.20	E16393 (92)	Saker	K.685	K.L.F.147	49894	16.1.56	Accident repairs. Service. Wiper blade. Water hose. Replace o/s top.
S.21	E16384	Peabody	Pilot	L.X.G.674	—	16.1.56	Fit new cover.
S.22	E16375	Richardson	91P.1639	A.U.R.861	51496	16.1.56	Service. Fit new reflector. Fit new pilot light bulb. Adjust brakes.
S.23	E16383	Langake	P.3259	H.R.O.351	40068	14.1.56	Torque tube. Brakes. Exhaust blow. New front bumper. Repair bonnet.
S.24	E16505	L. Davis	J.1	H.X.C.578	23901	17.1.56	Fit modified pedal ass. Fit new brake hose. Rebound strap. Repair p-tank.
S.25	E16413	Smith P Newport	SIM.804	T.M.X.198	67260	18.1.56	Tune. Balance wheels. Check brakes.
S.26	E16469	Godfrey Balham	T.181.46380	—	—	19.1.56	Strip & overhaul engine.
S.27	E16530	Gould	P.3261	U.1.4444	04611	27.1.56	Steering. Clutch judder. Decoke. Speedo. Wiper blades. Rad boiling.
S.28		Barber		K.KE 59	32788	23.1.56	Service. Speedo. o/s indicator. Front bumper. Replace oil filter tube.
S.29	E16379	Green	M2X.3013	Y.M.O.688	59743	23.1.56	Brakes. Service. &
S.30	E16380	Woodford	K.696	K.X.C.162	24048	23.1.56	Renew brake king pins & bushes.
S.31	E16385	Scott Miller	P.24002	A.K.C.461	20744	23.1.56	Shuddering at back end. Change wheels round.
S.32	E16386	Le Mesurier	91P.1635	L.G.K.36	52548	25.1.56	Tune engine. Brakes. Steering. Fit wiper blades. Trafficators.
S.33	E16382	Parton	91P.1952	L.O.E 822	49677	25.1.56	Wheel wobble.
S.34	E16411	Stamp	M2X.3016	X.M.E.322	26193	26.1.56	Fit new tappet blocks.
S.35		Car Sales		S.L.L 804	—	26.1.56	Fit licence plates. Check levels.

No	Invoice	Name	Type	Reg. No	Mileage	Date	
36	E16399	Car Sales	M2x 2295	M.L.x.158	21099	24.1.56	Repair Gearbox
37	E16466	Dr Morris	Tilley	1.G.4 408	—	27.1.56	Weld Wing
38	E16389	Morpeth	M.664 G	L.W.B.743	64914	24.1.56	Rear Spring Broken Leaf. Brakes. Steering Column Bush Tube. O/S Rear Bumper. Door Handle.
39	E16434	Whaley	YIK 510	J.U.C.310	60206	30.1.56	Fit Exchange Steering Column. Dynamo Belt. Check Flywheel Teeth.
40	16418	Craddock	91P.1954	F.P.H.300	41164	2.1.56	Repair Gearbox. Brakes. Hand Brake Cable.
41	E16415	Shires	91P.1548	K.4.M 669	31491	2.2.56	Check Screen Wipers. Clean Plugs. Service Heater. Check Brakes. Knock From Engine.
42	E16446	Fischer	91P.2041	L.X.Y 399	—	2.2.56	Change Engine Oil
43	E16406	Rer. Mr Whaley	7IM 659	K.M.B.874	10080	2.2.56	Repair Gearbox.
44	E16417	Hurlingham Car Sales	91K 2080	B.C.U.14	23393	7.2.56	Ecko Rings.
45	E16766	Drury & Drury	P.2305	M.X.A 555	—	7.2.56	Check Petrol Pump. Fitting New Push Rod. Changing Wiper Rubber
46	E16421	Peabody Builders	Rover	G.R.F 940	—	8.2.56	Change Engine Oil. Check Hand Brakes.
47	E16422	Berryman	Talbot 10	D.X.R 618	16430	8.2.56	O/S Rear Wheel & Hub.
48		Liley	7IM 290	J.O.C 63	39954	8.2.56	Check Carburettor
49	E16503	Peabody Builders	Pilot	L.X.L 285	...	11.2.56	O/S Front Wing Insurance. Brakes Service Tube etc...
50	E16405	Burgess	8IM 1024	K.A.H.894	84301	13.2.56	Gearbox. Check Brakes. Steering.
51	E16420	Leather	P.2252	M.L.U 872	—	13.2.56	Check House on Steering
52	E16605	Lambert	91P.1552	D.V.G.440	46494	13.2.56	Accident Repairs.

No.	Invoice	Name	Type	Reg No	Mileage	Date	
53	E16504	Peabody	Minx	K.L.A.180		14.2.56	Accident Repairs.
54		Sanderson	SIM.493	T.M.E.3	35401	15.2.56	Steering King Pins. Shock Absorbers. Balance Wheels.
55	E16449	Wallace	SIM.831	F.U.A.649	26950	15.2.56	Recoil Engine. New Voltage Regulator.
56		Swan	M.1069	K.P.X.1.	90413	15.2.56	Clutch Judder. Wheel Wobble. Play in Steering Box. Check Batteries.
57	E16501	Car Sales	P9.4504	M.O.G.160	7412	16.2.56	Gearbox. Service. Prepare Car For Sale.
58		Peabody	Armstrong			17.2.56	Fit Two New Tyres.
59		Car Sales	7IP.1823	H.K.J.831	983	17.2.56	Gearbox. Brakes. Oil Leak on Engine. Rectify Gear Change Mechanism.
60	E16468	Godfrey Balham	Kew 2R1103.			22.2.56	Overhaul Engine.
61	E16469	Prudence	P1506.	V.M.X.875.	44362	22.2.56	Wheel Change o/s Rear for Spare. Steering. Check Heater. Clutch Slip. Screen Wipers.
62	E16574	Car Sales	7IK.	H.J.K.120		23.2.56	Strip & Clean Gearbox.
63	E16607	Graham	P1504	K.H.F.599	29257	28.2.56	Tune. Service. Brakes. Check Rear Lights o/s Indicator.
64	E16581	Leather	72587 64. L.H.D.			28.2.56	Strip & Overhaul Engine.
65	E16472	Fletcher	7IM.267	E.D.R.131	4653	29.2.56	Service. Change Oils. Brakes. Clutch. Bodywork Repairs.
66	E16776	Drury & Drury	P9905	H.L.A.555	8364	1.3.56	Driver's Side Trafficator. Linkers Faulty. Etc.
67	E16653	Muir	N2X.3089	M.J.U.186	10345	3.3.56	Clean Car.
68	E16461	Griffiths	SIM.803	K.L.K.58	9001	5.3.56	Water Gauge. Brakes. New Bulb. Check Cab. Shudder on Eng.
69	E16478	Berriguya	SIM.862	H.A.A.166	10232	5.3.56	Service. Tune. Shockers.

No	Invoice	Name	Type	Reg No	Mileage		
S 40	E16464	TURNER RILEY.	71M 421.	M.P.J. 219	94761.	5.3.56	SERVICE RADIATOR.
S 41	E16459	DR MORRIS.	71L 124.	T.C.Y. 708	21464	5.3.56	SERVICE CHECK CARBS. BRAKES. CLEAN PLUGS.
S 42	E16463	PHILLIPS.	P 1588.	H.O.T. 631.	34039	5.3.56	REGRIND CRANKSHAFT BEARING.
S 43	E16460	LEATHER.	P 2252.	M.L.U. 870	—	5.3.56	CHECK PETROL PUMP. CHANGE PUSH ROD.
S 44		SAMPSON.	91K 9008.	M.L.P. 117.	29274.	6.3.56	FOCUS LAMPS. CYLINDER HEADS. ADJUST BRAKES.
S 75	E16516.	Blackburn.	Talbot 10.	DXL 613	4000.	7.3.56	SERVICE.
S 76		MICHAELSON.	91P 2055.	LEL 646.	38124	7.3.56	FRONT SPRING THRUST WASHERS.
S 77	E16454	PEARCOY	PILOT	LXG 1677		7.3.56	TUNE CARBURETTER
S 78		CHONG.	71M 629 G.	K.L.O. 128	43991	9.3.56	SERVICE. DYNAMO BELT. CHECK STRAP. ANTI SWAY BAR BRACKET. 6X 90
S79	E16455	CRAIG.	91P 3044	L.Y.Y 914.	46754.	9.3.56	RECON ENGINE. REFIT HEATER PIPE. SERVICE. D
380.	E16458	Col Parker.	P.1643	A.U.G. 722	54631	9.3.56	REPLACEMENT STEERING COLUMN.
S 81	E16553.	Godfrey Baldwin	T120 9050.			14.3.56	Strip and overhaul Engine.
S 82	E16679	CAR SALES.	SIM 853	K.L.L. 138	20393.	15.3.56	COLLECTING CAR.
S 83		GREEN	M2X 3013	Y.M.D. 688	61035	15.3.56	PETROL PUMP.
S 4	E16457	TODD.	91P 3340	KGA. 165	10442.	15.3.56	FRONT SPRING CHECK SHOCK ABSORBERS.
85		Leighton Refrigeration Ser.	New Anglia.		300	16.3.56	300 MILE SERVICE.
86		CAR SALES.	91P 1823	HKJ.631		19.3.56	BODY REPAIRS. COMPLETE OVERHAUL.

No.	Invoice No.	Name	Type	Reg No	Mileage	Date	
8.87	E16462	Scott Miller.	P 24009.	HKC 461	22046	19 3 56	5,000 Mile Service. Fit Two New Tyres Balance Wheels.
88.	E16552	Godfrey Balham.	T181 - 49 TYPE		—	19 3 56	Replace Broken Crankshaft.
89.	E16590	Wymer.	91P 1672.	L.G.K 678.	42156.	20 3 56	Exhaust Ignition Electric Clock.
90.	E16766.	Drury + Drury.	P 3205.	MXA 555	9089	21 3 56	Flat Spot. Fit 2 New Tyres. Trafficators. New Cable on Rev Counter.
91.	~~E16676~~	Car Sales.		S.L.K 976	—	21 3 56	Collect Car.
92.		White.	91P 2117.	H.G.K. 409	40028.	21 3 56	Hand Brake Cable.
93.	E16612.	Cox.	Zephyr.	213 DHX	5,000	21 3 56	Service. Air Cleaner Loose. A/S Front Brake.
94.	E16623	Bailey	91P 1834.	CCH 509.	15191	22 3 56	Tune Engine. Adjust Brakes. Front Ends. Steering. Check Greasing.
95.	E16510.	Car Sales.	81M 853.	K.LL 138.	20392.	22 3 56	Clean + Polish Car.
96.	E16509.	Colly's Garage.	81M 1053B.	KLY 854.	49133.	24 3 56	Estimate for Rectifying Wheel Camber.
97.	E16677	Car Sales.	Anglia	S.L.K 977	40.	24 3 56	Collect Car From Brixton.
98.	E16673	Gray.	91P 1862.	HCV 430.	29728.	26 3 56	Check Steering. Brake Hose. Rad. Hose. Fan Belt. Check Spirals.
99.	E16536.	Wilcott.	71K 1948.	J.Y.W. 44	—	26 3 56	Bodywork Accident.
100.	E16524.	Franklin	Zephyr.	S.L.V 169	300	27 3 56	300 Service. Panel Light. Steering Wheel.
1.	E16523.	Fischel.	91P 2041.	LGY 399.	53991	27 3 56	Fit New Silencer.
2.	E16508.	Car Sales.	71M 530.	IL 4287	71534	26 3 56	Wash Car. Adjust Brakes.
3.	E16528	Jefferson.	71L 300.	L.HT 839	66449	28 3 56	Service. A/S Tail Pipes. Exhaust Gasket.

No	Engine	Name	Type	Reg No	Mileage	Date	
T.4	E16525	Brangwyn	FIM 869	HAA 106	68445	28.3.56	Bodywork Flat Spot Vibration
T.5		Barlow	—	LXN 5		28.3.56	Check Petrol Pump
T.6	E16543	Scott Miller	P.34009	HKC 461	—	29.3.56	Fitting New Dynamo Belt
T.7	E16524	Elliot	7IM.1433P	SLW 582	73093	29.3.56	Cylinder Head Gasket
T.8	E16514	Miller	Anglia	229 HMY	450	3.4.56	500 Service. 100E 226698
T.9	E16520	T. Franaszczuk	Anglia	SLY 977	~~100E 233231~~ 100E 233231	13.4.56	500 Service
T.10	E16522	Lightfoot Refrig Scout	Scout Thames	709 HMV	1494	4.4.56	2nd Service
T.11		Bergman	Anglia	SJJ 405		4.4.56	2nd Service
T.12	E16511	Flint	91P.2238	NOE 334	22603	4.4.56	Replace Tool Shocker. Check Shockers. Recon Engine Frame Filter. Check Brakes. Three Branch Manifold
T.13	E16630	Muir	42X 3089	HUU 181	30985	4.4.56	Service Change Oils
T.14	E16549	Zvar	91K 2149	LCL 443	—	4.4.56	Wheel Wobble. Engine Tune. Adjust Belts. i/s Indicator Repairs
T.15		Samuels	Zephyr	SLL 976	423	4.4.56	Service (1st) Screen Wipers. Check Charge Rate. Noise on Rear
T.16	E16599	Todd	91P 2240	KCA 165	11371	4.4.56	Wander. Speeds Wipes. Check Brakes. Rubber on Doors
T.17	E16600	Staup	42X 3016	XME 332	34283	4.4.56	Engine Miss
T.18	E16583	Leather	P.2252	HLU 879	—	4.4.56	Check Leak on Steering Box
T.19	E16571	Car Sales	81N1058B	UHC 938	87675	7.7.56	K/Pins. Shackles. Brakes. Perch Bolt. Exhaust
T.20	E16574	Green	42X 3013	YMD 688		5.7.56	Service. Adjust Brakes. Short on

No	Invoice	Name	Type	Reg No	Mileage	Date	
21	E16609	Graham	P.1504	K.N.F.599	30099	9.4.56	Rectify Fuel Starvation.
22		Car Sales	91P 1823	N.K.J.631	4834	9.4.56	Bodywork.
23	E16592	Scott Miller	P2. 4002	NKC 461		9.4.56	Bodywork.
24	E16598	Winter	P.17.61	L.L.M.565	42176	9.4.56	Repair N/S Door. Fit Screen. R/H Indicator. Check Brake Linings. Tune. Adjust Clutch. Change Round Wheels. Service etc.
25		Stock Engine	B/L1369/4			10.4.56	Overhaul Engine.
26		Long	Armstrong	C.U.K.504		10.4.56	Fit Generator.
27	E16664	Peabody	Rover	G.R.F.970		11.4.56	Rectify Brakes.
8		Meier	Anglia	P.X.E.104	500	11.4.56	First Service.
29		Porter	81M1053B	K.L.Y.854	19235	11.4.56	Change Shock Absorbers.
		Car Sales	91P 1843	H.W.S.853	59243	12.4.56	Prepare Car For Sale.
	E16598		81M804	T.H.X.198	70492	17.4.56	Check Steering. Brakes. Tune Engine. Service. Top up Shockers. Balance Wheels. Check over Car.
32	E16551	Rose Garage	91P 1734	L.P.X.419	20849	17.4.56	Recon Engine. Pack Front Springs. New Rubber Doors + Stear. Check For Any Nec. Work.
		Hayne	91P1551	K.Y.M.794	131814	17.4.56	Accident Repairs.
	E16594	Richards	91P 1870	L.V.F.363	56906	18.4.56	Exhaust. Service. 9,500. Change Round Wheels.
		Car Sales	91M 563	FWM 453	46751	21.4.56	Gearbox. Brakes. Clutch.
	E16740 E16546	Drew	91P 1680	LGK 100		23.4.56	Steering. Brakes. Check Track. Estimate For Accident Repairs.
34	E16568	Peabody	Zodiac	824 DTW	11169	23.4.56	Service. Check Brakes. Clutch. Radio Repair.

No.	INVOICE	NAME	TYPE	REG No	MILEAGE	DATE	
T.38		CAR SALES	POPLAR	OXL 168	93,009	23.4.56	REPAIR INDICATOR LIGHT.
T.39		Murray	91M.065g	LWB 664	54,904	24.4.56	Rear Spring.
T.40	E16587	Mr Letto	P2285	MLK 400	44,864	24.4.56	Check front radius end brackets - tune engine - flat spot. Check rings and replace if necessary. Check rear steering box check for water leak.
T.41		SAMPSON	91K.2028	MLP 117	71,212	24.4.56	ENGINE KNOCK. FAN BELT. TUNE. ADJUST BRAKES. FOCUS HEADLAMPS ETC.
T.42	E16631	Richardson	91P 1629	NUB 861	52,998	25.4.56	Service. Check trafficators (right) does not work. Engine missing. Drain out anti freeze. Check electric leads inside light does not function when doors open. One electric lead short under bonnet.
T.43	E16589	LYMER	91P.1679	LGX 648	—	26.4.56	SERVICE. BRAKES.
T.44	E16572	Jacobs	212 3004	16429	27409	26.4.56	Service clean engine, check gearbox, repair rev counter, repair speedo, new hood, new screenglass etc. —
T.45	E16625	SHAW	212.5100	OVM 949	23100	27.4.56	Change Petrol Pipe.
T.46		SOUTHWELL	91P 2169	NKA 727	32001	30.4.56	FUEL PIPE. MASTER CYL. SILENCERS. GEAR CHANGE.
T.47	E16601	STAMP	M2X 3016	XME 222	34670	30.4.56	CORN RINGS FLYWHEEL RING GEAR.
T.48		WALKER	91P. 1658	LGX 641	65374	1.5.56	SERVICE. BRAKES. STEERING. EXHAUST TUNE ENGINE.
T.49	E16626	Turner Riley	91M 421	MPJ 219	99699	2.5.56	Check Petrol Pump.
T.50		Pearce	91P 1290	WMC 579	19,992	2.5.56	Check Steering.
T.51		CAR SALES. PILOT	E74	WTD 387	53631	5.5.56	CORD RINGS. CHANGE TIRE (CUSTOMERS)
T.52	E16627	JUKES	91P 2232	NNE 400	33358	7.5.56	SERVICE. BRAKES. CLUTCH. STEERING. EXHAUST. OIL FILTER. BATHAMPS CHANGE ROUND WHEELS.
T.53	E16611	GIBBS	91P 1754	LLC 45	05189	1.5.56	NOISE ON TAPPET.
T.54	E16602	GODFREY	T.181	4033C		4.5.56	STRIP & CLEAN ENGINE.

No	Invoice	Name	Type	Reg No	Mileage	Date	
T 55	E16675	GODFREY BALHAM	T 181 - 4442 C			7.5.56	STRIP & CLEAN ENGINE
T.56		CAR SALES	81M 1040B	J.S.P 851	31744	7.5.56	RECTIFY WIPERS
57	E16628	Harding	P1904	L.H.S 350	74919	11.5.56	CHECK AM. SWOP CAR. FLAT SPOT CHECK BRAKES. DECOKE ONLY RAISE WH SIDE TAIL PIPE
58		WILKES	81M 857	K PO. 65	46614	11.5.56	CLEAN CARB
59		BARRY	91P 1583	K L V 880	35519	14.5.56	TUNE ENGINE SERVICE
60	E16621	PIKE	81M 751	V.H.N 207	72319	14.5.56	COKO RINGS. ADJUST BRAKES. THRUST WASHERS. CHECK CLUTCH
61		MASTERS	91P 2237	SRA 337	A7020	14.5.56	TUNE ENGINE. CLUTCH JUDDER
62		CAR SALES	81M 853	KLL 138	21888	15.5.56	BRAKES. STEERING. BIGENDS
63		KEIGHLEY	91P 1593	K 40 689	—	17.5.56	CHECK GEAR CHANGE
64	E16624	ELLIOT	ZEPHYR	SXA 362	100	18.5.56	FIT PARTS
65		CAR SALES	71M 633F	JLW 582	74500	18.5.56	CYLINDER HEAD GASKETS
66	E16662	D? MORRIS	71L 124	JGY 408	23439	22.5.56	BROKEN PERCH BOLT
67		Car Sales	P1943	H.W.S 853	59764	23.5.56	STEERING. GREASE KING PINS. ADJUST BRAKES. REFIT HANDBRAKE. CHECK SHOCKERS EX BLOW. FIT H/S DASH PANEL. CLEAN ENGINE. RELINE PLAY FROM STEERING BOX
68	E16785	BARTLETT	M.1005B	974 CPL	11042	23.5.56	FRONT SHACKLE BUSHES. DROPPED DOORS ADJUST HAND & FOOT BRAKES. TUNE ENGINE. SERVICE CHECK LEVELS. GENERAL CHECK + REPORT ON CAR
69		FRAHASZCZUK	ANGLIA	S.L.X 944	1,000	23.5.56	1,000 SERVICE WING MIRROR
70	E16714	SAMUELS	ZEPHYR	S.L.X. 946	02872	24.5.56	SERVICE CHANGE OILS
71	E16671	WILCOXS	GEARBOX	—		24.5.56	REPAIR GEARBOX

No	Invoice	Name	Type	Reg No	Mileage	Date	
72	E16684	Car Sales.	Jaguar.	S.X.P.527	—	25-5-56	Fit Number Plates.
73.		Biddell	99S 1913.	L.X.Y.15.	25071.	25-5-56	Repair Clutch. Check Gearbox.
74		Rootham Service Station	5337-25			25-5-56	Make up Engine.
75.		Car Sales.	Popular	S.X.L 289	—	28-5-56	Test Run. Underseal. Fit Flash Indicators.
T76.	E16710	Mr Jones.	Popular.	SUL 318.	3871	29-5-56	1st Service. Door. Mirror.
T77.	E16670	Mr Richards.	91P 1872	LVF 363.	53794.	29-5-56	Noise on Rear. Check Kingpins. Reline Brakes. Raise Spot Lamps.
T78.	E16669	Michaelson	91P 2055.	LEL.646	4080 y.	30-5-56	Rear Spring.
T79.		Ballantine.	71K 519.	HLT 575	21037.	30-5-56	Service. Brakes. Wipers. Retread Tyres. Body Rattles
~~T80~~		~~Club Events~~	~~8/10/572~~	—		~~30-5-56 Overhaul Engine~~	
T80.	E16620.	Whaley	71K 510.	TUC 310.	60,897.	31-5-56	Tune Engine. Check Fuel Pump.
T81.	E16648	Mr Back.	71M LH 271A.	DBA 77B	7747.	1-6-56	Steering. Tune Engine. Brakes. Clutch Judder. Rattle.
T82.	E16665	Peabody.	Rover.	GRF 970.	18040.	1-6-56	Rear Axle.
T83.	E16678	Turner Riley.	71M 421.	HPJ 319.	1028.	2-6-56	Cyl Head Gaskets.
T84.	E16682	Mr Todd.	91P 2270.	KGH 165.	12618.	4-6-56	Check Steering & Speedo.
T85.	E16622	Pearce.	91P 1890.	WAC 579	21666.	4-6-56	Steering Wander.
T86.	E16633	Hudson.		CVG 438.	259257	4-6-56	Steering. Tune Engine. Shockers. Brakes. Clutch. Remove Damper. Rectify Leaks on Steering
T87	E16683	Mills.	81M 1087B	SRE 801	52306	4-6-56	New Big Ends

No	Invoice	Name	Type	Reg. No	Mileage	Date	
T88	E16672	Stamp	M2X.3016	X.M.E.222	38500	5-6-56	Recon. Steer ride
T89	E16634	Farrell	81M.879	OMK.935	13173	5-6-56	Recon Engine
T90	E16680	Robinson	Poplar	SXL.989	300	6-6-56	Service (300) Miles
T91	E16676	Peabody	Pilot	LCX.644	54889	9-6-56	Recon Engine
T92	E16646	Mr Longshoot	91P.1906	OVK.395	18483	8-6-56	Check Brakes: N/S door lock. O/S handle: Check Fuel System: Service: Change Oils: Heater. Mirror: Exhaust: Decoke: Check Chassis Bolts etc.
T93	E16681	S/L Gray	91P 1862	NCV 430	31531	8-6-56	Door Handle: Fan Belts: Sway Bar: Ignition: Engine Oil: N/S King Pin
T94		Car Sales	P 9252	MLL.872	16,231	9-6-56	Prepare car for Sale
T95	E16642	White	71M.095	H.P.D.140	58764	11-6-56	Wheel Wobble
T96	E16687 86	Graham Muir	M2X 3089	MUU.180	32224	11-6-56	Gear Box: Towing
T97		Hamilton	81M 877	JVF 17	56103	12-6-56	New Hood: Collect Car: Repair N/S Wing: Check Steering: N/oil
T98	E16661	Peabody	Pilot	LXL 265	96031	12-6-56	Starter Ring
T99	E16711	Berryman	Anglia	SJJ 405	—	12-6-56	Service. Fit Filter
T100	E16755	Miller	81M 714	EY 8941	63886	13-6-56	Accident repair
U1	E16684	O'Flaherty		TJL 314	JLH 3	35471	18-6-56	Check Rear Axle: Check Suspension, Shocker & Steering etc: Balance Wheels: Tighten Fan. Front Spring Clip
U2	E16674	Craddock H.P.	P3			15-6-56	Wipers: Batterys: H/Brake Cable
U3	E16785 84	Drury	P2 3058	MXA 555	12106	18-6-56	Fit Engine: Reline Brakes: New Window: Over-Rider: Side Grille: No-Plate: Door Handle: Speedo: Bonnett Shoe: Rad Leak: Rear Tire: Seal Bulkhead: New Mat: Fit Flashers
U4	E16668 67	Goldie	Zodiac	SXA 894	571	19-6-56	Fit Accessories

NO:	INVOICE NO:	NAME:	TYPE:	REG: NO:	MILEAGE:	DATE:	
U5:	E16715	SAMUELS:	ZEPHYR:	SLX976:	4160:	20-6-56:	WATER PUMP: RAD LEAK: TUNE ENGINE: BRAKES:
U6:		HARDING:	GIP 1904:	WHD350:	38459:	20-6-56:	SILENCER: ENGINE RUNS BADLY: CLUTCH JUDDER:
U7:		BAPTE:	GIP 1582:	KLV 880:	37811:	20-6-56:	CORD RINGS: DECOKE:
U8:	E16666	RICHARDSON:	GIP: 1629:	NUB 861:	54053:	21-6-56:	SERVICE: DENTS IN REAR PANEL:
U9:		~~BARRY~~ Shelton.	PILOT:	KLD757:	60223:	25-6-56:	RECON ENGINE: PUMP: STEERING:
U10:	E16747	PRUDENCE:	GIP 1506:	UMX 875:	47475:	25-6-56:	STEERING: EXHAUST: CLUTCH: AERIAL: WIPERS: WINDOW: DOOR RATTLES: RECELL LOOSE:
U11:		CAR SALES:	ANGLIA:	SXP 549	481	26-6-56:	FIT ACCESSORIES:
U12:	E16723	MR L DAVIS:	J11	HXC 578:		26-6-56:	ACCIDENT: REPAIRS:
U13:		TATHAM:	7JH 140:	HUD 781:	63109:	28-6-56:	FUEL STARVATION: TANK CAP: DIPSTICK:
U14:	E16706	CHAMBERLAIN:	7JH 570:	FFH ~~570~~ 927	58536:	28-6-56:	GEARBOX: CLUTCH: STEERING:
U 15:	E16718	JUKES:	GIP 2282:	NNE: 700	35864:	28-6-56:	NOISE ON ENGINE: SCREEN: WASHER:
U16:	E16689	DR JOHANS:	MBX: 3015:	MLW 940:	47037:	28-6-56:	CHECK ENGINE: CHANGE ENGINE OIL: FLUSH RAD: FRONT SHOCKERS: DOOR RUBBERS: HOOD COVER: RADIO & HEATER:
U17:	E16663	Mr Heatley	Gear-box			28-6-56	Gear-box. repair.
U18.	E16660	Peabody.	Hillman Minx.			28-6-56	Fit replacement cut-out regulator.
U19:		REIS:	8JH 1070B:	TOP 851:	22593:	2-7-56:	FRONT SPRING: EXHAUST:
U20:		WHITE:	7JL 755Q:	LKX 145:	58264:	2-7-56:	BRAKES:
U21:	E16725	SCOTT:	P87 4505:	TZ 300:	38865:	1-7-56:	STEERING: BRAKES: COACHWORK: CLUTCH: SPOTLIGHT: WINDOWS: OIL LEAKS: SERVICE: HEATER NOISY:

NO	INVOICE NO	NAME	TYPE	REG NO	MILEAGE	DATE	
U22	E16719	SMITH: C/O PEABODY:	CONSUL:	DCP 648	31550:	2-7-56	REMOVE N/S/F SUSPENSION UNIT: NEW TYRE:
U23	E16739	GREEN:	MBX 3013:	YMD688	65752:	3-7-56	SERVICE: FAN: BRAKES:
U24		CAR SALES:	ERJ 521:	GIP 1903:	72157:	4-7-56	PREPARE CAR FOR SALE:
U25	E16716	ROBERTSON:	POPLAR:	SXL 289:	939:	8-7-56	1,000 MILES. SERVICE:
U26		SHIRES:	GIP 1548:	KYM 669	35609:	10-7-56	TAIL PIPE: O/S/R HUB:
U27	E16712	DR COX:	ANGLIA:	SXP 549:	308:	10-7-56	500 MILES SERVICE: WING MIRRORS:
U28		LE MEASURER:	P 1635:	LGK 30:	56734:	11-7-56	NOISE ON N/S: REBRPH WINGS & BOOTLID: CHECK BRAKES, KING PINS & SHOCKERS: TIGHTEN SCREEN: WASHER CABLE: CHECK CLUTCH: TUNE ENGINE
U29	E16724	RICHARDSON	GIP 1689:	NUB 861:	55079:	11-7-56	DENT IN REAR: EXHAUST SYSTEM: N/S MUD FLAP:
U30	E16720	Todd.	GIP 2270:	KSH 165:	13791:	12-7-56	SERVICE: RIDEMASTER: CHECK OIL LEAKS: CHECK BRAKES: WATER PUMP OR HOSE: SPORTS COIL: RADIO.
U31	E16721	CORFIELD:	GIP 1815:	WMC 515:	18761:		MODIFIED THRUST WASHERS: CHECK STEERING: BALANCE FRONT WHEELS:
U32	E16713	GOLDIE:	ZODIAC:	SXH 894	1118	16-7-56	1000 MILES: CHECK LEVELS: CHECK BRAKES: FIT ACCESSORIES: SPARE WHEEL CARRIER LOOSE:
U33	E16733	PIKE:	BIH 751:	UMV 207:	77853:	16-7-56	SERVICE: BRAKES:
U34	E16777	BROWN:	BIH 869:	KAT 226:	89394:	16-7-56	ACCIDENT REPAIRS: BONNET HANDLE: SERVICE:
U35	E16709	JONES:	POPLAR:	SUL 318:	1,000:	17-7-56	1,000 SERVICE: FIT CLOCK:
U36		SAMUELS:	ZEPHYR:	SLX 976:	5,000:	17-7-56	RAD: 5,000 SERVICE: CHANGE ROUND TYRES: O/S SPOTLAMP: GB PLATE. INTERIOR LAMP: DOOR RATTLES:
U37		COX:	ZEPHYR:	313 DHX:	13811:	17-7-56	COLLECT CAR: 5,000 SERVICE: TUNE: SLOW RUNNING: MAT: REVERSE LAMP: WIPERS: CLOCK: LICENCE HOLDER:
U38	E16707	JONES:	GIP 1880:	PPA 880:	31863:	18-7-56	TUNE: FUEL PUMP: GEARSHIFT: WATER LEAKS: SERVICE: PUNCTURE: EXHAUST: HEATER

No:	Invoice:	Name:	Type:	Reg No.	Mileage:	Date:	
039:	E16722	ABERDEEN:	91P 3148:	LLT 488:	35195:	18-7-56:	TUNE: SERVICE: H/BRAKE: EXHAUST: N° PLATE: SPOTLAMP: M/LAMP:
070:	E16717	MORRIS:	71L 187:	FGN 708:	25192:	18-7-56:	DECOKE: N/S/F WING: SERVICE:
071	E16741	CHURCHILL:	91P 1652	KYP 637:	68846:	18-7-56:	5,000 MILES SERVICE: TUNE ENGINE: CHECK STRAP: VENT WINDOW:
042		DREW.	91P 1630:	L.G.K 100	——	19-7-56	CYLINDER HEAD GASKET.
043:		CAR SALES.	ANGLIA.	——	——	19-7-56	BRING IN CAR.
044:	E16739	FRANASZCZUK:	ANGLIA:	SLX 977:	3456:	20-7-56:	2,000 SERVICE: CHARGE RATE:
045:		PARSONS:	6179:	JYN 272:	21921:	20-7-56:	KINGPINS & BUSHES:
046:	E16742	VAN KETTPEN:	81H 874:	TT 0794:	37818:	23-7-56:	CLUTCH: REAR SPRING:
047:	E16732	PEARSON:	81H 1032:	NPH 871:		23-7-56:	GEARBOX: STEERING: SERVICE: FRONT: TUNE: BRAKES: ENGINE: SILENCER:
048:	E16738	JEFFERSON:	71L 360:	LHT 839:	69790:	23-7-56:	SERVICE: RATTLES:
049:		SCOTT MILLER:	P7002:	NKC 761:	26824:	23-7-56:	PLUGS: H/BRAKE:
050:	E16708	FARRELL:	81H 879:	UMK 735:	17631:	23-7-56:	KINGPINS: TAIL LAMP: ENGINE:
051:		HOPPER:	91P 2267:	STO 224:	49904:	23-7-56:	DOOR HANDLES: SERVICE: ADJUST BRAKES:
052:	E16761	GRAHAM:	61P 1504:	KNF 599:	31576:	23-7-56:	FUEL PUMP: SERVICE: BRAKES: CHECK OVER CAR:
053:	E16760	SMITH & NEWPORT:	81H 804:	TMX 198:	76600:	24-7-56:	IGNITION:
054	E16759	SHIRRS:	91P 1548:	KYH 669:	36027:	24-7-56:	TUNE ENGINE: CHANGE OILS:
055:	E16785	SOUTHWELL:	91P 3189:	NKH 727:	34094:	26-7-56:	SCREEN: CARB: RINS:

JobNo	Invoice	Name	Type	Reg No	Mileage	Date	Labour
U56		JONES	91P1880	PFF 830	31879	26-7-56	ACCIDENT REPAIRS
U57		SURGETTE MUIR	MBX2089	MUU 186	33223.7	26-7-56	SWAY BAR. WOBBLE. CLUTCH JUDDER. NO PLATE BOX DISTRIBUTOR RADIO.
U58	E16734	MR TAYLOR	BIM872	JAO 308	53905	26-7-56	STEERING WANDER.
U59	E167	Galilie	ZODIAC	SXA 894		30.7.56	CHANGE ENGINE OIL - NEW FILTER - BRAKES. HAND BRAKE - CHECK ENGINE TUNE - HELPHOS LAMP - WHEEL DISCS - FIT - FAN - STRAP OIL (CHECK RADIO) FINS IN BOOT - WING MIRRORS WITH COVERS, YELLOW BULBS, S. BULBS,
U60		SAMUELS	S+				
U60		SAMUELS	ZEPHYR	SLX 976	6,300	31.7.56	BRAKES RADIATOR. JUDDER. 40 M.P.H.
U61	E16769	Mr Richards	91P1872	LVF 363	61,710	31.7.56	CHECK PETROL PUMP. - KING PINS - FIT MODIFIED THRUST WASHERS.
U62		Car Sales M.R. Rogers	91P2272	JFY 499		81.7.56	KING PINS & BUSHES.
U63		CAR SALES	SAFARIA	M.X.A. 554	—	31.7.56	CHANGE POINTS. CHECK & CLEAN. DISTRIBUTOR.
U64	E16763	Mr James	91L689	KAR.612	40432	2.8.56	Gear box and exhaust repair.
U65		GODFREY		T1814653C		2.8.56	STRIP & CLEAN OVERHAUL ENGINE
U66	E1676X	PEARSON	71L652	900 25	33695	7-8-56	STEERING. THRUST WASHERS. CLUTCH. CARB. BONNET HANDLES
U67		WARREN	ROVER	SRF 970	842539	7-8-56	WATERPUMP. STEERING.
U68	E16764	DET. INSP. HEDDON		HAA 4	32669	7-8-56	SPRING. SUSPENSION. BRAKES.
U69		DAVIES	WOLSELEY	9KK 848	37513	7-8-56	DECOKE.
U70		DAVIES	CARTINA	KXC 598	32742	7-8-56	K PINS. THRUST WASHERS. 3 WHEELERS. Nº PLATE.
U71		FISCHEL	91P3041	LXY 399	56835	8-8-56	EXHAUST RATTLE. BRAKES. PLUGS. STEERING.
U72		SMITH	81M1030	KXR294	35337	8-8-56	CLUTCH.

U73	TODD:	91P 2270	KGH 165:	13971:	3-8-'56:	WATER PUMP:
U74:	BLANCHARD:	—	CRT 218:	400941:	8-8-'56:	KING PINS & BUSHES:
U75:	PHILLIPS:	91P 1588:	HOT 631:	35917:	9-8-'56:	STERLING COLUMN BUSH: N/S/R HUB:
U76:	DR. ROLLS:	91P 1975:	HWS 853:	60853:	9-8-'56:	GREASE: EXHAUST FLEX:
U77	Mr. Green.	M2X 3013	YMD 688	—	10-8-56	Check and Test Petrol Pump, changing pump, changing fan and Dynamo Belts, Adjusting front Brakes.
U78 E16780:	CHEEK:	71L 146:	LKX 146	50903:	10-8-'56:	COLLECT CAR: SUMP: STARTER MOTOR:
U79:	JEFFERSON:	71L 360:	LHT 839:	70327:	13-8-'56:	KING PINS & BUSHES: EXHAUST BLOW
U80:	JUKES:	91P 2380:	NNE 400:	38938:	13-8-56:	BONNETT: OIL CAP: DOOR LOCK O/S:
U81 E16772	FIDDIAN:	8H 1072:	KUW 576:	61916:	13-8-56:	RECON ENGINE: KING PINS: EXHAUST:
U82 E16774	CURRAN:	71K 622:	KUW 565:	12051:	15-8-56:	N/S OIL SEAL: EXHAUST N/S: CHECK ENGINE TUNE:
U83:	MARSHALL WILSON:	ANGLIA:	RGN 547:	7116:	15-8-56:	STARTER: SERVICE:
U84:	PIKE:	8H 751:	UHV 207:	82862:	15-8-56:	H/BRAKE CABLE:
U85:	PHILLIPS:	91P 1588:	H.O.T. 631:		15-8-56	REPLACE BRAKE DRUMS.
U86:	CAR SALES:	P 2252:	M.L.U. 872:		15-8-56	FITTING WING MIRRORS:
U87	LE ROSSINIER:	91P 1635	LGK 80:	57538:	15-8-'56:	STERLING COLUMN BKT: WASHER CABLE: KNOCK ON N/S: NEW TYRE: BRAKES: RADIO: DYNAMO BELT:
U88 E16773	HOPPER:				15-8-'56:	CHECK BRAKES: FIT THRUST WASHERS:
U89	MILLER:	ANGLIA:	229 HDX:	5,059:	15-8-'56:	5,000 MILES SERVICE:

Job No	Invoice No	Name	Type	Reg No:	Mileage	Date	Labour
U90:	E16779	FOREMAN:	91P2364	MXK 373	79950:	13-8-56	GEARBOX. CHANGE ALL OILS: FILTER. TUNE ENGINE: PUMP: SPEEDO: BRAKES:
U.91.		Dr JOHNS.	H3X.3015.	MLW.940.	47906.	17. 8. 56.	SERVICE CHANGE OIL. TUNE. WATER LEAK. BRAKES. WASH CAR. REPAIR BONNET. ETC
U.92.		RICHARDSON	91P 1629	HUB 861		17.8.56.	SERVICE. CHANGE OIL. STARTER MOTOR.
U 93		Columbia Axle	—	—	—	17 8 56	Columbia Axle.
U.94.		WATERMAN.	POPULAR.	632.AME.	55690	18.8.56	SERVICE. CHANGE OILS. PLUGS. BRAKE LININGS.
U95:		CAR SALES:	—	6088:	7757	20-8-56	EXHAUST: GEARSHIFT: DRIVE SHAFTS: PROP SHAFT: WIRING LOOM:
U96:		PEABODY:	PILOT.	LXL265:	99891:	20-8-56	ACCIDENT REPAIRS:
U97:		ROLLS:	91P 1973.	HWS 853	613081	21-8-56:	GEARSHIFT MECHANISM:
U98:		TURNEDGE:	PILOT:	FNM 768:	1147:	21-8-56	TUNE ENGINE:
U99:		UPPERTON.	91P1517:	KNF 752:	33753:	21-8-56:	N/S AXLE CASE: TUNE ENGINE: STICKING THROTTLE:
U100:		BALL-WILSON.	PREFECT:	KUW 603:	61158:	22-8-56:	5,000 MILES SERVICE: LIGHTS:
V1:		SAMUELS:	ZEPHYR.	SLK 976:	7136:	22-8-56:	RADIATOR: BRAKES:
V2:		MILLS:	81M 1087:	SRE 801:	67400:	22-8-56:	5,000 MILES SERVICE: HEADLAMPS: O/S/R WHEEL SPAT:
V3:		JONES:	71M 773:	DFR 376:	47107:	23-8-56:	GENERAL CHECK OVER OF CAR: TUNE ENGINE: SERVICE: CHANGE OILS ETC:
V4:		DORMER:	71K 154:	JGP 474:	45020:	25-8-56:	CHECK BRAKES: STEERING: TUNE ENGINE: SERVICE CHANGE OILS:
V5:		GOLDIE:	ZODIAC:	SXK 897:	4090:	27-8-56:	FIT COIL, GENERATOR: TEMP GAUGE:
V6:		SOUTHWELL:	91P 3189:	NKK 727:	—	27-8-56:	ACCIDENT REPAIRS: PUNCTURE: TEST:

JOB NO.	INDICE NO.	NAME	TYPE	REG NO:	MILEAGE	DATE	LABOUR
V7:		HEDDON.	—	MHHH	52970.	27-8-56	WHEEL WOBBLE.
V8:		KNIP.	9/P/883:	LXF 746:	48792:	27-8-56	ACCIDENT REPAIRS.
V9		CAR SALES	MONTE CARLO	SALOON.	—	27-8-56	BALANCE WHEELS.
V.10.		BRASFORD.	RECTIFICATION.	M.Z. 7880	—	27-8-56	ATTEND TO COMPLAINT.
V.11:		PRICE:	9/P8259:	GRV III	45422:	27-8-56	6,000 MILES SERVICE: TUNE: CHARGE RATE: O/S INDICATOR: THROTTLE & CHOKE: BULB: EXHAUST: GEAR CHANGE: HORN NUT: STAND: BRAKES: STEERING: K/PINS: ROOF LAMP: BUMPER BOLT: SPOT LAMP: BONNETT:
V.12:		WINSTON.	9/P 1761	LLH 505	43323	28-8-56	TUNE ENGINE: CHECK BRAKES, CLUTCH, FUEL PUMP, WASHER, INDICATORS, WATER JOINTS & FAN BELTS: FIT AERIAL FOCUS LAMPS BACK SEAT CLOCK: REAR WINDOW
V.13:		DAVIES:	J110	HXC 578:	—	28-8-56	SWING ARM BUSH.
V.17:		DICKSON.	9/P1623:	DVG 779:	36019:	28-8-56	TUNE ENGINE: SWIVEL BAR:
V.15:		GODFREY.	KEW. 2/1444. Dodge engine.			28-8-56	STRIP & OVERHAUL ENGINE
V.16.		GODFREY.	T120/9050 Dodge engine.			28-8-56	BROKEN CRANKSHAFT.
V.14.		H^d GRIFFITHS	M.802.	K.H.K. 28	—	28-8-56	CHECK WIPERS.
V.18.		CAR SALES.	ZEPHYR.	—		28-8-56	COLLECT CAR.
V.19.		REB.	81H/1070:	JGP857	25108:	28-8-56	SERVICE CHANGE OILS: PLUGS & POINTS: WHEELED UP: SILENCER & TAIL PIPE O/S: N/S: LAMP.
V.20.		HOUCHIP.	71L 789:	CES 616	52920:	28-8-56	ACCIDENT REPAIRS:
V.21:		NIEKRASZ:	9/P 1783:	DJD 345:	44377:	30-8-56	TUNE ENGINE: FUEL PUMP: SERVICE: CHANGE OILS:
V.22:		RICHARDS:	9/P1872:	LVF363:	627601	30-8-56	NEW BUMPERS & FRONT IRONS: FUEL PUMP & LINES CHECK:
V.23:		HOGG:	71K 644:	HRU 815:	40061:	1-9-56	K/PINS: THRUST WASHERS: BALANCE WHEELS: SHACKLES: NEW FRONT SHOCKERS:

JOB NO.	INVOICE NO.	CUSTOMERS NAME:	CHASSIS NO:	REG NO:	MILEAGE:	DATE:	LABOUR:—
V24		UPPERTON	91P 1517	KNF 752	33786	3-9-56	CAR SHUDDERS BADLY IN 1ST: REVERSE JUMPS OUT:
V25		TITCHENOR	8IH 79D	MNN 622	25938	3-9-56	RECTIFY STEERING:
V26		S/L GRAY	91P 1862	NCV 430	36047	4-9-56	RECTIFY STEERING: FLAT SPOT:
V27		LAWLER	7IH 687	EUX 371	835	7-9-56	CHECK FRONT S/A: CHECK CLUTCH: CHECK H/LAMPS: WHEEL WOBBLE: CHECK SHACKLES ETC:
V28		SUNN	91P 2118	FBA 50	46704	5-9-56	DOOR HANDLE: STEERING: RADIO: BRAKES: HH 42 B BADGES:
V29		CAR SALES	PREFECT	TSH 969	35	5-9-56	FIT ACCESSORIES ETC:
V30		COX	ANGLIA	SXP 579	1067	5-9-56	1,000 MILES SERVICE:
V31		MASTERS	91P 3237	GEH 334	54362	6-9-56	SEAT BOX:
V32		ROLLS	91P 1943	HWS 853	61695	7-9-56	ACCIDENT DAMAGE:
V33		HERRIOT	8IH 726	MPH 177	64065	7-9-56	ENGINE TUNE:
V34		WATERMAN ~~ROBINSON~~	POPULAR	632 AHE	56675	7-9-56	FIT NEW ENGINE & HOSES:
V35		MILLS	8IH 1087	SRE 861	54447	10-9-56	HEADLAMPS: GRILLE: THROTTLE: WOBBLE: WHISTLE FROM ENGINE
V36		PEABODY	PILOT	LSX 677	60228	10-9-56	BRAKES: TYRES: SHACKLES:
V37		MILESON	91P 1792	LLC 44	11004	10-9-56	STEERING: BRAKES: THROTTLE SPRING:
V38		CAR SALES	8IH 530	IH 4278	77481	10-9-56	HANDBRAKE: BATTERYS:
V39		GOODWIN	POPULAR	SLU 154	8511	11-9-56	WIPERS: INDICATOR 'A' SERVICE:
V40		HEATLEY	ANGLIA	743 FMP	6661	12-9-56	6,000 MILES SERVICE: SILENCER:

Job No	Customer	Type	Reg. No	Mileage	Date	
V.41	Car Sales	91P 1582	K.L.V. 880	—	8.9.56	Clean & Check Car.
V.42	White	7M 566	MNW 477	44603	11.9.56	Fit Lights; Exhaust.
V.43	Ball. Willson	Anglia	R.G.N. 547	07505	12.9.56	Service. Bodywork.
V.44	Todd	P.9970	K.G.A. 165	15257	13.9.56	Speedo - Check Gearbox - Grease.
V.45	Russell	Anglia	RLF 548	13687	13.9.56	Accident Repairs; Wipers.
V.46	Niekrasz	91P 1783	DJD 345	44638	13.9.56	Gearbox.
V.47	Car Sales	7IL 317	JLH 3	372615	17.9.56	Prepare Car for Sale.
V.48	Car Sales	Anglia	—	—	17.9.56	Deliver Car to South Side.
V.49	Car Sales	7IK 485	JKD 874	31830	17.9.56	Prepare Car for Sale.
V.50	Horris	7IL 127	JSN 708	26705	18.9.56	Gearbox; Rear Lamp; Clutch.
V.51	Haas	8IH 1058	UHC 938	88374	19.01.56	Wander.
V.52	Car Sales	Zephyr	T.G.T 401	77.	19.9.56	Change Speedo Cable. Interior Light.
V.53	Rees	8IH 813	HRU 994	57585	20.9.56	Water in Sump; Gearbox; Steering Box Leaks; Exhaust.
V.54	Woodford	7IK 696	KXC 162	27133	20.9.56	Wheel Wobble; Trafficators; Spot Lamp; Screen Washer; SU Pump; Brakes.
V.55	~~Rea~~ [Waterman]	Popular	AHE 632	—	21.9.56	Rear Lamps; Engine; Bumper.
V.56	Sim Rees	91P 1548	KVM 669	—	21.9.56	Window; Carb; Door Lock.
V.57	Newport	8IH 804	THX 198	790717	22.9.56	Brakes; Tune Engine.

V58:	MURRAY	PREFECT:	PBY75.	7.9.5	2-9-56	1st SERVICE:
V59:	BROWN:	8H 869:	KAT 226:	90771:	24-9-56	GEARBOX:
V60:	DR DAVIES:	9/P 1681:	HUS 202:	36983:	24-9-56	GEARBOX: STEERING: EXHAUST:
V61:	GOLDIE	ZODIAC:	SXH 894:	4543:	26-9-56	BRAKES:
V62	CAR SALES	PREFECT	—	—	26.9.56	DELIVER CAR.
V63	CAR SALES	PREFECT	—		26.9.56	DELIVER CAR.
V64:	MICHEALSON:	9/P 2055:	LEL 646:	45709:	26-9-56	DISTRIBUTOR: STEERING:
V65:	BIDDELL:	A2:	LXY 15:	27285:	27-9-56	GEARBOX: DRIVE SHAFTS:
V66:	CAR SALES:	ANGLIA:	—	—	29-9-56	COLLECT CAR & PREPARE FOR SALE: STARTER:
V67:	CAR SALES	7IL 772:	LSY 397	45396:	1-10-56	EXHAUST: GRILLES: PREPARE CAR FOR SALE:
V68	CAR SALES	P. 3084.	HUJ 760	26,045	2.10.56	PREPARE CAR FOR SALE
V69:	MORRISON:	9/P 1959:	NTB 208:	7077:	2-10-56	FIT SIDE LAMP: DECOKE: SERVICE: WINDSCL. WIPERS: FUEL GAUGE: TAIL LAMP: DOOR STRIKERS: WIRING: TYRES: RUBBERS IN DOOR: BRAKES:
V70:	COX:	ZEPHYR:	2.3DHY	15988:	2-10-56	1,000 MILES SERVICE: TAPPETS: CARB:
V71:	WILLERBY:	ANGLIA	PL061	21435:	3-10-56	5,000 MILES SERVICE: RATTLE ON FRONT:
V72:	DAVIES:	J110:	HXC578	—	3-10-56	ACCIDENT REPAIRS:
V73:	BERRYMAN.	ANGLIA:	STT 405:	7655:	3-10-56	REAR AXLE:
V74.	OSBORNE:	8H 871:	THX5:	77723:	4-10-56	REAR AXLE:

V75	PIKE	81M751	UMV307	84205	8-10-56	DENT IN WING: N/S/R SHOCK ABSORBER: TRANSMISSION: STEERING: BRAKES: LIGHTING: SERVICE
V76	CAR SALES	91P1799	KNX847	63803	8-10-56	SILENCER: STEERING BUSH: INDICATORS
V77	COX	ANGLIA	SXP549	1988	8-10-56	1,000 MILES SERVICE
V78	WILLIS	91P1587	KMP622	619	8-10-56	WANDER
V79	FEIN	POPULAR	596 CMH	—	9-10-56	UNDERSEAL: SPOTLAMP: PARKING LAMP: SERVICE: CHANGE OILS (CONVERSION): O/S/F: S/F:
V80	JOHNS	112X3015	ALW940	50138	9-10-56	O/S HEAD: HEATER HOSES: SERVICE: LIGHTER ELEMENT: BONNETT: WIPER BLADES:
V81	CAR SALES	81M874	TT 67-94	41336	11-10-56	NOISE ON ENGINE
V82	CAR SALES	ZODIAC	—	—	12-10-56	PREPARE CAR FOR SALE
V83	COURT	112X3119	YHD692	42981	12-10-56	CHECK STEERING: CHECK BRAKES: F
V84	ROLLS	91P1973	HWS853	—	12-10-56	1,000 MILES: EARTH STRAP: BADGE BAR: YELLOW BULBS: BRAKES:
V85	BALL-WILSON	PREFECT	KUW603	61881	12-10-56	FIT REAR LAMPS: FIT BONNETT RUBBERS:
V86	BASSETT	POPULAR	XPE984	—	12-10-56	ACCIDENT DAMAGE
V87	ROBINSON	POPULAR	SXL889	3767	13-10-56	SILENCER
V88	WATERMAN	POPULAR	682 AME	58237	13-10-56	SERVICE: TYRE CHANGE:
V89	BUNDELL	PREFECT	RUW494	8392	15-10-56	1,000 MILES SERVICE: CHANGE OILS: FILTER: ADJUST CLUTCH & BRAKES: POINTS & PLUGS: HUBS: NOISE IN GEAR BOX:
V90	RICHARDSON	91P1689	NUB861	55989	15-10-56	SERVICE ETC: TRAFFICATOR:
V91	CAR SALES	ZEPHYR	PLK516	11698	15-10-56	SERVICE: CHANGE ENGINE OIL:
V92	GOLDIE	ZODIAC	SXA894	—	16-10-56	SERVICE: RAD BLIND: CHANGE ROUND WHEELS

W10:	BARRETT:	91P1592:	HGJ·99:	1231:	30-10-56	ACCIDENT REPAIRS:
W11	SHIRES:	91P1578:	KYH669	37510:	31-10·56	WHEEL STUDS: PUNCTURE: INTERIOR LAMP: PLUGS: CLUTCH: ACCIDENT (ESTIMATE):
W12	CARSALES (CLAPHAM)	~~~~	KBC178 ~~~~	~~~~	2-11-56	PREPARE CAR FOR MONTE CARLO RALLY
W13:	CARSALES (CLAPHAM):	PREFECT:	RGY808:	19553:	2-11-56	FIT LAMPS WIRING:
W14:	BARRON.	91P3071.	HCY863:	35537:	2-11-56	WHEEL TRAMP: CHECK BRAKES: CLUTCH JUDDER
W15	HEBDEN:	S	H4H4:	33969:	5-11-56	CHECK TRACK: RECON ENGINE: RECON COLUMN: CHECK REAR SPRING: FOCUS LAMPS
W16:	HILESON:	91P1798	LLC47:	12181:	5-11-56	ENGINE RATTLE O/S/R WHEEL:
W17.	HUSIK.	81M873:	FUF470:	4532:	5-11-56	WHEEL WOBBLE: STEERING COLUMN: ENGINE TUNE: SHACKLE BUSHES:
W18:	JEFFERSON	71L360.	HHT839	73118:	7-11-56	BRAKES: SERVICE: PLUGS:
W19:	DR JOHNS	112X3015.	HLW940:	51790:	7-11-56	SERVICE CHANGE OIL X100 SPRH UDDR CAR: NEW PLUGS: DISTRIBUTOR: RADIO: CARB: HOSE CLIPS: ANTIFREEZE.
W20:	SAMUELS:	ZEPHYR:	SLX976:	—	8-11-56	ACCIDENT REPAIRS:
W21:	SHIRES:	91P1548:	KYH669:	37576:	8-11-56	ACCIDENT REPAIRS:
W22:	CARSALES:	ANGLIA:	TGT717:	30:	8-11-56	PREPARE CAR FOR SALE:
W23:	KIRKLAND	ZODIAC:	YPB69:	14774:	9-11-56	REAR AXLE:
W24:	DOLPHIN:	91PR187.	XHF656:	37889:	13-11-56	STEERING: CLUTCH:
W25:	FISCHEL:	91P3041:	LXY399:	60789:	15-11-56	KNOCK ON ENGINE: EXHAUST:
W26	HAWKES	PREFECT	S·L·L·204		15-11-56	ENGINE MOUNTING.
W27:	ARTHUR.	71K149.	DFR259.	62782	15-11-56	ACCIDENT: 1ST GEAR: CLUTCH JUDDER:

W28	MURRAY	PREFECT	PBY175	—	23-11-56	ACCIDENT DAMAGE
W29	ROLLS	91P1973	HWS853	63588	27-11-56	1,000 MILES SERVICE
W30	TODD	91P2370	KFH165	16897	19-11-56	DISTRIBUTOR: TUNE: EXHAUST: SPEDO SERVICE: ANTIFREEZE: SEAT ROADMASTER SPRING
W31	PANTON	ZODIAC	BMP7	1085	20-11-56	1,000 MILES SERVICE: DOOR, ARMREST + PAINTWORK
W32	CHOONG	71M627	KLO133	73997	20-11-56	TUNE ENGINE: CHARGE BATTERYS: SERVICE CHANGE OILS
W33	SAMUELS	ZEPHYR	8LX976	10778	21-11-56	TUNE ENGINE: SERVICE: BRAKES: ANTI-FREEZE: N/S/F DOOR
W34	BATTER (NOVELS)	POPULAR	HDW154	9736	23-11-56	CHECK FOR NOISE IN ENGINE: TOW CAR
W35	TALBOT	PREFECT	TQH969	2067	23-11-56	1,000 MILES SERVICE
W36	MILLER	CONSUL	779HHX	8197	23-11-56	1ST SERVICE: CHANGE ENGINE OIL
W37	GRIFFITHS	81M802	KNK28	98913	23-11-56	AMMETER: WOBBLE WASHERS: HEADLAMP: TUNE ENGINE
W38	WATERMAN	POPULAR	632 AHE	60168	24-11-56	DYNAMO
W39	SCOTT MILLER	SAFARI	NKC461	81175	27-11-56	TOW IN CAR: RADIUS RODS
W40	DR COX	ZEPHYR	213DHM	17082	26-11-56	1,000 MILES SERVICE: ANTIFREEZE: TAPPETS: FOCUS LAMPS
W41	CAR SALES	91P3084	HUT760	86050	27-11-56	FIT ENGINE
W42	DR KEIGHLEY	91P1593	KLO689	78857	27-11-56	R/D BLIND: BUMPERS: PANEL LAMP
W43	RADIO TRADING CO	POPULAR	TSY645	528	27-11-56	1ST SERVICE: FIT MIRROR + STAY
W44	CHARLTON	71M640	HBB836	40393	28-11-56	RATTLE
W45	DENNY	91P1663	LGP258	35748	29-11-56	THRUST WASHERS: SERVICE: ADJUST BRAKES

							TANK READING:
W46	~~HALES~~ CAR SALES:	7LK718:	TCRS860:	47752	1-12-56:	TUNE REAR LAMPS: INDICATORS: CURTAINS:	
W47	GREEN:	RBX3013:	YHD688	78886	3-12-56:	SERVICE: EXHAUST: LAMP: BRAKES: BATTERIES: KINGPINS:	3/4 FULL:
W48	SOUTHWELL:	9LP2169:	NKH727:	36158:	5-12-56:	PAINTWORK O/S SPOTLAMP: HORNS: INDICATOR: TAIL PIPE: FUEL STARVATION 40MPH:	MIDWAY BETWEEN 1/2 9 3/4:
W49	WARNER:	9LP2060	NRL837	34004	5-12-56:	ACCIDENT REPAIRS:	JUST UNDER 1/4 FULL:
W50	FISCHEL:	9LP2041	LXY399		8-12-56	RECTIFY WHEEL RUBBING:	
W51	RICHARDSON:	9LP1629:	NUB801:	56684:	8-12-56:	SERVICE: O/S INDICATOR:	BETWEEN 1/2 9 3/4:
W52	JONES:	9LP1830:	PLH830:	83105:	10-12-56:	EXHAUST: BRAKES:	3/4 FULL:
W53	FREEMAN:	7LK485:	JKD874:	23129:	10-12-56	CHECK ENGINE:	3/4 FULL:
W54	HARDING:	—	WHD850:	—	8-12-56:	FIT NEW REAR BUMPER:	—
W55	MR BERGS MONTEFIORE	ANGLIA:	DJK638:	329:	10-12-56:	1ST SERVICE:	FULL:
W56	DR JOHNS	RBX3015:	HLW940:	53867:	11-12-56:	SERVICE: AFKL2: SWING ARM BUSH: BRAKES: REAR LAMP:	1/2 FULL:
W57	PANTON:	ZODIAC:	BMP7:	—	12-12-56:	TOUCH IN PAINTWORK:	
W58	MRS BALL-WILSON:	ANGLIA:	RGN547:	9146:	13-12-56:	SERVICE: CHECK STEERING: FIT CARB CONVERSION KIT: PLUGS:	JUST OVER 1/2 FULL:
W59	BALL-WILSON:	PREFECT:	KUW603:	62718:	12-12-56:	CLEAN OUT BATTERY ETC: CHECK CARB: PLUGS: ANTI-FREEZE: SERVICE: BONNET RUBBERS:	JUST OVER 1/2 FULL:
W60	CAR SALES:	7LL372:	LSY897:	45419:	14-12-56:	REPAIR EXHAUST CHECK BRAKES: REMOVE PLATES:	
W61	OLDFIELD:	AUSTIN:	UPD688:	16303:	17-12-56:	SERVICE:	
W62	G.B.KENT:	POPULAR:	564DHX:	59587:	19-12-56:	'C' SERVICE:	

W63.	RADIO TRADING CO.	POPULAR.	TSY 645.	1360.	20-12-56.	1,000 MILES. SERVICE.	
W64.	CRADDOCK.	91P 1957.	FPN 300.	46811	27-12-56.	ENGINE: OIL: STEERING: BUMPERS: HUBCAPS: GRILLE: SPEEDO: BATTERIS: BRAKES: DYNAMOS STARTER: CARPETS: CHECK ENGINE: CHECK DOORS ETC. R+SRRA-1: REVERSE LAMP: FILLERS:	JUST UNDER A FULL:
W65.	FARROW.	8IH 879.	JHK 735.	17903.	27-12-56.	TUNE ENGINE.	JUST OVER RESRVE:
W66.	SLADE-H.U.K.	H2X 3089.	HUU 186.	37007.	28-12-56.	DISTRIBUTOR.	
W67.	WATERMAN.	POPULAR.	632 AME.	160921	29-12-56.	'C' SERVICE.	
W68.	CAR SALES.	CONSUL.	SYU 947.	93.	1-1-57.	COLLECT & PREPARE CAR FOR SALE.	
W69.	SCOTT-MILLER.	SAFARI.	NKC 461.	—	2-1-57.	FUEL PUMP: TIGHTEN HEADS.	
W.70.	CAR SALES.	P2 4513.	T.G.T. 403.		2-1-57.	CHECK HOLE PARTS OF CAR.	
W71.	PANTON.	ZODIAC.	BMP 7.	2165.	5-1-57.	OIL IN AXLE: TAPPETS: BAD STARTING: NO PLATE:	
W.72.	LISTER.	ANGLIA.	T.G.T. 686	1,000.	7-1-57	1,000 MILE SERVICE	
W.73.	FEN	POPULAR	596. C.M.H	.	7-1-57.	SERVICE CHANGE OILS. FIX 2 WIPER BLADES	
W.74.	WOOD-WRIGHT	ZEPHYR.	P.L.K. 516	12669	8-1-57.	O/S DRIVERS DOOR. SERVICE. OIL. LEAK. CHECK O/S REAR DOOR CLUTCH	
W.75.	GRAHAM.	91P. 1504	K.H.F. 599	33, 336	8-1-57	NEW DOOR HANDLE. SERVICE, CHECK WIPERS.	
W.76	GOUGH + Co	PILOT.	L.L.C. 417	33709	8-1-57	TUNE ENGINE.	
W.77	MICHEALSON	91P 20551.	L.E.L. 646	49314.	9-1-57.	THREE BRANCH MANIFOLD, SILENCERS, EXHAUST PIPE.	
W78.	GRIFITHS.	8IH 808.	KNK 28.	90466.	9-1-57.	FIT NEW BATTERYS: CHECK FUEL PUMP	
W79	SEBAG-MONTEFIORE	ANGLIA.	DTK 632.	1041.	9-1-57.	1,000 MILES SERVICE.	

						FUEL:
W80:	ROLLS:	91P 1943:	HWS 853:	65022	20-1-57:	ENGINE WINDSCREEN TYRE: BLIND: TAP GAUGE, THROTTLE PEDAL: LH DOOR STICKS: RH DOOR RUBBER: HEATER RH DOOR HANDLE: SILENCER: REAR SHOCK ABSORBERS:	EMPTY:
W81:	G.B. KENT:	ANGLIA:	TLL 985:	371:	14-1-57:	1st SERVICE: WING MIRRORS:	
W82:	BULL:	71H 469:	JOL 616:	57437:	14-1-57:	WATER LOSS: LEAK ON PUMP N/S:	
W83:	HEATLEY:	ANGLIA:	743 FMP:	—	14-1-57:	ADJUST TAPPETS: SERVICE:	
W84:	CAR SALES:	ANGLIA:	—	27:	2-1-57:	PREPARE CAR FOR SALE: PRE-DELIVERY CHECK:	½ FULL:
W85:	CAR SALES:	71L 772:	L.G.Y. 397:	—	2-1-57	PREPARE CAR FOR DOCKS. ✗ January 1958 - letter from Bill Chisholm, Los Angeles asking for information.	
W86:	MICHEL:	CONSUL:	SYU 947:	A96:	14-1-57:	WATER LEAKS: FILLER CAP: 1st SERVICE:	
W87:	TODD:	91P 2270:	KCH 165:	—	17-1-57:	FIT NUMBER PLATE BOX:	
W88:	STOCK ENGINE:	—	—	—	17-1-57:	STRIP & OVERHAUL:	
W89	MAIR	112X 3089	M.U.U 186:	37265	17-1-57	RAD. BLIND, H/S EXHAUST, IGNITION, FIT RADIO, SERVICE, WIPER BLADES, ETC.	
W90:	CAR SALES:	71H 457:	LUH 89:	63985:	21-1-57:	FIT NEW BRAKE PIPES: RECTIFY CHOKE CONTROL: CHARGE BATTERIES:	
W91:	CAR SALES:	—	SMH 107:	56681:	22-1-57:	PREPARE CAR FOR SALE:	
W92:	CAR SALES:	112X 3119:	VHD 698:	44037:	22-1-57:	PREPARE CAR FOR SALE: DELIVER & COLLECT TO & FROM SOUTH SIDE CLAPHAM	

Design:	Jodi Ellis Graphics
Printer:	Interpress Ltd., Hungary
Page Size:	290 mm x 230 mm
Text paper:	135gsm Magno Gloss
End paper:	170gsm Woodfree Offset
Dust Jacket:	157gsm Glossy Artpaper with matte scratch-free lamination
Casing:	Foil stamping on front and spine, on black Geltex, over 3 mm board
Chapter Heads:	24 pt. Gill Sans Nova Inline Regular
Main Body Text:	9.5 pt ITC Avant Garde Gothic Pro Book
Captions:	8 pt ITC Avant Garde Gothic Pro Medium